IRISH WHISKEY

John Jameson, founder of John Jameson and Son Limited,
(the Irish Distillers' Bow Street Distillery)

IRISH WHISKEY

A History of Distilling, the Spirit Trade
and Excise Controls in Ireland

E. B. McGUIRE

GILL AND MACMILLAN · DUBLIN
BARNES & NOBLE BOOKS · NEW YORK
a division of Harper & Row Publishers, Inc.

First published in 1973

Gill and Macmillan Ltd
2 Belvedere Place
Dublin 1
and in London through association with the
Macmillan
International Group of Publishing Companies

Published in the USA in 1973 by
Harper & Row Publishers, Inc.
Barnes & Noble Import Division

Gill and Macmillan SBN: 7171 0604 7
Barnes & Noble ISBN: 06 4947017

Printed and bound in the Republic of Ireland by
Cahill & Co Limited, Dublin

CONTENTS

CONTENTS

FOREWORD

Mr E. B. McGuire had a long and distinguished career in Customs and Excise. This book fully reflects his erudition and detailed knowledge of a complex subject.

There can be little doubt that it will be the definitive history of the distilling industry in Ireland and of the manner in which our present system of Excise controls evolved. Additionally, his work will be of great interest to all those in the distilling industry throughout the world and the trade it serves: it will also be a most valuable source document for future historians.

We congratulate Mr McGuire on a notable achievement and are extremely pleased to have been able to assist in its publication.

Frank O'Reilly, *Chairman*
Irish Distillers Limited
Dublin

PREFACE

So many industrial and economic histories have been written that another addition requires explanation. The Irish distilling industry has been briefly mentioned in a few technical and economic works during the past hundred years, but a comprehensive account has not been attempted since Samuel Morewood included Ireland in his massive book on inebriating liquors published in 1838. Yet the industry has for centuries been at the heart of Irish social life, and for a large part of that time an important factor in Irish politics. The story of the inns and taverns has been even more neglected. Corruption, illicit distilling, lawlessness, political jobbery, antagonism to English rule, are all accentuated in government attempts to control the manufacture and consumption of Irish whiskey. Revenue needs versus sobriety led to disastrous administrative blunders and also to spectacular emotional movements to persuade Irishmen to keep sober. These turbulent times for the industry have long since passed, to be replaced by the uncertainties of trade cycles in much wider markets, the aftermath of two great wars, and competition from Scotch whisky and other beverages. This history covers these aspects and also the parallel development of distillery apparatus, techniques and skill from the advent of usquebaugh to the high quality whiskey of 1970.

It may be wondered why this gap in Irish history was not filled long ago. The usual research difficulties face the historian. There is scarcely any information before the nineteenth century about individuals or their distilleries, but because of the government concern for revenue, there is a wealth of statistics and other records in official documents, probably more than for any other industry. A possible reason for the neglect of historians may be the formidable problems presented by the interaction of rigid government regulation with the technical distilling processes and the complexities of marketing. Close association for many years with these problems has equipped me to attempt to fill this gap in Irish history.

This work was first suggested to me by Professor K. H. Connell of The Queen's University, Belfast, who guided me in the early stages into the methods of historians and gave me sound advice on presentation. I must also acknowledge the help of the librarians of the Linenhall Library, Belfast, where so much of the research was done, Queen's University Library, and the Belfast Public Library. I am grateful for the facilities extended to me in the Customs and Excise Library, London, and the Public Record Offices in Dublin and Belfast. When the Irish distilling firms became aware of my work they generously invited me to visit their establishments, made available information from their private records, and gave me every encouragement. I had help from a number of friends, but I am specially indebted to H. J. MacGovern, formerly of the Customs and Excise, Dublin, who carefully read the final text and made helpful suggestions. If there are errors of fact or flaws in presentation, I, alone, am responsible.

E. B. McGuire
Belfast, February 1972

INTRODUCTION

DISTILLING and marketing spirits is unique among Irish industries in several respects. Governments have regarded the industry as a fit subject for taxation far higher in relation to value than any other manufactured commodity. Though a main source of revenue, the consumption of spirits cannot be looked upon as a necessity to life, but despite taxation, demand never diminished and until this century, there were no appreciable periods of trade depression; on moral grounds marketing has been restrained by laws and attacked by temperance societies; high taxation generated extensive fraud by distillers and corruption among revenue officials; and its main domestic competitor, beer, received preferential treatment both in manufacture and marketing by revenue laws designed specially to divert public taste away from spirits. These features resulted in rigid government controls being imposed at all vital stages of manufacture and severe marketing restrictions. No other industry, even brewing, has had to contend with anything like these restraints to normal industrial development. The spirit trade survived only because, in Ireland, public demand could not be suppressed and because governments could not afford to lose the revenue derived from it. The dilemma of sobriety versus revenue is well expressed by McCulloch and quoted with approval in a report to parliament in 1834. He wrote:

'There are, perhaps, no better subjects for taxation than spirituous and fermented liquors. They are essentially luxuries; and while moderate duties on them are, in consequence of their being generally used, exceeding productive, the increase in price which they occasion has a tendency to lessen their consumption by the poor, to whom, when taken in excess, they are exceedingly pernicious. Few governments, however, have been satisfied with imposing moderate duties on spirits; but partly in view of increasing the revenue and partly in view of placing them beyond the reach of the lower classes, have almost invariably loaded them with such impressively high duties as to have entirely defeated both objects. The imposition of such duties does not take away the appetite for spirits; and so no vigilance of the officers or severity of the laws has been found sufficient to secure a monopoly of the market to the legal distillers, the real effect of the high duties has been to throw the supply of a large proportion of the demand into the hands of the illicit distiller, and to superadd the atrocities of the smuggler to the idleness and dissipation of the drunkard.

Perhaps no country has suffered more from the excessive height to which duties on spirits have been carried than Ireland. If heavy taxes, enforced by severe fiscal regulations, could make a people sober and industrious, the Irish would be the most so of any upon the face of earth. In order to make the possessors of property join heartily in suppressing illicit distillation, the novel expedient was here resorted to, of imposing a heavy fine on every parish, townland, manor-land or lordship, in which an unlicensed still was found; while the unfortunate wretches found working it were subjected to transportation for seven years. But instead of putting down illicit distillation, these unheard of severities rendered it universal, and filled the country with bloodshed and even rebellion.'[1]

As the story unfolds it will be seen that the Irish distilling industry emerged from extensive domestic distilling towards the end of the seventeenth century and that for most of the next century its main competitor was imported spirits, especially rum. Legal manufacture overtook imports at the end of the century, but because of ill-conceived revenue laws, distilling techniques and the emergence of large scale units did not occur until the middle of the nineteenth century. At about this time Irish beer was improving in quality, large breweries were being erected and beer supplanted imported spirits as the main competitor to Irish spirits.

It is an advantage when examining the development of any

1. *Inquiry into the Excise Establishment and into the Management and Collection of the Excise Revenue throughout the United Kingdom*, 7th Report, Part I, Parl. Pps. 1834 (7) xxv, pp. 105–6. *McCulloch's Dictionary, Practical, Theoretical and Historical of Commerce and Commercial Navigation*, see 1854 ed. pp. 1223–4.

industry to have some knowledge of its techniques and in no industry is this more important than in distilling where the problems of manufacturing and marketing, the excise duties, and revenue laws interacted so intimately to mould its development. So much was this so that distilling and the excise cannot be separated. A short account of the processes and equipment in distilleries is given before the history of the industry. It is based mainly on conditions in the nineteenth century as information of earlier distilleries is meagre, but basic features would not differ materially at any period. Raw materials had to be fermented whether the apparatus was crude or sophisticated. It is hoped that the description of processes and plant, though far from exhaustive, will enable the reader to understand more easily the problems that arose at different times, the ways they were solved and the relationship with the revenue laws.

One particular feature was the spur given to invention by these revenue laws. The evolution of a standard for measuring spirits and the development of the hydrometer and saccharometer considerably aided the distiller in making and marketing spirits and the revenue authorities in assessing duties fairly. A chapter has been given to this important subject.

The history of an industry is illuminated if the fortunes of some of the leading firms can be traced. Unfortunately there are few extant records of distilleries that are of any value. Before 1823 there were no really large firms and until the nineteenth century was well advanced fraudulent practices were widespread, even amongst the best known distillers, and were openly admitted, so that full records were unlikely. Added to this was the destruction of records as firms changed hands or discontinued, culminating in the disastrous loss of so many records when the Four Courts in Dublin was destroyed during the civil strife of 1922. A little information can be gleaned from records which have survived and are now in the Public Record Offices in Dublin and Belfast, but knowledge of firms must rely heavily on excise records and on evidence given before parliamentary inquiries. These sources are no more than indirect information and must often be treated with reserve.

For practical purposes distilling in Ireland means the manufacture of whiskey from cereals, mainly barley. Sometimes molasses, sugar and possibly potatoes have been used to make

raw spirit intended for further processing to make British brandy,
gin or imitation rum, but this branch of distilling was of minor
importance. The name 'whiskey' derives from a corruption of an
old gaelic word that became 'usquebagh' in the eighteenth
century laws and corresponds with 'aqua vitae' also used in those
laws. It is now common usage to spell the Irish product 'whiskey'
and the similar Scottish product 'whisky'.[2]

References to statutes before 1801 are to Acts of the Irish
parliament unless an English statute is specially indicated. After
1922 the Acts of the Dublin parliament are identified by the year
and number. The citation of Acts of the parliaments of the
United Kingdom and Northern Ireland follow the lines officially
used. Examples are:

United Kingdom
    Before 1963—6 Geo. 5, c.18
    From 1963—1965, c.18
Northern Ireland
    Before 1943—6 Geo. 5, c.18(N.I.)
    1943 to 1962—1944, c.18
    1963 onwards—1965, c.18(N.I.)

2. Usquebagh is sometimes spelled 'usquebaugh'. This distinction is made on
the labels of whiskey bottles and in advertisements. See also O. A. Mendelsohn,
Dictionary of Drink and Drinking, London, 1965, p. 367. 'Whiskey' is the spelling
generally used in the United States whatever the source. The Cork Distilleries
Company is an exception to the spelling tradition. They use 'whisky' for their
brands.

CHAPTER I

DISTILLERY PROCESSES

THE object of fermenting and distilling is to produce ethyl alcohol, but when a pot still is used small quantities of other alcohols and their ethers are also produced in varying proportions according to the raw materials used. It is these extraneous substances which give a beverage its characteristic flavour.[1]

The raw material for making spirits must be either naturally rich in sugar, such as grape juice, or must be capable of being saccharified. The starch in grain seeds and in potatoes, beet, beans and similar plants can be converted into suitable sugars, but there are objections to many of these articles because of the flavour of the spirit produced or the techniques of brewing and distilling, and the choice of materials is, therefore, limited. Irish whiskey distillers have always used barley normally as the main ingredient of a mixture of cereal grains. Oats are generally part of the mixture as this is considered to give the whiskey a more desirable flavour. Bear or bigg, an inferior barley, was also used, specially in the first half of the nineteenth century. It was imported from south-west Scotland though some was also grown in parts of Ulster, particularly in County Down where it was called four or six rowed barley.[2] Other starchy grains used are rye, maize, and

1. Textbooks on distilling alcohol go into much detail on the small quantities of higher alcohols and other substances produced during fermentation. Most of these by-products are grouped together under the term 'fusel oil' of which the chief constituent in whiskey manufacture is amyl alcohol. Fusel oil has a greater intoxicating power than ethyl alcohol and if excessive amounts are present an unpleasant flavour is imparted to the beverage. For the practical value of these substances to a distiller see *Truths about Whiskey*, Dublin 1878, published by John Jameson, William Jameson, John Power and George Roe, all Dublin distillers, pp. 3, 18, 21.

2. *Inquiry into the Revenue arising in Ireland, 5th Report, Parl. Pps. 1823* (405), vii, p. 320. *Inquiry into the Excise Establishment and into the Management and*

wheat, though wheat has to be used with caution as there is a strong tendency for its starch to form into a paste when mixed with hot water and this would impede fermentation.[3] During periods of food shortage distillers were encouraged to use molasses or sugar; the process is cheaper, but the spirit is a poor substitute for whiskey and had no market in Ireland. This spirit is, however, suitable for making gin and other flavoured beverages.[4]

Thus the choice of materials is the distiller's first problem and it is not so easy as it might appear. The flavour of whiskey is influenced by the proportions of the different cereals used, but it is also influenced to a lesser extent by different varieties of the same cereal and the quality of the grain. When a mixture of different cereals is used price becomes another consideration. Probably the distiller before the middle of the nineteenth century was satisfied if his grain was reasonably sound and the price low. The modern Irish distiller, however, especially if he is using a pot still, goes to a lot of trouble to get the best grain he can find and price is less important. In recent years he has drawn wholly on locally grown grain for his pot still whiskey. But until the early years of this century he sometimes went farther afield to England or foreign countries, particularly if a bad summer or some other reason had resulted in some crops not becoming fully ripened. Poor barley may not germinate satisfactorily during malting and poor grain generally may adversely affect flavour. So it may be no economy to buy cheaply. When grain is bought it is first thoroughly dried and then stored till needed.[5]

Whiskey distillers stress the need for an ample supply of suitable water and site their distilleries accordingly. The Dublin distillers, for example, prized the waters of the rivers Vartry and Tolka.

Collection of the Excise Revenue, 7th Report, Part I, Parl. Pps. 1834 (7) xxv, pp. 58, 210, 311–2, 447. M. Donovan, *Domestic Economy,* Dublin, 1830, i, p. 53. J. Owens, *Plain Papers,* London, 1879, pp. 325–7. Bear is also spelt 'bere'. See 2 and 3 Will. 4, c. 29, section 2 where the same allowance on malt spirits required a greater quantity of bear or bigg than barley.

3. S. Morewood, *A Philosophical and Statistical History . . . of Inebriating Liquors,* Dublin, 1838, p. 660. J. Scarisbrick, *Spirit Manual,* 2nd ed. Wolverhampton, 1891, p. 106.

4. See, for example, 48 Geo. 3, c. 78 and c. 118, and the special inducements contained in 10 and 11 Vict., c. 6.

5. *Royal Commission on Whiskey and other Potable Spirits; Evidence,* 1908 (Cd. 4181) pp. 91–2, 237–8, 272, 412.

Similarly in Scotland numbers of pot still distilleries are concentrated in Highland districts such as the vicinity of the river Spey. It seems that the water best suited for making whiskey is soft and has certain minerals dissolved in it and these conditions occur in peaty districts. Possibly these conditions could be imitated by a chemist, but this is generally denied by distillers. In any case chemical imitation would add to costs.[6]

All the processes of manufacturing spirit require fuel. In Ireland peat fuel is freely available in areas where there are also suitable water supplies and before the nineteenth century a good deal of Irish whiskey was made in these districts. Coal, however, is a more efficient fuel and as distilling units became larger at a time when inland transport remained difficult, coal replaced peat and the principal distilleries were centred on the ports, especially Dublin and Cork where there was also a substantial local market. Some small distilleries, however, using local peat, survived into the early nineteenth century in the boglands of the north and west.[7]

Before a distiller can begin making whiskey he must first malt some or all of his grain in order to change the starchy material into sugars that yeast can convert into alcohol. If some grain only is malted the enzymes generated will, during the brewing process, carry on the conversion in a mixture of malt and raw grain producing the typical whiskey of Ireland since 1800. If only malted grain is used the product is malt whiskey common in Ireland before 1800 and the usual spirit from illicit stills till about 1830. Malt whiskey made in pot stills is the customary spirit of Scotland, but since the 1860s most of it has been blended with a spirit obtained from a different type of still which extracts most of the flavouring essences. Our ancestors preferred a heavy whiskey and called this lighter product, sometimes disparagingly, 'neutral or silent spirit'. To-day, if the spirit is derived wholly from cereals, it is called 'grain whiskey'. The action of malt can also convert other starchy materials such as potatoes, and on rare

6. *Truths about Whiskey, op. cit.,* pp. 25–6; *R.C. on Whiskey; Evidence, op. cit.,* p. 210, 236.

7. *Irish House of Commons Journal,* Appendix, 7 June 1782, pp. 523–32. lists 871 licensed stills and their situation. *Irish Revenue Inquiry, 5th Report, 1823, op. cit.,* pp. 288, 348. The distilleries in 1802 and 1822 are listed on pp. 367–9. S. Morewood, *History of Inebriating Liquors, op. cit.,* p. 725.

occasions this was tried in Ireland. Morewood mentions that Jameson of Fairfield near Enniscorthy began distilling from potatoes in 1832 but stopped because of local opposition to this use of a staple food. In 1845 Robinson of Lisburn sought permission to distil from malt and potatoes, stating that the blight disease in potatoes at that time did not affect the farina which could be converted into saccharine matter. His application was refused because of his bad revenue reputation. These are isolated cases and potato spirit was not made in Ireland either legally or by illicit distillers before the present century.[8]

Before a duty was imposed on malt in 1785 distillers malted both barley and oats, but when the duty was levied it was assessed on volume and as oats swell much more than barley when steeped, malting oats became prohibitive. Illicit distillers, however, frequently used oats which, it was said, produced a better flavoured whiskey. No other grains were malted.[9] The malt duty brought with it close revenue control over malting operations, precise regulations concerning the construction of malting floors, and limited time factors for the different operations. Making good malt requires considerable skill and in the nineteenth century 'the determination of the form and measurement of the apparatus by which it is produced constitutes a part of the law of the realm; and the whole process is embarrassed by legislative restrictions of such a nature as to prevent the likelihood of improvement'. To this comment by Donovan in 1830 it should be added that from 1785 to 1825 the distiller paid duty on his malt in addition to the spirit duty. He was later given relief by way of an allowance on malt spirit and finally an exemption

8. The sugars in malt are maltose and dextrin (see, for example, W. H. Nithsdale and A. J. Manton, *Practical Brewing*, Glasgow, 1924, p. 33). *Excise Revenue Inquiry*, 7th Report, Part I, 1834, *op. cit.*, pp. 71–2, 379. On p. 307 the report gives only two small malt whiskey distilleries in Ireland; at Gorton, Co. Tyrone and Bushmills, Co. Antrim. S. Morewood, *Inebriating Liquors, op. cit.*, p. 699. *Belfast Historical Excise Records*, Custom House, Belfast, Mss Book No. 5, p. 88. On pp. 30, 53, Maxwell of Portaferry made sugar from potatoes for a short time in 1844. *Royal Comm. on Whiskey; Evidence* 1908, *op. cit.*, p. 162. Blending of spirits began about 1860; p. 303, sulphuric acid was also used instead of malt to convert starch. This was not done by Irish distillers.

9. The malt duty was imposed by 25 Geo. 3, c. 3. *Irish Revenue Inquiry, 5th Report*, 1823, *op. cit.*, pp. 269, 312, 319, 336. *Excise Revenue Inquiry, 7th Report, Part I*, pp. 205, 396, 406. A Barnard, *The Whisky Distilleries of the United Kingdom*, London 1887. The malt houses in each Irish distillery are described.

from the duty, but to safeguard the revenue from fraud, the distiller's maltings remained under close supervision and subject to the regulations applying to brewers and maltsters. In 1880 the malt duty was repealed and control over the raw materials for distilling spirits disappeared.[10]

Malting is the germination of grain causing some of the starch to be converted into sugar by enzymes present in the grain and also a considerable increase in these enzymes which are known collectively as the diastase of malt. This increase is available to continue the process of conversion and is therefore vital to future operations. Little change took place in the last century in the apparatus used or in the operations of malting. There were, of course, minor changes to overcome difficulties. For example, kiln drying directly by the hot gases from the furnace was apt to cause charring and thus diminishing the value of the malt, and in the early nineteenth century drying was sometimes accomplished by the hot air around the flues passing up through the malt.[11]

The grain is put into a cistern to steep. It is covered with water for a short time when unsuitable matter is dissolved from the husks and any light barley floats to the top. The malt laws allowed this to be done once only. This light barley has a poor malt value and to exclude it from revenue assessment it was skimmed off. The first water is drained off and the grain again covered. It remains in steep for at least forty hours, often sixty hours or more according to the quality of the grain and the season, the steep taking longer in cold weather. As a rough test the maltster of the nineteenth century considered steeping sufficient if a grain broke into a pulpy state when squeezed along its length between the finger and thumb.

After steeping the grain is transferred to a 'couch frame'. When the malt laws were in force this frame was a long narrow floor

10. M. Donovan, *Domestic Economy, op. cit.,* i, p. 77. 6 Geo. 4, c. 58, section 2 granted allowances. Exemption was given in 1855 by 18 and 19 Vict., c. 94, section 5. The malt duty was repealed by 43 and 44 Vict., c. 20, section 3.

11. Authoritative accounts of nineteenth century malting processes are given in the report of the *Committee appointed to consider the present state of the laws relative to the distillery of spirits . . . in Scotland,* 1799. App. M. pp. 365, *et. seq.;* M. Donovan, *Domestic Economy, op. cit.,* i, pp. 77–84; W. H. Johnston, *Inland Revenue Officer's Manual,* Loftus publication, London, 1873, pp. 265–9; Nithsdale and Manton, *Practical Brewing, op. cit.,* pp. 11–14. The revenue controls are described in the *13th Inland Revenue Report,* Parl. Pps. 1870 (c. 82) xx, pp. 235–6.

enclosed on three sides somewhat like a long box with one end missing. The steeped grain is piled at one end of the frame and the malt laws required that the depth should not exceed thirty inches. For some thirty to forty hours there is no appreciable change, then the temperature begins to rise, germination starts and the grain dries on its surface. The grain is now spread in the frame. The temperature continues to rise and rootlets appear at the base of the grain. After about two or three days the grain becomes moist on the surface or 'sweats' and the acrospire, or sprout, appears growing inside the husk in the opposite direction to that of the rootlets. While this is happening the temperature is maintained at about 60°F by repeatedly turning over the grain and spreading it more and more thinly in the frame. Damage to the rootlets and acrospire must be avoided for, if the grain dies, mould may appear. Couching takes about five days.

When the grain is spread to a depth of about six inches it is called a 'floor'. During flooring the temperature is allowed to rise to 70°F or a little more and growth continues till the acrospire reaches the length at which the maltster deems that growth should be stopped. Usually this length is about three-quarters of the length of the grain. By this time the greater part of the moisture absorbed in steeping will have been dissipated and the rootlets will be withering. This empirical decision to stop growth is critical for future fermenting operations because as the acrospire grows starch is being converted into sugar to nourish the growing plant, but a point is reached when the drain on the store of sugar begins to exceed the conversion from starch. The maltster's aim is to stop growth at this optimum point. This is also the point when the excess of diastase needed to carry on conversion of starch in the mash is at its greatest. Grain on the floor may need sprinkling with water if germination is flagging or if it is being forced, but when there was a revenue control of malting this practice was first prohibited, then allowed subject to restrictions designed to prevent the introduction of grain after the revenue account had been raised. During the whole process of flooring, which takes about eight days, the grain is regularly turned over so as to maintain an even temperature and growth.[12]

12. Sprinkling was prohibited in 1802 by 42 Geo. 3, c. 38, section 30 to prevent the clandestine introduction of a batch of grain to replace grain taken from the

After flooring, malting is complete and growth in the green malt is stopped by kiln drying. The object is to kill the grain without destroying the diastase and to drive out all remaining moisture. In the nineteenth century and earlier, without the modern aids of control, considerable skill was needed during kiln drying to prevent scorching. The distiller requires a pale malt. The earliest kilns were crude, consisting of a floor of fine wire mesh or of perforated tiles under which a fire was lit. Under such conditions some scorching was inevitable and the malt also became tainted with smoke. At the turn of the eighteenth and nineteenth centuries the furnace gases in the better malt houses were conducted through flues under the kiln floors and drying was done by hot air rising from them, the heat being regulated by fans. Some distillers continued to use direct heat from peat fires on the grounds that it gave spirits a peaty flavour, but this result is debatable. The malted grain is spread thinly over the kiln floor and mild heat is allowed to pass up through the floor. This heat is slowly increased for pale malt to about 120°F over a period of two or three days and during this time the malt is frequently turned to prevent scorching. It is then lightly raked over to remove the rootlets which are marketable for cattle food as malt combs or culms. An improved modern method is to pass hot air under pressure up through the kiln floor. Using this arrangement a layer of malt on the floor can be over two feet thick instead of a few inches and the malt is continually stirred. The malting process is now complete and the malt can be bagged and stored, though it is often first mellowed in the air for a day or two.

The whole process of malting, calling for so much skill and care, can be compared with the rough and ready methods of illicit malting in the period when illicit distilling was rife. Then it was common for the illicit maltster to soak a sack of grain in bog water, spread it over his cabin floor to germinate and then dry it over a makeshift fire. The only result would be some good malt and a good deal of poor or useless malt. So long as only malt was used, or only a small admixture of raw grain, fermenta-

---

cistern before it was properly steeped. Following a departmental inquiry in 1828 the prohibition was relaxed by 11 Geo. 4, and 1 Will, 4, c. 17, to allow sprinkling after a few days following steeping. See J. Owens, *Plain Papers, op. cit.,* pp. 327–8.

tion would be sufficient to produce enough spirit to be worth while at duty free values.[13]

The value of malt and the various raw grains in terms of the spirit that can be produced cannot be assessed with any precision since there are so many variable factors in the distillery processes. When drawback was allowed on malt used in distilling, the rate of drawback was based on the assumption that one bushel of malt produced two gallons of spirit. It was found, however, that there is a greater yield from a mixture of raw grain and malt, and it could be as much as two and a half gallons to the bushel. Spirit production is generally estimated in relation to the specific gravity of wash rather than the quantity of raw materials.[14]

In the manufacture of whiskey there are two distinct major processes, brewing and distilling. The brewing process is essentially the same as in the manufacture of beer, but there is one important difference. In making beer the fermented material is the brewer's final product and he is concerned with the retention of some sugar as well as its alcoholic content. The distiller, on the other hand, is mainly interested in producing as much alcohol as he can as well as developing flavour. A brewer skims off yeast to stop fermentation before it would exhaust itself naturally, whereas the distiller, whose main object is to produce spirit, will continue fermentation as long as it will last. Both, of course, try to get good quality grains.

A pure malt whiskey, as the name implies, is made entirely from malt, but in Ireland mixed grain pot still whiskey has been favoured except for a short period at the end of the eighteenth century.[15] Illicit distillers did, however, make malt whiskey until about 1830 when some of them began using some raw grain. One reason may have been that the malt in earlier years was

13. *Select Committee to consider extending the functions of the Constabulary in Ireland to the suppression of Illicit Distillation*, Parl. Pps. 1854 (53) x, p. 30.

14. *Irish Revenue Inquiry, 5th Report*, 1823, *op. cit.*, p. 269. *Excise Revenue Inquiry, 7th Report, Part I*, 1834, *op. cit.*, p. 213. *Report from the Board of Excise to the Treasury on the use of barley, malt, sugar and molasses in Breweries and Distilleries*, Parl. Pps. 1847 (26) lix, pp. 337–41. The results of an earlier investigation by the excise laboratory. See also W. H. Johnston, *Excise Officer's Manual*, *op. cit.*, p. 299. On pp. 397–403 is an abstract of the malt laws in 1873.

15. The use of raw grain in distilling was prohibited when the malt duty was imposed in 1785 (see 25 Geo. 3, c. 3, section 32). *Irish Revenue Inquiry 5th Report*, 1823, *op. cit.*, p. 268. This report was misleading when it stated that the use of raw grain was of modern origin and a consequence of the high duty on malt.

frequently so badly made that the addition of raw grain would have seriously impaired fermentation. Although mashing is easier with some grains than others, any raw grain rich in starch may be used to make whiskey. Because of mashing problems and to get the best results the distiller uses well known and well tried cereals of which barley is the best. Some malt is essential and normally constitutes not less than about one-fifth of the mixture of raw materials in the grist. Malt, always more costly to the distiller than raw grain, was particularly so during the period of the malt duty; distillers then, in consequence, reduced the proportion of malt in the grist as much as they dared, some of them even going as low as one-tenth. Enough diastase must be generated to convert the starch in the mash so there is a limit to which the malt may be reduced or full fermentation may be in jeopardy.[16]

W. H. Johnston, an excise official writing in 1873, gives examples of the composition of the grist used by an Irish pot still distiller working on a large scale. At this time malt was still subject to revenue control. The use of maize in the fourth brew was not normal because this cereal imparts a distinctive flavour to whiskey, acceptable in the United States, but not popular elsewhere. Probably the maize flavour would be slight and largely lost in subsequent blending. The proportion of rye is also unusual for a pot still whiskey intended for the home market. After the removal of controls over malt in 1880 Irish distillers used far more and at present the proportion of malt is in the region of 40 per cent or more. Rye and maize are not now used for making Irish pot still whiskey.[17]

Total bushels	2,000	1,600	1,360	2,000	560
Per cent of malt	14	15	15	12	14
barley	40	39	38	46	50
oats	16	16	19	14	22
rye	30	30	28	16	14
maize	—	—	—	12	—

16. *Ibid.*, pp. 285, 297, 314, 340, 359. *Excise Revenue Inquiry, 7th Report, Part I*, *op. cit.*, pp. 71–2, 211.

17. Johnston, *Inland Revenue Officer's Manual, op. cit.*, p. 280.

Eighteenth century Irish still, from S. Morewood, *Inventions and Customs in the use of Inebriating Liquors*, London, 1824, p. 356.

The last brew was not distilled, but was used for later mashings of grist.

The first operation is to grind the materials. The distiller's object is a grist where the materials will become intimately mixed and the texture of the grist will be fairly open. For this purpose raw grain is finely ground and malt coarsely ground. The texture is further helped by the malt husks which are not finely broken up in the grinding process.

The brewing arrangements vary in detail in different distilleries, but the object is the same. The grist is infused with weak wort from an earlier brew, or with hot water, three or four times in order to take up as much soluble matter as possible. The stronger infusions are drained off and fermented and the weaker runnings used to infuse a subsequent brew. A number of descriptions of brewing processes are given by writers at different times during the nineteenth century and they differ only in minor detail from present day practice. Typical is that given by W. H. Johnston in 1873.[18] In his description water, heated to about 150°F, or 'liquor' as it is called in brewing practice, is introduced into the mash tun or kieve through the false bottom. The malt is first added and thoroughly agitated by 'oars' or by machinery. The barley, oats and any other materials are then quickly added. Moderate stirring continues to ensure that the materials are thoroughly mixed, any clots are broken up and the mash prevented from setting. The cellular structure of the starch breaks down, and allows the diastase of malt to convert the starch into a glucose suitable for fermenting. A little more hot water may be added to complete the process which takes some two hours. In a successful mashing, with two or more infusions, about four-fifths of the starch in the grist will be converted into sugar. The resulting solution is called wort or pot-ale though the latter term is now used only when referring to illicit distillation.[19]

18. *Ibid.*, pp. 278, *et. seq.*, see also Donovan, *Domestic Economy, op. cit.*, i, pp. 217–26. Morewood, *Inebriating Liquors, op. cit.*, p. 660 *et seq.*, Scarisbrick, *Spirit Manual, op. cit.*, 75, 79–80.

19. The term 'pot ale' is often loosely used. In Irish statutes it meant wort, or wash in any stage of fermentation. See, for example, 3 Geo. 3, c. 21 of 1763. This is the meaning used in police reports of seizures of illicit materials. C. McCoy, *Dictionary of Customs and Excise*, London, 1938, defines pot ale as fully fermented wash and quotes 48 Geo. 3, c. 81. *The Royal Comm. on Whiskey; Final Report*, 1909 (Cd. 4796) and in the evidence of scientists in 1908 the term is used to mean

The quantity of water used in mashing is of some importance as it will affect the degree of concentration of the wort though this can be controlled, within limits, by boiling off an excess of water or by dilution. This concentration is measured by its specific gravity in relation to water the latter being referred to as 1,000°. Until the middle of the last century there was an alternative measure also related to water, but referred to the weight in pounds per barrel. In practice only the last two figures of the gravity are quoted. Thus a specific gravity of 1,055° is quoted as 55°. A dilute mash favours the conversion of starch, but takes longer, a matter of some importance in the period between 1780 and 1823 when rapid work was stimulated by the distillery laws. On the other hand a highly concentrated wort may not be completely fermented when the yeast is exhausted. The most suitable gravities for a mixed grist are from 45° to 55° and a little higher when using malt only.[20] The first infusion is drained off and takes with it most of the saccharine matter. Two or three further infusions at slightly higher temperatures are passed through the mash tun in a similar manner to remove most of the remaining soluble material. Sometimes the second running is mixed with the first to make up the wort which is collected in a receiving vessel called the underback. The remaining runnings are very weak and are conveyed to a copper for heating and used as liquor for subsequent brews.

Clearly, unless the distiller has considerable freedom in the management of this process the ultimate produce may be seriously affected and indeed, until the nineteenth century was well advanced and the malt laws relaxed, the distiller was badly handicapped. Legislation and the excise supervision of these operations in the interests of the revenue gave rise to many complaints by distillers in the first half of the nineteenth century.

---

the residue after distillation, that is, the spent wash. This does not accord with common usage though some dictionaries define it in the same way.

20. At the *Irish Revenue Inquiry, 5th Report,* 1823 and the *Excise Revenue Inquiry, 7th Report, Part I,* 1834, distillers and revenue officials expressed a variety of opinions on the best gravities. In 1823 the range allowed was settled as between 30° and 80° by Geo. 4, c. 94, section 44. For the yield of wort see *Irish Revenue Inquiry, 5th Report,* 1823, p. 268 and Scarisbrick, *Spirit Manual,* 2nd ed. *op. cit.,* pp. 76–8. Unhealthy yeast affects fermentation; it is liable to disease and attacks from parasites (p. 83).

Rigid legal control by excise officers of processes that could not be controlled precisely amounted to harassing. This difficulty has long since disappeared.[21]

From the underback the hot worts are passed over a cooler, of which there are several forms. The temperature is quickly reduced to between 65°F and 80°F because worts at this stage are in a condition which favours infection by deleterious bacteria and wild yeasts and it is imperative to bring the worts into contact with yeast without delay. When this occurs wort is then referred to as distiller's wash. Brewer's yeast is used at the rate of 1 to 2 per cent of the wort. Usually the yeast is spread in the bottom of the fermenting vessel and the wort then run in, but some distillers ran in the wort first. The yeast is broken up before meeting the wort so that it will more easily spread through the wash. Sometimes the yeast is mixed with a little wort before being put in the vessel and the term 'barm' was used for this mixture as well as for yeast. Some distillers also added 'lob' during fermentation. This is a mixture of strong wort and yeast which is allowed to ferment and when in full fermentation it is added to the wash. In Scotland lob was called 'bub' and this term is now used throughout the industry. Some distillers feeling that the addition of lob or bub spoiled the flavour, felt obliged, nevertheless, to add it if fermentation became stubborn.[22]

Yeast, a low form of plant life rather like a fungus, grows by budding and abstraction from sugars in the wash in right conditions, otherwise it is quiescent. Fermentation results from the presence of enzymes or ferments in yeast. It begins slowly and gradually increases until it becomes very active and then dies away as the sugars in the wash are converted into alcohol. Yeast cannot survive if the concentration of alcohol reaches about 19 per cent of the wash. If the distiller finds the yeast is becoming exhausted too soon he may try to revive fermentation by adding

21. *Inquiry into Fees, Perquisites and Emoluments . . . in certain Public Offices in Ireland, 5th Report,* Parl. Pps. 1806–7 (124) vi, p. 141. Donovan, *Domestic Economy, op. cit.,* i, pp. 217–20. Johnston, *Inland Revenue Officer's Manual, op. cit.,* p. 281. Some of the complaints appear in the *Excise Revenue Inquiry, 7th Report, Part I,* 1834, *op. cit.,* pp. 190, 193, 199, 425.

22. *Irish Revenue Inquiry, 5th Report,* 1823, *op. cit.,* pp. 298, 312, 352, 538 (item 23). *Excise Revenue Inquiry, 7th Report, Part I,* 1834, *op. cit.,* pp. 196, 377. Morewood, *Inebriating Liquors, op. cit.,* p. 660. Johnston, *Inland Revenue Officer's Manual, op. cit.,* p. 281.

yeast or bub. During decomposition of the sugars carbon dioxide is given off, but no use was made of this by-product in the nineteenth century.[23]

During fermentation small quantities of higher alcohols are also generated, and some oxidation occurs giving rise to yet other substances, among them acetic acid. If unchecked, or if the wash is not distilled soon after it is ready, further chemical changes would lead to some decomposition which would render the wash useless. The distiller, therefore, excites fermentation rapidly to minimise the formation of acetic acid. He cannot avoid it altogether, but early in the last century, it was discovered that by closing the top of the fermenting vessel to exclude air the formation of acetic acid and other undesirable reactions were much retarded and this became the standard practice of many distillers. Here again, ill-conceived excise controls could seriously hamper the distiller.[24]

The specific gravity of alcohol is less than that of water and much less than that of wash. It follows, therefore, that as alcohol is formed in the wash and carbon dioxide given off, the specific gravity of the wash falls. It has also been established that there is a definite relationship between the fall in gravity and the alcohol content of fermenting wash. This phenomenon, known as attenuation, became an important feature of the distillery laws and the revenue controls over a distiller's operations after 1823. Thus while the gravity of wash is not, by itself, a measure of its spirit content, a comparison of gravities taken at different stages of fermentation is a good indication of the alcohol formed. It is sufficiently close for the law to levy a charge for duty based on the attenuation between the beginning and ending of fermentation. Until 1823 revenue officers took no cognizance of attenua-

23. There are a great number of different 'races' of yeast, many of them harmful to a distiller's fermentation. The enzymes function as a catalyst. Carbon dioxide is now used as 'dry ice' as well as for other purposes. Among many authorities on these points are: J. Scarisbrick, *Spirit Manual, op. cit.,* pp. 82–4; L. W. Marrison, *Wines and Spirits,* Penguin series, London, 1957, p. 74; W. H. Nithsdale and A. J. Manton *Practical Brewing,* Glasgow, 1924, pp. 43 *et seq.* In a paper read in December 1902, Dr A. L. Stern showed that yeast fermentations are most active between 55° and 77°F (*Journal of the Federated Institutes of Brewing,* Vol. viii, No. 6, p. 696). For the distilling aspects see Johnston, *Inland Revenue Officer's Manual, op. cit.,* p. 281.

24. Donovan, *Domestic Economy, op. cit.,* p. 220. Johnston, *Officer's Manual, op. cit.,* pp. 281, 285. Marrison, *Wines and Spirits, op. cit.,* p. 67.

tion and any official assessments were based on the quantity of wash distilled regardless of any gravities. Following a government inquiry in 1823 a charge for duty was raised in Ireland and Scotland on attenuation at the rate of 1 per cent of proof spirit for each 5° attenuation. This was extended to the rest of the United Kingdom in 1825. It was a presumptive charge to be levied only if it exceeded the actual spirit produced.[25]

Full fermentation takes three or four days. If the concentration of the wash is not too great full attenuation will be complete when the gravity is reduced to that of water or slightly lower. It cannot go any further because unfermented heavier matter remains in the wash which counterbalances the alcohol. If the concentration is too great, full fermentation of all fermentable sugars may not occur with consequent loss to the distiller. Such losses were common before 1823 when distillers working on high gravities were not always able to re-activate a flagging fermentation. As one authority put it, 'once the head of yeast falls in the tun, neither the further addition of yeast nor increase of temperature will succeed in resuscitating the fermentation'.[26] If working gravities are reasonable, however, additions of yeast or bub may revive a dying fermentation, but in a well run distillery this situation does not often occur. These are not the only problems concerning the concentration of wash. A wash of low gravity is fully fermented sooner than one of high gravity since the attenuation is less, but the lower the original gravity the more is the formation of acetic acid favoured. Just as the presence of about 19 per cent alcohol inhibits further fermentation, so do extremes of temperature. A temperature of 70°F or slightly higher is most suitable for fermentation.[27] Thus the distiller has quite a range of

25. *Irish Revenue Inquiry, 5th Report*, 1823, *op. cit.* 4 Geo. 4, c. 94, section 46; 6 Geo. 4, c. 80, section 71. See also *Handbook for Officers of Excise*, Loftus publication, London, 1857, pp. 133–45. The present law is contained in 15 and 16 Geo. 6, and 1 Eliz. 2, c. 44, section 95 for Northern Ireland and 43 and 44 Vict.,c.24 for the Republic of Ireland.

26. Donovan, *Domestic Economy, op. cit.*, i, p. 226. The vagaries of fermentation are described by Morewood, *Inebriating Liquors, op. cit.*, p. 660. The reasons for using high gravities despite loss of spirit will be explained in the history for the period 1788 to 1823.

27. *Excise Report to the Treasury on the use of barley, malt . . . in distilleries*, 1847, *op. cit.* Experiments by Dobson and Phillips in 1847 found that fermentation ceased at 187°F. An important investigation and report on the attenuation of wash

choices in his working. Fermented wash made from cereals will
contain from 10 to 15 per cent or more of ethyl alcohol if the
brewing has been efficient. It also contains other volatile substances in small quantities collectively known as fusel oils and, if
a pot still is used, traces of these substances will give the spirit its
distinctive flavour.

The wash is transferred from the fermenting vessels in batches
to a large vat called a wash charger from which it is conveyed to
the wash still. Before 1823 only one still was used for all distilling,
but since then, there have been stills specially set apart for distilling
wash and different stills for subsequent distillations.[28] The distilling
process extracts spirit from wash because of the different boiling
and condensing temperatures of alcohol and water. Anhydrous
alcohol boils at 173°F and water at 212°F. Mixtures will vaporise
at intermediate temperatures but there will always be a larger
proportion of alcohol in vapours at the lower end of the scale.
There is a limit, however, for a mixture of more than approximately 96 per cent alcohol will, if heated, condense in the same
proportions. It is known to the chemist as an azeotropic mixture.
In a pot still wash is boiled in the body of the still, the vapour
passes up through a still head and then on to a coiled pipe immersed in water, called the worm. The still head is exposed to the
air and will be cooler than the rising vapours so that some
condensation will take place and this condensate, which will be
chiefly water, will fall back into the still. If, therefore, a still head
is lengthened or shaped to give greater exposure to the surrounding air more water will be extracted and returned to the
still leaving a richer vapour to be condensed in the worm.
Designers of stills have experimented with this phenomenon and
in fact it is the basic principle of the continuous still.[29]

---

was made in 1852 by Professors Graham, Hofman and Redwood to the Board of
Inland Revenue (see Johnston, *Revenue Manual, op. cit.,* p. 285 and Scarisbrick,
Spirit Manual, op. cit., p. 101).

28. The effective duty before 1823 was on the content of each still and no
distiller could therefore afford to have stills specialising on further distillation. See
49 Geo. 3, c. 99, section 8 which levied a charge on every still.

29. *The Historical Development of Distilling Plant.* A paper read by A. J. V.
Underwood to the Institute of Chemical Engineers on 22 February 1935. The
worm is, of course, a condenser, but another arrangement was to pass incoming
cool wash over the pipe containing the vapours. This both pre-heated the wash

Before 1823 the distillery laws distorted manufacturing processes but since then distillers have been fairly free. Normally the
body of the still, or kettle, is filled to about two-thirds and
heated, the furnace being controlled to ensure that the wash does
not boil too violently. In recent years steam coils have replaced
furnaces in Irish pot stills. The vapours given off will always
contain some secondary products as well as ethyl alcohol, but if
boiled too violently a greater and unwanted proportion of these
volatile substances will reappear in the distillate. All alcohol in
the wash will have been extracted when about one-third of the
contents of the still has been evaporated and at this stage the
temperature of the spent wash will be slightly above the boiling
point of water. If the heat has been well controlled the greater
part of the oily less volatile substances and acetic acid will still be
in the wash when all the spirit has been extracted. The spent wash
and exhausted grain from brewing have a value as cattle food
and their sale is a welcome help in reducing the distiller's costs.[30]

The first distillation was known as singlings in Ireland and in
Great Britain as low wines of the first extraction. When the
distillery laws for the United Kingdom were standardised the
term singlings disappeared from formal use.[31] The strength of low
wines can, of course, vary considerably, depending on the rapidity
of working and whether the flow of the extract is quickly cut
off when spirit ceases to come over. Since 1823 the low wines
have been collected into a special receiver and, after excise
assessment, transferred to another vessel to supply a second still
for distilling into spirits. In the second distillation the first runnings
contain a high proportion of unwanted volatile substances and
are run into a feints receiver. These runnings are known as foreshots and the term 'feints' is used for them and all other rejected

---

and condensed some of the vapours. See the evidence of a distiller in 1834 who
was passing the wash pipe through an intermediate still charger (*Excise Revenue
Inquiry, 7th Report, Part I*, 1834, *op. cit.*, p. 195, item. 3). See also S. Young,
Distillation Principles and Processes, London, 1922, p. 128.

30. Spent wash was referred to as 'draff' or 'still bottoms' by some writers in
the nineteenth century. Sometimes it is called 'lees' as in wine residue, but this
term is normally applied to the residue from the low wines still.

31. *Irish Revenue Inquiry, 5th Report*, p. 257. Some of the Acts before the Union
used the term low wines. For its general use in laws see 43 and 44 Vict., c. 24,
section 3.

runnings. When the distiller considers that the proportion of unwanted substances is sufficiently reduced he switches the flow to a spirit receiver allowing it to proceed till the strength starts to drop. When he thinks this has gone far enough he switches the distillate to the feints receiver. When the distillate contains no spirit, the remaining contents of the still are run to waste. The feints are fed back to subsequent distillations. In Irish practice from the mid-nineteenth century a third distillation on the same lines reduced still further the proportion of fusel oil and improved the flavour of the spirit.[32]

Wash has a tendency to froth during distillation and if boiled too violently this froth may rise and go over with the vapour to clog up the worm. In extreme cases it could cause the steam pressure to rise and risk bursting the still or alternatively it may even cause some of the wash to siphon out of the kettle. These accidents are unlikely in modern stills equipped with safety valves, but was a real risk in the past. Between 1780 and 1823, when the distillery laws favoured rapid distillation, frothing and fouling were serious problems. To prevent them distillers put soap into their stills. After 1823 when the incentive for rapid working was removed, the practice continued on a reduced scale of about 1 lb of soap to 800 gallons of wash. Soap is decomposed by the acetic acid formed in the wash, the fatty parts melt, spread over the surface and inhibit frothing. Some distillers thought that soap affected the flavour of the spirit, but this is doubtful if the quantity of soap is not excessive and boiling is not too violent. A few distillers also added charcoal claiming that it reduced the amount of fusel oil coming over. The final spirit from pot stills from the mid-nineteenth century was in the region of 35° to 40° over proof. Soap is no longer used in Ireland.[33]

32. The strength of low wines was usually from 60° under proof or stronger. Before 1823 Irish law defined feints as spirits below 85° under proof. (*Irish Revenue Inquiry, 5th Report*, 1823, p. 558, item 19). Later it was any spirit run into a feints receiver. See *Truths about Whiskey, op. cit.*, p. 29 on the further distillation of whiskey. See also p. 2 where whiskey is defined as 'a spirit which is distilled from barley or oats, and malt or from a mixture of them, in a pot still, which brings over together with spirit, a variety of flavouring and other ingredients from the grain.'

33. *Irish Revenue Inquiry, 5th Report*, 1823, *op. cit.*, 296–7, 318. Morewood, *Inebriating Liquors, op. cit.*, p. 667. Donovan, *Domestic Economy, op. cit.*, i, 227. Salt and oil of vitriol were also used to cleanse the spirit. Whiskey from three distillations may run off at strengths approaching 50° over proof.

COFFEY'S DISTILLING APPARATUS

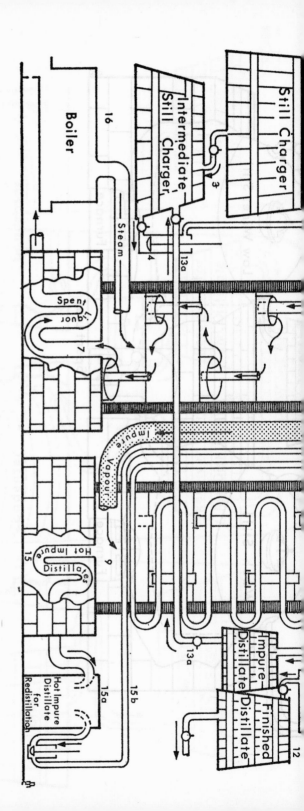

Order of process.—1. Vat for crude liquor. 2. Charger for Still. 3. Additional Charger. 4. Pump. 5. Pipe conveying liquor to be distilled. Col. No. 2 containing No. 5 Pipe, impure Vapour from Col. 1 and spirit plate where hot distillate is drawn off. Col. No. 1 containing liquor descending from diaphragm to diaphragm and ascending steam from boiler. 6. Liquor spreading over diaphragm. 7. Spent liquor. 8. Vapour from steam and liquor to bottom of Col. 2. 9. Vapour ascending to Col. 2. 10. Plate where hot product condensed is drawn off. 11. Hot product condenser. 12. Finished product 13. Impure product for re-distillation. 13ᵃ. Impure product condensed is drawn off and conveyed by 13 and 13ᵃ to Still Charger 15. 14. Uncondensed vapour to be condensed in 14ᵃ and conveyed by 13 and 13ᵃ to Still Charger 15. Impure spirit liquid for re-distillation through 15ᵃ and 15ᵇ to Col. No. 1. 16. Steam boiler. Drawing adapted from *Evidence before the Royal Commission on Whiskey and Other Potable Spirits, 1908.*

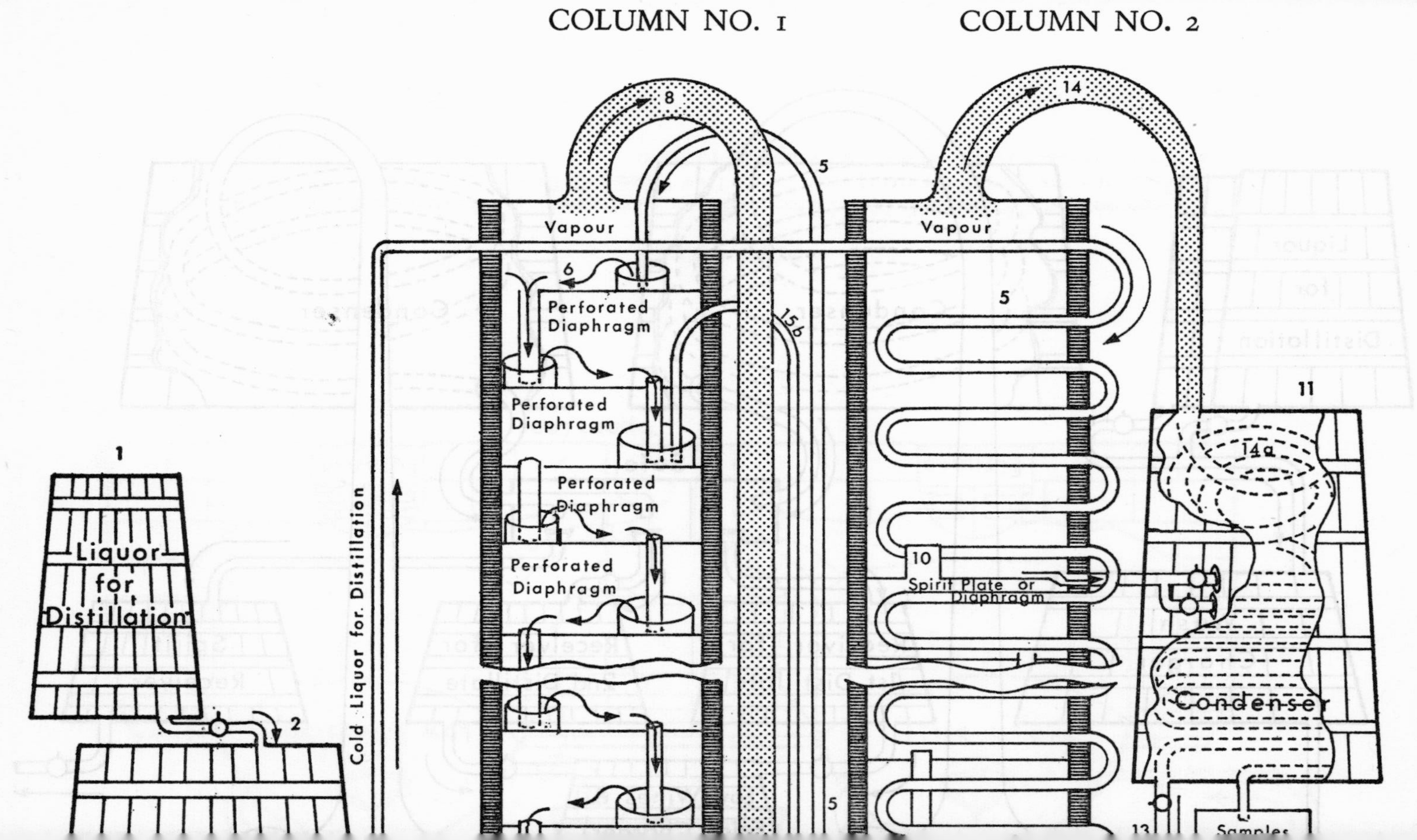

COLUMN NO. 1   COLUMN NO. 2

Liquor for Distillation

1

2

Cold Liquor for Distillation

Perforated Diaphragm

Perforated Diaphragm

Perforated Diaphragm

Perforated Diaphragm

Perforated Diaphragm

6

Vapour

8

15b

5

5

10

Spirit Plate or Diaphragm

5

Vapour

14

13

Sample

Condenser

14a

11

In the late eighteenth and early nineteenth centuries scientists and distillers were trying to evolve a still combining the distillations in pot stills and thus saving fuel. Several types of stills were devised where wash was fed in continuously and alcohol separated off. Aeneas Coffey, an Inspector General of Excise in Ireland who later turned distiller, invented such a still which, after early imperfections had been corrected, proved the most satisfactory and was installed in a number of Irish distilleries. It is still used, especially in Scotland, and is often referred to as the 'patent' still. The Coffey still, patented in 1830, was economical in fuel and labour costs and produced in one operation a distillate directly from wash of more than 60 per cent over proof and very little fusel oil. After improvements in the last century the patent still settled down in its present form producing a spirit of from 66 to 68 per cent over proof. Because of the azeotropic nature of stronger spirit this is very nearly the highest strength that can be obtained by normal distilling. The extract of the patent still therefore contains much less fusel oil. If diluted it tastes insipid. Its principal use is in blending with pot still whiskey. If molasses or other non-cereal materials are used, the chief market to-day is in industry or science.[34]

The treatment of the distillate from a patent still follows a similar pattern to that of a pot still. Spent lees are discarded. Foreshots contain some of the secondary highly volatile substances which have condensing points differing slightly from those of strong ethyl alcohol. Less volatile substances appear as the still is being worked off and the strength drops away. Foreshots and tailings are run into a feints receiver and are than fed back into the wash after sufficient dilution to ensure that the wash will not become too rich in alcohol. If it becomes too rich there is a danger of spirit being lost with the spent wash.

The government of the Irish Republic set up a company in 1938 to make highly purified spirit from potatoes. It is made in an improved continuous still, free of fusel oil, and intended for

---

34. Johnston, *Revenue Manual, op. cit.,* p. 290. Underwood, *Development of Distilling Plant, op. cit.,* pp. 23–4. Absolute alcohol had been obtained in the laboratory before the 19th century, but was not made on an industrial scale till the end of the century. It can be made in a continuous still, with the aid of benzine, by utilising the azeotropic properties of mixtures. Scarisbrick, *Spirit Manual, op. cit.,* p. 91. *Royal Comm. on Whiskey: Evidence,* 1908, p. 176.

B

industrial purposes. The spirit is raised to strengths above 70
over proof by special distillation using benzine as an 'entrainer'.
Benzine and water mix to form an azeotropic liquid with a
boiling point different from a mixture of alcohol and water. This
difference enables water to be abstracted from high strength
spirit. The principal outlet is blending with petrol for motor fuel.
Thus this distilling is completely outside the business of distilling
firms.[35]

New whiskey is harsh and fiery, but, if it is stored for a number
of years in oak casks, subtle and imperfectly understood changes
occur in the minute quantities of ethers, higher alcohols and
other secondary constituents in the spirit. This maturing gives it
a pleasant aroma and makes it smoother to the palate. At one
time the public taste demanded fiery whiskey and indeed it was
sometimes adulterated with oil of vitriol to enhance this effect
as well as to mask dilution.[36] Discriminating consumers, however,
came to prefer a more matured whiskey. Also the fusel oils in
immature whiskey were said to generate violence in intoxication
and some members of parliament pressed for maturing to be
compulsory. As the last century progressed the preference for
matured whiskey grew until by the close of the century all
reputable distillers and dealers matured their whiskey before
marketing it. In 1915 legislation made it obligatory for whiskey
to be at least three years old before it is sold for consumption.
The best Irish whiskey is now matured in cask for much longer.
If the spirits are further manufactured the rule does not apply.
Spirits of any age can, of course, be sold in bond. The Act of
1915 was a war-time measure to reduce stocks coming on the
retail market and was not primarily in the interests of health or
to preserve quality. Maturing adds to the costs of production
since storage space must be provided and the distiller has to wait a
long time for a return on his manufacturing expenses though
there is some compensation from the added value of the whiskey.
The burden of these years for maturing is greatly mitigated by
provisions for storage in warehouses and deferring payment of the
duty, a system first allowed in Ireland in 1804. The three year

35. *Industrial Alcohol Act,* 1938, No. 23.

36. *Truths about Whiskey, op. cit.,* pp. 3, 21. Scarisbrick, *Spirit Manual, op. cit.,*
pp. 95–6. Marrison, *Wines and Spirits, op. cit.,* p. 232. *Irish Revenue Inquiry, 5th
Report,* 1823, *op. cit.,* p. 318.

restriction on delivery from bond also applies to the produce of continuous stills though because it is almost free of fusel oils, long maturing is not so necessary. Grain whiskey does nothing to speed maturing of the whiskey with which it is blended, but in a blend it dilutes the fusel oils of the pot still whiskey and gives a smooth milder taste in a shorter time. Whiskey only matures while it is in casks and after bottling maturing ceases.[37]

Whiskey coming off the still is colourless. In the nineteenth century, especially in the earlier years, the best whiskey was stored and matured in sherry casks as this was thought to give it an additional and desirable flavour. The sherry absorbed in the wood, however, also slightly coloured the spirit and as the public taste for such whiskey grew it became necessary to colour all whiskey whether or not sherry casks were used. Sometimes small quantities of wine were used to colour whiskey, but more often colouring matter such as caramel was employed. In time distillers found that a standard colour for their particular brand was better for marketing purposes and as the colouring from sherry casks was variable the addition of colouring matter became general practice.[38]

After the introduction of grain whiskey from continuous or patent stills, blending with pot still whiskey became an art that developed considerably during the latter part of the nineteenth century. Before that time blending by distillers was not the custom. Casks were sold to retailers as filled at the distillery. In the mid-nineteenth century bonding facilities were extended to allow buying and selling in bond enabling spirit dealers, who bought casks from various distillers, to blend different whiskeys before paying duty and to market the product under their own trade names. As will be seen later this was an important development in the spirit trade. As with colouring, distillers began to aim at a distinctive uniform flavour for their brands and blending became necessary not only with grain whiskey, but with different distillations even from the same pot still which may not always

37. *Parliamentary Debates*, (Hansard) 2 July 1879, cols. 1209 *et seq.* 5 and 6 Geo. 5, c. 46. See also *All about Whiskey*, Dublin, 1957, p. 6. Published by the Irish Pot Still Distillers Association. 44 Geo. 3, c. 104. Marrison, *Wines and Spirits, op. cit.,* p. 232. *Royal Comm. on Whiskey: Evidence, op. cit.,* p. 69.

38. *Truths about Whiskey, op. cit.,* p. 45. The distillers also stated that sham whiskey was made by adding sherry to silent spirit.

be identical in character. Small changes occur for a variety of reasons. There may be differences in the quality or variety of the grain used in the various batches, or in the malt; fermentation may not be exactly the same in each case; or the still may not be operated in the same manner. All these factors can give rise to small variations in the final spirit. Irish whiskey marketed under the name of a distiller normally consists of spirits made in his distillery and if the spirit is solely from pot stills it is sometimes referred to as a straight or self whiskey. The term blended whiskey usually refers to mixtures of spirits from different distilleries or blends of pot still and grain whiskeys. The terms 'grain spirit' or 'grain whiskey' originally meant pot still spirit made from a mixed grain mash. For the past hundred years it has become customary to use the terms for spirit obtained by distillation in continuous stills from cereal grains.[39]

In the last century, when retailers served their customers direct from the cask, distillers sometimes found that their branded casks were refilled with inferior whiskey by unscrupulous dealers thereby injuring their reputation and redress was not easy. John Jameson and Son, Dublin distillers, experienced this kind of fraud and cited a case in 1875 which they claimed was frequent and affected their good name.[40] One way of defeating such impostures was to bottle matured whiskey at the distillery, or while it was still under the distiller's control in a bonded warehouse, and to seal the bottles with a distinctive capsule that would be destroyed when the bottle was opened. Reputable dealers, too, could protect their blends in a similar manner. All this became possible when the law governing bonded and distillers' warehouses was extended in the 1860s to permit bottling in bond and exempting from duty the losses in the operation. As spirit duties rose towards the end of the century this inducement to bottle whiskey in bond before putting it on the retail market became stronger. At the present time the delivery of a cask from bond for consumption is extremely rare.[41]

39. The use of these terms is merely a trade custom and they sometimes appear in trade advertisements.

40. *Truths about Whiskey, op. cit.,* pp. 96–9. *Royal Comm. on Whiskey, Evidence,* 1908, *op. cit.,* p. 52.

41. Bottling in bond for export was allowed in 1864 by 27 and 28 Vict., c. 12 and this was extended to bottling for the home market in 1867 by 30 and 31 Vict., c. 27.

Bottling is a relatively simple operation. It consists merely of reducing the matured whiskey to the desired strength and running it into bottles of standard sizes. Sometimes considerable care is taken in the choice of the water used for reducing. Filling was done by merely holding one bottle after another under a cock inserted in the store cask and this primitive method could still be seen until quite recently in small warehouses. In distilleries and modern large warehouses, however, bottling is done on a mass production scale, using large supply vats, filters, and bottling and labelling machinery. These have developed since about the middle of the last century.[42]

The reputed 'peaty' or 'smoky' flavour of Irish whiskey has been attributed to the use of peat as fuel for the kilns when drying malt and in distilling. But as most legal distillers in the nineteenth century used coal, any peaty flavour was, more probably, acquired from the water used. The distilleries in Scotland are also mainly in peaty districts and a similar flavour might be expected in Scotch whisky. Persons in the vicinity of Highland distilleries where the malt whiskies are highly flavoured would easily notice the difference between the local and other whiskies, and to a lesser extent this would apply to drinkers in Islay. Apart from them, the truth is that today most people have not got such discriminating palates, especially as the quality of all well-known whiskey is now so high. For such people the differences between properly matured pot still whiskey would be hard to distinguish wherever it is made, particularly as a pure malt pot still whiskey is rarely available except, perhaps, in the north of Ireland. A more sensitive palate would notice a difference between a malt and mixed grain whiskey. They might more easily distinguish between a blend of pot still and patent whiskey and a self whiskey because there will probably be rather less flavour in the former and hence is regarded as milder. In general the public preference more often depends on the label on the bottle than on its contents. The custom of adding aerated waters to whiskey, a practice that has grown since the beginning of this century, has also blurred differences in flavour.

42. A large bottling plant with the most modern equipment has been erected on the outskirts of Dublin very recently by the Dublin distillers. Another modern plant was installed at Bushmills in 1968. Large plants operate in some Scottish warehouses dealing with the very big export trade. Barnard, *Whiskey Distilleries, op. cit.*, Bottling plants are advertised.

Illicit spirit, or poteen, in the earlier part of the nineteenth century was a malt spirit. Peat fuel was used for malting and distilling and it was said to derive its particular flavour from this fact. This may be true to a limited extent, but the flavour of poteen must also have been influenced by inefficient malting, crude apparatus, haphazard methods of fermentation and a 'rule of thumb' control of distillation. Good quality poteen must have required great skill and some luck and most poteen must have had a variety of strong flavours in addition to a peaty taste.[43]

A number of flavoured and sweetened beverages are made from the plain spirit coming from a distillery. Before the nineteenth century the distiller made these drinks himself and also made a purified strong spirit, known as spirits of wine, for industrial and scientific uses, but in 1805 these further processes were confined to specialised rectifiers and compounders. In 1807 the rectifier and the compounder were treated as separate trades but the distinction disappeared in 1828. Thereafter rectifying and compounding have been conducted on the same premises and, since 1880, all the products, except spirits of wine, have been called British compounds for revenue purposes. In the Irish Republic the word 'British' has been dropped.[44]

The early nineteenth century Irish rectifier used a small pot still in much the same way as a distiller distilling low wines. He made two products: spirits of wine and unsweetened flavoured beverages. Spirits of wine was made by adding crude alkali potash, known as 'grey salts', to the raw spirit. Pearl ash or carbonate of potash, referred to as 'white salts', might also be added. These substances have an affinity for water and help to strengthen the distillate. Foreshots and tailings would remove most of the fusel oil and sometimes charcoal was put into the still as a further purifier. Two or three such distillations resulted in a strong rectified spirit. The advent in the 1830s of the continuous still

43. *Irish Revenue Inquiry, 5th Report, op. cit.*, p. 308. On p. 378 there is a classified list of distilleries in 1823 showing the kind of fuel used. *Excise Revenue Inquiry, 7th Report, Part I,* 1834, *op. cit.*, p. 71, 190. Donovan, *Domestic Economy, op. cit.*, i, pp. 252–5. *Royal Comm. on Whiskey; Evidence,* 1908, *op. cit.*, pp. 88, 203, 210, 353, 370.

44. 45 Geo. 3, c. 104, section 12. The trades were separated in 1807 by 47 Geo. 3, sess. 2, c. 19, section 3. This was repealed by 9 Geo. 4, c. 45 which applied the English law to Ireland. 43 and 44 Vict., c. 24, section 3 defines British compounds.

and its subsequent legal recognition in distilleries undermined the rectifier's market for spirits of wine. To make beverages one distillation is generally sufficient. Depending on the particular drink the rectifier added a variety of ingredients to the raw spirit. Common ingredients were juniper berries, corriander seed and aniseed and, perhaps, flavourings that were guarded trade secrets. After suitable steeping the mixture was distilled and the aroma and flavouring imparted by the ingredients would be carried over in the distillate.When the law distinguished between a rectifier and compounder the latter made a sweetened product. Like the rectifier he distilled raw spirits, sometimes with other ingredients, and then added sugar, honey or other sweetening matter and, perhaps, flavouring essences to make liqueurs and similar drinks. Cheap British brandy was said to be no more than diluted rectified spirit coloured with burnt sugar. Rectifiers and compounders also made medicinal preparations and tinctures from raw spirit.[45]

In Ireland rectifying and compounding never approached the scale of whiskey production. The local market was limited and the main hope for Irish rectifying houses was the large English gin market, particularly in the early nineteenth century. This lucrative outlet was denied to them by the revenue laws of both countries until 1858 and by that time it was too late for the Irish rectifier, working on a small scale, to have any hope of success against the large houses in England with their well established markets.[46]

The only other manufacturing process of any importance was making methylated spirits which was authorised in 1855. Potable spirits were denatured by adding impure methyl alcohol, render-

---

45. Johnston, *Officer's Manual, op. cit.*, pp. 300–1. See *Inquiry into Fees . . . in certain public offices in Ireland, 5th Report*, Parl. Pps. 1806–7 (124) vi, p. 222 where a Dublin rectifier said that he made imitation rum, brandy and geneva by distillation, and shrub by compounding rectified spirit with an equal quantity of water, fruit juices and sugar. 6 and 7 Will. 4, c. 72 deals with certain difficulties over the rates of duty on tinctures and medicinal compounds. 6 Edw. 7, c. 20, defines tinctures, includes flavouring essences and perfumed spirits.

46. *Inquiry into Fees in Ireland, 5th Report*, 1806–7, *op. cit.*, pp. 204–5 shows the number and sizes of stills in distilleries and rectifying houses. The latter were working on a much smaller scale. See the *Excise Revenue Inquiry, 7th Report, Part I*, 1834, *op. cit.*, pp. 189, 200–2 and *Part II*, Parl. Pps. 1835 (8) xxx, p. 56, where rectifiers describe their difficulties in entering the English market.

ing the spirit nauseous. Such spirit could be used duty free in
industry. Irish distillers did not undertake methylating to any
significant extent before this century nor did more than one or
two independent methylators operate in Ireland. Apparently the
demand was mainly satisfied by imports from England.[47]

47. The methylating Act was 18 and 19 Vict., c. 38. The annual *Inland Revenue
Reports* show no more than one methylated spirit maker for most years. Sometimes there were none. During the present century a great many industrial uses
for alcohol have been discovered. It is a raw material for chemical conversion
into various solvents, for example, and revenue laws have had to be adapted
accordingly.

CHAPTER II

DISTILLERY APPARATUS

LITTLE is known about the apparatus used by distillers before the latter part of the eighteenth century, but from Acts of parliament and the journals of the House of Commons some knowledge can be gleaned. It is clear, for instance, that each distillery operated on a very small scale and that some vessels served more than one purpose. When a minimum spirit duty was levied on the size of stills a better picture of these early distilleries can be seen. During the period of these laws, from 1780 to 1823, distillers exercised considerable ingenuity both in the brewing and distilling processes in order to exceed this minimum because ineffectual excise controls enabled the distillers to evade duty on the excess spirits produced. The result was improvements and adaptations of apparatus.[1] For the rest of the nineteenth century the distillery laws permitted more freedom for these changes, new types of apparatus were invented and the modern distillery emerged. There were similar conditions in Scotland and it can be assumed that knowledge of new methods or apparatus in either country would be diffused in both countries so that changes in Ireland, particularly in stills, cannot be treated in isolation.[2] Most changes would be gradual, perhaps a series of minor improvements, and in many instances it would be impossible to fix the time of a particular change or where it happened. Thus the manual stirring of mash by 'oars' was replaced by mechanical rakes and these were probably manually

1. The Acts imposing and repealing the duty on stills were 19 and 20 Geo. 3, c. 12 and 4 Geo. 4, c. 94.

2. The interaction of distilling practices in Ireland and Scotland is shown in government inquiries, especially in the *Inquiry into the Revenue arising in Ireland, 5th Report,* Parl. Pps. 1823 (405) vii.

operated until the introduction of power either by windmill, water or steam.[3] Occasionally the time of a major change can be determined. Thus the invention of the Coffey still can be fixed from the date of the patent, but even in this case there is no evidence of who or what distillery first used it, though its general use in several distilleries a few years later is established by a government return. These points will be elaborated when describing the history of the distilling industry, but as a preliminary it will be convenient to describe the plant of a distillery with particular reference to the nineteenth century. This should reduce the need later to explain technical terms and interpolate descriptions though at the risk of some repetition.

Malting, the distiller's first process, is as ancient as making ale. Little information is extant about malting before the late eighteenth century, but it is likely to have consisted of merely steeping barley, spreading it roughly on any sheltered floor to germinate and drying it in some kind of oven. Very like the processes of the illicit maltster of the nineteenth century.[4] Improvements in methods and utensils were probably imported from England by some distillers and maltsters where, from 1697, there had been malt laws that prescribed utensils and processing. Much more precise information on Irish malting became available from 1785 when a malt duty was imposed. The terms of the law would almost certainly have drawn on English experience and been fitted into existing Irish practices. For economy in administration and revenue safety minimum sizes and construction specifications were prescribed for the vessels used.[5]

3. A windmill was in Roe's distillery in Dublin before steam power was introduced. (*Truths about Whiskey,* Dublin, 1878, p. 7, published by four Dublin distillers, John Jameson, William Jameson, John Power and George Roe.) J. O'Brien, *Economic History of Ireland from the Union to the Famine,* London, 1921, p. 414. states that the first steam engine made in Ireland in the first decade of the nineteenth century was designed for use in a Drogheda distillery.

4. For a description of illicit malting see *S.C. to consider extending the functions of the Constabulary in Ireland to the suppression of Illicit Distillation,* Parl. Pps. 1854 (53) x, p. 30.

5. The English statute imposing a malt duty of 6d a winchester bushel in 1697 was 8 and 9 Will, 3, c. 22. Under section 4 cisterns were to be gauged. In 1702 the English statute, 1 Anne, stat. 2, c. 3, refers to altering the kiln or the cistern. In 1712, 12 Anne, c. 2 forbad compressing material in the cistern or the couch. Subsequent Acts built up various excise regulations that clearly accorded with trade practices. They were repeated in the Irish Act of 25 Geo. 3, c. 3, expanded

The four distinct stages in malting are steeping, couching, flooring and kiln-drying. The cistern for steeping the barley in the nineteenth century had to be rectangular, with perpendicular sides, a flat bottom with a slope, or drip, of not more than half an inch per foot to the draining hole and a total depth of not more than forty inches. It had to be large enough to contain twenty-five barrels of barley. Couching and flooring were done in a vessel or frame. The frame had to be rectangular with rigidly supported sides that would not alter in shape when filled with grain. One side of the couch frame could be removable. When the grain was finally spread thinly for germinating it was called a floor. The specification for kiln floors was prescribed in 1795. They had to be constructed with floors of iron wire mesh or perforated plates. The mesh or perforations were too small for malt to pass through, but enabled hot air surrounding the flues to pass upward through the spread malt. After 1880, when the malt duty was repealed, maltsters were free to construct their plant in any way they wished, but visits to long established distilleries show that the old usages have not changed much. Turning over the malt in the kilns, an arduous job in fairly high temperatures, has been made easier by using mechanical rakes or using a forced draught of hot air, but couching and flooring are very much as they were a century ago.[6]

Materials for the grist have to be broken down. Malt is crushed or bruised rather than ground as the object is to detach the husk and reduce the malt to fairly large particles. Raw grain, however, is finely ground in order to permeate the malt in the mixture. The coarser crushed malt also helps to keep the mash open and

---

and adapted to Irish conditions by 35 Geo. 3, c. 41, sections 30–32 and finally assimilated with the regulations in Great Britain by 7 and 8 Geo. 4, c. 52 in 1827. The change from kiln drying by direct hot furnace gases to indirect drying by hot air controlled by fans occurred towards the end of the eighteenth century (*Report on Distilleries in Scotland,* 1799, app. M).

6. M. Donovan, *Domestic Economy,* Dublin, 1830, i, pp. 77–84, describes the restrictions on the construction of vessels. See also W. H. Johnston, *Inland Revenue. Officer's Manual,* Loftus publications, London, 1873, pp. 265–9; and *13th Inland Revenue Report,* Parl Pps. 1870 (c. 82)x, p. 235. The malt houses of J. Jameson and Son, Dublin, or at Bushmills distillery, county Antrim, are good examples of present methods. See also an article on malt in the *Encyclopaedia Britannica* where modern mechanical methods are described that differ materially from the old methods.

stops it from 'setting' or forming a paste which would inhibit proper fermentation. Fine grinding of raw grain presents no problem, but crushing malt properly is not so easy. Originally common mill stones were used for malt, but this was only partially successful for no matter how carefully the space between the mill stones was set some malt was powdered and some almost escaped bruising. Grooved metal cylinders were also tried and were probably superior to mill stones. It was found from experience that smooth iron or steel rollers were best for the process and, in fact, this method was enforced by regulation for brewers.[7] Modern milling machines can be adjusted to grind to any desired size of particle.

The plant used in both the brewing and distilling processes altered a great deal in the eighteenth and nineteenth centuries. Changes in methods and improvements in the brewing apparatus in distilleries ran parallel with those in breweries since the processes are alike. Thus the manufacturer of a patent wort cooler, for example, would bring it to the notice of both distillers and brewers. On the distilling side the changes in techniques and apparatus have been greater. The oldest apparatus, the pot still, consisted of a container or kettle set over a fire with a head fitted to the top. From the head the rising vapours were conveyed to a worm, a spiral pipe immersed in cold water, where the vapours were condensed. This basic arrangement has remained, but there have been considerable changes in operating methods and in the shape and size of stills. At the present time most Irish whiskey comes from pot stills. Using a pot still is a batch process since the residue of each charge of a kettle must be emptied and the kettle refilled before further distilling. By 1830 a suitable still was evolved whereby distilling was continuous and the still itself was completely different in appearance to the pot still.

In the eighteenth century the kettle of the pot still was often used for brewing processes, heating water for mashing, mashing and fermenting, draining off the wash and, after cleansing, returning the wash for distillation. The distillate was collected, the still cleared of residue and the low wines returned for a second distillation. All this was possible with the small scale of

7. Donovan, *Domestic Economy, op. cit.,* i, p. 217, describes these developments. See also Johnston, *Officer's Manual, op. cit.,* p. 278.

the operations of that period. From 1780 to 1823 the distillery laws encouraged distillers to work as rapidly as possible and as the spirit duty was usually assessed on the still capacity, its use for brewing became too costly. After 1823 the spirit duty was based on actual production and this permitted distillers to use separate stills for distilling wash and low wines.[8] Much larger stills resulted and to feed them required a larger brewing plant with separate vessels for each brewing stage. Thus in the nineteenth century each process had its own specialised utensils and a description of the apparatus in this period can be adapted to explain earlier distilling practices. Some of the terms for these vessels may be a little confusing. The vats used in the brewing processes were referred to as tuns or backs in the earlier laws, and distillers and officials giving evidence before government inquiries generally called the vessels for fermenting wash the wash backs. Later nineteenth century laws referred to them as fermenting vessels. The mashing vessel is always referred to either as the mash tun or by its older name the mash kieve, and the wort from this vessel is collected in the underback. Possibly the term 'tun' derives from the large wine tun which may have been used as a brewing vessel at a time when distilleries were very small. Normally tuns or backs were, and many still are, coopered vessels, and, like casks, made of oak though this is not essential, and in the latter half of the nineteenth century cast iron vessels were used in a number of Irish distilleries. Wash backs were not usually made of iron probably because of the possibility of the metal being attacked by acids during fermentation and also because wooden vessels do not dissipate heat so rapidly.[9]

During the mashing process the mash must be continually stirred and in the small distilleries of the eighteenth and early nineteenth centuries this was done by hand operated 'oars'. After 1823, with larger distilling plant, power was essential.

8. These changes will later be described in detail.

9. A. Barnard, *The Whisky Distilleries of the United Kingdom*, London, 1887. Examples are given of iron mash tuns, underbacks and worm tubs and other vessels on pp. 402, 427 and 428 and in some of the advertisements. The derivation of the term 'tun' is conjecture. A wine tun was regarded as 252 gallons in 18th century revenue accounts (see, for example, *Irish House of Commons Journal*, 25 November 1769, statistics on p. 334).

Large mash tuns were fitted with power driven rotating rakes. Some of these mash tuns later in the century had a capacity of up to 100,000 gallons. These large vessels were fitted with a false bottom made up in sections for easy removal and perforated so that the worts could be drained off to the underback. After removing the spent grains, the false bottom was taken out and the mash tun cleansed.[10]

From the underback the worts were transferred to coolers in order to reduce the temperature as quickly as possible to a point suitable for fermentation and thus minimise the danger of infection from air-borne bacteria. At the same time some aeration is needed. The early cooler, which may still be seen, consisted of a large floor over which the wort flowed to an outlet leading to the wash backs, and cooling was hastened and partly controlled by a current of air from ventilators or by fans. In the latter part of the nineteenth century various patent refrigerators were also used. Their principle was to allow the wort to flow over pipes in which cold water was circulating or vice versa. There were other variations of heat exchangers, but the object was the same, to cool and aerate the wort quickly.[11]

Fermentation is a slow process requiring some three or four days during which an even temperature must be maintained. This must have been a problem before 1823 for in small scale operations temperature could drop fairly quickly. After that year with much larger wash backs, as large as 20,000 gallons capacity even in 1834, this was not so difficult, but was still a

10. Donovan, *Domestic Economy, op. cit.,* i, p. 224. A. Barnard, *Whisky Distilleries, op. cit.,* p. 372. Marrowbone Lane distillery had two mash tuns each of 100,000 gallons. The mash house is illustrated. An advertisement by Llewellins and James illustrates a cast iron mashing machine. F. Acum, *Treatise on the Art of Brewing,* London, 1821. In a preface is an illustration of a wooden mash tun with stirring rakes and an iron underback as used in a brewery. Irish distilleries were not likely to use very elaborate machinery till after 1823 when the law permitted them to use larger vessels.

11. *Inquiry into Fees, Gratuities, Perquisites and Emoluments received in Public Offices in Ireland,* Parl. Pps. 1806–7 (124) vi, p. 141 describes coolers. See also Johnston, *Revenue Manual, op. cit.,* p. 281. S. Morewood, *A Philosophical and Statistical History of Inebriating Liquors,* Dublin, 1838, p. 660; J. A. Nettleton, *The Manufacture of Spirit,* London, 1893, pp. 41–3 and a description of cooling tanks on p. 106; Barnard, *Whisky Distilleries,* makes several references to coolers and refrigerators, for example on pp. 402, 411, 436. The patent refrigerator most used in Ireland is illustrated in the advertisement of R. Morton and Co.

problem and distillers in the first half of the century complained that the distillery laws made no allowance for winter and summer working when daily temperatures affected fermentation. To overcome this, attemperating coils were sometimes fitted in wash backs and through these coils either warm or cold water circulated and controlled the temperature of the wash. Distillers referred to bub in various government inquiries and the distillery laws restricted its use as an aid to fermentation. Its manufacture required no special apparatus. All that was needed was a special vessel set aside to ferment small quantities of wort which, when in violent fermentation, were added to wash backs. When fermentation of wash was complete, the wash was run into a wash charger, a vessel similar to a wash back and from which the wash was piped to the still house. In some cases there was a further vessel interposed between the wash charger and the wash still called an intermediate still charger. This was simply a head tank to ensure a constant supply of wash to the still and was specially useful with the continuous still.[12]

Any kind of enclosed copper or other vessel can be used as a still kettle and in the history of distilling the kettle has had a variety of shapes. Not much is known of the kind of stills used in Ireland before the nineteenth century, but the wording of statutes does indicate something approximating to the familiar onion shape of modern pot stills. The usual reference in these laws was to 'stills, alembics or black pots'. Alembic probably means the form of distilling apparatus used by the chemist, a spherical body and a tube bent over to take off the vapours. The term 'black pot' might mean anything other than the alembic, perhaps a small copper.[13] After 1780, when a minimum spirit duty was levied on the still content and there were regulations governing certain features in its construction, the picture gets

---

12. *Inquiry into the Excise Establishment and the Management and Collection of the Excise Revenue throughout the United Kingdom, 7th Report, Part I*, Parl. Pps. 1834 (7) xxv, p. 196. Barnard, *Whisky Distilleries*, p. 355 refers to wash backs at John's Street distillery, Dublin, as circular timber vessels fitted with attemperating coils. Intermediate still chargers are referred to on pp. 402, 406, 411. The *Irish Revenue Inquiry, 5th Report*, 1823, *op. cit.*, p. 555, item 1 lists the various vessels used in the early nineteenth century.

13. Barnard, *Whisky Distilleries, op. cit.* Facing p. 1 is an illustration of a still of 1729 which approximates in shape to the modern pot still. Alembics and black pots are referred to in an Irish statute in 1731, 5 Geo. 2, c. 3, section 3.

clearer. For the next forty years distillers showed considerable ingenuity in adapting their stills to very rapid work and the shape of the kettle became a cylinder of large diameter and little height until the law required the diameter to be not greater than three times the height.[14] Since 1823 distillers have been free to develop their stills both in size and shape. The kettle of the pot still became spherical with a slightly concave base and set in the brickwork of the furnace under it. Later in the nineteenth century some stills were heated by steam coils inside the kettle instead of by fire, an improvement which reduced the risk of residue burning. In the coal fired distillery this danger was countered by scouring chains revolving by mechanical contrivances. There were other devices such as a safety valve to prevent an accidental rise in pressure damaging the still. There was also, of course, a charging cock and another for empting the still of spent wash as well as a man-hole to permit cleaning. Until the latter part of the nineteenth century many distillers added soap to prevent frothing by merely throwing it in, but later illustrations of wash stills show the modern soap box fixed outside the still from which a tube entered the kettle permitting liquid soap to be added while the still was operating.[15] Soap is no longer used in Irish stills.

The still head is fitted to a hole in the top of the kettle and like the kettle there were a variety of shapes before 1823 from a large diameter straight pipe to a conical shape which became

14. *Select Committee to inquire into the Regulations governing drawbacks . . . in Great Britain and Ireland,* Parl Pps. 1809 (199) iii, p. 296. A 500 gallon still is described as 70 inches diameter at the bottom, 74 inches at the top and 24½ inches deep. S. Morewood, *Inventions and Customs in the use of Inebriating Liquors,* London, 1824, p. 356, gives an illustration of an old Irish still similar to that described in the report of the Select Committee. The law regulating dimensions was passed in 1804, 44 Geo. 3, c. 103, section 2. See also the *Report on Distilleries in Scotland,* 1799, p. 453 giving a description of Millar's still at a time when Scottish distillery laws were similar to those in Ireland. In this still there were several outlets for vapours from a flat kettle and all leading into a still head. A charge of 16 gallons was distilled in less than 3 minutes.

15. Barnard, *Whisky Distilleries, op. cit.,* p. 413 refers to two stills in a Cork distillery heated internally by steam coils. The advertisement by Daniel Millar and Co., Dublin coppersmiths, depicts a pot still set in the brickwork of the furnace showing the safety valve and other fittings. *Irish Revenue Inquiry, 5th Report,* 1823, *op. cit.,* p. 295, refers to a pot still in Roscrea in 1818 that was heated by a steam jacket. See also A. J. V. Underwood, *The Historical Development of Distilling Plant,* in a paper read to the Institute of Chemical Engineers on 22 February 1935, p. 23, which refers to scouring chains in the eighteenth and nineteenth centuries.

the standard later. During distillation some vapours condense on the walls of the head and drip back into the kettle and since the temperature of the head is fairly high this condensate contains practically no alcohol. Consequently some distillers regard the shape of the combined kettle and head as having some bearing on the quality of their product. From about 1870, the cone has usually been very wide where it joins the kettle and an anti-collapse valve has also been fitted since an error in operating might cause a vacuum in the still. Until the early part of the nineteenth century the junction of the kettle and head was sealed by paste made up of linseed meal and water and enabled the head to be easily removed when these small stills were being cleaned. The large stills after 1823 had a man-hole in the breast of the still for this purpose and the head was riveted to the kettle.[16]

In a certain Highland distillery a visitor will see a pot still with the head slightly tilted. There is a story told among distillers that in the last century a tipsy coppersmith erecting a still set the head askew. The distiller obtained such an excellent whisky that the error was never corrected. When this still was worn out the distiller insisted that the replacement must be exactly the same. He was, apparently, afraid to risk the quality of his highly prized whisky. The story may not be wholly true, but other distillers have often patched up stills till they could be patched no more for similar reasons and the story is a striking illustration of the concern of some distillers for the shape of their stills.

Illustrations of nineteenth-century pot stills sometimes show the top of the still head turning down and joined to a pipe leading to the condensing worm. This structure, which could help to arrest foam, is sometimes referred to as the 'beak' or 'swan neck' from its appearance and like the joint between kettle and still head was sealed by linseed meal paste and later by riveting.[17] In

16. Donovan, *Domestic Economy, op. cit.*, i, pp. 229–32, describes the pot still of 1830 and sealing the joints, p. 235 refers to the early condensation in the head. Johnston, *Inland Revenue Officer's Manual*, 1873 *op. cit.*, p. 290, also mentions efforts to cause more condensation in the head. Some present day distillers are sensitive to the relation between still design and quality to the extent of patching up a worn still rather than replacing it for fear that a new still may not be quite the same. Still head characteristics are examined by S. Young, *Distillation Principles and Processes*, London, 1922, p. 128.

17. In 1812 an Act, 52 Geo. 3, c. 48, section 8, required the still content to be measured from a point where the neck of the head turns down at 45° to the

some Irish distilleries the still head was short and of large diameter. The vapour pipe was long and passed through a trough of water on its way to the worm. Some condensation of water and less volatile by-products would occur at this point. Also if any froth or liquid bubbled out of the still kettle it would be trapped. A thin return pipe was fitted to convey these liquids back to the still. If desired the distiller could ignore this refinement by closing a cock on the return pipe. This kind of vapour pipe is known as a 'lyne arm' and can still be seen in the large distilleries in Dublin and Midleton.

The worm itself is immersed in cooling water in a worm tub, the diameter of the coils getting smaller as the pipe reaches the bottom and emerges on its way to the spirit safe. Until 1823 spirit could be run direct from the end of the worm to a receiving vessel, but the distiller was free to interpose an arrangement of sampling jars, if he wished, in order to control his distillation. He could arrange for a can to be placed in a pit under the pipe to the receiving vessel to obtain his samples and it is probable that this is the origin of the term 'can-pit'.

From a distiller's sampling point the can-pit became a controlling point for the excise officer in 1823. The sample jars were enclosed in a box with glass sides, known as the spirit safe, and secured by revenue locks. Each jar was set in a sump from which the overflowing spirit could be drained off. The pipe from each still led directly into the safe, discharged into a separate jar and was drained off through an exit pipe. By a system of control cocks the emerging spirit could be diverted at will to a low wines, feints or spirit receiver. The distiller did not now have access to his extract but by placing a hydrometer and thermometer in each jar he could keep a continuous check on the strength and appearance of his spirit. This arrangement for securing the worm's end or tail of a still was a key point of control for

---

worm. This bend was not always present and an old Irish still depicted by Morewood shows a right angle bend (*Inebriating Liquors,* 1838, p. 657). Modern low wines stills leading to a condenser usually have a right angle lead from the still head. Barnard, *Whisky Distillers, op. cit.,* pp. 58, 101, 360 illustrate the variety of shapes of still heads and also the straight right angled pipe to the worm. On p. 60 he describes a special low wines still head designed for partially condensing the rising vapours. See also *Royal Commission on Whiskey and other Potable Spirits Evidence,* Parl. Pps. 1908 (Cd. 4181), pp. 4, 55, 62, 66, 129.

both distiller and the excise and still operates in every distillery.[18]

Receivers are merely large vats and, since 1823, wholly enclosed and secured by revenue locks. From as early as 1717 the capacities of these vats were measured so that increases and decreases of low wines could be ascertained. The precise method of assessing charges is not known, but in time the wet dip was used and, with a proper calibration of the vessel, a dip will disclose the liquid contained within a very small margin of error. When the receivers were enclosed the law prescribed the size of a small aperture in the cover through which was fitted a dip rod and by this means the quantity contained can be read off at any time without opening up the receiver.[19] Dip rods are now permanent fittings, counterbalanced by a weight, and cannot be wholly withdrawn from the receiver. Following on experiments in Carrickfergus in 1818 an indicator was evolved. This was a device which prevented the charging and discharging cocks of a receiver being opened at the same time and also recorded each turning of either cock, but it was not made a compulsory fitting till 1853.[20] From the low wines and the feints receivers the spirit was conveyed to a low wines and feints charger which supplied the low wines still. When a third distillation took place there was a similar arrangement and the still was sometimes referred to as the spirit still.[21] The final destination of spirit was the spirit store which needs no explanation. This was first made compulsory in 1805, but was not put under close revenue supervision until 1853. In the store were vats or casks from which the finished spirit was delivered either for consump-

18. Enclosing the spirit safe in 1823 applied only to the worm from the low wines still, 4 Geo. 4, c. 94, section 26. Evidence at the *Excise Revenue Inquiry, 7th Report, Part I*, 1834, on pp. 151, 402, 425 showed a weakness in revenue control and in 1860 the spirit safe system was extended to all distillations by 23 and 24 Vict., c. 114, section 23. These arrangements remain today. The can-pit room is a special feature of Power's Distillery, Dublin.

19. 4 Geo. 4, c. 94, section 20. There was, of course, a manhole secured by revenue lock to enable samples to be drawn and to permit cleaning.

20. *Experiments in Distillation by the Excise Department*, Parl. Pps. 1821 (538) xix, pp. 369–71. 16 and 17 Vict., c. 37, section 32. The indicator is fully described by J. Owens, *Plain Papers*, London, 1879, p. 287. The indicator is not now used in Northern Ireland.

21. Barnard, *Whisky Distilleries*, uses this term. See pp. 422, 424, 436.

tion or to a bonded warehouse. Delivery for consumption is now extremely rare.[22]

In the early years of the nineteenth century the excessive amounts of coal used in distilleries gave rise to several inventions designed to reduce fuel consumption. Excise officials conducting experiments in 1821 reported that under the rapid distilling system in Ireland at that time about seven-eighths of the fuel used could be saved with slower processes.[23] This was certainly an incentive for invention, but there was a move towards improved methods apart from the special circumstances in Ireland. The main trend of these inventions was to obtain continuous distillation from wash to spirit in one operation and Morewood records inventors in several countries, two of them in Ireland, Joseph Shee of Cork and M. Stein of Clonmel. Shee used four pot stills in series, the first heated by fire and the others by the hot vapours from the first still.[24] It was not strictly a continuous still and its main purpose was to conserve fuel. Sir Anthony Perrier of Cork was among the early inventors of a truly continuous still. His patent granted in 1822 was to allow the wash to flow in a thin stream over a heated surface with baffles and to blow steam through it, the steam taking off with it the spirituous vapours. Underwood in an historical paper on distilling techniques considered that amongst the most important advances leading to the continuous still was an invention by Adams. In this arrangement there was a series of egg shaped containers. Wash entered the first container and passed on to others. Meanwhile steam entered the last container and bubbled up through the incoming wash and over to the next container and so on, the vapour getting richer in alcohol on its journey and the wash weaker. The final vapour emerging was then condensed.[25]

22. 45 Geo. 3, c. 104, section 27; 16 and 17 Vict., c. 37, sections 8, 9.

23. *Distilling Experiments*, 1821, *op. cit.*, p. 372. See also the *Newry Magazine*, vol. iv, March–April, 1818, p. 53 where it states that the expense of making spirit was 6d. a gallon of which 4d. was for coal. This excluded the cost of materials.

24. S. Morewood, *Inebriating Liquors*, 1838, *op. cit.*, pp. 635 *et seq.*, see also Underwood, *Historical Development of Distilling Plant*, *op. cit.*, 23–4. In a *Return of Licensed Distillers*, Parl. Pps. 1851 (386) liii, on p. 269 a Shee apparatus is shown as in operation in Cork. Donovan, *Domestic Economy*, *op. cit.*, i, pp. 235–6 describes several patent stills.

25. Underwood, *Distilling Plant*, *op. cit.*, pp. 24, 27.

According to Morewood the first successful attempt to construct a continuous still was made in the first decade of the nineteenth century by St Marc in France who brought his idea to England in 1823 but failed to get it accepted. After improvements the patent was sold to J. B. Sharp and this still found its way to Ireland. In this still spirit was made in one distillation by passing steam through incoming wash and it was claimed that by eliminating the bad vapours arising from direct fire a purer spirit was obtained. One of these stills was at work in Belfast in 1834.[26] There were other inventions, particularly in France, and eventually in 1830 Aeneas Coffey, a former senior excise official in Ireland, patented a still that soon came into general use in several Irish distilleries and its use spread to Scotland. An improved version is used today to distil grain whiskey for blending.[27] Coffey may have been influenced by a successful continuous still evolved in France in 1813 by Cellier-Blumenthal for the same principle and some of the features of the latter still were repeated in the Coffey still, particularly the first version of it. The Cellier-Blumenthal still had the usual kettle for the wash, but instead of a still head there was a long cylindrical column, the upper part of which contained perforated plates. There were condensers for spirit vapours for which the cooling agent was the pipe conveying the incoming new wash which was thus pre-heated. Warm wash entered near the base of the column, below the perforated plates, and fell down into the kettle over a series of curved plates to ensure close contact with the rising vapours. These vapours partly condensed on the cooler plates towards the top of the column and this distillate dropped back towards the kettle while the rising vapours bubbled through the perforated plates. Since water condenses at a higher temperature than alcohol the vapours got richer in alcohol as the vapours rose to the cooler upper plates and the liquid falling back from the hotter plates would be almost exhausted of alcohol. At a point near the top of the column the strong vapours were tapped off and passed through a condenser. In order to maintain

26. S. Morewood, *Inebriating Liquor*, 1838, *op. cit.*, p. 635. *Excise Revenue Inquiry, 7th Report, Part 1*, 1834, *op. cit.*, p. 383. Evidence of the excise collector, Lisburn.

27. Coffey's patent was No. 5974, 1830. The neutral spirit from a patent still is also suitable for making gin and other spirit compounds (*28th Inland Revenue Report*, 1884–5 (c. 4474) xxii, p. 52).

a continuous supply of wash two kettles were used, when the wash in the first was stripped of spirit the supply was switched to the second and the first kettle emptied.[28]

The first Coffey still almost duplicated the Cellier-Blumenthal still, the differences were little more than improvements. The still had one column, the lower half of which had perforated plates and the upper half had no plates. The new wash entered the top of this column in a pipe that wound to and fro as it descended in the upper half of the column. This cold wash was heated as it condensed some of the rising vapours. The heated wash then spread over the perforated plates and percolated to the base of the column where it fell into the upper of two kettles, keeping this kettle fully charged with liquid. As in the Cellier-Blumenthal still vapours in the upper part of the column became rich in alcohol and vapours condensing in the lower and hotter parts would be stripped. Heat was provided by a steam coil in the lower kettle and from time to time spent wash from the upper kettle would be run into the lower in order to maintain a liquid level over the steam coil. The strong vapours in the upper or rectifying part of the column were tapped off through a condenser.[29]

The early Coffey stills were not entirely satisfactory. One fault was that they were made of iron and when in contact with the wash, the acids generated during fermentation attacked the iron, producing hydrogen and gave a bad flavour to the spirit.[30] Improvements were made. The kettles disappeared and the still took its present form of two columns, one for stripping the wash of spirit, called the analyser, and a second, called the rectifier, for concentrating the spirituous vapours and removing unwanted fusel oils. The columns were of rectangular cross-section and made of wood. Each column was divided into a number of chambers or frames by metal diaphragms perforated with small holes. The pipe conveying incoming cold wash entered the top of the rectifier and was heated as it passed to and fro through each chamber to a point near the base. From there the pipe led to the top of the analyser where the heated wash was discharged on

28. Underwood, *Distilling Plant, op. cit.,* p. 24.
29. *Ibid.,* p. 28.
30. *Excise Revenue Inquiry, 7th Report, Part* I, 1834, *op. cit.,* p. 422.

to the first perforated plate. Each plate had a dropping tube projecting a short distance up so as to provide a shallow liquid level. The liquid then flowed over and down the tube into a cup on the next lower plate which formed a seal. It overflowed the cup and spread over this plate and so on from plate to plate down the analyser column. Meanwhile steam entered the base of the column and rose through the perforations. As it bubbled up through each shallow layer of wash the vapour became stronger and stronger with spirit since in the hotter parts at the bottom of the column water would condense, but alcohol would not. By the time the steam had reached the top of the column it was carrying with it the alcohol in the wash while at the bottom there would only be spent wash which was drained off. This spirituous vapour then passed to the base of the rectifier. As it rose in the rectifier through plates similar to those in the analyser it came in contact with the pipe conveying incoming cool wash and a condensing action followed. Again at the base both the vapour and the wash pipe would be hot and alcohol would not condense, but some water would condense. As the vapour rose to the cooler parts of the rectifier this action would continue with the condensate becoming richer in alcohol till near the top it would be a very strong spirit. At this point there was a solid plate called the spirit sheet with one or more vapour passages. Above this sheet were more perforated plates with dropping tubes and the condensed vapour, which would now be strong spirit, fell back on the spirit sheet and was drained off to be cooled in a refrigerating condenser. At the top of the rectifying column was a pipe that permitted incondensable gases to escape. The vapours entering the rectifying column were similar to the low wines from a pot still and contained the same fusel oils and other unwanted products. The condensing points of these substances differ from spirit hence the condensing action in the rectifying column will strip them from the vapours at different stages. These stages are called 'fractions' by distillers. The spirit sheet was therefore placed at a point when the rising vapours are almost wholly spirit. The condensed fusel oils falling back towards the base of the column were drawn off and as they would contain a small amount of alcohol they could be pumped back and mixed with the wash. This outline of the Coffey still is intended only to explain the principle on which it works and auxiliary apparatus is excluded. For example there were relief valves on the plates in case excess pressure built up and there were arrangements for passing aldehydes, the gases not condensed in the rectifying column, through a condenser and refluxing the liquid back into the system. Present day Coffey stills differ very little from those used a century ago.[31]

Coffey made a special point that the flow of wash into the still should be sufficiently rapid to prevent sediment settling, particularly when thick grain wash was being used. There was a danger of the analyser becoming choked. However, this and other variants of continuous stills depended for efficient working on a regulated supply of steam and for this condition distillers had to wait till Savalle invented the steam regulator in 1857. The spirit coming off the early Coffey still was about 60° over proof, but by the middle of the century the strength was usually 66° over proof or stronger. It is not possible to get an absolute alcohol by ordinary distillation, for a spirit exceeding about ninety-six per cent. of alcohol boils and condenses as a liquid with a single constituent.[32]

Improved continuous stills were designed in the late nineteenth century, principally in Germany and France, to produce a spirit practically free of fusel oil. A full description of such a still would be long and complicated and, in any case, there are numerous variations. They all use the basic principle of the Coffey still. In the first column, or analyser, steam enters the base and bubbles up through descending wash, but the diaphragms, or plates, are not perforated as in the Coffey still. Each plate is pierced with a number of holes fitted with short chimneys. Over each of

31. The Coffey still is described by a number of authorities. A few of them are Morewood, *Inebriating Liquors,* 1838, *op. cit.,* p. 650; Johnston, *Inland Revenue Officer's Manual,* 1873, *op. cit.,* pp. 290–4; Nettleton, *The Manufacture of Spirit,* 1893, *op. cit.,* p. 134; C. Simmonds, *Alcohol,* London, 1919, p. 87; A. J. V. Underwood, *Distilling Plant, op. cit.,* p. 28.

32. Underwood, *Distilling Plant, op. cit.,* pp. 24, 28. The *28th Inland Revenue Report,* Parl. Pps. 1884–5 (c. 4474) xxii, p. 51 gave the average strength from Coffey stills as 60° over proof. This is an average and at that time these stills were capable of producing higher strengths. J. Scarisbrick, *Spirit Manual,* 2nd ed. Wolverhampton, 1894, p. 92, gave strengths from 66° to 69° over proof but the latter figure is perhaps, a little too high. J. Reilly, *Distillation,* London, 1936, chap. 5 on pp. 694 *et seq.* explains the behaviour of azeotropic mixtures which would make strengths above 69° over proof doubtful from a Coffey still.

these is a cowl with a serrated edge almost touching the plate. Between the plates is a dropping tube projecting above the plate which determines the depth of the layer of wash in the same manner as a Coffey still. Incoming wash flows over the plate. Rising steam reaching the cowl or bubbler cap is forced down and out through the serrated edge, which breaks up any large bubbles, and up through the layer of wash to the next plate. Some condensed vapour is left behind and the excess liquid drops to the next lower plate, sometimes called a deck. Thus the Coffey still principle occurs of a rising vapour getting richer in alcohol as it reaches the upper parts. In this case, however, the spirituous vapour is condensed before passing to the next column.

The usual sequence is to discharge the low strength spirit from the analyser into the upper part of an aldehyde column. Then follows the same process as in the analyser. The rising steam is so regulated that the vapours leaving the top carry off most of the secondary constituents that are more volatile than ethyl alcohol. These vapours are condensed and may be further treated before being fed back into the wash. Spirit taken off near the top of the aldehyde column is fed into the top of a rectifying column. It descends, as in the analyser, from plate to plate against rising steam. A stripping column may be interposed before rectifying to increase the strength of the feed into the rectifier. In the rectifier the low volatile constituents still remaining are tapped off continuously at the lower levels and collected in a separate vessel. This fusel oil will contain some alcohol and water. It is sprayed with water in a decanter where the oil floats and is run off, the balance being returned to the system. The resulting spirit will have a strength approaching 70° over proof with only the merest trace of fusel oil. Even this trace can be eliminated, if desired, by allowing the strong spirit to percolate through vessels containing activated carbon. Conversely, the distiller, if he wishes, can include some fusel oil by altering the take off point.

There are a number of condensers in the system and arrangements for refluxing, or returning, a small part of condensates to the column for various reasons, for example, to maintain a liquid level. New cold wash can get some pre-heating in one or more condensers by acting as a cooling agent. Additionally it can be specially heated in a steam heated vessel. The wash can get a further boost in a heat exchanger through which hot spent wash is discharged from the base of the analyser. Since 1950 stills of this kind have been erected in Dublin and Midleton.[33]

During this century a satisfactory method has been evolved for producing absolute alcohol by a continuous process. Like the improved still described the arrangements are complicated and there are variations; so an emasculated explanation must suffice. A single dehydrating column, the upper part of which is fitted with bubbler plates, produces absolute alcohol from spirit of about 68° or more over proof. Its principle depends entirely on the azeotropic nature of mixtures. Normally the entraining agent introduced to extract the water from the spirit is benzine, but a small quantity of petrol can be added. Boiling points are crucial. Benzine boils at about 80°C and ethyl alcohol at 78.3°C. The binary azeotropic mixture of strong spirit boils at about 78.3°C; benzine and water at 69°C; and alcohol and benzine at 68°C. A ternary mixture of alcohol, water and benzine boils just below 65°C. In operation benzine and spirit are fed into the upper part of the column and hot vaporised spirit enters at a point a short distance up from the base. As the hot vapours pass through the descending benzine and spirit the more volatile ternary and binary mixtures are driven off by the heat exchanging process leaving dehydrated alcohol in liquid form at the base. Tight control of temperatures is essential. The bottom zone in particular must be maintained at about 78°C at which dry alcohol will be just below boiling point. The right quantity of the entraining agent is also important. If there is too little some water will remain in the alcohol; if too much there will be traces of benzine. The latter may not be so important if the alcohol is intended for blending with motor fuel, as in Ireland. There are arrangements for extracting water and spirit from the entrainer, returning the former to the ordinary distilling units and cycling the cleaned entrainer back to start its work anew. There are also various regulators, coolers, pressure and vacuum valves and so on to ensure that the critical operations in the dehydrating column work efficiently. Stills for producing dry alcohol were erected in Ireland in 1938.[34]

33. References to purer continental spirit are in the report and evidence of the *Select Committee on British and Foreign Spirits,* Parl. Pps. 1890 (316) x, pp. 528-9, 531.
34. Industrial Alcohol Act, 1938, No. 23.

Very little information is available about the apparatus used before this century by Irish rectifiers and compounders. They used pot stills similar to those used by distillers for low wines though rather smaller. After the invention of continuous stills for distilling from wash, stills of a similar character were built to designs specially suited for further distilling spirits. One had a kettle in which spirits and ingredients were heated and the vapours passed up through a rectifying column designed on the same principle used in the continuous spirit still.[35]

35. In 1807, 47 Geo. 3, sess. 2, c. 19, section 4, limited rectifiers' stills to 200 gallons capacity and compounders to half that size. *The Revenue Review*, Vol. III, March, 1903. A journal published in Falkirk and circulated amongst excise officials. On p. 5 is a drawing of Carter's rectifying still. The kettle has a still head similar to the rectifying column of a Coffey still.

CHAPTER III

ASSESSING SPIRIT

THE complete miscibility of water and alcohol in all proportions has always presented a problem to those who make spirituous beverages, those who trade in them and to the revenue authorities. Clearly without some fairly simple means of assessing the spirit content of a liquid a distiller could not easily manage his operations so as to avoid weak or undesirable feints getting into his finished product. A merchant buying spirit could not be sure that the spirit being sold to him as a certain quality had not been watered down. The revenue authorities could not levy a duty on the spirit contained in a beverage and would be forced to tax it on the liquid quantity with only a secondary regard to its strength. These different interests all combined about the middle of the eighteenth century in an attempt to evolve a satisfactory method of measuring the alcohol in a liquid which could be used in the ordinary commercial transactions of everyday life. The chemist in his laboratory had earlier discovered means of doing this by weighing, but neither his methods nor his apparatus were practicable for the distiller, trader or revenue officer.[1] What was sought was a convenient way of measuring by volume.

The problem arises from the different physical properties of alcohol and water. When the temperature rises alcohol expands more than water so that the density of a mixture will depend not only on the proportions of the two liquids, but also on its temperature. This phenomenon presents no serious difficulty in the laboratory where measurements are made with weighing apparatus, but in a distillery, a warehouse or at the dock side this

1. For a scientific exposition of the problem of obtaining the alcohol content in a mixture with water see W. T. Brannt, *A Practical Treatise on the Raw Materials and Distillation and Rectification of Alcohol*, London; pp. 38 *et seq.* is a chapter on alcoholometry.

kind of testing would be much too cumbersome. Another property of these liquids is the molecular penetration of alcohol into
water when they are mixed. If one gallon of alcohol is mixed
with one gallon of water the result will be something less than
two gallons though the total weight will not change. A simple
analogy would be adding a bucket of sand to a bucket of pebbles
where the result would be rather less than two buckets of the
mixture. This penetration of alcohol will also vary according
to the proportions of the two liquids. A very small proportion
of alcohol would add almost nothing to the bulk of the mixture;
also with a large amount of alcohol and a small quantity of
water not much of the bulk would be lost in penetration. This
penetration thus changes the density of the liquid. Hence any
instrument used to assess the spirit content of a beverage with
reference to its volume will have to take into account different
densities of varying proportions of alcohol and water at every
degree of temperature. A hydrometer was eventually evolved
which will do this with the help of a book of tables for each
degree of temperature, but it took nearly a century of experiment
and inquiry.

Another problem which presented itself, especially in earlier
times, was fixing a standard from which to measure the proportions in a mixture. This was more particularly a problem affecting
the revenue authorities and those trading between Great Britain
and Ireland, but whatever standard was fixed it would have to
be one which the distilling industry and merchants dealing in
spirits could conveniently adopt. The percentage of alcohol
would, at first sight, seem the obvious standard, but at the time
when the hydrometer was being evolved nobody could, with
certainty, say that they had been able to produce alcohol
absolutely free of water, so that the density of absolute alcohol
was uncertain. Fom this it follows that the relative densities of
mixtures would be uncertain. So it came about that a standard
called proof spirit was arbitrarily fixed and stronger or weaker
spirits were then referred to as being so much over or under
proof. This had the advantage that no matter how pure an alcohol
the distiller or chemist produced it could be referred to as a
certain degree over proof without any complications in relation
to other mixtures. The method was not scientific, but was a
practical solution for all commercial and revenue purposes. In

the early years there were changes in the standard of proof, but it has remained constant for nearly 150 years.[2]

In the earliest days spirits were used as a specific against disease, and indeed this belief in the curative properties was still prevalent in Ireland until the middle of the last century, particularly during the terrible years of the great famines of 1845 to 1847.[3] Quality for this purpose was judged by the strength of the spirit rather than its flavour and it was early noticed that the product of two distillations was stronger than one and that spirit thrice distilled was stronger still and therefore more potent in warding off disease. Spirit is, however, colourless so that without instruments to measure the alcohol content reliance had to be placed on crude tests, taste, or smell, all very unsatisfactory methods. Other properties of alcohol were soon brought into use to supplement and then supplant these methods.

Among the earliest tests was the inflammable nature of alcohol. Scarisbrick, quoting from a sixteenth century Dutch source, says that a test employed then was to soak a piece of linen in the spirit. If the linen burnt, the spirit was good, if it did not the spirit had no virtue. Another early test was to add oil to the spirit and the spirit was considered strong if it floated on the oil.[4] A later test was to set fire to a sample of the spirit after weighing it. When the alcohol had burnt off the sample it was again weighed. If the residue weighed less than half the original sample the spirit was regarded as strong.[5] Still later came the gunpowder test which gave a little more accuracy. In this test some gunpowder was moistened with the spirit to be tested and a light applied. If the gunpowder burnt slowly the spirit was good. If

2. The present proof standard was fixed in 1816 by 56 Geo. 3, c. 140 for excise duties and two years later for the customs (Sir N. Highmore, *The Excise Laws*, London, 1923, 3rd ed., i, p. 480). Proof is expressed in different ways, but all in relation to proof equalling 100. Thus a spirit can be said to be 70 per cent of proof or 30 per cent under proof which conforms with the way variations from proof are shown in the 1816 Act. The same strength is also expressed in degrees, thus 70° of proof or 30° under proof. Frequently in trade or revenue documents it is shown merely as 30 under proof, the percentage being understood.

3. J. Forbes, *Memorandums made in Ireland in 1852*, London, 1853, ii, pp. 45, 98. *Select Committee on Drunkenness*, Parl. Pps. 1834 (559), p. 558.

4. J. Scarisbrick, *Spirit Assaying*, Wolverhampton, 1898, p. 7. *Handbook for Officers of Excise*, Loftus publication, London, 1857, pp. 81–92.

5. F. G. H. Tate, *Alcoholometry*, London, 1930, historical introduction, p. x. Scarisbrick, *Spirit Assaying, op. cit.*, p. 7.

it burst into flame the spirit was deemed to be strong. If, however, the gunpowder merely spluttered and burnt with difficulty the spirit was weak. This test at least left some room for judgment between these various points, for example, by observing how quickly it flared up. This test became known as the proof test and Tate expresses the view that the term is derived from 'proving' or testing the spirit and not from the 'poof' of the explosion when strong spirit was tested.[6]

Another test used by both revenue officers and the trade was known as the bead test, or the crown or proof vial test. In this test some spirit was placed in a phial and shaken. Beads will form on the edges at the surface under these conditions and an experienced observer can estimate the strength from the time it takes for the beads to disappear. Scarisbrick states that the strength can be estimated by this method to within 10 per cent. Variants of this test appear to have been used as late as 1853 by illicit distillers in Ireland. Golding Bird, collector of excise, Londonderry, giving evidence before a select committee of the House of Commons, stated that the illicit distiller estimated his extract by pouring it into a vessel held very low and calculated the strength from the bubbles formed and from this he calculated the quantity of water to be added to make the spirit fit for his market.[7]

All these tests were crude and only partially successful for the purpose of commerce. They were thoroughly unsatisfactory when the duty on spirits became one of the principal sources of revenue. Here was a good example of revenue needs waiting upon scientific advance. A means had to be found for testing spirit easily, speedily and with moderate accuracy if the revenue was to be collected fairly. Without such means cheating in trade and against the revenue authorities was bound to be widespread with all its ill effects on civic morality.

The fact that spirit is lighter than water attracted the attention of scientists and they looked again at the experiments of Robert

6. Tate, *Alcoholometry*, p. x.

7. *Handbook for Officers of Excise, op. cit.*, p. 83. An extract is quoted from A. Highmore, *The Excise Laws*, 1796, giving details of this method of trying the strength of spirits. Illicit distillers used this method in 1854. See *S.C. to consider extending the functions of the Constabulary in Ireland to the suppression of Illicit Distillation*, Parl. Pps. 1854 (53) x, p. 48, evidence of G. Bird. Scarisbrick, *Spirit Assaying, op. cit.*, p. 8.

Boyle recorded in a paper read before the Royal Society in 1675.[8] Boyle noticed that the greater the proportion of alcohol in a liquid the lower was the specific gravity and he designed a glass instrument consisting of a bulb and stem. A little mercury was placed in the bulb which caused the instrument to float with the stem upright. This instrument floated higher or lower in the liquid as the spirit content was small or large. By marking the stem an indication of this spirit content could be observed. The instrument was known as an aerometer. This form of instrument, considerably modified, was to become the type of hydrometer and saccharometer in use today, the first for assessing the alcohol content in spirit and the other for measuring the attenuation of wash. The hydrometer can only be used successfully if the spirits do not contain obscuring matter such as sugar in liqueurs or other compounds. For obscured spirits an accurate assessment of the spirit content must be obtained by actually distilling a sample.

Boyle's instrument was an instrument of constant volume and had a very limited range. Other similar instruments appeared later and Tate quotes the instrument made by Thomas Tuttal about 1700 and advertised as a 'Waterpoise to try the strength of liquids' which he thinks the earliest instance of a hydrometer on sale by an instrument maker. What was wanted was a floating instrument of variable weight and the earliest attempts aimed at an instrument with a fixed mark on the stem. When placed in the spirit, weights were added to sink it till the mark cut the liquid level thus ascertaining the specific gravity. Such aerometers were fragile and troublesome in use.[9]

Charles Leadbetter describes a stronger type of aerometer used in the middle of the eighteenth century. It was made of ivory similar to Boyle's instrument in shape and indicated the specific gravity by the distance it sank in the liquid. The stem was divided into degrees. He also described a balance for determining the specific gravity. On one side of the balance was a leaden globe and the other had a weight counterbalancing the globe.

    8. *Phil. Trans.*, Vol. 10, No. 115, 21 June 1675, pp. 329–31. A reference to Boyle's instrument also appears in *Pepys' Diary* on 9 December 1668 wherein he writes 'He did give me a glass bubble to try the strength of spirits with'.

    9. Tate, *Alcoholometry, op. cit.*, pp. xiii–xiv.

This weight was removed and the globe was sunk in the liquid. Counterbalancing weights were added till the balance was in equilibrium. The difference between the original counterbalance and the added weights gave the specific gravity. 'Hence because the densities are, as the specific gravities, we find the ratio of the densities of the fluids at the same time', that is, the various weights indicated different densities.[10]

The idea of using a balance as described by Leadbetter was pursued in various forms. Thus Sir James Murray of Dublin showed Morewood, collector of excise at Naas in the early nineteenth century, a device whereby a small vessel of known capacity was filled with liquid and suspended from an arm, like a steel yard, marked off in divisions each side of a proof point. The vessel containing the liquid under test was moved along the arm till the arm remained in balance at the level and the strength read off according to the distance from the fulcrum.[11] All such arrangements for using a balance were too cumbersome for the general use of the distiller or revenue officer and though this method became an accurate way of testing spirit in the laboratory it was never adopted generally.

Scientists set their minds to evolving a satisfactory hydrometer and eventually one was invented by John Clarke in 1725. It was made of metal and therefore not easily damaged and became a standard instrument in 1730. The Royal Society was addressed in 1730 by J. T. Desaguliers about the new hydrometer made by Clarke. He described this as an aerometer and said that 'such an instrument does indeed show the different specific gravities of all waters and wines'.[12] It was shaped like Boyle's aerometer and had a number of weights to enable it to be used with a wide range in strengths. There were additional weights to make rough corrections for temperature. In 1746 Clarke published a work titled *The Hydrometer or Brandy Prover* which Tate considers as probably the earliest English work on the hydrometer.[13] Distillery officers of excise were consulted by Clarke in his investigations and he undoubtedly made a great advance on the existing method of ascertaining strengths by the proof vial.

10. C. Leadbetter, *The Royal Gauger*, London, 1755, p. 203.
11. Tate, *Alcoholometry*, p. xiii.
12. *Phil. Trans*, 1730, Vol. 36, No. 413, p. 277.
13. Tate, *Alcoholometry*, p. xiv.

C

The excise department in England made use of the instrument and caused a number of improvements, but for complete accuracy at all proportions of alcohol and water and at all temperatures an ever increasing number of weights were necessary until in 1815 some 140 weights were used, 11 of which were for differences of temperature. There was also a very complicated nomenclature for describing strength which was based on the number of parts of water to be added or extracted to bring the spirit to proof. After many years of semi-official recognition Clarke's hydrometer received legal recognition in England in 1787 on a yearly basis till 1801 when this was made permanent for the United Kingdom. In Ireland the law at first only applied to imported spirits.[14]

Clarke's hydrometer, though a great advance, did not satisfy the need for a simple instrument of sufficient accuracy for the ordinary purposes of trade and revenue. In 1802, William Speer, supervisor and assayer of spirits in the port of Dublin, wrote a paper on the deficiencies in the existing methods of assaying spirits. It was the substance of a report he had made a year earlier to the Chancellor of the Exchequer. He condemned Clarke's hydrometer and the Irish hydrometer which was similar, but which he says differed in its readings to the extent of 9° above English proof. He attributed this chiefly to a lack of a definition of proof so that the indication of proof on the hydrometer was 'just what the maker of the hydrometer pleased'. He rightly pointed out that this was a serious obstacle to trade between Ireland and England, since the proof quantities of spirits in transit would not agree in the two countries and thus affect not merely the commercial side of these transactions, but the duty to be paid.[15]

During the latter part of the eighteenth century the English Board of Excise gave serious consideration to the defects in the

14. *Ibid.*, p. xvii. Scarisbrick, *Spirit Assaying, op. cit.*, p. 61. The provisional use of Clarke's hydrometer was first authorised in England by 27 Geo. 3, c. 31 (English statutes). Its use was made permanent for the United Kingdom by 41 Geo. 3, c. 97, but until 1823 it was used only by the customs in Ireland. Later it will be shown the effect these laws had on the trade of Irish distillers with Great Britain.

15. W. Speer, *An Enquiry into the causes of Errors and Irregularities . . . in ascertaining the strengths of Spirituous Liquors by Hydrometer, London, 1802*, pp. 10, 16. This paper greatly influenced the Government to institute measures to get a more satisfactory hydrometer.

methods for assessing spirits and eventually invited Sir George Banks, President of the Royal Society in 1787 to carry out an investigation. The Society, appointed Sir Charles Blagden to undertake the work with the assistance of George Gilpin, clerk to the Royal Society. Sir Charles Blagden referred to the terms of this appointment in his first report in 1790 where he states: 'In consequence of an application by the Government to Sir Joseph Banks, President of the Royal Society, for the best means of ascertaining the just proportions of duty to be paid by any kind of spirituous liquor that should come before the officers of excise, I was requested by that gentleman to assist in planning the proper experiments for that purpose, and to draw up the report on them when they should be finished.' Gilpin conducted exhaustive experiments over a period of four years and three reports were submitted to the Society.[16] These experiments did not produce a satisfactory instrument for assessing spirits, but they did throw a great deal of light on the problem. In particular the reports gave a very accurate account of the physical properties of alcohol and Gilpin not only obtained an alcohol which was almost absolute, but constructed tables showing specific gravities over the whole normal range of temperature for different percentages of alcohol in a liquid. The reports also showed the need for a fixed standard of proof and preferred such a standard for non-scientific purposes than referring strengths to a percentage of alcohol. All subsequent investigations in the United Kingdom relating to hydrometers and to proof have their roots in these reports.

The development of instruments such as Clarke's hydrometer enabled the measurement of the alcohol content in a liquid to be made with fair accuracy, but there still remained the problem of fixing the standard of proof. For trade purposes it was vital that the meaning of the term 'proof' could not be disputed and in the case of trade between Ireland and Great Britain it was very desirable that proof meant the same thing in both countries. A standard of proof was also necessary for the revenue authorities as the rates of duty rose and became more closely associated with the percentage of alcohol in spirits.

16. *Phil. Trans.* Vol. 80, No. 18, p. 321, 22 April 1790; Vol. 82, No. 22, p. 425, 28 June 1792; 19 June 1794, Vol. 84, No. 20, Part 2, Tables of specific gravities. See also Speer, *Hydrometer Errors, op. cit.,* pp. 25–31.

At the time Speer of Dublin sent in his report to N. Vansittart, Chancellor of the Exchequer, in 1801, there was a standard of proof which the Board of Excise had fixed as a mixture of the strongest spirit obtainable with an equal quantity of water to which was added one part of water to six of the mixture. The weight of one wine gallon of this mixture was 7 lb. 13 oz. and was to be reckoned as 1 to 6 or in Clarke's nomenclature as 1 in 7, that is 1 part of water added to 6 parts of the mixture or a spirit containing one-seventh part added water.[17]

Naturally such an untidy definition raised anew the question of using the actual percentage of alcohol as the standard, but the government adhered to the views of the Royal Society in the latter's reports of 1790 and 1792. These views were re-inforced by a committee of the Royal Society who further investigated the proof standard and reported on 12 February 1833: 'With regard to the substance called alcohol, upon which the excise duty is levied, there appears to be no reason, either philosophical or practical, why it should be considered as absolute. A definite mixture of alcohol and water is as invariable in its value as absolute alcohol can be. It is also invariable in its nature, and can be more readily and with equal accuracy be identified by that only quality or condition to which recourse can be had in practice, namely, specific gravity. A diluted alcohol is, there-fore, that which is recommended by us as the only exciseable substance; and as, on the one hand, it will make no difference in identification, and on the other, will be a great commercial advantage, it is further recommended that the standard be very nearly that of the present proof spirit.'[18]

The report of the Royal Society in 1833 was a confirmation of a standard of proof legally defined in 1816 and arrived at con-currently with the development of the hydrometer.[19] Following on Speer's report in 1801 and agitation from others, an Act was passed empowering the Treasuries in Great Britain and in Ireland

17. Speer, *Hydrometer Errors*, pp. 7, 14. The proof was defined in England by 2 Geo. 3, c. 5 and Clarke's hydrometer was first officially recognised in 1787 by 27 Geo. 3, c. 31 (English statutes).

18. This report was made by Prof. Faraday. See *Handbook for Officers of Excise*, 1857, *op. cit.*, pp. 91-2, 123-4; John Owens, *Plain Papers*, London, 1879, pp. 283-5; Tate, *Alcoholometry, op. cit.*, p. 43.

19. Proof was legally defined in 1816 by 56 Geo. 3, c. 140.

to order existing hydrometers to be discontinued and the use of others in their place.[20] Accordingly on 20 July 1802, before making an order, the Treasury directed the Board of Excise in London 'to consider and report upon the Act for establishing a new hydrometer'. In reply the Board of Excise reported: 'We wait in expectation of seeing or hearing from the Gentlemen of the several Boards who are prepared to attend the Investigation. But till they arrive we conceive we cannot under your Lordships' Order proceed in the matter and we take this occasion of apprizing your Lordships of these Circumstances in order that such further directions may be issued as your Lordships shall deem expedient. That no time, however, may be lost we have directed an Advertisement on the subject to be prepared of which we subjoin a Copy proposing to cause it to be inserted in the Public Papers unless we receive your Lordships' Orders to the contrary.'[21]

Advertisements duly appeared in August 1802 inviting inventors to submit hydrometers and stipulating that the instruments must meet the following three conditions:

1. The intervals on the stem indicating the strength must show small and equal differences in strength and be as evenly spaced as possible.

2. Allowance must be made for different temperatures.

3. The reading of the hydrometer must be uniform whatever the proportion of alcohol in the mixture, that is, a liquid must be shown as containing a given quantity of proof spirit whether it be diluted or condensed.

It was also made plain that any system strongly deviating from current practice would not be favoured as there was no desire to dislocate seriously either trade or revenue methods.

The first obstacle facing inventors was the confusion of the term 'proof'. Legal proof was supposed to be a mixture of a specific gravity of ·916 at 60°Fahr. Some investigators had shown proof to be something different. The English and Scottish Boards of Excise fixed a gallon of proof spirit as weighing 7 lb. 13 oz. The English Board of Customs fixed the weight at

20. 42 Geo. 3, c. 97.

21. *Excise and Treasury correspondence 1801–4*, Customs and Excise Library, London, ref. 19. 8. 1802, f. 442.

7 lb. 12 oz. The Irish Board of Excise differed from both. More-over there was no standard gallon.[22] Speer quotes three imperfections of the existing definition of proof.[23]

1. The spirit defined is not proof, but another spirit.

2. The difficulty of procuring an exact gallon measure and quotes Ramsden in a publication of 1792 as stating that makers of hydrometers differ on this point by 7½ per cent. The gallon, he says, should be 231 cubic inches, but despite an effort by a committee of the House of Commons in 1758, the construction of a vessel containing exactly 231 cubic inches could not be satisfactorily made.

3. No temperature was mentioned in the definition.

Vansittart informed George Quin, one of the inventors, that proof would be regarded as a mixture of a specific gravity of ·920 at 60° Fahr. and the other inventors worked to this standard.[24] Hydrometers were submitted by Dring and Fage, the makers of Clarke's hydrometers, Atkins and Co. of London, Miss M. Dicas of Liverpool, whose father had made the hydrometer adopted in the United States of America and used by some distillers in Ireland and Scotland, George Quin, William Speer, Miller and Adie of Edinburgh, Mrs. Catherine Andoe, the widow of a Bordeaux distiller, Bartholemew Sikes, a secretary of the English Board of Excise, and by others. Vansittart had directed that the Boards of Excise and of Customs in England and the Revenue Boards in Scotland and in Ireland were to co-operate with distillers and others in this matter and accordingly a committee of the various interests was set up to judge the merits of the instruments submitted. The Irish authorities were represented by Saunders, an instrument maker who made a saccharometer in use in some Irish distilleries. The investigation work was mainly carried out by Dr Wollaston.[25]

Most of the instruments examined by the committee were on the lines of existing instruments which had been modified in an attempt to achieve greater perfection and were accompanied with slide rules to convert readings on the instruments into

22. Scarisbrick, *Spirit Assaying, op. cit.,* pp. 88–9.
23. Speer, *Hydrometer Errors, op. cit.,* p. 9.
24. Scarisbrick, *Spirit Assaying,* p. 89.
25. Tate, *Alcoholometry, op. cit.,* pp. 4–8.

proof. Sikes, however, in his capacity as an official of the English Board of Excise, had a very full knowledge of what was required and he had probably been an inspiration behind many of the improvements in the Clarke hydrometer. The instrument he submitted was a modified form of Clarke's hydrometer. He did not strive for perfection, nor did his instrument require a slide rule to interpret its readings, or indications as these were called. Instead he provided a book of tables, a table for each degree of temperature. By reference to the appropriate table it became a simple matter to convert the hydrometer indication into strengths related to proof spirit. The hydrometer, which is still in use, consisted of a hollow brass sphere with a tail below it which could hold a weight and a stem above with ten divisions marked off on it. Each weight equalled ten divisions so that by changing the weights a full range of different strengths could be measured. This simple method of using a book of tables made all the difference in facilitating assessment and the instrument was selected.[26]

Despite these investigations Clarke's hydrometer remained in use until 1816 when an Act was passed making the Sikes hydrometer legal. The Act also provided that the instrument would 'denote as proof spirit that which at a temperature of 51° Fahr. weighs exactly twelve-thirteenths of an equal measure of distilled water'. This is equivalent to a specific gravity of 0·92 at 60°F. The instrument was only authorised provisionally at first, but its legal use was made permanent in 1818.[27]

Following on experiments made by R. B. Bates tables of weights per gallon, corresponding to Sikes' hydrometer indications, were constructed and received legal sanction in 1853. The tables have been of great value to distillers, enabling them to assess strengths and proof quantities in casks merely from temperature, indication of the hydrometer and net weight. These tables continued in use until 1915 when they were supplanted by tables of weights per gallon constructed by Sir Edward Thorpe.[28]

26. Scarisbrick, *Spirit Assaying, op. cit.,* pp. 61, 66, 90. Tate, *Alcoholometry,* pp. 14–32. Sikes relied on the tables constructed by Gilpin of the Royal Society and presented in 1794.

27. 56 Geo. 3, c. 140; 58 Geo. 3, c. 28.

28. 16 and 17 Vict., c. 37, Sched. C; 5 and 6 Geo. 5, c. 89, section 19. The tables are given by Sir N. Highmore, *The Excise Laws, op. cit.,* i, pp. 578–82.

The only other improvements in the first Sikes hydrometer concern spirits of very high strengths which were beyond its range. This obstacle was overcome much later after unsuccessful efforts by George Phillips in the excise laboratory from 1858 to 1861. A Sikes 'A' hydrometer for such spirits up to 40°F was legalised in 1915 and in the following year a Sikes 'B' hydrometer was perfected for higher temperatures.[29] These improvements, however, had practically no effect on Irish distilling which was almost wholly confined to spirits of much lower strengths.

So far the assessment of alcohol content in a mixture with water had been examined, but many alcoholic beverages are made with other ingredients, especially sugar, and the presence of these ingredients would obscure a true reading of the hydro-meter by causing it to float higher in the liquid. Gin and British compounds are in this category.[30] The revenue authorities in the early nineteenth century had no way of assessing strengths in these cases other than actually distilling samples. They therefore arbitrarily assumed strengths and this had very serious affects on the manufacturers in Ireland of these beverages. It did, in fact, almost exclude Irish-made compounds from the English market.[31] In 1760 when Clarke's early types of hydrometer were in use, collectors of customs in England were directed to charge double the duty if imported spirits had in them syrups or other obscuring matter which defeated the hydrometer. When the hydrometer was made the only legal method of assessing spirit duty this obscuration presented a problem which was met by sending samples for tests to the excise laboratory, but this method did not receive legal sanction until 1881.[32]

Distilling wash is a mechanical operation to separate spirit from the rest of the fermented liquid and since the evolution of the

29. 5 and 6 Geo. 5, c. 89, section 19 (2). See also Tate, *Alcoholometry*, p. 54.

30. 23 and 24 Vict., c. 114, section 148 defined the different forms of spirituous liquors. 43 and 44 Vict., c. 24, section 3 embraced all British liqueurs, tinctures and medicinal spirits in the term 'British compounds'.

31. *Inquiry into the Excise Establishment and into the Management and Collection of the Excise Revenue throughout the United Kingdom, 7th Report, Part I*, Parl. Pps. 1834 (7) xxv, pp. 40–1, 189, 443 refer to this obstruction to trade. There are several other similar references. On p. 203 Coffey suggested a way to overcome the difficulty.

32. Tate, *Alcoholometry, op. cit.*, p. 77, cites the directions to the customs to charge double duty on obscured spirits. Testing the strength by means other than by the hydrometer were legalised by 44 and 45 Vict., c. 12, section 8 in 1881.

hydrometer for assessing the spirit content of a liquid depended on alcohol being lighter than water, it naturally followed that those concerned with the distilling industry should turn their attention to a similar device to measure the spirit content in the wort or wash. The saccharometer, shaped like the hydrometer, resulted. While it does not measure strength directly it enables an estimate to be made.

In a report on the distillery laws in Scotland in 1799, the committee compared the hydrometer with the saccharometer which it had been proposed should be used by excise officers. They pointed out that the hydrometer indicated the strength of spirit by showing how much lighter a liquid was when compared with water. A saccharometer, on the other hand, demonstrated the weight of wort compared with water. Dr Jeffray and other witnesses objected that all material in solution cannot be converted into spirit and that a saccharometer would show everything as compared with water. The committee, however, held that the value of the instrument was not that it showed the weight or gravity of wort, but that it showed the difference in weights occurring during and after fermentation, that is, the attenuation, so that suspension in the liquid of materials which do not ferment made no difference. The committee also held the view that there is a close relationship between this attenuation and the spirit content of wash.[33]

Before the eighteenth century the control of the operations of setting wort and its fermentation was a matter of guesswork and experience. There was no ready way of testing the concention or specific gravity of wort and the extent to which fermentation had proceeded when the yeast stopped working. An expert distiller could, of course, tell by the vigour of the fermentation and the time taken whether his fermentation had been successful.

The use of saccharometers seems to have become more widespread amongst distillers in Scotland than in Ireland in the eighteenth century and it is certainly doubtful whether English distillers used them at that time. The English excise do not appear to have used them to check distillery operations even as

33. *Report on Distilleries in Scotland,* 1799, especially app. M. An extract from this report appears in the *Inquiry into the Revenue arising in Ireland,* 5th Report, Parl. Pps. 1823 (405) vii, pp. 582–4.

late as 1823.[34] Because distillers found the saccharometer useful
for controlling their brewing operations it was not long before
excise officers made use of the same instrument as a check against
fraud. At first the saccharometer was not used by excise officers
to measure attenuation, but merely to test the gravity of wash
from time to time to see that no wash was introduced clandestinely. In Scotland penalties were incurred if the gravity of a
wash back increased between two such tests or if the gravity
was found to be higher than that declared by the distiller.[35] In
Ireland the gravity of the wash was not related to the spirit
produced until after 1823 so that the use of the saccharometer,
whilst valuable to the distiller, was merely an adjunct to revenue
control.

Under the circumstances described it is not surprising to find
that there were no standards for saccharometers and, in fact,
each instrument maker had his own standard. Nor did this
hinder the industry since each distiller would accustom himself
to the instrument of his choice. The instrument in general use
amongst Irish distillers was said by Aeneas Coffey to be a
saccharometer made by Saunders, a Dublin instrument maker,
though one important Dublin distiller stated that he used the
Dicas saccharometer. In Scotland the Allan saccharometer was
generally used as well as the Dicas instrument. In operation the
Allan saccharometer indicated in degrees the specific gravity of
wort or wash in relation to water which was regarded as 1,000,
that is, gravities would be shown as 1,050, 1,070, etc. The Dicas
and similar instruments showed the pounds per barrel of fement-
able matter contained in the wort and was less exact. Thus a
reading of 60 lb. meant that 36 gallons of wash weighed 60 lb.
more than the same quantity of water.[36]

Frauds in distilleries forced the attention of the revenue
authorities to look for a better means of controlling operations
and the initiative came from the Scottish Board of Excise. The

34. *Ibid.,* p. 343.

35. *Ibid.,* p. 352.

36. *Ibid.,* pp. 299, 323. The *Handbook for Officers of Excise, 1857 op. cit.,* p. 158
states that the Allan saccharometer was used. So the evidence points to the use in
Ireland of the Dicas, Saunders, and Allan instruments in the early nineteenth
century. S. Morewood, *A Philosophical and Statistical History . . . of Inebriating
Liquors,* Dublin, 1838, p. 684, also refers to the Allan saccharometer in Ireland.
He explains the principle of the Dicas saccharometer.

need in Ireland until 1823 was not so great because the method of levying the spirit duty depended on the size of stills rather than the quantity of spirit produced. In Scotland a similar system had been replaced by a direct charge on the spirit manufactured supplemented by an alternative charge based on the attenuation of wash. This alternative charge, which became known as a presumptive charge, arose from proposals made by Scottish excise officials to a parliamentary committee on Scottish distilleries in 1798 in which they expressed the belief that 'a table of attenuation can be formed by which the quantity of spirits may be very nearly ascertained'.[37] Their object was to put a limit on the extent of possible fraud, but the method depended entirely on the accuracy with which a saccharometer could measure decreases in gravity during attenuation and whether these decreases were in direct relation to the formation of spirit. The Treasury appointed three scientists, Doctors Hope, Thomson and Coventry, to examine the problem and in 1806 they made an extensive report confirming that there was a direct relationship between decreases in gravity and the formation of alcohol. In the same year it was enacted that the distiller in Scotland would be charged additional duty if there was any increase in the gravity of wash as 'ascertained by an instrument called a saccharometer'.[38] Thus the saccharometer became officially recognised and in the next few years the attenuation charge in Scotland became established.

The use of the saccharometer, having progressed beyond the stage of a valuable instrument to a distiller, to an official method of raising a charge for duty, it became essential to standardise the instrument. The earliest saccharometer is said to have been invented by Richardson, a brewer in Hull, in 1784.[39] By 1806 a number of saccharometers were on the market, but the Allan instrument emerged as the prototype for the modern saccharo-

37. *Irish Revenue Inquiry*, 5th *Report*, 1823, *op. cit.*, p. 261. J. Scarisbrick, *Spirit Manual*, Wolverhampton, 1894, 2nd ed. p. 99.

38. 46 Geo. 3, c. 102, section 25 legalised the saccharometer in Scotland. Its use was extended to Ireland by 4 Geo. 4, c. 94, section 56. A history of the saccharometer is given in the *Handbook for Officers of Excise*, 1857, *op. cit.*, pp. 155–62. The experiments in 1806 are related by Scarisbrick, *Spirit Manual, op. cit.*, pp. 99–100. The three scientists received £600 for their labours (Customs and Excise Library, London, ref. *Treasury and Scottish Excise*, Mss N. 1817, 1805–1811, p. 117).

39. S. Morewood, *Inebriating Liquors*, 1838, *op. cit.*, p. 684.

meter. The original Allan saccharometer was constructed like a hydrometer with a three-sided stem and a set of divisions on each side. Seven weights were used and were applied at the top. Reading off the gravity was done by using the appropriate side of the stem in conjunction with the weights used. In 1822 the instrument was improved. The size was reduced and the stem altered to a flat stem with two scales. The weights were still applied at the top which made it troublesome to operate and gave rise to inaccuracies.[40]

About this time William Brettel Bate evolved a saccharometer which overcame the difficulties and inaccuracies of Allan's saccharometer and in 1823 this instrument was adopted by the Treasury. In the same year the Excise Commissioners in Dublin ordered its use in Ireland. Bate's saccharometer is still used. It was designed to give the correct specific gravity of wort at a temperature of 60°F, but in the nineteenth century no adjustments for other temperatures were made. The instrument is made of brass and therefore not fragile in operation. It consists of an elongated hollow bulb with a flat stem above and underneath a simple arrangement for attaching weights. Since its principle depends on the volume of liquid displaced when floating, the divisions of the scale on the stem get smaller towards the top to allow for the additional displacement by the stem as the instrument sinks deeper into the liquid. The stem has thirty graduated divisions and there are matching weights for each 30° of gravity. In Bate's words: 'As the saccharometer could not be accurate without a distinct scale or set of divisions for each range of specific gravity, and as this would be perfectly accomplished if the instrument were furnished with a change of stems, each bearing a scale shorter than the preceding, so would the same perfection be attained by transferring the same stem to different instruments, each larger than the preceding in the same proportion.' Changing weights was equivalent to changing the instrument but using the same scale.[41]

40. *Handbook for Officers of Excise*, 1857, *op. cit.*, pp. 231–4. Before 1806 saccharometers indicated gravity as pounds per barrel. In that year Dr Thomson, a member of the committee that investigated attenuation, invented an instrument indicating degrees of gravity (*McCoy's Dictionary of Customs and Excise*, London, 1938).

41. *Excise Historical Records*, Custom House, Belfast, Mss. book No. 133, p. 133. Morewood, *Inebriating Liquors*, 1838, p. 684.

Both the hydrometer and saccharometer are flotation instruments relying on displacement of the liquid, but in the Sikes hydrometer the indications or readings are arbitrary and the strength of spirits is ascertained by the help of tables for each degree of temperature. Saccharometers give a direct reading of the specific gravity of a liquid. They do not measure its alcoholic content.[42]

Proof as a measure of strength is an arbitrary method, but most countries have found it necessary to adopt standards and hydrometers along lines similar to those in the United Kingdom. Exporters of Irish whiskey to those countries usually find it necessary to quote foreign standards in their dealings. In Commonwealth countries the British standards are generally used. In the important United States market the proof standard is a little different. A Federal regulation defines proof strength as a mixture at 60°F of 50 parts by volume of absolute alcohol and 53·73 parts water giving 100 parts of proof spirit owing to the contraction on mixing. At 60°F the American hydrometer reads 100° for proof spirit and 200° for absolute alcohol. As a comparison 30° under proof in this country is equivalent to 80° proof in the United States.[43]

---

42. It is customary to record a gravity in degrees. Thus a gravity of 1,050, water being 1,000, is shown as 50°. Gravities below 1,000 are shown with a minus sign. Thus 998 would be written —2°. All brewers use saccharometers and beer is classified by the original gravity of the unfermented wort. This is often regarded erroneously as the alcoholic strength of the beer, but the original gravity merely indicates the degree of attenuation that is possible. A high original gravity can, and normally does result in a strong beer; it does not show how strong.

43. *Encyclopaedia Britannica*, 1968, xviii, p. 624.

CHAPTER IV

THE EXCISE ADMINISTRATION

BEFORE the seventeenth century there was no organised excise department, the taxes on spirits were farmed and the government interest was entrusted to a few appointed men sometimes referred to as Commissioners. When a direct tax of 4d. a gallon was imposed in 1661 an excise department came into existence but, apart from collecting the duty, had very little to do with the distiller. From the early eighteenth century, however, the excise department became more and more involved in the manufacture and sale of spirits and it was during this century that all the later essential excise controls were devised and developed. By the end of the century distillers, rectifiers and sellers all had to notify their intention to start their trades; to register, or enter, their premises and plant in sufficient detail to enable an excise officer to identify exactly the place and the purpose of each utensil; to obtain a licence with a limited currency and renew it if the trade was to continue; to give prior notice to the excise before beginning certain key operations; to declare the quantity produced; to transfer spirits from place to place under a system of permits issued by the excise for each transaction; and to keep stock records. Thus the legitimate trade in spirits from distiller to consumer was channelled through a series of excise controls. Outside this channel the excise instituted measures to stop illegal manufacture and distribution and to prevent any such spirits from entering the stream of legitimate traffic.[1]

By the early nineteenth century the framework of excise controls was complete and thereafter it was elaborated and strengthened or sometimes altered to meet special circumstances. The excise officer had become intimately concerned in every

1. The points raised will be developed later.

stage of distillery activities and the excise laws had a great influence on the development of the industry. The spirit duty had become the largest single item in the national revenue and was therefore the constant concern of the Government. The reasons for the close excise supervision at all stages in spirit manufacture were summed up in 1834 in a report to parliament stating that 'it is obviously necessary, for purposes of revenue survey, that the officers of the department should have complete and general cognisance of a manufacture during every part of its process; that the business should not be conducted without a licence from the department; and that buildings, grounds or premises on which it is carried on, and the various implements, machinery, receptacles and vessels which are required for its production should be at all times subject to survey and inspection, and in many respects under the control of excise officers; and it is further necessary, in the case of many of the manufactures, that the mode of conducting the business, and the times of commencing and completing the several stages of the operation should be in great measure prescribed by the provisions of Acts of Parliament, the observance of which is enforced by severe penalties'. This was a general statement on excise duties but had particular reference to spirits.[2]

In 1661 an office of excise was established in Dublin and five Commissioners and a Surveyor were appointed as the first Board of Excise under the great seal of the Chief Governor. They were given powers to appoint clerks, searchers and other necessary staff and all were to take the oath of supremacy and oath of allegiance. This was a period when these oaths were deemed essential in Ireland. The new organisation was clearly modelled on the customs department, even to some of the titles such as searcher. It was totally without experience and in areas remote from Dublin and other main cities was operating in hostile

2. *Inquiry into the Excise Establishment and the Management and Collection of the Excise Revenue throughout the United Kingdom, 7th Report, Part I.* Parl. Pps. 1834 (7) xxv. p. 7. An instance of a change in excise controls was the abolition of the use of permits as part of the stock account system by spirit dealers in 1848 by 11 and 12 Vict., c. 121, sections 13–17. A greatly relaxed control by spirit certificates was substituted. This was extended to rectifiers and compounders in 1860 by 23 and 24 Vict., c. 116. *Digest of the Reports,* Parl. Pps. 1837 (84) xxx, p. 148. The total excise revenue in 1833 was £2·2 millions of which the spirit revenue was £1·8 millions.

country. No details are available of the excise centres set up to collect the duties, but distillers paid weekly whatever they decided to declare as their production, or compounded the duty for an agreed yearly sum which exempted them from all excise control. Gaugers were sworn and appointed to do such preventive work as searching premises or making test checks on distillers' declarations. This was the situation to the end of the seventeenth century.[3]

In 1761 the Revenue Board was re-affirmed as not less than five nor more than seven Commissioners of Customs and not more than five of them were also Commissioners of Excise. The Surveyor of 1661 had disappeared and the title was now given to subordinate officers. The character of the Board members had, however, completely changed. In the seventeenth and early eighteenth century the Board members were men of influence favoured by the Lord Lieutenant, but in the latter half of the eighteenth century they were members of parliament whose claim to their position on the Board was that they had promised their influence in support of measures the Lord Lieutenant might put to parliament. Public office was a customary method of buying parliamentary support and the post of Revenue Commissioner was amongst the most coveted prizes.[4] Thus in 1765 the Revenue Board was headed by Ponsonby, Speaker of the House of Commons. In 1790 the Excise Commissioners were John Beresford, J. Monck Mason, Sir Hercules Langrishe, Lord Donoughmore, R. Annesley, Lord Fitzgerald and Isaac Corry, all except Lord Donoughmore were members of the House of Commons and Beresford or Mason were usually the official spokesmen on revenue matters.[5]

3. 14 and 15 Car. 2, c. 8, sections 10, 34, 36, 42.

4. 1 Geo. 3, c. 7, section 17. J. E. Howard, *A Treatise on the Exchequer and Revenue in Ireland*, Dublin, 1776, ii, pp. 73–94 give the terms of the 'Commissioners of the Revenue's Patent' and the opening paragraph shows the persons responsible for both customs and excise and those for customs only. J. A. Froude, *The English in Ireland in the Eighteenth Century*, London, 1874; ii, pp. 58, 91, 109; iii, pp. 489–92. *Mss. Sources of the History of Irish Civilisation*, ed. R. T. Hayes, Boston, Mass., 1965. Sir Robert Walpole stated that 'all places in the Revenue of Ireland are at the disposal of the Treasury in England' (cited from *Hist. Mss. Comm. Rep., Egmont Diary*, ii, 1923, p. 107). This may have been a convention in the 1720s, but was certainly not the practice later.

5. *A Directory, November 1765*, Linenhall Library, Belfast, Ref. N. 6592. *The Treble Almanack*, Dublin, 1790, Lin. Library, Ref. N. 6599. See also *The Gentleman's and Citizen's Almanacks*, Dublin, for example 1793, p. 66.

The reasons for this corrupt system stemmed from the legislative processes under Poynings' Act of 1495, slightly modified in practice. The first stage was for the Lords or Commons to draw up the 'Heads of a Bill' for the desired law. This stage might be inspired by the Lord Lieutenant and put forward by one of his supporters in parliament. The 'Heads of Bill' was taken to the Lord Lieutenant who ordered it to be laid before the Irish Privy Council. They could agree, vary or suppress the Bill. If agreed or varied it was put in the form of an Act and sent to England with reasons for the proposed law. In London a committee of the Privy Council referred the Bill to the Attorney General. The Privy Council considered his report and at that stage the proposed Act could be either dropped or returned to Dublin under the Great Seal with or without amendment. The Lord Lieutenant then sent the returned Bill to parliament who considered any variations made to the original Bill. Parliament had no power to make any further changes and it went through the normal readings. If any variations defeated the purpose of the original Bill or were otherwise unacceptable the Bill was dropped. It will be seen that though the powers of the Irish parliament were rigidly curbed, the process allowed them to hit back by blocking legislation desired by the Government. To counter this the Lord Lieutenant blatantly bought support and the price was as blatantly demanded by influential members. Blocking a revenue Bill was a specially potent weapon, not necessarily because the Bill itself was objectionable, but to put pressure on the Lord Lieutenant to send some other measure to London.[6]

At that time there were two kinds of revenue, hereditary and additional. Parliament had no power over the hereditary revenue, some of which was the original excise duty on spirits, but in the eighteenth century this was insufficient, and parliament granted additional duties for short periods, for most of the century for two years at a time. On one occasion the Lord Lieutenant attempted to carry on solely with the hereditary revenue by reducing expenditure and parliament replied by preventing government economies. As the spirit duty was one of the main

6. Howard, *Exchequer and Revenue in Ireland, op. cit.,* ii, pp. 233–6. Froude, *The English in Ireland, op. cit.,* ii, pp. 56–63.

sources of revenue and most of it was an additional duty, it became a part of the political game and the distillers' interests were sometimes secondary.[7]

Townsend, the Lord Lieutenant in 1770, exasperated by many gross frauds on the revenue held the Revenue Board responsible. He dismissed the whole Board and many of those in offices depending on the Board's patronage. The new Board was filled by men of alleged probity who were naturally his supporters in parliament. This move generated hostility and more support was needed. By judicious choice of men with a good following he could get this by creating new posts. So in 1772 he hit on the idea of separating the Customs and Excise and having two Boards, seven for the customs and five for the excise, thus multiplying the number of lucrative posts. This did not pass unchallenged. The House of Commons debated a resolution to refuse consent to alter revenue laws that would have the effect of increasing the number of Commissioners. The resolution was lost as there was sufficient support to carry the motion to divide the Boards. One member congratulated the Lord Lieutenant 'upon your Excellency's prudent distribution of lucrative posts and seats in the House'. Technical difficulties in paying customs duties and excise import duties troubled merchants and in 1774 the Boards were re-united. Enough has been written to demonstrate the kind of leadership in the excise department in this period and this, together with the patronage which spread all through the ranks, would do much to account for some of the legislative and administrative mistakes that occurred as well as for the official corruption at all levels.[8]

Froude relates some of the demands made on the Lord Lieutenant. Ponsonby, speaker of the House of Commons and a Revenue Commissioner, desiring to ensure his future, wanted appointment for life for himself and his brother as examinators of customs. Hely Hutchinson got a pension and was appointed

7. Howard, *Exchequer and Revenue in Ireland*, op. cit., i, p. 30. Froude, *The English in Ireland*, op. cit., ii, pp. 78, 80. The hereditary revenue ceased in 1793 and was substituted by a Civil List under 33 Geo. 3, c. 34, section 15.

8. Howard, *Exchequer and Revenue in Ireland*, op. cit., i, p. 63 and ii, p. 98. Froude, *The English in Ireland*, op. cit., ii, pp. 40, 91, 100, 110. *Irish House of Commons Journals*, 11 February 1772; 27 May 1772. The King's letter re-uniting the two Boards appears in the minutes for 16 November 1773.

Provost of Trinity College, Dublin, but this was not enough. He wanted to provide for his two sons and get his wife made a viscountess. His sons, aged sixteen and seventeen years, were duly appointed searchers at Strangford at £1,000 a year. The rewards spread to the posts of collector, for example in 1765 Sir Edward Newenham, M.P., was the excise collector for county Dublin and Sir Hercules Langrishe, M.P., was the excise collector for Kilkenny. Langrishe improved on this by getting a post on the Board in 1790 and by that time he should, at least, have learned something of his trade.[9] These rewards came to be regarded as a right, but at times the very gentlemen who so willingly profited found their position irksome. They guarded their 'rights' but did not like the accompanying duties. In 1781 Ponsonby complained that 'it was notorious that gentlemen could not hold places under the Government and act in opposition'. Newenham lamented that 'places should be forfeited for acting conscientiously, but it would be so till placemen and pensioners were by law excluded from parliament'. They were themselves placemen, but perhaps as they were actively engaged in the excise administration and not in sinecure jobs they did not look upon their positions in that light. Newenham a year later was still complaining that 'was there ever a man of them found to vote in parliament in opposition to government that did not suffer for it'. Another member cynically remarked that 'you cannot hope to abolish corruption in an age of corruption'.[10]

In 1790 there was another move to increase the Board by two more Commissioners and there were the same objections to more placemen which, as before, did not succeed. The debate in this instance gave a glimpse of the work of the Commissioners. It appears that in 1771 the seven Board members met at 11 a.m. and all their work was done by 2 p.m. In 1790, because of additional taxes their hours were from 10 a.m. to 4 p.m. and sometimes extended to 5 p.m. Comparison was made with England where it was said there were twenty-three Commissioners, but Grattan drew attention to one important difference

9. Froude, *The English in Ireland, op. cit.*, i, p. 632, and ii, p. 169. *The Directory 1765 op. cit.*, and *Treble Almanack, 1790, op. cit.*

10. *Parliamentary Register of Debates*, ed. Byrne and Porter, i, p. 42, 8 November 1781; p. 374, 28 May 1782; p. 403, 10 June 1782.

when he said that 'in England revenue commissioners were examined at the bar of the House, but in Ireland they sit amongst us'. There were, of course, many other posts, some without any tangible duties, outside the revenue department and it was pointed out that no less than one-eighth of the revenue was divided amongst members of parliament, placemen and pensioners. An Act of 1793 finally put an end to the system and thereafter any person taking up a salaried office under the Crown was ineligible to be a member of parliament. It did not affect the existing parliament and for some undisclosed reason it specifically excluded collectors of customs or excise in Dublin. The abuses of the system had at last become intolerable to the majority of members as well as the Lord Lieutenant.[11]

Before leaving the eighteenth century it is worth considering the relationship of the Revenue Board with the Government. There was no Prime Minister in the sense of the post in England. There was a Chancellor of the Exchequer who introduced the budget, but there is no evidence that he had any authority over the Revenue Board as was the case in England. He would have found it difficult to exercise any such authority when all the Board members were government spokesmen in the House, and one member was even chairman of the committee of ways and means. The Chancellor's function was to relate expenditure to revenue and he had to rely on the Revenue Board for the revenue without much authority over its management. The only apparent control over the Revenue Board was by the Privy Council who had the somewhat absurd power of examining and approving any instructions issued by the Board to the excise service.[12]

At the time of the Act of Union, 1801, five of the nine Revenue Commissioners acted separately as Commissioners of Excise, but were also Commissioners of Customs. After the Union the separation of customs and excise was made more complete under

11. *Ibid.,* x, pp. 69–70, 78, 1 February 1790; p. 154, 8 February 1790; and xii, p. 272, 6 March 1792 when in debate it was disclosed that the Government took over the office of weigh maker from the Cork corporation and appointed 3 members of parliament as joint holders of the office on salaries, thereby increasing the Crown influence in parliament. 33 Geo. 3, c. 41 ended any salaried office being held by a future member of parliament.

12. Howard, *Exchequer and Revenue in Ireland, op. cit.,* ii, p. 98. *Parl. Register,* x, p. 156, 8 February 1790; xv, p. 104, 12 February 1795 is one example of the budget speech.

directions from the Lord Lieutenant and in 1806 this arrangement was put on a statutory basis. It conformed with the revenue arrangements in Great Britain where the customs and the excise were two distinct departments and the Irish change was the first step in eventual amalgamation.[13] The Act gave powers to appoint Commissioners of Customs and 'certain other persons not exceeding seven nor less than five in number to be Commissioners of inland excise and taxes' in Ireland. An administrative decision in 1821 reduced the number to five, but allowed the reduction to become effective as vacancies arose.[14] In 1823 all existing royal patents for England, Scotland and Ireland were revoked and a new consolidated Excise Board was set up for the whole United Kingdom with its headquarters in London and included two Irish members, William Plunkett and the Hon. James Hewett. There was an interim period from 1823 to 1830 to ease the change during which a subordinate Board continued to sit in Dublin under a chairman who was one of the London Commissioners, but this Board derived all authority from the London Board. The Irish Board ceased to exist in 1830, but to smooth the change still more a Commissioner from London officiated in Dublin on a yearly basis until 1834 and from that time the excise business in Ireland was directed from London, initially under seven Commissioners.[15] The Board of Stamps and Taxes was consolidated with the Board of Excise in 1849 to become the Board of Inland Revenue. This Board functioned until 1909 when the excise was detached and merged with the customs to form the present Board of Customs and Excise.[16]

13. *Inquiry into the Collection and Management of the Revenue arising in Ireland, 2nd Report,* Parl. Pps. 1822 (565) xii, pp. 23–4. 46 Geo. 3, c. 58.

14. Treasury Warrant, 23 April, 1821. Copy in the Customs and Excise Library in London.

15. 4 Geo. 3, c. 23. Measures for consolidating the Boards in the three countries were enacted by 7 and 8 Geo. 4, c. 53. *Irish Revenue Inquiry, 7th Report,* Parl. Pps. 1824 (100) xi, p. 3 explains the subordinate status of the Irish Board. The *5th Report,* 1823 (405) vii, p. 371, describes its judicial powers. See also *Excise Revenue Inquiry, 20th Report,* Parl Pps. 1836 (22) xxvi, p. 212. *Report of the Board of Excise committee . . . upon the observations of the Excise Revenue Inquiry, 20th Report, Parl. Pps.* 1837 (96) xxx, pp. 417, 449 and *Detailed account of the Excise Establishment, Ireland,* Parl. Pps. 1823 (203) xii, p. 625.

16. *13th Inland Revenue Report,* Parl. Pps. 1780 (c. 82) xx, p. 338. Sir N. J. Highmore, *The Excise Laws,* 3rd ed., London, 1923, i, p. 5 (note). The present Board of Customs and Excise resulted from the Excise Transfer Order, 1909, made under 8 Edw. 7, c. 16, section 4.

After the Union in 1801 when the Irish excise department became part of the system in Great Britain the responsible minister in parliament was the Chancellor of the Exchequer who exercised his supervision through the Treasury. The Excise, therefore, was a sub-department of the Treasury. The Treasury had not the means at their disposal, nor would it have been desirable, for any day to day control, but they could exercise a general supervision over running costs or criticise obvious deficiencies. During the first years of the transitional period an Irish member acted as an Irish Chancellor of the Exchequer and dealt with matters concerning the excise in Ireland.[17] The Treasury's over-riding control remained until 1922 when the Irish Free State was created. Thereafter there was no change in Northern Ireland, but in the Republic of Ireland the excise came under the Minister for Finance.

In the first four decades of the nineteenth century the working of the Board of Excise seems to have been a very leisurely affair and apparently their main function was to sign orders prepared for decision by committee clerks. They met daily from 10 a.m. to 3 p.m. and during 1821 signed 39,420 excise orders, each one signed by three Commissioners. The Chairman and Deputy Chairman attended alternately for six months in each year and each Commissioner felt entitled to three months' holiday. They also received £165 a year as Commissioners of Excise Appeals, but there were only eight appeals in the thirteen years to 1824. This appeal court also had a paid registrar and doorkeeper. There were other offices under the Board with no duties whatever. For example, there was the 'Equaliser of duties and Inspector of hereditary revenue', though this revenue had ceased to exist since 1793. Another office was Surveyor of Kenmare river at £300 a year.[18]

---

17. *Excise Revenue Inquiry, 20th Report*, 1837, *op. cit.*, p. 305. The Board of Excise was regarded as a sub-department of the Lord High Treasurer's department. Close Treasury control did not exist and attempts to secure economies had failed. *Parl. Debates* (Hansard) listed an Irish Chancellor of the Exchequer. See, for example, the debate on 31 January 1809 when Newport spoke as Chancellor of the Exchequer on grain distilling in Ireland.

18. *Irish Revenue Inquiry, 3rd Report*, Parl. Papers, 1822 (606) xiii, p. 933. *7th Report*, Parl. Pps., 1824 (100) xi, p. 15. *15th Report*, Parl. Pps. 1824 (141) ix, p. 186. See also R. B. McDowell, *The Irish Administration, 1801–1914*, London, 1964, p. 8 regarding sinecures and plural offices.

During this period each Revenue Commissioner, including the Chairman, had equal powers and all decisions were those of the Board as a whole, an arrangement which came in for severe criticism in 1836 as a 'divided and intangible responsibility'. It was stated that 'the responsibility of the Board, as a Board, is of no value whatever, and as to the Commissioners, individually, not one of them is responsible for the acts of the Board, as where others participate with him in all he does, and as much may be done in which some member of the Board has not acted; so that, in fact, the appointing of a Board of several Commissioners with equal powers, as head of a sub-department for revenue purposes, completely sets aside all responsibility'.[19] What troubled the critics was that no single person acted as the head of the department and responsible to the Treasury for its work and they compared this with the French department for 'Contributions Indirectes'. They strongly recommended a similar system with one person as head of the excise department responsible to the Treasury and ultimately to the Chancellor of the Exchequer, with assistant Commissioners each with a defined duty, the Board as a whole only deliberating on important matters. The Excise Board agreed that a Chairman assisted by Commissioners each one responsible for a particular section of the work of the department would be an advantage, especially with the Treasury acting as a court of appeal against decisions considered too rigorous. Many years later this arrangement evolved with a Board exercising its duties 'subject to the authority, direction and control of the Treasury' and the appointment of an accounting officer for all departmental affairs.[20] The Treasury did not act as a court of appeal in the normal sense and an aggrieved

19. *Excise Revenue Inquiry, 20th Report*, 1836, *op. cit.*, p. 308. See also *S.C. to inquire into the Regulations in the Customs and the Import and Export Departments of the Excise: Warehousing System, 10th Report*, Parl. Pps. 1821 (25) x, pp. 331, 336. A Treasury direction dated 2 February 1822 to fix individual responsibility seems to have been ignored.

20. *Excise Revenue Inquiry, 20th Report*, 1836, *op. cit.*, pp. 309–11. *Report of the Board of Excise committee on the 20th Report*, Parl. Pps. 1837 (96) xxx, pp. 566–8. See also *A return of recommendations . . . carried into effect*, Parl. Pps. 1842 (75) xxvi. The accounting officer was appointed under the Exchequer and Audit Department Act, 1866 (29 and 30 Vict., c. 39). See 53 and 54 Vict., c. 21 as to the over-riding authority of the Treasury. At the present time the Chairman of the Board is the accounting officer.

person resorted to the courts of justice in matters relating to the
spirit duties.

To manufacturers and traders subject to excise duties the way
the Board functioned was particularly important and in no
industry was this more so than in distilling and selling spirits
which was so rigidly controlled by law and by directions issuing
from this Board. In 1836 'the whole of the laws and regulations
which constitute the general system of excise is by Act of parliament vested in the Commissioners appointed by royal letters
patent'. They administered numerous Acts of parliament, issued
general orders to the excise service and tried to ensure through
their inspectors and by correspondence and reports that the staff
throughout the country were efficiently carrying out their
orders.[21] In the early part of the nineteenth century the Board
of Excise became wholly immersed in a great mass of detail
nearly all of which had already been adequately considered by
subordinate staff. It is not surprising, therefore, that distillers
complained about delay in getting decisions and sometimes
receiving no reply to their petitions and that the Board was
accused of tending to stick to routine. Even a reply rejecting a
complaint gave no reasons, the Board's view being that they
risked legal action. This gives a suspicion that cases were dealt
with hurriedly or that reasons would have doubtful validity.[22]

These criticisms in reports to parliament led to considerable
reform and a description of the Board at work in 1862 shows
that there was now a responsible head of the department and
that the business reaching the Board had been sifted through

21. *Excise Revenue Inquiry, 20th Report,* 1836, *op. cit.,* pp. 294–5. Between
1801 and 1831 some 400 Acts had been passed affecting the whole excise making
a total of 620 Acts current at the time, many of them relating to spirits. The
general orders of the Excise Board were sent to the excise collectors who copied
them for distribution (p. 260). *Belfast Historical Excise Records,* Custom House,
Belfast, contain these orders for the years 1824–51 in Mss. books 132–138. In
later years the orders were printed and a summary of their contents appears in
Ham's Inland Revenue Year Books, published by Effingham Wilson, London,
from 1879.

22. *Excise Revenue Inquiry, 20th Report,* 1836, *op. cit.,* pp. 295–6. An astonishing
list of the duties of the Commissioners is given, including such details as examining abstracts of outdoor officers' records and diaries to correspondence with the
Customs department and from traders and officers, and to sanctioning proceedings in the Court of Exchequer or recommending revision of the law. Examples
of complaints appear on pp. 299, 567 and in *7th Report, Part I,* 1834, *op. cit.,* pp.
179, 456. See also *Report of the Board of Excise 1837, op. cit.,* pp. 554–5, 557.

various stages so that the full Board only dealt with matters of moment. In 1870 the Board of Inland Revenue reporting on excise business were able to state that there was a vast difference in the mode of doing business with the public in the thirty years between 1838 and 1868, 'nor is the growing demand for attention on the part of the taxpayer at all to be wondered at. On the contrary the wonder is that people should formerly, and even within recent period, have submitted to the treatment which they received'. They referred in their 1870 report to the criticisms of the Commissioners of the Excise Revenue Inquiry in their 1836 report and found it incredible that the Board of Excise at that time were recommended to give answers when traders asked about the excise laws, the rule then being never to communicate directly, but to instruct an excise officer to give a verbal reply. This restricted intercourse, they stated in 1870, enabled the revenue department to levy crown dues with a smaller and less educated staff. There is not much information about the internal working of the Board after the mid-nineteenth century, but a re-organised department had settled down to function much in the same manner as at present. There was a Chairman as a single head of the department and each Commissioner took charge of a particular field with the detailed and routine work being done by subordinate staff. Minor policy decisions would be made by senior officials responsible to a Commissioner and the whole Board would be involved only in major policy.[23]

Another strong criticism in 1836 was that the Commissioners themselves were not qualified to deal with the matters brought before them, particularly in relation to distilleries, as none of them had any technical knowledge or practical experience and it was recommended that practical men from the excise service should be recruited to the Board. The suggestion was that at least one member should come from amongst the excise collectors and another from the legal side. The Board at that time were gentlemen of standing and not career civil servants and it was alleged that because of a lack of technical knowledge they were at the mercy of the staff and that its business was run by 'some

23. *S.C. to inquire whether it would be practicable to consolidate any establishments governed by the Boards of Inland Revenue and Customs,* Parl. Pps. 1862 (370) vii, p. 141. *The Board of Excise Report, 1837, op. cit.,* p. 564. The Board rejected the charge of sticking to routine. *13th Inland Revenue Report,* 1870, *op. cit.,* p. 339.

clever and subordinate officer' who by 'his long experience and abilities was necessarily a preponderating influence'. This was naturally rejected by the Board of Excise, but they did admit that this situation could arise. After the establishment of the Civil Service Commission in 1855, members of the Board were men who had worked their way up over many years in the civil service, usually in the excise department, and were well qualified to assess the reports and recommendations put before them.[24]

The need for expert technical advice did not become a problem before 1823 when in Ireland the spirit revenue depended on the size of stills. Nevertheless the Irish Revenue Commissioners had taken powers to experiment in distilling in 1785, but there is no record of them using these powers. After the Union the excise department undertook distillery experiments in 1821 at Carrick-fergus and also took over Roe's distillery in Dublin for 6 months, but these were to test and evolve better ways of excise control by mechanical means. The excise also had their own distillery in St Katherine's dock in London where seized spirits were re-distilled for sale.[25] For any scientific investigation the department called in outside help, for instance in early efforts to perfect the hydrometer and saccharometer, or establishing the standard of proof spirit. There was no machinery for regular checks by chemists or trained officials on the day to day operations in distilleries. Surveying officers would, of course, through experience, become expert to a limited extent, but they would be unlikely to undertake with accuracy such matters as the analysis of obscured spirits or of ascertaining the original gravity of wash.[26] The need for a scientific official first arose in relation to tobacco, but soon extended to other excise revenues, especially spirits and malt. In 1843 George Phillips, an excise official who

24. *Excise Revenue Inquiry, 20th Report,* 1836, *op. cit.,* pp. 258, 310. *Board of Excise Report,* 1837, *op. cit.,* p. 565.

25. 25 Geo. 3, c. 34, sections 74, 78. *Experiments in Distillation by the Excise Department,* Parl. Pps. 1821 (538) xix. *Irish Revenue Inquiry, 5th Report,* 1823, *op. cit.,* p. 329 and *16th Report,* Parl. Pps. 1824 (429) ix, p. 201. J. Owens, *Plain Papers,* London, 1879, p. 498.

26. Two examples of the problems connected with spirits were obtaining a satisfactory hydrometer and fixing a legal definition of proof spirits. They are described by J. Scarisbrick, *Spirit Assaying,* Wolverhampton, 1898, pp. 61, 89 and F. G. Tate, *Alcoholometry,* London, 1930, p. 43. Another example concerned obscured spirits and is described with a suggested solution in the *Excise Revenue Inquiry, 7th Report, Part I,* 1834, *op. cit.,* p. 203.

had studied chemistry, was established by the Board of Inland Revenue in a laboratory in London and was soon engaged on examining the values of materials used in distilling, methods for ascertaining the original gravity of wash and various other basic technical problems. In 1875 the customs department set up a similar laboratory and in 1894 both laboratories were put under one official but kept as separate units. Excise officers were recruited and trained in routine chemical analysis of revenue samples and qualified chemists for more intricate work. In 1909 the two units were merged when the two departments were amalgamated and in 1911 the laboratory was detached to become a separate department serving all government departments, though the bulk of its work still concerned the revenue. A subordinate branch was established in Dublin to save delay in dealing with routine analyses. In time the status of the laboratory and its scope grew until it undertook scientific inquiries into major problems such as the development of the saccharometer, improving the hydrometer, constructing tables for assessing spirit by weight and similar projects. There was no longer need to call in outside help.[27]

The Irish Board of Revenue, in 1772 responsible for both the customs and the excise revenues, worked with a very small staff in Dublin. There were only four secretaries and nine clerks to deal with correspondence, keep records, compile returns when called for by parliament and similar work. There was a solicitor paid £350 a year, out of which he paid his own clerks, who did all the legal work which was principally prosecutions in the court of exchequer. There were no officials at headquarters, either customs or excise, from the 'outdoor' service, commonly referred to as the surveying branch, to give practical advice on the actual work of collecting duties, surveying distilleries and other revenue controls. The Board relied for such advice on four surveyors-general, one for each province, who visited collectors and examined the work of officials, and who reported to the Revenue Board on the efficiency of the staff and made

27. *13th Inland Revenue Report*, 1870, *op. cit.*, pp. 340–2. J. Scarisbrick, *Spirit Manual*, Burton-on-Trent, 1891, p. 77. *Report of the Government Chemist* for the year ending 31 March 1912. *Tobacco Year Book*, London, 1920. A survey of the Government Laboratory by J. Woodward. W. H. Johnson, *Inland Revenue Officer's Manual*, Loftus publication, London, 1873, p. 34.

recommendations if they thought any changes were necessary.[28]

During the transition period after the Union, the subordinate Board in Dublin did not deal with all the work arising in Ireland, some of it was done in London, and only a small staff worked locally. Eventually all headquarters work was done in London, but for many years after the abolition of the Irish Board, a solicitor continued to function in Dublin, probably because the London solicitor would be unfamiliar with Irish legal procedures. The Irish solicitor caused criticism and complaint, especially from some distillers, because he was said to bring far more cases before the court of exchequer instead of before magistrates, thus causing greater expense. His interest was obviously the fees he got. His powers were eventually curtailed and he came under the control of the solicitor in London.[29] The arrangements for providing the Board with practical and technical advice was put on a more satisfactory basis. A few senior excise officials drawn from the surveying branch were stationed at headquarters in London. They paid periodic inspection visits to different parts of the country and at other times were available to discuss with the Board or its senior staff any problems arising. These advisory officials had the cumbersome title of surveyor-general-examiners. One of their important duties was to sift out members of the surveying branch most suitable for promotion. In due course the advisory branch evolved into an organised office under a chief inspector and its personnel was interchangeable with the collectors.[30]

The surveying branch comprised by far the largest number employed by the excise department. They were located in towns and country, sometimes in particular premises such as a distillery or warehouse, and were engaged in the actual work of assessing and collecting the revenue. In the eighteenth and early nineteenth

28. *Mss. List of the Commissioners of H.M. Customs, appointed by patent dated 3 February 1772*. Linenhall Library, Belfast, ref. N. 2060. Howard, *Exchequer and Revenue of Ireland, op. cit.*, i, pp. 73–4.

29. *Irish Revenue Inquiry, 7th Report*, Parl. Pps., 1824 (100) xi, pp. 15–16. *Excise Revenue Inquiry, 7th Report, Part I*, 1834, *op. cit.*, pp. 379–80. *20th Report*, 1836, *op. cit.*, pp. 189, 206, 212, 580.

30. *Irish Revenue Inquiry, 5th Report*, 1823, *op. cit.*, p. 321. The title in Ireland was inspector-general. *Excise Revenue Inquiry, 20th Report*, 1836, *op. cit.*, 563. The English title was adopted in 1826. By 1890 the simpler title of inspector was used (see *Ham's Inland Revenue Year Book*, 1890, *op. cit.*, p. 268).

centuries Ireland was divided into districts each in the charge of a collector. There were about thirty-five such districts in Ireland, the number varying slightly from time to time. The collector was responsible to the Board for the collection of duties and the discipline of the staff. The district in turn was divided into surveys, each under a surveyor, and each survey was sub-divided into rides or walks staffed by gaugers. In 1824 the corresponding English titles were adopted, districts were called collections, surveys became districts and the rides or walks were renamed divisions. The titles of the officials were collector as before, supervisor, and ride or division officer. The term gauger disappeared as an official title.[31]

The integration of the staffs in Ireland and Great Britain was complete by 1831. The last headquarters office in Dublin was discontinued on 1 March 1831 and all officers were required to serve in any part of the United Kingdom. To seal the integration it was ordered that one-third of the officers in Ireland were to be English and to give effect to this order twenty-eight supervisors and 108 officers were to be transferred to Ireland and a like number of Irish officers were to go to England. There was also to be an interchange with officers in Scotland. A common seniority list was drawn up. There was, as might be expected, some resistance to these wholesale movements and the full assimilation of the staffs proceeded in a leisurely fashion which drew some criticism in 1836 in a report to parliament.[32] Nor were the Irish distillers pleased about the influx of English officials. A group of Dublin distillers alleged in 1832 that Ireland was covered by English and Scottish excise officials who operated the laws harshly and with partiality and that they were persons 'imbued with vulgar national prejudices'. These criticisms probably had some substance, especially those directed against the

31. *Board of Excise Report*, 1837, *op. cit.*, p. 524. In 1837 the surveying branch constituted over nine-tenths of the whole staff of the excise department. The proportion was of this order for the rest of the nineteenth century (see *13th Inland Revenue Report*, 1870, *op. cit.*, p. 375 and *Ham's Inland Revenue Year Books*). *Belfast Historical Excise Records, op. cit.*, Book 132, ref 1025/24. An order dated 3 August 1824 changed the official titles. As travel conditions improved so the number of collections grew less and by 1900 there were only 8 collections.

32. *Belfast Historical Records, op. cit.*, Book 132, reference G.B. 409,25; Book 133, p. 120, ref. GB. 561/29 dated 30 June 1829; and pp. 149–50 ordering the closure of the central office in Ireland for surveyor-general-examiners. *Excise Revenue Inquiry, 20th Report*, 1836, *op. cit.*, pp. 303–4.

incompetence of English officials working in distilleries for there
were so few distilleries in England that many of them could have
had very little experience. The laws were also different. By 1860,
however, the numerous distillery Acts in the three countries
were consolidated for the whole United Kingdom and all
criticism of the amalgamation of staffs died down.[33]

In view of the corruption that riddled the excise service in the
eighteenth and early nineteenth centuries it is worth examining
the method of recruitment, the qualifications required of candi-
dates and the salaries paid, especially to the junior grades. Before
the Union all appointments were in the hands of the Revenue
Board and were by nomination. The lowest grade was supernumerary gauger and was a kind of apprenticeship for promotion
as occasion arose to the rank of gauger. In 1772 the supernumerary
gauger received £30 a year and the gauger £40. The next grade
above was surveyor at a salary of £70 a year. After that there
was very little opportunity to rise higher. Collectors, whose
salary varied according to the importance of their districts, were
direct appointments from outside the excise service. Information
on the qualification for new entrants is not available. After the
Union and until the consolidation of the Revenue Board in
Ireland with the Excise Board in England these conditions
continued except that the nomination of a candidate was the
prerogative of the Irish Treasury.[34] Following the full integration
of the excise services of the United Kingdom there is much
fuller information. The system in England was adopted and a
new recruit was termed an expectant. At first he got no pay
and was regarded as a pupil for six weeks or until he got a
certificate of competence, and Irish pupils had to travel to
England for this training. The satisfactory pupil was made a
supernumerary at £52 plus an allowance of £38 when employed.
Nomination was looked upon as a kind of perquisite. At first
the Treasury had the right of nominating half the new entrants
and the Board of Excise the other half, but the size of the Board

33. *Excise Revenue Inquiry, 7th Report, Part I,* 1834, *op. cit.,* 29. The incompetence of English officers is referred to on pp. 176, 207, 417. The consolidating
distillery Act was 23 and 24 Vict., c. 114.

34. *Mss. List of H.M. Customs,* 1772, Linenhall Library, *op. cit., Excise Revenue
Inquiry, 20th Report,* 1836, *op. cit.,* pp. 275. By 1823 the gauger's pay had risen
to £80 a year (*Detailed account of the Excise establishment in Ireland,* Parl. Pps., 1823
(203) xii, pp. 625–6).

was being reduced and as the number of Commissioners fell so their share of the nominations was taken up by the Treasury.[35] This was the raw material for the excise surveying branch. The step from expectant was to supernumerary or to assistant, an intermediate grade in the United Kingdom that did not exist in the former Irish excise, and led to the rank of gauger, now renamed a division officer or a ride officer. The former had a round of duties in an urban area called a 'walk', and the latter in the country. Promotion to these posts until 1843 was by an application to the Excise Board and it was the practice to get the application supported by a member of parliament or other prominent person.[36]

Promotion to the supervisor grades followed a process known as 'taking out the official's character'. This meant a close examination of his books and a collector's report on his conduct. There was first a training grade of examiner leading to supervisor of a district. A district might contain both rides and walks and it was the supervisor's job to ensure, by selective checks on the work of officers and activities of traders, that duties were being properly assessed. In the early years of the century when collusion between officers and distillers to practise fraud was rampant the supervisor was clearly in a key position. An honest supervisor was a hazard to distillers, but if corrupt the risk was almost eliminated. As a surveyor under the Irish board before 1800 the salary was £70 a year. In 1837 it was £200 and by modern standards he was grossly overworked.[37]

35. *Excise Revenue Inquiry, 20th Report*, 1836, *op. cit.*, pp. 270, 275–6. By 1836 an expectant was paid £50, he had to be between 19 and 30 years old, healthy, free from debt and if married his family was not to exceed 2 children. *Belfast Historical Excise Records, op. cit.*, Book 136, p. 91. An order dated 9 December 1837 required an expectant to pay for his instruction. J. Bateman, *The Excise Officer's Manual*, London, 1840, pp. 247–54. The instruction fees were 20/– to the supervisor and 42/– to the instructing officer.

36. *Belfast Historical Records, op. cit.*, Book 132, ref. 1025/24. Before 1824 the grade was known as supernumerary gauger. *Excise Revenue Inquiry, 20th Report*, 1836, *op. cit.*, pp. 270–2. Bateman, *Excise Officer's Manual, op. cit.*, pp. 248–9.

37. *Mss. List of H.M. Customs*, 1772, Linenhall Library, *op. cit., Excise Revenue Inquiry, 20th Report*, 1836, *op. cit.*, pp. 270–2, 347. *Report of the Board of Excise*, 1837, *op. cit.*, pp. 413–4. *Belfast Historical Records, op. cit.*, Book 136, pp. 139–40. An order dated 10 January 1839 rescinded an order of 1824 requiring daily visits to distillers, 'it appearing that since such order was issued the number of entered distilleries has greatly increased in Ireland. . . .' In future the number of visits was left to the supervisor's discretion. See also *13th Inland Revenue Report*, 1870, *op. cit.*, p. 212.

After the Union the higher posts of surveyor-general-examiner and collector were opened to the Irish supervisor and he was eligible for the former after three years or to collector after five years, but one of these qualifying years had to be on distillery work. A qualified supervisor desiring promotion sent a petition to the Excise Board. Thereafter the process of 'taking out his character' followed, only in this instance the examination of his books extended to all the records of the officers in his district since he was held responsible for picking up errors and the action he took. Later in the century written tests were held before the books were examined, first by the collector and if this preliminary examination was satisfactory there was a further written examination in London. If the examination hurdle was achieved, the books were examined by senior members of the surveying branch and his 'character' then read to the Board for their approval.[38]

Surveyor-general-examiners were based in London. Their task was to examine records of the work done in the collections, to visit and inspect officers on their work and give technical advice to the Board on the management of the revenue. During the 'corrupt era' the inspection work was sometimes criticised and distillers in Ireland in 1834 complained to a parliamentary inquiry that the inspections were ineffective. This headquarters branch eventually became the present chief inspector's office. The salary ranged in 1836 from £300 to £550 a year in relation to four grades.[39]

Not much is known about the work of collectors in the eighteenth century and as some, or perhaps most of them, had other interests, it is probable that some junior official acted for them. A few excise collectors, for example, were also members of parliament. The collector was, of course, responsible for collecting the duties and the work of the staff in his district, but

38. Bateman, *Excise Officer's Manual*, op. cit., pp. 250, 275–7. J. Owens, *Plain Papers*, London, 1879, p. 519. *13th Inland Revenue Report*, 1870, op. cit., pp. 212–3. After the experiences of inefficiency and corruption earlier in the century the authorities were trying to make sure of those promoted to the higher ranks.

39. *Excise Revenue Inquiry, 20th Report*, 1836, op. cit., 253, 258–9, 266. *Board of Excise Report*, 1837, op. cit., pp. 491–4. These officials were regarded by the Board as the highest class of superintending officer under any supreme administrative authority *13th Inland Revenue Report*, 1870, op. cit., p. 213.

it is more likely that the revenue duties received special attention and the staffing very little. Howard gives an account of the business of a collector, and it seems that in 1776 the arrangements for paying excise duties in the previous century still operated, that is, traders attended the excise office weekly. The collector notified the Commissioners weekly and monthly of his receipts and rendered a quarterly account to the Accountant General. The procedure for remitting the cash itself seems to have been very lax and there was a long list of collectors who had died or been dismissed with large sums of collected duties still outstanding. Some of this money was recovered from their estates. There were also cases of outright embezzlement. The situation became so notorious that in 1765 the law prescribed that collectors or other officers defacing or destroying their accounts, or not delivering them to the Revenue Commissioners on demand or within twenty-one days, would be guilty of a felony and liable to a death penalty. After 1765 no more is heard of new outstanding balances arising. The drastic penalty may have been a deterrent, but the officials most affected were men of high standing and influence, such as Sir John Eccles, excise collector in Dublin, and Sir Richard Cox of Cork. There is no record of a conviction and it is unlikely that the mere mulcting of the government till by this method would be pressed to the extreme. The collector before the Union was responsible for both customs and excise revenues except in large ports or inland districts, where the work was separated, though the subordinate staff for the two revenues was always distinct.[40]

After the Union the English arrangements for collecting duties governed the collector's work. He was still the administrative head of the area of his collection, responsible for collecting the money and remitting it to the Exchequer, maintaining discipline and efficiency and keeping the Board informed on matters relating to the management of the revenue. In 1836 his salary ranged from £350 to £600 a year depending on the importance of

40. 5 Geo. 3, c. 16, sections 25–6. Howard, *Exchequer and Revenue of Ireland, op. cit.,* i, pp. 84, 99. *Instructions for collecting Customs and Excise duties,* Parl. Pps. 1805 (23) vi, pp. 202–5. These refer to balances still outstanding in 1799 and steps taken to recover them. *Parl. Debates,* 17 February 1809; 30 May 1810. These debates refer to the alleged embezzlement of £23,000 by the collector at Cork. See also *Mss. List of H.M. Customs,* 1772, *op. cit.,* which shows the jurisdiction and staff of each collector's district.

D

his collection. His activities were largely dictated by an old English statute which enacted that no trader should be required to travel further than the nearest market town to pay his duties.[41] The resulting procedure conjures up an interesting picture of a regular event in the life of a market town in the nineteenth century. The collector would receive advices from his staff on the assessments made on each trader and would post these in his books. At the beginning and again in the middle of each quarter, the collector would set out on a round of the towns accompanied by an assistant carrying his portmanteau. At each town he would hold a 'sitting' and in the early part of the century this would usually be held on the premises of a publican. The local excise staff would attend at the sitting and all traders in the vicinity and liable for duties would arrive and pay cash. The debt would then be discharged from the books. Any argument would be settled on the spot. The collector would then move on to the next town, his portmanteau getting heavier with the cash as the round progressed. Carrying so much cash was a hazard during troubled periods and the collector would rely for some measure of protection from the clerk and also a supernumerary and driver accompanying him, but this did not stop the Board questioning the expense of taking round the supernumerary. The collector, Lisburn, defended the practice of taking three people with him in 1844. He replied that he travelled at stated times, carrying public money and this was unsafe in Ireland. It seems a niggling criticism from London. This system of rounds had one good point. The collector was in close contact with his staff, traders and the community generally. He could examine local excise records, hear complaints from distillers or others and if necessary visit a distillery. On the other hand this travelling was a wearisome and time-consuming task and the collector must have been hard pressed to do all the office work at his headquarters. By 1880 the system ceased and duties were paid by post or directly at the collector's headquarters.[42]

41. 12 Car. 2, c. 23 (English statutes). *Excise Revenue Inquiry, 20th Report, 1836, op. cit.,* pp. 270–2. *13th Inland Revenue Report,* 1870, *op. cit.,* p. 213.

42. The procedure outlined operated in Ireland from about 1840. Before that the duty assessment was made up each Wednesday for the previous distilling period and paid on Saturday. See *Inquiry into Fees, Perquisites and Emoluments . . . received in certain Public Offices in Ireland, 5th Report,* Parl. Pps. 1806–7 (124) vi, p. 148; *Irish Revenue Inquiry, 5th Report,* 1823, *op. cit.,* p. 310; J. Bateman,

One of the most serious problems in the early nineteenth century was the corruption of excise officers and their connivance of fraud by distillers, and the hopeless position of any distiller who tried to be honest. This canker also permeated through all stages in the spirit trade, particularly through fraudulent permits. The problem led to parliamentary inquiries and debates and persisted for many years after these inquiries had resulted in the abolition of recognised fees, a euphemism for bribes, paid by distillers to officers and making such practices a misdemeanour. Accounts written at the time and reports of official inquiries leave no doubt whatever that the main reason for so much corruption was the inadequate salaries paid, which in turn would not attract suitable recruits. One member of parliament considered that it was sufficient proof of corruption that the officers were alive for without bribes they would starve. He said the salaries paid to gaugers and surveyors in 1809 were settled in the reign of Charles II and, in fact, the figures he quoted were the same as the salaries paid in 1772 and probably much earlier.[43] In the same debate on Irish frauds Sir John Newport quoted the case of a surveyor who received twenty guineas a month for each still in his survey and though he openly admitted this he was later promoted. The Chancellor of the Exchequer replied that 'owing to the inadequacy of salaries, an universal system of corruption had formerly existed among revenue officers in Ireland and that out of thirty-two excise officers examined by the Commissioners in Inquiry thirty of them had confessed that they had received similar presents. They justified it as being a constant practice and known to be so by the Board who employed them and who took no measures to stop it'. He went on to say that the officer concerned gave the Commission of Inquiry every information in his power, was a good surveyor and was promoted on his merits.[44] Earlier in 1805 the Chancellor of the Exchequer

---

Excise Officer's Manual, op. cit., p. 254; *13th Inland Revenue Report, 1870, op. cit.,* p. 213. C. McCoy, *Dictionary of Customs and Excise,* London, 1938, p. 198. From 1880 duties could be remitted by post. The Lisburn collector's reply is in *Belfast Historical Records, op. cit.,* Book 5, p. 10.

43. *Mss. List of H.M. Customs,* 1772, Linenhall Library, *op. cit.,* Parl. Debates 30 May 1809, col 789. In 1806 receiving fees from distillers was made a misdemeanour by 46 Geo. 3, c. 88, section 40.

44. *Parl. Debates,* 30 May 1809, cols. 787-9.

had stated that there was extensive corruption owing to low salaries and said that one distiller paid £1,200 a year to revenue officers. An inspector-general of excise admitted that frauds on the extensive scale prevailing in 1807 would not be possible without the collusion of officers. These frauds were not confined to distillery operations, but to the sale of official permits which enabled illicit spirit to enter the legitimate market. Bribery was also a regular feature with rectifiers and compounders. All this was confirmed by the testimony of distillers and rectifiers.[45] In effect the government were really allowing the trade to subsidise the low pay of officials. In the official accounts, the cost of the revenue service was kept lower at the expense of encouraging dishonesty.

Permits were issued to cover the transfer of spirits from the distiller to his customers and movements thereafter. To counteract the permit frauds and also to speed up the procedure of transfer, a grade of permit writer was introduced in 1807 with a status about the equivalent of an officer. He was employed in towns where there was a busy spirit trade. In the country the officer continued to issue permits. At that time the permit was also the basis of official stock records and when spirits were transferred there was no other advice between the officers concerned. Thus a distiller getting a permit to send out spirits could use it more than once without detection and in this way illicit spirit entered the stream of legal spirit. Time limits for the transfer were circumvented. A permit issued for a distant place and a time limit of a day or more set for the journey, enabled a distiller to transport one or more consignments to nearby places before the proper consignment was sent out. Another fraud was the sale of permits by officers, the counterfoil in his record of issue being filled in to suit the distiller's stock after the transaction was over. Where both a permit writer and an officer in different offices were concerned with one transaction, it was hoped that permit frauds would be too difficult. There were also many complaints of delay due to the time taken to get permits on busy market days and the introduction of permit writers was intended to meet these complaints. The grade was

45. *Parl. Debates,* 13 March 1805, col. 9. *Inquiry into Fees in Ireland, 5th Report,* 1806–7, *op. cit.,* pp. 195–6, 201, 209, 220–1. McDowell, *The Irish Administration, op. cit.,* p. 82.

abolished in 1860 when the permit system was altered on the introduction of spirit certificates for use by dealers and rectifiers.[46]

In this atmosphere of corruption laws designed to prevent fraud were useless where both officer and trader were in collusion. The more rigid and restrictive these laws became the more was their object defeated, for this merely put further weapons in the hands of officers to harass any trader who did not bribe sufficiently; and the officers could do nothing else in order to live decently on their meagre salaries. The distiller who might try to avoid bribing would be obstructed or penalised in a dozen different ways; offences against the distillery laws without any fraudulent intent could be magnified until his competitive power against less conscientious distillers would be seriously weakened. Openly acknowledged corruption is not eliminated at a stroke, the habits become entrenched and continue beyond the needs which were their reason. Official salaries were raised, fees were made illegal, but in 1834 the same story of corruption and underpaid officers appears in the evidence before another government inquiry. The salary of an officer was now £100 a year and the supervisor's £200; certainly an improvement, but the total income of a distillery officer earlier was £40 salary plus distillers' fees and this was rather more than the new salary. Supervisors were similarly placed.[47] Distillers still complained that they had to practise fraud in order to stay in business and some of them asked for special punitive measures against fraudulent distillers in order to protect those who tried to be honest. Again inadequate official salaries were stated as the primary cause of the trouble. Nor is it surprising to find that dishonesty in the excise service had spread upwards to senior officials in this age of corruption, though here low salaries were no excuse and only isolated cases came to light.[48]

46. Owens, *Plain Papers*, op. cit., p. 394. *Inquiry into Fees in Ireland, 5th Report,* 1806–7, op. cit., p. 156. *Irish Revenue Inquiry, 5th Report,* 1823, op. cit., p. 325. *Excise Revenue Inquiry, 7th Report, Part* I, 1834, op. cit., p. 180, item 15 and p. 181. *Belfast Historical Excise Records,* op. cit., Book 5, p. 11. The excise collector reported on the great demand on permit writers in Belfast on the principal market day, Friday, when they could not cope with the work in the proper time. *13th Inland Revenue Report,* 1870, op. cit., pp. 269–70.

47. *Excise Revenue Inquiry, 20th Report,* 1836, op. cit., pp. 270–2.

48. *Ibid.,* pp. 277, 456. Two collectors defaulted in 1823 and 1832. *Board of Excise Report on the 20th Report,* 1837, op. cit., 524–6. The Board agreed that salaries were too low and that the poverty of officers was a strong temptation.

88 *Irish Whiskey*

By 1870 corruption on the grand scale was no longer evident. Salary scales had been improved and the officer now received from £120 to £150 a year and the supervisor from £210 to £250 without any appreciable change in the cost of living. This improvement in itself was not likely to have eradicated corruption though it probably attracted a better type of entrant. Pensions were also put on a better footing. Before 1812 officers could pay 6d. in the pound of their salaries into a charity fund and could get a pension when sixty years old equal to their salary if their services where meritorious. This replaced an earlier arrangement of providing a sinecure post. A general superannuation fund was established in 1824 free of contributions. In 1829 parliament imposed contributions. In 1859 this fund was abolished and a superannuation Act passed for all civil servants under which a pension of two-thirds the salary was paid after forty years service. Another feature of this period was the decline in patronage and the rise in examination tests before entry until finally, in 1855, the Civil Service Commission was established. Thereafter entry into the civil service was conditional on passing independently conducted tests. All these measures combined to lift the standards in the civil service and wholesale corruption in the excise disappeared. The excise did not immediately come within the full scope of the Civil Service Commission. The Treasury and Excise Board held on to their privileges of nomination until 1870, but nominees were subject to independent examination before appointment.[49]

The excise authorities faced a major problem in their efforts to suppress unlicensed distilling which reached astonishing proportions in the late eighteenth and early nineteenth centuries. At first the gauger protected by soldiers was the only real defence, but the military protection was restricted to ensuring the gauger's safety and they were no help in the actual seizure of unlicensed stills. Gaugers used hired men to assist them. In 1788 privately raised armed parties were authorised to combat illicit distillers in small areas in Ulster and Connaught and succeeded in suppressing the practice where they operated.[50] Eventually in 1818 an official

---

p. 267–8 describes frauds at Midleton and Kilkenny distilleries. See *Excise Revenue Inquiry, 7th Report, Part I*, 1834, pp. 200, 256–7, 435–6.

49. J. Owens, *Plain Papers, op. cit.*, pp. 110, 502–8. The Superannuation Act of 1859 was 22 Vict., c. 26.

50. *Irish Revenue Inquiry*, 5th Report, 1823, *op. cit.*, pp. 335–6. *Excise Revenue Inquiry, 7th Report, Part II*, Parl. Pps., 1835 (8) xxx, pp. 84–5.

force of revenue police was established. They were armed, accoutred and trained on the lines of rifle regiments and posted in small parties in areas notorious for illicit distilling. At first each party was under the charge of an excise officer. Their sole work was still hunting to begin with, but they later did subsidiary jobs such as checks against illicit malting. In 1824 lieutenants were appointed to replace the excise officer and thereafter the supervision of the revenue police was in the hands of their own inspectors and a rather tenuous check by collectors.[51] In areas where the revenue police operated the ordinary excise officer tended to regard illicit distilling as outside his province, but a combination of excise officer and military protection did continue in many places and quite a large military force was ear-marked for this duty.[52] The revenue police were re-organised in 1836, a more stringent test of fitness was imposed and a training depot set up in Dublin. The police even had their own band. Internal discipline was also tightened. The result was that wholesale illicit distilling to an extent which could affect the legal industry declined to the point when the economics of using a special force was questioned, and in 1855 the force was disbanded and the work was undertaken by the constabulary. Since then illicit distilling has never been a threat to the legal distiller.[53]

After the turmoil of the nineteenth century the present century has been tame. The most important event was, of course, the creation in 1922 of the Government of Northern Ireland, and the Irish Free State. The former is subordinate to that in London and the British excise department continues to function as before.

51. *Ibid.*, pp. 59, 85, 88, pp. 63–4 describes the control of revenue police. *S.C. on extending the function of the Constabulary in Ireland to the suppression of Illicit Distillation*, Parl. Pps. 1854 (53) x, p. 366.

52. *Excise Revenue Inquiry, 7th Report, Part II*, 1835, *op. cit.*, pp. 70–1 *Return of Excise Officers*, Parl. Pps. 1816 (231) ix, p. 414. The troops cantoned for assisting the excise is given. There were 104 stations with over 2,500 soldiers under the command of a Field Officer. Sixty-two stations were in the northern command.

53. The constabulary assumed responsibility under 17 and 18 Vict., c. 89. *S.C. on Constabulary functions*, 1854, *op. cit.*, pp. 6–10, 38, p. 238 shows the revenue police in 1852 as 151 officers and 947 men. On pp. 375–7 is an extract of army orders for assisting revenue officers. See *13th Inland Revenue Report*, 1870, *op. cit.*, p. 235. *Historical Excise Records*, Custom House, Londonderry, Books 41–3 contain orders and decisions concerning the detailed work, movements and money matters relating to the revenue police in that collection. The drums of the revenue police band are in the Customs and Excise Library in London.

Licensing to sell spirits is, however, one of the functions transferred and is subject to Northern Ireland legislation. By arrangement, however, the collector of customs and excise acts as agent
and the British staff collect the licence duties for the Northern
Ireland Government. In the Irish Free State a Revenue Board was
constituted and charged with the management and collection of
all revenues. This Board, answerable to the Minister for Finance,
consists of a Chairman and two Commissioners, one of whom is
responsible for the excise administration in the twenty-six
counties. The structure of the excise service has not changed and
such changes as have occurred in distillery laws have been towards
easing their impact on distillers. This relaxation has been evident
in both parts of Ireland, particularly in the last ten years. Thus
the political upheavals of the early 1920s have not had any serious
direct effect on distillers, but distillers in the Republic of Ireland
may find that there is a closer contact between them and the
Revenue Board and Government than formerly and a situation
which is, perhaps, more desirable.[54]

54. 13 Geo. 5, sess. 2, c. 1, sec. 2 and Article 74; and c. 2, sec. 5. The corresponding Irish Acts were 1922, Nos. 1 and 5.

CHAPTER V

EARLY HISTORY

Before 1700

THE art of distilling spirits is believed to have been discovered about the eleventh century in Mediterranean countries and that the spirits were used chiefly for curative purposes. There is no authentic record to show when knowledge of distilling reached Ireland; or indeed, whether distilling was independently discovered.[1] Some writers have claimed that the invading soldiers of Henry II found the Irish drinking aqua vitae and that usquebagh was a beverage in common use in the twelfth century. The 'common use' is unlikely, but Irish monks returning from pilgrimages may have brought distilling knowledge with them and distilled spirits in monasteries for medicinal reasons. A few scraps of information about spirit drinking appear a century later.[2] Evidence of spirituous beverages in Ireland gets stronger at the beginning of the fifteenth century, but even in 1450 the wording of a statute that 'Irish wine, ale or other liquor' was to be sold by the King's measure properly sealed, that is, by 'the

---

1. A. J. V. Underwood, *The Historical Development of Distilling Plant*, a paper read before the Institute of Chemical Engineers, 22 February 1935, p.1. F. G. Tate, *Alcoholometry*, London, 1930, p. viii, spirits were distilled for medicinal purposes by monks. The *Encyclopaedia Britannica* gives a period earlier than the eleventh century.

2. S. Morewood, *A Philosophical and Statistical History . . . of Inebriating Liquors*, Dublin, 1838, pp. 615–6; J. Scarisbrick, *Spirit Manual*, 2nd ed., Wolverhampton, 1891, p. 44; The Department of Agriculture and Technical Instruction, *Ireland, Industry and Agriculture*, Dublin, 1902, p. 494; *Thom's Directory of Manufacturers*, Dublin, 1908, p. 434. *The Irish Year Book*, 1909, issued by the National Council, Dublin, p. 151 states that there is no real evidence of 12th century distilling. *The Ulster Journal of Archaeology*, Belfast, 1858, p. 285 quotes an extract from the 13th century *Red Book of Ossory* giving a recipe for making aqua vitae from wine indicating that distilling was not common. On p. 284 there is an account from the *Annals of the Four Masters*, of a chieftain, Richard Magranell, dying in 1405 from a surfeit of aqua vitae. See also P. W. Joyce, *Social History of Ancient Ireland*, Dublin, 1906, p. 350.

gallon, pottle, quart, pint and half-pint', indicates that spirits were no more than 'other liquor'.[3] There is other evidence that distilling was not commonly practised before the fifteenth century. Vessels, including an ancient worm, have been found in bogs and appeared to have been used as stills ranging from half gallon to 100 gallons in size. None of them suggest a date earlier than 1400 judging from the materials, solder used and their condition, but they lend support to a probability that distilling operations were purely domestic.[4]

A century later spirit drinking had become sufficiently widespread to warrant legislation to curb it because of its consequent social evils, for a statute in 1556 states that 'aqua vitae a drink nothing profitable to be daily drunken and used is now universally throughout the realm of Ireland'. A licence from the Lord Deputy under the Great Seal was required before making the spirit and infringement carried a penalty of £4 with imprisonment. Peers, gentlemen owning property worth £10, and borough freemen were permitted to make aqua vitae without this licence.[5] The picture is that of innkeepers with small stills to meet local needs while in larger households distilling was part of the domestic duties. It does not indicate any substantial distilleries, but it does show a probability of innumerable small stills widely distributed throughout the country, a feature which may have had an important bearing on illicit distilling in later centuries. The Act of 1556 made no reference to a licence duty but some charge was probable.[6] The machinery for enforcing the spirit licences or any other laws at the time was utterly inadequate. Wardens of the peace were named for every county following the statute of Kilkenny in 1367 and in the sixteenth century were still nominally operating, but by then Ireland was in a state of anarchy. Laws, at least those of the Dublin government, were not even nominally observed beyond the Pale, so it is not possible to assess the extent of distilling except by inference.[7]

3. 28 Hy. 6, sess. 2 (Drogheda), c. 3.
4. *The Ulster Journal of Archaeology*, 1859, pp. 38–40.
5. 3 and 4 Philip and Mary, c. 7, sections 1–2.
6. Carew, *Book of Howth, Miscellaneous*, ed. J. S. Brewer and W. Bullen, London, 1868, p. 390. The King's revenue in Ireland in 1537 was under £5,000 so any licence revenue would be to no consequence.
7. J. A. Froude, *The English in Ireland in the Eighteenth Century*, London, 1874, i, pp. 31, 35, 47.

The English Government in Ireland, regarding spirit drinking as amongst the causes of unrest, issued a direction in 1580 that in Munster martial law was to be applied to 'idle persons . . . aiders of rebels . . . makers of aqua vitae . . .' and the provost marshal was commanded to make a monthly return of persons executed.[8] This edict merely diverted drinking from home-made spirits to smuggled imports for later in the same year there is a complaint from Munster that 'great quantities of aqua vitae and wines were being imported which defeated the customs'. The numerous bays and creeks in Cork and Kerry plus the temper of the people would frustrate any attempt to prevent smuggling.[9] Laws and edicts to restrain drinking aqua vitae or usquebaugh were so ineffective or badly enforced that the Lord Deputy received a long letter in 1584 asking that the 'statute for making aqua vitae be put in execution, which sets the Irishry a madinge, and breeds much mischiefs'.[10] There is no indication of an established distilling industry, but rather of retailers making the spirit they sold, and household distilling, with competing imports when distilling was held in check. There is even no sound evidence that there was any considerable distilling from cereals, for wine might have been used. It is likely that either was used according to its availability, and the term usquebaugh applied generally. At this period the spirit favoured was not the plain spirit, or whiskey, which was probably harsh and unpalatable, but a compounded spirit. About 1600, Fynes O. Moryson, secretary to the Lord Deputy, wrote a description of Ireland in which he praised the medicinal value of 'aqua vitae, vulgarly called usquebaugh', and its superiority over spirits made in England because it was compounded with raisins and other ingredients. He also mentioned the drunken orgies that occurred at feasts and markets. Wine competed with spirits at these orgies. Attempts had been made in 1569 to stop excessive imports of wine and in addition to a customs duty an import licence was required. In 1586 an Act complained about the abundance of wine imports and the lack of a navy to ensure that imports arrived only at approved cities and ports. Clearly usquebaugh was not yet a national preference,

8. Carew, *Calendar of State Papers, 1575–88*, ed. Brewer and Bullen, London, 1868, p. 197, item 251. If any monthly returns were made they are not recorded.

9. *Ibid.*, p. 285, item 440.

10. *Ibid.*, p. 398, item 572. Clause 9 of the letter.

though its popularity must have been growing fast. A historian wrote in 1633 that the 'Irish eat raw meat which boyleth in their stomachs with aqua vitae which they swill in after such a surfeite, by quarts and pottles'. This colourful statement sounds more like a traveller's tale, but it does indicate considerable spirit drinking.[11]

By 1611 a practice was well established of granting patents to individuals giving them a monopoly to make aqua vitae in a particular area. The patentee paid an agreed sum for a licence covering a fixed period, usually for not more than seven years. Crown officers watched the patentee to ensure that a fair licence fee was paid at each renewal. During the currency of the licence the patentee could permit others in his area to make spirits at whatever charge he could exact. In 1611 the licence periods of many of these patentees were running out and there were suggestions for reform. One was to reduce the number of patentees by granting only one licence for each county. The opportunity was taken for a review of the system by the Attorney General who recommended that licence renewals should be at an enhanced price. He estimated this would bring in about £500 a year.[12]

Probably because of this review future monopolies consisted of farming all revenues on a larger scale and occasional references to the old system disappear after 1625. The scale grew for in 1669 the whole revenue was farmed to John Forth, a London alderman, for £219,500 and in 1676 to Sir James Shean and ten others for £240,000. Home-made spirits would only be a small part of these totals, but the system was observing a dictum following the review of 1611 that 'aqua vitae and wines are to be put on the same footing as wines. Licences granted under the great seal of Ireland are to be granted so that some reasonable profit may be raised by some indifferent fines and rents to be agreed and compounded for by such persons as shall use the trade'. No rates of

11. Edmund Spenser and others, *Ireland under Elizabeth and James I*, ed. H. Morley, London, 1890, pp. 420, 428. The Acts in 1569 and 1586 were 11 Eliz., sess. 4, c. 1. and 28 Eliz., c. 4. Edmund Campion, *History of Ireland,* Dublin, 1633, p. 18. See also A. E. Longfield, *Anglo-Irish trade in the 16th century*, London, 1929, chap. IX.

12. Carew, *Calendar of State Papers*, 1603–24, *op. cit.,* p. 99, item 70. The longest grant was for seven years. On p. 130, item 81 the Auditor General's certificate of the state of the revenue shows that grants for making aqua vitae in 1611 only amounted to 11s. 8d. There are no details, but it may have been that this small sum was arrears from an earlier year.

licence duty or any other levy were prescribed either by law or by the government. As before the farmer compounded for a fixed sum and it was left to him to recover it with a profit. He employed his own agents whose actions were backed by law. Thus the small patentees had been replaced by men of considerable influence.[13] This large scale farming came in for much criticism in 1640. Earlier the House of Commons objected to 'the universal and unlawful increasing of monopolies, to the advantage of the few, to the disprofit of his Majesty and the impoverishment of the people'. This criticism was levelled at the extortions of agents employed by the farmers. Another criticism was that the law only punished the makers of aqua vitae for infringements, but that the patentee, without warrant of the law, extended his licence power to buyers and sellers to his private gain. The farmer was only concerned with collecting money, not with the activities of distillers. Sir William Petty was against farming, but he discloses that because of incompetent and dishonest officials the rent paid by farmers was three times that obtained by direct government control. He also attacked the Crown supervising officers and claimed that the evils of placemen and perquisites under farming were three times as great, so that the Treasury profit was, in his view, a national loss.[14]

In October, 1641, at the beginning of the revolt of Irish chiefs, the Dublin government was in so parlous a state that it could not raise £50 and the Lord Lieutenant was reduced to visiting towns and cities to raise money by pledging the customs revenue. Distillers and sellers of spirits must have been practically immune from levies or control of any kind, but there is some evidence that the rebel government did attempt to levy some kind of duty

13. G. E. Howard, *A Treatise of the Exchequer and Revenue of Ireland,* Dublin, 1776, i, Preface, p. xlvii. Carew, *Calendar of State Papers 1603–24, op. cit.,* p. 207, item 120. See *Calendar of State Papers, 1615–25,* ed. C. W. Russell and J. Prendergast, London, 1880, for examples of the last few licences under the Lord Deputy's seal on p. 152, item 342 and p. 170, item 377. Disputes about patents appear on pp. 532, 540.

14. *Irish House of Commons Journal,* 7 November 1640. A Remonstrance, item 7. *Economic Writings of Sir William Petty,* ed. C. H. Hall, Cambridge, 1899, i, pp. 195–7. G. O'Brien, *Economic History of Ireland in the 17th century,* Dublin, 1919, pp. 60, 93, 201–2. R. Dunlop, *Ireland under the Commonwealth,* Manchester, 1913, i, p. 135, item 141. Farming the excise revenue was approved on 12 February 1652 by the governing Irish Commissioners. *The Ulster Journal of Archaeology,* 1858, p. 288.

and grant immunity from taxes to those providing munitions. When the rebellion ended, the Articles of Peace, signed in Kilkenny on 17 January 1648, make a reference to excise duties and infer a levy on spirits. One of these articles abolished monopolies and arranged for the appointment of Commissioners 'to set down the rates for customs and imposition to be laid on aqua vitae'. These Commissioners were also given power to collect arrears of excise duty and levy additional duties to meet the debts of the Catholic Confederacy incurred before 1648. There had been a long delay between agreeing the Articles and signing the treaty and a year later Charles I was executed, the agreement was disclaimed, and as a result there seems to be no record of the duties being collected. The terms of the treaty do indicate, however, that a distilling trade was emerging and that there were probably, but not certainly, individuals making spirit primarily for sale to retailers. A small degree of specialisation was arising.[15] Ireland was soon to enter yet another period of war and so far as distilling is concerned its progress and extent are guesswork. It would be fair to assume that distilling was common in all parts of the country, that the stills and utensils would be small and primitive by later standards, and that there was no sharp distinction between legal and illegal distilling.

The retail outlet for spirits would be alehouses, inns and similar places and their owners were brought under official control by an Act in 1634 because of their excessive numbers and because many of these places were established 'in woods, bogges and other unfit places . . . and that those that keep alehouses for the most part are not fitted or furnished to lodge or entertain travellers . . .' Beer must have been the popular drink at the time for it was the main target of the Act, but the Act is important for spirits because it set the pattern for later controls over retailing all liquors. The Act prescribed that none shall sell beer without a licence and that the Lord Deputy was to nominate Commissioners in every county from justices of the peace and other fit persons. These Commissioners were to consider applications for licences, decide on the number to be granted and the suitability of places for selling beer, as well as the sufficiency and probity of the applicants. A

15. E. Borlase, *History of the Irish Rebellion*, London, 1680, pp. 27, 211. John Milton, *Prose Works*. ed. J. A. St. John, London, 1875, ii, pp. 158 et. seq., p. 172.

licence was valid for one year and the licensee had to enter into recognisances with one surety for £10, to observe the assize of bread, ale and beer, and sell at reasonable rates, in order, no doubt, to curb any abuse of the partial monopoly conferred by the grant of a licence. The licensee was not to harbour suspects or a neighbour's servants, nor permit 'ill-behaviour'. Lodging a stranger was limited to twenty-four hours unless he was over-taken by illness. There was a licence duty of 5s. 6d. in English currency and the premises were to be advertised by displaying a sign, stake or bush.[16]

The revenue yield from customs duties had long been based on quantity and value so it is not surprising that a similar type of excise duty on spirits would be levied as soon as this became practicable, or in the words of an Act in 1661 to 'gather the said customs, excise and new import that shall grow in the said tyme'. Duties of this kind have been referred to as 'growing duties' ever since.[17] By the time of the restoration of Charles II a distinct distilling industry was in being and sufficiently large to attract to itself a duty on the quantity produced. From 24 December 1661 a duty of 4d. a gallon was levied on home-made spirits. There were corresponding duties on imports of 1s. a gallon on spirits 'perfectly made' and 4d. a gallon if made from 'wine or cyder'. The distinction is not clear, but it may be presumed that the lower rate was for inferior quality, perhaps of low strength from a single distillation. These rates gave the Irish distiller considerable protection against imports, including spirits from Great Britain, and although the difference was enough to give an incentive to smuggling there is no official evidence of any marked increase in illegal imports. There may, of course, have been a great deal of misdescription at import and claims that perfectly made spirits were spirits of lower quality. With no accurate means of assess-ment the customs officers would have to rely on crude tests such as taste, so a good deal of haggling and bribery would probably

16. 10 and 11 Car. 1, c. 5. See also *H. C. Journal*, 8 June 1640. Anyone versed in the present licensing laws will recognise several features of the Act. Un-licensed retailers used similar signs to advertise their shebeens as late as the mid-nineteenth century. (*S.C. to consider extending the functions of the Constabulary in Ireland to the suppression of Illicit Distilling*, Parl. Pps. 1854 (53) x, p. 56.)

17. 14 Car. 2, sess. 3, c. 1. See C. McCoy, *Dictionary of Customs and Excise*, London, 1938, p. 97.

reduce the protection of the higher duty.[18] The Act made a clear distinction between distillers, who could sell to retailers, and innkeepers, victuallers and others who could only distil for sale to their customers. If the latter sold to another retailer both seller and buyer were liable to a penalty of double the duty. Clearly there must have been a very large number of persons distilling spirits, but it is not known how many were specialised distillers.[19] The enforcement provisions were very weak. There was no provision for distillers or importers to register or enter their premises with the newly set up excise authorities, but powers were given for gaugers to search the premises of any importer, or still houses and out houses by day or night, to gauge vessels and take an account of any aqua vitae or strong waters that they found. There were also penalties for concealing or using vessels without prior notification.[20]

Under the Act of 1661 Excise Commissioners were established with powers to appoint gaugers and searchers. A new system of excise taxation and a new department began without experience except such as could be learned from the customs, without a trained staff and without any knowledge of the numbers needed to police and collect the duties efficiently. Staff of some kind would be necessary in a number of widely separated towns and not concentrated in a few places as in the customs. It was, in fact, the first attempt to set up a civil department where most of its members would be remote from immediate control. These difficulties were recognised from the beginning for the Act provided that distillers, innkeepers and similar persons making aqua vitae or strong waters could compound the duty for twelve months at a sum adjudged as fair by the Excise Commissioners, provided a bond was given with sureties for the due payment of this sum in monthly instalments. These persons were then exempted from all excise control. They could make as much as they liked and feel fairly safe that the compounded figure would not be increased since there was no check on their production and

---

18. 14 and 15 Car. 2, c. 8. Section 4 imposed the excise duty, and section 7 the customs duty. The latter was levied as 1s in the £ and is related to a Book of Rates annexed to the Act where 'strong waters' are valued at £1 a gallon and spirits made from wine or cyder at 6s. 8d. a gallon. It is possible that the latter duty was a preference to spirits made in Great Britain.

19. *Ibid.*, sections 32, 38.

20. *Ibid.*, sections 10, 34–5.

apparently making excess spirits was not an offence.[21] Those who did not compound were to attend the excise office every Monday and enter the quantity and quality of the spirits made during the previous week, thus following the system used for customs duties where an importer attended the custom house, entered his imports and paid the duty. Distillers living more than three miles from an excise officer were permitted to attend fortnightly.[22]

Unlike the Act of 1634 for retailers the Act of 1661 did not require a distiller to exhibit any sign proclaiming his trade which indicates that the sign was not primarily for revenue reasons, but rather to pin-point houses to which the justices should give special attention as probable centres of mischief. The gauger, therefore, had first to find out where distilling was being done before he could operate any checks. In towns this would not be too difficult. He could go the rounds of persons known to have stills who had not compounded for the duty and very likely hear of any new-comers to the trade, but the gauger's task would be very difficult even a short distance from urban areas. Thus the collection of this revenue depended mainly on the doubtful honesty of distillers and any effective checks relied heavily on the vigilance, integrity and often the courage of the gauger; all amounting to a very insecure basis for collecting this tax. To bolster the gauger in his onerous task the Act directed that sheriffs, mayors, sovereigns and constables were to assist the excise, but these officers had no organised force, other than calling on the military, to give this help even if they felt any keen desire to do so. Doubtless it was expected that the gauger would get help from the magistrates and gentry, or at least their neutrality, since they would have com-pounded for the duty for their domestic distilling and should normally support a law that did not press on them. When evasion was discovered the gauger could bring his case before the magis-trates where conviction could well depend on local prejudice rather than the facts, but a zealous gauger could easily be in personal danger if he attempted prosecution, so it is probable that most of the duty in the non-compounded section was the result

21. *Ibid.*, section 36.

22. *Ibid.*, sections 30, 32. It is not clear what is meant by 'quality' of spirits produced, but it may refer to spirits of the first or second distillation. The former would be very low grade, but there may have been a demand for it at a cheap rate.

Irish Whiskey

of an understanding with the distiller. In country areas it is very unlikely that the spirit laws were obeyed except perhaps by token payments.[23] In this period of Irish history a normal dislike for paying taxes was reinforced since a large part of the nation regarded all laws as being imposed by an alien power and tax agents as a natural enemy. Even some loyal legislators were unhappy about the situation where any proposed Irish law depended on English sanction, though they found means of turning this against the English government. In this environment the gauger's task was an unenviable one and this continued for fifty years.[24]

The revenues from the duty on spirits levied in 1661 were granted permanently to the King and were part of the hereditary duties. As such the duty was outside the power of parliament to alter, which was another reason for their dislike by the Irish parliament. Later increases in the spirit duties were limited to one or two years and these additions were intended to supplement the hereditary revenue to meet exceptional expenditure. As might be expected, parliament exploited the arrangement from time to time so that future spirit laws during the eighteenth century became a 'pawn in politics'. Sometimes their passage through parliament was obstructed for reasons that were not remotely concerned with spirits or distilling.[25]

Official revenue figures in the seventeenth century were meagre and the quantities of domestic spirit charged with duty are not distinguished. Even if available they would not give a reliable picture of the industry where distilling and retailing were so often conducted on the same premises and where the quantities

23. *Ibid.*, section 60.

24. The legislative procedure was governed by Poynings' Act of 1495 (10 Hy. 7, c. 4). G. E. Howard, *Exchequer and Revenue in Ireland, op. cit.*, ii, pp. 233–6 explains how the Act operated in practice and how dependent the Irish parliament was on English approval of its Bills. The most potent weapon in Irish hands was its power to reject a Bill if English amendments were deemed undesirable. J. A. Froude, *The English in Ireland, op. cit.*, gives instances where money bills, to which there was no fundamental objection, were rejected, or rejection threatened, in order to force other issues. (See, for example, ii, pp. 56–63, 78–80).

25. Howard, *Exchequer and Revenue in Ireland, op. cit.*, i, p. 30. G. O'Brien, *Economic History of Ireland in the 17th Century, op. cit.*, pp. 87–8, 197–200, 232–3. J. A. Froude, *The English in Ireland, op. cit.*, ii, p. 78–80. The hereditary revenues were abandoned in 1793 by 33 Geo. 3, c. 34, section 15 and a Civil List substituted to meet royal expenses.

not paying duty, yet not breaking any law, are quite unknown. Illicit distilling would merely consist of a person making spirit and not presenting himself at an excise office to declare the fact. He could become legal or illicit as the fancy took him or as the gauger pressed him. Those who compounded would account for a fixed quantity in any official records regardless of what they made. In these circumstances it is not possible even to estimate how much spirit was made. It would, however, be fair to assume that there was a great deal of distilling at innumerable houses and hostels and probably a large number of distilleries for sale working small stills.

The Act of 1634 for controlling alehouses selling beer by means of licences had been extended in practice to all liquors, apparently without any legal sanction, for in 1641 parliament 'desired the abolition of retailing wine and aqua vitae by licence which is not warranted by law'.[26] This criticism seems to have rebounded for in 1665 an Act extended the licensing system to spirits and centralised its administration. From 29 September 1665 every person selling aqua vitae, usquebaugh, wine or any other liquor had to obtain a licence. The Lord Lieutenant appointed Commissioners who replaced the County Commissioners responsible under the 1634 Act. The new Commissioners had a similar range of duties, that is, they issued licences only to persons whose character and premises were satisfactory. A licence ran for three years and the duty was fixed by agreement, but the annual sum was limited to not less than 10s. nor more than £10 in Dublin or £5 elsewhere, payable in two moieties. The Commissioners, who were quite separate from the Excise Commissioners managing the revenue from distillers, appointed their own collectors and clerks and these officers were entitled to a fee of 1s. for each licence.[27] It is not known if this fee was supplementary to a salary and if the Commissioners relied on collectors when inquiring into the suitability of applicants for licences. Indeed it must be clear that the Commissioners could not, themselves, make all these inquiries. The Act was intended to curb and channel drinking habits, so that the fee itself would be enough to undermine the purpose of the Act, for there would be an urge by the

26. *Calendar of State Papers, 1633–47*, ed. R. P. Mahaffy, H.M. Stationery Office, 1901, entry for 11 May 1641.

27. 17 and 18 Car. 2, c. 19.

collector to push through as many licences as possible. The way was also open for attempts by applicants to bribe the collector to favour their cases. There was no provision for registering or entering licensed premises with the new authority, it being presumed, doubtless, that all retailers would be anxious to get a licence, but a licence had other disabilities such as compulsory entertainment of travellers, indeed these disabilities could be repulsive to many innkeepers, for example, soldiers could be quartered on them. In their zeal to gather in licences the licensing authority clashed with the excise when they tried to license distillers who sold to customers at their distilleries, a practice of long standing. The licensing Act was a badly devised law and its results probably the opposite to its intention.[28]

After 1700

Eighteenth-century Ireland 'in theory was law-ridden ... Ireland in fact was without any laws save what was recognised by the habits of each district'. This applied to distilling as much as to every other aspect of Irish life. Some fragmentary information about the distilling industry appears in the journals of the House of Commons, some insight into distillery practices can be gleaned from Acts of parliament, and general trends can be seen in official statistics. But before 1780 statistics and information on the structure and prosperity of the distilling industry are far too inadequate to trace its progress satisfactorily. To do this it would be necessary to know the number and sizes of stills at frequent intervals, their distribution and their individual production. It would also be useful to know something about the spirit market, the number of retailers, whether there was an export trade and the full extent of competition from imports. It will be seen that on rare occasions revenue returns reveal worth while facts, but all that can be traced with certainty are the legal framework and the duties that applied to the industry. There are figures for spirits distilled and imported

28. *H. C. Journals.* On 15 October 1695, seven Dublin distillers complained that the licensing commissioners had summoned them as retailers requiring them to take out a licence despite a judgment in 1657 that a distiller selling only in his own shop was not a retailer. They added that if licensed they could have soldiers quartered on them. The result of quartering soldiers in a distillery can well be imagined.

from the beginning of the century, but as Ireland was 'a country where laws had lost all energy, magistracy all authority' these statistics represent only a fraction of the total. There is no way of even estimating how much was lawfully distilled in private households, clandestinely distilled by legal and illicit distillers, and how much was smuggled into the country.[29] The excise authorities, however, gained experience as the century progressed and evolved better controls, spurred by the growing importance of the spirit revenue and the social necessity to control spirit shops. These improvements and better official records make it possible to get a much more complete picture by the end of the century.

Distilleries

Under the spirit laws of 1661 the excise authorities were merely passive revenue collectors and without experience or qualified staff they could not have been otherwise. A rise in the spirit duties from 4d. to 7d. a gallon in 1715 and to 8d. in 1717 no doubt prompted revision of the mode for collecting this duty, and after over fifty years the excise were better placed to take more active measures.[30] Fundamental changes in excise management were enacted in 1717. They probably had little influence at first on distillery practices or on the number and size of stills, but these changes inaugurated an excise system which was to grow and have a very great effect on the industry. The old system of compounding for the duty, or collecting it on the basis of a mere declaration of spirits made, was swept away. In its place the duty depended on an excise assessment of the wash and low wines used by the distiller. Gaugers now had to keep an account of wash and low wines and assess duty on decreases during distillery operations on the following ratios:

(a) If the spirits were made from malted or unmalted corn or any other grains the assessment for spirit was to be based on one-ninth of the wash used or one-third of the spirits of the first extraction, that is, the low wines.

29. Official figures for quantities distilled appear in appendices of the *H. C. Journal* on 9 February 1780, p. 108; 27 January 1791, p. 53; and 1 February 1791, pp. 123–4. See Froude, *The English in Ireland, op. cit.,* i, pp. 477, 622 on ineffective laws.

30. 2 Geo. 1, c. 1, section 1; 4 Geo. 1, c. 2, section 4. There was an increase of 3d. a gallon for one year only in 1692 under 1 Will. and Mary, c. 3, section 3.

(b) If made from sugar, molasses or decayed wines the assessment was on one-sixth of the wash or one-half of the low wines. The distiller was charged duty on the higher of these assessments in each case.[31] The reference to unmalted corn shows that a parliamentary commission in 1823 was not well informed on this point when they reported that the use of raw grain in distilling was of modern origin.[32] A saving clause was retained from the 1661 Act enabling the gauger to check spirit stocks, but it had little practical value. The principle of charging duty at a point prior to the final product and relying on the gauger's stock checks as a reserve power underlaid all excise administration of distilleries for the rest of the eighteenth century. It failed miserably after 1780 when there was an attempt to impose a minimum duty based on the still capacity, with the system of 1717 still operating as the official method of assessment.[33] An interesting innovation in the Act of 1717 was a customs duty on 'brandy and spirits over proof'. Though there was, as yet, no precise definition of proof, this points to the use of a hydrometer of some kind in Ireland. The short step of applying a proof standard to home-made spirits did not take place until 1761 and then only in relation to exports.[34]

One important result of the Act of 1717 was the change in the excise gauger's duties. Occasional visits and inadequate checks of distillers' declarations were now replaced by frequent attendances to measure the wash and low wines used. He had, in fact, to keep a running account of the distillers operations, and assess duty. His role had changed from a passive observer to an active participant in the distiller's business and he had to know something of distilling techniques. He now notified both the distiller and excise collector of his assessments, which could be challenged, and in turn the collector would send returns to the Revenue Board. This was the beginning of a regular and more informative system of

31. 4 Geo. I, c. 2, section 9.

32. *Inquiry into the Collection . . . of Revenue arising in Ireland, 5th Report*, Parl. Pps. 1823 (405) vii, p. 268.

33. 19 and 20 Geo. 3, c. 12, section 20 prescribed that an assessment on the still content charged four times in 28 days was to be the minimum. Assessment on the wash or low wines was to be the charge unless it was below that on the still content.

34. 4 Geo. I, c. 2, section 4; 1 Geo. 3, c. 1, refers to proof in relation to excise drawbacks for exports.

excise accounting and of reliable statistics of home-made spirits legally produced. There were a number of defects so far as the excise was concerned. Thus there was no obligation for a distiller to register his premises or to inform anyone of his intended operations and there were weaknesses in some technical aspects of taking an account, but these were rectified as they became obvious.[35]

Despite ineffective enforcement the excise authorities plodded on and laws were passed to improve the machinery of control even if it laboured in operation. In 1719 it was enacted that no distiller must start work or deliver spirits to customers after dark unless the excise gauger had been notified and had attended. Obviously there must have been noticeable operations at night.[36] In 1731 another hopeful Act attempted to stop distilling in areas where gaugers could not exercise any control, for in the preamble it states 'whereas distillers of aqua vitae and other strong waters for sale, frequently fix their stills, alimbecks and black pots in mountainous parts of the kingdom remote from any market town with intent to avoid the payment of excise . . .' and then proceeds to enact that from 25 March 1732, stills were to be erected only in premises in market towns or within two miles of them. This, if observed, would give the gauger a chance to do his work with reasonable safety. Private stills not exceeding twelve gallons content kept in the owner's house for his own use were exempted.[37] This latter clause discloses that a significant amount of distilling was still of a domestic nature and akin to baking bread.

The Government, on the advice of the Board of Excise, may persuade Parliament to enact laws strengthening the administration and stopping up loopholes, but ingenious distillers continued to find ways of evading the duties. Acts passed from time to time all too often disclosed that the excise were not keeping abreast with distillers' practices. A clause in a distillery law in 1741 opened with a phrase occurring in some form in a number of later Acts. Correcting an obvious defect in the Act of 1717 it stated that 'whereas great frauds have been committed by distillers of aqua

35. Howard, *Exchequer and Revenue in Ireland, op. cit.,* i, pp. 84, 99. The accounting system is outlined.

36. 6 Geo. 1, c. 8, section 6.

37. 5 Geo. 2, c. 3, sections 13–14.

vitae and strong waters by filling their stills with private wash and luting the same so that the officer . . . cannot take account of the wash in the said still, but is obliged to make his . . . charge according to the decrease appearing in the public stock of the wash of such distiller; which decrease bears but small proportion to the quantity of wash contained in the stills'. Evidently some distillers used undisclosed wash to fill their stills and showed only a token decrease in the wash under the gauger's observation. He was unable to check what was in the still. From 24 June 1742, therefore, the duty charge on the decrease in wash could be increased by a charge on the still content. One-seventh of the content was deducted for liberty to work the still.[38] The effect of the measure was that an officer would regard a still containing wash as full less one-seventh and charge the distiller with spirit duty on one-ninth of this quantity for corn wash or one-sixth for wash made from sugar, molasses or decayed wines. This seemingly administrative detail was to have the utmost significance for distillers after 1780. The excise now had to measure the still capacity. This, together with the working tolerance, was the basis for calculating the minimum spirit duty between 1780 and 1823 and which, in turn, caused drastic changes in the whole industry.

The excise administration's lack of foresight in distillery matters was well illustrated in 1743. At that time an excise officer had no right to force an entry into a distillery in the distiller's absence. On the approach of the gauger to take stock of the spirits the distiller could lock up and disappear. There was no power to insist on the distillery being opened by an employee. The position was so misunderstood that an Act to correct the difficulty merely required a distiller to allow the stock of his spirits to be taken and provided for a penalty of £1 a gallon for any excess spirits found. The Act did not state that the distiller should arrange for anyone else to open the premises if he was not available. Two years later the law caught up with the real difficulty of the disappearing distiller. It was prescribed that for the purposes of taking stock the term 'distiller' included a wife or servant.[39]

A new trade known as 'sugar bakers' emerged during the first half of the eighteenth century. These were persons who made

38. 15 Geo. 2, c. 3, sections 4–5.
39. 17 Geo. 2, c. 17, section 4; 19 Geo. 2, c. 4, section 5.

fermented wash for sale to distillers. Their origin is obscure and they were not under excise surveillance. Some of them may have been small scale brewers who began this trade as a sideline. Others may have been bakers who made wort to cultivate yeast for baking bread and switched to distiller's wash occasionally. These sugar bakers did not loom large on the distillery scene before 1780, but between 1780 and 1823 they became a specialised trade and they must have been an important factor in the steep rise in production at the few distilleries that survived in that period. The sugar bakers enabled the small distilleries of the eighteenth century, often with little capital, to instal just sufficient brewing plant to meet a minimum demand. Indeed sugar bakers would make possible a distillery without any brewing plant; a vat to receive bought in wash might suffice. Stills can be worked faster, but brewing cannot be hurried so the reserve of wash from a sugar baker was a great convenience when demand fluctuated.[40]

In the mid-eighteenth century no gauger, however efficient and honest, could be reasonably sure of assessing the full duty. An Act of 1751 after quoting a long list of previous efforts to defeat frauds then stated that 'distillers and makers of low wines or spirits for sale frequently take in wash privately prepared and charge stills in the officer's absence and by such means run off great quantities of wash, low wines, and spirits'. Week-end distilling was prohibited. In this Act sugar bakers first received attention though they still did not come under excise control. It was decreed that the distiller was to give the gauger twenty-four hours' written notice before receiving 'decayed wines, sugar waters or any other kind of fermented wash'. Thus the law at least made certain practices illegal. It did not necessarily stop them.[41] The contest between the distiller and revenue laws, the latter blocking up holes as fast as the distiller made new ones, went on for the rest of the century. The distiller appeared to have no civic sense of responsibility and the revenue authorities often made onerous regulations that were a forcing house for either evasion or bankruptcy. The anarchic state of the country and

40. Several sugar bakers are shown in the *Dublin Directory List of Traders, The Gentleman's and Citizen's Almanack,* for example there are two on p. 65 of the 1796 edition.

41. 25 Geo. 2, c. 9, sections 1–3.

corruption in all walks of life merely gave the laws a spurious stringency. Nevertheless these laws and the experience gained were the basis for much of the modern distillery laws.

Before 1757 there was no limitation on the size of stills and it is a sign of the progress of the industry from its primitive beginnings that the Government had become concerned about the use of small stills in distilleries. An Act of that year complained that distillers concealed small stills to make spirits illegally, and with bad materials, which were sold at low prices 'to the manifest encouragement of drunkenness and all sorts of disorders.' From 1758 the prescribed minimum for stills was fixed at 200 gallons content. This minimum is not large, but it does indicate that a modest capital was needed to establish a distillery. Stills kept by private persons for their household use were exempted, but to prevent abuse, if such stills exceeded twelve gallons, the owner was deemed a distiller and if less than 200 gallons they were seized.[42] It would be interesting to know how this worked if the owner of a large mansion and estate, and possibly also a magistrate, possessed a still of, say, thirty gallons to supply his household and estate servants. These limitations on the size of stills were strengthened in 1759 by a clause in a consolidating Act which stated that 'no brazier is to make stills, alimbecks . . . between 12 and 200 gallons content'.[43]

In 1761 the excise at last got the essential power of requiring distillers to enter their premises and plant, powers which were modest at first, but were improved in later years. The gauger no longer had to discover for himself who was distilling. It was enacted that every still above twelve gallons was to be registered with the excise before being set to work. The Act required a distiller to register and enter his still with the excise office for his district, the entry to show his name, the content of the still and the place where it was installed. After entry, a certificate of registration was issued. If an unentered still was discovered it was forfeit together with any wash and spirits found on the premises. A clause also required fermenting vessels to be not less than 400 gallons capacity. This minimum was aimed at distillers keeping wash in small and easily concealed vessels for clandestine dis-

42. 31 Geo. 2, c. 6, sections 8–11.
43. 33 Geo. 2, c. 10, section 82.

tilling.[44] Apparently the law was not completely satisfactory in relation to the small twelve gallon private still. It can be inferred that the intention of allowing such stills for use in the country houses had now extended to their use in all kinds of other places. Furthermore the existing law did not stop a private house from having several twelve gallon stills, all exempt from the excise duties, and it would not always be easy to prove their existence or that the product was not wholly for use of the household, so in 1763 there was a restriction to one still not exceeding twelve gallons and there was a limit of not more than sixty gallons of pot-ale or wash at one time. In addition these small stills were to be entered with the excise who were also to be notified before a still was set to work.[45] There must still have been a good deal of exempted domestic distilling working parallel with licensed distilling paying duty.

A short Act in 1759 throws light on some of the practices of distillers at that time. After stating that pernicious, cheap and intoxicating ingredients were being used in spirituous liquors which encouraged immoderate drinking, the Act prohibited distillers using any ingredient except malt, grain, potatoes and sugar. It specifically prohibited 'potash, lime, bog-gall or any other unwholesome or pernicious material or ingredient' and provided for a maximum penalty of £50. The prohibition did not extend to usquebaugh or strong waters used for medicine. The Act infers that distillers were using potatoes, but this could not have been a regular practice for there are no references to their use by licensed distillers either in the eighteenth or nineteenth centuries. Some potato distilling may have been done by illicit distillers. A curious clause in this Act provided that the proceeds from fines were to be divided equally between the first prosecutor, usually the informant, and the Protestant Charter Schools.[46]

Among the efforts to patch up defects in the law one is worth mentioning as it was the forerunner of the distillery spirit store, a prominent feature from the early nineteenth century. Distillers before 1775 had been in the habit of storing their spirits in various places pending sales, some of these stores being remote from the

44. 1 Geo. 3, c. 7, sections 7–8.
45. 3 Geo. 3, c. 21, sections 5–6.
46. 33 Geo. 2, c. 9.

distillery. This naturally made it difficult for the gauger to keep track of the spirits made and it was easier for distillers to manipulate the spirit stock to conceal malpractices. Thus a distiller would claim that some of these stocks were not new spirit, but returns from customers as unfit when, in fact, they were rectified spirit or perhaps spirit that had never been assessed. In 1775 it was therefore enacted that all spirit was to be kept in one place near the distillery in casks of not less than 100 gallons capacity and easily accessible to the gauger. There was an interesting, though not important measure in 1778 that throws some light on a distiller's side lines. He was no longer allowed to brew small beer, a product he could easily make with his existing apparatus.[47]

Production and Competition

Statistics of spirit production merely record the quantities paying duty, but significant quantities were reaching the consumer which were not included, most of it evading the duties. Howard quotes a Revenue Commissioner who estimated in the 1770s that not one-third of the revenue was being collected.[48] He was referring to all customs and excise revenues, but it is fair to assume that whatever the extent of evasion, it would be of the same order for home-made spirits. Home-made spirits not included in statistics would come from three sources. First there would be supplies from domestic stills which were legal if used solely in the household, but it is probable that small quantities would be made in the domestic still by servants and sold in the neighbourhood unknown to the master of the house. This might have led to fanciful stories of poteen-making in country mansions. The second source would be the unlicensed distiller mainly operating in remote districts and supplying a local clientele. It was said in 1770 that 'when the mountains are occupied (by troops) the revenue will increase by forty or fifty thousand a year'. This was an exaggerated guess for it was the equivalent of the revenue actually collected.[49] The third source would be illegal manufacture by registered distillers. In 1765 there were 946 registered stills of 200 gallons content or over scattered in market towns throughout

47. 15 Geo. 3, c. 15, sections 18–19; 17 and 18 Geo. 3, c. 8, section 4.
48. Howard, *Exchequer and Revenue in Ireland, op. cit.,* i, Preface, p. viii.
49. Froude, *The English in Ireland, op. cit.,* ii, p. 97 (footnote).

Ireland.[50] It will be shown that when a minimum duty was imposed in 1780 there followed a large rise in the quantities charged with duty, a heavy fall in the number of distilleries and a great increase in illicit distilling. This indicates that before 1780 very substantial quantities of illegal spirits were coming from registered stills and this was the most likely source of the bulk of the spirits not appearing in official statistics. These legal distillers would have a ready outlet amongst their normal customers. Despite these deficiencies, however, official statistics can be used as a fairly reliable guide to trace the expansion of the industry and how it fared in its competition with other alcoholic beverages, since the statistics of these beverages suffered from similar disabilities.

Official figures from the customs department of the quantities of imported spirits had long been recorded and now, resulting from distillery assessments under the Act of 1717, there was similar information for home-made spirits. The returns for 1720 show 136,075 gallons distilled and 327,082 imported to cater for a population estimated at just over 2 million.[51] To these figures must be added the contribution of smuggled and illicit spirits. This quantity is unknown since enforcement of the spirit laws both for home-made and imported spirits was not possible in large areas. In 1719 'law, indeed, all over Ireland was a phantom, which few had cause to fear who defied it'. It was a period of various illegal societies such as tories and rapparees and 'hearth money collectors and civil officers went about in peril of their lives.'[52] The spirit revenue was well below the amount which could have been collected by an honest and moderately efficient administration even after making allowances for the disturbed state of the country. The unfortunate distillers were severely beset by the competition from imports both duty paid and smuggled and, to a lesser extent, by illicit distillation. Probably all distillers practised some illicit work to redress the balance against them and

50. *H. C. Journal,* 22 November 1765.
51. *Ibid.,* 10 December 1765; Appendix dated 1 February 1791, pp. 123-4. *The Irish Census,* 1821, Parl. Pps. 1824 (577) xxii, p. 421. The 1720 population is an estimate based on returns by hearth money collectors. K. H. Connell, *The Population of Ireland,* Oxford, 1950, using additional evidence, gives a higher estimate of 2·8 million. See also T. W. Freeman, *Ireland,* London, 1950, p. 123.
52. Froude, *The English in Ireland, op. cit.,* i, pp. 408 *et sq.* on unpublished crime, and pp. 425, 453.

probably all of them bribed or were in some kind of collusion with the gaugers. It was an age of corruption so it is unlikely that distillers would be different.

In the early part of the century brandy from the continent was, in the main, favoured by people of wealth and influence and whiskey by the rest.[53] 'Smuggling carried not the faintest stigma' so it may be presumed that this would apply to illicit distilling. Froude, writing on conditions in 1730, recounts the results of the English laws which paralysed the Irish woollen industry. These laws resulted in extensive smuggling of wool to the continent and the ships returned laden with spirits that were smuggled into the country. 'The entire nation, high and low, was enlisted in an organised confederacy against the law. Distinctions of creed were obliterated and resistance to law became a bond of union between catholic and protestant.' Magistrates and justices dismissed cases of smuggling brought before them. 'Cargoes of spirits were landed at the Dublin quay. If notice was given to the commissioners (of revenue) they turned the other way.'[54] Distillers in the large ports where distilleries of any size were most likely to be established would, in this environment, be driven to illegal practices in order to survive, though doubtless without much reluctance. In country areas remote from ports distillers had a better chance, but such distilleries, relying on local fuel, were not likely to be large. The operation of the distillery laws, however, could not have been irksome since the excise gaugers were unable to enforce them and could only do their work on sufferance.

The flood of imports continued and in 1730 official returns show that 538,316 gallons were imported whilst home-made spirits only reached 134,738 gallons. By 1735, however, imports had fallen to 383,301 gallons and home made spirits had risen to 209,045 gallons. No reason is given for the drop in imports and whilst there may have been an actual fall it is equally possible that

53. A number of writers record drinking habits and it is clear that spirits, whether home made or imported also met severe competition from wine in the early eighteenth century. See W. A. Lecky, *A History of Ireland in the 18th Century*, London, 1896, i, p. 287 where he quotes from early 18th century writers, especially from Bishop Berkeley's book *Querist*, 1735; also C. Maxwell, *Country and Town in Ireland under the Georges*, Dundalk, 1949, pp. 21, 25.

54. Froude, *The English in Ireland, op. cit.*, i, pp. 448–9; Lecky, *History of Ireland in the 18th Century, op. cit.*, i, pp. 291, 346, 358, 360.

a greater quantity evaded the customs duty for this was the period when ships were returning with spirits after smuggling wool exports. By 1755 imports totalled 919,133 gallons and home-made spirits 498,304 gallons so the Irish distillers were increasing their share of the home market. An interesting feature of the imports in 1735 was the appearance of rum from the West Indies as a separate item and accounting for 148,570 gallons or nearly 40 per cent. Rum imports grew rapidly and reached their peak in 1771 when over two million gallons were imported representing 85 per cent of all imported spirits and the chief competitor to the Irish distilling industry for the spirit market. This increase in rum also indicates a massive change in tastes from brandy to rum, helped considerably by preferential duties. Meanwhile the quantities of home-made spirits, mostly whiskey, were also rising, but remained well below imports and they did not in fact overtake imports until the end of the eighteenth century. These figures do not, of course, take into account illicit and smuggled spirits, but they do show the trend in drinking habits and the competition between imports and home-made spirits. It is also fair to assume that the efficiency of revenue officers in the customs and the excise did not differ materially. The revenue authorities in the face of all the difficulties and considerable dishonesty among subordinate staff merely accounted for part of the total spirits, but probably the major part.[55]

The net revenue yields from spirits for each excise district show the preponderance of Dublin as a distilling centre where the yield was between four and five times that of the next largest centre, Coleraine. The figures show that in 1755 the main distilling towns were in the north and east of the country and at or close to ports. In the south and west and in inland districts distilling was on a small scale. Even in Cork, later to become an important distilling city, the net revenue in 1755 was only £118 compared with Dublin at £4,993 and Coleraine at £1,267. Dublin had a large local market, but apart from this special circumstance there is no

55. *H. C. Journal,* 10 December 1765; Appendices on 9 February 1780, pp. 107–8; 27 January 1791, p. 53; 28 January 1791, p. 81; and 1 February 1791, pp. 123–4. Froude, *The English in Ireland, op. cit.,* ii, pp. 40, 91, describing the dishonesty of officials, and pp. 76, 97, 460 giving facts of smuggling and illicit distilling. See also C. Maxwell, *Country and Town under the Georges, op. cit.,* pp. 129–30.

obvious reason for the uneven distribution of distilling in the rest of the country. Important factors would be access to fuel and grain, drinking habits and illicit manufacture. At or near ports distillers could either import grain or buy it inside the country so any famine conditions did not mean cessation of distilling, and they could also buy grain at competitive prices. Fuel is essential and at the ports distillers could import coal direct whilst the country distiller had to rely on turf or costly transported coal. Spirits made more cheaply at the ports could be more easily transported than its coal equivalent and better situated distillers could therefore compete with the inland distiller in his own local market. It would be unwise, however, to press this advantage, for transport facilities in the first half of the eighteenth century were poor and all bulk transport difficult. There was, in fact, no general market for spirits, but several different markets each with its own problems and customs. The ports, for example, would feel the main impact of competing imported spirits and wines. In some places, such as Cork and Waterford, local beer was popular. These factors may well have accounted for low spirit production in places like Waterford, Cork, Limerick and Galway, particularly the last city where there was a long established wine import trade. Another explanation for uneven distribution of distilling is that the excise returns of revenue may give a distorted and incomplete picture for there may have been a greater concentration of illicit distilling in districts showing a low revenue yield. It is also possible that in places like Cork extensive smuggling of foreign spirits may have prevented the rise of a thriving distilling industry. A true assessment of Irish distilling whether legal or not cannot be made in isolation, imported spirits whether paying the customs duties or smuggled must be taken into the reckoning; they competed directly for the favours of the spirit drinker.[56]

A hazard facing distillers was failure of crops in Ireland from time to time leading to greater imports of grain for food and livestock, and this in turn gave rise to agitation to restrict the use

56. *H. C. Journal,* 29 October, 1757. Other leading districts in the revenue return were Armagh, Cavan, Lisburn, Strabane and Londonderry. These figures are interesting because most of these areas were later infested with illicit distillers and legal distilling was almost extinguished (see K. H. Connell, *Illicit Distilling,* Historical Studies, III, 1961).

*James Power, founder of John Power and Son Limited
(the Irish Distillers' John's Lane Distillery)*

James Murphy, son of James Murphy who founded Midleton Distillery in 1825, was born in 1839 and died in 1901

of scarce grain and the drain of money to pay for imports. In 1758 nearly 400,000 gallons were distilled and charged with duty, but scarcity conditions arose and distilling was prohibited during the winter of 1758-9. A similar prohibition was imposed for 1765-6, but in this case there was a saving clause whereby the prohibition could be relaxed by proclamation if famine conditions were not imminent, thus giving the administration power to reduce the loss of revenue that would follow a prohibition. A relaxation would also tend to reduce illicit distilling for illicit spirits would certainly fill any trade gap left by a shortage of legal spirit. The spirit revenue was now large enough to cause any government to be very hesitant to stop distilling, especially as supplies of illicit spirit would render the prohibition useless. The prohibition of 1758-9 reduced the quantity legally distilled to 225,217 gallons in 1760, but the industry was buoyant and by 1765 it had more than recovered to 715,475 gallons and by 1770 production had risen to over 800,000 gallons.[57]

Discouraging distilling when famine threatened naturally led to attempts to use the industry to encourage agriculture when good crops depressed prices. In 1759 a drawback was authorised of two-thirds of the duty for spirits exported if prices of bere and barley fell below 6d. a stone. This was increased in 1765 by 3d. a gallon. In 1775 the drawback was the whole of the duty if bere and barley prices were not above 9d. a stone. These measures are important because they set a precedent for future years, but at the time the effect was negligible. Thus in 1774 only £727 was paid in drawback out of a spirit revenue of over £70,000. This was to be expected for the only worthwhile market was in Great Britain and it was closed to Irish distillers. This market was not opened until effect had been belatedly given to Pitt's 'Resolutions for Commercial Intercourse between Great Britain and Ireland', presented to parliament in England in 1785.[58]

57. *H. C. Journal*, Appendices, 1780, p. 108; 1791, pp. 123-4. The prohibitions were imposed by 31 Geo. 2, c. 2, section 2, and 5 Geo. 3, c. 3, sections 2, 8. The spirit revenue in 1757 was nearly £14,000 (*H. C. Journal*, 29 October 1757).

58. 33 Geo. 2, c. 10, section 57; 5 Geo. 3, c. 16, section 10; 15 Geo. 3, c. 15, section 22. Howard, *Exchequer and Revenue of Ireland, op. cit.*, ii, pp. 252-3 give tables of duties and drawback totals. *H. C. Journal*, Appendix for 1780, p. 106 shows that only 10 gallons were exported in 1779. *Parl. Debates* (Hansard), 22 February 1785, cols. 317-8. Spirits did not immediately benefit because of fears that foreign spirits might be smuggled into England through Ireland (Debate on 12 May 1785, col. 579).

E

The principal competition met by distillers in 1779 still came from imported spirits, especially rum. A direct trade had developed with the West Indies and ships carried Irish goods there to return with rum and sugar.[59] Although distilling had expanded to about eight times its production at the beginning of the century, the quantities imported had also risen and in 1777 legal home-produced spirits were still only about half the quantity imported. Rum imports in the 1770s were about 80 per cent of all imported spirits due to the influence of persons with considerable financial interest in West Indian estates. Import duties favoured it. For example, when additional import duties on spirits were imposed in 1775 they did not apply to 'spirits the growth and produce of His Majesty's sugar colonies of America', and the result was that rum even had a preference over spirits from Great Britain. The rum import duty did provide a good margin of protection for Irish distillers, but despite this during the latter half of the century rum was by far the main competitor for the Irish market and the legal Irish production did not reach the level of rum imports till after 1780. So great was the taste for rum, even into the nineteenth century, that distillers and rectifiers made imitation rum from raw whiskey.[60]

Wine imports in 1715 were almost 1·2 million gallons or about ten times the gallons distilled legally. In 1763 wine imports had only risen to nearly 1·4 million gallons. By 1777 the gallons distilled had almost reached the levels of wine imports.[61] It must, of course, be remembered that quantity alone is not a fair comparison. It takes no account of alcoholic strength and, gallon for gallon, spirits would be of the order of at least five times stronger

59. *Parliamentary Register of Debates*, P. Byrne and J. Moore, Dublin, xi, p. 73. J. Beresford, Revenue Commissioner, in a debate on 2 February 1791. Direct imports were possible after the relaxation of the English navigation laws by 19 and 20 Geo. 3, c. 11, though there was some direct trade, other than in spirits, before the Act.

60. *H. C. Journal*, 1780 appendix, pp. 107–8. Additional import duties were imposed by 15 and 16 Geo. 3, c. 7, sections 4–5, 4d. a gallon on rum and 6d. on other spirits. Rum from 'His Majesty's sugar colonies of America' was exempted from this increase. For the interest of West Indian property owners see the report of the *Select Committee on the use of Sugar in Distilleries*, Parl. Pps. 1808 (178) iv. There are a number of references to making imitation rum. See, for example, *Inquiry into the Fees, Emoluments . . . received in Public Offices in Ireland*, 5th Report, Parl. Pps. 1806–7 (124) vi, p. 222.

61. *H. C. Journal*, 16 December 1715; appendices 1769, p. 334; 1783, p. 57; 1791, p. 81.

coming off the still than the strongest wine. Thus between 1700 and 1780 while wine imports rose only very slightly, spirits distilled had increased from 136,075 gallons in 1720 to 1,229,416 gallons in 1780. The distiller was far more than containing the competition from wine.[62]

Beer, the remaining competitor for the Irish liquor market, also made no serious inroads. There is not much information about breweries in the period 1700–1780, but it can be inferred from a return in 1790 that there were a large number scattered through most parts of Ireland with a moderate concentration in Dublin and Cork. There were also hundreds of retailer-brewers in all parts of the country. There is no indication that any of these breweries was large and this would be improbable.[63] Home-brewed beer was so poor in quality that, far from competing with spirits, brewers could barely maintain their market. Howard in 1776, deploring the low state of Irish brewing, wrote that 'there being hardly a village, nay, even a large town or city . . . where Irish ale or strong beer is to be had which the poorest wretch can with safety admit into his stomach; nothing but English porter, which they of circumstance only can purchase' and this often adulterated.[64] Despite this deficiency in quality there was, in the middle of the eighteenth century, a market of between 700,000 and 800,000 barrels of local and imported beer, including small beer, but this fell to less than 500,000 barrels by 1780.[65] Though local beer predominated, it was having its own troubles from competing English beer of better quality. The latter was making headway in the 1770s assisted, according to Dublin brewers, by liberal drawbacks when exported from England and by the Irish method of charging duty by the barrel. At the time the English gallon was larger than the Irish gallon, hence an English barrel of thirty-two gallons contained thirty-six Irish gallons thus giving the English brewer four gallons free of duty. The Irish brewers also complained that they had to bear an import duty on hops.[66] The basic trouble however, was quality and this

---

62. *H. C. Journal*, Appendix 1791, pp. 53, 123–4.
63. *Ibid.*, Appendix 1792, pp. 190–1.
64. Howard, *Exchequer and Revenue in Ireland, op. cit.*, i, p. xxxix.
65. *H. C. Journal*, Appendices, 1791, p. 81; 1796, pp. 377–80.
66. The standard barrel for beer was 32 Irish gallons (see 4 Geo. 1, c. 2, section 4). It was changed in 1791 to 42 gallons by 31 Geo. 3, c. 16, section 23. J. Beresford

was considerably influenced by the Irish beer duties. Strong beer was the real competitor to beer imports and, in the liquor market, to spirits. The difference in excise duty between strong and small beer depended on its price and not on any measurable physical property. As the duty on strong beer was, for most of the century, as much as six times the duty on small beer a good deal of fraud occurred, usually by mixing the two beers after assessment.[67] Such short sighted dishonesty could have no other result than a losing battle against imported beer and home-made spirits. Without government support for beer drinking, which will be described later, Irish brewing would have been in a very parlous state.

Some comparative figures taken from various returns presented to parliament illustrate the growing competitive power of home-distilled spirits. Rum was not separately distinguished in official statistics before 1732. The beer statistics include small beer and as strong beer was the real competitor these figures obscure the full domination of spirits. Thus in the twenty years 1771–1790 while all home-brewed beer was in the region of 600,000 barrels, strong beer varied between 360,000 and 460,000 barrels annually. For comparison with spirits the alcoholic strength of strong beer attenuating from, say, 50° to 10° gravity, would be in the region of 8 or 9 per cent of proof spirit. Spirit off the still would be from 25 to 30 per cent over proof or some fourteen times stronger. The revenue returns for 1725 and 1731 show the yield from beer duties but not the quantities. Wine is excluded from the table as imports were almost static.[68]

explained the advantages enjoyed by English beer (*Parl. Register, op. cit.,* xi, 2 February 1791, p. 79). See also Howard, *The Exchequer and Revenue of Ireland, op. cit.,* i, p. xl.

67. Beer or ale was treated as strong if the price exceeded 6s. a barrel. This was raised after 1780. The excise duty in 1717, under 4 Geo. 1, c. 2, was 6d. a barrel for strong beer and 1d. for small beer. In 1775, under 15 and 16 Geo. 3, the duties were 2s. and 4d. The ratio of the duties varies slightly between these years. The proportion of strong to small beer paying duty was about 4 to 1. Thus in 1777 the higher duty was paid on nearly 473,000 barrels and the lower duty on 110,000 barrels (*H. C. Journal,* 5 November 1783, app. p. 77). The 1717 Act prohibited mixing under sections 5–6, but it was practised extensively as late as 1791 (*Parl. Register, op. cit.,* xi, 2 February 1791, p. 74, statement by J. Beresford).

68. The statistics appear in the *H. C. Journals* in the minutes of 10 November 1765 and appendices for 1780, p. 108; 1783, p. 77; 1791, pp. 81, 120, 123–4; and 1796, pp. 377–80. As hydrometers and saccharometers were not used the gravities and attenuation of beer, and the strength of spirits, are not known. The figures given are what were likely and are intended merely for a rough comparison.

Year	Excise Duty	Spirits (Gallons)			Beer (Barrels)	
		Distilled	Imported		Home Brewed	Imported
			Rum	Total		
1725	8d.	134,080		327,194		
1731	8d.	174,791		336,923		983
1754	8d.	561,230	987,112	1,473,370	796,152	20,055
1767	10d.	354,964	1,677,541	2,577,056	705,704	29,487
1777	1/2d.	1,115,352	1,680,233	2,297,703	583,538	71,796

Transit permits

In the eighteenth century the excise authorities adopted a system long used by the customs for keeping a control over dutiable goods in transit. A distiller desiring to send spirits to a retailer or dealer made a written request to the gauger giving full details of the consignment and destination. The gauger then issued a let-pass or permit showing these details and this document certified that the spirits had paid duty, thus protecting them from seizure during transit. There were no independent official advices between the excise officers at each end of the transaction and the permit became the basis for debiting and crediting the spirit stocks of sender and receiver. Many frauds were perpetrated, ranging from outright forgery to the misuse of genuine permits. An Act of 1765 tried to counteract some of these frauds, especially the double use of permits, but the repeated reference to these frauds as late as the first half of the nineteenth century indicates that this effort was not very successful. It was said that permits were used to transport spirits and were then returned to the distiller who surrendered them as not used 'because the goods were returned or for some other false reason' and fresh permits were issued. By this means the stock of the receiver was officially increased while the debit from the distiller's stock was cancelled. From 1766 the arrival of goods on a permit was to be notified to the gauger who was to examine the consignment, take up the permit, note the stock account and issue a certificate that duty had been paid. Thereafter any further movement of the spirits would

require another permit. The certificate now became the basic
document of the merchant's stock record. The laxity of the
system can be judged from a direction that permit forms were to
be printed, so it seems that sometimes it was just a written note,
easily forged or altered without risk when there was no official
verification between the gaugers at the despatching and receiving
ends. The importance attached to permits is evident from the
penalty of seven years transportation for forgery or the fraudulent
use of genuine permits.[69]

Marketing

There is no mention of retailers distilling the spirits they sold
to consumers in any official returns during the eighteenth century.
Probably some of them did continue to distil in the early years
of the century, but in 1717, when the gauger began checking the
wash and low wines used, this control would become irksome
for such small scale manufacture. If any retail distilling did linger
on the growing excise controls would discourage it. Finally when
the minimum size of stills was fixed at 200 gallons in 1757 the
capital needed for distilling would extinguish any legal distilling
by retailers. Distillers could sell direct to consumers, but it is
unlikely that this trade was of any consequence. After 1700 any
fringe of distilling retailers may be ignored and the division
between distilling and retailing regarded as complete.

Spirit retailing had been licensed since 1665, but the revenue
yield was unimportant. It was only £1,882 in 1703 and rose to
£3,882 in 1730.[70] Revenue, however, was secondary to control
in the interests of law and order. Distillers were, naturally,
interested and perhaps concerned about the stringency of licensing
controls for the domestic consumer was almost their only market.
There is no evidence that distillers owned licensed houses though
this may have occasionally happened when, for example, ownership was forced on them to recover bad debts. There is no
recorded instance of any distiller using tied houses as a deliberate
policy.

69. 5 Geo. 3, c. 16, sections 6–8. These rules applied to all dutiable goods, but
were fraudulently manipulated for spirits and were the subject of complaints
by distillers, especially at the parliamentary inquiries in 1823 and 1834. See also
33 Geo. 2, c. 10, section 50.

70. *H. C. Journal,* 9 December 1737, app. p. 99.

The Licensing Commissioners appointed under the Act of 1665 had either been ineffective or reluctant in their duties and they had been taken over by the Board of Excise as a natural extension of their control of distilleries. They were accused by Bindon in 1732 of usurping the functions of the Licensing Commissioners and the Excise Board admitted that their officers were indeed collecting the licensing revenue contrary to the law. The Excise Board did not know when or why this happened. They thought that the change occurred during the confused period after James II abdicated in 1688. They justified their position by stating that they did not think magistrates could do this work so well as officers of excise appointed for the purpose.[71]

David Bindon presented a scheme to the Lord Lieutenant in 1732 for returning licensing powers to magistrates. The scheme was opposed by the Excise Board in a letter on 2 April 1736 pointing out that the Board had been given these powers by an Act of 1732. Bindon's scheme for granting licences gave considerable detail to prove that statistics of population and the number of licences showed extensive evasion and advocated returning the work to magistrates. Many of Bindon's conclusions must have been obvious to the members of parliament. For example, he referred to the licence revenue of 1700 and went on that 'it may be presumed that soon after the revolution (of 1688) which bred so much confusion in this country, the public revenue was not managed with all the care it was capable of . . .', a naive or masterly understatement. Some of his facts are interesting. He stated that in 1672 there were not more than 5,000 houses in Dublin of which 1,180 were alehouses; in 1700 there were at least 1,354 alehouses and in 1730 out of a total of 11,280 houses there were 1,492 alehouses. The figures for 1672 are consistent with those given by Sir William Petty for 1685.[72] Bindon was not without self interest for he offered to undertake the administration of the licensing laws at a remuneration of 1s. in the £ of the licence duty collected. Apparently parliament at that time was not fully aware that the revenue and social aspects of licensing liquor retailers are opposed and that the problem would be more

71. *Ibid.,* 28 November 1737, app. p. 90.
72. *Ibid.,* 19, 28 and 30 November 1737, app. pp. 81–94. Some of Bindon's statistics were challenged by the Board of Excise and appear to have been very inaccurate.

effectively solved if each aspect was the province of a separate
body, the excise collecting the revenue and the magistracy controlling the grant of licences, a position which eventually emerged
and has remained ever since. An Act of 1737 confirmed the
power of the Excise Board and their collectors continued to
issue licences.[73]

Attempts were regularly made to curb spirit drinking in the
interest of public morals. In 1735 licensed retailers were precluded
from using the courts to recover a debt exceeding 1s. incurred
for drink sold on credit. The unlicensed liquor shop, or shebeen,
regarded as a den where revolts and crimes were hatched, received
similar attention in 1759. Any debt contracted was void, though
doubtless the shebeen owner would have his own means of
ensuring payment.[74] Brewers, who had been unable to combat
successfully with the competition from distillers, tried to use the
objections to spirit drinking by seeking government support to
help them force their inferior beer down Irish throats. Dublin
brewers petitioned parliament in 1760. They complained that the
low prices of spirits must indicate evasion of duty and they
stressed the drunkenness among the lower classes resulting from
the popularity of cheap spirits. The brewers, naturally, ignored
their own malpractices which corresponded to those practised by
distillers, with the added illegality of mixing strong and small
beer after assessment and evading up to six times the proper duty.
They asked that the great consumption of spirits should be stopped
either by a prohibition or limiting the number of dram shops.
They were, of course, really asking for the government to surrender part or all of the spirit duty and must have known full well
that illicit spirits would flow as a result, thus largely nullifying
any prohibition. The revenue drop might, of course, be made
good by an increase in the duties on beer! Parliament pronounced
that keeping spirits at a high price would greatly contribute to
the health, sobriety and industry of the common people, all of
which sounds satisfying, but means nothing. The brewers were
side tracked but a rise in spirit duties seemed likely.[75] The duty
did rise in 1761 by 2d. to make it 10d. a gallon, clearly a rise for

73. 11 Geo. 2, c. 3, section 7.
74. 9 Geo. 2, c. 8; 33 Geo. 2, c. 10, section 89.
75. *H. C. Journal,* 8 March 1760. See note 67 relating to mixing beers.

more revenue, and not for any moral reasons.[76] Shortly after the
brewer's petition, parliament discussed the retail trade and resolved
that the small sums paid for licences to retail spirits greatly contributed to the multiplicity of licensed traders, a rather obvious
conclusion. This prompted some members to ask that licence
duties should be raised and thus increase the price of spirits, but
the motion was defeated in favour of another enjoining all persons
granting licences to make strict inquiry into the character and
suitability of applicants for licences, which was no more than a
reminder to the Excise Board of their licensing duties.[77]

Duty paid home-made spirits in 1765 were 715,475 gallons and
legal imports 2,141,415. At this period of bribery, lax behaviour
of officials and a Revenue Commissioner's estimate that only one-
third of the revenue was collected, a conservative estimate of all
spirits consumed would be in the region of five million gallons.
The liquor market was also receiving about 700,000 barrels of
beer and nearly 1·4 million gallons of wine from legal sources
plus an unknown quantity of illegally brewed beer and smuggled
wine. Thus the total of all alcoholic liquors was large in relation to
a population officially estimated at over $2\frac{1}{2}$ millions. Drunkenness
was so common as to cause concern amongst merchants, not on
any moral grounds, but because of damage to their trades when
their workers were so often tipsy. The merchants of Dublin presented a petition to parliament in 1771 complaining particularly
about 'the consumption of spirituous liquors being a cause of dis-
tress, universal corruption of manners and want of industry
amongst artisans'. As a support for their complaints they referred
to the scarcity of corn owing to bad harvests and its consumption
by distillers which aggravated the scarcity. No mention is made of
the use of corn by breweries. The Viceroy, probably considering
the evils of excessive spirit drinking on a wider front than the
distillers' profits, supported the petitioners and the heads of a
Whiskey Bill were prepared under which it was proposed to
suspend distilling and make a general attack on drunkenness. The
Bill was rejected in London because the Treasury said that the
country could not afford the loss of revenue.[78] Four years later a

76. 1 Geo. 3, c. 5.
77. *H. C. Journal*, 21 March 1760.
78. *Ibid.*, March 1771. The heads of the Bill were introduced in parliament
on 8 March and sent to London by the Viceroy on 12 March 1771. See Froude,
The English in Ireland, op. cit., i, pp. 593–4 and ii, p. 105.

minor attack was made on immoderate drinking by transferring some of the tax burden on licensees to the drinkers, though naturally this transfer already occurred wherever possible. This more direct attack was to raise the spirit duties by 4d. to 1s. 2d. a gallon and to reduce licence duties. The licence duty had been fixed in 1765 as a minimum of £4 and a maximum of £10 in Dublin and £5 elsewhere, the sum actually paid being agreed between each licensee and the Board of Excise. From 1775 the licence duties were fixed at £3 to £5 in all places. The grounds advanced for this licence duty reduction were that many retailers could not afford to pay the former duty, but the measure was more likely to increase the number of retail shops.[79] With more liquor shops there would follow more drunkenness and more revenue, more inefficiency in industry, more harm to the economy and more crime. It was the perennial government problem. The revenue was badly needed, so was a sober, industrious and law-abiding nation; the elusive solution was to balance the two to the least disadvantage.

An Act of 1779 introduced a still licence duty, an apparently innocuous measure to ensure at least a minimum revenue from distillers. Its effects were so far reaching on the pattern of the distilling industry and on the excise administration that it marks a distinct change in the industry's history. From 1661, when an excise duty was imposed directly on spirits, to 1779, techniques had improved and distilling had expanded enormously, much faster than the increase in population which, according to officially accepted estimates, had approximately doubled. Imports of spirits had also increased at least six fold in the same period. There were no corresponding increases in wine or beer. Illegal supplies to the liquor market give much the same picture. Illicit distilling was matched by smuggled spirits and between them contributed substantial quantities. Wine smuggling was unlikely to have been significant except in Dublin and Galway where there existed a special demand. Beer is bulky in relation to the duty and smuggling was unlikely, but whether illicitly brewed or smuggled the quality was poor. Because of its low alcoholic content the cost of beer would be greater in terms of satisfying the consumer. Thus

79. 15 and 16 Geo. 3, c. 8, section 5; 15 Geo. 3, c. 15, sections 16, 22. Whiskey was said to sell at 1s. a quart retail at this time, which seems low for legal spirit (R. Twiss, *A Tour of Ireland*, Dublin, 1776, p. 112).

spirits had become the national preference and the Irish distiller's main competitor was the spirit importer. During the latter years of this period a commercially acceptable hydrometer had been evolved and was commonly used for the import trade. It could help distillers in their distilling operations and was probably used for many domestic transactions. The saccharometer, so useful in controlling fermentation, had yet to come, though experiments were occurring in Great Britain.[80]

The excise administration had progressed from a primitive organisation relying on a declaration of production by a distiller or the alternative of compounding for the duty, to a large department spread over all the main towns where officials themselves assessed the duty, first on the decreases in wash or low wines and then, in 1742, on the contents of stills as well. Registration or entry of distillers was enacted; stills were confined to market towns; a system of permits for transporting spirits was imposed on lines similar to those used by the customs; and distilling operations were prohibited until the gauger was notified. All these provisions were designed to defeat frauds, but holes were still found in the revenue net however much these laws curtailed irregular practices. There remained the spirits coming from illicit stills usually situated in remote mountainous regions. In 1779 there was no adequate excise force or constabulary to meet this problem.[81] There was the background of inefficient or corrupt officials, wholesale patronage, poor leadership and a low civic morality in all classes of society. In addition there were the periodic upheavals of rebellion, and widespread lawlessness at other times by a peasant population who looked upon the government as alien, and spirit laws would be regarded no less a burden than any other laws.

80. F. C. Tate, *Alcoholometry*, London, 1930. A paper read before the Institute of Chemical Engineers, historical introduction, pp. xiv–xviii. On wine smuggling see L. M. Cullen, *The Galway smuggling trade in the Seventeen-thirties*. Journal of the Galway Archaeological and Historical Society, 1962, vol. xxx.

81. Law enforcement depended on high constables authorised in 1733 by 7 Geo. 2, c. 12, assisted by petty constables appointed under 23 Geo. 2, c. 14. It is very unlikely that they would regard suppressing illicit distilling as part of their duties. In any case they were of poor calibre, part time, and received very small salaries. See P. Froggart, *The Census of Ireland, 1813–15*. Irish Historical Studies, III, 1965, pp. 231–3, and *Peel and Police reform in Ireland, 1814–1818*, Studia Hibernica, No. 6, 1966.

The change in 1717 from a direct excise duty on each gallon of spirit to a roundabout method of measuring the wash and low wines used, may arouse curiosity. No reasons were made public for adopting this indirect method. Doubtless it was thought that assessment at an early stage would counter fraud more easily. But there were other factors. Fermenting and distilling, and the apparatus used, would differ in the various distilleries. With variations in production efficiency the ratios to relate wash or low wines with the resulting spirit would be approximations culled from practical experience. The low wines charge would correct deviations from the expected produce from the wash. If a good distiller extracted too much from his wash, he paid on the low wines. Similarly this low wines charge might pick up any wash clandestinely introduced. The system inhibited any experiment to get the maximum output from the ingredients used. It also encouraged distillers to extract as much spirit as they could from the low wines and doubtless many distillers ran over excessive fusel oils. An assessment on the spirit itself would have avoided these problems, but with no official hydrometer and no proof standard any direct charge would have to ignore strength. The skilled distiller in the eighteenth century could produce more spirit from a given quantity of wash than his less efficient competitor, but his spirit need not be greater in volume, it could be stronger. He could, therefore, dilute his spirit after assessment to the lower level of others and gain in quantity. Thus a direct duty on the spirit without regard to strength would bear unevenly between one distiller and another. The excise view would more likely be that the skilled distiller was getting some spirit duty free.

CHAPTER VI

THE MIDDLE PERIOD
1780–1823

CHANGE in an industry is usually a slow process. Even when the cause is known it is not always possible to fix a point when the change began. The Irish distilling industry in the last two decades of the eighteenth century was a remarkable exception. An alteration to the distillery laws in 1779 resulted in a rapid and almost dramatic upheaval of the industry. An attempt was made to limit the extent of evasion of the spirit duty by prescribing a minimum revenue from each still. This minimum was based on the estimated number of times a still could be worked off in twenty-eight days.[1] The new regulation came into force in September 1780 and for the first year the minimum was well within the compass of any distiller so that the effects of the change on the industry were negligible. A year later the minimum was raised. The effect was immediate and a quarter of the legal distilleries ceased. The process of raising the minimum charge continued until 1823 when the system was so discredited that it had to be abandoned.

When the Act of 1779 was passed there was no intention to supplant the existing method of assessing the spirit duty on decreases in the stocks of wash or low wines. The House of Commons journals do not indicate any serious discussion during the passage of the Act, nor is there any record of comments from distillers. The minimum duty clause was buried in a long revenue Act covering the whole field of customs and excise and it seems that the change and its implications escaped notice. The revenue authorities gave no indication that the minimum charge was anything more than an effort to reduce evasion. It was to become an uncontrollable monster. It caused the number of legal distilleries

---

1. 19 and 20 Geo. 3, c. 12. The minimum still charge is in section 20.

to fall catastrophically. The design of stills, working methods and
the quality of the spirit were all affected. Evasion in legal distilleries was not checked and the number of illicit distilleries
greatly increased. This minimum still charge fostered official
corruption to a point where a regular system of fees, indistinguish-
able from bribes, was openly condoned by the Revenue Commissioners. Any distiller who did not conform to the customary
dishonest practices could not survive. Prosecutions resulted only
from some outrageous fraud, or a refusal to satisfy the demands
of a greedy gauger over-reaching the conventional bribes, or
merely an occasional show of authority regarded by the distiller
as just part of his overhead expenses.

The Act of Union had no immediate impact on the distillery
laws or on the internal spirit trade, but it did affect the trade in
spirits between Ireland and Great Britain. It is, therefore, convenient to examine the period to 1823 in two parts, under the
Irish government before 1801, and under the United Kingdom
government afterwards.

A – BEFORE THE UNION

Distilling

When the revenue Bill was presented in 1779 there were said
to be 1,152 registered distilleries and when the Act came into
force in 1780 there were 1,228. By 1790 the distilleries had fallen
to 246, but the quantities distilled, or more correctly the quantities
charged with duty, rose from 1·2 million gallons in 1780 to three
million gallons in 1790.[2] From the administrative standpoint,
therefore, one good result was a greater concentration of the
industry. Against this advantage, however, must be put the
numerous illicit distilleries that took the place of the small legal
stills.

How did the attack on evasion by the method of a minimum

2. *Parliamentary Register of the History of Debates . . . in the House of Commons,*
ed. P. Byrne and J. Moore, Dublin, xi, p. 73, 2 February 1791. Statement by J.
Beresford giving the number of stills for different years. The greatest contraction
occurred between 1781 and 1784 when the number of stills fell from 1,212 to 345.
S. Morewood, *A Philosophical and Statistical History of Inebriating Liquors,* Dublin,
1838, p. 631. The quantities distilled are listed in a paper presented to parliament
and appear in the *House of Commons Journal,* 27 January 1791, app. pp. 52–3.

still charge arise, rather than adopting some other way? Evasion might have been reduced by a larger excise staff or a drive for more efficiency and against corrupt gaugers. As has been seen the assessment for duty was a fixed ratio of spirit to the quantity either of wash or low wines used. More important for the present purpose, a still in use was treated as full less a tolerance for liberty to work it. The distiller did not declare the quantity of spirit he made and the gauger did not measure it. A variety of frauds were common. Wash was clandestinely made or bought from sugar bakers and distilled at night or at weekends. Feints, at that time weak unwanted spirits, were removed from stills and replaced by low wines in the gauger's absence and then distilled at the first opportunity. Stills were declared as filled with wash when they actually contained low wines. The hydrometer might have uncovered some of these frauds, but it was not commonly used by gaugers. The gauger did have a reserve power. He could have a suspected still worked off in his presence and measure the resulting spirit, but there is no evidence that this power was exercised.[3] The prescribed procedures to defeat fraud were not effective because of inefficient officials. The excise authorities must have been convinced that the quantities evading duty were very large and that their staff were too unreliable to stop or curtail it. Hence the idea of a minimum duty must have arisen.

The still content was already part of the precautions for assessing the duty so it was, therefore, only a short step to use this content as a basis for a minimum charge on the assumption that in a given period the still could be worked off a certain number of times at least. From 29 September 1780 a licence duty covering twenty-eight days distilling was imposed on each still on the basis of four charges of low wines at the ratio of three gallons of low wines equalling one gallon of spirit. Thus a minimum revenue was assured before distilling began. The gauger made his assessments on decreases in wash and low wines and the distiller paid this duty for the first three weeks. On the fourth week he paid on the assessments and if the total assessments did not reach the licence duty he paid the balance. There appears to have been no intention whatever that the still licence duty was to supplant the normal

---

3. 19 and 20 Geo. 3, c. 12, section 18 quotes existing practice and authorises the hydrometer used for testing imports to be used for testing feints.

assessment and indeed four charges of the small stills then used was a low figure. It was common practice for distillers to use their stills as coppers or for mashing during the brewing period, or even fermenting wash, by removing the still head. The still charge system took this into account, because if a distiller had separate vessels for these purposes it would free his still and his minimum was therefore increased to six charges in the twenty-eight days. To safeguard the revenue when the still was silent the distiller had to provide at his own expense fastenings for the still head, furnace doors, and all cocks on the still, and to pay the cost of the locks and keys used by the excise officials to secure these fastenings.[4] To offset any advantage a small still might have over a large still in rapidity of working, as well as to foster the use of large stills, there was a rebate of the still licence duty of 6 per cent for stills of 1,000 gallons content or more and 3 per cent for stills from 500 to 1,000 gallons. The minimum size of stills remained at 200 gallons.[5]

Increased revenue yields after 1780 support the view that the quantity prescribed for the still licence was greater than the former excise assessments. The still licence duty therefore made inroads on the spirit that had been evading duty. In the new circumstances the distiller would be anxious that the excise assessments were kept below the still licence charge and he would be encouraged to treat the gauger liberally so as to ensure that perfunctory assessments and lax attendance would continue. There was no effort by the Revenue Board to instil greater efficiency in its staff and with more duty being paid the gauger ran little risk of official displeasure if his assessments did not result in additional revenue. It is not surprising, therefore, that in a very short time assessments on wash and low wines became secondary in the excise control. Thus the still licence duty instead of being a minimum became the normal charge. The prescribed standards for assessment were repeated and changed from time to time for

4. *Ibid.*, sections 19–22. *Inquiry into Fees, Gratuities and Emoluments . . . in Ireland, 5th Report*, Parl. Pps. 1806–7 (124) vi, p. 182 explains the method of paying the duty.

5. *Ibid.*, section 30. See also *Report from the Committee on Distilleries in Ireland*, Parl. Pps. 1812–13 (269) vi, p. 6; A. Coffey, *Observations on E. Chicester's Pamphlet titled 'Oppressions and Cruelties of Irish Excise Officers'*, London 1818. Coffey, an inspector general of excise, explains on p. 70 that two 500 gallon stills can produce more spirit in a given time than one 1,000 gallon still. See also p. 71.

they still had a value even if they rarely resulted in an actual levy. They were used to calculate the minimum spirit production from the gross content of the still. The allowance for liberty to work was deducted from the gross still content and the balance treated as low wines capable of producing spirit in the ratio laid down in the current law. Thus in 1780, when distilling low wines, one-twelfth was deducted and the balance divided by three to give the spirit from one charge. This figure multiplied by four gave the gallons liable to the still licence duty.[6] In the following years, therefore, there were four variables affecting the duty; changes in the allowance for liberty to work, the ratio of low wines to spirits, the number of charges in a period, and the rate of duty. Even the period of twenty-eight days was thrice altered.

With the gauger's assessment being supplanted by the still licence duty the distiller had every inducement to work his still as fast as he could and produce as much spirit as possible within the twenty-eight days of his licence. This resulted in considerable quantities of spirit escaping duty. The government faced with distillers beating the assumption of four charges in twenty-eight days, responded by increasing the number of charges. The distillers worked faster and the number was again increased and so the race continued until it escalated into an undignified competition; the distillers working their stills faster and faster regardless of wasteful methods and the legislators lagging behind with increases in the number of charges. Even the shape of stills was changed. They were specially designed to distil rapidly to produce in quantity rather than quality. Distillers who did not have the capital or skill, or those with markets too limited to take the quantities needed to keep the stills at work, disappeared. As many of these unsuccessful distillers were in country districts unlicensed distillers filled the gap.[7]

The race between the distillers and excise legislation developed quickly. In 1781 an Act was passed 'for the better regulation and

6. 33 Geo. 2, c. 10, section 84 enacted the ratio of 3 gallons of low wines to one gallon of spirits. 19 and 20 Geo. 3, c. 12, section 18 allowed one-seventh for wash and one-twelfth for low wines for liberty to work the still. See also *Inquiry into the Revenue arising in Ireland, 5th Report,* Parl. Pps. 1823 (405) vii, pp. 260, 284, 376–7.

7. *House of Commons Journal,* 15 February 1782. Donegal distillers asked for the law to be modified as four charges were too many for 28 days in their case. They alleged that the produce was more than could be sold in the market. They

collection of his Majesty's revenue and for preventing frauds therein'. The number of still charges was raised and a distinction was made according to size. Stills of 1,000 gallons or over were assessed at six charges of low wines; under 1,000 and not less than 500 gallons, seven charges; and smaller stills, eight charges. To offset any disadvantages that large stills might suffer in relation to small stills and also to encourage distillers to invest in larger stills the rebates were increased to 10 per cent for stills of 1,000 gallons and upwards and 5 per cent for stills not less than 500 gallons.[8] Some interesting information emerges in this Act. In some distilleries the practice of using the still for brewing wash had continued because in such cases stills had to be set up to the breast in a furnace of brick or stone. Disputes between the distiller and excise officials must have been frequent because distillers were to be supplied with a 'minute book . . . to prevent frauds and mistakes'. In this book the distiller recorded the times and details of proposed operations and the gauger entered the essential facts of his inspections. Any disagreement could thus be resolved on the spot. A more elaborate form of this important book is still used and is known as the 'specimen'.[9] Spirits for the home market could be any strength without affecting the duty, but strength now became a feature of spirits exported on drawback. The rates paid were related to a minimum strength of 5° or 10 per cent under hydrometer proof. The strengths were probably ascertained by customs officers. Drawbacks at this time were unimportant, but the distillery gauger was just a little nearer to using the instrument.[10] It will be seen later that when the English market was opened after 1800 Irish distillers could gain an advantage when exporting because strength was important for drawbacks, but was ignored for the domestic market.

---

also asked for steps to be taken against private stills. On 13 and 15 February 1782, country distillers complained that the new laws were driving the industry into a monopoly and encouraging private stills.

8. 21 and 22 Geo. 3, c. 15, sections 17–19, 35, 36.
9. *Ibid.*, sections 15, 39. The term 'specimen' was first used in 1791 (31 Geo. 3, c. 16, section 149).
10. *Ibid.*, sections 2–4. H. C. *Journal*, app. p. 106, 9 February 1780. A return of exports shows only 20 gallons in 1760, 5 gallons in 1770, and 10 gallons in 1779. After 1800 exports became important.

The first two years of the still licence duty had a considerable effect on the structure of the distilling industry and clearly indicated the future trend. The number of licensed stills fell from 1,228 to 904 and the ratio of gallons charged with duty to the total still capacity of all entered stills rose from 4·2 to 1 up to 9 to 1, so despite its defects, the new system was bringing much more spirit under revenue charge. Four still charges a month was easily accomplished by a moderately skilful distiller so the increased return is a good indication that before 1780 evasion in licensed distilleries must have been very great indeed. The increased legal production of whiskey had also overtaken imported spirits, indicating a growing preference for whiskey, and probably some improvement in quality in relation to imports, despite more rapid distilling.[11]

A revenue Act in 1785 increased the still charges for stills between 500 and 1,000 gallons from 7 to 8 and smaller stills from 8 to 12. It also gave an additional inducement to distillers to increase the size of their stills. The rebates of the still licence duty were increased to 16 per cent for stills of 1,000 gallons content or above and 8 per cent for stills down to 500 gallons. Of course, if the distiller made enough spirit in excess of the still charge, and this was assessed and charged by the gauger, the rebate would be absorbed. There is no doubt that the excise authorities were now relying on the still charge rather than the vigilance of their officers. The rebates themselves were not having any very marked effect in encouraging larger stills. In 1782 out of 871 stills there were only six over 1,000 gallons and nineteen between 500 and 1,000 gallons.[12] What matters to a distiller is a size most economical to work in given circumstances, capital available, layout of premises, access to fuel, coal or turf, the size of his market and so on; rebates were a marginal consideration.

A number of other provisions concerned revenue security when stills were shut down and later re-started. One of them prescribed a penalty of £50 if a still was warm twenty-four hours after it was supposed to have ceased operating. Another trick was to

11. *Parliamentary Register, op. cit.,* xi, pp. 71–83. A speech by J. Beresford, a revenue commissioner, on 2 February 1791. *H. C. Journal,* 27 and 28 January 1791, app. pp. 52–3, 81, show the quantities distilled and imported.

12. 25 Geo. 3, c. 34, sections 58–60, 63. *H. C. Journal,* 7 June 1782, app. pp. 523–532.

insert objects in a still so that it would be under gauged. If a still was found to be more than four gallons above the official content it was to be seized.[13] The dry and tortuous language of clauses is sometimes very revealing.

The distillers' reaction to the increases in still charges in 1785 was to step up the speed of distilling and get more spirit. The gauger's assessments, now referred to as his survey and account, were not likely to gather in the duty on the excess spirit. In 1791, therefore, another attempt was made to equate the still licence duty with an approximation of the distiller's production. The licence period was reduced to twenty-five days and the number of still charges again increased to thirteen for stills of 1,000 gallons and upwards, fifteen for stills of 500 gallons or more and twenty for smaller stills. An interesting new regulation decreed that coppers and other vessels were not to have narrow mouths thus making it easy to convert them into stills. Some distillers must have speeded up their production by unorthodox ways. There was another regulation that had an important bearing on illicit distilling. A licensed distiller had to work his still for a minimum of 112 days a year or pay the still licence for that period. This was a short sighted rule for it dealt a severe blow to the small country distillery with a limited market. As if to make sure that the blow would be effective, all new stills were to be 500 gallons or over and a distiller's bond with substantial sureties was demanded. To ram home this attack on small distilleries some clauses involved further capital outlay. Minimum sizes were prescribed for fermenting vessels and low wines receivers. The construction of coolers was to conform with an official specification and a spirit store had to be erected near the distillery.[14] No doubt these were praise-worthy efforts to reduce evasion, to encourage only men of substance into the industry and to concentrate production into fewer units and thus simplify excise supervision. The capital outlay could be calculated from the physical changes in distilleries, but there were other considerations which made the total costs to the country great indeed. In Dublin and other urban areas these new rules were probably desirable, but the effect in rural areas was disastrous. It is from this period that there was an incredible

13. 25 Geo. 3, c. 34, sections 52–7, 71. *Inquiry into Fees, 5th Report*, 1806–7, *op. cit.*, p. 209.

14. 31 Geo. 3, c. 16, sections 39–41, 47–9, 63–70.

upsurge of illicit distilling coinciding with the disappearance of the small country distilleries.

Two other aspects of the 1791 Act are worth mentioning. A beginning was made to free from duty distilling not connected with drinking. This exemption was to grow to very large proportions in the next century, especially after methylation was permitted. In 1791 the small stills used by chemists and scientists were exempted from the still licence charge provided no spirit was made. There appears to have been no objection to recovering spirit used in experiments. The other measure was another attempt to bolster the gauger's survey and account so as to make it more effective. Distillers were manipulating wash, their own and wash bought from sugar bakers. The gauger on his visits could never know whether he was seeing the same wash examined on a previous visit or some other brew, and whether to record a decrease or not. He had no saccharometer to help him and only by special vigilance or luck could he detect a distiller running a charge of wash that had never been assessed. For this reason a time limit for fermenting wash was imposed though it is doubtful if this measure was very fruitful.[15]

Until 1797 distillery laws were embedded in long and complex revenue Acts ranging over the whole field of customs, shipping regulations, hearth money and all excise duties and licences. How distillers could keep abreast of the laws affecting their trade is a mystery. Nor were the excise officials in any better position. One suspects that only the major points were observed. In that year there was a sensible innovation. A single Act drew together all the scattered law relating solely to distilling, both legal and illicit. Rectifying and licensing for sale were similarly isolated in later Acts. This legislative improvement had one defect that might have been avoided. It included clauses subject to frequent change, such as the rates of duty, and the Act was in consequence valid for only one year. In the next century this was rectified and distillery Acts were confined to the more lasting regulations leaving transient features for separate treatment.[16]

15. *Ibid.,* sections 59, 78–9. Section 74 brought sugar bakers under excise control. Their sugar wash was charged with spirit duty unless sold to distillers.

16. 37 Geo. 3, c. 16. This Act expired on 24 June 1798 and was re-enacted with a few modifications. 23 and 24 Vict., c. 114 and 43 and 44 Vict., c. 24 were the main consolidating Acts of the nineteenth century.

By 1797 rapid distillation had outstripped the still licence charges of 1791 and there were further increases. The number of charges in twenty-five working days was raised to twenty for stills of 1,000 gallons or more, twenty-three for stills down to 500 gallons and thirty for smaller stills. The minimum annual period for working was reduced from 112 days to 100 days. This relief for small distilleries with limited markets was both insufficient and too late. The damage had been done. Illicit distilleries had become well established and there was little chance of a revival of small legal distilleries.[17]

Most of the other regulations in this comprehensive Act of 1797 were only of academic interest to the distiller. Thus attempts to strengthen assessments of wash used by a time limit for distillation were ineffective. With a still rushing through wash or low wines as fast as possible there was very little hope for a gauger to measure decreases with any accuracy. By now assessments by survey and account had virtually collapsed.[18] Another useless regulation made it an offence for a distiller to obscure spirits or feints by adding materials that would defeat hydrometer checks. In a system where, in the official view, the duty depended on decreases in wash or low wines and where the strength of spirits was disregarded, hydrometers were not normally used by gaugers and, indeed, some of them did not know how to use them.[19] Some of the impressive distillery law had little relation to the facts. Another Act in 1797 to regulate rectifying included distillery clauses to cater for stills in the licence system of 1,500 gallons and upwards. For stills of 3,000 gallons content or more the still licence charge for twenty-five working days was fifteen charges; for stills down to 2,500 gallons sixteen charges; down to 2,000 gallons seventeen charges; and down to 1,500 gallons eighteen charges. This refinement was no doubt intended to ease the position of distillers in these categories who could not be

17. 37 Geo. 3, c. 16, sections 5, 18–20.

18. *Ibid.*, section 39 set a time of 7 days for grain wash. See *Inquiry into Fees in Ireland, 5th Report*, 1806–7, *op. cit.*, p. 148; and *Irish Revenue Inquiry, 5th Report*, 1823, *op. cit.*, p. 259.

19 37 Geo. 3, c. 16, section 36. *Inquiry into Fees in Ireland, 5th Report*, 1806–7, *op. cit.*, pp. 182, 219, 221, 223. One official complained that the law made frequent references to the hydrometer and to computing strengths, which generally were not understood. Another, employed at a distillery, said he never used the hydrometer.

expected to work as rapidly as those with smaller stills, but it also displayed an expectation that much larger stills were likely to be operated. This optimism was to be disappointed for there is no record of any still of 3,000 gallons in the whole period to 1823 when the still licence system was abandoned. It was rare to see a record showing any still above 2,000 gallons and the popular size ranged between above 400 gallons to under 1,000 gallons.[20]

The Irish parliament made a last effort in 1800 to relate the still licence charge to actual production. When computing the size of a still the still head was to be included. Using a still head of ample proportions would be tantamount to enlarging the kettle and more wash could be used in each batch distilled without fouling the still. It would nullify the allowance for liberty to work the still. Clearly some distillers had designed still heads with this in view. The change made little difference. For a short time it may have curtailed the excess spirit produced, but this loss was soon overtaken by still greater speed in working. Another clause prohibited a distiller from possessing more still heads than stills. Probably these extra heads were fitted to coppers or other vessels where a fire could be applied, thus converting them into stills for clandestine distilling when gaugers were absent, for example, at night. A clause akin to this prescribed that a distiller with more than one still must have a difference of at least two inches in the diameter of the necks of each still so that still heads could not be easily transferred from a working still to another which was ostensibly out of action, nor could there be any confusion as to the number of still heads to stills. There was a precautionary measure requiring the dipping place of a vessel to be at its uppermost part, thus preventing wash or low wines being added beyond the point where they could be measured. These and similar sections in distillery Acts indicate the various fraudulent practices of the period which enabled so much spirit to evade duty.[21] There was one important omission in the Act of 1800. The prohibition against the use of raw grain was not re-enacted leaving the distiller free to use only so much malt as was needed to generate fermentation with raw grain. As malt paid duty the distilling industry lost no time in switching over to a mixed malt and

20. 37 Geo. 3, c. 46, section 29.
21. 40 Geo. 3, c. 67, sections 3, 9–10, 48.

grain spirit which was the characteristic Irish whiskey of the
nineteenth century.

The 1785 Act gave the Revenue Commissioners authority to
erect their own stills for experimental purposes and employ
persons to work them. They could also demand pot-ale or
molasses wash from any distiller for use in an experimental still.
Before 1785 the excise department had no means of obtaining
technical data to help them draft revenue laws other than
observing, as best the officers could, the practice in distilleries.
With the pressure on distillers to accelerate the output of stills,
the revenue authorities were feeling the need to undertake
independent investigations to find out just how quickly and how
efficiently stills of various sizes could work. They do not, however, appear to have made full use of their powers until about
1820 when they took over Roe's Dublin distillery for six months.
The only information about this occupation relates to a claim for
£25,000 compensation which was rejected as exorbitant.[22]

The Malt Duty

Recurrent periods of corn scarcity were a real threat to the
prosperity of both distiller and brewer and in the past there had
been temporary prohibitions against using corn for distillation.
These corn scarcities were often local and aggravated by poor
transport conditions. Dublin, the largest distilling centre, was a
special problem. Bounties were paid for the land carriage of corn
to Dublin to enable country farmers to compete for the Dublin
market against imported corn, but the effect produced was a
shortage in the city because the policy generated favourable
conditions for exporting. The excise were involved in this
agricultural policy. As far back as 1759 there had been a drawback
of spirit duty for exports when the price of beer and barley did
not exceed 6d. a stone, in order to encourage growing. In 1785
excise collectors were required to obtain returns of bere and
barley bought by maltsters whose malt also got the land carriage
bounty.[23] Some of these measures were connected with efforts to

22. 25 Geo. 3, c. 34, sections 74, 78. *Irish Revenue Inquiry, 5th Report*, 1823,
op. cit., p. 329. See also *Experiments in Distillation by the Excise Department*, Parl.
Pps. 1821 (538) xix, p. 372, describing tests made at Carrickfergus distillery.

23. 33 Geo. 2, c. 10, section 56 granted the drawback on bere and barley.
25 Geo. 3, c. 62, sections 1, 8 deal with malt and the bounty. *Parliamentary Register,*

control malt prices and stop fraudulent trading. In 1738, in an attempt to defeat fraud, malt had to be sold by weight. This proved a failure so from 1784 sales had to be by the winchester bushel. Ten years later the measure for sale was the barrel and the Revenue Commissioners fixed the price if the free market price exceeded 12s.[24] Thus the distiller had his raw material regulated whether it was raw corn or malt and had to face periodic threats to suspend distilling in order to ease corn scarcity with no corresponding restriction on imported spirits.[25] It is a measure of the public demand for whiskey that the industry not merely survived but thrived.

The regulation of corn, and especially malt, inevitably raised the possibility of a tax as a means of reducing the demand for malt and perhaps diverting more grain for food. It would make spirituous liquors and beer dearer and there would be the added supposed advantage of levying a tax at an earlier stage in spirit manufacture. The probability of such a tax must have been discussed amongst distillers as well as in government circles. Indeed distillers, brewers and maltsters must have been consulted because drafting a law to suit Irish conditions, and its subsequent administration, would be a complex task even though the authorities could draw on English experience, where a malt tax had been imposed as long ago as 1697. In 1785 Dublin distillers, no doubt hoping to influence any government decision, presented a petition to parliament advocating 'that if a malt tax was established in lieu

---

i, 12 and 13 February 1782. Debates on the frauds arising from the bounty for the land carriage of corn.

24. *H. C. Journal.* There are a number of petitions about corn prices. The general demands were to keep prices below 12s. a barrel, to use the hundredweight so as to correspond with Great Britain, and to permit imports. Some of these petitions are in the minutes for 1 December 1783 from Newry, 3 December 1783 from Belfast, 8 December 1783 from Londonderry and a few others in 1784. The unit of sale was first fixed by 11 Geo. 2, c. 11 and altered by 23 and 24 Geo. 3, c. 24 and 34 Geo. 3, c. 10, section 115.

25. *H. C. Journal.* On 13 March 1784 Dublin distillers petitioned against the Heads of a Bill to stop distilling at certain times and country distillers complained about the effect a stoppage would have on farming, pointing out that cattle depended partly on spent wash and spent grains which would cease without distilling, but, of course, the grain would not be diminished if there were no distilling. It was also said that there would be substitution of foreign spirit for whiskey and that imports would gain a preference in the public taste leading to a permanent loss in the domestic market. There is some substance in this argument and whiskey was gaining ground over imports at the time.

of the present excise on ale and spirit, it would in great measure prevent clandestine distilling'.[26]

They could hardly have expected this petition to succeed so alternatively they suggested reductions in spirit duties so as to absorb a malt tax, in effect to exempt them from the tax. On the same day that this petition was laid before parliament the Chancellor of the Exchequer introduced a tax on malt, as he said, to promote distilling and brewing and therefore encourage agriculture. The logic of this reasoning must have surprised members of parliament. The new malt tax was 2s. 6d. a barrel of twelve stones and he estimated that one barrel would produce six gallons of spirit. The distiller was to be compensated for the duty by a rebate of 6d. a gallon off the spirit duty and a repayment of the whole of the malt duty on proof of its payment. There were similar provisions for brewers. The real reason for the tax now emerged. It was clearly not imposed to produce revenue. The Chancellor of the Exchequer explained that the full malt duty would fall only on the unlicensed distiller 'for as the quantity privately distilled that pays no duty much revenue is lost' he would now be caught with tax on his malt.[27] However it is viewed, this was an extraordinary measure directed against the illicit distiller and it should have been obvious that the main result would be illegal malting and evasions in entered malt-houses, thus adding considerably to the difficulties of the excise. It did, nevertheless, give the excise powers to supervise malting and thus attempt to control distillery operations from the earliest stage.

Before introducing the malt tax Bill the Revenue Commissioners had made their own inquiries into the malting industry. They had conducted a survey and in a parliamentary debate a Revenue Commissioner disclosed that in 1785 there were 3,604 maltsters in Ireland, all of whom had been asked to furnish a return of their average annual production of malt. Returns were received, probably of a conservative nature, from 3,304 maltsters and showed a total of 1,405,090 barrels. He added that this total

26. 8 and 9 Will. 3, c. 22 (English statute). *H. C. Journal*, 22 February 1785.

27. *Parliamentary Register*, iv, pp. 310–11. The budget speech on 22 February 1785. See *H. C. Journal*, 22 February 1785. The malt duty and consequent regulations occur in a general revenue Act, 25 Geo. 3, c. 3. Section 13 defines a barrel as 4 bushels of corn and a winchester bushel as $272\frac{1}{4}$ cubic inches.

after being distilled or brewed should have yielded a revenue of
£525,878 whereas the actual yield was only £164,529.[28] It is not
clear whether malting done by distillers and brewers was included,
but that there was a large revenue leak is evident and is an
indication of the extent of clandestine distilling and brewing,
much of which it is safe to assume was conducted in registered
premises. With this new malt tax all malthouses came under
surveillance with all the trappings of the excise machinery of
control; entered premises, gauger surveys, official assessments and
transit permits. All that distillers and brewers could hope for,
apart from tax relief, was that restrictive regulations to counter
frauds would not be too onerous and costly.

In the first years of the new malt tax distillers were not seriously
affected. There was no increase in the total duty borne by spirits
and the only disadvantages were restraints in freedom of malting
and the cost of adapting or altering the plant, if necessary, to meet
the excise regulations. For instance, the cistern and drying floors
had to be above a specified size, the course of manufacture was
prescribed in some detail, for example separate steepings were not
to be mixed, malt in the cistern or couch was not to be rammed
or treaded down so as to cause errors in gauging; and notices
had to be handed to the gauger before wetting grain.[29] One
clause in the Act did, however, specially affect distillers for they
were prohibited from using any unmalted grain. The Act of 1785
did provide an easy method of raising the spirit duties for it was
now only necessary to reduce or revoke that remarkable abatement of the malt tax and, in fact, the Revenue Commissioners
agreed in parliament in 1791 to stop the malt drawback of 5d. a
gallon on spirits. From 1785 onwards any consideration of the
spirit duties must take into account the malt duties paid by the
distiller.[30]

28. *Parliamentary Register,* vii, pp. 118–9. J. Beresford on 7 February 1787.

29. 25 Geo. 3, c. 3, sections 9, 11, 18, 28–9. These restrictive laws were necessary
for any hope of effective excise control.

30. *Ibid.,* section 32. This provision was designed to protect the malt drawback
for it would be very difficult to disprove a claim for the malt used to make spirit
if a mixture of malted and unmalted grain were permitted. In 1791, under 31
Geo. 3, c. 16, section 153, this abatement of the malt duty was repealed and
thereafter malt duty merely added to the duty on spirits. See also *Parl. Register,* xi,
2 February 1791, p. 82. The spirit duties were imposed by 31 Geo. 3, c. 1,
sched. F.

It is not easy to explain the government's intentions when the malt tax was imposed for there are contradictions. There were periodic scarcities of corn and objections to corn imports because of the outflow of capital. Grand juries and other bodies were urging action against immoderate drinking. A malt tax, if it had any effect at all, would discourage the use of corn for making spirits and relieve shortages of food grains. Yet when the Chancellor of the Exchequer introduced the malt duty he stated that it was intended to encourage agriculture by maintaining or increasing the demands of distillers and brewers. He therefore compensated both distillers and brewers to the full extent of the malt duty and reduced the liquor duties. There is no evidence to indicate that the malt tax had any significant effect on agriculture in so far as the tax was concerned with legitimate distilling and brewing. There might have been some undesirable effects for if legitimate maltsters formerly supplied illicit and licensed distillers evading the spirit duties, future supplies would tend to come from illicit malting. This would be certain to create counterparts to the illicit distiller or cause the latter to do much more of his own malting. The Government made no positive steps to restrain spirit drinking so the market for spirits was unaffected by the Act. The excise were saddled with a duty every bit as difficult to administer as the spirit duty and involving a large staff. It may be that there were ideas of eventually having a single tax for all alcoholic liquors imposed at a very early stage, a sort of adaptation of the theories of the physiocrats, but this is conjecture. It would have the merit of concentrating excise control solely on the maltster.[31]

Theoretically this concentration sounds well, for the brewing stage in making spirit is much the same as in making beer, but there is one important difference; the distiller carries his fermentation as far as he can while the brewer, who is making his final product, does not, and this alone is a serious complication which would probably lead to different rates of malt duty for making spirit and beer. Also the two products would be tied together and this would create difficulties in any efforts to check spirit drinking

31. Duties were charged on both malt and beer until 1796 when the beer duty was repealed and the whole duty levied on the malt by 36 Geo. 3, c. 2, section 12 and schedule G. *Parl. Register*, xi, 2 February 1791, p. 78. Beresford explains the need to train many excise officers because of the malt tax.

and encourage beer.[32] While these ideas may have been in the minds of the revenue authorities the most probable reason for the malt duty was that stated by the Chancellor of the Exchequer; to undermine the illicit distiller. This was clearly supported by J. Beresford, a Revenue Commissioner, in his speech in the House of Commons on 7 February 1787.[33] In a few years it was plain that the consequence of the Act of 1785 was the exact opposite for illicit malting was perhaps more widespread than illicit distilling.[34] The excise relied on the permit system to prevent illicit malt reaching distillers, but means were found to evade these regulations and bring outside malt into the production stream without the knowledge of the gauger, or with his connivance. In an effort to close gaps in the revenue defences the malt laws became more and more complicated and the distiller became increasingly hedged in with restrictions.[35]

In the early years the amount of malt duty to be charged was easily ascertained for the gauger merely visited the malt house, measured the grain in the cistern, and calculated at a fixed rate the quantity of malt, or alternatively the maltster could opt for the revenue account being raised on the dry weight of the finished malt if this was less. Four months grace was allowed for paying the duty.[36] The effect of this procedure was that the distiller paid

32. There was no attempt to assess the alcoholic strength of beer or obtain the specific gravity of the wort which would indicate probable strength. Saccharometers were not used. The only difference in the duty was whether beer was classed as beer and ale or as small beer and this depended on its price which in turn led to fraud. A malt tax would roughly graduate the duty according to strength (See especially *Parliamentary Register*, xi, pp. 74–5, 2 February 1791). The beer duty imposed by 15 and 16 Geo. 3, c. 7, section 2 was 2s. a barrel of 32 gallons if the price exceeded 6s. and 4d. if less.

33. *Parliamentary Register*, iv, 22 February 1785, pp. 310–11 and vii, 7 February 1787, pp. 118–9.

34. *Inquiry into the Management and Collection of the Excise Revenue in the United Kingdom, 10th Report*, Parl. Pps. 1834 (11) xxv, conclusions on p. 591.

35. *Ibid.*, p. 593 refers specially to large breweries making their own malt. There are a number of references to clandestine malting. See also *7th Report, Part 1* of this inquiry, Parl. Pps. 1834 (7) xxv, pp. 108–11 relating to malt for distilling and app. 61, pp. 208–17 concerning malt drawback frauds by distillers. *13th Inland Revenue Report*, Parl. Pps 1870 (c. 82) xx, p. 237 describes difficulties in suppressing some of these frauds and p. 235 gives a picture of the various excise checks in force in 1870 as a result of a century of legislation.

36. 25 Geo. 3, c. 3, sections 2, 4, 14–15. The four months' grace extended to distillers and brewers making their own malt. They paid the duty and reclaimed it if they could prove the connexion between the spirit or beer that had paid duty and the malt used.

1s. 2d. a gallon on his spirit when it was made and four months later he could claim a rebate of 6d. from the spirit duty and 2s. 6d. a barrel or the whole of the malt duty. Spirits made in excess of the still licence charge and which had evaded any additional charge did not, of course, qualify. This arrangement led to a complaint in parliament that the distiller, in effect, paid about one-third more than the final spirit duty in the first instance which became a credit for a future duty charge. The Revenue Commissioners agreed that this was true, but said that this was the strongest tie on the distiller to use only duty paid malt. A sad commentary on the effectiveness of the revenue control.[37] By these various means the net duty on spirit was reduced from the official rate of 1s. 2d. shown in government statistics to 8d. a gallon.

The malt duty arrangement of 1785 could not last. The temptation to raise more revenue by wiping out abatements to distillers and brewers would be much too strong for any government to resist for long. In 1791 the abatements were abolished and the spirit duty restored to the full 1s. 2d. a gallon. The malt duty of 2s. 6d. a barrel was equivalent to adding another 5d. a gallon on corn spirit, using the official estimate that a barrel of malt would make six gallons of spirit. Thus the total duty on spirits rose from a net 8d. to 1s. 7d. a gallon, or the same as the rate levied on spirits distilled from molasses. This parallel of rates was maintained in subsequent tariff charges. Official reports and revenue returns can be misleading. They show spirits and malt separately so that neither the rate of spirit duty nor the revenue yield tells the whole story. The malt duty also applied to beer thus complicating any attempt to ascertain the full revenue yield from distilling.[38]

Despite the prohibition in 1785 distillers continued to use mixtures of raw grain and malt in their grist. This resulted in fraudulent claims for rebate of the malt duty which were difficult to uncover. From 1790, therefore, 'any aqua vitae, spirits or

37. *Parliamentary Register*, vii, pp. 118–9, 7 February 1878. The fact that duty on malt had to be paid and then later refunded may appear an unnecessary and cumbersome procedure and this is true for a distiller making his own malt, but not so with supplies from a maltster and the onus of proving duty payment would fall on the distiller. In 1791 the period of grace for paying duty was shortened to one month by 31 Geo. 3, c. 16, section 110.

38. 31 Geo. 3, c. 1, sched. F. 31 Geo. 3, c. 16, section 64 prohibited mixing molasses and corn wash and section 153 repealed the abatement of the malt tax.

strong waters made . . . from corn or grain unmalted' carried a penalty of seizure of the grain and utensils. Henceforth the only legal spirit was either malt whiskey or spirits distilled from molasses and other saccharine material. The latter were of no consequence.[39] Mixing grain and malt was not the only fraudulent practice concerning the grist. Until 1791 a distiller could freely move malt from his malt house into the distillery. When the rebate ended this left an opening to manipulate receipts on permits from maltsters with his own malt, thus confusing the gauger and evading the malt duty. To counter this the malt house and distillery were treated as separate premises and movements of all malt to the mill in the distillery required a permit.[40]

The distiller making his own malt found himself involved in 1794 in another race with the revenue laws similar in character to the still licence charges. He now had to take out a maltster's licence. Evasion of the malt duty was probably extensive due not so much from defective regulation as ineffective revenue officers and the excise resorted to the same method as they did with distillers; they fixed a minimum charge. It began with a yearly charge of twelve barrels of malt for each 100 square feet of drying floor, fixing the barrel as twelve stones. As in the case of distilleries, the maltster worked more rapidly than the law allowed for and the excess was not being brought under charge for duty so in the following year the minimum was raised to sixteen barrels and two years later to twenty-four barrels and so on till by 1813 the minimum had reached eighty barrels.[41]

In 1796 the duty on beer was repealed and in its place the duty on malt was increased to 5s. 3d. a barrel. As there was no relief to distillers this rise in the malt duty, coupled with the prohibition against using unmalted grain, was equivalent to raising the duty on malt spirit by 10½d. a gallon on the basis of one barrel producing six gallons. This made the effective duty 2s. 4½d. or the same as the duty fixed by the same Act for spirits made from sugar, molasses or decayed wine.[42] The total duty was now more

39. 30 Geo. 3, c. 6, section 49.
40. 31 Geo. 3, c. 16, section 137.
41. 34 Geo. 3, c. 10, sections 105, 114. The successive rises in barrels per 100 square feet of floor were imposed by 35 Geo. 3, c. 41, section 51; 37 Geo. 3, c. 33, section 35; 45 Geo. 3, c. 53, section 23; 46 Geo. 3, c. 57, section 2; and 53 Geo. 3, c. 74, section 2.
42. 36 Geo. 3, c. 2, section 12 and sched. G. *Parliamentary Register*, iv, pp. 310–

than double the rate in 1770 when a rise of 4d. to 1s. 2d. a gallon was said to have resulted in a marked increase in clandestine distilling so there is a strong presumption that the changes in 1796, which were greater, would have the same effect.[43] Later in 1796 another Act stopped the malting of wheat or oats. No reasons were given, but it is unlikely to have been a revenue measure and probably had more to do with conserving food. Apart from the relative prices of various cereals the only effect on the distiller would be in the flavour of his whiskey. He was not allowed to have wheat or oats on his premises which was a foolishly rigid prohibition, for distillers, like other businesses using horse transport, needed some oats and in 1799 they were allowed to keep up to eight stone.[44]

Production

The tempo of the competition between legislation and rapid distilling though slow at first was developing speed by the end of the century. It was to become much faster in the first quarter of the next century, but already the effect on the future structure of the industry was clearly emerging. This is an appropriate moment to look at the results of the 1779 Act and subsequent legislation and see how far the industry had concentrated. In the first two years 25 per cent of the distilleries had ceased and by the end of the century only 15 per cent of the licensed distilleries remained. Lengthy returns of stills, their capacities and the excise districts in which they were situated, were laid before the Irish House of Commons on a few occasions and selected extracts can give a fair picture of the changes. In some cases, as in Strabane district, the industry appears to have been eliminated since the returns show no distilleries. These official figures obscure the real facts. Drinking habits and demands do not change so quickly and distilling in these areas, far from ceasing, had merely transferred from licensed to unlicensed production.[45]

11, 22 February 1785, gives the official estimate of 6 gallons of spirit from a barrel of malt. This addition of the malt duty is generally overlooked.

43. *Parl. Register*, xi, p. 76. J. Beresford on 2 February 1791.

44. 36 Geo. 3, c. 35, section 6; 39 Geo. 3, c. 41, section 4.

45. *H. C. Journal*. The tables are extracted from returns in appendices on 7 June 1782, pp. 523–32; 7 February 1792, pp. 140–4; 26 February 1796, pp. 372–6. The influence on unlicensed distilling is examined in a separate chapter.

This steam engine, in Irish Distillers' John's Lane Distillery, dates from 1886. It is kept in perfect condition and every year on the first day of the new whiskey season it is started up

Turning malt in a malt house

Excise District	1782			1791			1796		
	No.	Range (Gallons)	Large	No.	Range (Gallons)	Large	No.	Range (Gallons)	Large
Armagh	74	200–231	—	13	202–258	—	9	200–542	—
Clonmel	47	200–479	—	24	221–600	—	24	215–1,036	2
Coleraine	39	200–263	—	8	220–510	—	5	206–510	—
Cork	8	203–1,000	1	3	343–1,979	2	10	542–2,021	6
Drogheda	27	225–424	—	10	255–1,086	3	9	308–1,094	3
Dublin	52	212–1,038	2	38	229–1,626	12	49	500–1400	24
Kilkenny	13	220–276	—	8	501–548	—	11	212–584	—
Lisburn	2	217–248	—	1	212	—	2	536–1,007	1
Maryborough	74	210–500	—	23	215–1,525	3	13	220–1,200	1
Naas	74	212–784	—	20	220–570	—	18	218– 567	—
Strabane	72	200–258	—	8	217–563	—	None	—	—

Large stills are those of 1,000 gallons or more.

In the whole of the north west there were very few licensed stills; there were no stills in Londonderry district for example. Belfast, which was in the Lisburn district, had no still till after 1791, but had two fairly large stills in 1796. One outstanding feature is the rapid growth of distilling in the Cork district and this is clearly shown by comparing the total content in gallons of all licensed stills in each of the three main centres in 1796 with earlier years:

	1782	1791	1796
Clonmel	12,313	10,399	10,965
Cork	2,662	3,400	11,825
Dublin	17,282	25,828	39,134

By far the greatest number of stills in 1782 were in the range of 200–250 gallons. One interesting feature in 1782 was the number of women distillers. In the Galway excise district, for example, there were five women amongst the eleven licensed distillers. This may well have been a surviving relic of the time when

F

distilling was often a domestic chore. Under the mounting
pressure of the still licence duty women distillers disappeared.
In 1791 there was a significant increase in size and most stills
were in the range of 500–600 gallons and by 1796 this range
predominated. In the whole country in 1782 there were 851
licensed stills, 6 of them of 1,000 gallons or more; in 1791 the
total was 238 of which 24 were 1,000 gallons or above; and in
1796 out of a total of 214 stills, 42 were over 1,000 gallons. Not
only were there fewer and larger stills, but the ratio of gallons
charged with duty to the total still capacity had risen from 9
to 1 in 1782 to 24 to 1 in 1790. In the same period the spirits
legally distilled in licensed distilleries rose from 1,707,295 to
2,926,795 gallons while imported spirits rose to only 1,472,822
gallons. Thus Irish distilleries were producing more from fewer
stills and had secured two-thirds of the domestic market since
there was hardly any export trade. Dublin dominated the
industry which was to be expected for it had easily the largest
local market. In country areas there had been a great decrease in
the number of small stills. The desire of the Government to
concentrate the industry into fewer hands was being achieved
without, at this stage, any serious repercussions on the production
of the industry as a whole.[46]

There were good reasons for presuming that illicit distilling was
increasing and that the discontinuance of the smaller stills was a
major influence. Before 1787 the only real risk to such distillers
was action by an excise gauger and was negligible unless he got
military support. In that year seven gentlemen got authority to
raise small armed parties and apparently succeeded in driving
illicit distillers out of the districts in which the parties operated.
In a parliamentary debate it was stated that there were preventive
surveyors in certain districts where illicit distilling was prevalent
and they received 20 per cent. of any increase in the excise
revenue in the area in which they operated, but this may have
referred to the privately run parties. Even with this meagre

46. *Parl. Register,* xi, pp. 71 *et seq.,* speech by J. Beresford on 2 February 1791.
Statistics of spirits distilled and imported appear in the *H. C. Journal,* appendices
27 and 28 January 1791, pp. 52–3, 81. See also app. 8 March 1800, pp. 701–2,
showing the preponderance of Dublin distilling with 30 licensed stills and nearly
1·5 million gallons paying duty out of a total of 4 million gallons. The Galway
distillers appear in the 1782 appendix, p. 527.

offensive, which only amounted to a local deterrent, the illicit distiller would be unlikely to use a large still and in the first years of this special but puny effort to stop him it is very probable that many of the discontinued stills in the 200–250 gallon range went over to unlicensed distilling. Later, when a much larger and organised force, the revenue police, was established, stills which were easily portable or concealed were a necessity and even a 200 gallon still would be too large for safety.[47]

The still licence duty and restrictive laws had been ruinous to a great number of distillers unable to cope with the changed conditions and not all of them could turn to illicit distilling. There was a steady demand for whiskey and the greater part of it would be in cities and towns where illicit distilling would not so easily remain undetected. In this environment the licensed distillers that survived did a thriving business and seemed immune from industrial depressions. Nevertheless each distiller had to fight hard to maintain his market. The distillery laws pressed severely on all of them and the fierce competition within the legal trade had not diminished. There was also the pressure, potential or actual, of lower priced poteen. These factors forced distillers to resort to considerable evasion of the spirit duties. The legal whiskey marketed in 1797 had risen to 4·6 million gallons to meet the demands of an estimated population of nearly five million.[48] This quantity, however, was only a fraction of the total consumption. There are no means of ascertaining this total even approximately. Illicit distillers certainly supplied substantial quantities, but there are good grounds for assuming that the bulk came from legal distilleries. Some idea of the quantities evading duty in licensed distilleries can be had from statements by distillers in 1805. John Forbes, a distiller, said that he worked a 540 gallon still and his weekly payment for the still licence

47. *Parl. Register*, x, p. 146. J. Beresford on 8 February 1790. *Inquiry into the Excise Establishment and . . . Excise Revenue in the United Kingdom, 7th Report, Part II*, Parl. Pps. 1835 (8) xxx, pp. 83–4.

48. *The Irish Census, 1821*, Parl. Pps. 1824 (577) xii gives an estimated population of 4·2 millions in 1791. K. H. Connell, *The Population of Ireland, 1750–1845*, Oxford, 1950, estimates the population at 4·6 millions. The numbers were rising and for the limited purpose of comparing the expansion of distilling with population increases an estimate for 1797 of nearly 5 millions is close enough. *H. C. Journal*, 4 March 1800, app. p. 703 shows the 1797 production of spirit. See T. Newenham, *Statistical and Historical Inquiry into the Population of Ireland*, London, 1805, p. 223.

charge was for 2,075 gallons, but his average production was 5,000 gallons. Roe, a Dublin distiller, was charged 5,000 gallons on a 1,560 gallon still, but his actual output was 9,000 to 10,000 gallons. John Stein, who worked a 500 gallon still, was charged 3,500 gallons a week but his average extract was 6,500 gallons. These statements were made quite openly in evidence before a parliamentary inquiry and emphasise the inadequacy of the still charge system as well as the breakdown of the method of survey and account by gaugers. It can be assumed, therefore, that Robert Haig, another distiller, was near the truth when speaking about licensed stills that 'for some years past considerable quantities of spirit have been made which were more than double the quantity chargeable by law, or for which duty was paid'.[49]

In each of the last three years of the Irish parliament distillery Acts were passed which continued all the main provisions of the 1797 Act and added a few refinements. Some changes were also made in the duties. In 1798 the malt duty was raised to 6s. a barrel adding another 1s. to the duty on malt spirit at the official rating of a barrel producing six gallons, but there is reason to believe that distillers were getting more than this quantity for the distillery Act of that year provided for an extract of seven gallons when assessing duty on the malt used. The duty on molasses spirit was raised to 3s. and on corn spirit to 2s. plus the 1s. for malt.[50] In 1799 these duties were again increased to 6s. 6d. a barrel on malt, 2s. 6d. a gallon on malt spirit and 3s. 7d. a gallon on molasses spirit. Drawbacks on export, except to Great Britain, were raised accordingly and exporters had to use casks of 100 gallons or larger which would make it just a little more difficult to smuggle them into Great Britain after claiming drawback. There was also an additional drawback of 4d. a gallon on exports when the price of barley was not above 13s. 6d. a barrel.[51] Irish distillers received considerable protection against imports for the import duty on rum was 4s. $1\frac{3}{4}$d. a gallon and spirits from Great Britain paid 5s. $2\frac{1}{4}$d. a gallon. Other import duties were higher.[52]

49. *Inquiry into Fees in Ireland, 5th Report,* 1806–7, *op. cit.,* pp. 153, 194.

50. 38 Geo. 3, c. 5, section 26 and sched. G; and c. 51, section 26. Small increases in duties had been imposed earlier in 1794 and 1795.

51. 39 Geo. 3, c. 8, sections 24, 29–32 and sched. G; c. 66, sections 9, 12.

52. 38 Geo. 3, c. 5, schedules A and C.

In 1800, Irish distillers were further handicapped in making whiskey. Malting and distilling malt spirits were prohibited from 7th April to 1st November, but incentives were offered to encourage distilling from sugar by way of a drawback of 19s. 7¼d for every eight gallons distilled, with appropriate safeguards against claiming this drawback when other materials, especially molasses, were used. There are good grounds for concluding that these measures were influenced by persons with interests in the sugar plantations of the West Indies rather than to counteract any food shortages and this was clearly brought to light in later years when circumstances were similar.[53]

At the end of the century the domination of the liquor market by Irish whiskey and the concentration of distilling in Dublin are demonstrated by official returns in 1795:

Spirits (gallons)				Beer (barrels)		
Distilled		Imported		Home-brewed		Imported
Total	Dublin	Total	Rum	Beer	Small Beer	
4,262,036	1,490,781	610,809	498,946	539,512	169,911	72,398

In the spirit market rum was still the main competitor with nearly 10 per cent of the total, but was falling away rapidly and by 1797 had fallen to 125,123 gallons. Other spirit imports had fallen even more. Beer, its consumption encouraged by the Government, might have affected the spirit trade, but both home-brewed and imported beer had made no advance on the quantities twenty years earlier. Wine consumption had also remained stationary.[54]

53. The prohibitions were enacted by 40 Geo. 3, c. 6, section 1; c. 28, section 2; c. 58, sections 1, 2. The Act permitted the Governor to extend the prohibition, but this power does not appear to have been exercised. Distilling sugar was encouraged by 40 Geo. 3, c. 55. The influence of West Indian sugar planters was made clear by the *Select Committee to inquire how far it may be practicable to confine distilleries to use sugar and molasses only; and what provision can be made for the relief of growers in the British West Indies*, Parl. Pps. 1808 (178) iv. T. Newenham, *A View of the National, Political and Commercial Circumstances of Ireland*, London, 1809, p. 211, considered that the demands for corn by distillers and brewers was no hardship in a country where the staple food was potatoes, but this view would be valid only in rural areas. See *Parliamentary Debates*, 6 May 1811, cols. 789–94.

54. The figures are extracted from returns in *H. C. Journal*, 26 February 1796, app. pp. 378, 380 and 1800, app. pp. 567, 703. The average annual wine consumption appears in *Thom's Directory*, 1866, p. 855.

Rectifying and Compounding

From the earliest times of distilling, the plain spirit from stills had been further treated by adding other ingredients. About 1600 Fynes Moryson mentioned that raisins and other fruits or flavouring were used and references in several Acts show that distillers continued to process their raw spirit by further distillation with various ingredients, or by merely adding essences.[55] There is no evidence to show clearly the rate of the changes in public taste, but there is a strong presumption that in early times the raw immature spirit from the still needed flavouring to make it palatable. In time the plain spirit improved, probably because larger foreshots and tailings of the distillate were extracted, and it became more popular till in the end whiskey became the principal beverage. Rectified and compounded spirits, known by a variety of names such as Irish brandy and shrub, receded in demand. There was another small market for rectified spirit which came from chemists and scientists who wanted a stronger spirit, as strong in alcohol as possible, for extracting plant essences, preserving specimens and the like. Additional distillation would be necessary for this purpose and the product was referred to as spirits of wine.

Until 1798 all these processes might be performed by a distiller from his duty paid stock, but in addition there had grown up a distinct class of rectifiers and compounders who bought their spirit, their raw material, from distillers. The excise gauger did not concern himself with rectifying for, after all, the duty had been paid. He might, as has been shown, become suspicious that a still in a distillery supposedly rectifying actually contained wash or low wines, but that was the full extent of his interest. It is clear, however, that a rectifier could easily use his still to make spirit. He only needed wash and as he was not surveyed he was not so likely to be detected. In 1797, therefore, an Act was passed which removed the ease of evasion in a rectifying house, but still permitted distillers to continue to rectify and compound. Rectifiers had to enter their premises and put up signboards, their stills were licensed, and in general they had to conform with the restrictions applied to distillers. At first the minimum

55. E. Spenser and others, *Ireland under Elizabeth and James I,* ed. H. Morley, London 1890, pp. 420–425.

size of their stills was not less than forty gallons content, but this was raised in the following year to eighty gallons with a permissive clause allowing the Revenue Commissioners to license forty gallon stills. Distilling from grain or molasses was, naturally, prohibited and spirits for rectifying or compounding had to be bought direct from a licensed distiller.[56] There were other regulations to ensure that the still was only at work with the gauger's knowledge and there were specific provisions about the construction of fastenings, turning keys and cocks. When at work the rectifier had to charge his still to at least seven-tenths of its capacity and work it off within eighteen hours, and the distillate had to pass through an open safe so that the gauger could see exactly what was being produced. It was intended to make it difficult to run through a succession of small quantities some of which may escape observation and thus make it possible to process illicit spirit.[57]

There were restrictive rules concerning the strength of spirits sent out to customers, probably to ensure that material had been added and the strength thereby reduced for there seems no other reason. Irish brandy and other rectified or compounded spirits were not to be stronger than 1 in 8 under hydrometer proof by Clarke's hydrometer, or about 13° under proof by the Sikes hydrometer now used. Spirits of wine were of course, excepted, but could only be delivered to a store where they could be segregated from other spirits. They were not defined and were sometimes referred to as double spirits, but were probably in the region of 30° or more over proof. They were defined by law in 1818 as not less than 42° over proof. Frequently, the product from a rectifying house would contain sugar, syrup, honey, fruit and similar ingredients either put into the original spirit before re-distilling or added afterwards, or perhaps the only operation would be to add ingredients to the original spirit. In all these cases the spirit would be obscured, that is, attempts to ascertain

56. 37 Geo. 3, c. 46, sections 1–3, 6–9; 38 Geo. 3, c. 52, sections 2–3, 9. The still licence duty was 50s. for each 10 gallons of the still content. Distillers were not stopped from rectifying until 1805 by 45 Geo. 3, c. 104, section 12. *Inquiry into Fees, 5th Report*, 1806–7, *op. cit.*, p. 210. An inspector general of excise stated that rectifiers worked their stills at night distilling plain spirits. Shrub was a compound with a whiskey or rum base.

57. 37 Geo. 3, c. 46, sections 10–19, 22.

the strength by hydrometer would be defeated. For these obscured spirits the rectifier had to mark on the cask the quantity and strength of the contents and his stock was credited with having used only 100 gallons of raw spirit for every 150 gallons of his product. The gauger allowed for this in his quarterly stock-taking. In 1798 the strength on delivery of all compounded spirits was reduced to 1 in 5 under hydrometer proof, or about 22° under proof by Sikes' hydrometer. These details of strengths were to become a subject of complaint later when rectifiers were seriously obstructed in their efforts to enter the extensive English market.[58]

It is one thing to make laws to protect the revenue, but unless the excise officials see that they are effective the laws merely become a record which may mislead readers into regarding the trade as severely restricted. In fact there is ample evidence that these laws were not enforced. The gauger was supposed to unlock the furnace doors and see the rectifier's still charged, but he often did neither and allowed the rectifier to keep the key, thus the still could be worked at any time. Hydrometers were not used despite the elaborate clauses about delivery strengths. The allowance in stocks of fifty gallons for every 100 gallons of raw spirit received, was sometimes included in the stock account as a credit of raw spirit instead of a credit for rectified spirit. Thus the rectifier could work in with distillery frauds by using up spirits which had evaded duty, and often the rectifier was connected with the distiller in his business. The gaugers were not wholly to blame since the law was intricately worded, said to be based on English practice which nobody knew, their superiors did not understand the Acts, and the Board of Excise issued no explanatory instructions. Even in 1822 such directions as were issued

58. *Ibid.*, sections 23–6; 38 Geo. 3, c. 52, section 21 reduced the delivery strength to 1 in 5 under proof. These strengths are expressed in terms of Clarke's hydrometer. A strength of 1 in 5 means one part water added to four parts of proof spirit and could also be expressed as 1 to 4. Proof at that time was a mixture of the strongest spirit obtainable and water in the proportion of three to four by volume. Temperature was ignored. See W. Speer, *Enquiry into the causes of Errors by Hydrometer*, London, 1802, pp. 7, 14; *Inquiry into Fees in Ireland, 5th Report*, 1806–7, *op. cit.*, pp. 164–6, the evidence of rectifiers, and p. 223 where spirits of wine is described as 30 per cent over proof. *Irish Revenue Inquiry, 5th Report Supplement*, Parl. Pps. 1823 (498) vii, p. 667 explains complaints about delivery strengths. Some equivalents between Clarke's and Sikes' hydrometers are given in 58 Geo. 3, c. 28, section 4.

were merely a recapitulation of Acts.[59] Rectifying and compounding developed in Cork and Dublin. In 1807 there were 13 rectifying houses in Cork, 10 in Dublin and only one each in Limerick and Waterford. The sizes of the stills ranged from 78 gallons to 593 gallons.[60] The market was almost wholly domestic in 1807, but the evidence of rectifiers at a parliamentary inquiry clearly shows that they were striving to get into the huge English gin trade.

Marketing

The legislative arrangements for isolating the different aspects of the revenue and its regulation, begun in 1797 by the distillery and rectifying Acts, were continued in 1800 by consolidating all the scattered law relating to permits. They were used for imports, exports and a range of articles subject to excise duties when they were in transit. Irish spirits exceeding four gallons needed a permit when conveyed between traders. All other clauses in this permit Act applied generally.[61] Forging or falsifying permits carried a penalty of seven years transportation. The permits were used as the official data for taking stock at a trader's premises. As a result of various frauds this Act was replaced by an Act in 1819 which in turn was superseded by an Act in 1832 considerably strengthening the law relating to the use of permits and which operated throughout the nineteenth century.[62]

Rising spirit production is an unsatisfactory indication of the prosperity of the distilling industry. It must be related to the size of the liquor market and the supplies reaching it from the liquor trade as a whole. Any attempt to estimate the number of actual consumers of alcoholic beverages would involve too much guesswork. The alternative is to compare populations at different years with liquor supplies. The method is crude but sufficient to show trends. No proper census was taken in the eighteenth

59. *Inquiry into Fees in Ireland, 5th Report*, 1806–7, *op. cit.*, pp. 164, 219–223, *Irish Revenue Inquiry, 3rd Report*, Parl. Pps. 1822 (606) xiii, pp. 707 *et seq.*, give a number of examples of the kind of instructions issued.

60. *Inquiry into Fees in Ireland, 5th Report*, 1806–7, *op. cit.*, p. 205.

61. 40 Geo. 3, c. 68, sections 1, 23.

62. *Ibid.*, sections 2, 4, 11, 22. Other provisions of the Act were mainly concerned with customs duties. The permit Act of 1832 was 2 and 3 Will. 4, c. 16. The use of permits as the basis for official accounts ceased when official internal documents were used, probably beginning about this time.

century, but officially accepted estimates gave a population of
2·8 millions in 1785 rising to 4·2 millions in 1791. Connell in
1950 estimated the rise from 4 millions to nearly 4·6 millions and,
on the evidence he examined, his figures are more likely.[63] In the
same period Irish spirits charged with duty rose from 1·2 million
gallons in 1780 to nearly 3 million gallons in 1790 to which must
be added the very substantial quantities that escaped the duty.
Spirit imports rose from just over 1 million gallons in 1780, nearly
two-thirds of this was rum, to nearly 1·4 million gallons in 1790
of which nearly three-quarters was rum. Beer and ale, the other
main competitors for the liquor market, also increased. In 1780,
429,000 barrels were brewed and 40,000 imported, while in 1790
this had risen to 434,000 barrels brewed and 109,000 barrels imported.[64] These figures show that the Irish distiller was increasing
his stake in the domestic market and since his exports were
negligible, he was well on the way to dominating it. The figures
also confirm the views of contemporary writers and parliamentary
statements that excessive drinking was a feature of Irish life. The
quantities of alcoholic beverages of all kinds being consumed,
particularly whiskey, was increasing faster than the rise in population. This led to a growing demand by influential persons, both in
and out of parliament, for measures to curb immoderate drinking
and were specially directed against the taverns and spirituous
liquors. Drinking was so commonplace that even prisoners in the
new Dublin gaol sent out for their liquor.[65] In 1778 a House of
Commons committee was set up to examine the way in which the
Dublin magistrates issued certificates enabling persons to obtain
excise licences to retail spirits. A number of petitions were
presented to parliament on drunkenness, one of which described
taverns as 'hellish dens'. In the House of Commons excessive
drinking was described as 'highly injurious' and was the subject
of lengthy debates on five successive sittings.[66] A report on the

63. *The Irish Census, 1821.* Parl. Pps. 1824 (577) xxii. K. H. Connell, *The
Population of Ireland, op. cit.,* p. 25. T. Newenham, *Statistical and Historical Inquiry
into the Population of Ireland,* London, 1805, p. 226 gives his attempt to estimate
the number of consumers.

64. *H. C. Journal,* 27 and 28 January 1791, appendices pp. 53, 81.

65. *Ibid.,* 9 March 1771; 7 March 1778; 15 June 1782 where there is a report
in an appendix, of the new gaol in Dublin.

66. *Parliamentary Register,* vi, 11 February 1786, pp. 132–3; xi, 26 January–
2 February 1791. Debates on excessive drinking. *H. C. Journal,* a number of
petitions are recorded, for example, from the grand jury in Dublin on 14 February

immoderate consumption of spirituous liquor was made on 5 February 1791, but perhaps the most authoritative statement on this whole question of production and consumption of both spirits and beer was made by J. Beresford, a Revenue Commissioner, in a Commons' debate. Against all the evidence he made a case that drinking habits were not increasing. Grattan certainly did not support this view, but Beresford was probably defending the revenue rather than dispassionately discussing the moral aspects of the problem.[67] Irish drinking habits in 1780 seem to have escaped Arthur Young who was otherwise so astute an observer. He makes few references to drinking and except for wakes and one mention of the Irish love of whiskey, appears to think that the nation was generally of sober habits, but he may have been comparing Ireland with the England he knew.[68] The truth is that most of the Irish people were miserably poor and drink with convivial friends was an easy and almost the only relief from worldly cares.

With so large a public demand for alcoholic drinks many leading men thought that the best solution was to wean public taste away from spirits by making beer and ale more attractive through a reduction in price and making it easier for retailers to obtain a licence to sell these drinks. Something was done in both directions. As already noted brewers got some advantage by the repeal of the beer duty and its replacement by an increased malt tax whilst the distiller paid both the spirit duty and the whole of the malt tax. Further efforts were concentrated on favourable licences to retail beer. In 1792 a committee of the House of Commons received a clause in a new licensing Bill to permit a rebate of the licence duty in relation to the proportion of beer sold to spirits.[69] In the same year there were two debates on this

---

1785 and 28 February 1786; from the grand jury and high sheriff of Kildare on 15 April 1788; the Quakers on 21 January 1789; and from Roscommon on 21 January 1791. See also J. A. Froude, *The English in Ireland in the Eighteenth Century*, London, 1874, ii, p. 460.

67. *Parl. Register*, xi, 2 February 1791, pp. 69 *et seq.*; and xii, 5 March 1792, p. 258. *H. C. Journal*, 5 February 1791. See also C. Maxwell, *Country and Town under the Georges*, Dundalk, 1949, pp. 21, 129.

68. Arthur Young, *A Tour of Ireland*, London, 1780, Part I, pp. 99, 209 and Part II, pp. 22, 77.

69. *Parl. Register*, xii, 23 February 1792, p. 52. The Chancellor of the Exchequer was indifferent to arguments favouring beer. In his view 'it is of little consequence

theme in the House of Commons. It was alleged that the attempts
to divert the public taste towards beer was succeeding and, while
the quantity of distilled spirits was rising, this was at the expense
of rum imports and was not an absolute rise in spirit consumption.
In one of these debates Irish beer was said to be inferior to English
beer and should be improved in quality if it was to attract the
public taste. The debate became interesting and a Government
spokesman was explaining that they were examining English
efforts to restrain gin drinking when he was interrupted by an
announcement that the roof was on fire. The House adjourned
hurriedly.[70]

The whole weight of government control over selling spirits
was concentrated on the place where it was retailed for consumption on the premises. Dealers selling large quantities and
shops selling small quantities for consumption off the premises
were not licensed in 1779 unless they held stocks which were
considered might indicate retailing. If a dealer kept more than
sixty-three gallons in his stock he was deemed a retailer and had
to get a licence, a regulation which would be difficult to explain
even though wholesale factors were not included. It must have
caused endless disputes. The probable reason for the rule was that
public houses at that time sold from the cask and that normally in
such a place there would be more than one cask, hence anyone
with more than a hogshead in his shop was, in the eyes of the
excise, retailing spirits for consumption on the premises. At the
other extreme, the law in 1779 regarded any place with more than
one gallon as a retailing house. This rule would exclude dealers
otherwise it would not make sense, but it did permit stocks of less
than a gallon without licence and doubtless this catered for sales
in grocers shops' for customers to take home. The retailer's licence
duty in 1779 still remained at the modest rates of £3 to £5 fixed
in 1775.[71]

The growing concern about intemperance was directed to its
harmful effects on morals and industry. In the House of Commons
in 1791 a member alleged that there were only about 8,000 spirit
licences in Ireland, and parish returns showed 640,000 houses of

---

to the morals of the people, if they will get drunk, what they get drunk with'.
H. C. Journal, 23 February 1792.

70. *Parl. Register*, xii, 2 February 1792, pp. 50–5, 252.

71. 15 Geo. 3, c. 15, section 16; 19 and 20 Geo. 3, c. 12, sections 37–8.

which some 90,000 sold whiskey so that about one house in seven was a whiskey shop and only a few paid the licence duty. No details are given and these figures may have included grocers who were not in the same class as the taverns, though perhaps many of the grocers permitted customers to take a dram in the shop.[72] This exaggeration, however, does not materially affect the conclusion that the licensing arrangements were not functioning satisfactorily. In the debate Grattan outlined several proposals to the government with the object of raising the price of spirits to a point not high enough to encourage import smuggling, but sufficiently high to put the price beyond the labourer. He favoured reducing the price of beer by removing the beer tax and keeping a moderate tax on malt. Raising spirit prices was an ambitious proposal. Customs controls were more effective by 1791, but the rapid distiller making excess spirits and the illicit distiller were far from being under control. Such spirits were bound to find their way into retailers' premises. The proposal to repeal the beer tax, as already shown, was adopted in 1796. Among his licensing proposals Grattan wanted spirit licences to be granted only at a quarter sessions, the licence duty to be considerably higher and recognisances entered into by licensees for order and regularity in licensed premises. He asked that grants of licences should only be made to persons of proved suitability and that if later they were shown to be unsuitable a magistrate could suspend the licence and the next quarter sessions withdraw it; also that magistrates should have powers of summary conviction for unlicensed selling.[73] Most of his proposals eventually became law, but the background should be appreciated. The whiskey shop was a part of the daily life; it was not looked upon as a blight on the nation by the majority, but this majority had no vote or political power and those who had the power could get all the drink they wanted elsewhere. The wealthy had their own private stocks and there is no evidence to show that they set a good example in sobriety. These attacks on taverns, therefore, were generally unpopular and it is not surprising that the shebeen continued to flourish.[74]

72. *Parl. Register*, xi, 2 February 1791, p. 68.
73. *Ibid.*, pp. 69–71.
74. 'Shebeen' originally referred to ale which had not paid duty, hence shebeen houses or shebeens where such ale was sold. As spirits were usually sold as well, all unlicensed retail houses were known as shebeens. See 31 Geo. 3, c. 16, section 36.

In 1791 a new licensing Act was passed which was a vicious attack on the poor man's 'club'. The preamble of the Act stated that 'whereas the use of spirituous liquors prevails to an immoderate excess, to the great injury of the health, industry and morals of the people; and whereas the laws now in being for regulating licences . . . have been found insufficient . . .', it then imposed penal increases. In Dublin and for two miles beyond the Circular Road the licence duty was £20. In the area up to five miles it was £15. In Cork, Waterford and Limerick the duty was £20 and in the counties of these cities, that is, their suburbs, the duty was £15. In all other cities and towns it was £6 and in country areas £4. Magistrates' certificates were required before a collector of excise could issue a licence and it was a condition that the retailer should have at least two hearths for customers.[75] One curious clause reflects popular entertainment of the period. It prescribes that a ball-court, cock-pit or skittle alley was deemed to be a place retailing spirits and would be treated as selling spirits without a licence unless licensed for both beer and spirits. Wholesalers had to pay a fee of 2s. 8½d., were required to sell one gallon or more, and give bond with two sureties in a penalty of £50. It seems an odd figure to fix for a fee. Other clauses repeated existing laws, including one which prescribed that debts under 20s. for credit drinking were not recoverable in the courts.[76]

A further effort to restrain spirit drinking was made in 1792. Retail licences were only granted to innkeepers, tavern keepers and victuallers if they also sold good strong beer or ale for retail at reasonable prices, and they were not permitted to sell spirits before 1 p.m. on Sundays or before sunrise on other days. These restrictions did not apply to coffee houses where spirit was also sold. Meals had to be available at inns and taverns. The policing of these clauses must have been a problem. Beer could be sold at any time, but not spirits, so the fact that a public house was open was no indication that the law was being broken. Grocers, who had been licensed as such since 1785, were not permitted to sell spirits if they carried on any other kind of business on their

75. 31 Geo. 3, c. 13, sections 1, 8–13. The condition requiring two hearths was probably aimed at the shebeen type of house which would frequently be a lowly cabin. By disqualifying such houses the effect might well have been to encourage them as shebeens.

76. *Ibid.*, sections 18, 26, 31.

premises. In Dublin the chief constable or his assistants could remove from public houses anyone found drinking between midnight and 7 a.m. There was a special incentive to sell beer in Dublin, Cork, Waterford and Limerick where the licensee could obtain a reduction of the licence duty in the following year of one-sixth if he sold 75 or more barrels of beer, one-fifth for 100 barrels and one-third for 200 barrels or over, thus giving effect to a clause received in committee when the House of Commons was debating the Bill.[77] An arrangement was instituted for parishes in Dublin to appoint overseers of licensed premises. These overseers had powers similar to the chief constable and were responsible for seeing that drinking places were conducted in an orderly manner. Denominations other than the established church were not given any such powers.[78] There were other measures to stop such abuses as paying workmen's wages on licensed premises, paying wages in part by spirits, or stopping wages to recover drinking debts. Unlicensed selling carried heavy penalties, up to £40 in Dublin and £20 elsewhere. The rest of the 1792 Act contained existing law with a few revisions.[79]

The licensing Act of 1792 did not apparently achieve its object. It looked a good Act for the purposes intended, but no law is any use unless it is either universally desired or properly enforced. The 1792 Act was neither. In a House of Commons debate on 25 November 1793, it was alleged that the licensing laws were not working properly 'because of the non-attendance or supineness of magistrates'. In Dublin it was said that there were 504 licences, but only forty-three of the licensees had a magistrate's or justice's certificate and for the whole country out of about 5,000 licences only 1,446 had certificates. It is not clear what this member really meant because an excise collector could not legally

77. 32 Geo. 3, c. 19, sections 3–6, 26, 33. *H. C. Journal*, 23 February 1792. Dublin grocers petitioned about injury to their trade by the Act of 1791 and the regulations made under it. They were certainly confused by section 17 of the 1791 Act which seemed to prescribe that sales under 1 gallon was retailing for consumption on the premises. Grocers were first licensed as such by 25 Geo. 3, c. 8, and the licence was issued by the excise collector without reference to the justices. The Act did not mention spirits, but the presumption is that the grocer sold small quantities which were not to be drunk on the premises. The grocer's licence was 20s. in Dublin and 10s. elsewhere and covered sales of tea, coffee and similar goods (30 Geo. 3, c. 11).
78. 32 Geo. 3, c. 19, section 27.
79. *Ibid.*, sections 18, 31.

issue a licence unless he had some form of certificate. There was a reserve power enabling the Revenue Commissioners to grant licences without a magistrate's certificate in cases where the certificate was refused unreasonably. It was rarely exercised, but on one occasion fifty-one licences were issued by the Commissioners when a county Down magistrate refused all applications without giving reasons. There was also a saving clause in the 1792 Act to say that if there was no assembly of justices the collector could issue a licence on the strength of a certificate from a single justice. This may have been the basis of the complaint for in such a case there would be no adequate inquiry into the character of the applicant or the suitability of his premises.[80] In 1796 a licensing Act strengthened this weakness by requiring an applicant to give notice before the July sessions of his intentions and this was followed by a special licensing sessions which set the pattern still in being.[81] The same Act extended to the whole country the arrangements for vestries to appoint overseers. The law for licensed grocers became more explicit. Provided a grocer was licensed as such the excise collector could issue a grocer's spirit licence without charge for the sale of not less than one pint which must not be consumed on the premises. The grocer had to give bond with two sureties for £50. Presumably a pint was more than a customer was likely to consume immediately in the shop. With supplies being drawn from a cask, detecting consumption on the premises would be a difficult task.[82] Thus three kinds of trader had emerged which in modern terms would be called the on-licence, off-licence and dealer.

In the following year, 1797, there was another licensing Act correcting minor defects and making small changes in procedure. It also gave a little more emphasis on the sale of beer and ale. A licence to sell wine or ale for consumption on the premises could be issued by the collector of excise without any justice's certificate or any other formality. Under these licences any quantity of bottled porter could be sold, but there was a limit on

80. *Ibid.*, section 10. See also *Parliamentary Register*, xi, 28 January 1791, p. 48; xiii, 25 November 1793, p. 469. The 1792 Act changed the licensing year from 25 March to 29 September.

81. 36 Geo. 3, c. 40, sections 13–15.

82. *Ibid.*, sections 35, 44. The rebates of licence duty for selling beer in major cities allowed by the 1792 Act were extended to the whole country by section 41.

a sale from bulk of one gallon of wine and ten gallons of ale or beer.[83] Spirit licences on the other hand came in for further formalities and the machinery for their issue was changed. Special licensing sessions of the courts were to be held between July and September and the grant of a certificate was conditional on the applicant making an oath of allegiance which reflected the growing disaffection in the country that led to the rebellion the next year. The applicant having obtained a certificate then produced it to the excise collector, paid the licence duty and had his certificate endorsed. He then went to the clerk of the peace for his licence, but before he could get it he had to produce a collector's licence to sell beer. The licence itself specified precisely where spirit sales were permitted and any sales in other rooms or places were deemed unlicensed.[84]

The sale of spirits was truly being circumscribed with in narrow limits and it needed a persistent man to pursue so restricted a trade, but his troubles did not end there, for two years later the heavy licence duties to sell spirits were further increased. In Dublin the duty was raised by 50 per cent to £30; fortwo miles around the city it was £20; and up to five miles, £15. In Cork, Waterford and Limerick there were similar increases to £20 in the cities and £15 in the suburbs. In nine other towns, now including Belfast, the duty was £15, in all other towns £10 and in country areas £6. Licence duties might almost be used as a measure of the importance and growth of towns. There was also a new licence of 20s. for retailing mead or metheglin, but there is no evidence that these beverages had any significant sales.[85] So far as laws could go, beer sales were being promoted and spirit sales severely handicapped. If these laws had been really effective distillers would have had great difficulty maintaining their market against the loaded competition from brewers. The public taste for spirits was, however, stronger than the law as the continued rise in spirit production proved. Attempts to force up the price of whiskey to a point beyond the reach of the poorer

83. 37 Geo. 3, c. 45, sections 2–3.
84. *Ibid.,* sections 12–14, 31. In Dublin the excise collector issued the licence. Under section 48 any person having more than 2 quarts of spirits on his premises was deemed to be retailing. This led to difficulties over private houses.
85. 39 Geo. 3, c. 40, sections 1, 3. The last licensing Act of the Irish parliament, 40 Geo. 3, c. 54, made no further changes except to curtail Sunday sales.

classes had failed and had only given added incentive to every form of evasion. The illicit distiller and the shebeen thrived in this fertile soil. It is worth noting that distilling was forbidden in 1796 and 1797 without seriously affecting the trade and that when the Irish parliament ceased in 1801 the quantities legally distilled were running at over 4 million gallons a year.[86] Irish whiskey was now the problem of the new United Kingdom parliament.

B—AFTER THE UNION

The Act of Union in 1800 had no immediate effect on distillers or rectifiers, but it did offer the prospect of a better export market.[87] The disappearance of the Irish Revenue Board was a gradual process, a subordinate Board continuing in Dublin until 1822. In London, the Irish revenue laws were enacted separately and were presented by an Irish member referred to as the Irish Chancellor of the Exchequer.[88] The same basic distillery laws continued with modifications from time to time, some of them important. The industry continued as before to face attacks from brewery and temperance interests; attempts to prohibit distilling or to force distillers to use sugar in times of scarcity of cereals; and the competiton from the illicit distiller, though it will be shown that the illicit distiller was not wholly harmful to the legal distiller. Spirits for the Irish market charged with duty were 4·7 million gallons in 1802 and 3·6 million in 1823. Apart from four exceptional years, when distilling was temporarily prohibited, this figure varied between 3 million and 6·4 million gallons and

86. *H. C. Journals.* A note in the heading of the revenue accounts presented on 24 May 1800, app. p. 988 states that distilling had been stopped. The quantities distilled appear in a return on 4 March 1800, app. p. 701.
87. 40 Geo. 3, c. 38 (Irish Statutes) and 39 and 40 Geo. 3, c. 67 (English), Article 6 provided for spirits from Great Britain to be imported into Ireland at 3s. 7d. a gallon without reference to strength. Irish spirits entering Great Britain were to be charged 5s. 1¼d. a gallon at a strength of 1 to 10 over proof, or 7° over proof by Sikes' hydrometer, and in proportion for stronger spirits. If sweetened or otherwise obscured, they were rated at the highest strength at which they could be made. This rule virtually excluded Irish rectified or compounded spirits.
88. *Irish Revenue Inquiry, 7th Report,* Parl. Pps. ᵀ1824 (100) xi, p. 3. *Parliamentary Debates* (Hansard). The Irish member presenting Irish budgets was officially listed as the Irish Chancellor of the Exchequer; for example, see the preface showing the ministers of the Crown in 1809 and the debate on 21 March 1809, col. 762.

in addition there were considerable exports. In the same period imports of spirits from Great Britain were negligible. Imports of other spirits ranged from 1·8 million in 1802, mainly rum, to only 43,000 gallons in 1820. So despite attacks the distilling industry remained healthy.[89]

Distilling

The central feature of the period 1800 to 1823 was the frequent changes in the number of charges in the still licence system and the ancillary methods of bolstering this system; a necessary consequence of the complete collapse of the excise gaugers' efforts to assess the spirit duty and the increasing ingenuity of distillers who were always able to put through their stills more charges than the number fixed by the licence. The official method of assessment by survey and account continued, calculating the equivalent spirit at ratios specified in the law. A charged still was regarded as full less a deduction for liberty to work. Though this assessment was rarely levied its use as the basis of calculation was important, for the spirit equivalent of low wines and the allowance for liberty to work were used to calculate the still licence charge. Thus from 1798 to 1804 liberty for working a still for low wines was one-twelfth the content and five gallons of low wines was equivalent to two gallons of spirit, hence a still was treated as eleven-twelfths full and the spirit two-fifths of this, or eleven-thirtieths of the content. This figure multiplied by the number of charges gave the gallons chargeable for the still licence duty. In 1805 the spirit equivalent to low wines was changed to one in three thus altering all the still licence duties. In 1806 this equivalent was again changed, reverting to five gallons of low wines to two gallons of spirit and liberty to work altered to one-tenth of the still content. The latter figure was again altered to one-eighth in 1807. This remained static till the end of the still licence system in 1823, the calculation of the duty being seven-twentieths of the content multiplied by the number of charges and the current rate of duty. In 1809 the assessment on wash was

89. *Irish Revenue Inquiry, 3rd Report*, Parl. Pps. 1822 (606) xiii, p. 1282; *4th Report*, Parl. Pps. 1822 (634) xiii, p. 1407. Exports fell considerably after 1809. *5th Report, 1823, op. cit.*, pp. 373–4. *Inquiry into the Excise Establishment and into the Management and Collection of the Excise Revenue in the United Kingdom, 7th Report, Part 1*, Parl. Pps. 1834 (7) xxv, pp. 66–7.

repealed and the duty was charged on the low wines actually produced instead of the quantity used; probably to stop irregular manipulation between these two points. In 1812 a special Act authorising small stills to be licensed and provided for assessments in their case to be based on one gallon of spirit to ten gallons of wash or two gallons of low wines.[90]

So much for the regulations governing assessment, but with distillers putting through charges in a single still three, four or more times a day from wash to spirit even the most zealous officer could not keep track of the quantities used and inevitably the still charge continued to be the actual charge for duty. Nevertheless the authorities clung to the official line and in a final effort an Act of 1813 provided for the surveyor and gauger to receive a proportion of any excess duty arising from assessments above the still licence duty, and for distillers to be charged only half the duty on this excess if they declared it. This extraordinary bonus followed a recommendation by a senior excise official, giving evidence before a Select Committee, to halve the excess duty and shows how far these assessments had failed.[91] It was stated in evidence in 1806 that officers and distillers co-operated so that assessments would not exceed the still licence charge and as officers were in the pay of distillers this is not surprising, especially as this pay exceeded more than the bonus offered. Well might a Select Committee report in 1808 that 'there would, it appears, be considerable difficulty in framing regulations, or inducing officers suddenly to change that relaxed conduct, and in many cases corrupt behaviour, to which they have been un-fortunately too much addicted'.[92]

90. The relevant Acts are 44 Geo. 3, c. 103; 45 Geo. 3, c. 104, section 46; 46 Geo. 3, c. 88, section 47; 47 Geo. 3, sess. 2, c. 17, section 8; 49 Geo. 3, c. 99, section 28; 52 Geo. 3, c. 48, section 38; 56 Geo. 3, c. 111, sections 18–19. In 1805 under 45 Geo. 3, c. 104, section 47 the gauger was required to charge double duty on a disproportionate decrease of wash or low wines in relation to the spirits declared as produced. This was repealed in 1807. See appendix to this chapter regarding the manipulation of accounts at the end of each licence period.
91. 53 Geo. 3, c. 145, sections 1–2. *Report from the Committee on Distilleries in Ireland*, Parl. Pps. 1812–13 (269) vi, pp. 3, 8–9. See also *Irish Revenue Inquiry, 5th Report*, 1823, *op. cit.*, p. 259.
92. *Inquiry into Fees received in Ireland, 5th Report*, 1806–7, *op. cit.*, pp. 190, 194–6, 201, 209. *Report of the S.C. on the use of Sugar in Distilleries*, Parl. Pps. 1808 (178) iv, p. 9. *Parliamentary Debates*, 30 May 1809, cols. 787–9. See also *Irish Revenue Inquiry, 5th Report*, 1823, *op. cit.*, p. 259 where the Commissioners

A parliamentary inquiry in 1823 reported that following the first imposition of the still licence system 'it was soon found that distillers could produce more than was thought'. This is amply demonstrated by the frequent increases in the number of still charges, but there were also changes in the stills themselves as distillers sought the most advantageous size and design to suit rapid working. In addition the reduction in the number of stills, so noticeable in the later years of the eighteenth century, continued. The real decline in numbers is masked after 1809 because small stills were licensed in an effort to combat illicit distilling. They would not otherwise have been erected. Thus in 1822 of the 40 stills licensed, 18 did not exceed 101 gallons content. The following table shows the changing pattern of the industry before 1823:

Year	No. of Stills	Content in gallons			
		Less than 499	500–749	750–1,000	1,000 and over
1802	124	27	58	1	38
1807	30	—	21	—	9
1818	33	17	9	2	5
1822	40	26	14	—	—

The only still to exceed 2,000 gallons was worked by Walker and Browne of Cork in 1802. It had disappeared by 1807 and thereafter the largest stills were in the region of 1,500 to 1,600 gallons.[93] After allowing for the special licensing of small stills the table clearly shows the emergence of the 500 gallon still as the most favoured. Increases in the number of still charges per month for this size, therefore, give a fair picture of the incredible race between distillers and legislation:

	1800	1804	1805	1806	1806	1807	1809	1813	1815	1816	1817
Charges	23	34	50	56	74	84	91	125	144	172	189

report that the gauger's survey was ineffectual and practically no duty resulted from it.

93. *Ibid.*, pp. 258, 367–9. *Inquiry into Fees in Ireland, 5th Report*, 1806–7, *op. cit.*, p. 204. S. Morewood, *History of Inebriating Liquors*, 1838, *op. cit.*, p. 725. The stills

The same kind of increases occurred in other sizes, for example, a still of 200 gallons content was subject to 30 charges in 1800 and 272 in 1817 and for a still of 1,000 gallons the number rose from 20 to 154 and even these increases were not enough to cover the spirit that distillers could produce.[94]

Dublin continued to be by far the principal distilling centre and Cork easily next in importance. Of the 38 large stills in 1802, 27 were in Dublin and 5 in Cork. The figures for 1807 show only 3 large stills in Dublin as against 5 in Cork, but in the range 500 to 1,000 gallons there were 10 in Dublin and only 1 in Cork. By 1818 Dublin had 4 large stills, Cork one large still and there were none in any other towns. In 1822 the five largest stills in Ireland were all 750 gallons and all in Dublin.

The unsuitability of large stills in this period is clearly shown by the changes made in some distilleries. Edmond Grange, the most prominent distiller in Dublin in 1802, owned four distilleries. He operated four stills exceeding 1,000 gallons each and one of 558 gallons content. By 1807 he had disappeared from the scene and none of these stills was being worked. It is possible that the premises of one distillery in Bow Street had been taken over by John Jameson who was working a 538 gallon still. Jameson had increased the size of his still to 1,256 gallons by 1818, but by 1822 the size had been reduced to 750 gallons. Jameson and Stein of Marrowbone Lane had a 1,206 gallon still in 1802. By 1822 Stein had dropped out and James Jameson remained, working a 750 gallon still. Nicholas Roe owned a distillery in Pimlico, founded about 1784. He was probably related to Richard Roe who had worked a distillery in nearby Earls Street from 1777 to 1789. Roe's distillery was to become very large towards the end of the nineteenth century, but in 1802 there was one still of 1,165 gallons, increased to 1,575 gallons in 1807, but by 1818 the still used was only 751 gallons. James Power, a distiller and innkeeper at 109

shown in official returns are those actually licensed on 29 September and there may have been others temporarily silent. At that time of the year few, if any, would be silent.

94. *Parl. Debates,* 7 May 1806, cols. 38–9 show that the 500 gallon still was considered the most advantageous. The Acts prescribing the still charges for a 500 gallon still were: 38 Geo. 3, c. 51 (Irish statutes); 44 Geo. 3, c. 103; 45 Geo. 3 c. 104; 46 Geo. 3, c. 56, and c. 88; 47 Geo. 3, sess. 2, c. 17: 49 Geo. 3, c. 99; 54 Geo. 3, c. 88; 55 Geo. 3, c. 111; 56 Geo. 3, c. 111; and 57 Geo. 3, c. 110.

Thomas Street from about 1796, was trading in 1804 as James Power and Son. John Power is shown in the Dublin directory as a distiller at John's Lane, Thomas Street, in 1802 so the family business was expanding. At John's Lane there was a 1,536 gallon still. Power was amongst the earliest to realise the advantages of the small still and in 1807 he was working a 523 gallon still. In 1818 his still was 751 gallons. His trade must have prospered, but rather than increase the size of his still he erected more stills and in 1823 he was working three stills of 750 gallons, 509 gallons and 500 gallons. In Cork the distillers Walker and Browne used a 2,179 gallon still in 1802, the largest in Ireland at the time. By 1807 Browne had left and Francis Walker persisted with large stills. In 1818 he worked two stills each of 1,530 gallons. Like other distillers he eventually changed to smaller stills and in 1822 he worked two stills of 750 and 501 gallons. The same story of reducing sizes occurred in all other places, sometimes the reduction was very considerable. Thus in Belfast there were two distilling firms in 1802, Rowan, Montgomery and Co., working a 1,020 gallon still and Porter, Tennant and Co., with a 1,011 gallon still. By 1807 there was only one still of 504 gallons worked by Henry Rowan. James Shaw had taken over the distillery by 1818 and used a still of 503 gallons which he changed to a 300 gallon still by 1822. The story is similar in Roscrea where George Birch in 1807 had a 1,769 gallon still. John Birch changed this by 1818 to 306 gallons. He reduced this still further to 101 gallons in 1822. The same trend is seen in the distilleries in Newry, Dundalk, and other towns.[95]

In the hope that it would be 'expedient for the more effectual suppression of illicit distillation' an Act in 1809 authorised the licensing of small stills between 50 and 200 gallons content in notorious poteen districts. For stills in the range 190 to 200 gallons 144 still charges were prescribed and this number rose by no less than fifteen stages to 280 charges for stills between 50 and 60 gallons. The charges for each size of still were supposed to correspond with the habits and practices of illicit distillers. The optimistic official view was that a licensed distiller could now

---

95. Details of still sizes appear in the references given in Note 93. Distillers' addresses are shown in the *Directory of Merchants and Traders* in the annual *Gentleman's and Citizen's Almanacks,* published in Dublin.

successfully compete with the poteen maker and that some of the latter might be induced to license their stills. Not only was the schedule of still charges complicated by fragmenting the whole range into numerous changes in still sizes, but the problem was not squarely faced. Illicit distillers normally worked stills of 50 to 60 gallons content, sometimes smaller, but rarely as large as 100 gallons. Hence licensed stills between 100 and 200 gallons would have no influence in solving the problem. They did, however, fit tidily into the mainstream of still licences for larger stills. For smaller stills, which might have had some effect, the number of charges fixed was too high. In 1812 these defects were partly remedied by reducing the lowest size of legal stills to 44 gallons and confining to two stages the number of still charges for stills below 100 gallons. For stills between 65 and 100 gallons there were 65 charges, and 90 charges for smaller stills. There was no relaxation for stills over 100 gallons. In the following years any chance of the policy for small stills succeeding was shattered by progressive increases in still charges. By 1817 stills between 100 and 200 gallons bore 304 charges. This meant that a single still had to put through enough wash to low wines and then distil to spirits nearly eleven times every day continuously for twenty-eight days. This assumes that the still was filled with low wines for each charge, but distillers working rapidly usually only partly filled the still. Thus the still might well be charged with low wines a score of times each day. A mere recounting of these facts is enough to give a picture of the hectic daily rush that must have prevailed. Stills under 100 gallons had an advantage under the Act of 1817 as they bore only 200 charges. To keep stills going to meet the number of charges required the support of a sizeable brewing plant and a capital investment that would deter any poteen-maker turning over to legal distilling. As a belated recognition of this fact there was a reduction to ninety charges for stills below 100 gallons if the brewing vessels were limited in number. It will be shown that these attempts for the 'effectual suppression of illicit distillation' made no impression. Despite the onerous number of charges imposed legal distillers were able to make excess spirits. Clearly the still licence system was driving all distillers to using small stills.[96]

96. 49 Geo. 3, c. 99, section 27; 52 Geo. 3, c. 48, sections 1, 4, 50; 57 Geo. 3,

Despite regulations requiring notices to start or stop distilling; the details required when taking out a licence which included the still dimensions; and even the licensing of braziers who made stills; the distillers found various ways of getting round the rules and the excise laws were constantly being amended to stop the revenue leaks as they came to light as well as the normal changes where existing laws pressed unduly. The Government were faced with a dilemma. They wanted to encourage larger distilling units and at the same time their main hope of combating illicit distilling was to encourage small stills. For large stills the bounty in 1800 was 16 per cent for stills exceeding 1,000 gallons content and 8 per cent if they exceeded 500 gallons, but the latter had become the favoured size whilst really large stills were shunned. This policy had been criticised in parliament in 1806 and again in 1809 and was clearly not working as desired. To meet these criticisms the sizes of stills to qualify for the bounties were raised in 1806 by 500 gallons and in 1810 bounties were finally abandoned.[97] Small stills permitted in 1809 were not to be erected within five miles of a large still, nor could a distiller working with a still of 500 gallons or more also have a smaller still. Thus the small still was to be isolated from the large and the two policies to encourage larger units and to discourage illicit distilling were kept distinct. In 1810 this separation was discontinued.[98] Another criticism concerned the fuel used. Coal was better than turf and distillers using turf felt aggrieved. In 1810 stills from 100 to 1,000 gallons content using turf received an allowance from the still licence duty of quarter of the full charge. In 1819 this was extended to all stills.[99]

---

c. 110, sections 2, 6–10. *Committee on Distilleries in Ireland*, 1812–13, *op. cit.*, p. 12. *Irish Revenue Inquiry*, *5th Report*, 1823, *op. cit.*, p. 379.

97. 37 Geo. 3, c. 16, section 38 (Irish statutes); 46 Geo. 3, c. 88, section 77; 50 Geo. 3, c. 15, section 5. *Parl. Debates*, 7 May 1806, cols. 38–9 and 25 February 1809, col. 1047.

98. 49 Geo. 3, c. 99, sections 23–6. See also 47 Geo. 3, sess. 2, c. 17, sections 2–3 relating to stills between 200 and 500 gallons. A special Act (52 Geo. 3, c. 48) prescribed regulations for small stills and the preamble states the purpose of the Act. The separation of large and small stills was repealed by 50 Geo. 3, c. 15, sections 6–7. See *Parl. Debates*, 1 March 1810, cols. 653–7, where government policy on this aspect is discussed.

99. 55 Geo. 3, c. 111, section 2; 57 Geo. 3, c. 110, section 3. *Irish Revenue Inquiry*, *5th Report*, 1823, *op. cit.*, pp. 376–7.

So far the changes mentioned have referred to furthering policy and removing grievances, but there were other changes forced on the Government by the distillers themselves and were chiefly concerned with the construction of stills. Rapid distilling had long ousted the practices of using a still as a copper or for any other brewing purpose and every distiller had perforce to use a copper solely for hot water and a separate mash kieve. He also constructed his still so as to expose as much of the vessel to the fire as possible, and made a concave bottom to concentrate as fierce a heat as he could to evaporate the wash or low wines rapidly. A still developed which was a flat circular vessel of large diameter and little height with a large diameter head and a scraper in the still to keep it from furring and stop residues burning. In Scotland where a similar still licence system operated, ingenious methods were discovered and there is little doubt that some were adopted here; so much so that the Board of Excise would not license Scotsmen to work small stills.[100] Morewood describes an Irish still of the type evolved in this period of still charges. The still looks like a large shallow cylinder with a man working the scraping machinery and another tapping the head to stop it getting foul.[101] These efforts to beat the number of charges of the licence were countered in 1804 by requiring that the diameter of a still kettle at the top was not to exceed three times the height measured from the bottom to the mouth of the still. This was later applied to small stills when they were encouraged in 1812.[102] In 1823 when the still licence system was being critically examined the possibility of relating the still charges to the area of the base

100. *Ibid.*, p. 379. A Treasury minute dated 29 May 1812 directed that Scottish distillers were not to be permitted to work small stills. *The Report on Distilleries in Scotland*, Parl. Pps. 1799, describes a 40 gallon still of unusual design capable of being partly charged, the contents distilled and the still emptied in less than 3 minutes. It is described on p. 392 and drawings appear on p. 453. See also S. Morewood, *A History of Inebriating Liquors*, 1838, *op. cit.*, p. 633 and *Irish Revenue Inquiry, 5th Report*, 1823, *op. cit.*, p. 376. The use of stills for brewing is said to have ceased in 1780, but is more likely to have faded out gradually some time later.

101. S. Morewood, *A History of Inebriating Liquors*, 1838, *op. cit.*, p. 657. *S.C. to inquire into the Regulations which govern the drawbacks and countervailing duties* . . . Parl. Pps. 1809 (199) iii, p. 296. A typical 500 gallon still kettle was described as 70 inches in diameter at the bottom, 74 inches at the top and 24½ inches deep.

102. 44 Geo. 3, c. 103, section 2; 52 Geo. 3, c. 48, sections 8–9. *Inquiry in Fees in Ireland, 5th Report, op. cit.*, p. 144. The rule restricting the width was intended to retard rapid work and on the assumption that the effect of fire on the sides of a still was about one fourth the effect on the base.

instead of the content was discussed.[103] Other devices for beating the still charge concerned the auxiliary vessels. Coppers could not, by an earlier Act, have a narrow mouth enabling them to be easily converted into a still, but apparently this was not enough and in 1805 they were not to be placed near the worm. The still was to be situated in a line between the copper and the worm. The construction of coolers was specified and backs and coolers were not to be smaller than the still in the hope, no doubt, that this would hinder a quick run through of a small quantity. It seems that these rules were still not sufficient for in 1814 the law prescribed that none of these vessels were to be so constructed as to be steam tight, nor connected in any way with the worm. Another measure to curb rapid distilling was to forbid pre-heating wash. Distillers apparently had been heating wash before charging the still and thereby reducing the time needed for evaporation. This measure also prevented distillers economising on fuel.[104]

It has been shown that the official method of assessing the spirit duty from the gauger's account and survey had collapsed, that the minimum charge based on the still content had become the actual charge, and that in an attempt to get the proper revenue it had been necessary to tailor this charge to a variety of distilling practices and sizes of stills. The result was an exceedingly cumbersome structure of assessments. No doubt distillers and the excise would understand this structure, but to anyone else the still licence system must have been bewildering. From a simple four charges per month on every still in 1780 there had emerged in the last few years of the system five distinct classes of stills, and in each class there was a range of charges depending on the size of the still. It would be difficult to devise a more complicated system. The five classes were:

1st Class.
Stills assessed at the highest rate and using coal.

103. *Irish Revenue Inquiry, 5th Report,* 1823, *op. cit.,* pp. 312, 375. In item 7 on p. 555 it states that the widest point must not be at the bottom of the still, thus stopping any attempt to emulate Miller's still in Scotland (see Note 100).

104. 45 Geo. 3, c. 104, sections 23–5; 46 Geo. 3, c. 88, sections 5, 7, 22, 24, 58; 54 Geo. 3, c. 88, sections 16–17. To forbid pre-heating was a particularly foolish measure. It might help to maintain some resemblance between the still licence duty and the spirit produced, but it also discouraged any attempts to invent means of saving fuel, and coal had to be imported against an outflow of capital.

2nd Class.

As in Class 1, but using turf fuel, the licence being abated by two-sevenths.

3rd Class.

Stills not exceeding 100 gallons content assessed at reduced rates and working with coal.

4th Class.

As in Class 3 and using turf, the licence being abated by two-sevenths.

5th Class.

As in Class 3 and working with restricted utensils, the licence being assessed on 90 charges in 28 days.

This was not all. Distillers in 1806 had to work their stills for a minimum of 224 days a year or pay still licence duty. They could cease after 168 days on giving notice, but could not then re-start during the rest of the year. For stills under 100 gallons the minimum was 168 days.[105]

So far the effects of the still licence system have been described. In this period, however, distillers had to contend with a variety of other regulations that hampered their operations and some had undesirable results on the quality of their spirit. Like the changes in the number of still charges these regulations were imposed autocratically and administered by a Revenue Board concerned solely with revenue. Except when the revenue yield was threatened the health and prosperity of the industry was disregarded by the Government, but with the corrupt background at the time this is understandable even if unwise. Distillers themselves might have wielded more influence, but they were not organised and were in cut-throat competition amongst themselves. Unlike brewers and other industries there was no distillers' guild to mould trade practices and represent their interests as a body.[106] Only occasionally did a few distillers get together to petition parliament on a particular issue. Though most of these regulations were designed to prevent fraud, some were part of public policies, such as conserving food in times of famine or

---

105. *Irish Revenue Inquiry, 5th Report,* 1823, *op. cit.,* p. 259; 46 Geo. 3, c. 88, sections 49, 51; 52 Geo. 3, c. 48, section 50.

106. *The Gentleman's and Citizen's Almanacks* list the guilds of Corporations. For example, in Dublin there were 25 in 1792.

favouring the use of sugar to help the West Indian economy. A few of these regulations persisted long after the still licence system was abandoned because of their intrinsic value to the revenue authorities, though their impact was softened to fit better into distillery practices.

There was a long comprehensive distillery Act in 1806 which re-enacted the provisions of previous laws, gave some added powers to the excise and clamped further restraints on distillers, some of which involved them in capital outlay. The details required before a licence was issued were expanded. For instance, the distiller had to send the Excise Commissioners in Dublin a drawing of his still for their approval, his entry had to include coppers, kieve and other utensils and his store room. His fermenting backs were to be as large as his largest still, though existing backs could continue in use until replaced, he was to give an oath not to use his copper for distilling and generally keep the rules, and he had to give bond in a penalty of £5 per gallon of the still content. He was not permitted to brew beer, but only pot-ale from corn or grain malted or unmalted, nor must he possess beer except for his personal use. He was also required to assist the gauger, set up casks for gauging and supply ladders and lights. Without such assistance there would be little chance of a gauger being able to check stocks.[107] The gauger too was given further powers. He could, for example, order the water to be drawn off the worm so that it could be inspected with the object of detecting any pipe which may be tapped off before the spirit emerged at the end of the worm. The Act repeated earlier powers enabling the officer to enter the distillery and adjoining houses or search such houses in order to detect hidden pipelines or other irregularities. The former regulations for giving notices when starting or stopping operations were also repeated. To curb corruption or taking fees it was made a misdemeanour to accept bribes.[108] These examples are sufficient to show that the distiller was fast being encompassed by regulations and his activities put into an official strait-jacket beyond that of any other industry, but no other industry was at this time so important to the revenue of the country.[109] Other industries, if they did attract government

107. 46 Geo. 3, c. 88, sections 1, 5–7, 15, 26–7, 32–3.
108. *Ibid.*, sections 34, 36, 38, 40–6, 51.
109. *Parliamentary Debates*, 1804, Appendix p. iii. Revenue returns for the year

attention, were usually either aided or hampered in relation to sea-borne trading; there was little interference with their internal working. Even brewing did not have such onerous regulations. Nevertheless the distilling industry remained vigorous.

So far the effects of the distillery laws have been examined only in the way they affected distilling processes, but they also had repercussions on the use of grain and in the brewing processes. In the first place because a distiller had to work his stills for a minimum number of days a year, or pay the duty for this period, he had to buy sufficient grain early in the distilling year whatever the state of the market. His ability to buy when the market was favourable was curtailed. His freedom to use malt was also regulated. Because of the malt duty and because, since 1800, he could use raw grain, as little malt as possible went into the grist, just enough to complete conversion and maintain the quality of his spirit. Furthermore, this mixture produced more spirit than could be made from malt alone, and as the malt duty was a serious addition to the spirit duty there was every inducement for a distiller to make a mixed grain whiskey.[110] There was also an inducement to introduce malt that had not paid duty. Malt received from outside sources was controlled, however ineffectively, through the permit system, but distillers had malt houses in their distillery premises. In 1808, therefore, it was enacted that permits were required to move malt from the distiller's malt house to his still house.[111] As a further check

---

ending 5 January 1803 show a gross revenue of £3,715,111 of which the customs was £1,626,794 and excise £1,716,412. The customs revenue mainly on consumer goods would not, in most cases, fall directly on Irish domestic industry. In the same year over 4½ million gallons of spirit were charged at 3s. 9½d. a gallon (English currency), plus the duty on the malt used (*Inquiry into Fees, 5th Report, 1806–7, op. cit.,* pp. 162, 202–3). In 1819 the excise revenue was £1,833,474, of which spirits accounted for £1,306,402 (*Return of Revenue Accounts,* Parl. Pps. 1819 (209) ix, p. 315 and *Irish Revenue Inquiry, 3rd Report,* Parl. Pps. 1822 (606) xiii, p. 958.)

110. *Irish Revenue Inquiry, 5th Report,* 1823, *op. cit.,* pp. 268, 288, 340. The report states that it was thought that spirit could not be made with malt and raw grain, but distillers had long known that it could be so made. It had been the common practice in distilleries before the malt duty was imposed in 1785. Raw grain had then been prohibited to protect the malt drawback. See *Report from the Committee on Distilleries in Ireland,* 1812–13, *op. cit.,* p. 3 where it is suggested that distillers should be compelled to use a certain proportion of malt in order to compete with illicit distillers. Some malt was, of course, necessary.

111. 48 Geo. 3, c. 79, section 4.

distillers were to keep an account of all malt used and this was related to spirit production. Later in 1813 this was changed to an account of the malt actually put into the kieve or mash tun. He was expected to produce twenty-four gallons of spirit for every barrel of malt used and if he fell short he paid additional malt duty. Assuming that a barrel of malt produced six gallons of spirit and that added raw grain produced only slightly more per barrel, these regulations attempted to tie the distiller to a ratio of about one barrel of malt to three of grain in the grist. It is very unlikely that this ratio was observed and in 1816 the regulation was repealed.[112]

With rapid distillation the distiller would be busy with a succession of brews to keep his still going for it took him two to four days to make wash. He would often add a completed brew to the remnants of a former brew to clear his vat for another brew. In this rush of processes the gauger had a hopeless task trying to keep track of each brewing for the purpose of raising a revenue account on the decreases in wash. Nor could he detect additions to the wash after his checks. Sometimes he relied on tasting. One distiller described in 1806 how the contents of wash backs were moved forward and the backs refilled with new wort when the gauger was away. To meet these manipulations of the wash an Act in 1806 required distillers to keep each brewing separate, to use each brew in proper sequence, and to distil a brew within six days of mashing.[113]

The saccharometer was in common use by distillers. They checked fermentation as it proceeded and it was a valuable aid in determining when to start distilling for with rapid distilling it did not pay the distiller to ferment his wash fully. As wash

112. 54 Geo. 3, c. 88, sections 6, 8 and 56 Geo. 3, c. 111, section 22. In 1798, 38 Geo. 3, c. 51, section 26 required a distiller to produce 7 gallons of spirit per barrel of malt, but when relating the duty on corn spirit to molasses spirit the ratio of 6 gallons to a barrel of malt was used. See also *Inquiry into Fees, 6th Report*, Parl. Pps. 1808 (4) iii, p. 463. This report refers to 14 gallons of spirit, but it must relate to post-1800 when the use of raw grain was permissible. Examples of the proportions of malt and various grains used in later years are given by S. Morewood, *History of Inebriating Liquors*, 1838, *op. cit.*, p. 660. See also *S.C. on Drawbacks and Duties on Spirits*, 1809, *op. cit.*, p. 221. English distillers used about one-third malt in their grist.

113. *Inquiry into Fees in Ireland, 5th Report*, 1806–7, *op. cit.*, pp. 146, 153, 181, 196. 46 Geo. 3, c. 88, sections 55, 57. See also *Irish Revenue Inquiry, 5th Report*, 1823, *op. cit.*, p. 559, item 23.

approaches full fermentation the action gets slower and the cost
of waiting would exceed the value of the extra spirit possible.
Furthermore the six day limit for brewing and distilling took no
account of winter and summer temperatures or weather conditions which could effect the speed of attenuation, though a skilful
distiller should have been able to keep within the limit.[114] The
saccharometer which was such a help to the distiller was denied
to the gauger to make similar checks until 1813 and even then its
use was very limited. He disregarded attenuation as a means of
estimating spirit production and used the instrument merely as a
check to see that new wash was not introduced clandestinely. If
the specific gravity was higher than on a previous survey the back
was deemed to contain new wash. For this limited purpose the
fact that there were different makes of saccharometers in use with
no standard instruments was no handicap.[115]

Distillers at this time used a strong wash usually in the region
of 60° to 80° of gravity although it was generally admitted that
a weaker wash produced a better quality spirit, especially if
distilled slowly, but the time factor was against a weak wash. Also
strong wash produced more but coarser spirit per gallon. On the
other hand it required more yeast from brewers to ferment it
rapidly, it was more difficult to ferment satisfactorily and some
distillers resorted to using lob to boost fermentation. All these
factors militated against any distiller who was not well skilled in
his art.[116] The wasteful use of grain with these methods may be
estimated from a distiller's statement that he formerly got eight

114. *Inquiry into Fees, 5th Report,* 1806–7, *op. cit.,* pp. 153, 191. *Irish Revenue
Inquiry, 5th Report,* 1823, *op. cit.,* pp. 259, 308, 323 and *5th Report Supplement,*
Parl. Pps. 1823 (498) vii, p. 688. *Distilling Experiments by the Excise Department,*
Parl. Pps. 1821 (538) xix, pp. 372–3.

115. 54 Geo. 3, c. 88, section 15 authorised the use of the saccharometer. See
Inquiry into Fees in Ireland, 5th Report, 1806–7, *op. cit.,* pp. 153–5 and *Irish Revenue
Inquiry, 5th Report,* 1823, *op. cit.,* pp. 300, 322–3. An important report on the use
of the saccharometer in Scotland appears in the 1823 report on p. 582 *et seq.* The
instrument favoured by some Irish distillers was the Saunders, others and some
excise officials preferred the Dicas instrument, which measured the specific
gravity in pounds to the barrel instead of degrees related to the gravity of water.

116. *Inquiry into Fees, 5th Report,* 1806–7, *op. cit.,* p. 155. *Distilling Experiments,*
1821, *op. cit.,* p. 373. *Irish Revenue Inquiry, 5th Report,* 1823, *op. cit.,* pp. 298–9,
308, 312, 340, 345, 352. Bub is an alternative term for lob and is now generally
used. It is warm wort in a state of high fermentation. See also *S.C. on Drawback
and Duties on Spirits,* 1809, *op. cit.,* p. 289. Extra yeast was estimated to add 1¼d.
a gallon to the costs of spirits, and lack of full fermentation another 6d.

gallons of spirit per barrel of grain, but in 1806 he only produced 5 to 5½ gallons. It was claimed that a better spirit could be made if some malted oats were used, but when steeped, oats swelled so much more than barley that the malt duty, based on the gauge by the excise officer, rendered the use of oats prohibitive.[117]

The speed at which stills were run off would, if no corrective measures were taken, have had some very undesirable effects. Little time was available to keep the bottom of the kettle free from sludge and a constant scouring by chains was essential to prevent burning. Excessive fusel oil and other unwanted products of fermentation went over to the worm giving a bad flavour unless considerable foreshots and tailings were taken off and run back into subsequent distilling, but this nevertheless led to further waste which would have been largely avoided with a slower process. Violent evaporation led to much frothing which choked the head and worm. This was counteracted by the excessive use of soap which was said to injure the quality of the spirit. One senior excise official stated that a 300 gallon still used nearly a ton of soap every month. To cleanse the spirit salt went into the still. Many distillers used vitriol for this purpose as it was said to stay at the bottom of the still. These were some of the many efforts to offset the defects of rapid distilling, all of them trying to correct a basically inefficient method of production forced on distillers by unwise legislation which was only partially enforceable.[118] An example of rapid working in 1806 was given by a distiller with a 1,560 gallon still. He said he could make his wash in thirty hours and run off over 1,000 gallons of it in fifty minutes, that is, distil to singlings, recharge the still and take off finished spirit. A feat which would seem incredible today. In 1823, two English excise officials reporting on Irish distilleries described the working of a 500 gallon still. It was charged with 250 gallons of wash which was run off in fourteen minutes. Six such charges produced 375 gallons of low wines which were run off in twenty-six minutes. Allowing thirty-four minutes for delays and running off

117. *Inquiry into Fees, 5th Report,* 1806–7, *op. cit.,* p. 179. *Distilleries in Ireland,* Parl. Pps. 1812–13 (269) vi, pp. 7–8. *Irish Revenue Inquiry, 5th Report,* 1823, *op. cit.,* pp. 312, 336.

118. *Distilling Experiments,* 1821, *op. cit.,* p. 373. *Irish Revenue Inquiry, 5th Report,* 1823, *op. cit.,* pp. 283, 297, 340. S. Morewood, *History of Inebriating Liquors,* 1838, *op. cit.,* p. 672.

feints the time from wash to spirits was 144 minutes. They calculated that on a six and a half day week there would be 65 charges or 260 a month and that at a 10 per cent produce from the wash the resulting spirit would be 39,000 gallons, whilst the still licence charge would be 33,075 gallons. They thought, however, that the produce would be more like 12 per cent of the wash and that the spirit produced would be 46,800 gallons, giving the distiller a surplus of 13,725 gallons which he could dispose of clandestinely. The strength of the spirit was usually 24° over proof though spirits up to a strength of 31° over proof were obtained by cutting off tailings earlier in the process.[119]

In outward appearance the distiller was so hedged in with excise controls that evading the revenue would seem to require considerable astuteness. An excise minute book was placed in his distillery in which he recorded a declaration of the corn to be used and the hour of each mashing, but the law said this record was to be in bushels, a measure not used by distillers who worked by weight and the result was that this entry was a mere formality ignored by the gauger. The gauger was directed to take dips of the cooler on his surveys, but the dips were inaccurate in a vessel which could have a variety of depths. So again the dips were a formality. To make any kind of assessment of wash the gauger must know the number of mashings each day, but as one of them admitted he rarely had this essential information. He visited the distillery three times a day if he did his job faithfully, but visits were often 'stamped', that is, they were recorded in the minute book on a subsequent visit, but were never made. In any case his visits were at fixed times, rarely at night, and at the convenience of the distiller. His superior, the surveyor, visited daily and never at night. With this kind of control, far from being astute, a distiller would be stupid if he could not evade the laws with impunity.[120]

What were the irregularities practised? In the malt house the distiller could do little. He could trample down the steeped malt

119. *Inquiry into Fees in Ireland, 5th Report*, 1806–7, *op. cit.*, p. 153. *Irish Revenue Inquiry, 5th Report*, 1823, *op. cit.*, pp. 323, 552–3. See also p. 559, item 27, where it is stated that stills were usually only charged to half their content.

120. *Inquiry into Fees, 5th Report*, 1806–7, *op. cit.*, pp. 146, 148, 150, 181. *Irish Revenue Inquiry, 3rd Report*, Parl. Pps. 1822 (606) xiii, p. 727. An excise order in 1811. See also p. 812 where the Excise Board state in 1815 that a number of officers had been dismissed for insobriety.

to reduce the gauge by depth and similar malpractices, but the process was too slow to do much more. He could, however, bring in malt on a large scale by manipulating permits.[121] In the distillery the frauds began before operations even started. Before a licence was granted the still and backs were gauged by a senior excise official, who was paid a fee by the distiller, and who used a five gallon measure to ascertain the content of the still or back. For the latter vessel he tabulated the capacity at each inch of depth so that the contents could be read off on a dip rod. Distillers got round this by inserting copper coloured tiles or blown bladders in order to reduce the excise measurement of content. They later inserted blocks below the dipping place to reduce the dip and therefore the inches of liquid depth as shown by the dip rod. Backs were also found to have been enlarged after the official gauging and most of the principal frauds emanated from the management of the wash. There were also cases of enlarged stills after gauging, and underground vessels for wash.[122] Another irregularity concerned accidents to the distilling plant. In 1806 the law allowed duty to be abated if distilling was stopped by fire or accident. This was repealed in 1808 and in its place a distiller was permitted to deposit with the excise a duplicate still for replacement if needed and abatement of duty was limited to cases of fire or severe structural damage. It was stated that 90 per cent of the accidents, such as a still bursting, were faked, and were followed by fabricated affidavits with the officer's collusion in order to get the abatement of duty.[123] These were some of a number of fraudulent practices.

121. *Inquiry into Fees, 6th Report,* Parl. Pps. 1808 (4) iii, p. 463. A decrease in the malt used in distilleries was thought to be due to an increase in illicit malting and the 'ignorance, neglect and corruption of officers'.

122. *Inquiry into Fees, 5th Report,* 1806–7, *op. cit.,* pp. 153, 155, 209. The Commissioners of the inquiry suggested using 'dry' inches instead of a wet dip to ascertain the contents of fermenting backs. In any case froth in a fermenting back would prevent an accurate wet dip. At the present time a dry dip is used and the rod has a cork float at its tip. The dry dip was another method of fraud later when a gauger and distiller in collusion at Kilkenny altered dips of, say, 23 inches to 123 inches. (*Excise Revenue Inquiry, 7th Report, Part I,* 1834, *op. cit.,* p. 268.)

123. 46 Geo. 3, c. 88, section 52; 48 Geo. 3, c. 81, sections 1–5; 49 Geo. 3, c. 99, section 30. 55 Geo. 3, c. 12, sections 13–14 removed the provision to deposit a spare still with the excise. See also *Inquiry into Fees, 5th Report,* 1806–7, *op. cit.,* p. 209.

Production

As in the previous century distillers had to face from time to time laws prohibiting distilling of grain, but there was now a difference for although there were often shortages of food grains there was an undercurrent of political or other reasons. There had always been famines in Ireland, but they were usually of a local nature. There had, for instance, been at least seven famine years between 1800 and 1821 where crops had failed in one or other of the provinces. Only in 1816 was the famine widespread and even then it was not total, and this was followed by a request in parliament to suspend distilling. In Ballina there had been riots where four people were killed and twenty-seven wounded due to the scarcity of food and attempts to move grain elsewhere.[124]

While there might be justification to curtail distilling corn spirit when the food scarcity is real there were also attempts to stop the use of grain in favour of sugar, which even excluded molasses, and which had no justification except the interests of West Indian property owners. These latter persons did succeed in prohibiting grain distilling in England, but a parliamentary inquiry deemed it inexpedient to extend the measure to Ireland, the main reason being that it would not work. The prohibition would merely increase evasion in distilleries and illicit distilling, especially the latter. In an early attempt to stop grain distilling it was said that Dublin distillers got corn wash from brewers under the pretence of getting barm. No faith was placed in the ability or willingness of excise officers to enforce a prohibition.

Illicit distilling had reached such proportions in 1808 that there were only two licensed stills in Ulster and three about to be licensed in Connaught. A surveyor general of excise with considerable experience of private distilling said that in these two provinces not one-fiftieth of the spirit consumed paid duty. In the face of such evidence any attempt to force sugar distilling would simply mean a loss of revenue and no saving in grain. Furthermore, sugar had to be imported whereas the Irish distiller had grain within easy reach. So except for one short attempt, parliament confined itself to encouraging, without much success, the use of sugar by relaxations in the duty. There is no doubt that

124. G. O'Brien, *The Economic History of Ireland from the Union to the Famine,* London, 1921, p. 227. *Parliamentary Debates,* 10 February 1817, Col. 309 and 5 March 1817, col. 883.

the threat of a great increase in illicit distilling considerably affected government policy and in this way the private distiller became the ally of the licensed distiller. Foster, the Irish Chancellor of the Exchequer in the London parliament summed up the attitude of the Irish people in 1810 when he said 'distillation we will have, revenue from it you may give up. It is vain for gentlemen connected with the West Indies to affect to consider the abundance of illicit distilling in Ireland as proceeding from remissness with which the laws for its punishment are enforced'. A year earlier, reviewing the results of a prohibition Act in favour of sugar in 1808 he said that during the year six million gallons were distilled of which not one gallon came from sugar in the whole nine months of the prohibition.[125]

Prohibition measures because of food scarcity were on a different footing and were usually steps which any government should take when the subsistence of the nation is threatened. Even in this matter, however, some English interests tried to stop Irish distilling to ensure grain imports into England rather than for any concern for the welfare of Irish people. One member of parliament in 1809 gave his opinion that the real reason for prohibiting corn distilling was that England wanted Irish grain and he got some support. Others, however, thought that the removal of the prohibition would encourage corn growing and lead to better supplies to England. Foster, himself, supported this view.[126] The first suspension of both malting and distilling from grain after the Union was in 1801 to last up to 31 December, but power was given to the Lord Lieutenant to allow malting and distilling at his discretion after 1 October, presumably when the success of the crops was known. Some later Acts were only partial. In 1803 for instance, the Lord Lieutenant could prohibit distilling from oats or oatmeal if he considered it advisable. All corn distilling was stopped in 1809 and again in 1812 to the end of 1813. Apparently these prohibitory measures were futile and

125. *S.C. on the use of Sugar in Distilleries,* Parl. Pps. 1808 (178) iv, pp. 3, 8–9, 70, 72, 74. Distilling from molasses was prohibited in 1808 by 48 Geo. 3, c. 81, section 7. *Parliamentary Debates,* 25 February 1809, col. 1044; 21 February 1810, col. 499; and 22 February 1810, col. 549. Distilling from sugar was specially encouraged in 1813 by 53 Geo. 3, c. 52 during a prohibition against distilling from grain imposed in the same year by c. 7.

126. *Parliamentary Debates,* 23 February 1809, cols. 1128, 1132; 13 February 1810, cols. 390–9; 22 February 1810, cols. 547–8.

none was imposed during the more severe famine in 1816. The results appearing in the returns of gallons charged show that in 1800 only 275,013 gallons paid duty, there was no spirit charged with duty in 1801, in 1809 duty was paid on 71,628 gallons and on 1,809,849 in 1813. The gallons paying duty in other years range from 3½ to over 6 million. These figures of duty paid spirit do not give the whole picture. Foster's remark in 1810 relating to attempts to force distilling from sugar was based on his own first hand knowledge of Ireland and would apply equally to prohibitions. Furthermore, duty free warehousing began in 1804 so that some of the spirit charged with duty would have been distilled earlier. Hence the quantity charged before 1804 would be the yield of the still licences, not what was actually distilled. After 1804 the quantity would be swelled by deliveries from warehouses.[127] Sometimes during food scarcity the people themselves might enforce a stoppage as already mentioned in the case at Ballina. The same action might be taken even with illicit distillers where it is said that on one occasion during a period when grain distilling was prohibited 'the people themselves went in bodies to take them down (the stills) because they were working on oats and meal'.[128]

The rate of duty for corn spirit in 1800 was 2s. 6d. a gallon in Irish currency. Thereafter the rates are quoted in English currency in returns put before parliament. In 1802 it was 2s. 10¼d. and rose in 1803 to 3s. 6¾d. and to 4s. 1d. in 1804. In 1810 it fell to 2s. 6½d. in a move to help distillers to compete with illicit distillers, but rose again to 5s. 1¼d. in 1812 and 5s. 7¼d. in 1813. Except for 1815 when it rose to 6s. 1½d. it remained at 5s. 7¼d. till 1823. For molasses spirit the rate rose and fell in sympathy with the duty on corn spirit plus the added malt duty, except in 1809. In that year a special rate of 2s. 10½d. was in force for spirit made from sugar

127. The prohibitions were imposed by 41 Geo. 3, c. 16; 44 Geo. 3, c. 11; 48 Geo. 3, c. 118; 49 Geo. 3, c. 7; 53 Geo. 3, c. 7. The figures for duty paid spirits are taken from the *Excise Revenue Inquiry, 7th Report, Part 1, 1834, op. cit.,* pp. 66–7. The statistics show 3,575,430 gallons for 1808 as compared with Foster's statement in parliament in 1809 that 6 million gallons were distilled. The discrepancy would arise from the quantity warehoused and also the year ending may not be the same. Thus the official figures for duty paid spirits in the previous year, 1807, were 5½ million gallons. Foster may have included part of this year. Duty free warehousing was allowed in 1804 by 44 Geo. 3, c. 104. See also *Irish Revenue Inquiry, 5th Report Supplement,* Parl. Pps. 1837 (7) xxv, p. 664.

128. *S.C. on the Use of Sugar in Distilleries,* 1808, *op. cit.,* p. 75.

only. The malt duty was 7s. 7d. a barrel in 1803 and rose by stages to 14s. 3d. in 1823. There was a special addition to the corn spirit duty in 1808 of 10s. for every six gallons which could later be recovered on proof of the malt used, no doubt as an aid to the excise to ensure that all malt had paid duty. This was repealed in 1810. Drawbacks on export were correspondingly adjusted.[129] Population figures for the period 1800–23 rose steadily from 5,216,000 to 6,802,000, and gallons distilled averaged about four and a half million a year, so that, related to legal spirit, there appears to be a slight fall in *per capita* consumption.[130]

The prices of legal spirit varied slightly in different parts of Ireland, but were about 9s. a gallon duty paid in 1823 of which the duty was 5s. 11½d. (Irish currency) including the added malt duty estimated at about 4d. One distiller said that this price was only possible because of his profits from spirit that evaded the duty which he sold at 6s. to 7s. a gallon, the difference below the full price being due to the risk to the dealer of seizure and penalties. Competing illicit spirit varied considerably depending chiefly on the distance from the market, but it generally sold at 2s. to 4s. 6d. below the price of legal whiskey. Belfast was an exception where it actually reached 10s. to 12s. a gallon. Illicit spirit was distilled more slowly than legal spirit at this time and a number of witnesses at the inquiry in 1823 considered it better quality, though this view was probably coloured by a desire to get the rate of duty reduced. Evasion in licensed distilleries was said to amount to a third by one distiller, a fifth by an official witness and, as a compromise, a quarter by the Commissioners of a Parliamentary Inquiry who also reported that in their opinion illicit distillers accounted for no less than 6 out of every 10 gallons consumed, a very high and questionable estimate.[131]

129. *Excise Revenue Inquiry, 7th Report, Part I,* 1834, *op. cit.,* pp. 66-7. *13th Inland Revenue Report,* Parl. Pps. 1870 (c. 82) xx, p. 387. The special addition of 6s. per 10 gallons was imposed by 48 Geo. 3, c. 78 and repealed by 50 Geo. 3, c. 15. The low duty on spirit made from sugar was imposed by 49 Geo. 3, c. 33. The malt duty is quoted as a rate per bushel in the revenue returns.

130. *13th Inland Revenue Report,* 1870, *op. cit.,* p. 204. Population figures are taken from the *Irish Census, 1821.*

131. *Irish Revenue Inquiry, 5th Report,* 1823, *op. cit.,* pp. 260, 284, 297, 308–9, 313, 318, 323, 652. Ten years earlier duty paid whiskey prices were considerably higher. Thus on 7 August 1813 they were quoted at 16s. to 18s. 6d. a gallon (*Belfast Commercial Chronicle*).

The complete distortion of normal distilling processes resulting from the still licence system was accompanied by a great waste of grain and fuel and the extravagant use of labour. Because even partially fermented wash needed some 30 to 50 hours to prepare and distilling took only a fraction of that time, capital outlay on brewing plant was larger than would have been essential without the urge for rapid distilling. It must also have been a major problem to maintain the plant in good repair during the furious rush of production. J. Jameson, a Dublin distiller, said in 1823 that in the previous year with a 750 gallon still, the largest then used, he worked off 13 or 14 fermenting backs, of about 100 to 150 gallons of wash to the inch of depth, continuously for 6 or 7 months a year.[132] Strong wash was used because there was a greater yield of spirit in a shorter time even though it was admitted that a weaker wash, not below 40° gravity, would result in better quality spirit. It was not fully fermented and fermentation hurried by excessive yeast was a further waste. The official ratio in 1823 of wash to spirit was ten gallons of wash to one gallon on spirit, but even with imperfect fermentation distillers admitted a yield of 12 per cent. In England similar wash slowly and fully fermented yielded up to 19 per cent, and attenuation was carried from a high gravity down to the gravity of water or even lower instead of between 6° and 10° as in Ireland. Malt was used as sparingly as possible by Irish distillers usually being about a fifth of the grist though the quality would have been improved under existing conditions with a higher proportion.[133] Speed, however, was all important. A fierce heat was kept going, stills were charged at least two or three times with wash, each charge run off, the spent wash and sludge cleared, charged again with the resulting low wines, the spirit run off and the stills cleared for the next distillation as fast as the labour could handle the work. It is no wonder that the spirit contained excessive oils and other injurious ingredients and that special

132. *Ibid.*, 5th *Report Supplement*, 1823, pp. 688–9.
133. *Distilling Experiments*, 1821, *op. cit.*, p. 372. *Irish Revenue Inquiry*, 5th *Report*, 1823, *op. cit.*, pp. 312, 322, 342–3, 345, 629. M. Donovan, *Domestic Economy*, London, 1830, i, p. 225. With a high gravity wash extra yeast is essential for 'once the head of yeast falls in the tun, neither the further additions of yeast nor increase in temperature will succeed in resuscitating the fermentation' and yeast is killed as alcohol is formed. On pp. 227–8 he indicates that third distillations were being done in Ireland in 1830.

precautions were needed to prevent the still fouling or burning.[134]

Perhaps the most spectacular waste was in fuel and labour. Coffey, reporting on distilling experiments in 1821 wrote 'incredible as the facts may appear, our experiments have fully shown us that one-eighth part of the fuel consumed in working a still in Ireland under the present rapid system would be sufficient to distil the same quantity of spirits under a slow system'. This great waste would vary with the size of the still, the smaller the still the greater the waste and inflation of costs, though this was compensated by more rapid production. Since coal was the best fuel the system favoured the establishment of distilleries at ports. Some coal from Kilkenny would help inland distilleries, but the help was limited. A noteworthy effort to cut fuel costs was made in Roscrea by Birch who had a 100 gallon still using turf. He was having difficulty in getting enough suitable turf. He put a jacket round the still and instead of heating with direct fire he passed steam round the still. The steam also heated two coppers. He claimed to cut fuel costs by 80 per cent. Despite determined opposition from conservative Dublin distillers the Board of Excise in 1818 allowed Birch to experiment under the supervision of a chemistry professor and experienced excise officers. The Board rejected the idea on the grounds that it would facilitate illegal manufacture since existing law forbad pre-heating wash, an essential feature of the fuel saving, and no doubt they thought it would be too easy to convert other vessels into stills. It is easier to divert a steam pipe temporarily than surreptitiously light a fire.[135]

The numbers employed in distilleries were reported in 1822. In thirty-seven distilleries there were 3,318 men, 11 women and 18 children. The highest number was in Maryborough district where three distilleries employed 689 men and the lowest in Armagh where two stills only employed twenty-eight men.

134. *Distilling Experiments*, 1821, *op. cit.*, p. 372. *Irish Revenue Inquiry, 5th Report*, 1823, *op. cit.*, pp. 279–80, 318.

135. *Distilling Experiments*, 1821, *op. cit.*, pp. 372–3. *Irish Revenue Inquiry, 5th Report*, 1823, *op. cit.*, pp. 287–8, 290, 294–6, 318, 348. The Roscrea experiment mentioned on p. 295 is more fully described by S. Morewood, *History of Inebriating Liquors*, 1838 *op. cit.*, p. 634 and by A. J. V. Underwood, *Historical Development of Distilling Plant*, p. 27, a paper read before the Institute of Chemical Engineers on 22 February 1935.

These figures would include persons who were not actually operating the stills. The stills themselves were estimated to require four times the labour force which would be needed if slow distilling were practised. Compared with some industries employment in distilling was unimportant to the country. In a distillery of this period there would be a skilled distiller, normally the owner, a foreman of limited skill and labourers. Distilleries with a large output would have a few skilled tradesmen such as a cooper and a smith. The distiller would rely on calling in copper smiths and other specialists for major repairs. No figures are available for excise staff employed on distilleries, but in 1806 there were 20 surveyors, 42 gaugers and 24 supernumeraries controlling 30 stills, most of them in the range of 500 to 600 gallons content, and 25 rectifiers with smaller stills.[136]

Before 1800 the distillery laws, debates in parliament, petitions and the accounts of travellers all indicated widespread illicit distilling, but its extent was guesswork. After 1800 it was still guesswork, but there were returns of seizures of stills and materials and the evidence of excise officials and others which supported estimates of the quantities illicitly distilled. In 1806 this estimate was a third of all spirit produced and in 1808 there were said to be 'upwards of 3,000 illicit stills in Ireland'. In 1823 a legal distiller thought that illicit stills accounted for between a half and two-thirds of all spirit in Ireland, but his opinion would be biased.[137] The effects of all this illicit spirit on the legal distilling industry was uneven. In Ulster and Connaught legal distillers had great difficulty in getting established despite encouragement to set up small stills. An Act in 1814 even offered half of the townland fines to anyone establishing a still not exceeding 1,000 gallons content in an illicit distilling area. Those who tried to start legal stills were undersold. In other areas, particularly large cities, distillers competed successfully, aided by considerable clandestine distilling, and the illicit distiller never

136. *Distilling Experiments*, 1821, *op. cit.*, p. 373. *Irish Revenue Inquiry, 4th Report*, Parl. Pps. 1822 (634) xiii, pp. 1644–68 and *5th Report*, 1823, *op. cit.*, p. 341.

137. *Inquiry into Fees, 5th Report*, 1806–7 *op. cit.*, 166, 170–1. S.C. on the use of Sugar in Distilleries, 1808, *op. cit.*, p. 72. *Irish Revenue Inquiry, 5th Report*, 1823, *op. cit.*, pp. 301, 370. Statements on the proportion of illicit to legal whiskey should be treated with reserve, some illegal whiskey from licensed distilleries may be included in these estimates. Moreover, distillers were pressing for a reduction of the duty.

took root.[138] The large demand for spirituous liquors, however, meant that there was a potential danger at all times that illicit distilling would quickly arise if legal distilling was stopped or even checked for any length of time. This was well understood by the Government and there is no doubt that legal distillers were saved from severe restrictions because of the certain expansion of illicit distilling which would result and that the sacrifice of revenue for a desirable object would be of no avail. On those occasions when legal manufacture was attacked, illicit distilling did, in fact, rise or fall in relation to the restraints imposed, or with the rise or fall of the spirit duty. The practices and methods of illicit distilling were, apart from evading penalties, little affected by distillery laws, and the history of the poteen maker does not fall neatly into periods. It is better, therefore, to discuss illicit distilling separately.

Exports

The large quantities of spirit from licensed distilleries that evaded duty affected measures taken to control the export trade when it was opened after 1800, and gave rise to various laws designed to combat these revenue leaks, especially in relation to dishonest excise officials. It is sufficient at this point, however, to record the verdict of a report to parliament in 1807 that distillers profited little from their malpractices in marketing this spirit for 'besides the risk of seizure and penalties, a deficiency of produce and considerable waste of all kinds of materials was attendant on the hurry and confusion with which the whole process was necessarily carried on; and in the end he was obliged to sell his private spirits frequently at two shillings under the market price of permitted spirits, and could not legally recover their value from the purchaser'.[139] Small quantities were taken out of the distillery by day by employees and if under one gallon they did not require a permit. Large quantities were removed

138. *Committee on Distilleries in Ireland*, Parl. Pps. 1812–13 (269) vi, pp. 7, 18. The Act granting half the fines was 54 Geo. 3, c. 150, section 8. *Irish Revenue Inquiry*, 5th Report, 1823, op. cit., p. 655. Guinness, the Dublin brewer, said that poteen had no sale in that city, but that illegal whiskey was coming from the licensed distilleries.

139. *Inquiry into Fees in Ireland*, 5th Report, 1806–7, op. cit., p. 157. Permitted spirits here means spirits delivered under cover of an official permit.

at night by gangs who could not be challenged except with
military support.[140] A more usual way of disposal, however,
was by the manipulation of permits, a single permit covering
a legal delivery being used a second or third time before its
surrender in order to cover the transport of illegal spirits; or
sometimes actually purchasing a blank permit form from an
excise officer who would later fill in his counterfoil and adjust
his accounts to cover the fraud. These monstrous frauds were
only possible through the collusion and connivance of officers
'whose corrupt intercourse with distillers appears to have been
general'.[141] The flood of illegal spirits on to the domestic market
reacted on the export trade through prices and the manipulation
of alcoholic strengths.

Before the Act of Union efforts had been made in both
countries to free the trade between them of legal restrictions, but
the intercourse of spirits had not received the benefits of the
various Acts for a number of reasons. England was afraid that
Ireland, with its lower customs duties, might be used to tranship
foreign spirits and smuggle them into England. There were also
technical difficulties, the different modes of collecting the revenue,
standards of strength, assessing fair drawback rates and, so far
as England was concerned, the fact that whiskey was a finished
product whereas spirit from English distilleries had to be rectified. So Irish spirit only entered Great Britain on the same footing
as any other foreign spirit and the result was that virtually no
export could take place before 1800.[142] Article 6 of the Act of
Union stated that Irish spirit could be imported into Great Britain
at a duty of 5s. 1¼d. a gallon at a strength of 1 to 10 over proof,
or 7° over proof by the Sikes hydrometer, and in proportion
for stronger spirits. The way was opened, therefore, for Irish
distillers to enter the market in Great Britain, though as will

140. *Irish Revenue Inquiry, 5th Report,* 1823, *op. cit.,* pp. 324, 339.
141. *Inquiry into Fees, 5th Report,* 1806–7, *op. cit.,* pp. 154, 156, 183, 209. *Irish
Revenue Inquiry, 5th Report,* 1823, *op. cit.,* p. 325.
142. *Parliamentary Debates.* A series of long debates took place in London on
22 February 1785 following the introduction of resolutions by Pitt for commercial
intercourse between Great Britain and Ireland. See particularly 12 May 1785,
col. 579 referring to drawbacks and the smuggling of West Indies spirit through
Ireland. Other references of special application are 24 May 1785, col. 712 and 25
July 1785, col. 940. On 2 July 1804, col. 1030, Foster, the Irish Chancellor of the
Exchequer, refers to the total lack of exports to Great Britain before 1800.

be seen this trade did not develop so easily as the law made it appear. There were reciprocal measures for spirits from Great Britain to enter Ireland, but there was little demand for them and except for a flow from Scotland, when a drawback anomaly favoured them, these imports had practically no effect on Irish distillers.[143] The duties and export drawbacks on spirits, the estimated malt used, and the modes of assessing them were different in each of the three countries. In Ireland, as already explained, the spirit duty was collected as a still licence charge and the malt used was regarded as equivalent to 10d. a gallon when the malt duty was 10s. a barrel, a generous estimate for distillers exporting to Great Britain. In England the spirit duty was assessed on the wash calculated at nineteen gallons of spirits at 8° over proof for every 100 gallons of wash, the minimum size of stills was 3,000 gallons content, an account was taken of the spirit made and run into a receiver, and locks were used to prevent unauthorised additions of wash after the account had been taken.[144] Malt drawback was calculated at export on the basis of one-third malt used in the grist. In Scotland until 1816 a still licence system similar to the Irish system operated, but without the same arrangement for the officer's survey and account. In 1816 the still licence was abandoned and duty was assessed on the attenuation of the wash during fermentation. Until 1815 there was a complication, because lower rates of duty applied to stills in the Highlands, but so far as Ireland was concerned imports came from Lowland districts and it was on these rates of duty that Scottish drawbacks were eventually based.[145] The ultimate goal was a single system of distillery

143. *Irish Revenue Inquiry, 3rd Report,* 1822, *op. cit.,* p. 1282. Imports from Great Britain were negligible except during 1808 to 1810 when they reached a maximum of 226,000 gallons. Irish exports to Great Britain in the year ending 5 January 1802 were 227,000 gallons of which 198,000 went to England. By 1805 Irish exports had reached 1,157,000 gallons, nearly all to England. After 1810 exports were small or nil for a few years because of prohibitions on distilling in England, but began to rise after 1820. See also *4th Report,* Parl. Pps. 1822 (634) xiii, p. 1361 and *5th Report Supplement,* 1823, *op. cit.,* pp. 719-21.

144. *Irish Revenue Inquiry, 5th Report,* 1823, *op. cit.,* pp. 263, 342. 46 Geo. 3, c. 83 fixed the malt drawback equivalent at 10d. a gallon.

145. *Irish Revenue Inquiry, 5th Report,* 1823, *op. cit.,* pp. 261, 265 and comparisons of excise controls on pp. 555-62. The Highland and Lowland rates of duty are shown in the *Excise Revenue Inquiry, 7th Report, Part I,* 1834, *op. cit.,* p. 42.

laws and duties for the whole United Kingdom. This was accomplished for Ireland and Scotland in 1823, but it was not until 1858 that the whole United Kingdom came under a unified system and rates of duty.[146]

Irish spirits exported to Great Britain in 1801 qualified for a drawback of 3s. 7d. a gallon representing the whole of the spirit duty of 2s. 4½d. (British) or 2s. 6d. (Irish) plus an addition for the duty paid on the malt presumed to have been used. Stills exceeding 500 gallons content received abatements from the spirit duty of 16 or 8 per cent which were not deducted in the drawback and there were also large quantities which escaped duty altogether and which reduced the distiller's marketing costs. Hence the Irish distillers were favourably placed to compete in the English market if whiskey could be made acceptable to English consumers. However there was no immediate advantage as distilling from grain in Ireland was prohibited in 1801 and consequently drawbacks ceased. When this was lifted Irish exports at once responded and in 1803 reached over a million gallons. There was, naturally, a reaction from English distillers and in 1804 the allowance of 16 or 8 per cent had to be repaid on spirits exported. The excess spirits evading duty could not very well be estimated and there were countercharges that evasions occurred in Great Britain.[147] The withdrawal of the still allowances made no real difference to the Irish export trade which remained in the region of a million or more gallons annually till 1807. A more important advantage to Irish distillers, however, was in spirit strengths. The Irish distiller paid duty on his spirits without regard to strength and he usually marketed

146. The Act of Union implied an ultimate union of revenues and provided for interim arrangements. *Parliamentary Debates*, 23 November 1814, col. 486. The Irish Chancellor of the Exchequer stated his aim to equalise duties in Ireland and Great Britain and the modes of collection. On 2 April 1815, col. 956 he raised the Irish malt duty to 19s. a barrel, the rate current in Great Britain. See also *13th Inland Revenue Report*, 1870, *op. cit.*, p. 220.

147. *Inquiry into Fees in Ireland*, 1806–7, *op. cit.*, p. 161. Spirits imported from Great Britain were charged at a higher rate of duty than the excise on Irish home-made spirits and in addition, the drawback on exported Irish spirits exceeded the duty paid because of manipulated strengths and because the 10d. a gallon allowed for malt much exceeded the duty on the malt actually used. *Parliamentary Debates*, 2 July 1804, cols. 1030–4. The exclusion of the still bounties from drawbacks was raised in a debate on the *Irish Spirit Warehousing Bill*, and this was done by 44 Geo. 3, c. 104, section 15.

it at about 24° over proof by Sikes' hydrometer. In Great Britain the import duty was calculated at 1 to 10 over proof by Clarke's hydrometer, equivalent to 7° over proof by Sikes. The Irish distiller could, therefore, dilute his spirit after paying duty, export the same number of gallons on which duty had been paid and have a surplus free of duty for the Irish market. It was claimed that this surplus amounted to a gallon for every three exported and, as the English distiller was supposedly unable to evade duty so easily, the Irish distiller was able to undersell the English distiller in his own market.[148] Trade between Ireland and Scotland resulted in a hopeless muddle where the drawback laws were heavily weighted against the Irish distiller in both markets and Scottish distillers were, in effect, subsidised at the expense of the revenue of Great Britain. In 1809 intercourse of spirits between the three countries was so distorted by ill-devised laws that parliament appointed a select committee to inquire into all aspects of trade.[149]

The English excise duty in 1809 was 7s. 3d. a gallon for spirits at a strength of 7° over proof and in proportion for higher strengths plus 11½d. a gallon for malt used. At export, drawback of the whole 8s. 2½d. was paid and Irish spirits imported into England paid a similar countervailing duty. In Ireland the spirit duty was 4s. regardless of strength and 1s. 8d. for the malt used calculated at a barrel of malt being equivalent to six gallons of spirit and one third of the grist being malt. Drawback on Irish exports and the countervailing duty on English imports were the full 5s. 8d. Thus there was apparently free trade between the two countries, but besides the different regulations for strength the select committee reported probably correctly, that the Irish malt calculation was inaccurate giving the Irish distiller an advantage in the English market. The English distiller had no corresponding advantage and no inducement to export to

148. There are a number of references to the delivery strength of spirits from Irish distilleries. See, for example, *Irish Revenue Inquiry, 5th Report,* 1823 *op. cit.,* pp. 285, 323, 562 (item 50) and *5th Report Supplement,* 1823, p. 666. *Parliamentary Debates,* 14 June 1811, col. 626, it was alleged that an Irish distiller could make 100 gallons up to 130 by adding water, export 100 gallons to England and retain 30 gallons as a clear bonus.

149. *S.C. to inquire into the Regulations governing the drawbacks and countervailing duties on the Import and Export of spirits made in Great Britain or Ireland from one country to the other.* Parl. Pps. 1809 (199) (235) iii, pp. 199–201.

Ireland. The committee also referred to the 'imperfect state of the collection of duty in Ireland'. They might have added that the two markets were not the same. English spirit was not palatable unless rectified and Irish tastes did not favour such spirit to any significant degree. Possibly Irish whiskey was not popular in England, but it could be used by rectifiers to produce flavoured beverages.[150]

Trade between Ireland and Scotland was on an entirely different basis. In both countries the popular beverage was whiskey. In 1809 the Scottish excise duty was 5s. 1½d. a gallon for spirit at a strength of 1 to 10 over proof plus 10d. a gallon for the malt used. Irish imports paid duty at the full 5s. 11½d. Trade in the reverse direction from Scotland was favoured by an incredible bonus. The Scottish distillers discovered that Article 6 of the Act of Union made no distinction between English and Scottish spirits and that the latter were thus entitled to the English drawbacks of 8s. 2½d. As duty had only been paid at 5s. 11½d. this gave the Scottish distillers an advantage of 2s. 3d. a gallon paid out of the revenue of Great Britain.[151] A number of suggestions were made to meet the difficulty. It was suggested that there should be a uniform strength in each country for computing the duty and that exports should conform to the strength for duty of the importing country, leaving the regulation for the home market to go its own way. Another idea was to isolate distilleries making spirits for export from those making for home consumption and that exports should pass through duty free warehouses thus avoiding all drawbacks on spirits. The malt drawback difficulty was to be overcome by assuming the malt used to be one-third of the grist.[152] The Government had to consider the thorny problem of changing the provisions of the Act of Union which was bound to raise criticism, so they shelved the matter by the simple expedient of prohibiting all trade in spirits between the countries in order to amend 'defective legislation'. This also coincided with the prohibitions in Great Britain of the use of grain in distilleries in favour of sugar, so

---

150. *Ibid.*, pp. 198–9. See also *Irish Revenue Inquiry, 5th Report, 1823 op. cit.*, pp. 263, 303, 638.
151. *S.C. on drawbacks and countervailing duties, 1809, op. cit.*, p. 199.
152. *Ibid.*, p. 201.

that it was natural for a demand to arise to stop Irish imports. Irish members of parliament responded that this prohibition violated the Act of Union.[153]

Drawback difficulties were not the only hindrance to Irish exports. English raw spirit all went to rectifiers who were closely associated with English distillers and the latter obstructed rectifiers from getting Irish spirits in order to keep up their prices. Irish spirit, however, was palatable and did not, therefore, depend entirely on English rectifiers. In 1817 an Act prohibited the sale of raw spirit in England and Irish spirit was deemed raw thus narrowing their market to rectifiers. There were urgent representations and the Act was repealed. The Irish distillers did not benefit, however, as the English Board of Excise ruled that as Irish spirit was not raw it was therefore on the same footing as rectified spirit in England and as such could not go into consumption stronger than 22 per cent under proof. At this strength Irish whiskey, under the drinking habits of the time, would not be acceptable unless flavoured or compounded, but this process was not allowed in Ireland before export. So Irish spirit, in order to enter the English market, still had to go to English rectifiers.[154] There is a strong suspicion of conspiracy between English distillers and high excise officials to exclude Irish spirits. This gets some confirmation from one Irish distiller who sent a trial consignment to Scotland where the Excise Board's ruling was not applied although the laws in this respect were the same and in addition Scotch whiskey was marketed at 7° over proof as in England. Apparently the Excise Board were acting rigidly within the law and it was necessary to present a Bill in parliament

153. The following references exemplify the drawback muddle. 47 Geo. 3, sess. 1, c. 20 suspended trade in order to amend defective legislation. The suspension was continued by sess. 2, c. 62; 48 Geo. 3, c. 43; 49 Geo. 3, c. 7 and c. 105. As well as the drawback difficulties there were suspensions on the grounds of grain shortages. Trade was resumed, but only through a duty free warehouse (51 Geo. 3, c. 121). It was again suspended by 52 Geo. 3, c. 45; and 53 Geo. 3, c. 7. *Parliamentary Debates*. There are numerous debates on this subject. 3 January 1809, col. 241; 13 February 1810, cols. 390–9; 10 May 1811, cols. 1176–8; 14 June 1811, cols. 626–7; 6 June 1814, cols. 428–9; 25 May 1814, col. 1026. See also *Irish Revenue Inquiry, 5th Report Supplement*, 1823, *op. cit.*, p. 665.

154. *Irish Revenue Inquiry, 5th Report*, 1823, *op. cit.*, p. 303. *5th Report Supplement*, p. 667. A Cork distiller claimed that Irish whiskey spoiled if reduced to 22° under proof. At that strength it would not be considered suitable for making punch, apparently a favoured drink.

in 1820 to overcome the difficulty.[155] Thereafter Irish whiskey was not handicapped by duties and drawbacks.

Warehousing

A most important landmark in the history of Irish distilling occurred in 1804 when an Act permitted Irish distillers to deposit their spirits in customs warehouses without paying duty. These warehouses were owned and managed by the customs department for storing dutiable imports until they were either exported or paid duty on delivery for home consumption. The extension of this privilege to Irish spirits was to facilitate exports, but it also avoided drawback difficulties.[156] There was no compulsion on distillers to use the warehouses and they could, if they wished, export direct on drawback, but there were obvious advantages in using the warehouses. It saved private storage space, and capital was not locked up in duty pending export and the receipt of the drawback. There were disadvantages for the distiller who lost control of his spirits and he had to pay duty on any losses arising during storage whether the spirit was exported or delivered for home use. The distiller was allowed to examine his goods once a week and he could remove his spirits from one customs warehouse to another if it was more convenient.[157] A distiller intending to warehouse his spirits had to give notice between three and six days beforehand and give five days notice before exporting them and he was only allowed four months warehousing. If the spirits were not exported in that time the excise could sell the spirit to recover the duty. When the spirits were leaving the distillery the excise officer attended, noted the decrease in the stock and issued a permit. On arrival at the warehouse the storekeeper issued a receipt which the distiller had to produce to the distillery officer.[158] These rules were enlarged in the following years and by 1822 detailed accounts, including the strength of the spirit, were recorded. Spirit had to be in casks of

155. *Irish Revenue Inquiry, 5th Report,* 1823, *op. cit.,* p. 291. *Parliamentary Debates,* 6 July 1820, col. 286. The probability is that the English distillers found this loophole in the law and the Excise Board took no steps to get the law amended till strong protests arose.

156. 44 Geo. 3, c. 104.

157. *Ibid.,* sections 10–12. See *Parliamentary Debates,* 2 July 1804, cols. 1030–4 for a discussion on the *Irish Spirits Warehousing Bill.*

158. 44 Geo. 3, c. 104, sections 3–4, 7, 13.

100 gallons or more and not less than 1 to 10 over proof which conformed with the standard in Great Britain. After four months storage, instead of the excise selling the spirit, interest at 10 per cent of the duty was charged and a small charge was levied for storage. Except for charging duty on natural loss during storage, and seizure if there were any loss not due to wastage or accident, the regulations were not onerous though the long notice before depositing or exporting seemed unnecessary.[159]

The system of warehousing spirits in customs warehouses at the principal ports continued till 1812. Under this arrangement not only did the distiller lose control of his spirit, except for a weekly visit, but the excise authorities also had no check on the management of the warehouse. If there was any pilfering whilst in the customs charge the distiller was liable to have all the spirit in the cask seized. The customs were not specially interested in distillers, as were the excise, and it is more than probable that there were times of intense rivalry between the two departments. In 1812, therefore, the excise department were authorised to provide warehouses at ports where there was a licensed still of 100 gallons content or more and the customs control ceased. No changes were made in existing warehouse regulations.[160]

Payment of duty on deficiencies during storage was patently an unfair charge as casks of spirit suffer loss from evaporation and sometimes from small leaks not easily detected, especially as the distiller had so little opportunity to inspect his casks. Until 1811 he also had to pay for losses in transit which might well be ruinous by the time the ships of that period reached Great Britain. In 1811 a natural loss during transit not exceeding 3 per cent was allowed on the quantity and strength shown on a

159. See 46 Geo. 3, c. 88, sections 102, 105 and *Irish Revenue Inquiry, 3rd Report, 1822, op. cit.*, p. 731 which gives the substance of a general order to the excise service dated 1812. The rent charge in 1823 was 3d. a cask per week (*5th Report, 1823, op. cit.*, p. 340). The interest charge of 10 per cent of the duty was first levied after 60 days of storage. The time of storage was extended to 4 months by 47 Geo. 3, sess. 2, c. 17, section 10.

160. 52 Geo. 3, c. 30. *See S.C. to inquire into the Regulations for the conduct of business in the Customs and the Import and Export Department of the Excise, Warehousing System, 10th Report*. Parl. Pps. 1821 (25) x, p. 334. Unlike Great Britain, the construction of docks and warehouses in Ireland was undertaken by the Revenue Board owing to the difficulty of getting corporations or companies to undertake the work. This may have been due to lack of capital rather than enterprise. It was a situation unsuitable to the best development of trade.

certificate issued by the Irish excise at the time of export. Thus
the Irish distiller had amongst his other handicaps in the English
market, the cost of these losses and his freight charges. In that
year also he lost his option of direct export on drawback and
all spirit for Great Britain had to pass through a Crown warehouse.[161]

Despite its defects during its first years the extension to home-
made spirits of warehousing duty free was one of the most
important measures affecting the distilling industry. As the
nineteenth century progressed the warehousing system was
perfected to suit the needs of the industry, fair account was taken
of natural losses, distillers had complete control of their stocks
within the limits of reasonable revenue security, and operations
were permitted to prepare the spirits for the market. As the
rates of duty rose so the value of duty free warehousing became
greater. Duty free warehousing became essential for both the
distiller and the revenue.

Rectifying and Compounding

Rectifiers and compounders who were separately distinguished
from distillers in 1797, were further distinguished in 1805 when
distillers were forbidden to rectify or compound their spirits.[162]
In 1807 there was another separation and rectifiers were distinguished from compounders. A rectifier was defined as a person
distilling spirits of wine or imitation foreign plain spirit such as
brandy. A compounder was a person distilling and compounding
with sugar or other ingredients. A rectifier was allowed a still of
between 80 and 200 gallons and a compounder was limited to a
still between 60 and 100 gallons. Neither was to do the operations
of the other, nor have in stock any spirits not proper to his trade.
The allowances for rectifiers remained unaltered, that is, for
every 100 gallons of raw spirit received he was credited with 150
gallons of rectified spirit in his stock which was liberal when it is
borne in mind that in some cases, such as making spirits of wine,

161. The transit loss was allowed by 51 Geo. 3, c. 121, section 5. Section 3
restricted exports to warehoused spirits. See also *Irish Revenue Inquiry, 5th Report,
1823, op. cit.,* p. 305 where a Cork distiller complains of the charge on losses and
said that, in addition, his freight cost was 16s. 3d. a puncheon of 120 to 140
gallons from Cork and 10s. from Dublin.

162. 37 Geo. 3, c. 46 (Irish Statutes); 45 Geo. 3, c. 104, section 12.

the resulting quantity would be less. The compounder was allowed a 20 per cent increase in stock for added sugar, syrup or other ingredients which may well have been rather tight. The licence duty at 50s. for each ten gallons of still content imposed in 1797 was raised to 10s. a gallon. In 1815 they were required to give bond in a penalty of £500 with two sureties on a condition not to distil wash nor sell raw spirit.[163]

The excise methods of control remained, in general, as in 1797. When the still was silent the furnace door and discharge cock were locked. Before starting twelve hours' notice was required in towns and twenty-four hours in the country. The still was to be charged to at least seven-tenths of its content in the officer's presence who then locked on the still head. The resulting product was added to the rectifier's stock. The rectifier was not allowed to deliver his spirits at a strength exceeding 1 in 5 under proof, or 22° under proof by Sikes, except spirits of wine which could be delivered in quantities not exceeding 120 gallons a day to any one person. If a compounder, ingredients would obscure a true reading of the hydrometer, so the casks had to be marked with the true strength.[164] These are the bare bones of the excise regulations and if observed any large scale fraud would have been difficult. The regulations, however, were not put into effect except in the 'most immaterial provisions'. Officers' visits were made to suit the rectifier or compounder; they rarely saw the still charged or locked down and the trader usually kept the key, or had a skeleton key; and they never checked delivery strengths which the law said should not be above 22° under proof, in fact they did not use a hydrometer. Thus the rectifier or compounder was an easy avenue for the distiller to dispose of spirits made in excess of the still licence charge. The crudest fraud was to use the still at night to distil wash and make spirits like a distiller, which would not be assessed for duty. Another large leak was to manage the allowance credited in the stock for rectified or

163. 47 Geo. 3, sess. 2, c. 19. *Inquiry into Fees in Ireland, 5th Report, 1806–7, op. cit.*, p. 222. A Dublin rectifier said that his raw spirit when rectified gained 10 per cent in strength and lost 12 per cent in quantity when making imitation rum, brandy or geneva. His spirits of wine, called double spirit, was usually run off at 40° over proof. The licence duty was raised to 10s. a gallon by section 3 of the Act of 1807. 55 Geo. 3, c. 19, sections 26–7 imposed the bond conditions.
164. *Inquiry into Fees in Ireland, 5th Report, 1806–7, op. cit.*, pp. 163, 210.

compounded spirits that is, 50 gallons for every 100 gallons of raw spirit received. A rectifier could receive 100 gallons on permit, add 50 gallons of illegal spirit and deliver the whole 150 gallons on an official permit as rectified spirit. As there was no hydrometer check the fraud was simple and could be done openly. Some used spirit to make shrub or other compounds, but allowing for this the estimated margin for fraud was put at 37½ gallons for every 100 gallons received in stock.[165] It is little wonder that distillers had a close association with rectifiers and compounders.

Rectified and compounded spirits never became popular in Ireland and the prospects of trade with England, where there was a large market, never matured because of the various obstructions already mentioned. In 1807 there were twenty-three rectifying houses, but in the last few years to 1823 the number fell to eleven. The sizes of the stills before these were restricted in 1807 were mainly between 100 and 250 gallons content. There were only three over 500 gallons, the largest being 616 gallons in Cork. All except two of the rectifiers were in Dublin and Cork. A Cork distiller did attempt about 1820 to break his way into the English market by establishing a rectifying house in London which he intended to supply from his distillery and thus side-track the monopoly of the English distillers. The latter bought him out by a compromise in which they agreed to buy 4,000 puncheons of spirit a year from the Cork distiller at one-fifth a gallon above the English price so long as the supply from Ireland did not exceed 4,000 puncheons. That was the only recorded attempt of any significance to enter the English market for gin and similar beverages. All other Irish exports either went to English rectifiers or to Irish immigrants. Rectifying for export was not allowed in Ireland where the regulations required all exports to be warehoused at 25° over proof, thus ruling out the rectifier's low strength spirits. No doubt this was to circumvent the possibility of distillery spirits of high strength being diluted after assessment and part only being shipped.[166] In

165. *Ibid.*, pp. 164–5, 210, 218, 222–3.
166. *Ibid.*, p. 205. *Irish Revenue Inquiry, 5th Report,* 1823, *op. cit.,* pp. 264, 303, 638. *5th Report Supplement,* 1823, *op. cit.,* 667–8, 721. Exports from Ireland after 1809 had to pass through a warehouse and by 50 Geo. 3, c. 111, section 7, spirits were not to be less than 25° over proof when warehoused. This ruled out rectified

addition there was a prohibitive import duty into Great Britain where sweetened or otherwise obscured spirits were charged at the highest strength at which they could be made which was far above the actual strength.[167]

Marketing

From the Union to 1823 the pattern of the licence duties to sell spirits was unchanged though the rates themselves rose by about a third. The rates in force in 1802 and 1818 for spirit retailers were:

	1802	1818
1. Dublin, Cork, Waterford and Limerick	£30	£40
2. Within 2 miles of Dublin and in the other city counties	£20	£33
3. Within 5 miles of Dublin and in 8 other towns	£15	£22
4. All other cities and towns	£10	£11
5. All other places	£6	£11

In 1818 Belfast was included in the second category. The third category was changed to the Dublin excise district and 28 other cities and towns. The number of licences issued in 1802–3 were 10,180 and in 1818 there were 8,709.[168] In 1804 these spirit licences were transferred from the excise to the stamp duty office. The change made no practical difference to the trade, but

or compounded spirits other than spirits of wine. The restriction on the sizes of stills imposed in 1807 remained till 1825 when 6 Geo. 4, c. 80, section 103 fixed a minimum of 120 gallons.

167. At the time of the Union rectifiers received spirits from distillers at about 24° over proof, but were not permitted to send out their finished product at a strength exceeding 22° under proof by 38 Geo. 3, c. 52, section 21 (Irish Statutes). The import duty into Great Britain was at the strength before rectifying or compounding because it was not possible to ascertain the strength by hydrometer when these spirits entered that country. Use of the warehousing system might have overcome the difficulty, but the strength of spirits from the rectifier prevented warehousing. Nothing was done to meet the problem See *Irish Revenue Inquiry*, 5th Report, 1823, *op. cit.* p. 316. The numbers of rectifiers are given in *Inquiry into Fees in Ireland. 5th Report*, 1806–7, *op. cit.*, p. 205, and *13th Inland Revenue Report*, Parl. Pps. 1870 (c. 82) xx, p 429.

168. *Accounts presented to Parliament*, Parl. Pps. 1806 (162) (191) xiv, p. 337 and 55 Geo. 3, c. 19, schedule annexed to the Act: The duties were repeated in the Licensing Act of 1819, 59 Geo. 3, c. 106. The inclusion of places in a higher category clearly indicates their growing importance. In Dublin there was a special £7 hotel licence (56 Geo. 3, c. 111, section 23). *13th Inland Revenue, Report 1870*, *op. cit.*, p. 433.

probably did remove some interest in their control by the excise officers and brought in the clerk of the peace who now received the duties and issued stamps.[169] In the following year an effort was made to strengthen local control over spirit drinking. The general sessions in April were to fix a date for a special licensing session and if they failed to do this, licensing was to be dealt with at the July session. The grand jury had the duty of determining the number of houses to be licensed in each barony and if they did not, then the justices granted licences at their discretion. Thus the revenue authorities could no longer issue licences to retail spirits purely to support revenue receipts. No major changes were made in the licensing laws for retailers. The bounty or rebate of licence duty in proportion to the beer sold in relation to spirits sales was continued on the same basis as in the licensing Act of 1796.[170]

There was another revision of the licensing laws in 1815. Spirit licences were transferred back from the stamp duty office to the excise department. It had never been clearly explained why these licences had ever been the province of the stamp office who had no interest in them, but it is a small indication of the muddled administrative thinking of the time. The procedure to obtain a licence remained on the same lines, that is, a retailer first applied to the clerk of the peace and the justices then inquired into the applicant's character and sufficiency of the sureties to a bond at £25 each. The result of the application was recorded in a Crown book and, if satisfactory, the clerk issued a certificate enabling the applicant to get a licence from the excise.[171]

The conditions of a retailer's bond of £50 with two sureties gives a lucid outline of the regulations. It stated that a keeper of a victualling house, inn or tavern must provide strong beer and victuals of good quality at reasonable prices and supply all travellers. He must not sell any spirits on Sunday or wine or beer on Sunday before 2 p.m. He must not sell drink at an unreasonable hour except to travellers. He must not permit the payment

169. 44 Geo. 3, c. 103, sections 10–11.

170. 45 Geo. 3, c. 50, sections 2–3, 7–8, 67–8. In 1810 the Board of Excise refused to pay these rebates on the grounds that the conditions were not observed (*Irish Revenue Inquiry, 3rd Report*, 1822, *op. cit.*, p. 717).

171. 55 Geo. 3, c. 19, sections 3, 28–30. See also *Parliamentary Debates*, 16 June 1815, col. 865.

of wages on his premises, nor allow an unlawful assembly, nor admit armed persons unless they were lawfully allowed to carry arms. And he was not to sell spirits which had not paid duty.[172] Certain persons were specifically excluded from the retail trade. Distillers, rectifiers, compounders and anyone who was not a victualler, innkeeper or tavern-keeper was incapable of having a licence. Grocers were excepted. The retail licence permitted sales up to twenty-five gallons at a time, but except in the main cities with their city counties, there was a reduction in the licence duty if this limit was reduced. Thus a licencee in an area where the full duty was £22 permitting sales up to twenty-five gallons, could obtain his licence for £15 with a limit of twenty gallons or £11 with a limit of ten gallons. These were mainly rural areas where the full licence duty fell much more harshly than in towns where trade was greater. In the country where the shebeen would normally flourish there was an even greater reduction and a licence could be had for £7 if sales did not exceed a gallon at a time—a rather ineffective gesture. Nowhere in parliamentary debates or government inquiries is there any indication about the control of these rules. At the time there was no effective police force, or any other enforcement agency, to check sales and it is more than doubtful if they could have been checked even if there had been any such agency.[173]

At the beginning of the century grocers were not eligible for a retailer's licence, but paid a special licence duty of £3 in Dublin and £2 elsewhere. This enabled them to sell spirits for consumption off the premises in quantities of not less than two quarts. This favoured position was withdrawn in 1813 when their licence duties were raised to about three quarters of the full retail licence duty. For example a grocer's spirit licence in Dublin, Cork, Waterford and Limerick was £30. In 1818 they were allowed to sell less than two quarts, but the licence duty was further raised to the same level as a retailer.[174] This was a heavy burden for

172. 55 Geo. 3, c. 19, section 37.

173. *Ibid.,* sections 45, 47. The reduction of duty for limited sales was continued in the Licensing Act, 59 Geo. 3, c. 106. It was not until 1822 that a country-wide police force was authorised by 3 Geo. 4, c. 103 and then for purposes of keeping the peace, not for enforcing licensing or revenue laws.

174. 44 Geo. 3, c. 26, schedule F; 45 Geo. 3, c. 50, section 19; 47 Geo. 3, sess. 2, c. 12, section 19; 53 Geo. 3, c. 103, section 4; 58 Geo. 3, c. 57, see sections 2–3.

what is now known as an off-licence. The most likely explanation
is that surreptitious drinking on the premises was a common
practice and therefore it was fair to tax the grocer as heavily as
the spirit retailer. The grocer did have the advantage that his
licence did not need the justices' approval. The remaining outlet
for the distiller was through the factor or dealer. In 1805 they
were combined for licence purposes. They were not permitted
to sell less than two gallons and had to give a bond of £500 with
two sureties of £250 each. The licence duty in 1805 was £20.
Two years later the dealer and factor were again separated, the
factor being defined as a person selling spirits on commission in
quantities of not less than fifty gallons and his licence cost £20.
The dealer selling two gallons or over was subject to a varying
licence duty ranging from £25 down to £10 according to the
retail licence area.[175]

The legal framework in which the spirit licence trade operated
only gives the obstacles facing a distiller selling his products in
his local market. It does not show what success he achieved.
Indeed these obstacles were formidable, especially the rates of
licence duties and the magisterial control of drinking. In a
country of over five million people some five million gallons of
spirit were charged with duty annually and there was also an
unknown quantity escaping the duty which was estimated to be
at least as much again. If children, persons who did not drink
spirits—beer drinkers for example—and better class people who
did not normally frequent taverns were excluded it would be a
fair assumption that some ten million gallons a year were consumed annually by about two million persons or the equivalent
of thirty bottles of present day size per person, in the form of
glasses drunk on the premises in the majority of cases. The number
of retail licences were in the region of 8,000 to 10,000, that is each
tavern or inn dispensed an average of at least 1,000 gallons a

See also L. MacNally, *The Justice of the Peace for Ireland*, Dublin, 1810, i, 2nd
supplement, p. 150 and 1st appendix pp. 10–11.

175. 45 Geo. 3, c. 52, section 16; 44 Geo. 3, c. 26, schedule F; 47 Geo. 3, sess.
1, c. 18, schedule A; 55 Geo. 3, c. 19, schedule. Under 47 Geo. 3, sess. 1, c. 35,
section 1, these licences did not require a justice's certificate and the Board of
Excise had power to delegate the issue of such licences.

year.[176] Distillers sold their spirit at about 9s. a gallon at 24° over proof and it was retailed at what was known as 'phial proof' after one part of water was added to two parts of spirit giving a strength in the region of 22° under proof.[177] A glass of whiskey sold at about 2d. in 1812. The size of this glass is not known, but the modern measure in Ireland is about ten and a half glasses to the bottle or sixty-five to the gallon. It is probable that, without a precise measure, the glass of the early nineteenth century was more generous and fifty to the gallon is a likely figure. On this basis a 'phial proof' gallon sold for 8s. 4d. and 150 gallons for £62 10s. The retailer would buy 100 gallons for these sales at 9s. or a total of £45 giving a profit of £17 10s. So a retailer in Dublin or Cork, for example, had to sell over 300 gallons or 15,000 glasses to recover the licence duty. Clearly only a retailer with the exceptional facilities could make a living at this rate solely from legal spirit.[178] The licence duties were indeed a savage attack on spirit drinking and only added further incentive to the shebeen and unlicensed drinking at the spirit grocer's shop. No doubt that was the main reason for imposing the full licence duty on the latter from 1813 owards.

The retailer, as well as the dealer, could recoup himself by buying from distillers spirit which had evaded the duty where the price was from 2s. to 2s. 6d. below the price of duty paid

176. See note 168. T. Newenham, *Statistical and Historical Inquiry into the Population of Ireland*, London, 1805, p. 229, made estimates of spirit consumption in 1804 on the basis of 6 persons per house ranging from paupers to houses with 1 hearth for the lower classes, 2 to 3 hearths for the middle classes and 4 or more up to 114 hearths for better and upper classes. He assumed, for example, that a middle class house of 3 hearths consumed 24 gallons of home made spirit and 4 gallons of foreign spirit. It was an ingenious attempt to assess spirit drinking, but there were too many unknown factors to treat it as a reliable guide. It has the merit of giving a pattern of drinking habits in the different social classes. The Irish gallon at that time was just over 6 per cent larger than the imperial gallon.

177. *Inquiry into Fees in Ireland, 5th Report*, 1806–7, *op. cit.*, p. 195. *Irish Revenue Inquiry, 5th Report*, 1823, *op. cit.*, pp. 297, 309.

178. *Parliamentary Debates*, 10 May 1811, col. 180. Sir J. Newport alleged that in Cavan 'a man could get completely drunk for 4d.' Some private records in Belfast show that between 1811 and 1816 a glass of whiskey was 2d. *S.C. on Drunkenness*, Parl. Pps. 1834 (559) viii, p. 394. In 1834 a glass of whiskey in Belfast cost 1½d., but by that year the smaller imperial gallon was the standard and the glass and other measures may have been reduced accordingly. Prices seem to support this view, but there was also a drop in the price per gallon to 7s. and the figures quoted rather support about 9 glasses to the bottle, assuming six bottles to the gallon. Retailer's profits would include sales of beer.

whiskey, and this trade was openly admitted by distillers.[179] He
could also buy spirit from illicit distillers at rates ranging from
4s. to 6s. 6d. a gallon depending on the locality and, to a lesser
extent, on quality.[180] The retailer did, of course, get some profit
from beer sales, but even the effort to encourage beer sales by
rebates of licence duty was frustrated by the Board of Excise in
1810 who refused these allowances on the grounds that the retailers had not complied with the conditions. Beer was not
supplanting whiskey in the taverns for as Peel said in 1817, 'In
Ireland whiskey is not a luxury to the lower orders. In that damp
climate and from long habits it was almost an article of the first
necessity.'[181]

Permits

The avenue for illegal spirit to dealers and retailers hinged
largely on the permit system on which the excise control of
spirits after sale by a distiller was mainly based. The permit laws
were consolidated in 1819 repeating much of the earlier regulations with a few refinements. A transit of spirit began with the
consignor giving the excise a request note with full details of
the spirits and their destination. The officer then issued a permit
with similar details and inserted the time allowed for the transit
which could be extended if there was some accidental delay.
The casks themselves had a ticket pasted on them showing the
content and description of spirits. Within twenty-four hours of
arrival the consignee lodged the permit with the officer and was
given a certificate in exchange which covered this addition to
his stock for three months, but this time could be extended if
necessary. Dealers were to keep a stock record in which receipts
and deliveries should be related to the certificates held.[182] The
machinery for controlling spirits after leaving the distillery seems
sound, but in the end the best rules depend on the people who are
to operate them and all concerned, excise officers, distillers and

179. *Irish Revenue Inquiry, 5th Report,* 1823, *op. cit.,* pp. 298, 313.

180. *Ibid.,* pp. 283, 309, 318.

181. *Irish Revenue Inquiry, 3rd Report,* 1823, *op. cit.,* p. 717, under a reference
G. O. 53/1810. *Parliamentary Debates,* 5 March 1817, col. 887.

182. 59 Geo. 3, c. 107, sections 6–7, 13, 15, 17–19. The penalty under section
40 for counterfeiting or making moulds to print permits was 7 years transportation which is an indication of the importance of permits in the system of excise
control at that time.

dealers, co-operated to defeat the system and allow a steady flow
of illegal spirits to find cover under spurious permits. Unlike
illicit spirits or illegal spirits removed clandestinely, once spirits
got the cover of a permit they were ostensibly duty paid. At the
dealer's premises the excise officer did not take a regular stock
and therefore he had no satisfactory check of sales so that no
matter how accurate his check on receipts his control was largely
useless. An excessive decrease in stock left room for irregular
receipts and in some cases, when an officer got to know that the
stock was lower than it should be, he actually sold a permit to
a distiller enabling him to unload spirits produced in excess of
the still licence charge. The distiller then showed in his books a
decrease arising from sales and at the dealer's end the ultimate
physical stock was restored to agree with his stock account. There
were other variations to these manipulations such as alterations
and erasures on permits which in 1819 caused the Board of
Excise to threaten disciplinary action against any officer accepting
such a permit and issuing a certificate.[183] The basic weakness of
the permit system at this time was reliance on the document for
both a cover against seizure during transit and its use as a key
document for stock accounts. Later in the century the latter
purposes faded out and the excise used their own advices between
the places of despatch and receipt of spirits when this was deemed
necessary. With the expansion of the warehousing system permit
frauds became rare.

Competition

The competition against whiskey by other spirits, mainly rum,
fell away during the period 1800–23. Imports from Great Britain
were unimportant. In the year ending 5 January 1802, net imports
of brandy, geneva and rum were 1·6 million gallons and home
made spirits were 1 million gallons. In 1812 net imports were
only 43,000 gallons while home-made spirits had reached 6·5
million gallons. This was an exceptional year, but in the following
year the figures were 0·2 million imported and four million home
made. In 1822 net imports showed a deficit of nine thousand
gallons, more being exported from warehouses than imported,

---

183. *Inquiry into Fees in Ireland, 5th Report,* 1806–7, *op. cit.,* pp. 208–9. *Irish
Revenue Inquiry, 3rd Report,* 1822, *op. cit.,* p. 802.

thus decreasing domestic stocks while home-made spirits amounted to 3·4 million gallons. Irish distillers had almost completely taken over the local market for spirits.[184]

The other competing beverage, beer, did not make any head-way either. Brewers' licences in 1820 were 224 plus a large number of retail-brewers. The quantities brewed are not available as the duty was charged on the malt used. Before 1800 the malt used by distillers and brewers and charged with duty averaged just over 4·5 million bushels. From 1800 this figure fell to a little over 2·5 million.[185] Thus 'the attempt to impose a taste for beer on the Irish in place of their taste for spirits does not seem to have been successful'. One reason in some localities was that malt liquor was more expensive and also that whiskey was regarded as wholesome and medicinal. Beer drinking was mainly confined to Dublin, Meath and beyond where it met the markets of the Cork brewers. Very little beer was drunk in the north and west of Ireland.[186] A factor favouring spirits rather than beer was the evolution of large distilleries from widespread domestic distilling. There had never been the same evolution with brewing beer and such beer as did come from breweries in Ireland was of inferior quality compared to the beer imported from England. Morewood in 1838 expressed surprise at this situation as he said that beer was so easy to make and he estimated that a small brewery could be established for as little as £267 and £40 a year expenses apart from materials. Such a brewery could have an output of thirty barrels a week. The fact is, of course, that the

184. The figures are taken from the *Irish Revenue Inquiry, 5th Report, 1823, op. cit.*, pp. 373–4. J. Jameson's stills are listed on p. 378.

185. *13th Inland Revenue Report, 1870, op. cit.*, pp. 384, 415. The figures for malt would include malt for distilleries.

186. T. Newenham, *A View of the National, Political and Commercial Circumstances of Ireland*, London, 1809, p. 225. He thought that in some parts of Munster 40 times as much beer was drunk as spirits. He probably referred to quantity and not alcoholic content. In alcohol, 40 pints of porter might well have been the equal of 4 pints of whiskey or even less as the relative strengths are not known. Other evidence supports his case that beer was a preferred drink, but he appears to have been anxious to further his argument with a mild exaggeration. F. Wakefield, *An Account of Ireland, Statistical and Political*, London, 1812, i, p. 743. W. S. Mason, *A Statistical Account of Ireland*, Dublin, 1814, i, p. 121. Remarks about Ardstraw, Co. Tyrone. G. O'Brien, *Economic History of Ireland from the Union to the Famine*, London, 1921, p. 346. *Irish Revenue Inquiry, 5th Report, 1823, op. cit.*, pp. 657–8. Carriers for Guinness took beer to Meath and the surrounding country and brought back butter. Some beer reached parts of Connaught.

brew is the final product and it needs considerable skill and
experience to produce good beer. The distiller has not got this
worry; he merely wants a maximum spirit content from his
brew.[187] That there were 224 brewers for sale in 1820 and only
forty licensed distillers is no guide to the size of their respective
markets even though the largest still used was only 750 gallons
content. A distiller producing spirit by rapid distillation would
make far larger quantities of wort than a brewer of comparable
scale. Witness, for example, James Jameson of Dublin working
a 750 gallon still in 1822. He was working off 13 or 14 wash
backs continuously and they measured from 100 to 150 gallons
to the inch of depth. At this time no brewer reached production
of wort on this scale. The market for beer was too limited to
encourage the erection of very large breweries and the export
market had yet to be developed.[188] Wine only managed to
maintain its market till 1810 with an average annual consumption
of just over one million gallons, but it fell away until by 1850
consumption was about half a million gallons.[189]

The end of the Still Licence System

'The abuses in the collection of the Irish revenue were of so
extensive a nature that they could only be reached by a parliamentary commission.' So ran the minute relating to the Irish
Revenue Inquiry Bill. The Bill was concerned with all the Irish
revenue, but revenue from spirits and malt was very much in
the mind of the Government. The reports of this commission
appearing from 1822 onwards were to make drastic changes in
distillery laws and distillers' practices.[190]

Before leaving this account of the still licence system it is worth
recording the views of a committee appointed to consider the
laws relating to distilleries in Scotland when a similar licence
system operated. They reported in 1799 that 'Among the principal
Merits ascribed to it are, 1st, the Secure Receipt of the whole

187. S. Morewood, *A Philosophical and Statistical History of Inebriating Liquors,*
Dublin, 1838, pp. 623, 629.
188. *Irish Revenue Inquiry, 5th Report Supplement,* 1823, *op. cit.,* pp. 688–9.
189. *Thom's Directory,* 1866, p. 855.
190. *Parliamentary Debates,* 15 June 1821, col. 1193. The relative Act was 1 and
2 Geo. 4, c. 90. The Inquiry had wide powers, could take evidence on oath, could
order the arrest of anyone refusing to answer or telling lies and could suspend
any revenue officer obstructing their enquiries.

licence Duty without Risk and almost without Expense; 2nd, a free and comfortable Exercise of his calling by the Distiller, redounding in its Consequence to the Popularity of Government, and thereby in no small degree to the Advantage of the Public; 3rd, the alledged Diminution (certainly but ill made out in Proof or Argument) of the Temptation to, and loss of Smuggling; 4th, the Spur it affords to industry and invention in the progressive improvement of an useful Art not otherwise to have been attained or expected; 5th, its Tendency to increase the total Amount of the Article manufactured, and consequently (when the Fact of such Increase should come to be ascertained, and the Amount of the Annual Licence Duty thereupon augmented) to produce, independent of Cheapness of Collection, a greater Receipt at the Exchequer than could have been raised under a similar Rate of Duty by Survey.' There was apparently no alternative survey and assessment as in Ireland and as a result of this report a survey system was grafted on to the licence system, but, as in Ireland, eventually both systems had to be abandoned.[191]

191. *Report of the committee appointed to consider the present state of the laws relative to the distillery of spirits and the duties payable thereon in Scotland,* 1799, p. 11. Their conclusions were naive and remote from realities.

APPENDIX

The still licence charges in 1809 set out in the table annexed
to 49 Geo. 3, c. 99 are an example of the complicated system of
collecting the spirit duties. The still content in gallons is the
gross content.

Content	Charges	Content	Charges
3,000 and over	58	Under 180	168
Under 3,000	60	170	176
2,500	62	160	184
2,250	64	150	192
2,000	67	140	200
1,750	69	130	208
1,500	72	120	216
1,250	76	110	224
1,000	82	100	232
750	91	90	240
500	100	80	250
400	115	70	260
300	129	60	270
200	144	50	280
190	160		

In 1809 the still content for duty was the gross content less one-
eighth for liberty to work. In 1810 this charge was reduced by
a quarter if turf was used for fuel. There was also a bounty of
16 per cent of the still licence duty for stills of 1,500 gallons or
more and 8 per cent for 1,000 gallons or more until discontinued
in 1810.

The Irish Revenue Inquiry, 5th Report, 1823, gives a classified
list of distillers on p. 378 showing monthly charges. A 500 gallon
still is shown as liable to 33,075 gallons a month. At the time
one-eighth was allowed for liberty to work and five gallons of
low wines was regarded as equal to two gallons of spirit. Hence

H

the monthly charge was seven-twentieths of 500 multiplied by
189, the number of charges for this size of still. The duty was
paid weekly. During the first three weeks duty was paid on the
gauger's assessments. At the end of the fourth week all the
assessments were totalled up and if the duty fell short of the still
licence charge the distiller paid on the balance. Usually the
fourth assessment was manipulated so that it would not exceed
the still licence duty. (See *Inquiry into Fees in Ireland, 5th Report,*
1806–7, pp. 148, 182 and *Irish Revenue Inquiry, 5th Report,* 1823,
p. 322.)

CHAPTER VII

THE NINETEENTH CENTURY
1823–1900

THE year 1823 was a momentous year for the distilling industry in Ireland. The whole system of still licence charges was swept away and an Act gave distillers freedom to develop their stills and, within the limit of reasonable revenue security, to adjust their practices to produce good quality spirit efficiently. The basic features of this Act are still in force.[1]

The large market arising from the popularity of whiskey in Ireland should, in normal circumstances, have offered the prospect of a steady and profitable trade to an efficient distiller and should have attracted new capital. During the 40 years before 1823, however, as the number of still charges for spirit duty rose so competition became fiercer, technical development and economy in production were disregarded, quality was secondary to quantity, and fraudulent practices were forced on distillers. For distillers it finally became a matter of survival rather than profit. As two excise officials testified in 1823, 'no matter how good a distiller, unless he can work rapidly he would be ruined in Ireland'. In this environment there was a drastic weeding out of distillers lacking skill or capital and no encouragement was given for new men to enter the industry. As the charge was levied on every still, no distiller could afford to set aside special stills for low wines. The same still had to distil both the wash and the low wines. There was also a varying charge per gallon on the spirits produced depending on the size of the still and the fuel used. Nor was there any discernible or uniform system for apportioning the still charges for the different sizes of stills. The only answer the Government had to meet the inability of the excise to collect the duty by assessment was to increase the still charges, which

1. 4 Geo. 4, c. 94. This Act was in great measure the result of an inquiry in 1823 (see *Inquiry into the Excise Revenue throughout the United Kingdom, Digest of Reports*, Parl. Pps. 1837 (84) xxx, p. 166).

merely led to distillers producing a greater quantity of inferior spirit. Clearly the system had nothing to recommend it.[2]

The Commission of Inquiry set up by parliament in 1821 did not confine themselves to an exhaustive investigation of the distilling industry in Ireland; they also examined the distillery laws and their operation in England and Scotland to see if a uniform system could be evolved for the whole United Kingdom. In England distilling was in few hands operating large stills and geared to rectified spirits so they considered that Irish conditions were unsuitable for assimilation with England.[3] In Scotland, however, conditions were similar. The product, whiskey, was the same; the distilling units were small; and between 1806 and 1816 a similar still licence charge had operated. Irish officers were sent to Scotland and Scottish officers brought to Ireland to study the respective systems. The Irish officers submitted a report in which they gave unqualified praise to the Scottish system of separating the brewing and distilling periods, but were critical of other aspects which permitted fraud, and some absurdities such as locking the discharge cocks of vessels open at the top. The Scottish officers prepared a detailed comparison of every aspect of excise control in each country.[4] In Scotland the duty was charged on the spirit produced, but there was also a basis for charging the duty on the attenuation of the wash as found by the saccharometer. The latter charge resulted from a report by a committee considering Scottish distillery laws in which they stressed the phenomenon that decreasing gravity during fermentation had a fixed relationship to the spirit content of the wash.[5] There were also recommendations to relieve the distillers of the malt duty by way of drawbacks and to calculate the spirit duty on the English wine gallon at proof.[6]

It was clear to Irish distillers that considerable changes in distillery laws were contemplated and they were by no means unanimous that this was desirable. There had been so many changes already that Dublin distillers petitioned parliament to

2. *Inquiry into Fees, Gratuities . . . received in certain Public offices in Ireland*, 5th Report, Parl. Pps. 1806–7 (124) vi, p. 144. *Experiments in Distillation by the Excise Department*, Parl. Pps. 1821 (538) xix, p. 372. *Inquiry into the Collection and Management of the Revenue arising in Ireland*, 5th Report, 1823 (405) vii, pp. 260, 348.
3. *Irish Revenue Inquiry*, 5th Report, 1823, *op. cit.*, pp. 256–7, 263, 265, 342.
4. *Ibid.*, pp. 261, 265, 352–5, 555–62.
5. *Ibid.*, pp. 582, 629.   6. *Ibid.*, pp. 268–9.

leave the laws static. There was also apprehension that new laws would involve capital costs in plant. Some also thought that the still licence system removed the power of excise officers to harass them, since so long as the still licence duty was paid the officer did not interfere much with their activities. A duty charge on the spirit made and security measures up to that point threatened official action at various stages in manufacture, and fastenings and revenue locks on intermediate vessels and cocks. Some senior excise officials also favoured retaining the still licence duty. Perhaps they felt that a direct charge on the spirit and the restraint on distillers at crucial points in processes would give the gauger greater opportunities to extort bribes.[7] The Chancellor of the Exchequer, however, with the report of the Commission of Inquiry into the Irish revenue before him, had no doubts and said, 'I cannot look at the distillery laws of Ireland without feeling that some alteration is necessary to remove the monstrous evils which grow out of them'.[8]

The Distillery Act of 1823 was passed 'to establish uniformity of practice in Ireland and Scotland with respect to the regulations and collection of the duty'.[9] The keystone of the new Act was a combination of the Scottish system of using the attenuation of wash to ascertain the spirit duty and the Irish prescribed but ineffective methods of assessing duty on low wines or on spirits as an alternative to the still licence charge. The perfection of a satisfactory saccharometer and hydrometer made the new system possible and the Act prescribed the use of the Allan saccharometer in general use in Scotland and the Sikes hydrometer legally authorised in 1816.[10] From 1823 there were three distinct assessments the highest being the operative charge. The first assessment

7. *Ibid.*, pp. 290–92, 307, 339. Not all senior excise officials favoured the still licence charge. Coffey suggested in 1821 that it should be abandoned even if this meant a loss of revenue. (*Experiments in Distillation*, 1821, *op. cit.*, p. 372.)

8. *Parliamentary Debates* (Hansard), 21 February 1823, col. 212.

9. Preamble to 4 Geo. 4, c. 94 and *Parl. Debates*, 8 July 1823, Col. 1458. The Chancellor of the Exchequer also said that a uniform system to embrace England was contemplated.

10. *Irish Revenue Inquiry, 5th Report*, 1823, *op. cit.*, p. 261 explains the Scottish system and p. 323 records evidence of the use of Allan's saccharometer. The Sikes hydrometer was legally adopted by 56 Geo. 3, c. 140, in 1816. The Irish Board of Excise, by an order of 3 December 1823 supplanted the Allan by the Bates saccharometer. (*Handbook for Excise Officers*, Loftus publication, London, 1857, p. 158.)

was on the attenuation of wash at the rate of one proof gallon of
spirit for every 5° attenuation on each 100 gallons of wash. Thus,
if 3,000 gallons of wash was set at 50° gravity and after fermentation the gravity had fallen to 5° the presumed spirit would be
9 times 30, or 270 proof gallons of spirit. The second charge was
levied directly on the quantity and strength of the first extraction,
or low wines, as found by dip measurements and the hydrometer
with a deduction of 5 per cent to allow for any inaccuracies in
assessment and loss in further distilling. The third assessment was
on the actual spirit produced and its strength. The English
wine gallon was the standard for quantities.[11] The spirit duty was
fixed at 2s. a proof gallon and as Irish distillers usually delivered
spirit at about 25° over proof this was equivalent to 2s. 6d. a
bulk gallon.[12] In case these three charges did not account for all
spirit produced there was provision for a further annual charge.
Account was kept of all wash and gravities during the licence
year and, assuming all wash attenuated to the gravity of water,
the theoretical total spirit was calculated and compared with the
spirit charged. If there was a deficiency the officer made a return
within a month of the expiration of the annual licence and charged
the distiller for the balance. No doubt this provision was meant
to counteract evasion, but in fact it was a failure. The charges
were duly raised, but rarely paid, and as many officers at that
time did not understand how to take gravities it was nearly
impossible to get the evidence required to bring cases to the
courts.[13]

The new method of charging excise duty brought with it
considerable changes in distillery practice. With no charge on
the still content and freedom to distil slowly, distillers no longer
had to devise stills with a view to rapid operation. They could
now experiment in designing stills to produce a better quality
spirit. They could also introduce additional stills specially for
distilling low wines, without incurring any excise duty. Most

11. 4 Geo. 4, c. 94, sections 44, 56–8, 129.

12. *Ibid.*, section 3. This was a considerable reduction in the rate of duty. From
1821 the rate had been 5s. 9d. an Irish gallon at the customary strength of 25 per
cent over proof, the equivalent of 4s. 10½d. an English wine gallon at proof.

13. *Ibid.*, section 60. See also *Inquiry into the Management of the Excise Revenue
throughout the United Kingdom, 7th Report, Part II*, Parl. Pps. 1835 (8) xxx, p. 76.
Digest of Reports, 1837, *op. cit.*, p. 182; and *Return of Deficiency Duties on Whiskey*,
Parl. Pps. 1834 (414) xlix, p. 677.

important perhaps, larger stills could be installed without incurring further levies and the way was open to larger and more efficient distilling units. There was, however, another side to this picture, for the new Act not only repeated the basic excise regulations of entry, licence, control of malt, permits and similar excise controls evolved in the eighteenth century, but a number of new restraints in freedom of manufacture deemed necessary to safeguard the revenue were introduced. Excise officers also became much more intimately concerned with the distiller's operations. They were involved in taking revenue accounts at three different stages in manufacture as well as a general supervision of all distillery activities. This was the pattern for the rest of the nineteenth century and became uniform throughout the United Kingdom.[14]

Since the Act of 1823 was the basis for all future distillery laws it is worth examination in some detail. Before this Act an Irish distiller required no licence apart from his monthly still licence to cover the spirit duty. Now he had to take out a yearly licence of £10 as a kind of registration fee and unrelated to the spirit he produced. This licence could be refused if his distillery was near a rectifying house, brewery or vinegar maker's premises as in each of these trades there would be similar processes and fraud might be difficult to prevent. If the distillery was more than a mile from a market town the licence was conditional on the distiller providing suitable lodging for the excise gauger. Having surmounted these provisions the distiller made the usual entry of his premises and plant accompanied by a flow diagram and drawings of his apparatus.[15]

These preliminaries completed the distiller was faced with restrictions on his apparatus. In no case could a still be less than forty gallons content. If no still exceeded 500 gallons the distiller

14. The United Kingdom distillery laws in 1900 are contained in the Spirits Act of 1880, 43 and 44 Vict., c. 24. The same method for charging duty is prescribed and the basic regulations are similar. In 1809, by 49 Geo. 3, c. 99, section 8, the full still licence duty was levied on every still in use in a distillery.

15. 4 Geo. 4, c. 94, sections 3, 13–14, 34, 36. A summary of the laws is given in the *Excise Revenue Inquiry, 7th Report, Part I*, Parl. Pps. 1834 (7) xxv, pp. 22–5. On page 284 a plea is made to begin the licence year before October so that farmers could plan production. In 1840 the licence duty was raised by 3 and 4 Vict., c. 17, section 8, to £10 10s. In 1910 under 10 Edw. 7 and 1 Geo. 5, c. 8, section 51, the licence duty was graduated in relation to production.

had to produce a character certificate signed by three justices, but the Excise Commissioners had power to refuse a licence, stating their reasons, if they considered its issue undesirable. There were no restrictions for larger stills which were further favoured by permitting such distillers to have additional stills under 500 gallons without a justices' certificate. A distiller could have one all-purpose still, but if he had more than one still he had to designate the purpose of each still and could not change. Thus if he had two stills for wash and one for distilling low wines, he could only use them for these operations; he could not, for example, use one of the wash stills for low wines. This rule was obviously designed to make it difficult to run a spirit charge without detection.[16] As a further aid to revenue security there were limitations on the number of vessels used in distilling. The distiller was limited to, and had to install, one wash charger and one spirit receiver. He also had to install a low wines receiver, a low wines and feints charger and a feints receiver with the option of an additional vessel in each class. Some distillers would probably have most of those vessels, but many would have to lay out capital to provide them. For example, probably a low wines and feints charger was not generally used. There was a change in the definition of feints which removed an unnecessary irrita-tion. Formerly feints had been defined as a spirituous liquor not exceeding 85° under proof. Under the new Act this rule had no significance and feints were defined merely as any spirits from a second or subsequent distillation run into a feints receiver. Feints could still be weak foreshots or tailings to be fed back to a later distillation as formerly, but so could perfectly made spirit intended for another distillation, for example to increase its purity and strength. It enabled distillers in later years to treat as feints the spirits used to manufacture absolute alcohol, and the Irish practice of three distillations became feasible. The advantage of the new rule at the time was that although the excise would take an account of such feints, this spirit would not have to pay duty while being regarded as feints. There were no limitations on brewing vessels and the distiller could have as many mash tuns, underbacks, coolers, fermenting vessels and the like as he wished.[17]

16. 4 Geo. 4, c. 94, sections 9–12, 35.
17. *Ibid.*, sections 18–19, 61.

In addition to these restrictions on vessels the distiller now had to conform to measures that prevented him having access to any products during the distilling period, but he could install devices that enabled him to control his operations. Not only were stills and vessels secured by revenue locks, but all pipes had to be closed, that is, each end had to enter or discharge directly into a secured vessel. The worm end, for example, led into a safe, sometimes called a can-pit. In this particular case the Treasury could authorise the worm end to discharge direct into a receiver. The pipes themselves had to be painted in distinctive colours throughout their length according to the liquid they conveyed, white for water, red for wash, blue for low wines or feints and black for spirit. These colours can be seen on pipes in any present day distillery. There were other obligations regarding apparatus, all designed to assist an excise officer in his survey of the plant. Some of them merely made law of existing practice in the better distilleries or gave such practices more precision. For example, a brass plate had to be fixed to mark the dipping place on each vessel and hence the reference point for the measurements taken to calibrate the vessel. Dip holes of a prescribed size had to be provided on receivers and dip rods fitted so that dips could be taken at any time by the officer or distiller without unlocking the hatch.[18] All these regulations involved capital expense, but though there were some misgivings amongst distillers before the Act was passed, the industry settled down to the new conditions without serious complaint so far as the Act related to distillery apparatus. This would indicate that apparatus in well conducted distilleries was easily adapted.

The actual production of spirit was, naturally, geared to the new rules for distillery apparatus and for charging the duty. The Act prescribed the course of manufacture and imposed restrictive rules on the use of malt and grain which penalised most Irish distillers. A distiller could either distil wholly from malt, as was customary in Scotland, or from raw grain with a necessary addition of malt to induce conversion of the starch, as was the custom in Ireland. He could not use both methods and had to declare his intention when taking out his licence. There was provision, however, to permit a switch between malt and mixed

18. *Ibid.*, sections 20, 26, 28, 36.

grain spirit after notifying the excise. The reason for this regulation was the drawback allowed on malt for part of the malt duty.
This was granted only to spirit made wholly from malt when it
was exported and there was also an allowance of 1s. a gallon if
it was for home consumption. Mixed grain spirit got nothing
for the malt used. Nor was this the only disability for grain
distillers. To safeguard the revenue from drawback frauds there
were special regulations which the grain distiller had to observe
along with the malt distiller. All malt had to be ground on the
distillery premises and removed under permit to the mash tun.
In making malt spirit the law demanded that there should be a
yield of at least two proof gallons for each bushel of malt which
was fair enough as a check on the drawback. The grain distiller,
however, had to account for a bushel of malt for every ten proof
gallons or pay a duty of 2s. 6d. a bushel on any deficiency. As
might be expected Irish distillers complained strongly about the
malt drawback.[19]

   Under the new law the brewing and distilling operations were
separated into two periods with a twelve hour interval from the
time when all wash had been collected in the wash backs and
wash charger to the beginning of distilling. Six hours' notice
was required before brewing started and the distiller entered in
the minute or specimen book the time of brewing and the details
and quantity in winchester bushels of the materials he intended
to use. He also specified the wash backs to be employed and, to
enable the gauger to keep track of wash being made, the distiller
was not allowed to mix the contents of different wash backs.
The gravity of wort before fermentation, referred to in later
Acts as the original gravity, had to lie between 30° and 80° by
Allan's saccharometer. During fermentation checks on gravity
were imposed. If any check showed a gravity 5 per cent greater
than that declared the whole content of the wash back was
deemed new wash and added to the duty charge. For a check
before fermentation had begun this 5 per cent tolerance was
generous. To assist more rapid fermentation a distiller was

   19. *Ibid.*, sections 17, 21, 90–4, 100. In the *Excise Revenue Inquiry, 7th Report,
Part I, 1834, op. cit.*, on p. 19 and in appendix 61, pp. 208–17 there are strong
complaints from Irish distillers. See also *Report of the Board of Excise on the Malt
Drawback*, Parl. Pps. 1831–2 (150) xxxiv, pp. 433, 439–49. The whole of the malt
duty was not drawn back, 3d. a gallon on spirits was retained.

permitted to make bub, but was limited to adding not more than 5 per cent of the wash to be excited. Receiving wash from outside sources was no longer allowed.[20]

It will be evident from this brief account of the brewing regulations that the authorities had tried to meet all the fraudulent practices they had experienced during the years of the still licence charge. They were attempting to ensure that the duty charge raised on the attenuation of wash would not be evaded. The rules appear to confine the distiller to a rigid routine and hamper his freedom, but in fact these rules did fit into the normal course of manufacture and the only real criticism, apart from the general one of official interference, is that the twelve hour break between brewing and distilling was either unnecessary or too long. It might be said to interrupt continuous manufacture and this is true, but at the time few, if any, distillers had sufficient distilling plant to cope with such manufacture. The break itself was controlled at the wash charger when the discharge cock was locked closed while brewing was in progress. When all wash had been assessed in the wash backs this cock was opened so that wash could flow to the stills. When the last of the wash had been conveyed the discharge cock was closed. Its opening marked the beginning of the distilling period which ended when all spirits and feints had been collected. The complete brewing and distilling period formed a convenient break to both distiller and the excise on which to base their accounts and records and this was the pattern for the rest of the century.[21]

The only regulations relating to actual distilling concerned notices in advance of operations, and, of course, prohibiting tampering with locks, fastenings and pipes. No others were necessary as the processes and conveyance between stills and various vessels were all enclosed. The worm end from each still

20. 4 Geo. 4, c. 94, sections 41, 43–44, 46, 49–50, 111. Bub is a preparation of wash and yeast in violent fermentation and is added to normal wash to promote fermentation. It was sometimes referred to as lob (see *Irish Revenue Inquiry, 5th Report*, 1823, *op. cit.*, appendix 92, item 23).

21. The brewing and distilling periods were defined and the interval reduced to 2 hours later in the century (43 and 44 Vict., c. 24, section 25). The opening and closing of the discharge cock of the wash charger was the effective point of excise control over the break between these periods. Extant records of distilling firms sometimes include 'period books' showing the materials used, gravities and final extract from each complete period. See for example the Comber distillery records in the Belfast Public Records Office, ref. D 1808/25/1.

was connected to a safe with glass sides and the distiller, by installing inside the safe, glass jars containing hydrometers and thermometers, could not only see his product flowing, but could exercise a continuous check on strengths of the extract from his wash or low wines stills. In the pipelines leading from the safe would be cocks enabling the distiller to divert the flow to different receivers. The low wines from the wash still would run into a low wines receiver, where the low wines charge for duty would be assessed. From the low wines still spirit would go to the spirit receiver and feints to its receiver. The low wines from the wash still and the feints from the low wines still would be pumped into a low wines and feints charger to feed the low wines still. When the period ended there would be some feints left which had not been fed back. An account of these was taken and the feints held over to the next distilling period. All these arrangements can be seen in any modern pot still distillery, but in 1823 they were innovations and required considerable changes in the practices used under the still licence system when one general purpose still was the rule. No distiller under the former system could have afforded the luxury of specialised stills.[22]

Having made his spirit the distiller had some restraints on its disposal. He was not allowed to add any material such as sugar or syrup which would obscure a true hydrometer reading; nor was he allowed to have any spirit on his premises that had not been distilled there. If he wished to sell wholesale those premises had to be more than two miles from the distillery. Retail selling was not permitted. On the other hand he had the valuable privilege of warehousing his spirits duty free.[23] These restraints were clearly intended to prevent the distillery becoming an avenue for introducing illegal spirits into the legitimate stream. Even warehousing, which was hedged around with rigid rules, was not entirely a benevolent gesture, for it reduced the incentive to evade duty. The duty was deferred till the distiller wanted to sell his spirit for consumption in the home market, and in the mean time the spirits were maturing and increasing in value while under excise surveillance.

22. *Experiments in Distillation*, 1821, *op. cit.*, p. 370. S. Morewood, *A Philosophical and Statistical History of the Inventions and Customs . . . in the manufacture of Inebriating Liquors*, Dublin, 1838, p. 657.

23. 4 Geo. 4, c. 94, sections 66, 119, 122, 131–2.

The new distillery laws of 1823 made considerable changes in the role of the excise officer. Under the still licence system, with distilling conducted at a furious speed, the gauger was faced with the impossible task of assessing the spirit duty on the decreases in the distiller's stocks of wash or low wines. The saccharometer, if it was used, was merely intended to uncover any surreptitious introduction of new wash. The hydrometer had no part in excise distillery control since no cognisance was taken of strength. The gauger, if he was zealous, concentrated his attention on preventing any spirit made in excess of the still licence quantity from escaping assessment. In this he relied heavily on stock accounts and control through permits.

Under the new system the gauger was confronted with many unfamiliar jobs in his distillery survey. For example, the minute book, or specimen, in which the distiller entered details of the materials used, the date and hour of brewing or distilling and the vessels employed, was now, as formerly, inspected by the gauger on each visit. This inspection was no longer a mere formality. The details declared by the distiller were now essential information for the gauger's survey. During the gauger's round he would check dips and make tests with the saccharometer or the hydrometer and these checks should be consistent with the time since the processes began. In order to calculate the attenuation charge for duty, wash gravities had to be ascertained before and after fermentation. Low wines and spirits had to be tested with the hydrometer to determine proof strengths and the proof gallons calculated. Cocks vital to the proper flow from wash to the final spirit were secured by revenue locks and the gauger had to unlock or lock these cocks at the request of the distiller and in conformity with distillery regulations, to permit the orderly sequence of processes. Since the distiller had no access to low wines or spirit receivers, if he wished to make his own checks, he arranged with the gauger for the hatches to be unlocked, drew samples and tested the hydrometer strengths. This had the advantage that there should be no disagreement. These are some of the new excise officer's duties and enough to show that the gauger of 1823 had suddenly become intimately concerned with all the principal activities in a distillery.[24]

24. *Ibid.*, sections 28–9, 108–10, 112, 114, 123 refer to the main regulations involving the gauger. Among the many accounts of the gauger's survey see

Naturally so complete a change in distillery laws could not be implemented in full immediately. Time had to be given for distillers to adjust their practices and install or alter their plants and, no less important, excise officers had to be trained. There must have been a very difficult transition period, but there is little information on this point. It does seem, however, that existing plant and other arrangements were allowed a period of grace. One extreme case is quoted by Morewood, the excise collector at Naas, where a brewery and distillery were on the same premises as late as 1834 'because they were there before the law forbad it'.[25]

The 1823 Act applied only to Ireland and Scotland, but a unified system for the whole United Kingdom was the ultimate aim and this was greatly helped when standard measures were prescribed in all three countries in 1824. The standard gallon and bushel were defined. The imperial standard gallon was equal in volume to 10 lbs. of distilled water at 62° Fahrenheit and 30 inches barometric pressure. The new standards came into force from 5 January 1826 for spirit duties and drawbacks.[26] Because the

---

especially the *Irish Revenue Inquiry, 5th Report*, 1823, *op. cit.*, pp. 321–3, and the *Excise Revenue Inquiry, 7th Report, Part I*, 1834, *op. cit.*, pp. 425–6. The revenue locks are interesting. Padlocks that had replaced wax seals were not satisfactory and were replaced in 1829 by a lock patented by Gottlieb. An improved version was introduced in 1868 and a modified type of this lock is still used. After locking, a label showing the time and vessel is placed over the keyhole and held in position by a metal flap secured in the lock by a spring clip. To unlock, the key must break through the label and when turned the flap spring is released and circular sprigs tear the label. J. Owens, *Plain Papers, op. cit.*, pp. 310–12, gives a desciption and historical account of revenue locks.

25. *Excise Revenue Inquiry, 7th Report, Part I, op. cit.*, p. 399. Another instance of a similar nature appears in the *Belfast Historical Records, op. cit.*, Book 5, p. 128.

26. 5 Geo. 4, c. 74, sections 6–7; 6 Geo. 4, c. 12 and c. 58. The Irish gallon was 217·6 cu. inches the English wine gallon 231 cu. inches and the imperial standard gallon 277·274 cu. inches. There were similar variations between the Irish and English winchester bushels and between both and the imperial bushel (J. Owens, *Plain Papers*, London, 1879, p. 364). The delay in applying the new standards to Irish distilleries is understandable. All vessels would have to be re-gauged and calibrated, and gauging instruments altered. The Irish Board of Excise ordered this re-gauging on 24 June 1825 (*Belfast Historical Records, op. cit.*, Book 132, refs. 5121/25 and G. B. 837/25). Earlier statistics do not usually show the standard used for quantities. If issued in Ireland the local standard can be assumed. If in England, as in the *13th Inland Revenue Report*, 1870, *op. cit.*, conversion has been done, but comparisons even though approximate are sufficient for most purposes. Currencies were in a similar position with a conversion factor of 13d. Irish equal to 12d.

application of these new standards would result in inconvenient fractions, the existing duties and drawbacks were repealed and replaced by approximate equivalents. The Irish rate for proof spirits was fixed at 2s. 10d. a gallon.[27]

In 1825 a Distillery Act extended to England the principles of the 1823 Act. There were some differences. For example, the minimum size for stills in England was 400 gallons and if under 3,000 gallons there had to be not more than two wash and two low wines stills, but the important provisions were similar particularly the method of charging duty at three stages. There were, however, a few clauses applicable to Ireland tucked away in this long Act of nearly 150 sections. In Ireland distillers were allowed to distil from potatoes, but must not distil from sugar at the same time. It is not an important provision, but indicates that there must have been some demand for potato distilling. There were special export clauses of more consequence. Exports of Irish spirits to Great Britain had to be from a warehouse which could be either a Crown warehouse or a distiller's entered warehouse built to a prescribed specification. These latter warehouses still continue. The warehoused spirits had to be either 25° or 11° over proof and in casks of not less than eighty gallons. The rigid rule on strengths seems unnecessary and came in for some criticism later. When these spirits were exported the English duty was charged. This was probably to ease excise accounting procedure between the two countries.[28]

English. Small fractions in some statistics show this conversion (see, for example the rates of duty in the *Excise Revenue Inquiry, 7th Report,* Part I, 1834, *op. cit.,* pp. 66–7).

27. 6 Geo. 4, c. 58, sections 1–2. *Parliamentary Debates,* 12 May 1825, cols. 573–81 on the assimilation of currencies. 22 April 1825, cols. 132–5. The Chancellor of the Exchequer explained the new English spirit duty. Formerly the duty had been 10s. 6d. a gallon at 7 per cent over proof, equivalent to 5s. 10d. an English wine gallon at proof. This in turn was equal to 7s. an imperial standard gallon at proof. Similar reasoning, with currency changes in addition, would apply to Irish rates. Spirits at strengths other than proof were converted to the equivalent quantity at proof to calculate the duty.

28. 6 Geo. 4, c. 80, sections 10, 47, 82, 92–5. *Excise Revenue Inquiry, 7th Report,* Part I, 1834, *op. cit.,* pp. 179, 187 are examples of complaints on the rigid rules regarding the strengths of spirits; complaints which were supported by senior excise officials (see. p. 121). The distiller's entered warehouse was a new development and was an alternative to the Crown or King's warehouse.

The Malt Duty

A further step in assimilating the regulations in the United Kingdom came in 1827 with a consolidated law for maltsters and applied equally to distillers. Buying malt from outside sources was a revenue danger and this was met by specially licensing maltsters and malt dealers who supplied distillers. They were required to issue a certificate with each delivery and no allowance for malt used could be paid without the cover of this certificate. Since nearly all Irish distillers made a mixed grain spirit this rule was largely of academic interest. The term 'grain spirit' at this period meant spirit made in a pot still from a mixture of malted and unmalted cereals. Towards the end of the century the term became customary for spirit made in a Coffey still from a mash of cereal grains. All the distiller's malt was kept under official lock and there were the usual notices when it was used. A corresponding Act in 1831 consolidated the laws for suppressing illicit malting. If these laws were little more than an irritant and added cost to Irish distillers the case was different in Scotland where malt spirit was the rule and with the help of malt allowances, plus evasion, they were able to compete successfully with the Irish distiller in his own market, especially in the north of Ireland.[29] The consolidated law caused considerable uneasiness amongst distillers, maltsters and officials in Ireland because the regulations were based on those applying in England and abolished the former rules where there was full excise control from the time barley entered the malt house till malt was put into the mash. The new rules replaced the survey and account method and the use of permits was supplemented by certificates issued by the maltster. It was claimed that fraud was made easier

29. 7 and 8 Geo. 4, c. 52, sections 49, 66–75; 1 Will. 4, c. 55. *Excise Revenue Inquiry, 7th Report, Part I,* 1834, *op. cit.,* appendix 61, sets out very fully the case for Irish distillers against their Scottish competitors relating to the use of malt. It also attacks the ineptitude and impugns the honesty of the Board of Excise. The distillers' statistics, taken from official sources, demonstrate considerable drawback frauds in Scotland. See also *Report of the Board of Excise on the Malt Drawback,* Parl. Pps., 1831–2 (150) xxxiv, pp. 433, 439–40, observations by Irish distillers on 21 July 1831. The distillers' case is set out in *Memorials addressed to the Treasury by Corn Distillers,* Parl. Pps. 1830 (370) xxii, pp. 257 *et seq.* The subject was debated in parliament. See *Parl. Debates,* 3 August 1831, col. 651, and 5 August 1831, col. 825, where the petitioners complained that 'in consequence of the malt drawback Scotch distillers could sell their whisky in Ireland 20 per cent cheaper than distilled there'.

to the detriment of the fair trader. This was confirmed later in a report to parliament which stated that malt used for distilling rarely paid duty. So it seems that Irish distillers had their own remedy to counter the malt drawback paid to distillers of malt whiskey.[30] The malt laws themselves had become 'one uncouth mass of legislation which shackled and impeded the trade and commerce of the country'. McCulloch pointed out that the law had 'no fewer than 83 clauses enforced by 106 penalties'. A joint committee of the trade and excise reported to the Government and the repeal of many of the clauses and penalties in the 1827 Act resulted in 1830.[31]

The malt duty at this period was 2s. 7d. a bushel and the drawback 2s. 4d., or, at the rate of two proof gallons per bushel, a drawback of 1s. 2d. a proof gallon. Despite the opposition of Scottish members of parliament this drawback was reduced to 8d. in 1832. Irish members wanted the drawback abolished.[32] The agitation to get rid of the drawback continued and in 1842 an inquiry was undertaken to see if its abolition would affect distillers or revenue adversely. The report from this inquiry quoted from a Select Committee of 1831 that 'the present system of allowing drawback on malt spirits affords great opportunities for fraud'. Irish distillers again took this opportunity to press for its abolition in Ireland even if it were continued in Scotland. There were at the time only four malt distilleries in Ireland, none very large, and producing about 70,000 gallons a year out of a total production in the region of eight million gallons. The drawback had not induced distillers to revert from grain to malt spirit because, as they said, the market was too small. The committee of 1842 concluded that abolishing the drawback in Ireland would not be prejudicial to the spirit trade or revenue and this was done, but the drawback continued in Scotland. To protect Irish interests Scottish exporters were required to repay the drawback on malt when sending spirit to Ireland.[33] In 1846 the first glimmer of hope for Irish grain dis-

30. *Excise Revenue Inquiry, 10th Report,* Parl. Pps. 1834 (11) xxv, pp. 588, 592–3, and *Digest of Reports,* Parl. Pps. 1837 (84) xxx, p. 172.

31. J. Owens, *Plain Papers,* London, 1879, pp. 332–3. The repeals referred to were enacted by 11 Geo. 4, c. 17.

32. 2 and 3 Will. 4, c. 29, section 2. *Parl. Debates,* 7 February 1832, cols. 511 et seq. and 29 February 1832, cols. 980–1.

33. *S.C. to inquire into the Effects upon the Trade in Spirits in Ireland by the Repeal*

tillers appeared when drawback at $1\frac{1}{2}$d. a gallon was allowed
for grain spirits exported and in 1855 the Government at last did
the only sensible thing and allowed all malt for distilling to be free
of duty whether for making malt or grain spirit. The distiller
was also allowed to use sugar and molasses free of duty.[34] Since
malt was the vehicle for levying a duty on beer there was a
revenue risk that distillers might divert duty free malt to breweries and in consequence the distiller was still not free from stringent
official control of his malt. Malthouses had to be specially entered
and the kiln adapted so that it could be officially secured while
malt was drying. There was to be a store room and a mill room
at the distillery with fastenings for revenue locks. Malt was
measured on removal from the kiln with allowances for cum-
mins or roots. There were other restraints and the customary
system of notices for each operation or movement. Distillers did
not finally get free from these rigid controls until 1880 when the
malt duty was abandoned and replaced by a duty on beer.[35]

The Spirit Duties

Efforts to raise the spirit duties in Ireland, so that eventually
they would reach the level in Great Britain, continued to be
hampered by the threat of the illicit distiller. It was the latter who
really dictated policy on duties. In the budget debate in 1834
the Chancellor of the Exchequer said that 'increasing the duty
on spirits would do no good whatever either in the shape of
increasing the revenue or of diminishing their consumption' and
many experiments had shown that a rise in the spirit duty encouraged illicit distilling. He gave examples. For instance, the
rise in the rate in 1826 to 2s. 10d. was followed by a fall in the
gallons charged from 9,262,313 in 1826 to 6,834,866 in 1827.
There may have been other causes for the fall in quantity such
as over production and stocks building up in warehouses, because

---

of the Malt Drawback, Parl. Pps. 1842 (338) xiv, pp. 425, 430, 432, 434. The report
of this inquiry was implemented by 5 Vict., sess. 2, c. 15. See also *Return of Spirits
Distilled,* Parl. Pps. 1842 (238) xxxix, pp. 545–6. The terms 'drawback' and
'allowance' both mean a refund of duty. They are used here to distinguish in the
Act drawback for exports and allowances for home consumption.
    34. 11 and 12 Vict., c. 122, section 14; 18 and 19 Vict., c. 94, sections 5, 9.
    35. 18 and 19 Vict., c. 94, sections 6, 11–12, 14–15, 18, 20–28; 43 and 44 Vict.,
c. 20, sections 1, 11.

between 1828 and 1830 the gallons charged recovered to around nine millions. Another reason for this recovery may have been more success in preventing evasion in distilleries. In 1830 the rate was twice increased, first to 3s. and then 3s. 4d., without any serious drop in revenue. Nevertheless the Chancellor of the Exchequer estimated consumption in Ireland to be twelve to fourteen million gallons a year and in consequence he proposed reducing the duty to 2s. 4d. a gallon in the hope that the gallons charged would rise to ten millions. In fact, the result was that over eleven million gallons paid duty in 1835. There is thus clear evidence that the policy of repressive measures against illicit distillers were not so effective as a low rate of duty and that until illegal practices in distilleries were brought well under control there was little hope of ever assimilating the duties in Ireland with those in Great Britain.[36] A rise in general prosperity in Ireland would, of course, have helped, but there was no sign at the time of this being likely. Detections of illicit distillation began to fall dramatically after 1834. Before 1834 the detection rate was 5,000 to 8,000 a year. In that year there were 8,192 detections; in 1835 the number fell to 4,904 and the next year to 3,323. By 1840 detections were down to 1,004, still a very large figure, but the trend was enough to encourage the Chancellor of the Exchequer to raise the duty cautiously by 4d. to 2s. 8d. Again there was a heavy fall in the gallons charged to less than seven and a half millions. He was following his principle stated in 1836 that 'the only plan is to fix the duty below the insurance on smuggling' and this point could only be fixed by trial and error.[37]

The detection rate for illicit distillation remained between two and three thousand a year except for the years 1841 and 1847 when it was much lower and the number of gallons charged

36. *Parl. Debates*, 25 July 1834, cols. 503, 508–9 and 22 January 1847, col. 290. 4 and 5 Will. 4, c. 75. *13th Inland Revenue Report*, 1870, *op. cit.*, p. 387. There are small discrepancies in this report when compared with the *Excise Revenue Inquiry, 7th Report, Part I*, 1834, *op. cit.*, pp. 66–7, due to a different basis. The former report refers to gallons charged, the latter to gallons that paid duty. It is interesting to note that when the duty was 2s. 10d. the price of whiskey in bond in Belfast was 3s. 6d. a gallon. (*Northern Whig*, 13 September 1827.)

37. *13th Inland Revenue Report*, 1870, *op. cit.*, pp. 387, 390. Between 1835 and 1839 the gallons charged were between 11 and 12 million gallons a year. In 1840 this fell to 7·4 millions. See also *Parl. Debates*, 6 May 1836, the budget speech, cols. 657, 669. 3 and 4 Vict., c. 17 imposed the duty.

also remained fairly constant between 7 and 8 million. In 1853, therefore, it was decided to add another 8d. to the duty making it 3s. 4d. and as results were, at least, not unsatisfactory, the duty was further advanced to 4s. and then in 1855 to 6s. 2d. a proof gallon. The last move reduced the gallons charged, but did not cause any significant rise in detections of illicit stills. The fall in gallons charged as distinct from gallons distilled, was general in the United Kingdom and the Chancellor of the Exchequer explained it as mainly due to the high price of corn and the failure of the continental wine crop resulting in a shortage of brandy. The latter reason led to increased exports of spirit which meant that distillers benefited, but the revenue did not.[38] The same trend continued, but the disparity between the gallons distilled and charged widened which may have been partly accounted for by increasing use of warehousing facilities. By 1858 it was thought safe to raise the Irish rate to 8s., then in 1860 to 8s. 1d. and finally to 10s. which were the rates in Great Britain, so that assimilation became complete. Both the gallons distilled and those charged fell for a few years to less than five millions. One reason was probably a rise in beer drinking.[39]

The main reason why it became possible to raise the duty to the level in Great Britain was the more effective action taken against illicit distillers by the incorporation of the revenue police into the Irish constabulary and giving the latter the duty of suppressing these distillers. Formerly the constabulary had not been active against illicit distillers and exhibited a strong distaste for the work. After 1854 this much larger and more widespread force became active and if detections are any guide, illicit distilling

38. *13th Inland Revenue Report*, 1870, *op. cit.*, pp. 381, 387, 390. In 1855 the gallons distilled were 8·3 millions and the gallons charged 8 million, but the latter figure referred to 1¼ years. In 1842 the rate was increased to 3s. 8d. by 5 Vict., sess. 2, c. 15, but reduced again to 2s. 8d. the following year by 6 Vict., c. 49. The rate of 6s. 2d. was imposed by 18 and 19 Vict., c. 94. The reasons for the fall in revenue appear in *Parl. Debates*, 22 February 1856, cols. 1232–3 and 19 May 1856, col. 341.

39. *13th Inland Revenue Report*, 1870, *op. cit.*, pp. 381, 387, 398. Barrels of beer brewed in Ireland rose from 926,000 in 1857 to 1,561,355 in 1869. Presumably the quantities are computed from the malt used. 21 Vict., c. 15, section 1 equalised United Kingdom rates at 8s. The rates of 8s. 1d. and 10s. a proof gallon were imposed by 23 and 24 Vict., c. 129. The 10s. rate remained unchanged till 1890 when it was raised to 10s. 6d. and in 1894 to 11s. (*43rd Inland Revenue Report*, Parl. Pps. 1900 (cd. 347) xviii, p. 385. See also *Parl. Debates*, 22 June 1849, col. 749.

was severely checked, though far from suppressed. The main point was that the rise in duty did not increase illicit distillation. This was well explained by the Solicitor General in the House of Commons when defending the duty of 8s. a proof gallon for the whole United Kingdom.[40] A common United Kingdom duty wiped out many of the difficulties of trade between the countries and the customs checks and assessments. The rate of 10s. was certainly high in relation to the value of spirits and the Chancellor of the Exchequer was following his declared policy when he announced that 'we are justified in extracting from spirits as large an amount of revenue as the article can afford provided always that we do not incur the evil of increasing illicit distillation'.[41]

Distilling

The distillery laws of 1823 for Ireland and Scotland and those of 1825 for England did not differ materially. The Commissioners for the Excise Revenue Inquiry in 1834 listed sixteen differences of a minor character and perhaps the only difference of any importance was that limiting the original gravity of wort which was higher in England. English distillers, however, were strongly opposed to a common distillery law chiefly on the grounds of expense as they had already been forced to incur capital expenditure following the 1825 Act. In fact, of course, an examination of the two Acts shows that this reason was barely valid and it is more probable that English distillers feared the regulations associated with distilling, especially warehousing, which if opened up to Irish and Scottish distillers they might make serious inroads into the English market. The Commission of Inquiry did examine proposed legislation for common regulations which incorporated a number of changes, and heard evidence and severe criticism from distillers in all the countries. They concluded that there should be no radical changes in distillery laws without a full

40. The merging of the two forces resulted from the report of the *S.C. of the House of Lords to consider the consequences of extending the functions of the Constabulary in Ireland to the Suppression of Illicit Distillation*, Parl. Pps. 1854 (53) x. 17 and 18 Vict., c. 89, sections 13–15 gave effect to their recommendations. *13th Inland Revenue Report*, 1870, op. cit., p. 390 gives the number of detections. The Solicitor General's observations appear in *Parl. Debates*, 22 April 1856, col. 1745.

41. *Parl. Debates*, 19 May 1856, col. 340.

knowledge of the effects these would have on other branches of the spirit trade such as rectifying and retailing.[42]

This did not rule out amending existing laws and their view was that 'from want of revision it is notorious that many parts of the existing excise laws have now become obsolete and inapplicable to the objects for which they were framed'. They made special reference to improvements in chemical science and stressed that excise controls should be more closely related to manufacturing processes. It was also pointed out that penalties were too numerous and severe, defeated their object, and often fell on acts innocent in themselves. These were general observations on the whole excise, but the Commissioners considered they applied particularly to spirits.[43] These criticisms tend to give a false notion and are not strictly fair so far as they relate to excise controls over distilling. The introduction in 1823 of the attenuation charge was a major adaptation of chemical knowledge to related processes and the consequent changes in other parts of the law must have called for intensive study of distilling practices. The excise themselves showed how live they were to improvements soon after the 1823 Act was passed, for within a few months they scrapped the use of Allan's saccharometer for a better and more accurate instrument made by Bates.[44]

The Commissioners of the Inquiry were on sounder ground in their condemnation of penalties which mainly fell on breaches of various restrictions, some merely irksome and due to excessive caution against fraud, though in fairness it must be stated that fraud in licensed distilleries was a common occurrence. A witness, admittedly biassed, told a Commission of Inquiry into drunkenness that, apart from places such as Innishowen where illicit distilling was rife, the illicit spirit being sold was small compared with the illegal spirit coming from licensed distilleries. The excise collector in Cork gave his view that the legal distiller will smuggle if he can and it is the excise job to catch him. Apparently there

42. *Excise Revenue Inquiry, 7th Report, Part I,* 1834, *op. cit.,* pp. 28, 33, 193, 195–8. The Government did not proceed with the proposed legislation.

43. *Excise Revenue Inquiry, Digest of Reports,* 1837, *op. cit.,* p. 156.

44. *Belfast Historical Records, op. cit.,* Book 133, p. 133 and Book 137, p. 71, gives a general order to the excise service, No. 54 dated 3 December 1823, directing the use of the Bates saccharometer. This repetition of an order issued some years earlier indicates that some officers were still using the Allan or some other instrument.

was no trust on either side. Nor could the excise staff be trusted and even the Board of Excise admitted that officers were corrupt. There is considerable evidence of distillery frauds in the reports of the excise collector of Lisburn between 1841 and 1849. His jurisdiction comprised south Antrim and north Down. Most of the distilleries were reported as fraudulent, even the largest in Belfast. The same story comes from Dublin. Distillers themselves could not have benefited much from these irregular practices for when all are fraudulent nobody gains and all must attempt corrupting the excise gauger or be harassed. Distillers in the Cork district realising this agreed amongst themselves not to undertake fraudulent practices.[45] In the years following 1834 there appears to have been little if any improvement till after 1840. Numerous legal restrictions were deemed essential, but by 1870 the Revenue Commissioners were able to report that legislative enactments 'have had for their main purpose the removal of restrictions upon distillery operations and upon commercial intercourse, as far as, by general experience, it was found that this could be done with safety to the revenue'. They listed six restrictions on manufacture which had been abolished and all this despite a considerable rise in the rate of duty.[46] The only criticism that might be made is that some of these reliefs were obvious long before they came into effect, for example, regulations for continuous stills were not enacted till 1860 though the stills themselves had been in use for nearly thirty years and were really illegal since no separate low wines were produced in their operation. During that period the department made its own rules for controlling 'illegal stills' and the Act of 1860 merely regularised the position.[47]

45. *Ibid.*, Book 5, pp. 17–18, 34–5, 88–9, 190 and Book 6, pp. 36, 62 are some of the references. *S.C. to inquire into Drunkenness*, Parl. Pps. 1834 (559) viii, p. 393. The evidence of Rev. John Edgar, Royal College, Belfast. *Excise Revenue Inquiry, 7th Report, Part I*, 1834, *op. cit.*, pp. 200, 257, 402–3, 457.

46. *13th Inland Revenue Report*, 1870, *op. cit.*, pp. 219–21.

47. *Belfast Historical Records, op. cit.*, Book 137, p. 11. A directive to the excise service on 4 March 1839 refers to distilling spirits 'by means of steam in patent stills conducted otherwise than according to law' and deals with revenue security in such cases; for example, shutting off steam, locking the safe pipe and so on. See also a *Return of Licensed Distillers in each Collection distinguishing stills not sanctioned by law*, Parl. Pps. 1851 (386) liii, p. 269. 14 Coffey stills and one Shee still apparatus are listed. These stills were legally recognised in 1860 by 23 and 24 Vict., c. 114, section 8.

More liberal rules were also evolved regarding the materials a
distiller may use and how he may use them. In 1823 he could use
either malt, or a mixture of malt with raw grain, or sugar and
related saccharine substances, but not at the same time and notice
was required when switching from one to the other. Mangel-
wurzel was permitted in 1823, but there is no indication that
this measure affected Irish distillers.[48] This separation of each type
of raw material resulted from the fact that different yields of
spirit were obtained from the same quantity and the difficulty
of preventing fraudulent substitution. There was also the pressure
from sugar interests who wanted nothing less than a prohibition
on grain distilling. On one occasion the Chancellor of the
Exchequer resisting this pressure reminded the Commons that
'nothing gave so great a stimulus to illicit distillation as putting
an end to legal traffic'.[49] In 1847 the Board of Excise reported
on an investigation into the comparative values of different
materials in relation to the resulting alcohol. This report was
invaluable when assessing the proper drawbacks for sugar,
molasses and treacle used in distilling. It gave the prime cost of
spirits at the various prices of barley and other materials and
confirmed the existing relationship for drawback that 1 cwt. of
sugar made $11\frac{1}{2}$ proof gallons.[50] In the same year an Act was
passed to extend to Ireland the same encouragement to use

48. 2 and 3 Will. 4, c. 74. In the *Belfast Historical Records, op. cit.,* Book 134,
pp. 73–4 there is an interesting record dated 29 February 1831, of a patent by
Robert Hicks for extracting spirits from the vapours arising from making bread.
Users of this apparatus were required to take out a distiller's licence, but there is
no record of any such spirit production. In Book 5, p. 88, there is a report on an
application from Lisburn to mix malt and potatoes, dated 12 November 1845,
in order to get spirit from diseased potatoes, then all too plentiful, but the applicant had a bad revenue record and the collector recommended refusal. See also
S. Morewood, *Inebriating Liquors, op. cit.,* p. 699 on an attempt to distil from
potatoes near Enniscorthy in 1832. It failed because of peasant opposition.

49. *Parliamentary Debates,* 7 May 1847, col. 953. A reference to the dangers to
revenue security if distilling from grain and sugar were not kept separate appears
in the debate on 22 January 1847, col. 290.

50. *Report from the Board of Excise to the Treasury on the use of barley, malt, sugar
and molasses in Breweries and Distilleries,* Parl. Pps. 1847 (26) lix, pp. 337–41. There
was an earlier investigation in 1806 in Scotland by Doctors Hope, Thomson and
Coventry into the proportional values of malt made from barley and from bere
or bigg (Customs and Excise Library, London, ref. *Treasury and Scottish Excise,*
No. 1817. 1805–1811, p. 117). The relationship between sugar and spirit was
defined by 52 Geo. 3, c. 3 and applied in England. At that time the still licence
charge applied in Ireland. See also *13th Inland Revenue Report,* 1870, *op. cit.,* p. 218.

sugar in distilling as was given in England, but as there was practically no demand in Ireland for such spirit and as there were the
usual safeguards of giving notice of its use, providing secure store
rooms and the like, there was very little chance of the measure succeeding despite the payment of an allowance of 12s. 10d. on every
$11\frac{1}{2}$ proof gallons, equivalent to a drawback of all the sugar duty.

Evidently the excise authorities were losing their fears of fraud
from substituting materials, for in 1848 distillers were at last
allowed to use mixtures of malt, grain and sugar and attenuation
charges were fixed for sugar only and for mixtures. The allowance of 12s. 10d. for sugar and molasses was reduced to nothing
by stages over the next three years. Under these circumstances
it is quite possible that sugar or molasses was used by some
whiskey distillers, but there is no information on this point.[51]
In 1860 all restrictions on materials were abolished and a distiller
was permitted to use any material for making wort or wash
provided the gravity could be obtained by a saccharometer.[52]
It is not easy to understand why for so long the excise authorities
insisted on segregating distilling with the different materials
except perhaps as an aid to checks on sugar drawbacks, but these
were already strictly controlled by restricting supplies, by checks
on receipt and the provision of secure store rooms kept under
revenue locks. Once materials are put into the mash tun the
normal checks on gravity should ensure the correct legal attenuation charge whatever materials are used. It seems that any
encouragement, as for example the use of sugar, was always
balanced or even cancelled by discouraging regulations.[53]

Apart from illicit distilling the problem of the gravity of
wash was a dominating theme in the report of the Excise Revenue

51. 10 and 11 Vict., c. 6, and 11 and 12 Vict., c. 100. The reducing allowances
were based on the cwt. of sugar or molasses and not on the spirit. They are set
out in a schedule to the latter Act. In 1856, 19 and 20 Vict., c. 51 added rice to
the materials permitted for distilling. Some molasses was being used for patent
still spirit in 1857 (*Royal Commission on Whiskey and other Potable Spirits, Final
Report,* Parl. Pps. 1909 (Cd. 1796), p. 7).

52. 23 and 24 Vict., c. 114, section 50.

53. 10 and 11 Vict., c. 6, sections 2–5 insist on sugar being received only from
a customs warehouse on an official certificate and placed in a store room under
revenue lock. Notice had to be given before receiving sugar and again when it
was to be used and the excise officer kept a sugar stock account. 11 and 12 Vict.,
c. 100 retained these provisions. Distillations from sugar and from mixtures were
still kept apart.

Inquiry Commissioners in 1834. One after another, distillers gave evidence of the frauds practised, of harassing by excise officials and of their difficulties in meeting the law's requirements. The law at that time was that the distiller had to declare the gravity at which he intended to set his wort and that it should lie between 30° and 80°. This declaration applied to each wash back and not to the average of the whole brew so that late runnings could be well below the rest of the wort. It was not difficult, therefore, for an excise gauger to find errors in the distiller's declaration even though there was no fraudulent intention. Apparently conviction in the courts was automatic. Several distillers pressed hard that there should be some provision for a valid defence that errors were unavaoidable and that fraudulent intent should be proved. As it was, distillers, rather than incurring the expense of defending themselves, paid the penalties without demur. They claimed before the Commission that much capital had been employed in various ways to secure the revenue and not in furtherance of their trade. In return they asked that the fair trader should be protected and at least be allowed to prove no fraudulent intent. These distillers said they were aware of extensive fraud and supported any measures for more drastic action against genuine illegalities.[54]

The fraud most commonly quoted was adding wort after the gauger had checked the original gravity and provided the result was not a higher gravity it would not be detected. Nearly all the witnesses said this fraud was much easier with gravities as low as 30° and suggested that the minimum gravity permitted should be raised to 50° or 60° as in England. The argument is not easy to follow for two reasons. First, any addition should increase the quantity in the wash back and would be detected by dipping, though this might escape notice if the addition were small and there was much froth. There might, of course, be a concealed vessel taking off wash surreptitiously. Secondly the gravity should fall with time, though the rate of fall may not be predictable. These objections, however, would apply whatever the original gravity. One ruse, which would be easier with lower gravities, was to insert a little yeast before declaring the gravity and getting

54. *Excise Revenue Inquiry, 7th Report, Part I, 1834, op. cit.*, pp. 180, 198–9, 426, 457. On p. 422 is a description of the difficulties in setting wort at a stated gravity,

a mild and unnoticed fermentation with a consequent fall in gravity but if care was not taken, or the gauger made his check too soon, for example, checking the wort on the coolers, the gravity would not have had time to fall. Apparently the majority of prosecutions resulted from this cause.[55] The Commissioners of the Excise Inquiry were so perplexed with these problems that they recommended abolishing the attenuation charge and raising instead a charge direct on the original gravity of wash.[56] This abolition would have raised new complications into which they did not inquire.

At the time of this inquiry, 1834, no simple means had been devised to ascertain the original gravity of wash once fermentation had begun and if fraud had occurred it could not be proved unless a gravity happened to exceed the distiller's declaration, that is, very soon after a little yeast had been irregularly added. The gauger's check on wash merely extended to the declaration and the penalty was for a gravity exceeding the declaration by more than 5°. The whole wash back was then deemed new wash and charged again. Distillers had been discovered keeping strong wort in the mash tun and underback, which were not under the gauger's survey, and pumping it up to wash backs after the gauger had made his checks. Some of the declared and partly fermented wash would have to be run off elsewhere to make room for the new wash. A subsequent check during fermentation might disclose no more than a small fall in gravity that might well be attributed to fermentation sticking.[57] Clearly some means

55. *Ibid.*, some of the evidence on gravity frauds appears on pp. 191, 200, 249, 285, 403–4, 451. The trick of adding yeast before declaring gravity is quoted on p. 113. As to the vagaries of fermentation see S. Morewood, *Inebriating Liquors, op. cit.*, pp. 660, 663, 668 and J. Scarisbrick, *Spirit Manual*, Burton-on-Trent, 1891, pp. 93–7. Obtaining a fair sample to check gravity was another problem and in 1839 officers were warned against distillers running heavy wort into the bottom of vessels and topping up this with weak wort. They were directed to use sinking jars. This is a corked can lowered to the bottom and the cork is then jerked out by a string thus obtaining a sample from the bottom of the wash back. (*Belfast Historical Records, op. cit.*, Book 137, p. 15. Order dated 15 March 1839.) The sinking jar is still used.

56. *Excise Revenue Inquiry, 7th Report, Part I, 1834, op. cit.*, p. 73. An alternative suggestion was to reduce the rate for the presumed product from 1 gallon at proof per 100 gallons of wash for each 5° attenuation to each 4½° attenuation, but this was considered too tight (p. 378).

57. *Ibid.*, p. 403. The penalty for exceeding the declaration by more than 5° is prescribed in 4 Geo., c. 94, section 49.

of obtaining the original gravity of wash was desirable from the revenue standpoint. Dr Ure put forward an idea in 1831 for testing for original gravity, but it was not simple enough to be of practical use. In 1847 a simpler and accurate method by partial evaporation was proposed which impressed the Board of Excise and they had it investigated by their chemical officers. The report of this investigation resulted in legislation in 1853 prescribing the method for obtaining the original gravity of wash by distilling a sample and using a table of degrees of spirit indication. There was a more precise penalty than merely deeming wash to be new wash. If the original gravity found by sampling exceeded the declaration by more than 3° the penalty was £200 plus 6d. a gallon on all the wash in the vessel. If these rules were faithfully observed by gaugers then the complaints of distillers that they did not get protection from fraudulent competitors was being met. There are good grounds for believing that this was the case for by 1853 allegations of widespread fraud had died down.[58]

There was another kind of fraud that could only be stopped by official vigilance. Breweries made wort and this could be clandestinely transferred to a distiller for running through his stills if it was known that the gauger would be absent long enough, or with the gauger's connivance. There was no reason, however, why a brewer should not also try distilling. He had the wort and vessels that could be easily converted. Furthermore, the excise control in breweries, though close, was considerably less than in distilleries, and cases of distilling in breweries were discovered.[59]

58. 16 and 17 Vict., c. 37, sections 38–9. A report addressed to the Board of Inland Revenue by Professors Graham, Hofman and Redwood on 16 August 1852 is in the Customs and Excise Library, London, ref. 1101. J. Owens, *Plain Papers*, London, 1879, p. 379. See also W. H. Johnston, *Inland Revenue Officer's Manual*, Loftus publication, London, 1873, pp. 285–7 and *Handbook for Officers of Excise*, Loftus publication, London, 1857, pp. 139–141. The method of obtaining the original gravity by saccharometer is clearly set out in section 37 of 43 and 44 Vict., c. 24.

59. *Belfast Historical Records, op. cit.*, Book 135, p. 132. Brewery officers were enjoined to keep a watch for unentered wort intended for distilling. Book 137, p. 150: Order dated 13 October 1842. 'It having been discovered recently that a brewer for sale had artfully contrived apparatus by the application of which he was enabled to use his copper as a still and other of his brewing utensils and conveyance pipes in the manufacture of spirits upon a very considerable scale ...' The order also stated that brewers used beer casks to dispose of spirits illegally made, probably through licensed distillers.

During the period 1823–60 the emphasis on the attenuation charge gradually receded. In reserve there was the annual deficiency charge to recover duty from errors or fraud arising during the year. It was the difference between the spirit actually assessed and the theoretical production of the year calculated on the assumption that all attenuations had been carried to 0° of gravity. This was palpably not the case. The charge was difficult to enforce; there were always considerable arrears in payment and, in the earlier years, officers were none too competent in their use of the saccharometer. The charge quietly disappeared by omission from the consolidation of distillery laws in 1860.[60] The attenuation charge of 1 gallon of proof spirit per 100 gallons of wash for every 5° attenuation was generous and unless a distiller was inefficient this rate of production was easily obtained. The Commissioners for the Excise Inquiry in 1834 reported that the presumed spirit from attenuation was fixed leniently to allow latitude for imperfect working by distillers with little capital and inferior skill. In time this presumptive charge has become a reserve which has rarely operated.[61]

The brewing operations in distilleries did not change materially in the years following the 1823 Act except in scale and the absence of furious speed and incomplete fermentation. Distilling operations, however, were affected more profoundly especially by the invention of the patent still where continuous distilling gave rise to greater capital investment and larger units. Compared with the small pot stills of the early years of the nineteenth century the patent still produced much larger quantities of

---

60. The consolidating Act was 23 and 24 Vict., c. 114. The deficiency charge, designed to pick up any duty evaded, was unfair in operation. In those years refinements in controlling fermentation were not so efficient as they later became. The use of bub, for example, was controversial. Control of temperature was more elementary for none of the distillers giving evidence in 1834 mentioned methods such as the use of attemperator pipes. In the circumstances attenuation down to water was due as much to luck as to skill. S. Morewood, *Inebriating Liquors*, 1838, *op. cit.*, p. 668 writes that alkalis such as carbonate of soda were sometimes added to assist fermentation and correct acidity.

61. *Excise Revenue Inquiry, 7th Report, Part I, 1834, op. cit.*, p. 36. In a modern distillery attenuation normally causes the gravity to fall to about water or slightly less and the charge on actual spirit is in the region of 8 per cent to 14 per cent more than the attenuation charge. *13th Inland Revenue Report*, 1870, *op. cit.*, p. 217 gives 8 per cent to 15 per cent as the usual excess. *The Revenue Review*, March 1901, pp. 17–20, a monthly journal circulated among excise officials. It quotes the excess as between 9 per cent and 17 per cent.

spirit of high strength. Because it lacked flavour this spirit was unsuitable as a popular beverage, but by blending it with spirit from pot stills a cheaper whiskey could be made. In turn larger pot stills were used, often in the same distillery, to provide the whiskey for these blends, and by the middle of the century the whole industry was transformed from a number of small distilleries competing desperately with each other and with illicit distillers, using every trick and fraud to keep in business, to a few well-established firms building up a tradition of respectability. No less important was the improvement in the excise administration and the decrease in corruption after about 1840 to a point where such cases were a rare exception.[62]

During the years following the changes in 1823 the distillery laws were adapted to the new emerging conditions, though in general these changes were made cautiously and lagged behind the need. The charge on the low wines, for instance, was a legacy of the days of the still licence duty. Like the attenuation charge it was really a reserve or presumptive charge, but it was not easy to assess accurately. Low wines coming from the wash still vary in strength and composition during the process, fusel oils being greater in the early stages, for example, and unless the low wines receiver is thoroughly roused before drawing the test sample a false reading results. In any case there would be some loss in the final distillation. An allowance of 5 per cent was given in the 1823 Act for such errors that could well lead to apparent losses. There is no information whether the low wines charge was ever

62. *Excise Revenue Inquiry, 7th Report, Part I*, 1834, *op. cit.*, p. 383. The excise collector, Lisburn, said that 2 patent stills by St. Marc were working in Belfast in 1833, but the common patent still used in Ireland was the Coffey, patented in 1830 (A. J. V. Underwood, *Historical Development of Distilling Plant*, paper read to the Institute of Chemical Engineers on 22 February 1935, p. 28). The strength of the spirit from a Coffey still at this period was about 60 per cent over proof. With the modern Coffey still the strength is usually 66 per cent or higher. Blending with pot still whiskey to reduce costs is condemned in *Truths about Whiskey*, published by four Dublin distillers, 1878, pp. 36–7. The neutral spirit from patent stills is very suitable for rectifiers (see, for example, *28th Inland Revenue Report*, Parl. Pps. 1884–5 (c. 4474) xxii, p. 52). *Return of Licensed Distillers, 1851, op. cit.*, p. 269, shows 4 distilleries which had both pot and patent stills. The evidence of an improved excise administration is not direct, but the earlier allegations in parliament and elsewhere no longer appeared. In the *Belfast Historical Records, op. cit.*, Book 5, p. 177, the collector reported in 1848 that 'the excise surveying department had in great measure been purged of unworthy officer's. See also *13th Inland Revenue Report*, 1870, *op. cit.*, p. 339.

levied, but the advent of the patent still made this charge redundant for this kind of still, as in this case wash entered the still and pure spirit emerged. There were no low wines. Nevertheless this charge remained in the distillery laws until finally abolished in the United Kingdom in 1945. This was official caution in the extreme. It still operates in the Republic of Ireland.[63]

A partial revision of the distillery laws enacted in 1853 dealt with the spirit receiver and spirit store. It seems that some distillers were using receivers that were wide and shallow, so much so that a proper gauge of the spirit in them was not possible if they were not filled. Such a receiver could contain a considerable quantity of spirit in the drip, or fall to the outlet, without completely covering the base and in the last runnings towards the end of a distilling period this situation could easily arise. It was therefore decreed that receivers must be filled to a depth of fifteen inches, sufficient to admit a proper gauge in the centre. Distillers who had such shallow receivers were permitted to continue using them till they could be replaced, so they were relieved of immediate expense.[64] Distillers also had to fix an approved apparatus to receivers which prevented the inlet and discharge cocks from being open at the same time and which also recorded each turning of a cock. This apparatus, called an indicator, was developed from experiments in 1821.[65]

In the eighteenth and early nineteenth centuries most distillers had a room or building set aside to store their casks of spirits and despatched casks from this stock to customers with covering permits issued by the gauger certifying that duty had been paid. In 1805 a spirit store was made compulsory and all the distiller's spirit had to be channelled through it in order to stop illegal

63. 4 Geo. 4, c. 94, section 57 permits the 5 per cent allowance. In England under 6 Geo. 4, c. 80, the allowance was only 3 per cent. The difficulties of getting a true specific gravity of low wines is stated in evidence in the *Excise Revenue Inquiry, 7th Report, Part I,* 1834, *op. cit.,* p. 285. In 1880 the low wines charge was dispensed with in cases where the distiller was able to run them into a charger also receiving feints (*Highmore's Excise Laws,* 3rd ed. H.M.S.O. 1923, i, p. 518, note). The charge was finally abolished in the United Kingdom by 9 and 10 Geo. 6, c. 13.

64. 16 and 17 Vict., c. 37, sections 5 and 6.

65. *Ibid.,* section 32. The first attempt to develop this apparatus is described in *Experiments in Distilling by the Excise Department,* Parl. Pps. 1821 (538) xix, p. 369. The indicator was in use for the rest of the nineteenth century. It is fully described by J. Owens, *Plain Papers,* 1879, *op. cit.,* p. 287.

deliveries direct from the spirit receiver. By the middle of the nineteenth century when much larger stills were in use the revenue reasons for a spirit store still applied, but the store or some similar arrangement had become essential to the distiller. During a distilling period a very large receiver would be needed to take all the distilled spirit, but with a store containing large store casks or vats, a smaller receiver could be filled, the quantity and strength checked and the contents transferred to the store. The receiver could then be filled again. There would be a small disruption in the flow of manufacture since only one receiver was permitted, but this could be timed with the disposal of spent wash or some similar operation. In the spirit store, casks for delivery or storage in warehouse were racked from the vats. The Act of 1853 again made the spirit store compulsory, which was no hardship to distillers. It now had to be secured by revenue locks, no spirit was to be received except from the spirit receiver, and all the spirit had to be cleared from the store within six days of the end of the distilling period either by paying duty or by warehousing. An excise officer had to attend the store daily to make revenue checks, to issue permits, and generally supervise deliveries. The distiller, therefore, had a legal right to full attendance. He was no longer at the mercy of any laggard gauger. An important innovation was the recognition that there was usually some waste of spirit in these operations and a deduction not exceeding 1 per cent was allowed for any deficiency between the quantity assessed in the spirit receiver and the quantity delivered from the spirit store. In the same Act allowances of a similar nature were granted for natural waste during storage in warehouses. It had taken distillers a long time to get the government to grant any allowance for spirit which had obviously not gone into consumption.[66]

There was one other change worth noting. A method had

66. 45 Geo. 3, c. 104, section 27 made the spirit store compulsory in Ireland, but it was not under close revenue control. The spirit store regulations of 1853 are contained in 16 and 17 Vict., c. 37, sections 8, 9, 11–16. Section 28 granted the waste allowance in warehouse. At times an excess may arise in the spirit store and this was allowed up to $\frac{1}{2}$ per cent. No allowance was granted and a penalty incurred if the excess was more than $\frac{1}{2}$ per cent or the loss more than 3 per cent (section 17). J. Owens, _Plain Papers_, 1879, _op. cit.,_ p. 469, writes that these allowances reduced the number of attenuation charges levied which had formerly been numerous.

A section of the Irish Distillers' Still House in their Bow Street Distillery. These stills, large copper kettles, have an approximate total capacity of 20,000 gallons each.

Interior view of a Mash Tun or Kieve showing the rake machinery

been devised of ascertaining the quantity of spirit in a cask by reference to the net weight and strength and this was adopted. It is more accurate than gauging, convenient in use where there are proper weighing and filling facilities and is the normal method in modern distilleries. There was one small relaxation from the regulation requiring the spirit store to be cleared in six days. The distiller was allowed to keep a single duty paid cask to facilitate any immediate delivery to a customer which for any reason could not be made from his warehoused stock.[67] These measures which might be dismissed as mere detail are significant in the sense that they clearly indicate that distilleries were now large well-conducted enterprises run on factory lines and were far removed from the small distilleries forty years earlier which were primitive in comparison and which were not so very much better than the illicit distilleries in the mountainous bogland.

An Act in 1860 consolidated existing excise laws for all the spirit industry from distilling to retailing. It clarified and improved existing regulations, made some minor concessions and recognised changes in distilling practices. Chief amongst these changes was related to the patent still which now, after thirty years in use, was legally recognised and as no minimum capacity could be prescribed as for pot stills, this was fixed as an apparatus capable of distilling 200 gallons of wash an hour.[68] The limitations on the number of associated vessels was re-enacted, but a distiller could instal a second spirit receiver provided he fitted indicators and used the receivers alternately.[69] The construction of utensils, fittings and cocks, the positioning of pipelines and cocks and the

67. 16 and 17 Vict., c. 37, sections 11, 37 and sched. C. J. Owens, *Plain Papers,* 1879 *op. cit.,* p. 470 gives an account of attempts made from 1766 to devise a method of ascertaining the quantity of spirit by weighing. The Act of 1853 was based on tables constructed by J. Harrison in 1852 for spirits at 25 per cent and 11 per cent over proof for each degree of temperature. Improved tables were prepared in 1854 and again in 1874. See *13th Inland Revenue Report,* 1870, *op. cit.,* p. 223, concerning the duty paid cask in the spirit store and comments on weighing casks instead of gauging them when raising the excise duty charge. Experiments had shown that gauging was more often against the distiller.

68. 23 and 24 Vict., c. 114, section 8. This was a modest size for a patent still and was equated with the capabilities of a 40 gallon pot still though the apparatus, if properly worked, would produce considerably more spirit.

69. *Ibid.,* sections 14, 85. Section 20 provides that the Excise Commissioners may require an indicator to be fitted to receivers, which implies that some receivers were not so equipped.

I

course of brewing and distilling were all prescribed in some detail. The interval between the brewing and distilling periods was reduced to 4 hours. Brewing ended when all wash had been collected in the wash backs. After distilling began the low wines still had to be worked off within thirty-two hours after the last of the wash had been transferred from the wash backs and wash stills worked off within sixteen hours. All the spirit was to be sent to the spirit store which had to be cleared within ten days instead of six days, and before any spirit was received from the next distilling period.[70] The usual notices to the excise were to be given when receiving and using sugar and for brewing operations. The 102 sections applying specifically to distillers were closely related to normal distilling operations and gave distillers considerable room to develop their techniques and plant. They could, for example, use any size or shape of still provided it exceeded the minimum of 40 gallons; they could brew quickly or slowly and could set their brews at any gravity they wished provided this was declared. The successful distiller in the future no longer relied on questionable methods, but on the demand for his particular whiskey which in turn depended on astute buying of materials, skilful management and selling ability; in short, the normal basis of success for any manufactured product. The revolution of the industry begun in 1823, was completed so far as actual distilling was concerned, but there were still a number of improvements needed in the subsequent course of the spirits to the ultimate consumer.

So far distillery law had set out in much detail what vessels, materials and other such matters that a distiller should observe. These were rigid rules requiring an Act of parliament to change them. The discretion left to the excise authorities was extremely small. It might well be desirable to prohibit a government department from making its own rules, but carried to extremes, especially in technical matters, it is more likely to penalise the persons subject to the laws and compromise is necessary. This was the case with distilling where, for example, the law had been openly set aside to permit the use of patent stills. In 1866 a beginning was made to devolve technical details to the Board of Excise. They were given power to authorise any vessels, utensils

70. *Ibid.*, sections 15–31, 65, 97.

or other apparatus in a distillery in addition to, or in lieu of those permitted by the Act of 1860.[71] This trend of delegation became more marked with the passing of the Spirits Act in 1880 which governed distillery administration in the United Kingdom until 1952. The 1880 Act reduced the interval between brewing and distilling to two hours, but otherwise made little alteration to the consolidating Act in 1860. The phrasing was more precise and much of the detail relating to the number and construction of vessels was relegated to a schedule. The Act is easily understood and is a model in this respect, especially when it is compared with the distillery laws of former years. A saving clause gave the Board of Excise power to make any regulations to meet the purposes of the Act. Such regulations did not need parliamentary approval and could apply to the industry as a whole or to meet a particular case. They could, of course, be challenged on the grounds that they went outside the bounds of the Act, but in general any regulations made were aimed at easing a distiller's difficulties.[72]

Production

There were no legislative changes of any consequence affecting distilling after 1880. The distillery regulations of 1820 were described as 'so stringent and so ill-contrived as to prevent the licensed distiller from producing spirit equal in quality in comparison with those of the smuggler'.[73] The changes since then had been dramatic. Despite a reduction in the number of distilleries and a fall of about a third in population, the spirits distilled in 1900 were $3\frac{1}{2}$ times the quantity charged with duty in 1823. This comparison is not precise for the spirits distilled in 1823 are not known and the official figure relates to charges on still capacity. Also illicitly distilled spirit was a substantial factor. Neither of

71. 29 and 30 Vict., c. 64, section 7.

72. 43 and 44 Vict., c. 24. Section 159 contains the saving clause. Its use has been confined to meet difficulties in individual distilleries, and the local regulations are known as indulgences. These are not published. Section 8 made one change. The lower limit of a 40 gallon still in the 1860 Act was not re-enacted as distillery practice had made it redundant. A still could now be any size, but with conditions if less than 400 gallons. *Parl. Debates,* 21 June 1880, cols. 514–5. The Government stated that the Spirits Bill contained no changes in existing law.

73. *28th Inland Revenue Report,* Parl. Pps. 1884–5 (c. 4474) xii, p. 52.

these causes, however, alters the fact that in 1900, with fewer distilleries, production was very much greater. After 1823 the spirits distilled is the best measure of the state of the industry. The quantities charged with duty or the revenue yield do not take into account spirits warehoused or exported to Great Britain or to foreign parts, but they do include spirits made in Great Britain and imported into Ireland, warehoused and subsequently delivered for home consumption.[74]

In the following statistics the number of distilleries merely indicates the producing points and the decline is simply a concentration into larger units.[75]

Year	Distilleries	Proof gallons Distilled (Millions)
1823	40	3·0
1830	79	8·7
1840	86	7·3
1850	51	8·3
1860	35	7·4
1870	22	6·6
1880	28	11·1
1890	29	11·8
1900	30	14·5

74. 10 Edw. 7, c. 8, section 8 and 3rd Schedule raised the duty to 14s. 9d. The consumption and trade figures with Scotland are taken from *24th Inland Revenue Report*, Parl. Pps. 1881 (c. 2967) xxix, p. 267 and *43rd Report*, Parl. Pps. 1900 (Cd. 347) xviii, pp. 388–9. The large exports to Scotland were probably patent still spirits intended for blending.

75. The statistics are taken from the *Irish Revenue Inquiry, 5th Report, 1823, op. cit.*, pp. 255, 369; *13th Inland Revenue Report, 1870, op. cit.*, pp. 381, 431; *28th Report, 1884–5, op. cit.*, pp. 188, 211; *34th Report*, Parl. Pps. 1890–1 (c. 6537) xxvi, p. 313; *44th Report*, Parl. Pps. 1901 (Cd. 764) xviii, pp. 455, 459. A. Barnard, *Whisky Distilleries of the United Kingdom*, London, 1887, gives details of 28 Irish distilleries. See also the yearly editions of *Thom's Directory*.

The quantity shown for 1823 is that charged with duty. In that year the largest concentration was in Dublin with five stills of 500 gallons capacity. Cork had three of 500 gallons and one of 200 gallons capacity and Limerick had one still of 500 gallons. The industry had contracted to quite a small scale. By 1850 Dublin and Cork were still the main centres. In Dublin there were five stills, one a Coffey still, and an output of 2·4 million gallons. In Cork there were seven stills, two of them Coffey stills and one Shee still, with an output of 1·5 million proof gallons. Next in importance was Drogheda with five stills, four of them Coffey stills, and an output of 1·3 million gallons. Belfast was becoming important. In 1823 there was only one still of a mere 53 gallons capacity. In 1850 there were five stills, one a Coffey still, and an output of 789,000 gallons. So these four centres produced nearly six million gallons out of a total of 8·3 millions. The distribution of the remaining stills was fairly widespread among the sixteen excise collections.[76] The increase of distilling in Drogheda is remarkable. In 1823 there was only one still of 300 gallons capacity. In 1830 the proof gallons distilled were 355,000 and by 1850 the town was producing over 1¼ million gallons. No reasons are quoted, but the probable explanation was easy access to malt and barley from the surrounding country, direct coal imports and the nearby large Dublin market. The Drogheda distilleries were really competing with the giants in Dublin and as communications improved and grain was more easily transported, Drogheda became more vulnerable. By 1884 there were no distilleries in the town.[77] The distribution of the thirty distilleries in 1900 illustrates the influence of the vicinity of a seaport on their location. There were six in or near Belfast, four in the Cork district, seven in Dublin, three in Londonderry, two in or near Coleraine and one each in Galway, Limerick, Wexford and Dundalk. The remaining four, all small, were in counties Kildare, King's county, the

76. *Irish Revenue Inquiry, 5th Report,* 1823, *op. cit.,* p. 378. *Return of Licensed Distillers in each Collection,* Parl. Pps. 1851 (386) liii, p. 269. *Return of Spirits Distilled in each Collection.* Parl. Pps. 1851 (380) liii, p. 459.

77. *Irish Revenue Inquiry, 5th Report,* 1823, *op. cit.,* p. 378. *Accounts relating to Proof Spirits distilled,* Parl. Pps. 1840 (623) xliv, p. 432. *Return of Spirits Distilled in each Collection,* 1851, *op. cit.,* p. 459. A. Barnard, *The Whisky Distilleries of the United Kingdom, op. cit.* There was no later revival in Drogheda (see *Ham's Inland Revenue Year Book,* 1900, published by Effingham Wilson, London. Distilleries are indicated in the staff lists on pp. 317–26).

county of Londonderry and Westmeath. Clearly direct imports o
coal and convenience for exporting were major factors. Irisl
exports to England in 1900 were 4,271,134 proof gallons.[78]

There is very little information about the rate of growth in
the size of distilling plant after 1823, but it seems to have occurred
very quickly. Morewood in 1834 wrote that legal stills ranged
from 500 gallons capacity to 20,000 gallons and he specially refer
to the large establishments in Cork and Midleton; to Clonmel
where there was a wash still of 20,400 gallons and a low wine
still of 13,000 gallons; and to similar large stills in Limerick and
Dublin. In some cases there were not only large stills, but mor
than one each of wash and low wines stills in the same distillery
All this would have been unthinkable in 1823. Shaw's distiller
in Belfast was working a Coffey still producing 523,000 gallon
in 1842 and in addition there was in reserve a wash still of 9,46
gallons and two low wines stills of 6,147 and 5,563 gallons.[7]
Barnard toured round twenty-eight Irish distilleries in 1887 and
recorded details of the plant, output, materials used, number
employed and other items of interest. Dublin dominated th
industry with six distilleries having a total output of 5·7 millio
gallons. The largest, owned by George Roe and Company c
Thomas Street, covered seventeen acres and the output was nearl
two million gallons a year. The other five Dublin distilleries wer
also very large. John Jameson and Son had an output of a millio
gallons and had two wash stills each of 24,000 gallons conten
Power's distillery and William Jameson's distillery each had out
puts of approaching a million gallons. The remaining tw
distilleries were recent, one being a converted spinning mill, bi
their outputs were substantial. Belfast was the next largest centi
in 1887 with three distilleries producing over four millio
gallons, mainly from Coffey stills. The other main centre, Cork
had fallen in production behind Dublin and Belfast. There wer
four distilleries producing about two million gallons in the Co
excise collection which included Midleton and Bandon. Tl
largest, at Midleton, produced one million gallons from a pate

78. *44th Inland Revenue Report, op. cit.,* pp. 457, 459, and *Ham's Year Boo
Excise.*

79. S. Morewood, *Inebriating Liquors,* 1838, *op. cit.,* p. 677. *Belfast Histori
Records, op. cit.,* Book 6, p. 83. A report by the excise collector, Lisburn, dat
5 October 1843.

still, a wash still of 31,648 gallons and two low wines stills of 10,000 each. The smallest distilleries recorded were at Bushmills and Coleraine, each with an output of about 100,000 gallons a year and each with one wash still in the range 2,500 to 2,700 gallons and one low wines still of 1,500 gallons.[80]

This account written in 1887 is sufficient to show how great was the revolution in distilling following the abolition of the still licence system in 1823 and how penal and restrictive was that system. In fifty years the industry had changed beyond recognition and the stills of 1823 were mere toys in comparison. To enter this new industry needed considerable capital and normally by means of a limited company. Deliberate fraud by distillers so openly practised at the beginning of the century was now unlikely if only because of the reformed excise service. Petty frauds were always possible by those working in the distillery, but they were now checked by the distiller as well as the excise.[81]

The changes in the distillery laws in 1823 were not the only reason for the nineteenth century revolution in the industry. These changes coincided with great improvements in transport. The Grand Canal had been cut through from Dublin to the river Shannon and other canals had also opened up inland water transport. Railway systems were spreading and roads improved as the century progressed. Engineering and other techniques were developing which provided better distillery equipment. Distilling, now freed from laws inhibiting improvements, benefited like other industries. Wider domestic markets could be reached and raw materials obtained from larger areas without crippling transport costs. The advantages enjoyed by distilleries situated at ports were reduced. Thus one distiller in the 1880s chartered a ship to import his coal which was then brought to Tullamore via the Grand Canal. The effect of these improved facilities within

---

80. A. Barnard, *The Whisky Distilleries of the United Kingdom, op. cit.* This account, published by *Harper's Weekly Gazette*, sets out the facts of each distillery in numbered sections. Most of these distilleries no longer exist, but something of the 19th century atmosphere still remains in the malt floors and other places, and even some of the implements in use in those distilleries still functioning. Visitors to Power's distillery in Dublin, for example, will see the can-pit room much as it was a century ago and it is a feature of this distillery.

81. *Parl. Debates*, 6 March 1899, col. 1348. To discourage petty pilfering it was the practice to allow distillery workers 2 drams a day free of duty. This was not legal, but the Board of Inland Revenue ignored the practice.

the industry was similar to that in some other industries. Larger
scale production was stimulated resulting in reducing unit costs
and intensifying competition. Those distilleries unable to take full
advantage of these factors were either squeezed out of business or
taken over by limited companies which sometimes worked more
than one distillery, where a large capital could help to survive
temporary trade fluctuations. For example, distilleries in Cork
and Midleton lost their separate identities when merged in the
Cork Distilleries Company.[82]

It is not possible to assess with accuracy the effect of larger
distilling units on agriculture. The demand for grain would be
related to the total spirit produced whatever the number or size
of distilleries. Larger distilling companies would, however, be in
a stronger position to bargain for lower prices. Their scale of
production and better techniques would make better use of the
grain and to that extent demand would be reduced. Furthermore,
the demand for Irish grain is obscured by imports. There had
long been a considerable grain trade with England, particularly
through Dublin. In the north of Ireland there was a similar trade
with Scotland. Sometimes grain for distilling came from farther
afield. Thus in 1875 Comber distilleries were buying Danubian
barley. In the latter years of the century patent still distillers were
using rye, maize and occasionally rice in their grists. The use of
these cereals in patent still production grew considerably in the
latter half of the century following the repeal of the Corn Laws
in 1846 which made them cheaper. Maize and rye give a good
spirit yield, but impart undesirable flavours in pot still distillation.
The bulk of the pot distiller's grain would, however, come from
local agriculture. A perspective of the place of distilling in the
agricultural economy can be estimated by comparing the total
grain production with the grain equivalent of the spirits distilled.
A quarter of malt would produce sixteen proof gallons at the
official estimate that a bushel yielded two proof gallons. A mixed
grist, customary in Ireland, would produce slightly more, probably not less than seventeen proof gallons per quarter in the mid-

---

82. On roads and canals see G. O'Brien, *The Economic History of Ireland in the
18th Century,* Dublin, 1918, pp. 359–62, and C. Maxwell, *Country and Town under
the Georges,* Dundalk, 1949, pp. 283, 305–6. On railways see J. C. Conroy, *A
History of Railways in Ireland,* London, 1928. References to the distilleries are given
by A. Barnard, *Whisky Distilleries, op. cit.,* pp. 387, 405, 409.

nineteenth century and a greater quantity in later years as techniques improved. Johnston, in 1873, estimated a yield of nineteen or twenty proof gallons for a mixed grist. Owens in 1789 put the yield at twenty proof gallons. In the following table the spirit yield has been calculated at seventeen gallons per quarter of mixed grains in 1850 and twenty proof gallons in later years. In these later years there is also a reduction in the grain equivalent of 10 per cent in 1875 and 20 per cent in 1900 as a rough allowance for the use of imported grain.

Year	Distilleries	Proof Gallons	Grain Equivalent	Grain production		Percentage distilled
				Oats	Barley	
			,000 qtrs.	,000 qtrs.	,000 qtrs.	
1850	51	8,293,037	488	10,342	1,684	4·4
1875	27	9,674,004	435	8,204	1,210	4·6
1900	30	14,480,871	579	6,266	807	8·2

The figures for barley include bere and rye. Distilling and brewing would absorb most from the barley crops. Clearly distillers provided only a minor market for farmers. The latter did, of course, benefit by using spent grains for cheap cattle food.[83]

Warehousing

The introduction and evolution of the warehousing system ran parallel with the great changes in distilling. These changes to large scale production would not have been possible without warehousing duty free. The principal advantage to the distiller was that he had no capital locked up in the duty while his spirit was maturing and increasing in value. This advantage was considerably enhanced during the nineteenth century when

83. Northern Ireland Public Record Office, ref. D 1808/25/4. The Comber distillery record of the weekly prices of Danubian barley. Ref. D 1435/2–3 shows specific transactions in grain with Scotland and England by D. and R. Taylor, Londonderry in 1847. The estimated yields per quarter are given by W. H. Johnston, *Inland Revenue Officer's Manual*, London, 1873, p. 299, and J. Owens, *Plain Papers*, London, 1879, p. 463. The grain statistics are taken from *Thom's Directories*. The spirits distilled are given in a *Return of Spirits Distilled*, Parl. Pps. 1851 (380) liii, p. 455; the *28th Inland Revenue Report*, Parl. Pps. 1884–5 (c. 4474) xxii, p. 188; and the *44th Inland Revenue Report*, Parl. Pps. 1901 (Cd. 764) xviii, p. 459.

operations such as bottling in bond and duty free allowances for natural waste were authorised by law. Against these advantages he had to provide warehouses built to a specification approved by the excise in relation to security and convenience of supervision and he did not have access to his stocks unless an excise officer was present.

Duty free warehousing was first allowed in Ireland in 1804 when Irish spirits could be lodged in customs warehouses owned by the Crown and interest was charged during storage. In 1812 the excise provided warehouses at the ports and these replaced the storage in customs warehouses. This arrangement was useful to the authorities. It helped to control exports to Great Britain where the duties and drawbacks were different, but it was a marginal advantage to distillers who were hedged around with restrictive warehousing regulations, especially those which did not allow for any loss during storage and those fixing the strengths at which spirit could be stored.[84] The Act in 1823 assimilating the distillery laws of Scotland and Ireland repeated the main provisions of existing Irish law, that is, that spirits could be warehoused duty free in an excise warehouse in casks of 100 gallons or more and at a strength of either 25° or 11° over proof. A rent of 1d. a week for every forty gallons was charged, but the Crown assumed no liability for any loss, even by fire. Delivery for home use was allowed, but only in the original cask and paying duty on the quantity when warehoused. If exported to places other than Great Britain an allowance was made for any leakage, waste or accident.[85]

84. 44 Geo. 3, c. 104. The intention of this Act was to assist exports, but section 10 also permitted delivery for home use. See also 46 Geo. 3, c. 88, sections 102, 105; 52 Geo. 3, c. 30, section 1; 55 Geo. 3, c. 111, section 7; and 57 Geo. 3, c. 110, section 20. In 1833 a fire in the Dublin Custom House warehouses destroyed a lot of spirits and it required a vote of £68,000 by the House of Commons to compensate merchants (see Parl. Pps. 1835 (481) xxxviii, pp. 539 *et seq.*, and 1837 (312) xxxix, pp. 213-9).

85. 4 Geo. 4, c. 94, sections 66, 72-82. Government reports and accounts by other authorities may give rise to some doubt concerning the time when Irish warehousing of home-made spirits began. Thus the *13th Inland Revenue Report*, 1870, *op. cit.*, p. 219, and *Highmore's Excise Laws*, 3rd ed., London, 1923, i, p. 520 both state 1823. Other writers have followed this lead. The Act of 1804, is however, clear. In 1823, J. Jameson of Dublin had 1,500 to 1,600 puncheons in warehouse (*Irish Revenue Inquiry, 5th Report, Supplement*, Parl. Pps. 1823 (498) vii, p. 688). The law of 1823 simply extended the Irish warehousing system to Scotland.

Two years later the English distillery Act included clauses applying to Irish distillers. Irish distillers were permitted to erect warehouses in distillery premises to a prescribed specification and subject to elaborate rules relating to locks, keys and general security. The warehouses were to be entered with the excise and were intended to store spirits for export to Great Britain. When exported either the full English duty had to be paid or the distiller paid the Irish duty and gave a bond to cover the residue of the English duty, to be paid on arrival in Great Britain.[86] Distillers in country towns would find this extension of warehousing a convenience, but would have to erect warehouses and, if exporting spirit, would still have to transfer their spirits to Crown warehouses at the ports. In places like Dublin the distillers had the option of building warehouses or using the Crown warehouses and paying rent. At that time, 1825, there were no public warehouses owned and managed by private persons or companies in Ireland so there was no alternative to the Crown warehouse or the distiller's own warehouse.[87]

The warehousing laws enacted in 1823 did not materially relax the various irksome regulations of earlier years. The distiller still had to warehouse his spirits at prescribed strengths and got no allowance for loss during storage, which was a serious hardship. Another irritating rule still required two days notice before depositing spirits in a warehouse and again when exporting them. These and other regulations were severely criticised by witnesses before a parliamentary inquiry in 1834. The critics even included senior excise officials. Thus Daniel Logie, a surveyor-general, pointed out that fixing prescribed strengths for warehousing spirits was an impossible provision. However near this strength spirits may be when deposited, during storage there were bound

86. 6 Geo. 4, c. 80, sections 82, 93–4. There was a flaw in these rules for paying duty in England. It seems that if any duty was paid in Ireland the spirits were committed for direct home consumption and could not be sent to an English warehouse (*Belfast Historical Records, op. cit.,* Book 5, p. 185, excise collector's report on his refusal to accept the Irish duty on a consignment exported from a Belfast warehouse to a warehouse in Liverpool).

87. *S.C. to inquire into the Regulations in the Customs and Import and Export Department of the Excise. The Warehousing system, 10th Report,* Parl. Pps. 1821 (25) x, p. 334. The committee reported that unlike Great Britain the construction of docks and warehouses in Ireland was undertaken by the Revenue. Apparently there was difficulty in getting corporations or companies to undertake this work.

to be losses from evaporation, absorption in the wood of the cask and perhaps a drop in strength due to absorption of moisture if the storage was damp. There was also the possibility of unavoidable leakage from, for example, a faulty stave, a loss that might be aggravated by the limited opportunities for a distiller to inspect his stock. Logie pointed out that the revenue checks on every cask should be sufficient to stop or discover abstraction, that official accounts were kept in terms of proof spirit and not in quantities at 25° or 11° over proof and that it was an unnecessary hardship to disallow genuine losses. The distiller was also permitted to deliver spirits at 10° under proof, no doubt a useful privilege in England, but at that time such spirit would be unsaleable in Ireland. Comparison was made with the treatment given to imported spirits where the duty was charged on the quantity delivered, any natural losses being written off. Furthermore, if imported spirit was to be delivered, an hour's notice sufficed instead of two days. It seems, however, that the law was not always observed in practice and two days was not insisted upon for home made spirits.[88] Another comparison with imports concerned the size of casks. Rum and brandy could be warehoused in casks of not less than twenty gallons instead of the minimum of eighty gallons for home made spirits. One distiller wanted to install vats to store his spirits, but this got no farther than a suggestion. In Dublin, there was a curious situation for it seems that at first no distiller's warehouses were approved. They were forced to use the Crown warehouse at the Custom House at a rent they considered excessive. These distillers complained that country distillers could store up to four or five years to mature their spirit at a fraction of the cost. Eventually the Treasury allowed distiller's warehouses in Dublin.[89]

The Board of Excise replied to all these criticisms. They defended the two days notice on the grounds that this time was necessary for a distiller to obtain full details of strengths, quantities and so on, and to mark his casks. It also enabled the warehouse keeper in the Crown warehouse and the excise officer to arrange

88. *Excise Revenue Inquiry, 7th Report, Part I,* 1834, *op. cit.,* pp. 121, 128, 179, 186. Deficiencies from natural causes were allowed for foreign spirits by 2 and 3 Will. 4, c. 84, sections 44–5.

89. *Ibid.,* pp. 179, 266, 455. The minimum size of cask was reduced from 100 gallons to 80 gallons by 7 Geo. 4, c. 49, section 7.

their business to suit receipts or deliveries from the warehouse. They did agree, however, that the notice time for exports could be shortened and this concession would make it easier for the distiller to arrange shipments. On the really important complaint that duty was charged on the warehoused quantity, making no allowance for loss, the Board said that English distillers did not have the right to warehouse and must pay duty on the spirit made. If losses were allowed to Irish and Scottish distillers they would have an unfair advantage. The point was also made that English distillers paid a much higher duty. These arguments were very weak and disclose excessive caution amounting to obstruction to any change. No mention was made that the case of English distillers was very different. They did not want warehousing, and were actually opposed to it. They delivered direct to rectifiers and there was no question of maturing. Also if Irish or Scotch whiskey did go to England the English duty was charged. On the point of warehousing at fixed strengths, the Board said that this was made law on the distillers' request to prevent disputes with warehouse keepers and others if a variety of strengths were allowed, but they did not produce evidence of this request. It may have been made before 1823 when strength had no bearing on the spirit duty. The complaint appears to have arisen from the practice, not sanctioned by law, of returning spirits from a warehouse to the distillery before delivery to a customer in order to adjust the strength by adding stronger spirit or by dilution. Stocks were debited and credited at actual strengths instead of the fixed strengths and thus giving rise to apparent stock discrepancies. It might be expected that a new system such as warehousing would, at first, have some unforeseen difficulties, but those described were so obvious that it should never have taken so long to put them right. As the century progressed these complaints disappeared with various amending Acts.[90]

Distillers, spirit dealers and others had long kept duty paid stocks in stores convenient to their markets and some private persons had built up businesses by storing such spirits on behalf of one or more distillers. Thus in 1848 there were twenty-two such stores in Belfast. Six of them served the needs of anyone wishing to use them and the others were reserved solely for

90. *Excise Revenue Inquiry, 7th Report, Part I,* 1834, p. 188.

particular distillers.[91] In that year the law sanctioned public warehouses for storing spirits in bond where a distiller so desiring could deposit his spirits till he intended to sell them, and suitable existing stores were bonded. Thus a country distiller could send his spirit to a public bond in Dublin. The warehouse proprietor had to give bond for the security of duty on all spirits deposited and was responsible to the distiller for their safety. The spirits were to be deposited in the name of the distiller, but he was allowed to sell his spirits in bond and the transfer of ownership did not necessarily mean delivery. This opened up a new trade of buying and selling in bond, a feature of the spirit trade ever since. Losses through accident while in bond could be remitted. Removal from one bonded warehouse to another was allowed in 1860 to any part of the United Kingdom and to either another excise or a customs warehouse, and could be made in twenty gallon casks. There were no limitations on the strength of plain spirits deposited, but limits of an elastic nature were retained for rectified or compounded spirits. There were severe penalties for fraudulently altering the quality, quantity or strength of spirits in warehouses.[92] Thus many of the complaints made in 1834 by distillers and resisted by the Board of Excise had been met.

The principal complaint had always been that there was no allowance for natural waste during storage and, despite the objections of the Board of Excise to granting some allowance, this was a genuine hardship accentuated by each increase in the rate of duty. During prolonged storage such losses could be

91. *Belfast Historical Records, op. cit.,* Book 5, pp. 191–2. The Lisburn collector reported that 13 of the 22 warehouses in Belfast, which were small, were suitable for general warehouses. These warehouses had been in existence when the Distillery Act of 1823 was passed and there was a vested interest till occupation ceased. Many of them received spirit from some particular distillery. The collector also reported that these warehouses barely met the city's needs. He suggested that the proposed new building to house the Customs, Excise and Post Office should incorporate a basement designed for warehousing. The present custom house shows that this was done. The report, dated 22 October 1848, was preparatory to the approval of general bonded warehouses. The custom house was erected a year later.

92. 11 and 12 Vict., c. 122, sections 3–6, 15–16, 24. Section 1 extended warehousing facilities to distillers in England. Removals between distillery warehouses was not allowed and in 1860 transfer to a buyer of spirits stored in a distiller's warehouse was restricted to one transaction only by 23 and 24 Vict. c. 114, section 106.

considerable, for example, an unavoidable loss of 10 per cent might arise in a large cask over two years in warehouse depending on the kind of storage, whether damp or dry, due to absorption of moisture, or evaporation, or a faulty cask. Such spirit patently never went into consumption. From the time of the 1848 Act this grievance was frequently brought up in parliament by Irish members, particularly by Lord Naas. Their main argument rested on the favourable treatment accorded to imported spirits in customs warehouses where such losses were allowed. Both home-made and imported spirits were subjected to the same security rules in bonded warehouses and there was no obvious reason for different treatment which amounted to discrimination against the domestic product. The Chancellor of the Exchequer, no doubt briefed by the Board of Excise, gave reasons. He favoured 'charging the home spirit duty at the worm's end' to make fraud more difficult. He argued that the customs duty on imported spirit was on an entirely different basis to the excise. The duty was charged in the customs at the last possible moment before consumption and also encouraged importers to make the United Kingdom a depot for re-exports. The excise, he said, was levied at the earliest time so that excise supervision terminated, and to allow losses in warehouse would leave the excise revenue wide open to fraud.[93] These were very weak arguments and easily demolished. For one of his reasons, the termination of excise control, he must have overlooked all the controls by permits and surveys right up to the moment that the spirit was sold to a person about to drink it. In 1850 another attempt was made to get these allowances. Lord Naas made the point that 'the allowances for decreases would doubtless greatly encourage and increase the practice of bonding, which is admitted the greatest possible safeguard to the revenue'. The spirits, he said, mature in bond and a better product is marketed. Allowances were granted when home-made spirit was exported which exposed the weakness of arguments against a general remission, but the

93. *Parl. Debates,* 28 August 1848, cols. 591–3. In Col. 593, Irish distillers were quoted as asking for the same treatment then given to imported foreign spirits and the allowances granted to importers by 8 and 9 Vict., c. 91, section 22. 6 Geo. 4, c. 112, section 30, permitted various operations in bond on imported spirits and section 38 granted allowances for waste for imported spirits. *Ham's Year Book,* 1925, *op. cit.,* warehousing section, p. 88, states that the officer may allow up to 10 per cent deficiency on a large cask stored for 2 years.

spirit trade alleged that even in this case the allowance was a sham since the distiller had to declare his intention to export when he warehoused his spirit and was thus deprived of any opportunity to sell such spirit in the home market.[94]

The distiller's case was up against the usual opposition of temperance advocates who lost no chance to obstruct any leniency to the spirit trade and, also, West Indian interests who did not want to lose their advantages with rum which in any case was losing public favour. The Irish members persisted and got some support from Scottish members whose distillers were similarly placed, and even conceded their case so far as to be willing to pay duty on losses between the worm's end of the still and the warehouse, but not when stored in a warehouse under the Queen's seal.[95] Eventually the long fight to correct so obvious an anomaly ended in 1853 when a Distillery Act provided for a scale of allowances for deficiencies in warehouse due to natural causes and related to the time of storage. The scale was not adequate, but the principle was recognised. The scale itself, for every 100 proof gallons, ranged from $\frac{1}{4}$ gallon up to seven days' storage to $2\frac{3}{4}$ gallons for a year and $\frac{3}{4}$ gallon for every six months thereafter up to five years, after that there was no further allowance.[96] The scale of allowances was revised in 1860 at approximately the same rates, but was extended to ten years. These were fixed scales and went a good way towards meeting legitimate grievances, but it was found that they did not meet all the various causes of loss. Apart from natural waste there were losses from such causes as porous wood or a cracked stave or slack hoops where an excise officer could be reasonably satisfied that the spirit was genuinely lost. Accordingly in 1864 it was enacted that duty was to be paid on the delivered quantity provided there was no improper deficiency. It was left to the excise department to draw up its own rules and since that time deficiencies within regulated limits have been allowed locally

---

94. *Parl. Debates*, 6 May 1850, cols. 604–7. In the *Belfast Historical Records, op. cit.*, Book 137, pp. 168–9, an order dated 11 January 1843 discloses an extraordinary regulation that required the English spirit duty to be paid on any deficiency arising in an Irish warehouse on spirits being despatched to England for export abroad.

95. *Parl. Debates*, 11 June 1850, cols. 1088–91, 1093–4.

96. 16 and 17 Vict., c. 37, section 28. On the competition from rum see *Parl. Debates*, 6 May 1850, col. 611.

and if beyond these limits the case has been decided by the Excise Board.[97]

By the middle of the century warehousing spirits was no longer merely a relief to the distiller by way of deferring the duty, it was rapidly becoming an important feature of the spirit industry. Permission to remove spirits under bond from one warehouse to another in any part of the United Kingdom, to move them between excise and customs warehouses and, in 1864, to permit delivery to the home market, and to allow sales while in warehouse, had all helped to change the whole marketing system. One consequence was pressure on the Government to enable the owners of spirits in warehouse, whether distillers or factors, to extend warehousing facilities to include operations on spirits to prepare them for the ultimate market, the sales to the dealer and retailer. The most desired operation was bottling and in 1864 this was allowed for spirits being exported or for use as ships' stores and involved the related operations of racking casks, reducing the strength, vatting and blending. An allowance for loss in vatting granted in 1860 was raised to 1 per cent and there was also an allowance of 2d. a gallon when actually exported.[98] Three years later home-made spirits could be bottled in warehouse for the home market and a deficiency up to 2 per cent allowed for losses arising in the operation. A minimum delivery of five dozen quart bottles was fixed.[99] Whiskey could now be made, warehoused, prepared for the market and sold to others before any payment of the duty. It could be transferred to any part of the United Kingdom or exported. So the owner of the spirit was able to defer paying duty until he had found his best market and then only paid on the quantity delivered to the home market.

So far as the spirit trade was concerned the warehousing system had, by 1880, met all their main trading needs. There were,

97. 23 and 24 Vict., c. 114, section 132 and 27 and 28 Vict., c. 12 sections 7–8. The rules for granting allowances locally, called ordinary and special allowances, are set out in the annual editions of *Ham's Inland Revenue Year Book*. See, for example, the 1900 edition, warehousing section pp. 86–7.

98. Unfettered removals were allowed by 27 and 28 Vict., c. 12, section 11. Sections 1–4, 6, 12, permitted bottling, vatting and export allowances.

99. 30 and 31 Vict., c. 27. The various Acts dealing with operations in warehouses, sales, stowage and related regulations were consolidated by 43 and 44 Vict., c. 24, sections 64 *et seq.*

however, internal stresses in the excise and customs departments, particularly the latter, in assimilating their rules and methods. A Treasury committee was set up to deal with these problems, and although a uniform system did evolve, it was not without considerable debate in parliament obviously inspired by officials who were adversely affected.[100] Reformers also attempted, unsuccessfully, to make use of the warehousing system and on at least three occasions private Bills were introduced to compel distillers to retain spirits in bond for a minimum of twelve months and thus ensure the marketing of a more mature spirit.[101] Irish distillers complained about the use of blending facilities in warehouses that enabled factors to buy Irish whiskey and then blend it with Scotch or with the neutral spirit from patent stills and market the blend as Irish thus, as they alleged, undermining the reputation of their product. The complaint was debated at length in the House of Commons in 1874 and 1876, but apart from the excise refusing to associate themselves with the label on the blend, it is not easy to see how the Government could, at the time, do anything effective short of an Act on the lines of the Merchandise Marks Acts of later years. Prohibiting blending in warehouse would not stop blending after duty was paid.[102]

There is very little information to establish how much use was made of the warehousing system by Irish distillers. There is a return to parliament in 1851 which does give precise information for the year ending on 5 January 1851, but all other figures in

100. *Parl. Debates*, 23 August 1881, col. 728; 6 March 1882, col. 178; 15 March 1882, col. 661. There were also other occasions.

101. *Ibid.*, 2 July 1879, cols. 1209 *et seq*. The Bill was introduced by an Irish member who alleged that excessive fusel oils in raw spirit caused violence in drunkards. In cols. 1225–6 the Government opposed the Bill giving one curious reason that such a measure would tie their hands should they wish to abolish spirit duties in the future. There were other weak reasons given as well. Other attempts were made on 10 May 1882 and 16 February 1883. In both cases the Bills were withdrawn. Perhaps the only real reason was the extra cost of excise supervision. In 1915 the Immature Spirits (Restriction) Act, 5 and 6 Geo. 5, c. 46 was passed under the pressure of war conditions. It required spirits to remain in bond for 3 years before delivery for home consumption and is still in force.

102. *Parl. Debates*, 26 June 1874, cols. 598–600; 4 April 1876, cols. 1185 *et seq*. In cols. 1189–91 Scottish members wanted to continue blending. The Scottish distillers were said to be marketing the blends as Irish whiskey. See also *Truth about Whiskey*, Dublin, 1878, published by John Jameson and Son and three other Dublin distilling firms.

the inland revenue records quote spirits in bond in excise warehouses and would include all spirits. Thus the figures for Ireland would include both whiskey and rectified spirits from all sources in the United Kingdom and spirits from overseas. The great use of the system can be inferred, however, from the large quantities in bond compared with the quantities produced in each year. In the 1851 return a few of the figures for the major distilling areas in 1850 are sufficient to show that warehousing was an important feature of the trade even before operations and allowances for loss in warehouse were granted. In Dublin, 266,000 proof gallons were charged duty at the still and 2,131,000 gallons bonded. In Cork, 290,000 gallons were charged and 1,223,000 gallons bonded. In Belfast, 223,000 gallons were charged and 566,000 gallons bonded. The proportions of gallons charged to gallons bonded were of this order for the other 14 excise collections.[103] In 1880 there were 20,781,000 proof gallons in bond in Ireland and in the same year duty was paid on 7,262,000 gallons of which 5,184,000 were retained for consumption in the country. The corresponding figures for bonded spirits in England were 7,288,000 gallons and in Scotland 18,832,000 gallons. By 1900 the quantities in bond in the United Kingdom amounted to 157 million proof gallons, so much in excess of annual consumption as to show that large stocks of spirit had been built up over previous years.[104] The development of the warehousing system for spirits was complete by 1880 and thereafter only minor changes occurred. In 1900 a large and thriving distilling

103. *Return of Spirits distilled in each Collection in Ireland.* Parl. Pps. 1881 (380) liii, p. 459.

104. *24th Inland Revenue Report,* Parl. Pps. 1881 (c. 2967) xxix, pp. 185, 267. On p. 185 the Excise Board report that 'the production of spirit has for several years been largely in excess of the consumption within the year'. The *44th Report,* Parl. Pps. 1901 (Cd. 764) xviii, p. 456 gives the quantities for 1900. The *28th Report,* 1884–5, *op. cit.,* p. 188, shows the growth of warehousing in Ireland over fifteen years (in millions of gallons):

	Distilled	Warehoused
1870	6·6	8·5
1875	9·7	14·6
1880	11·1	20·8
1885	9·3	20·0

The warehoused quantities are cumulative excesses and include imports from Great Britain. *Ham's Inland Revenue Year Book, op. cit.,* for 1900 warehousing section pp. 3–69 lists 144 wine and spirit warehouses in Ireland, 40 of them under customs supervision.

industry was in being and after the changes in 1823 it would be impossible to select any more important factor than warehousing duty free in bringing the industry to this flourishing position.

The cost of producing whiskey naturally varied according to grain prices. In 1834 some distillers said that costs without the duty were between about 2s. 1d. and 3s. 4d. a proof gallon and an excise inquiry in 1847 showed, for example, the cost of grain whiskey at 1s. 6d. when barley was 30s. a quarter and malt whiskey at 2s. 10d. when malt was 54s. a quarter.[105] These costs may have risen towards the end of the century, but it is unlikely that this would be substantial and it can fairly be stated that the duty of 10s. represented between three and four times the cost of production. Without duty free warehousing, therefore, distillers would either have to face crippling costs if they made for stock or, to keep the outlay on duty to a minimum, would have to distil only to firm orders from customers. The former, besides needing large capital would certainly have enhanced the price, while the latter would have meant uneven or perhaps spasmodic production, much uncertainty, large scale production would be difficult if not impossible and again a probable increase in price. With warehousing the distiller could sell in the home or export market or for ships' stores and there would be no outlay in duty unless he sold for home consumption. He could, for example, sell in bond to factors, dealers or merchants who made their own blends and this market has become very important. So also has the victualling of ships in the large ports.[106]

105. *Excise Revenue Inquiry, 7th Report, Part I, 1834, op. cit.,* pp. 440, 443. The costs were stated in terms of spirit at 25 per cent over proof and have been converted to costs at proof. There were other quotations within the range of 2s. 1d. to 3s. 4d. *Report from the Board of Excise to the Treasury on the use of barley, malt . . . in Distilleries,* Parl. Pps. 1847 (26) lix, p. 341. The investigation was into the comparative values of using various materials in brewing and distilling. Whiskey prices quoted earlier were about the same as in 1834; for example, *Northern Whig,* 13 September 1827, quotes Belfast distilled whiskey in bond at 3s. 6d. the imperial gallon. This also indicates the growing commerce of buying and selling in bond. Allowances must be made for the cost of storage, the increase in value of matured spirit and distillers' profits.

106. John Jameson and Son and other distillers, *Truth about Whiskey,* Dublin 1878, *op. cit.,* pp. 10, 41–3. Examples are given of blending Irish and Scotch spirits in bond to the detriment of Irish whiskey. See also *Parl. Debates,* 4 April 1876, cols. 1185 *et seq.* The ships' store trade is facilitated because a merchant can warehouse a large quantity duty free and draw off small quantities as required to victual ships.

With the setting up of general bonded warehouses in 1848 these advantages enjoyed by distillers were extended to all spirit merchants. There was, of course, the disadvantage that the distiller had to erect soundly built and well secured warehouses and the blender had to pay rent for the use of a general warehouse which was usually owned by another person or company. All bottling or other operations were closely controlled by the excise and there was no access to the building for receiving, operating on, or delivering spirits except during the hours when the officer was present.[107] To some extent this disadvantage would be offset by lower insurance costs, for premiums would now normally be based on duty free values. The disadvantages of warehousing to the distiller or merchant are not, therefore, serious and certainly the system does open the wholesale trade to persons of limited capital. Another advantage, coming from an unexpected quarter, is the excise supervision during warehousing hours. With so tempting a product as whiskey, pilfering is an ever present danger and excise accounting and controls do act as a check. Excise physical stock checks, insistence on proper stowage in strongly built secure structures may give the warehouse keeper some trouble and expense, but these official demands should fit into any efficiently run business.

Consumers of spirits, whether as a beverage or for further manufacture, should benefit from bonded warehousing for besides enabling distillers to keep prices lower they can also stabilise them. They can lay in large stocks, let them mature and by releasing them judiciously they can damp down price fluctuations. The use of general warehouses by any spirit merchant is a sufficient check to prevent any group of distillers imposing a complete monopoly, though of course if sufficiently powerful such a group would have a strong market influence. In any case there are always the competing claims of imports.

So far as the government is concerned the system has one very important advantage. The duty can be raised without causing any major upheaval in distilleries because the duty is charged at the

107. In large centres attendance would be the normal week-day working hours, but in a small country warehouse it would probably be on set days at fixed hours as became the rule later. In a general warehouse the warehouse keeper was responsible to the revenue for the duty and his liability to the owner of the spirits would be a matter of private treaty.

rate in force when the spirit leaves the warehouse for home consumption and not when it is deposited. This was important when the duty was raised to 10s. in 1860, but it became much more important in later years when the basic spirit duty eventually soared to nearly £14 a proof gallon.[108]

The warehouse has become the outlet to the market for almost all spirit, only a very small quantity going direct from the distillery store before 1915 and none since then being delivered for drinking. With large bonded stocks any threatened budgetary changes could give rise to undesirable practices. If a fall in the rate was anticipated the market could be starved. If there were any hint of a rise heavy deliveries could result, distorting the market and upsetting the even flow of the revenue. Forestalling did not necessarily affect distilling, it merely emptied the warehouses. The excise authorities drew attention to this from time to time, but nothing was done to check forestalling till 1915.[109] The government must, of course, bear some additional costs for the staff and equipment needed to supervise warehouses and cannot recover the duty on legitimate losses in bond. All this would not arise without a warehousing system, but apart from the broader aspects of encouraging industry, the expense of attempting to control and collect duty at the still had already proved far greater and very difficult. Moreover the bonded warehouse made possible later laws for ensuring that only matured or rectified spirit was delivered for home consumption. This in its turn made distillers look to markets at least three years ahead of the present.[110]

108. In the 1921 budget the spirit duty was raised to 72s. 6d. a proof gallon. By successive increases following the war of 1939–45 the duty rose in 1969 to £13 9s. 9d. a proof gallon. In the *28th Inland Revenue Report*, 1884–5, *op. cit.*, p. 57, the Board of Excise call attention to the immense importance of the warehousing system if there is any rise in the rate of duty.

109. *Ibid.*, p. 57. The Board estimated the stocks in the United Kingdom warehouses as equal to two years consumption and they reported that if there was any suspicion of a rise in the duty there would be considerable forestalling and a large drop in revenue until these excess stocks were exhausted. In 1915 under 5 and 6 Geo. 5, c. 89, section 15, the Treasury were given power to authorise the revenue authorities to restrict the delivery of goods for home use for a specified period before a budget, but not exceeding three months. See *13th Inland Revenue Report*, 1870, *op. cit.*, p. 223, where it reports huge forestalling in 1860.

110. The Immature Spirits (Restriction) Act, 1915, 5 and 6 Geo. 5, c. 46. The restriction was confined to plain spirits intended as a beverage.

Rectifiers and Compounders

The Act of 1823 excluded rectifiers and compounders from its provisions and they continued under the legislation of 1797 to 1807. They bought their spirits duty paid from distillers, re-distilled the spirits with a variety of ingredients, or added flavouring essences or syrups depending on the beverage required, or made spirits of wine. Until 1828 rectifiers and compounders were regarded as separate trades. A rectifier could not compound or hold stocks of compounded spirits and a compounder was similarly placed in respect of rectified spirits. The rectifier's province was making unsweetened beverages, such as imitation brandy and gin, or making spirits of wine for which there was a growing demand as a solvent for medicines, tinctures, and some industrial uses such as hat making and varnishes. His still had to be in the range of 80 to 200 gallons content. A compounder distilled and compounded spirits with sugar or other sweetening ingredients and also added flavouring and colouring and his still was smaller. A licence duty of 10s. for each gallon of still content was fixed in 1807 for both rectifiers and compounders.[111] In 1825 the law relating to rectifiers and compounders in England was revised and the distinction between them removed. They were required to possess a still of not less than 120 gallons and to get a licence costing £10. There were the usual regulations governing the working of stills, some being partly dismantled when silent and in general repeating the regulations in force in Ireland in previous years. All flavoured spirits were defined as British compounds, and were to be sent out at 17° under proof in quantities of not less than two gallons. A rectifier's premises could easily become a channel for distillers to dispose of illegally made spirits so the law prescribed that no customer was to receive more than one cask in one day. It seems a curious regulation because it did not prevent a customer going to more than one rectifier or using his friends to order for him. If the emphasis of this control was in the rectifying house it threw a lot of responsibility on the

---

111. 47 Geo. 3, sess. 2, c. 19, sections 3–6. *Excise Revenue Inquiry, 7th Report, Part I*, 1834, pp. 254, 261. Industrial uses included hat making and varnishes, but because of the duty some varnish makers were using naphtha, an impure methyl alcohol. The licence duty of 10s. a gallon of still content imposed in 1807 by 47 Geo. 3, sess. 2, c. 19, was so heavy relative to output as to be almost a guarantee that fraud would follow.

excise gauger to keep watch at all times as well as regular and accurate stocktaking.

In 1828 the laws relating to rectifiers and compounders in Ireland were repealed and they became subject to the laws in England. Irish rectifiers had complained that a delivery strength of 17° under proof made many of their products unsaleable in Ireland and the strength was raised to 7° over proof. They were still not satisfied and said that they were handicapped when competing with whiskey which a distiller could send out at 25° over proof. While there seems no good reason for this restriction there was not much substance in the complaint for it is doubtful if even the drinking habits of the time would cause many persons to drink undiluted whiskey at 25° over proof.[112] Spirits of wine was treated specially. It had to be stored separately from all other products and delivery per day to any one customer restricted to one permit for one cask not exceeding 100 gallons.[113] These restrictions on strength were relaxed in 1855 when rectifiers were allowed to send out their compounds at any strength that spirit could be sold by a distiller, though in later years there was a limitation of 11° over proof if compounds were deposited in warehouse for the home market.[114]

As in the case of whiskey, warehousing was a facility of great importance to rectifiers. They bought their spirit duty paid, made it into various compounds and they could then deposit the compounds in a bonded warehouse and get drawback of the duty. They got no compensation for spirits lost during manufacture. They could, however, take their finished product out of warehouse duty free for export or use as ships' stores or send them out for home consumption on paying duty. The warehousing rules for compounds evolved in much the same way as for whiskey. At first the compounds were only deposited in excise warehouses, then unsweetened compounds could be deposited in

112. 6 Geo. 4, c. 80, sections 103–13, 127; 6 Geo. 4, c. 81, section 2. 9 Geo. 4, c. 45, repealed previous Acts and applied the English laws to Ireland. See also the *Excise Revenue Inquiry, 7th Report, Part I,* 1834, *op. cit.,* p. 202, and *Belfast Historical Records, op. cit.,* Book 133, p. 112, where an order from Dublin on 4 May 1829 directed that rectifiers may send out spirits at any strength not exceeding 7° over proof. The licence duty was raised to £10 10s. by 3 and 4 Vict., c. 17, and again to £15 15s. in 1910 by 10 Edw. 7 and 1 Geo. 5, c. 8, section 43. The limitations on quantities delivered was imposed by 6 Geo. 4, c. 80, section 114.

113. 6 Geo. 4, c. 80, sections 114, 125, 127.

114. 18 and 19 Vict., c. 94, section 34; 41 and 42 Vict., c. 15, section 24.

customs warehouses and so by stages till by 1865 all compounds could be stored in customs or excise warehouses for export, ships' stores or home use and could be transferred between warehouses. Operations in warehouse developed in a similar way. Difficulties of checking the strength of obscured spirits, such as British liqueurs, were met in 1869 by a provision that a sample could be distilled to check a rectifier's declaration.[115] In 1875 warehousing facilities were extended to tinctures and medicinal spirits made by rectifiers and compounders, but there is no evidence that this was an important trade in Ireland.

The excise regulations for controlling the operations of a rectifier in 1807 remained as the base for all future controls. They were designed so that the gauger would be fully aware when a rectifier proposed to work his still, to ensure that at other times the still could not operate and when it was working it could only be used within restricted limits. These physical controls were augmented by checking and recording receipts of raw spirit and resultant products. Thus notices of working were required; furnace doors, still manholes and cocks were closed and locked or the still head removed when the still was silent; and when at work the still was to be charged to not less than seven-tenths of its capacity.[116] These regulations were repeated with some refinements in the consolidating Acts of 1860 and 1880. Occasionally doubts on definition arose. For example, a maker of British wine in Belfast in 1845 fermented fruit and sugar and then fortified the wine by adding 12 per cent of proof spirit. The excise collector submitted samples to four Belfast rectifiers who pronounced the wine to be a British compound.[117]

115. The various Acts are: 11 and 12 Vict., c. 122, sections 17, 20, 22; 16 and 17 Vict., c. 37, section 26; 23 and 24 Vict., c. 114, sections 142, 148; 28 and 29 Vict., c. 98, sections 1–12; 30 and 31 Vict., c. 27, section 5; 32 and 33 Vict., sections 8, 13. Section 7 of the last Act imposed a small charge of 5s. per £100 of duty on British compounds delivered for home use, no doubt to compensate for the cost of excise supervision. 43 and 44 Vict., c. 24, sections 86, *et seq.*, consolidated previous Acts. See also *13th Inland Revenue Report,* 1870, *op. cit.,* p. 219.

116. *Inquiry into Fees, Gratuities etc., received in Public Offices in Ireland, 5th Report,* Parl. Pps. 1806–7 (124) vi, p. 163. *Belfast Historical Records, op. cit.,* Book 6, p. 48, a report on 12 January 1843 records that a Belfast rectifier did not remove the still head and as the manhole and cocks were not locked on the assumption of this removal, fraudulent use was possible.

117. *Belfast Historical Records, op. cit.,* Book 5, pp. 55, 60–1. The trader was making ginger wine.

There is no knowledge of the total produce of rectifiers and compounders in Ireland, but there is information about their numbers. In 1825 there were 11 and this number grew slowly to 26 in 1840, 36 in 1850, 45 in 1860 and 1870. After that the number began to fall from 40 in 1880 to 13 in 1910.[118] The reason for this rise and fall can only be guessed. In relation to whiskey or beer or even imported spirits the Irish market would be small since the principal compounds, gin and British brandy, were not widely popular and would be more expensive because of the added manufacturing costs. It is also possible, or even likely, that towards the close of the century, larger units were ousting small scale manufacturing. Rectifying in Ireland was largely concentrated in Dublin, and this may be because of a greater number of persons accustomed to, or aping, English ways as well as a large population.[119] There is no evidence that British compounds had much appeal in the country areas. Making spirits of wine was on a different footing as it was intended for use in further manufacture. At first there was an absurd legal anomaly. A distiller was not permitted to deliver spirits at a strength greater than 25° over proof, but if he used a Coffey still the strength of the extract before the 1850s would be about the 60° over proof mark. If a rectifier desiring to make spirits of wine bought from such a distiller, the latter had to dilute his spirit down to 25° over proof and the rectifier then concentrated it to the strength of spirits of wine. By 1860 these patent stills were legally recognised, no limit in strength was imposed on deliveries from a distillery and that virtually ended the rectifiers' interest in making strong spirits for other persons to use in medicine or industry. He did, however, develop an interest in making medicines and tinctures for in 1875 rectifiers or compounders were permitted to warehouse tinctures or medicinal spirits.[120]

A major factor affecting the use of strong spirits in industry and for other purposes occurred in 1855 when an Act permitted spirits of wine to be adulterated with methyl alcohol and then

118. *13th Inland Revenue Report*, 1870, *op. cit.*, p. 431; *28th Report*, 1884–5, *op. cit.*, p. 211. *43rd Report*, Parl. Pps. 1900 (Cd. 347) xviii, p. 409.

119. *Excise Revenue Inquiry*, *7th Report, Part I*, 1834, *op. cit.*, p. 236. Of the 19 Irish rectifiers listed, 10 were in Dublin, the others in 7 different towns. See pp. 201–3 on the impossibility of exporting to the English market.

120. *Ibid.*, p. 421. 38 and 39 Vict., c. 23, section 10.

used duty free in the arts or manufacture. In Ireland making methylated spirits did not attract distillers or others and the various inland revenue reports record only one or two methylators with a production reaching 21,229 gallons in 1885 and only 51,000 gallons in 1914. Probably Irish industry relied more on methylated spirit imported from England.[121] The regulations for methylated spirit were revised from time to time and power was given to the excise authorities to alter the proportion of methyl alcohol or substitute some other denaturant if the proposed use of the spirit rendered this essential. In England methylated spirit, being duty free, was one way of defeating illicit distilling because illicit spirits were sought for by varnish makers and others, but these reasons did not apply in Ireland so much where illicit spirit was primarily intended as a beverage.[122] Retailing methylated spirits in quantities not exceeding one gallon for domestic uses was allowed in 1861, the retailers paying a licence duty of £2 2s. reduced in 1868 to 10s. There was some abuse, however, by persons who seemed able to overcome the nauseous effects of drinking it, so in 1891 mineral naphtha was added to retailed spirits and also colouring to distinguish this mineralised methylated spirits. Drinking methylated spirits was never a serious problem in Ireland, apart from an upsurge of this habit for a short time in the 1890s in Ballymena.[123]

121. 18 and 19 Vict., c. 38. A distiller's or rectifier's licence covered methylation, otherwise the licence was £10 10s. This would account for only one or occasionally two methylating licences in a year. The quantities quoted are for all methylating. The figures are taken from *28th Inland Revenue Report*, 1884–5, *op. cit.*, p. 148, and *5th Customs and Excise Report*, Parl. Pps. 1914 (Cd. 7574) xvii, p. 24. The *13th Inland Revenue Report*, 1870, p. 231, list a number of uses for methylated spirit and this list is greatly extended in the *5th Customs and Excise Report*, 1914, p. 26.

122. 2 Edw. 7, c. 7, section 8. *Excise Revenue Inquiry, 7th Report, Part I*, 1834, *op. cit.*, p. 261. *28th Inland Revenue Report*, 1884–5, *op. cit.*, p. 59.

123. 24 and 25 Vict., c. 91. Sir N. Highmore, *The Excise Laws*, 3rd ed., London, 1923, i, p. 549, historical note. In 1865 purified methyl alcohol was regarded as potable and free from unpalatable flavours and by 28 and 29 Vict., c. 96, section 27, anyone filtering and distilling methyl alcohol was deemed a distiller and his product regarded as low wines. Under 31 and 32 Vict.,c. 124, a methylator had to sell not less than 5 gallons and a retailer not more than 1 gallon at a time. The methylated spirit law was consolidated in 1880 by 43 and 44 Vict., c. 24, Part II. The number of retailers in Ireland was small. In 1869 there were 41 and by 1890 the number had only risen to 376 (*13th Inland Revenue Report*, 1870, *op. cit.*, p. 444 and *34th Report*, Parl. Pps. 1890–1 (c. 6537) xxvi, p. 365). *S.C. on British and Foreign Spirits, Evidence*, Parl. Pps. 1890–1 (210) xi, pp. 494–6.

Exports

The position in 1823, and for some years afterwards, for a distiller or spirit merchant desiring to export whiskey was that he had to export from a bonded warehouse in the casks originally deposited which were to be not less than eighty gallons content and the exporting ship not less than fifty tons. He also had to repay any malt allowances and give bond for the due arrival of all the whiskey at its port of destination.[124] Following representations from the trade, who stressed that rum could be exported in twenty gallon casks, this minimum was extended to whiskey in 1848.[125] There was no provision for exporting whiskey in bottles until bottling in warehouse was allowed in 1865. There were other minor irritating regulations in the early years. Two days notice of export from a warehouse was required along with a mass of details relating to the consignment 'which did not bear on revenue security'. Thus if the excise account of the spirit was different from the notice no penalty ensued. When casks were lodged in the warehouse for export they were gauged by the excise and again gauged when delivered for shipment. They were gauged yet again on arrival in England where a tolerance of two gallons was allowed for differences in gaugers' assessments. All this measuring merely fixed the time of any loss. The account for duty was based on the quantity originally warehoused and no allowance was given for any wastage or leaks on the journey. In these circumstances some of the excise gauging could well have been abandoned. For distillers there was always a danger that differences in excise gauging might show an excess and if so they were charged 7s. 6d. a gallon on the excess in 1834 and appropriate English rates in other years.[126]

124. 4 Geo. 4, c. 94, sections 73–5; 6 Geo. 4, c. 80, sections 92, 95–6, 99.

125. *Excise Revenue Inquiry, 7th Report, Part I,* 1834, *op. cit.,* pp. 93, 180, 266. 11 and 12 Vict., c. 122, section 19.

126. *Excise Revenue Inquiry, 7th Report, Part I,* 1834, *op. cit.,* pp. 69, 117, 180, 182, 186–7, 198, 266, 280. It was alleged by the excise on p. 282 that the tolerance was abused and casks made to take advantage of it. This would make nonsense to any expert gauger. Gauging is based on the assumption that a cask is elliptical on its length with the ends cut off, and round across the width. Calipers can measure the dimensions and a slide rule can give the capacity. Allowances are made for deviations from the perfectly shaped cask and it is in this small margin that differences occur between gaugers. Hand made casks, usually puncheons of about 140 gallons, could not be deliberately made to an accuracy of precisely 2 gallons below an ostensible figure.

Before spirits were delivered for shipment the English duty was charged on any deficiency arising in a warehouse and the Irish duty on the quantity actually shipped. On arrival in England the balance of the English duty had to be paid on the quantity shipped and losses in transit were ignored. This refusal to grant such losses was easily the strongest complaint by Irish shippers and was thoroughly justified. Thus the Lisburn excise collector reported on 30 December 1846 about a loss on voyage due to shifting cargo in heavy seas causing leakages. There was no claim in law and it was not allowed. Moreover, the lost spirit was charged at the English rates although it never arrived. It appeared from this report that the Treasury did on occasions authorise the remission of duty even though there was no legal support for this leniency. Apparently they regarded the charge on such a loss in the nature of a fine for careless stowage and is typical of the autocratic way that revenue laws were sometimes administered.[127] These regulations naturally gave rise to increased insurance premiums which, with freight charges, were a considerable handicap in the competition with English distillers. Leathem, a Londonderry distiller, disclosed a number of accounts of sales to England in 1831. In one of them he shipped 10 puncheons containing 1,347 proof gallons of which 1,303 proof gallons arrived, the difference being due to leakage and drop in strength. Duty at 7s. 6d. a gallon and the insurance costs of this loss amounted to £17 15s. 6d. or equal to about 3d. a proof gallon on the consignment. His total charges for freight and other items, but excluding duty, were £23 9s. 6d. When duties throughout the United Kingdom were equalised in 1860 all these differences between the countries disappeared and a shipment of spirits was treated in the same way as a removal by land between warehouses. Transit losses, however, even with these removals were

127. 6 Geo. 4, c. 80, sections 93–4. *Excise Revenue Inquiry, 7th Report, Part I,* 1834, *op. cit.,* pp. 69, 71, 115, 221, are some of the references to charging on transit losses. *Belfast Historical Records, op. cit.,* Book 5, p. 133. The excise collector refers to a loss previously allowed on a shipment from Cork to London and a comment on careless stowage. Similar rules applied to Scottish shippers and on p. 336 of the *Excise Revenue Inquiry, 7th Report, Part I,* the case is quoted of the loss of the S.S. Queen Charlotte bound for London. All the spirits were lost and the shippers, who had paid the Scottish duty, still had to pay the balance of the English duty. See *Part II,* 1835, *op. cit.,* p. 76. Remission of duty in such cases was recommended.

not legally allowed at first. The Act of 1860 merely permitted loss by accident in warehouse, but the Act of 1880 extended the powers of the Board of Inland Revenue to remit duty due for any unavoidable accident. Their internal rules for establishing a transit loss were very elaborate in the case of accidents in contrast with the simple rules, locally administered, for normal losses due to natural causes during storage.[128]

While the excise regulations did obstruct free intercourse of spirits and this was aggravated by additional costs to get Irish spirits on the English market, the real difficulty was to make whiskey a popular drink and replace gin. In this effort the Irish distillers were naturally the allies of those in Scotland who laboured under the same difficulties. There was always a small market amongst Irish and Scottish migrants, but in the first half of the century the main hope for Irish whiskey was the English rectifier. Provided they could undersell the English distiller this was indeed a large market which by the laws before 1860 was virtually closed to Irish rectifiers. The competition was severe and made worse by the association of some English distillers with rectifying houses, lax excise control, and frauds. Irish distillers did manage, however, to do remarkably well in the English market even though they faced a duty paid price of 9s. 6d. a proof gallon in 1834 rising to 10s. 8d. in 1856. In 1840 exports amounted to 320,000 gallons and by 1860 when United Kingdom duties were equalised, exports had reached over a million gallons a year.[129] After that year official statistics of the movement of spirit are not based on the country distilling it, nor on the type of beverage. Spirits shown as sent to England from Ireland would include English gin and Scotch whiskey sent earlier to Ireland

128. *Ibid., Part I*, p. 427. 23 and 24 Vict., c. 114, section 136, did not extend to losses outside a warehouse. 43 and 44 Vict., c. 24, section 115, gave the Board of Inland Revenue a general authority to remit duty in all cases if they were satisfied that any loss was genuine. *Ham's Inland Revenue Year Book*, 1900, *op. cit.*, warehousing section, p. 90, gives the rates of allowance remitted locally for transit losses. *The Statements of Evidence given before the Sugar and Coffee Planting Committee*, Parl. Pps. 1847–8 (518) viii, pp. 523 *et seq.*, gives examples of transit losses for Scotch and Irish spirits imported into London.

129. *Irish Revenue Inquiry, 5th Report*, 1823, *op. cit.*, p. 303. *Excise Revenue Inquiry, 7th Report, Part I*, 1834, *op. cit.*, pp. 34–5, 38, 443, and *Part II*, 1835, *op. cit.*, p. 55. *Return of Spirits distilled in each Collection of Excise*, Parl. Pps. 1842 (238) xxxix, p. 545. *Accounts of proof spirit distilled, removed and in bond*, Parl. Pps. 1861 (144) lviii, p. 521. *Parliamentary Debates*, 19 May 1856, col. 343.

and deposited in bond, and the same position arises with spirits sent from Great Britain to Ireland. Nevertheless the bulk of these removals would be spirits distilled in the exporting country. It is also clear from statements by Dublin distillers that by 1878 there was not merely a good market for Irish whiskey in England, but that they were very jealous of the reputation of their product. In 1871 over 979,000 proof gallons were sent to England and over 47,000 to Scotland. By 1900 Ireland was sending over 4 million gallons to England and over 681,000 gallons to Scotland. There were much smaller movements of imported spirits. Movement in the reverse direction was very much smaller. In 1871 Ireland received just over 7,000 gallons from England and over 18,000 from Scotland. By 1900 the figures were 43,000 gallons from England and 34,000 gallons from Scotland.[130]

A fair picture of the trade of Irish spirits with Great Britain can be obtained from official figures, but unfortunately this is not the case with trade to overseas countries. There are firm figures for spirits distilled and in some years the quantity bonded, but deliveries overseas from Ireland are much more blurred than for United Kingdom trade as a whole. Exports are shown simply as British and Irish spirits, or merely British spirits. This would include Scotch and Irish whiskey and compounded spirits, the latter almost entirely from England where gin was the main product. Nor can the Irish share of the trade be calculated from the figures available because exports from any one country would include imports from the rest of the United Kingdom and then exported. All that can fairly be assumed is that exports from Ireland would be roughly proportioned to the quantity distilled less the spirits retained for home consumption. Most of the difference would be consumed in Great Britain and the rest exported. The same would apply to the produce of Scotland and England. In 1850 United Kingdom exports of British and Irish spirits were 308,914 proof gallons of which 123,774 gallons went to the colonies, a very small proportion of the quantity distilled.[131]

130. J. Jameson, W. Jameson, J. Power and G. Roe, *Truths about Whiskey*, Dublin, 1878. *14th Inland Revenue Report*, Parl. Pps. 1871 (c. 370) xvii, p. 700; *44th Report*, Parl. Pps. 1901 (Cd. 764) xvii, p. 462.

131. *Return of proof spirits distilled etc.* Parl. Pps. 1851 (263) liii, p. 452. In Ireland alone the quantity distilled was over 8 million gallons. (*13th Inland Revenue Report*, 1870, *op. cit.*, p. 381.)

By 1861 this export figure had jumped to 2·2 million gallons of which over half a million went to Portugal, probably for fortifying wine, and nearly 450,000 gallons to U.S.A. In the same year Ireland distilled 4·8 million gallons, retained 4·2 million gallons and sent 645,000 gallons to Great Britain apparently leaving no surplus for export, but of the 4·2 million gallons account must be taken of spirits received from Great Britain and in that year this amounted to over 776,000 gallons most of it under bond. This example is enough to show how intermingled the figures are and the best that can be said is that Irish whiskey had a good reputation, that it probably had a favourable market among Irish immigrants in U.S.A. and Australia and that it did at least get a fair proportion of the trade. The Australian market, in particular, became very prominent in 1880 for a total of 1·7 million gallons of British and Irish spirits exported, 879,000 went to Australia.[132] The export market for home-made spirits expanded rapidly after 1880 and by 1905 total exports reached nearly seven million gallons and went on to exceed ten million gallons in 1914. The Irish share of this total is not known. In the year ending 31 March 1914 Irish distilleries produced 9,878,739 proof gallons. In the same period 2,730,694 proof gallons of British spirits were retained for home consumption in Ireland, 2,225,991 gallons sent to England and 395,437 gallons to Scotland. Figures of a similar nature showing a considerable surplus of distilled spirits over United Kingdom use are contained in the annual reports of the Revenue Board. Thus in 1900 over fourteen million gallons were distilled in Ireland and the United Kingdom absorbed nearly ten million. Even allowing for the lag in time of distilled spirits being bonded and delivered later at different times, it is clear that there was a regular annual Irish surplus which must have been exported overseas and that it was in the region of three or four million gallons.[133]

132. *5th Inland Revenue Report,* Parl. Pps. 1861 (2877) xxxi, pp. 114, 143; *13th Inland Revenue Report,* 1870, *op. cit.,* p. 381; *23rd Report,* Parl. Pps. 1880 (c. 2770) xxix, p. 94.

133. *43rd Inland Revenue Report,* Parl. Pps. 1900 (Cd. 347) xviii, pp. 393, 395; *52nd Report,* Parl. Pps. 1909 (Cd. 4868) xxvii, p. 22. See *Parliamentary Debates,* 11 June 1850, col. 1096. Exports of Irish spirits in 1849 were said to be 67,000 proof gallons. As exports to England were 823,138 gallons in 1850, the figure quoted must refer to exports overseas, but as the debate was about rum imports, the figure for 1849 may refer to the re-export of imported spirit. However, it is

This picture of Power's Bottling Plant was taken on the 14 June 1895

This Water Wheel at Irish Distillers' Midleton Distillery dates from 1852. It is still used and provides part of the power to drive the machinery in the Distillery

Since in the mid-nineteenth century England was by far the main potential market outside Ireland and gin was the popular spirituous drink, so the best opportunities for Irish distillers were either to sell to rectifying houses in England or to rectifiers in Ireland for export. The size of the market can be judged from English production in earlier years before assimilation of the revenues. In 1834 there were twelve English distillers serving 108 rectifiers and producing 7·7 million proof gallons at a duty paid price of 9s. 6d. a gallon. In some instances the distiller and rectifier were associated and raw spirit prices could be artificially depressed to exclude Irish or Scottish imports. Despite this, however, Irish whiskey did gain an entry into this market.[134] The other possible opening for Irish spirits was through Irish rectifiers and compounders, but the huge English market dangling before them remained unattainable, because of the excise laws and regulations, until much later in the nineteenth century. By then the combined effect of the grip on the market by English rectifiers and the increasing taste for whiskey left little chance of any large scale Irish manufacture of gin or any other compounds.

The law in 1825 and later years required the rectifier or compounder to pay duty on the spirit he used and there were no arrangements to get this duty back when the compounds were sent to England or even to warehouse them. If this was not enough there was another rule that on import into England compounded or rectified spirits paid duty computed at the highest strength that spirits could be made. This strength was not specified, but in practice was regarded as 43° over proof but, except for spirits of wine, the rectifier was not allowed to deliver spirits from his rectifying house exceeding 7° over proof. These penal laws were in force on the grounds that compounded spirits obscured the true hydrometer reading and the actual strength could not, therefore, be ascertained.[135] Coffey had suggested a method in 1834 for getting the true strength of compounded

---

a probable figure for whiskey. J. Owens, *Plain Papers,* London, 1879, p. 477, writes that large quantities of spirits were sent to wine producing countries at this time for fortifying wines. Irish distillers probably got some of this trade.

134. *Inquiry into the Revenue arising in Ireland, 5th Report,* Parl. Pps. 1823 (405) vii, pp. 263, 303–5.

135. 6 Geo. 4, c. 80, section 3. *Excise Revenue Inquiry, 7th Report, Part I,* 1834, *op. cit.,* pp. 40, 115, 189, 200 and *Part II,* 1835, *op. cit.,* pp. 55–6.

K

spirits by evaporating the spirit from a weighed sample, making up the sample to its original quantity by adding water and weighing again. The strength would be related to the increase in weight. Such a method would only be approximate because evaporation of all spirit without any other moisture would be impossible, but the method would have been a good guide. The suggestion was ignored. The establishment of a chemical laboratory in 1843 by the Board of Inland Revenue, equalising all United Kingdom spirit duties in 1858, the extension of warehousing in 1865 to permit compounds to be deposited on drawback, and the freedom to move spirits between warehouses in any part of the United Kingdom caused all the difficulties of import and export between Ireland and Great Britain to disappear, but it was too late.[136] Exports of compounds to foreign countries were negligible and as the Irish market was almost wholly for whiskey, rectifying and compounding remained on the fringe of the spirit trade.[137] There was a move in 1847 to permit rectifying and compounding in bond, with, of course, allowances for waste in operations, but the Chancellor of the Exchequer rejected the proposal as too dangerous to revenue interests. It certainly would have involved the revenue authorities in considerable problems if distilling and all the other operations were to be conducted under close revenue supervision, in premises secured by bolts and bars and under revenue locks.[138] There was a possible opening for Irish rectifiers in the manufacture of tinctures and medicinal spirits, but this was closed in 1836 when it was disclosed that this trade with Great Britain was causing revenue losses and that it was virtually impossible for English products to enter the Irish

136. *Ibid.,* Part I, 1834, p. 203. J. Woodward, *Survey of the Government Laboratory, Tobacco Year Book,* London, 1920. Warehousing of unsweetened rectified spirits for export was allowed in 1848 by 11 and 12 Vict., c. 122, sections 17, 20, and was extended to all rectified or compounded spirits for home consumption, export or ships' stores in 1865 by 28 and 29 Vict., c. 98, section 1.

137. *Accounts of proof spirit distilled,* 1861, *op. cit.,* p. 522, shows only 539 gallons exported in 1860 to countries other than the United Kingdom. *24th Inland Revenue Report,* Parl. Pps. 1881 (c. 2967) xxix, p. 267, records 314 gallons warehoused for export. The *44th Report,* Parl. Pps. 1901 (Cd. 764) xviii, p. 457, gives 574 gallons for export. It should be noted that the term 'warehoused on drawback for export' refers to rectified or compounded spirit as it was not open to deposit other spirits on drawback.

138. *Parliamentary Debates,* 20 May 1847, col. 1104. The Commons voted against the government on this issue, but to no purpose.

market. When the trade was re-opened countervailing duties were imposed at 7s. 9d. a gallon into England and 5s. 4d. into Scotland. These rates were reviewed from time to time until finally abolished when all United Kingdom spirit duties were equalised.[139]

The competition from foreign or colonial spirits never seriously affected Irish distillers either in their home market or the market in Great Britain. Foreign spirits were practically excluded before 1860 because of an import duty of 15s. a gallon which applied to imports into any United Kingdom country. Colonial spirits, mainly rum from the West Indies, were far more favourably treated, but so far as Ireland was concerned imports were small as the English import duty plus a surcharge of 4d. a gallon was charged. In 1847 it was stated that rum imports into Ireland were running between 11,000 and 13,000 gallons. As Irish spirit duties rose to the English level the possibility of rum competition increased, but public taste remained faithful to whiskey.[140]

A commercial treaty with France in 1860 alarmed all United Kingdom distillers for it provided for free trade in foreign spirits. The Chancellor of the Exchequer did, however, impose a surtax of 5d. a gallon on foreign spirits and 2d. on rum to counteract the cost to distillers of excise restrictions in their manufacture. At first it was proposed that the surtax should be 2d. for all imported spirit. For a long time distillers had met the competition from rum with equanimity. The cheaper labour costs in the West Indies were offset by higher transport costs. Spirits from Europe were a very different matter. French brandy had a highly favoured taste and, except for the fastidious drinker, was not far removed from whiskey. In other countries, Holland or Germany, the spirit was made from materials similar to those used at home. The

139. 6 and 7 Will. 4, c. 72; 5 Vict., sess. 2, c. 25, section 1 and Schedule; 6 Vict., c. 48, section 1 and Schedule. Rectifiers and compounders were allowed to warehouse tinctures and medicinal spirits on drawback in 1875 by 38 and 39 Vict., c. 23, section 10 which put these products on the same footing as other compounded spirits.

140. *Parl. Debates*, 25 July 1834, col. 525; 22 January 1847, col. 295; 11 June 1850, col. 1096. *5th Customs and Excise Report*, 1914, *op. cit.*, p. 23. Removals of foreign spirits between Ireland and Great Britain were small compared with those of home-made spirits. In that year Irish warehouses sent to Great Britain more than twice the quantity they received. p. 21. The consumption per head of home-made spirits in Ireland was over six times the consumption of imported spirits. See also *S. C. on Drunkenness*, Parl. Pps. 1834 (559) viii, p. 533.

distillers' pressure for an import protection of at least $9\frac{1}{2}$d. a gallon had the beneficial effect of forcing the excise authorities to re-examine their regulations and reduce or abolish various restric-tions so as to bring the distillers' costs down to the equivalent of 5d. a gallon. At the same time allowances were granted to exports of British plain spirits of 2d. a gallon and to compounded spirits at 3d. a gallon. To protect the revenue from loss 1d. was added to the excise duty to make it 8s. 1d., a pin-pricking addition because in the following budget the duty was increased to 10s. The allowance on the export of compounded or rectified spirit was raised to 4d. a gallon in 1881 and the import surtax on foreign spirits reduced to 4d. The export allowances were increased to 3d. for plain spirits and 5d. for compounded spirits in 1902.[141] The statistics for spirits distilled following the French treaty do not confirm the distillers' apprehensions. Foreign imports merely added a little more variety for the consumer.

Domestic Sales

While the export market to Great Britain and sales to rectifiers were important to the Irish distiller, in the end his prosperity depended on the retail outlets in the home market. It was here that main battle between sobriety and the revenue was joined and an outright mastery of either side could be very serious. In the first half of the nineteenth century vigorous and almost fanatical attacks were made on intemperance and this was a social evil that deserved attention, but the attackers went far beyond mere restraint and desired prohibition. At the same time licence duties, various restrictions, and police supervision, made life difficult for the innkeeper. The public taste, however, preferred whiskey and the authorities were in a dilemma similar to that facing them if they attempted to tax whiskey too much. In the place of the illicit still or evasion at licensed stills, restriction or suppression of retail outlets inevitably resulted in an increase of

141. 23 and 24 Vict., c. 129, section 4; 44 and 45 Vict., c. 12, section 16. *Parl. Debates*, 24 February 1860, cols. 1705–6; 19 May 1879, cols. 757–60. Some members of parliament complained that the French treaty resulted in some loss of control of taxation, but this is an inevitable consequence of tariff agreements. See also *28th Inland Revenue Report*, 1884–5, *op. cit.*, p. 53. The increased allow-ances in 1902 were granted by 2 Edw. 7, c. 7, section 5. Section 8 of this Act also permitted the duty free use of spirits in the arts or manufacture without the addition of a denaturant, under certain conditions.

shebeens where illicit drinking was a favourable background for other illegal activities.

Before 1825 there were four classes of licences to sell spirits; the spirit factor paying a licence duty of £20 and selling on commission not less than fifty gallons at a time, the spirit dealer selling two gallons or more with a licence duty ranging from £10 to £25 according to the town in which he operated, the retailer selling in quantities of less than twenty-five gallons for consumption either on or off the premises paying a licence duty varying from £7 to £40, and the spirit grocer who sold tea, coffee and other goods and could also sell spirits in retail quantities for consumption off the premises by paying the same licence duty as a retailer.[142] In all cases these licensed sellers received spirit under an official permit, kept stock accounts of receipts and sales which were checked by gaugers and penalties were prescribed for discrepancies. A Commission of Inquiry into the excise regulations commented in 1836 on the multiplied restrictions and regulations in the progress of spirits from the distiller to the consumer through the hands of rectifiers, dealers and retailers which a complete system of survey and permit involved. They drew attention to the time and attention that excise officers required for their surveys and registering permits. They concluded from the evidence they heard that it was easy for retailers to evade the regulations with their everyday sales over which the excise gauger had no control. They condemned the system and recommended its abolition 'reserving only to the excise a general power of examining spirits, either in stock or in transit, on receipt of such information as may justify a strong suspicion of fraud'. These were strong words which must have startled the authorities, but it was not until 1848 that the stock and permit system was abolished and permits became documents whose sole purpose was to protect spirits from seizure during transit.[143]

The urge for assimilating the revenue systems of Great Britain and Ireland from 1823 onwards extended to the sales of spirit. There was no pressing need for this as a different system in Ireland

142. 55 Geo. 3, c. 19, schedule; 56 Geo. 3, c. 111, section 23; 58 Geo. 3, c. 57, section 2. See also the *Irish Revenue Inquiry, 3rd Report,* Parl. Pps. 1822 (606) xiii, pp. 611, 714.

143. *Excise Revenue Inquiry, Digest of Reports,* Parl. Pps. 1837 (84) xxx, pp. 174–5. *13th Inland Revenue Report,* 1870, *op. cit.,* p. 269. 11 and 12 Vict., c. 121, section 12; 23 and 24 Vict., c. 114, section 170.

would not affect Great Britain, but, it may be supposed, this would look untidy to the official mind. The change, however, benefited the Irish licensee, but it was not complete as small differences between the systems in Great Britain and Ireland remained for the rest of the century. In 1825 all Irish licences were withdrawn and new ones issued at the English rates of duty. For spirit retailers this was a graduated levy based on the rateable value of the premises and a nearer approximation to the value of the extent of their trade. Spirit dealers were now licensed at a flat rate of £10. Spirit grocers had no counterpart in England. They had been licensed as grocers at £3 3s. and paid additionally for a retail licence to sell spirits for consumption off the premises. The new law allowed the spirit grocers to continue at duties related to the rent value of the premises and prescribed a method for arriving at a rent value for premises not rated for inhabited house duty. The differences between the old and new laws were appreciable and were fairer. Under the old law a public house in one of the main cities paid £40 whether it was a hovel or well appointed house in a good situation. After 1825 the licence duty ranged from £2 2s. if rated under £10 up to £10 10s. for a rateable value of £50 or more. Spirit grocers were discouraged. The licence as a grocer was reduced to 11s. but the additional spirit licence was approximately £3 3s. higher than the publican's licence. The only real advantage was that a spirit grocer did not require a magistrate's certificate before being licensed. It was merely a matter of applying to the excise. Other regulations, such as excise entry of the premises and exhibiting a signboard, remained as before.[144]

The regulations governing permits were consolidated in an Act of 1832. Nothing new was enacted. There were the former safeguards against forgery and permits were only granted after the spirit trader had lodged a request giving full details of the consignment to be removed and the address. The excise inserted a time limit for the transfer, but there was a provision protecting the spirits from seizure if there had been unavoidable delay. In 1848 dealers and retailers were relieved of the necessity to get

144. 6 Geo. 4, c. 81, sections 2, 4–5. *Belfast Historical Records, op. cit.,* Book 133, p. 29. An excise order directed that existing grocers' licences were to run out and then a beginner's licence issued at new rates. See also Sir N. J. Highmore, *The Excise Laws,* 3rd ed. London, 1923, i, p. 192.

permits. They were supplied with serially numbered blank certificates and could fill them in when despatching goods without recourse to any excise official. At the receiving end these certificates were to be immediately cancelled and handed over to the excise on the next visit of the gauger. The certificates could more easily be used than permits to cover the movement of illicit spirits, but the stock records of traders at both ends of the transfer were intended to counter such frauds, coupled with the possibility that cancelled certificates would be checked back to the delivery point.[145]

A licensing Act in 1833 set the pattern in Ireland for the next half century. It ensured that any third party interested in a new application for an 'on' licence would get at least twenty-one days' notice to lodge any objections at the quarter sessions. If an applicant succeeded he was issued with a court certificate and after giving bond for good behaviour he produced this certificate to the excise, paid the licence duty and his licence was issued. The licence ran for a year and could be renewed by the excise without the justice's authority on production of a certificate of good character signed by six householders in the parish. This provision was subject to some criticism in later years. As before, certain persons, such as distillers and rectifiers, were not eligible for a licence. Sales were forbidden between 11 p.m. and 7 a.m., except to travellers, and tipplers or gamblers could be removed from the premises either by a constable or by overseers appointed by parishioners.[146]

At about this period temperance reformers were becoming more vocal. In the *Belfast Newsletter* of 14 August 1829, the Reverend Dr Edgar of the Royal College, Belfast, appealed for temperance. He started a society for total abstinence and a similar society was formed in New Ross, but they directed their attention solely against distilled spirits. This unquestionably lessened the appeal of the campaign against drunkenness. 'An organisation which permitted to the wealthy the enjoyment of wine and at

145. 2 and 3 Will. 4, c. 16; 11 and 12 Vict., c. 121, sections 12–13, 16–18; 23 and 24 Vict., c. 114, sections 150 *et seq.* There were special regulations in 1848 for spirits delivered from a customs warehouse. A certificate endorsed by the customs officer was used instead of a permit.
146. 3 and 4 Will. 4, c. 68. *Parl. Debates,* H. L. 21 July 1835, cols. 787–8. Complaint was made about the unsatisfactory control over the issue of spirit retailers' licences.

the same time prevented the poor from indulging in the form
of liquor most popular with them was not likely to commend
itself to the majority of the nation.' Some twenty-five societies
were formed and got a little middle-class popularity and some
support from medical circles. In protestant areas the movement
was aimed at moderation rather than total abstinence and six
such societies were formed. In England total abstinence societies
had been active since 1832 and as a result of their influence the
Dublin Total Abstinence Society was formed in 1836. At their
October meeting 'moderation' societies were roundly condemned
by a judge of the King's Bench on the grounds that they were a
nursery for intemperance.[147] These activities naturally led to
lobbying members of parliament and some of the demands of
the reformers caused Cobbett to object in the House of Commons
about people 'coming to ask the House to pass laws to correct
social evils which no laws could correct'. In June 1834 there was
a long parliamentary debate on intemperance throughout the
United Kingdom and as a result a Select Committee was
appointed to inquire into the matter.[148] The Chancellor of the
Exchequer endeavoured to forestall the Select Committee in his
budget. He said that 'increasing the duty on spirits would do no
good whatever either in the shape of increasing the revenue or
of diminishing their consumption'. He observed that increases
in the spirit duty merely encouraged illicit distilling. His remedy
was to raise licence duties and spirit retailers' licences were increased by 50 per cent. No additions were made to licence duties
for wholesalers and spirit grocers. This drastic increase bore
severely on publicans with a limited clientele or where spirit
sales were only part of the business, hotels for example, so in the
following year retailers selling less than fifty gallons a year were
exempted from the increases.[149] This exemption, as might have

147. P. Rogers, *Father Theobald Mathew*, Dublin, 1943, pp. 33–6.

148. *Parl. Debates*, 27 May 1834, col. 1263; 3 June 1834, cols. 90 *et seq*. Some
alleged facts relating to drinking appear in the latter debate in cols. 94–5, 103.
In col. 118 there was the recurring plea to encourage beer to which was added
a plea to reduce the duties on French wine, tea and coffee. Tea at that time was
subject to an *ad valorem* duty later altered to a duty of 1s. 6d., 2s. 2d. and 3s. a lb.,
according to three grades, a tax far too high to compete with spirits even if the
whiskey drinker was in any mood to change (see debates on 14 May 1835, col.
1070 and 13 June 1835, col. 485).

149. *Parl. Debates*, 25 July 1834, cols. 503–25. 4 and 5 Will. 4, c. 75, sections
7–8; 5 and 6 Will. 4, sections 1–2.

been expected, led to allegations of fraud. It was said that 2,616 publicans had been exempted and their practice now was to show in their records sales up to forty gallons and, to avoid being caught through permits and stock records, the balance of the sales was made up with illicit spirit. Thus even exemptions encouraged illicit distilling.[150]

The main licensing Act of 1833 was amended three years later. It does seem strange that reliance was placed on a character report from six householders when a publican's licence was renewed. It would not be difficult for him to get this from relations or friends and this must have penetrated the official mind for in 1836 the licensee had to get another certificate from the chief constable or from two parish overseers. Hours of sale on Sunday were shortened by closing from 9 p.m. to 9 a.m. on Monday, and booths at fairs were forbidden to sell at night. Both these measures were obviously aimed at preventing week-end mischief, but another measure was closely related to the politics of the time. A retailer was forbidden to permit societies or assemblies declared illegal to meet on his premises. Nor could he permit other societies if an oath or any rite or ceremony was required before admittance. Flags or emblems of these societies were not to be displayed. The publican was also made liable for persons found drunk on his premises. The powers of magistrates, constables and overseers were repeated, but it seems that parishes had been laggard in appointing overseers and power was now given to the petty sessions court to appoint them if the parish neglected its duty. Naturally some of these measures did not satisfy reformers, particularly a mere shortening by 2 hours for drinking on Sunday. The Government appeared to be more concerned with law and order than intemperance as such. As one spokesman remarked 'it is out of the power of parliament to prevent the drinking of spirits on Sundays', people would go to much worse places, that is, the shebeens.[151]

The Select Committee of the House of Commons appointed to inquire into drunkenness reported in 1834 and the evidence given in Ireland is instructive if not convincing. Reformers in fanatical zeal attacked the spirit trade from every angle with very little reply from distillers or sellers, so much so that a picture is

150. *Parl. Debates*, 10 March 1836, cols. 168, 173.
151. 6 and 7 Will. 4, c. 38. *Parl. Debates*, 20 June 1836, col. 665.

presented of a country whose people were dissolute. Their case was so extravagant that it defeated its object which they declared to be a prohibition of the importation and manufacture of spirits except for purposes of arts or manufacture and, presumably, for scientific and medical uses.[152] Nevertheless, much of this evidence gave revealing glimpses of drinking habits of the time. The committee reported that 'among the remote causes of the intemperance which still prevails, may be enumerated, the influence of example set by the upper classes of society when habits of intoxication were more frequent in such ranks than among their inferiors in station; and the many customs and courtesies still retained from remote ancestry of mingling the gift or use of intoxicating drinks with almost every important event in life, such as the celebration of baptisms, marriages and funerals, anniversaries, holidays and festivities as well as in the daily interchange of convivial entertainments, and even the commercial transactions of purchase and sale'. The committee ascribed as the immediate causes of drunkenness amongst poorer classes, the large number of selling points, the reduction of the spirit duty, admixtures of illicit spirits and the pleasant surroundings of new establishments. They were emphatic on the evils of excessive drinking, its effects on health and so on, the loss of productive labour, indiscipline in the armed forces and, in their view, the inherited propensity for drink from intemperate parents.[153]

Some witnesses wanted fairs to be curbed or abolished and special mention was made of Donnybrook Fair in Dublin, and the festivities on Cavehill in Belfast on Easter Monday. At these times adulteration of spirits was common and was not an offence in Ireland.[154] A Dublin custom was severely attacked by one

152. S. C. on Drunkenness, Parl. Pps. 1834 (559) viii, pp. 323, 583.
153. Ibid., pp. 317-9, 545. Many of these strictures had been uttered 30 years earlier and refuted with statistical evidence. (T. Newenham, *Statistical and Historical Inquiry into the Population of Ireland*, Dublin, 1805, pp. 232-4.) A number of travellers and others mentioned drinking habits, but about the best descriptions are to be found in the writings of William Carleton, particularly his *Traits and Stories of the Irish Peasantry*, Dublin, 1846.
154. S. C. on Drunkenness, 1834, op. cit., pp. 398, 411, 768. *Belfast Historical Records*, op. cit., Book 5, p. 68. Examples of adulteration practised in 1845 are given with the comment that it was an offence in England but not in Ireland. J. Owens, *Plain Papers*, London, 1879, p. 179. 'Doctor' was a term used in Ireland for persons attending fairs and races to doctor liquors for publicans. *Royal*

witness. He alleged that in the large houses maids were given money instead of breakfast and they also received tips from guests. On Sunday mornings the maids gathered at St. Stephen's Green to meet husbands or male friends and squandered the money in drink. The inference is that all the money was squandered and that the meeting with relatives was an orgy. This is one example where the evidence was given in a manner weighted to present a particular picture without any facts as to its evil effects. It would have been very unusual if husbands and wives did not celebrate at a weekly meeting. It was also said that women were tempted to drink in spirit grocers' shops behind a screen of tea chests and there is probably some truth in this, but it did not necessarily mean that there was widespread dissipation to swell the grocer's profits.[155] At that time a day labourer received 6s. to 7s. a week and a farm worker a little less. Whiskey on sale was diluted by adding one part of water to two of spirits and sold at $1\frac{1}{2}$d. a glass or 7s. a gallon, but even at that price whiskey would be a luxury to any labourer with a family. The reformers got over this by stating that labourers were too poor and were not the main consumers of spirits. The drinkers were chiefly tradesmen and farmers and, presumably, artisans whose wages were about 23s. a week. It was claimed that the law against paying wages in a public house was evaded by paying in bank notes of high denominations amongst a group of workers, so that the workers then went to the public house to get smaller money and at the same time start drinking.[156] The revenue interest in a growing sale of spirits did not escape attack, but enough has been given to show that while every fact stated could, by judicious selection, be demonstrated as true there was no real case that the nation was wallowing in drink. To these total abstention reformers temperance was as much an enemy as insobriety, and the distilling industry had little to fear from them in 1834. It is, of course, probable that there was more excessive drinking than was good for the country and that it was more

---

Commission on the Liquor Licensing Laws: Evidence taken in Ireland, Parl. Pps. 1898 (c. 8980) xxxviii, p. 642. A publican in gaol, and in the prison governor's presence, gave his visiting son a recipe for whiskey to be sold at a fair. It was 2 gallons of new whiskey, 1 gallon of rum, $\frac{1}{2}$ gallon of finish (methylated spirits), 4 gallons of water and 1 drachm of copper sulphate.

155. *S. C. on Drunkenness*, 1834, *op. cit.*, pp. 397, 594, 598.

156. *Ibid.*, pp. 394–5, 402, 406.

noticeable in Dublin and other large centres, but prohibition would have been a far worse evil. Laws are useless unless they accord with public opinion.

The selling points referred to by the Drunkenness Inquiry were, in 1825, 122 dealers, 13,794 retailers and 314 spirit grocers. By 1836, two years after the report, there were 381 dealers, 18,836 retailers and 239 spirit grocers, which shows a significant rise in dealers and retailers, but this was a peak year for by 1845 the number of dealers had fallen to 330, a small decrease, but retailers had dropped to 14,184.[157] There appears to be no special reason for the rise in retailers in 1836 and it may have been partly due to the fifty gallon exemption of the increased licence duty allowed in that year if sufficient beer was sold, or merely to a slackening of standards by justices in granting certificates to new applicants for licences. The number of licences is not a reliable measure of the quantities consumed, but in those years this number does rise and fall with the spirits charged with duty. Thus, in 1825 over nine million gallons were charged, in 1836 the quantity was over twelve millions and in 1845 it had fallen to just over 7·5 millions. The duty in these years ranged from 2s. 4d. to 2s. 8d. a proof gallon. A small proportion of spirits would find its way into use in arts or manufacture or be exported, but most of it would be drunk in Ireland. There were other factors affecting these statistics. Population rose by over a million, a vigorous temperance campaign occurred after 1836 and in 1845 the effects of the famine were being felt. It is, therefore, not possible to say with certainty that excessive drinking was on the increase in 1836 and falling later, though the evidence points that way. One thing is clear. The witnesses before the Inquiry into Drunkenness greatly over-stated their case.[158]

157. *13th Inland Revenue Report*, 1870, *op. cit.*, pp. 433, 439, 441. *Excise Revenue Inquiry, 19th Report*, Parl. Pps. 1837 (83) xxx, pp. 11–12.

158. *13th Inland Revenue Report*, 1870, *op. cit.*, p. 387. *Census of Ireland, Part II*, Parl. Pps. 1892 (c. 6780) xc, p. 107. *S.C. on Drunkenness*, 1834, *op. cit.* On page 764 Prof. Edgar quotes statistics of licences issued that are far in excess of official figures. For example he stated that 18,815 retailers' licences were issued in 1825. On p. 556 the Rev. Carr of New Ross gives exaggerated figures for Clonmel and other places. He was the founder of a local temperance society (P. Rogers, *Father Theobald Mathew*, p. 32). On p. 549 Dr Dods quotes medical authority that excessive spirit drinking can cause spontaneous combustion of the body. These are typical examples of much of the evidence given. Official figures of licences and their distribution by counties is given in a *Return of Spirit Licences*, Parl. Pps. 1837–8 (717) xlvi, p. 567.

The real threat to the distiller's home market was, as always, legislative restrictions on sales for immediate consumption, chiefly in licensed houses, but also in the booths at fairs and races, in clubs and at particular functions where occasional licences were granted for one or two days. In all these instances the licensing authority and the excise were involved and the issue was clear cut between free marketing and legal obstruction. The temperance campaigns, however, were outside the control of either distillers or Government. These had not seriously affected the spirit trade before 1838, but in that year a total abstinence campaign began, led by Father Mathew, and lasted to about 1847. It was a much greater threat to the distiller at the time than any previous campaigns. It evolved from the total abstinence societies formed some ten years earlier that had only a local appeal. In 1838 the Cork Total Abstinence Society persuaded Father Mathew, a capuchin friar, to become its president. His drive and his journeys to many parts of the country, together with such inducements as giving medals to all who signed the pledge, brought in a multitude of adherents. The movement was non-sectarian and was supported by many Ulster protestants. It was claimed that five million people signed the pledge. This is patently an extravagant claim, representing some 70 per cent of the whole population and if true would have meant a collapse of the distilling industry, whereas in fact the gallons charged with duty ran at the rate of 7·5 millions from 1840 to 1850. In the same period the population fell by nearly two millions. Further, the brewing industry would also have collapsed. The probability is that many signing the pledge did so on an emotional impulse which did not last.[159] The great famine of 1845–6 undermined the movement. Many country people believed that spirits were a specific against cholera and other famine fevers. There

---

159. P. Rogers, *Father Theobald Mathew, op. cit.,* pp. 38–41. *13th Inland Revenue Report,* 1870, *op. cit.,* p. 387. W. Carleton, *Traits and Stories of the Irish Peasantry, op. cit.,* the story of *Art Maguire* written at the time of the Father Mathew campaign and biassed in its favour. *Belfast Newsletter,* 29 June 1841, reports Ulster support and gives an address from Belfast and Lisburn Total Abstinence Societies to Father Mathew at Banbridge. The report says that 10,000 received the pledge on 20 June 1841. Belief in miraculous healing powers drew many people to these temperance meetings (J. F. Maguire, *Father Mathew,* ed. R. Mulholland, Dublin, pp. 212–9, and *Belfast Newsletter,* 25 June 1841). See also *S.C. on Constabulary functions,* 1854, *op. cit.,* p. 51, and E. Curtis, *A History of Ireland,* London, 1936, p. 364.

was also unexpected opposition from some roman catholic quarters. Nevertheless, though the temperance halls dwindled, writers at the time thought that the movement had a lasting effect and immoderate drinking was never quite so rampant afterwards.[160]

The Commissioners inquiring into the excise revenues reported on licensing in 1837. They recommended that distillers and others with a fixed licence duty unrelated to the extent of trade should pay a graduated duty. They also condemned the arbitrary minimum of two gallons for deliveries by spirit dealers and suggested reducing this to one gallon so that dealers could supply families who would otherwise have to go to public houses for small quantities. They thought innkeepers and victuallers were unfairly treated by having to pay a licence duty on the annual value of their premises as if they were publicans, because spirit sales were only part of their business. They considered that the distinction between a wholesaler and dealer should be abolished. These were mild recommendations compared with their suggestion that excise licences should be completely separated from magisterial control and police supervision. This was advocating free trade for they considered that any person who wished should be able to buy an excise licence. Any question of character or proper behaviour should be a matter for common law and police supervision should be similar to that in any other business.[161] All the recommendations except the separation of excise licensing and police supervision were either adopted or met in other ways, but long after the report. The graduated distiller's licence, for example, was not enacted till 1910. Separation of the excise and police functions never became a legal fact. Magistrates continued to grant certificates and the excise licence followed, but in practice the two functions were separated. Unless

160. J. Forbes, *Memorandums made in Ireland*, London, 1853, i, pp. 282, 291. In ii, p. 271–2, Forbes writes 'the great banded army of Pledged Abstainers from intoxicating drinks has long been broken in pieces and the numbering of the host has come down from millions to thousands and from thousands to hundreds. They show, however, at the same time, that though the organisation has gone, the influence of the movement for good has survived its formal existence'. See also *S.C. to consider extending the functions of the Constabulary in Ireland to the suppression of illicit distilling*, Parl. Pps. 1854 (53) x, p. 66. Local official views were that the campaign adversely affected distilling. The Committee doubted this opinion.

161. *Excise Revenue Inquiry, 19th Report, op. cit.*, pp. 28–30, 33–7.

an applicant was legally disqualified the excise never opposed the issue of a magistrate's certificate. They centred their interest in receiving the proper duty and ensuring that no person sold spirits without a licence. The enforcement of good behaviour and hours of sale, the standing of a new applicant and suitability of his premises, were the province of the police and the magistrates relied on police reports when deciding on a new application.[162]

Complex as were the licensing laws it could not be expected that complications should arise in the excise divisions of the trade. Between the distiller or rectifier and the consumer the trade was arbitrarily divided into dealers, retailers and spirit grocers thus providing additional revenue security by a control over spirits at each stage and incidentally picking up some revenue from licences. In 1841, however, a curious anomaly came to light. The Dublin grocers pointed out to the Treasury that a grocer can sell from one pint to two quarts and a dealer from two gallons upwards. There was no provision for sales in between except from a public house. They asked for this to be remedied. The Treasury replied that a grocer's licence covered sales from one pint or more, but a dealer's licence was necessary if they exceeded two gallons. The Dublin grocers instructed the Treasury on the law and the Treasury then directed the Board of Excise to withdraw grocers' licences and issue retailers' licences, making them public houses without a justice's certificates. Kilkenny grocers objected strongly. As a spirit grocer a person could sell tea, coffee and other goods; as a publican he could not. The Treasury gave them the choice to remain on the two quart upper limit or become retailers. Meanwhile some grocers had taken out retail licences and then been convicted for selling groceries. The Treasury mitigated part of the fine, but no doubt to their dismay, the grocers went to law and won, thus nullifying the convictions. The excise appealed, but actually continued to take proceedings and won while the appeal was pending. The excise also won the appeal, but the Treasury repaid the fines less 10s. The grocers had a real grievance because in England at that time a retailer was allowed to sell tea and coffee. Years later the gap was bridged

162. A graduated scale for distillers' licences was enacted by 10 Edw. 7, and 1 Geo. 5, c. 8, section 43, and First Sched. A. Graduated scales for dealers and rectifiers were not adopted.

when dealers could get a retail off-licence by paying additional duty.[163] This is an example of the inflexibility of the official mind in those days. It seemed a fairly simple issue that should have been easy to settle.

Reformers made much of the malpractices of spirit grocers and the temptations they offered for women to drink spirits. It might be supposed from these reports that there were large numbers of grocers selling spirits, encouraging dram drinking behind a screen of tea chests and the like. In fact these grocers never became a dominant feature of the licence trade. Until 1872 the spirit grocer did not need a magistrate's certificate and he was not restricted in his hours of business so it is not surprising that persons failing to get a publican's licence sometimes became spirit grocers. There was little other inducement because there was no advantage in the licence duty. In 1836 there were 12,440 grocers licensed as such at 11s. of which only 239 had taken out licences to sell spirits and 136 of them were in the lowest category for premises under £25 rateable value. In the same year there were over 18,000 spirit retailers. In 1880 there were 516 spirit grocers and over 16,000 publicans.[164] Attempts were made from time to time to abolish the spirit grocer but he survived until 1910.[165] Extension of the law to permit dealers to get an additional licence to sell in retail quantities was a complete failure and very few were taken out so the spirit grocer was not affected. In 1910 the spirit grocer's licence was merged with the retail off-licence. A new arrangement allowed a dealer, who then paid £15 15s., to obtain a retail 'off'-licence at rates varying from £10 to £50 according to the annual value of his premises, and in that case his

163. *Memorial from Licensed Victuallers in Ireland*, Parl. Pps. 1841 (275) xxvi, pp. 210 *et seq.* In 1861 under 24 and 25 Vict., c. 21, dealers could get additional licences to retail. See also *Parl. Debates*, 6 May 1861, cols. 1611–2.

164. 35 and 36 Vict., c. 94, sections 83–6 required justices' certificates and hours of sale were restricted. See also C. Molloy, *The Justice of the Peace for Ireland*, Dublin, 1890, pp. 859 *et seq.* Statistics are taken from the *Excise Revenue Inquiry, 19th Report, op. cit.*, pp. 11–12 and *23rd Inland Revenue Report*, Parl. Pps. 1880 (c. 2770) xxix, p. 149. A statement that unsuccessful applicants for retail licences took out licences as spirit grocers appears in the *Excise Revenue Inquiry, Digest of Reports, op. cit.*, p. 269.

165. *Parl. Debates*, 4 August 1836, col. 910; 7 August 1871, cols. 948–9. These are two attempts. 2 Edw. 7, c. 18, section 2, stopped the issue of all new licences in Ireland. The licensing laws were revised in 1904 by 4 Edw. 7, c. 23.

dealer's licence duty was halved provided the total was not below £15 15s.[166]

Ether drinking was an interesting though unimportant development that arose mainly in the Cookstown area in county Tyrone. Early in 1847 leading surgeons began using strong sulphuric ether vapour as an anaesthetic and one of them described in the *Belfast Commercial Chronicle* a successful operation whilst a patient was inebriated by the vapour. Other surgeons had similar praise and it may be that ether drinking originated from this publicity. In evidence before a Royal Commission in 1898 a county inspector of police in Londonderry said that soon after the Father Mathew campaign a quack doctor had prescribed ether drinking as a prophylactic against famine fevers. The practice led to a good deal of drunkenness and had some advantages to those who indulged in it. An abnormal state of temperance had been created by the temperance campaign and ether drinking was not considered a breach of the pledge since it could be sold freely and was not recognised as an intoxicant by the licensing laws. A person could get drunk and be sober in about two hours without the usual unpleasant after-effects from whiskey drinking. It was possible to get drunk three or four times a day. At first ether was costly at 24s. a gallon, but not so much was needed as it was more potent. After 1855 it could be made with methylated spirits and this brought the cost down to 3s. 6d. The habit persisted in this area till the end of the century when the Poisons Act was applied first for labelling bottles and later all buying and selling came within the ambit of the whole Act.[167]

166. *14th Inland Revenue Report*, Parl. Pps. 1871 (c. 370) xvii, p. 702. Of the 538 dealers in 1870 none was licensed to retail. *23rd Report*, 1880, *op. cit.*, p. 149. Three dealers out of 610 took out retail licences. *52nd Report*, Parl. Pps. 1909 (Cd. 4868) xxvii, p. 33, shows only 10 additional retail licences among 556 dealers. The wholesale dealer's licence and spirit retailer's off-licence were fixed by 10 Edw. 7, and 1 Geo. 5, c. 8, section 43 and First Sched. (B).

167. *Royal Commission on the Licensing Laws: Evidence taken in Ireland*, 1898, *op. cit.*, pp. 600–1, the evidence of a county inspector of police. Letters on the first use of sulphuric ether appear in the *Belfast Commercial Chronicle* on 4, 18, 23 January, 3 February and later dates in 1847. Sulphuric ether is easily made by heating a mixture of alcohol and sulphuric acid, slowly pouring alcohol on the mixture and distilling it. When using methylated spirits very little methyl alcohol remains in the resulting ether. See *S.C. on British and Foreign Spirits*, Parl. Pps. 1890–1 (210) xi, pp. 449, 451, 495. Also K. H. Connell, *Ether drinking in Ulster*, Quarterly Journal of Studies on Alcohol, vol. 26, No. 4, 1965, New Brunswick, U.S.A.

The licensing laws became more and more complex as the century progressed and caused Gladstone to remark in 1868 that 'so great were the difficulties and so anomalous our licensing laws that every attempt which had hitherto been made to reduce them to something like order or principle had failed'.[168] The difficulties and anomalies, however, were due not so much to the general purpose of legislation as to the detail and drafting which provided a great deal of litigation; for example, defining the precise curtilage of licensed premises and the annual value for licence purposes. Difficulties also arose in defining the licensing authority and its powers. These were administrative problems involved in attempts to control drunkenness while at the same time preserving the liberty of moderate drinkers to buy conveniently, and avoiding too much damage to the revenue from spirits. Licensing affected distillers by curtailing their domestic market and in this environment competition laid a greater emphasis on quality.[169]

The Spirits Act of 1860 devoted a separate part to licensing. It clarified and repeated earlier laws and did not disturb the licensing authorities' powers under the Act of 1833. There were, however, attacks from time to time both on the licensing powers of the courts and on the excise levy. In 1862 there was a move to supplant the justices by more than one system of local option with special reference to systems in other countries. The question was again raised in 1864 and the law in the state of Maine, U.S.A., was specially pressed as a model for the United Kingdom. The reformers also wanted complete closing on Sunday, but as one Irish member remarked that if 'Sunday law' was attempted by Act of Parliament it would be broken at once. It appears that in Cashel the church was against Sunday drinking and the public abstained, but a law would be a different matter. These efforts did not succeed, but in 1878 opening was reduced by two hours.[170] Complaints against the excise licence duties in 1867

---

168. *Parl. Debates*, 24 March 1868, col. 157. Gladstone was referring to the whole licensing system for all intoxicating liquors.

169. *Royal Commission on Licensing Laws: Statistics,* Parl. Pps. 1898 (c. 8696) xxxvii, pp. 437–8.

170. *Parl. Debates*, 27 June 1862, col. 1188; 8 June 1864, cols. 1392 *et seq.*: (The reference to Cashel appears in col. 1422) 9 March 1869, col. 989. The Sunday hours recommended by the Select Committee were not imposed till 1878 by 41 and 42 Vict., c. 72.

centred on the valuation of premises for assessing the duty. In Ireland this valuation was normally the assessment for the Poor Law or if none existed, then the tenement valuation made by the Commissioners of Valuation applied. The objection was that the Board of Inland Revenue arbitrarily added 25 per cent since there was a monopoly interest inherent in the licensing system, and they were legally bound to fix a value for places not rated for inhabited house duty. One Irish member thought this addition simply increased the shebeens.[171] In 1862 and 1863 occasional licences for publicans to sell spirits at places other than their entered premises were put under the jurisdiction of the justices whose approval was required before the excise granted the licence for one day or for special night functions.[172]

In 1870 the government announced that a Bill would be introduced that would place mechanical difficulties in the way of indulging in intoxicating drink and that it would consolidate at least 40 Acts. This caused some apprehension amongst distillers and those in the licence trade who emphasised that large capital was invested. The Home Secretary did not reassure them by saying that the object of the Bill was to reduce drunkenness and legislation 'must operate prejudicially to the capital invested'. A Bill was introduced in 1871 and a very long debate ensued. As a result there was a temporary stop in the issue of any new licences till a revised Bill could be prepared. There was a clause for granting provisional licences subject to confirmation by the Chief Secretary.[173]

The long promised Licensing Act was passed in 1872, but a number of its sections did not apply in Ireland and a subsequent Act in 1874 filled these gaps. The Acts dealt mainly with hours of sale, offences against public order, the method of issuing licences and rules for legal proceedings. The only reference to excise licence duty concerned a reduction by one-seventh of the full licence if a licensee closed one hour earlier every night and a similar reduction if the public house was closed on Sundays. If both conditions were fulfilled the reduction was two-sevenths.

---

171. *Ibid.*, 29 November 1867, cols. 431–3. The law permitting the increase in value was 6 Geo. 4, c. 81, section 5. The Poor Law valuation was sometimes referred to as Griffith's valuation.

172. 25 and 26 Vict., c. 22, section 13; 26 and 27 Vict., c. 33, section 2.

173. 34 and 35 Vict., c. 88. *Parl. Debates,* 4 March 1870, col. 1247; 3 April 1871, col. 1062–1114; 2 May 1871, cols. 44–5.

Certificates authorising an excise licence were to be granted once a year at a quarter sessions or petty sessions ordered by the Lord Lieutenant. The annual licensing quarter sessions granted certificates for new licences and authorised transfers of existing spirit licences; the petty sessions dealt with renewals.[174] There were some changes to meet changing conditions. For example, the applicant for a new licence had to advertise the fact in the local press between two and four weeks before the licensing sessions and he no longer had to serve a notice on the church wardens. A special theatre licence was introduced. There was provision to protect owners of licensed premises where a manager in charge was convicted of an offence which endangered the licence. In the main Act there were clauses dealing with adulteration which were repealed and not repeated in the Irish Act, the reason being that this problem was transferred to the Sale of Food and Drugs Act of 1875 which amongst its provisions forbad the dilution of whiskey below 25° under proof.[175]

There were a number of attacks on the licensing laws after 1874, almost all of them on two aspects, the licensing authority and the hours of sale. In addition the House of Lords set up a committee to inquire into intemperance. The desire of many members of parliament was to reduce the number of public houses and several private bills were introduced with this object in view. Some members seemed specially keen to introduce some form of local option or, if that was too strong, to replace magistrates by a kind of licensing board on which ratepayers would be represented. None of these suggestions were adopted.[176] There was a

174. The principal Act was 35 and 36 Vict., c. 94. The Act with special reference to Ireland was 37 and 38 Vict., c. 69. Section 12 defined the licensing authorities. A good summary of the law with appropriate notes is given by A. Reed, *The Liquor Licensing Laws of Ireland*, Dublin, 1889. See also C. Molloy, *The Justice of the Peace for Ireland*, Dublin, 1890, pp. 859 *et seq. Parl. Debates*, 16 May 1873, col. 15 pointed out defects in the 1872 Act as it applied to Ireland and amending legislation was promised.
175. 37 and 38 Vict., c. 69, sections 7, 10, 12–13; 38 and 39 Vict., c. 63, sections 6, 8; and 42 and 43 Vict., c. 30, section 6. The dilution limit was not directly imposed, but the law provided that it would be a good defence to prove that dilution with water did not reduce the strength below 25 per cent under proof. The present home market minimum strength is 30 per cent under proof. Protection for owners against the results following a convicted manager became necessary with the growth of 'tied' houses connected with breweries, chiefly in England.
176. *Parl. Debates*, 19 June 1874, cols. 210–15; 17 May 1876 cols. 848 *et seq.*,

small legislative success in 1878 to reduce selling when an Act prohibited sales on Sunday except in Dublin, Cork, Waterford, Limerick and Belfast. In these cities hours of sale were restricted. While there is no proof, it is exceedingly doubtful if these restrictions were very effective.[177] In 1880 the licence duties were revised. The rate for publicans was still based on the annual value for Poor Rates, but if this was the same as the rateable value there was an addition of 20 per cent to bring it up to the licence value. The licence rates themselves rose by stages from £4 10s. for a licence value under £10 to £60 if the value was £700 or more. The spirit licence covered the sale of beer and wine for consumption on or off the premises. Rates were also fixed for inns and hotels, theatres, and six-day or early closing publicans.[178]

The Royal Commission on the Liquor Licensing Laws made its reports in 1898 after an exhaustive inquiry. Its opinion on the existing law was summed up as 'No one can appreciate how complex and how difficult the law is till they have tried to summarise it, however generally. The system of legislation by reference and definition is here exemplified to the full; you have to leap from statute to statute and section to section in a most bewildering fashion, and after all this the uncertainty is so great that even within the last few weeks cases have been decided or are pending on some most important points. But if the English law stands badly in need of consolidation and codification, the Irish law stands in even greater need'.[179] From the standpoint of the lawyer these remarks were true. Parts of many statutes from 1825 onwards were still extant or modified without repealing the original, for example, a licensing Act of 1871 refers back to an Act in 1828 and the room for legal argument was vast. From the standpoint of the prosperity of the distilling industry and its outlets through the licensed trades the principal concern is not the fine legal points, but how far the trade was restricted.

---

30 June 1876, cols. 715–34; 16 June 1880, cols. 159 *et seq.*, and col. 365 in which Gladstone is reported as saying that he was 'thoroughly and radically dissatisfied with the licensing laws'. There were other debates on 20 May 1881 and 14 June 1881.

177. 41 and 42 Vict., c. 72. Sales to lodgers was allowed and it can be assumed that this was interpreted with some elasticity.

178. 43 and 44 Vict., c. 20, section 43.

179. *Royal Commission on the Liquor Licensing Laws: Statistics relating to Licensed premises,* 1898, *op. cit.,* p. 207.

By far the majority of the difficulties in law dealt with individual
cases on the fringe of the main trade. Quibbles about the annual
licence value might cause some publicans to pay a slightly higher
licence duty, or a question may arise as to what constitutes a
bona fide traveller who wants a drink, or where a sale takes
place when an unlicensed restaurant sends out for drinks for its
customers. None of these is of much importance to the distiller
or the retail trade generally and none of them seriously restricts
trade though they might, in some cases, lead to shebeening.[180]

A more important aspect was the Royal Commission's report
on the numbers of public houses in relation to population and the
clear inference that these numbers should be reduced. They
reported this in some detail. The greatest density was in the range
of one public house to 300 persons and this density was most
numerous in the counties of Cork, Limerick and Tipperary and
in some of the towns. At the same time there was an upward
trend in the number of off-licences, particularly in Belfast where
the rise had been from 301 in 1886 to 731 in 1896. So it seems
that past legislation had not restricted the spirit trade very signi-
ficantly. One interesting feature was disclosed in the evidence
given for Londonderry which had been affected by the Sunday
Closing Act of 1878. Following the Act there had been an increase in spirit grocers and a decrease in police prosecutions for
drunkenness. A police witness attributed this to five causes;
among them the temperance missions, improved education and
the increased popularity of athletics, particularly cycling. He also
said that most drunkards in the city were women and in the
country, men.[181]

The Royal Commission also drew attention to clubs where
drink was sold to members. There were two kinds of club
neither of which came within the licensing Acts. There were
clubs where the members owned the club, appointed trustees
and a council or its equivalent to run the establishment, the drinks
sold were treated as a return of the member's contribution to the
purchase of the liquor in proportion to the quantity he bought,
and all profits were returned to club funds. The other kind were

180. 34 and 35 Vict., c. 88 refers back to 6 Geo. 4, c. 61. Sir N. J. Highmore,
The Excise Laws, 3rd ed. London, 1923. In vol. ii, hundreds of court decisions
are listed resulting in a formidable body of case law.

181. *Royal Commission on the Licensing Laws: Statistics*, 1898, *op. cit.*, pp.
438, 442, and *Evidence taken in Ireland*, 1898, *op. cit.*, pp. 598, 600.

proprietary clubs run for profit by a person or company. Any control over these clubs was by case law and not by legislation and for proprietary clubs' sales would normally be illegal. The only difference between the latter and a publican was that sales were restricted to members. This position was corrected in 1902 by a licensing Act applying to England and extended to Ireland in 1904. Clubs had to be registered with the clerk to the petty session and a copy of the rules lodged. A statement of purchases had to be lodged with the excise after the close of each year and a duty of 6d. in the £ paid on liquor sales.[182]

Many of the recommendations of the Royal Commission were adopted by the Acts of 1902 and 1904. Consolidation of the law was the government's aim and so far these Acts merely patched up outdated parts. Irish licensing was left undisturbed except to put a ban on the issue of any new licences unless there was an increase of at least 25 per cent in population in any area. In such cases a minimum valuation was prescribed for licence duty.[183]

Spirit consumption and competing drinks

It is now appropriate to see what effect all this legislation had on the licensed trade and whether in fact there was any significant decrease in public houses and in drinking. The following table shows a considerable drop in spirit drinking, a rise in public houses, and a fall in population.[184]

	Spirits charged '000,000	Public Houses	Population '000
1825	9·3 gallons	13,794	6,802
1850	7·4 gallons	13,885	6,552
1880	5·1 gallons	16,493	5,175
1900	4·7 gallons	17,596	4,457

The figures for 1880 and 1900 are the quantities retained for home consumption.

182. 2 Edw. 7, c. 28; 4 Edw. 7, c. 9. See also *Highmore's Excise Laws, op. cit.,* ii, pp. 413–8.
183. 2 Edw. 7, c. 18.
184. *13th Inland Revenue Report,* 1870, *op. cit.,* pp. 387, 439, 441; *23rd Inland Revenue Report,* 1880, *op. cit.,* pp. 92, 149; *43rd Inland Revenue Report,* Parl. Pps., 1900 (Cd. 347) xviii, pp. 388, 392, 404.

The years selected for comparison are sufficient to show a general trend. There were very considerable variations above and below in the intervening years. Moreover' in the years 1825 and 1850 the only figures available are for gallons at proof charged with duty which assumes that the spirit was consumed in Ireland. As there was a customs barrier between Ireland and Great Britain till spirit duties were equalised in 1858 this is a fair assumption. In the later years, however, the gallons charged could differ appreciably from the spirits retained for home consumption and the latter figure is given. Thus in 1880 the spirits charged were 6·9 million proof gallons, but 1·8 millions are not shown as retained for home consumption. This difference represents spirits sent to customers in Great Britain. It is a net difference because there was a smaller traffic in the opposite direction. The rate of duty is another factor. In 1825 it was 2s. 4d. a proof gallon, in 1850 it was 2s. 8d., but in 1860 it was 10s. and by 1900 it was 11s. The decrease in population must also be taken into account. After allowing for all these variables it is clear that consumption of spirits had declined substantially.[185]

A precise explanation for the decline is not easy. It could be due to more sobriety following persistent temperance missions and restrictive legislation aimed at the retail trade, a rise in educational standards, alternatives such as interest in athletics as suggested by the police witness before the Royal Commission in 1898, or a switch to beer and wine drinking, or a combination of all these factors. The rise in the number of public houses indicates that beer drinking was probably the main reason for the drop in spirit consumption. A licence to retail spirits for consumption on the premises covered the sale of beer and wine and also all these

185. *The Inland Revenue Reports* give details of the movement of spirits between Ireland and Great Britain. For example, in the *24th Report,* Parl. Pps. 1881 (c. 2967) xxix, p. 267, 7·3 million gallons of duty paid spirit came on the Irish market of which nearly 36,000 gallons came from Great Britain and after allowing for spirits sent to Great Britain and for some 20,000 gallons for methylation, the net figure for Irish consumption was 5·2 million gallons. Also shown is the large scale of exports to Great Britain compared with the quantities in the opposite direction, especially to England where 1·8 million gallons were sent and only 18,000 gallons received. The Scottish figures are even more remarkable since whiskey was the common beverage. 17,715 gallons came from Scotland but 247,843 gallons were sent there. Much of the export to Scotland was grain whiskey made in patent stills and used for blending (see J. Jameson and Sons and others, *Truths about Whiskey*, Dublin, 1878, pp. 9–10, and *Parliamentary Debates,* 4 April 1876, cols. 1185–6).

beverages for sale in retail quantities for consumption off the premises. There was a licence at a lower rate of duty for selling beer only, but the numbers taken out were very small. Thus though the number of public houses is not a clear indication of drinking habits it is a pointer that the influence of temperance missions and the other factors was limited. The number, however, is not entirely a satisfactory guide. There is no way of discovering the average trade in these public houses. The onslaught of various persons on the number of public houses in a particular village or street was more an expression of righteous indignation than an effective argument. If four such houses were in one street and then two were closed it probably meant no reduction in drinking, but merely a concentration of trade and perhaps some inconvenience to customers.[186]

Since the decline in spirit drinking was probably due in a large measure to a rise in beer drinking it would be instructive if statistics of beer production were examined. Here there is a difficulty. Before 1880 there are no revenue statistics for beer as the duty was levied on malt. After that date the duty was paid on beer, but like the proof gallon for spirits, the revenue statistics for beer are for barrels calculated at an original gravity of $55°$ and not on the bulk quantity.[187] Estimation of beer consumption in the earlier years is further complicated because the malt used by distillers would be included in the revenue figures. The malt duty until 1855 was charged and the distillers later got a drawback. After that year the revenue figures do show the malt used for distilling, but the quantities were approximately half the total. Thus in 1879, the last year of the malt duty, 3·5 million bushels of malt were made of which 1·7 millions were used by distillers. At the conversion rate presumed by the 1880 Act this would result in 1·8 million standard barrels of beer. In 1850 the malt charged with duty was 1·7 million bushels and, after allowing for malt used in distilleries, the figures show a

186. Examples of the arguments of zealous reformers are in the report of the *S.C. on Drunkenness*, 1834, *op. cit.*, pp. 400, 556. See also *Royal Commission on the Liquor Licensing Laws: Statistics relating to Licensed premises*, 1898, *op. cit.*, pp. 438–9.

187. 43 and 44 Vict., c. 20, section 13. The standard barrel for duty was 36 gallons of worts of a gravity of $1057°$, water being regarded as $1000°$. The standard for gravity was changed to $1055°$ in 1889 by 52 and 53 Vict., c. 7, section 3. It was presumed that 2 bushels of malt would produce a standard barrel.

substantial rise in beer production between 1850 and 1880. In 1900, some three million barrels of beer were made. This rise does not represent the extent of beer drinking in Ireland as it would include a very large export trade in beer which had been developed by the firm of Arthur Guinness, Son and Company, who dominated Irish brewing, and some exports by smaller firms. Nevertheless domestic sales of beer did rise in the last quarter of the nineteenth century, and rise considerably. No exact figures can be given and any statistics are bound to be blurred by movements of beer both to and from Great Britain.[188]

Drinking habits were changing by 1900. From the standpoint of the Irish distiller the important change was the rise in popularity of blends of pot still and Coffey still whiskey. The change stemmed primarily from Scotland and a large English market was developing in proprietary blends, but firms in northern Ireland were also important in this market. In the Irish intoxicating liquor market wine had made no headway. Beer had certainly made inroads into the whiskey trade, but the movement was still relatively small. Viewing the liquor trade as a whole there is no firm evidence that there had been any decline. Indeed the increase in public houses points to a rise in drinking. Despite the movement towards beer and the disturbing effects of blended whiskey on pot still distillers, the industry was prosperous. In 1900 it was producing 14·5 million proof gallons. In that year over four million proof gallons were sent to England and over 680,000 proof gallons to Scotland. It is also certain that Irish whiskey would have its fair share of the spirits exported abroad from the United Kingdom.[189]

188. Statistics of Guinness's sales in Ireland are shown by P. Lynch and J. Vaizey, *Guinness's Brewery in the Irish Economy, 1759–1876*, Cambridge, 1960, p. 230. This book also shows the slow expansion of the firm's Irish trade inland along the canal routes, with setbacks, some serious, until 1870, when home sales began to rise quickly. It can be assumed that other successful Irish breweries had a similar experience. *13th Inland Revenue Report*, 1870, *op. cit.*, p. 384 gives the quantities of malt charged with duty and the rates in force up to 1869; p. 229 shows the increase in consumption per head in the ten years 1860–9. See also M. G. Mulhall, *Dictionary of Statistics*, London, 1929. p. 555 gives the figures for consumption of beer per head of population from 1800 to 1880. The rate rises sharply in 1870. Details are not given on the source or method of arriving at these figures.

189. *43rd Inland Revenue Report*, Parl. Pps. 1900 (Cd. 347) xviii, pp. 363 *et seq*. See also *Royal Commission on Licensing: Evidence in Ireland*, 1898, *op. cit.*, pp. 605, 625.

CHAPTER VIII

THE PRESENT CENTURY

THERE were no marked changes in the early years of this century, either in the distillery laws or techniques, or in the rates of duty; but during the century the industry was seriously disrupted, like many other industries, by two world wars and the political changes in Ireland following civil strife in the early 1920s. In overseas markets distillers had to contend with the rise of local distilling protected by tariffs and with the prohibition era in the United States. As the century progressed the outstanding feature was the fantastic rise in the spirit duties which, in turn, increased prices to such an extent that the whiskey trade inevitably declined in favour of cheaper drinks, output contracted, many firms succumbed and others sought safety by amalgamation. The rise in popularity of blends of pot and patent whiskey, so noticeable in the latter part of the nineteenth century, continued with greater vigour, especially in the north of Ireland, and in Scotland. In the end Scotch blended whisky dominated both the United Kingdom and overseas markets. Pot still whiskey distillers in both countries contracted production, but kept a substantial market supplying their whiskey for blending and also marketing self whiskey for the connoisseur. Southern Ireland remained a stronghold for pot still whiskey, but exports were spread thinly around the world.

The political division of Ireland occurred in 1922 when the Irish Free State was constituted. The result was that the parliament in Dublin had complete legislative powers for the twenty-six counties of southern Ireland. In the six Ulster counties constituting Northern Ireland distillery laws and revenues remained under the control of the imperial parliament in London, but legislation and the revenues of the licensed trade in spirits were transferred to the subordinate parliament in Belfast.[1]

1. Saorstat Eireann 1922, No. 1, Article 74, and the corresponding United

Distilling

In both parts of Ireland the Spirits Act of 1880 remains the basis of the distillery laws. In the Republic of Ireland this Act is still on the statute book. In the United Kingdom the Act was repealed in 1952, but its provisions were incorporated in the Customs and Excise Act of that year.[2] There have been changes since then to ease the lot of distillers principally by statutory or departmental regulations. These were minor and few for the first fifty years or so, but recently the changes have been quite radical. At present far fewer revenue locks are used in distilleries, the emphasis of excise control being concentrated on those parts of the pipes and vessels actually used for conveying or receiving potable spirit. Earlier stages are no longer under lock and key. Distillers have much freer access to stocks in their warehouses. They are not bound to have an interval between brewing and distilling. In the United Kingdom a distiller can, if he wishes, by-pass both the spirit receiver and spirit store and run his product direct into warehouse vats; a concession of more use when making industrial spirit than whiskey. In general, stock accounts have risen in importance in relation to physical controls. The changes are not identical in both parts of Ireland, but the trend to relaxed excise supervision is nearly parallel. No wild malpractices have resulted. It has taken a long time to recognise the plain fact that distilling has been in the hands of large companies for very many years, companies of the highest commercial standing. The atmosphere of distrust by the excise, so noticeable in the nineteenth century, and so justifiable in its earlier decades, has no place today. Regulation and supervision are still essential for the proper operation of the revenue machine and its interests must be protected. The aim is to achieve this goal with the least possible interference with the distiller's activities. The distiller's co-operation is sought rather than demanded. The distiller can, and does, complain from time to time, but in these days he is normally in disagreement with government policy and not excise regulation. One result of these changes has been to transfer much

---

Kingdom Act, 13 Geo. 5, sess. 2, c. 1, Article 74. Also 1922, No. 5, which provides for the continuance of expiring laws.

2. 15 and 16 Geo. 6 and Eliz. 2, c. 44, secs. 93–121. Sec. 94 gives wide powers to the Commissioners of Customs and Excise to regulate by departmental orders. This allows more elasticity than earlier laws.

of the burden of preventing irregularities, such as pilfering, from excise officers to the distillers themselves.

So by 1970 production of whiskey and other spirituous beverages is a commercial undertaking practically unhampered by excise laws and more like any other manufacturing business. The laws merely prescribe tram lines along which production and marketing must run and are fitted into the normal distilling operations. If an excise control rubs hard in any particular way, changes are hammered out to ease the situation. Innovations to improve efficiency, such as the use of accurate flow meters in the spirit store or warehouse, do not have to overcome official suspicion. If a new method is workable and the revenue risk negligible that is enough. In general the distillers and revenue authorities work together more like a team than as bodies with opposing interests. It is also noticeable that successive governments have more and more come to recognise the value of the distilling industry not simply as a source of revenue, but as a major factor in the country's economy, particularly in the export market. Increasing revenue needs have made this attitude a difficult problem; how to nurse the industry and extract a large revenue.

The distilling industry was subjected to inquiries by a Select Committee of the Commons in 1890 and by a Royal Commission in 1908–9. Arguments centred on the constituents in fusel oil, the differences between pot and patent still whiskey and on maturing. In the earlier inquiry distillers were against any form of compulsory bonding before marketing, but opinion had changed by 1908 and many distillers, especially those in southern Ireland, favoured at least two years bonding of whiskey before delivery for home consumption. Grain distillers opposed this, claiming that their patent still spirit had so little fusel oil in it that it did not need long maturing. Certain exports, however, had to satisfy these conditions, exports to Australia for example; so distillers were not without experience of compulsory bonding and an official certificate of age would be a help to them. Nothing was done immediately, but in 1915 war conditions brought this to the fore.[3]

3. *Select Committee on British and Foreign Spirits,* Parl. Pps. 1890 (316) x, 1890–1 (210) xi; *Royal Comm. on Whisky and other Potable Spirits,* Parl. Pps. 1908 [Cd. 4181], 1909 [Col. 4796 and 4876].

Among the proposals made by Lloyd George in his budget speech in April 1915 was one to double the spirit duty to 29s. 6d. a proof gallon. His opening words were that 'every government that has ever touched alcohol has burnt its fingers in its lurid flames', and he was not to be disappointed. His reasons were that the sale of alcoholic liquors should be discouraged as this was having a bad effect on munition workers and instanced the ill effects of drinking raw spirit, especially on naval repair work on the river Clyde. In his own brand of logic he declared: 'I am not proposing anything today as a solution of temperance, as a promotion of sobriety, as an advancement of social reform. Whatever I propose, I propose as an act of discipline during the war, and for making war more efficiently.' His proposals also included increasing the permitted level of dilution for sale to the public from $25°$ to $35°$ under proof. Naturally members of parliament with little or no munition work in their constituencies raised objections, but the Irish reaction took a different line. W. O'Brien of Cork, after asserting that 'no more healthy tonic can be prescribed than Irish whiskey which had been allowed to ripen in casks for four or five years', then asked the Chancellor of the Exchequer to confine himself to remedy 'villainous adulteration' and sale of raw spirit reeking with fusel oil. He also pointed out the bad effect the rise in duty would have on distilleries with a declining market, and on barley growing. He pressed for the proposal to be dropped in favour of compulsory maturing in bond before release for sale. Lloyd George replied that arguments on the value of maturing and the merits of pot and patent still whiskey had been fully investigated in 1909 and that 'it is really a fight between Belfast and Dublin'. He was referring to the concentration of patent still distilling in the north of Ireland.[4]

The Irish party in the Commons was sufficiently numerous to combine with the Conservative opposition and could defeat the Government. Its opposition to the rise in duty and its advocacy of compulsory bonding caused Lloyd George to drop his proposal in favour of restricting deliveries to matured spirit. If his aim was no more than to cut back supplies and reduce excessive drinking the new measure, if not so effective immediately, would have an influence for good in the long run. A Bill to prohibit the

4. *Parliamentary Debates*, 29 April 1915, cols. 864 *et seq.* 42 and 43 Vict., c. 30 had fixed a minimum of $25°$ under proof.

delivery for home consumption of plain spirits, in effect this meant whiskey, was duly introduced and became law as the Immature Spirits (Restriction) Act, 1915. Whiskey had to be stored in cask in bond for at least three years. To cushion the effect of the Act the period was reduced to two years for the first year of its operation. Imported spirits were subject to the same restrictions, but allowance was made, subject to proof, for any period between distillation and importation. The Act exempted spirits intended for further manufacture, for example to make liqueurs or perfumes, or intended for scientific or industrial use, subject to a small surcharge on the rate of duty if the processes themselves were not exempted.[5]

Naturally compulsory bonding did not suit all distillers. Those using Coffey stills complained that their purer spirit did not need long maturing, whilst pot still distillers were more than happy with the Act. Belfast and Londonderry were badly hit as they were large production centres for grain spirit which was often sold to blending houses soon after manufacture, a lot of it to Scottish blenders. These distillers did not carry large stocks and had insufficient warehousing space for three years storage. Nor could most blenders suddenly expand their storage to accept spirit three years before marketing. The position was aggravated by heavy forestalling since the law to restrict this only applied to budget proposals. Another disruption arose because distillers selling as they made the spirit were caught short of stocks to meet forestalling demands and many of those with stocks took the opportunity to sell out at good prices and retire. It is said that some fifty blending firms in Scotland retired. During the passage of the Bill suggestions were made to allow immature spirit deliveries at higher rates of duty instead of compulsory bonding, or to restrict sales in munitions areas. The Government rejected both suggestions.[6] The patent still distillers did not give up when the Act was passed, for two months later a proposal was made to amend the Act so that the age of a blend should be decided by the average age of the spirit used. The rule was, and still is, that the age of a blend is determined by the youngest spirit used

5. 5 and 6 Geo. 5, c. 46. See *The Times*, 10 May 1915.

6. *Parl. Debates*, 4 May 1915, col. 1004; 12 May 1915, cols. 1680–97. Ross Wilson, *Seventy Years of the Scotch Whisky Industry*, articles in the *Wine and Spirit Trade Record*, see especially the issue of 16 September 1965.

whether the blend is confined to different pot still distillations or putting together whiskey from pot and patent stills. Clearly the patent still supporters hoped to circumvent the Act by such blending as using, say, some five years old pot still whiskey with one year old grain whiskey and calling the result three years old. T. M. Healy, the member for Cork, vigorously opposed the proposal, rightly saying that it would shatter the purpose of the Act. The proposal was defeated, doubtless to the satisfaction of the traditional distillers in Ireland and the numerous small pot still malt distillers in Scotland.[7]

The war of 1914–18 put a heavy strain on food supplies so it was inevitable that distilling should come under severe restrictions. The pot still distillers, whose sole outlet was the drink trade, caught the brunt. Grain distillers had alternative markets of considerable importance for war purposes. Their high strength nearly pure alcohol was essential for making propellants such as cordite because alcohol is easily converted into acetone by a distilling process. The fusel oil was also valuable. The grain distillers also made yeast in large quantities and used principally maize and rye, the former imported mainly from America, the latter home grown and its cultivation could be expanded. Before the war a great deal of yeast came from Denmark and Belgium. This source was closed to the nation's bread suppliers who then had to depend solely on the yeast from grain distillers in Ireland and Scotland.[8]

To harness the distilling industry to the war effort the government's first step was to set up an Advisory Committee on Alcohol Supplies in 1915. Most of its members were drawn from the industry. S. C. Bayne represented the Irish grain distillers and Andrew Jameson the pot still distillers. Another member was Sir Arthur Tedder from the excise department, father of Lord Tedder, Marshal of the Royal Air Force in the second great war. As a result of its war importance grain distilling was encouraged rather than restricted. Pot still distillers got no encouragement, but many were kept alive because without them there would

---

7. *Parl. Debates*, 13 July 1915, cols. 779–81.
8. *7th Customs and Excise Report*, Parl. Pps.1917 [Cd. 8428], p. 33 lists 5 patent still distilleries in Ireland making yeast in 1915. R. Wilson, *Scotch Whisky Industry, op. cit.*, 18 October 1965. The grain distillers provided fusel oil and alcohol and made acetone for munitions.

have been no whiskey either pot still or blended. Complete prohibition was not practicable. It would not have had public sanction so control was the alternative and a Central Control Board (Liquor Traffic) was formed. The Board restricted the sale of spirits, forbad anyone to stand a friend a drink and so on, and permitted dilution of whiskey to 50° under proof in munitions areas. Like a number of these orders it was unsuccessful. In May 1916 there was an Order in Council prohibiting the manufacture of spirit except under a permit issued by the Ministry of Munitions. On 15 August 1917 the Barley (Restriction) Order, 1917, was made by the Ministry of Food, prohibiting the use of barley except for food or seed. Maize and rye were not touched. This put pot distillation out of business and it ceased for two years. Any blending, therefore, now meant drawing on warehoused stocks of pot still whiskey which could not be replaced and thus would handicap the market when the war ended. A Cork member of parliament, for example, complained that the Order had led to unemployment in Midleton and Cork. This hiatus in distilling caused some casualties in distilling firms in Ireland, but perhaps the effect was more severe in the Scottish highlands. Another complaint was that a shortage of whiskey in Ireland was arising because Scottish buyers attended auctions in Dublin and Belfast, buying up Irish whiskey at 25° under proof and diluting it to 50° under proof for sale at normal prices in munitions areas. As well as the Barley Order, deliveries from bonded warehouses were restricted and J. A. Clynes, for the government, said they were imposed to avoid the risk of transferring consumption from beer to spirits. Beer was having its own war time troubles. It is no surprise, therefore, that a black market arose. Unusual labels appeared. Whiskey sold at £1 a bottle or more, which was double the normal price, and at a lower strength. Complaints and rumours abounded, some partly true, during these years of complete disruption of normal trading conditions.[9]

The full effect of compulsory bonding for three years was overshadowed by the various war time measures. When peace came the distilling industry returned as quickly as it was able to its old

9. *Parl. Debates*, 22 November 1917, col. 1345; 10 December 1917, col. 882; 18 December 1917, col. 1819. R. Wilson, *Scotch Whisky Industry, op. cit.,* 17 November and 15 December 1965.

L

habits. One of these was a recurring cycle of optimism and pessimism on the future market needs, with the added new obstacle to correct assessment imposed by the restrictions on delivering new whiskey. These restrictions did not directly affect pot still distillers since it was normal for such whiskey to be stored for a number of years to mature. Grain whiskey from patent stills was a different matter since it was often sold to blenders soon after manufacture. The United Distilleries Company, for example, had patent stills in Belfast and Londonderry and in 1908 their managing director stated that this spirit was marketed within a few months of making it. Blenders then vatted and bottled it with mature pot still whiskey for sale to the public. After 1915 not only did distillers or blenders have to provide much more storage space, but they had to foretell the fickle public taste and state of the market at least three years in advance; a handicap that few other industries have to face. If the distiller was too confident stocks built up and storage costs ate away profits. If the opposite, a shortage of stocks arose that could not be quickly corrected by expanding production, and there was a danger that in an effort to build up stocks on the basis of existing demand, the increase might prove unjustified. Thus an oscillation of whiskey supplies is inherent in the distilling industry and the 1915 Act simply accentuated the 'boom and bust' tendency. Pot still distillers were used to these fluctuations and probably worked on average figures over a few years, but the rise in blending gave them an alternative market in which their whiskey lost its identity and made it harder for them to assess the future. In times of gloom their distilling would be cut back or temporarily cease, only to find a few years later that a fortune awaited anyone with large stocks of mature whiskey. Sometimes the gambling nature of the business was too severe on the nerves and there was an urge to sell out while prices were high. Not surprisingly some distilleries failed whilst others merged into larger units, both to co-ordinate and control production and to become financially stronger in order to ride the statistical waves.[10]

The compulsory bonding period in the Irish Free State was

10. *Royal Comm. on Whisky*, 1908, *op. cit.*, p. 155. Examples of failures and the fusion of companies are given in historical accounts of various Irish distilling companies in Chapter ix.

increased in 1926 from three years to five years and applied by stages over the next two years. The intention was to enhance the reputation of Irish whiskey produced by pot stills. Certainly the extended period penalised most imports from Scotland and Northern Ireland for at that time most of these imports were blends of pot and patent whiskey and the grain spirit used would, in most cases, be just over the three years minimum. In the Dáil debate on the Bill the point was again made that Irish pot still whiskey needed five years or more to mature whilst the patent spirit used in blends 'if it does improve at all' practically ceases maturing after three years. Since patent spirit is cheaper to make a longer storage time would go some way towards reducing the difference in costs. In the domestic market the extended period undoubtedly helped the Irish distiller, but whether it was a wise move is questionable. It obstructed exports, especially to the United States. In that country the spirit laws prescribed that no spirit could be marketed that could not be sold in the exporting country. Three year old whiskey from the United Kingdom could be sold in the United States but whiskey from the Irish Free State had to be five years old.[11]

Irish distillers in 1926 were no doubt convinced that their whiskey was a better article for which American customers would be prepared to pay a little extra. But the United States had its own whiskey industry after prohibition ended and imports, especially Scotch whiskey, were well advertised and cost less. The Irish distiller could not compete successfully even if he resorted to blending because of the five year rule. In his home market imported blended whiskey was making serious headway. If the domestic market needed help, it is clearly better secured by a protective customs duty and this was done in 1964 at a time when imported spirits had reached more than a third of the quantity home made. Eventually in December 1969 the restricted period was reduced to three years at the request of Irish distillers. The legal change brought Ireland into line with the internationally recognised three year minimum and the period recommended for spirits by the Council of Europe.[12]

In the latter part of the nineteenth century ruinous competition

11. 1926 No. 26; *Dáil Debates*, vol. 15, 13 May 1926, cols. 2471–5.
12. 1964 No. 15; 1969 No. 29. *Dáil Debates*, vol. 208, 14 April 1964, col. 1549; vol. 242, 11 November 1969, cols. 614–5.

and production unrelated to market needs forced some distillers
to attempt some kind of control. Mere understandings between
distilling firms were not likely to succeed. The wisdom of
uniting and establishing larger firms so as to regulate output
and provide better resources to tide over fluctuations was first
realised in Cork when, in 1867, the Cork Distilleries Company
was formed to embrace the distillery at Midleton and four
distilleries in Cork city. In Scotland a similar merger of grain
distillers ten years later resulted in the founding of the Distillers
Company Limited. The next major Irish union occurred in 1890
when three large pot still distilleries in Dublin combined to
become the Dublin (Whiskey) Distillers Company. In 1902 two
Belfast and two Londonderry distilleries merged as the United
Distilleries Company. This was a powerful union with a combined output in 1908 of five to six million proof gallons of both
pot and patent whiskey. A smaller, but more lasting combination
arose during 1935–7 when the Old Bushmills Distillery Company
acquired the distilleries in Coleraine and Killowen. This company
has enhanced its importance since then by association with the
Charrington brewery group in England, thus giving ready access
for its whiskey into the numerous English tied public houses
of the brewing firm as well as a broader and larger capital base.
In the Republic of Ireland all the distilleries were amalgamated
in 1966 to form the United Distillers of Ireland, now known as the
Irish Distillers Group Limited. Each of the constituent firms is
represented on the Board of the new company and the identity
of their brands is preserved. There has been a major change in
policy. Whiskey is no longer sold in bulk. All the whiskey is
vatted and bottled in their own premises in Dublin and Cork.
These changes should help to maintain a high standard, provide
a controlled production policy and the use of common services
for more effective advertising and marketing, especially with
exports. In the modern world the days of the small individually
owned distillery are over. The capital needed to survive is far too
much.[13]

13. *Royal Comm. on Whisky, op. cit.,* 1908, p. 160. W. W. Ross outlines the
formation of the Distillers Company; p. 152, the formation of the United
Distilleries Company is described. *S.C. on British and Foreign Spirits,* 1890–1,
p. 412 gives information on the merging of the Dublin distilleries in 1890.
Particulars of the United Distillers of Ireland and the Old Bushmills Distillery
Company have been supplied by the firms concerned. The statistics are taken

The up and down production cycles were not the only spur to amalgamations. There was also a drift away from spirit drinking in the first forty years of this century, especially towards beer, and the very heavy spirit duties imposed in recent years must be regarded as a prime cause of the decline in the industry. Whiskey has become more and more an expensive luxury despite the rise in prosperity and increases in personal incomes. The decline has been reversed and perhaps the best possibility lies with exports, although other countries have also imposed penal duties on imported spirits. In 1900 over fourteen million proof gallons were distilled by thirty distilleries and Irish production has never since then reached this figure. The fall in demand has not been confined to Ireland. In Scotland, with its larger home market, a similar decline has been experienced and its results more spectacular. In this century most Irish distilleries were large and production could be cut back by shortening the distilling period. The Scottish industry consisted of numerous small pot still distilleries and a few large grain distilleries. A substantial reduction in demand in these circumstances led to many small distilleries closing either temporarily or permanently. Thus in 1900 there were 156 Scottish distilleries producing about thirty million proof gallons. By 1927 there were eighty-four producing sixteen million gallons and the downward trend went on mainly because of overstocked warehouses, to reach its lowest peace time point in 1933 when only fifteen distilleries were at work producing about six million proof gallons, mainly grain spirit for which there was also an industrial outlet. In this general decline many firms resorted to price cutting to stay alive and only aggravated the general despondency in the industry. It was in this period between the two great wars, especially the 1930s, that a number of Irish and Scottish distilleries ceased production. This was also the time of widespread unemployment and a luxury such as whiskey was bound to suffer. Any hope of recovery was squashed by the war of 1939–45 during which a variety of obstacles arose both in Ireland and in its principal market in England. In Southern Ireland there were occasional restrictions

from the *Reports of the Commissioners of Customs and Excise,* London, and *Reports of the Revenue Commissioners,* Dublin. Information about the Scottish distillers is largely drawn from articles by R. Wilson, *The Scotch Whisky Industry, op. cit.*

on malting barley because, to make full use of limited food supplies, barley was used in bread making. Also a close watch was kept on the export of whiskey and a quota system imposed in order to maintain sufficient supplies for the home market. In this background whiskey was not likely to succeed against beer or other cheaper drinks. During the long period of more than ten years to 1945 and the sustained depression in whiskey, a new generation of drinkers had arrived in the United Kingdom. If they desired an alcoholic beverage, it was more likely to be beer. It was cheaper and even though the alcohol content is very much less, it suited the pocket of the working man.[14]

Statistics of distilleries and production for the present century are not of much value because of the political division of the country in 1922. Up to 1927 official figures gave a full picture, but after 1927 production in Northern Ireland is included in the figures for England. In 1926 there were fourteen distilleries in the Irish Free State producing just over one million proof gallons and twelve distilleries in Northern Ireland producing nearly two million gallons. In the Irish Free State production fell heavily in the 1930s to reach its lowest point of 390,566 proof gallons in 1933, but recovered to 803,146 gallons by 1937. After 1937 the Irish figures include production by alcohol factories, but after allowing for this, distilling production recovered to more than one million proof gallons. In Northern Ireland, while there are no separate figures, whiskey production fell drastically owing to the closure of all the largest distilleries. By 1950 only the smaller pot still distilleries in Bushmills, Coleraine and Comber remained and Comber ceased distilling in 1953. The other two are not only still operating but are thriving. Production in the Republic of Ireland is also rising where amalgamation of the distilling firms and a vigorous marketing policy are giving new life to the industry. One important development since the war ended in 1945 has been the entry of Irish distillers into the compounding and rectifying business. A revival in the public demand for gin and a new interest in vodka did not escape the distillers.

14. *Annual Reports of the Customs and Excise. Dáil Debates,* vol. 85, 18 February 1942, cols. 1852–3; 11 March 1942, col. 2359; vol. 91, 16 November 1943, cols. 2075–6; vol. 93, 2 May 1944, col. 1886; 9 May 1944, col. 2342. These are some of the references to the control of barley and whiskey. See also R. Wilson, *The Scotch Whisky Industry*, especially the article on 16 August 1966.

Formerly they would have sold their spirit to rectifiers who would make and market these products. Now the distillers do this themselves, and sell under their own brand names. With these beverages, together with both pot and blended whiskey, distillers are in a position to satisfy most spirit drinkers with a high quality product.[15]

The Spirit Duties

Whether whiskey or any other spirituous beverage will be a popular drink depends largely on price. This in turn depends very much on taxation, both internal and in export markets. Quality is an important factor too, but most of the whiskey now made is of the highest standard, whether it is Irish or Scotch. They all suffer the handicap of very severe duties and in the present century the rise in excise spirit duties has been enormous. These increases must, of course, be related to the drastic fall in the purchasing power of money so that much of the burden is rather less than the apparent burden. Money incomes have also risen to balance much of this rise. Even making these allowances, however, the rise in duties has been substantial. Before 1914 the value of money and the level of wages had changed very little for a long time and the spirit duties had not changed very much. The rate had remained unchanged at 10s. a proof gallon from 1860 to 1890. It had only risen to 11s. by 1910. In that year it was increased to 14s. 9d. and this rise caused some gloom amongst distillers. They little knew then what the future was to be. After the first world war there were increases in three successive years from 1918 bringing the duty to £3 12s. 6d. a proof gallon. A general rise in prices and wages largely offset the effect of the rise in excise duties and there was a tranquil period until the second world war. In 1939 the spirit duty in the Irish Free State was increased to £4 12s. 6d. and remained at that level until 1946. In that year the duty was raised to £4 15s., in 1947 to £6 17s. and in 1952 to £8 16s. a proof gallon. After a respite of ten years there was a further spate which resulted in increases from £9 11s. 2d. in 1962 by five stages to £13 9s. 9d. in 1969. Thus the present duty is over twenty-six times that ruling when the century opened and, of course, all other costs incurred by dis-

15. *Customs and Excise Reports*, London, and *Revenue Commissioner's Reports*, Dublin.

tillers have also risen. Clearly these costs and duties combined with compulsory bonding for three years mean that very much larger capital is now necessary to carry on a successful distillery. The Northern Ireland distillers were subject to United Kingdom duties which were, for most of the time, slightly higher. The time has surely come when governments must decide whether the desire for revenue is likely to be defeated if the excise burden is further increased. Sobriety is now enforced by price. The 10s. bottle of whiskey in 1900 has now become about £2 15s. and would be higher but for the increased efficiency in production.[16]

Customs duties kept in step with these excise duties until 1964. Before that year there was a small margin of protection of 2s. 6d. a proof gallon levied on spirits not entitled to preferential treatment, a relic of the imperial preference on goods from British empire countries. In addition there was an addition of 5d. a gallon on all imported spirits to counterbalance the cost to home distillers of excise regulations. The importance of these protective margins has almost disappeared because of the fall in money values. In 1964 Irish distillers received a protection of £1 10s. a proof gallon levied on all imports of spirits. Whiskey wholly manufactured and consigned from Northern Ireland was specially exempted from this increase. This rise in the import duty gave distillers a good margin to maintain their domestic market from imports of Scotch whisky which was threatening to undersell them. In 1968 the protective duty margin was raised to £4 11s. 7d. for spirits from sources other than the United Kingdom.[17]

Industrial Alcohol Factories

Distillers have long been interested in making high strength spirits for industrial use, but in Ireland this has generally been a

16. Increases in the spirit duties before 1922 were enacted by 8 and 9 Geo. 5, c. 15; 9 and 10 Geo. 5, c. 32; and 10 and 11 Geo. 5, c. 18. The Irish increases were imposed by 1939, No. 33; 1946, No. 15; 1947, No. 33; 1952, No. 14; 1962, No. 15; 1965, No. 22; 1966, No. 17; 1968, No. 33; and 1969, No. 21. See also *Dáil Debates,* vol. 145, 21 April 1954, cols. 509–10; vol. 196, 13 June 1962, col. 147.

17. Customs duties are a little complicated as there are different rates for various kinds of spirits and whether imported in casks or bottles. The rates quoted are for unsweetened and unenumerated spirits imported in casks, that is, plain spirits. This is the basic rate from which other rates are derived. The increase of £1 10s. was imposed by 1964, No. 15. The higher rates for spirits other than from the United Kingdom were imposed by 1968, No. 37.

side-line to the manufacture of potable spirits, or as a necessary part in the production of yeast. In Cork, for example, such spirit is made and some of it subsequently methylated. A government venture, therefore, to set up distilleries for the sole purpose of making industrial alcohol, though not in the main stream of Irish distilling, deserves notice. Furthermore, this spirit is made principally from potatoes, a raw material that no distiller would use, and it would be illegal to label the spirit as 'whiskey'. Even the illicit distiller would not normally make his poteen from potatoes. The process would be more troublesome than using treacle or sugar and would require malt to convert the starch. Coming from his primitive pot still, potato spirit would have a flavour that would have no appeal except to those long accustomed to it. When this type of spirit is made in continuous stills, and especially if further processed to become absolute alcohol, it is tasteless and useless as a popular beverage, but is as good as spirit from any other source for industrial purposes.

An Act of 1934 led to the establishment of five industrial alcohol factories in 1937 and 1938. They were situated in Cooley in Louth, Carrickmacross in Monaghan, Carndonagh and Labbadish in Donegal, and Corroy near Ballina in Mayo. All were using continuous stills patented by the Société Anonyme des Usines de Melle. In 1938 a State-controlled company was formed to run the factories. The Cooley factory was sited in an area subject to potato scab which did not affect spirit production and was therefore specially helpful to local farmers. The terms of the Act indicate clearly that there was no intention to compete with distilling firms, but there was a saving clause that spirit could be diverted to normal commercial channels. If this happened, and there is no information that it did, the spirit would be subject to the duties and excise regulations applying to potable spirits. To ensure a strong market, the law provided that the petrol companies had to mix a proportion of this industrial alcohol in their motor fuel. The factories did not rely entirely on potatoes for, in some of the early years, substantial quantities of molasses were also used.[18]

During the war years this venture served a useful purpose by adding to the supplies of motor fuel. After the war output rose

18. 1934, No. 40; 1938, No. 23. *Dáil Debates*. Vol. 53, cols. 2165 *et seq.*, and vol. 69, cols. 1307, 1502–3.

for a time, exceeding a million gallons, but by 1952 the home market demand had almost ceased and the spirit was being exported to England for blending with petrol. There were, however, large distilleries in England making industrial spirit and, as they returned from war to peace conditions, the demand for Irish spirit declined until, by 1954, it had almost dried up. Since then some of the factories have been converted to make glucose or starch. At present two factories are working below capacity and probably finding it difficult to operate profitably. Perhaps the Government incursion into the distilling world was too ambitious, but for a number of years it did bring some prosperity to agriculture in poor areas and it did reduce dependence on imports.[19]

Blending

Very considerable controversy about blending has arisen in the whiskey industry over the past hundred years and has not entirely died down yet. Indeed at one time there was more than mere doubt whether most blends were entitled to be called whiskey. Before embarking on an account of this process the precise meaning of some terms should be stated. There are two kinds of blends. First there is the blend of two or more different pot still whiskeys, whether from different distilleries or different distillations in the same distillery. There has never been any question that such a blend was entitled to be labelled whiskey. The other kind is blending whiskey from a pot still with the whiskey made in a continuous still, and it is about this blend that all the arguments raged. At present the terms 'patent' spirit and 'grain' whiskey mean the same thing; the product of the continuous still. Up to about 1840 or 1850, however, grain spirit meant a pot still whiskey made from a mash of malted and unmalted barley, as distinct from a malt whiskey made solely from barley malt. In the story that follows the term 'blend' will, for convenience, refer to blends of pot still and patent or grain whiskey. This conforms with trade usage.[20]

19. *Dáil Debates*. Vol. 99, col. 563; vol. 144, cols. 186, 1600; vol. 147, cols. 1461–2; vol. 178, col. 281.
20. Irish whiskey made from a mixed mash in pot stills was referred to as grain spirits in 1834 (*Inquiry into the Excise Establishment and Collection of the Excise Revenue in the United Kingdom, 7th Report, Part 1*, Parl. Pps., 1834 [7] xxv, p. 72). The arguments about blending reached their peak when the *Royal*

The Coffey still came into general use in the early 1840s and most of the spirit made was probably used for making compounds or for industrial purposes. Some spirit was almost certainly added to pot still whiskey by some distillers. It would probably be regarded as a mild adulteration which their patrons would not notice, and the patent spirit was much cheaper to make. Our ancestors preferred a whiskey with a good strong taste, so adding patent spirit had to be done with caution and not advertised. This blending had a mellowing effect on some of the harsh immature spirit then generally sold and the practice slowly grew as palates became more discriminating. A new pot still whiskey could be made to approach the taste of a year old whiskey and cost a lot less to market. Leading distilling firms with famous names and brands regarded the blending practices as ruinous to the reputation of Irish whiskey and, where appropriate, were prepared to take legal action if their whiskeys were used in blends.[21]

The situation in Scotland was rather different and this difference had a great influence on the future of the Irish distilling industry. The majority of Scottish pot still distillers made malt whisky, but there were some in the Lowlands who used a mash of mixed grain as in Ireland. An important difference, however, was that the whisky was only twice distilled, whereas the Irish practice was to distil three times. Scotch whisky was, in consequence, heavier and more oily in taste than Irish. Another difference was that the Scottish pot still distilleries were smaller and much more numerous. Each distillery produced a whisky with its distinctive taste and satisfied a local market. Many of these whiskies, if allowed to mature for many years, were very fine indeed, but still only had a limited appeal. Away from the locality of the distillery the Scotch malt whisky was

---

Commission on Whisky and other Potable Spirits investigated the question in 1908.

21. The change in public favour to more mature and milder whiskey in the nineteenth century has already been explained, but the whiskey with a strong bite still sold readily among poorer people right into the present century. In this case price was all important (*See Royal Comm. on Liquor Licensing—Ireland*, Parl. Pps. 1898 [8980] xxxviii, p. 642, and *Royal Comm. on Whisky*, Parl. Pps. 1908 [Cd. 4181] p. 79, as examples). On the protection of reputation see *Truths about Whiskey*, published in 1878 by four leading Dublin distillers, and *Royal Comm. on Whisky*, p. 54.

at a disadvantage. A person ordering a drink would feel affronted if he got a whisky with a taste very different to what he had become accustomed. On the other hand Irish pot stills were, in most cases, larger, often very much larger; three distillations produced a milder whiskey; the differences between the various distilleries was, therefore, much less. This more uniform whiskey had a good deal to do with the dominance of Irish in the English market in the last century. In this background it is not surprising that some Scottish firms, with an eye on the English market, were eager to blend, not only whiskies from different pot still distilleries, but use in the blends the practically flavourless whisky from Coffey stills. The process had everything in its favour. The harsh and heavier pot still whisky was reduced without loss of spirit strength and large quantities could be marketed with a brand name associated with a particular flavour. As a result several large Coffey still distilleries were built about the 1860s and in 1877 six of these firms amalgamated to form the Distillers Company Limited. From then onwards blends of pot still and grain whisky gathered momentum in all whiskey markets.[22]

Most of the blending in earlier years was done by dealers who bought the pot still and grain whiskey from distillers, had their own bonded warehouses, did their own testing, bottled, and withdrew their cases as market demands arose. Some of these blending firms became very large. Thus two such firms in Belfast, Kirk, Greer and Company and Mitchell and Company, joined with a distiller to build a large distillery at Connswater in Belfast in 1886. Mitchells, for example, were founded in 1871, had branches in London, Glasgow and Dublin and in 1908 had a turn-over of half a million proof gallons of whiskey a year. Another firm of world wide reputation is W. and A. Gilbey, based in London, who were not only blenders, but became owners of pot still distilleries in Scotland, probably to safeguard supplies. At present they sell their own branded whiskey in Dublin and also compound gin and vodka, using a very interesting glass still. Grain distillers, who catered for these blenders, naturally became

22. The evolution of blending in Scotland is described by A. Drysdale and W. H. Ross both of the Distillers Company in reports of *S.C. on British and Foreign Spirits*, 1890–1, pp. 403 *et seq.*, and the *Royal Comm. on Whisky*, pp. 160–170. See also the important articles by R. Wilson on the *Scotch Whisky Industry* in the *Wine and Spirit Trade Record* from October 1964 to February 1967.

interested in this market which was so successful towards the end of the nineteenth century. The whiskey was cheaper and public taste for it was fostered by massive and effective advertising. There were abuses and sometimes profits were made by mis-representation, especially as blending extended to publicans who bought two or three casks and made their own concoctions. Brand names appeared which have since become widely known and in time a reputation for these became accepted. This largely undermined the small blender or publican, though the signs on some old public houses still maintain that the proprietor bonds spirits. Some blenders did in fact operate outside bonded ware-houses on duty paid spirits, a luxury that would be ruinous today. A development by the end of the last century and early years of this century was the incorporation of most large blending business into one or other of the combinations of distillery companies. This was especially so in Scotland where eventually the two largest distilling groups joined with the Distillers Company and blending and bottling grew into an enormous trade with a vast export market based on a few standard brands.

The story is somewhat similar with the grain distillers in Ireland, but there was one important firm of dealers, Dunville and Company, who built a distillery in 1869 and deliberately set out from the beginning to make and blend both pot and grain whiskey.[23]

Predictably the pot still distillers did not regard the grain spirit from continuous stills as whiskey. For centuries usquebaugh or whiskey had come from pot stills and for the pot still distiller spirits made by any other method was not whiskey. Blended spirits were considered, therefore, nothing more than alcohol con-taining a small amount of whiskey as a kind of flavouring essence and was not entitled to be marketed as whiskey. It was, for them, an adulteration rather than a dilution of whiskey. The term 'whiskey' had no legal backing so the only real offence would be a misdescription that would mislead the customer. Grain spirit distillers maintained that their spirit was also made from cereals and that they were using an improved method of production.

23. *S.C. on British and Foreign Spirits*, 1890–1, pp. 357, 403. *Royal Comm. on Whisky*, pp. 66–9, 152–3, 163, 201, 300 *et seq.*, 337–42. R. Wilson, *Scotch Whisky Industry*, especially the articles in July and October 1965 and January and February 1966.

In fact, of course, they were making a spirit with much less of the fusel oils that gave whiskey its distinctive flavour. Also the public in the United Kingdom had taken to blended whiskey which had a milder flavour and from about 1880 blends had made great inroads into the pot still whiskey trade. Certainly in the earlier years and until the outbreak of the first world war many of these blends contained only 10 to 20 per cent of pot still whiskey and sold, not because of preference, but because they were cheaper. Some Scottish blenders, defending the use of grain spirit, claimed that their processes required considerable skill. They blended various pot still whiskies of different origins with grain whisky containing a small controlled quantity of fusel oil. This was referred to as 'marrying' whiskies of different sources to get a desired flavour. There is some truth in this claim, especially the blending of the pot still whiskies, but there is also some exaggeration. By using up to 80 per cent or more of grain whisky there would not be much deviation in flavour. Since grain spirit had so little flavour materials such as maize and rye could be used. Making yeast was also a profitable side line because there was practically no effect on the spirit produced. Another encouragement for blending occurred in 1860 when the operation was allowed in bond, enabling great quantities to be blended and stored without paying duty. There were debates on the subject in the House of Commons from 1876 onwards and a Select Committee investigated the matter in 1890. The arguments went on simmering as to what is whiskey until the whole question was brought to a head in 1905 by a prosecution in London.[24]

The Islington Borough Council instituted prosecutions in November 1905 before the North London Police Court in two test cases under the Food and Drugs Act of 1875. They concerned the sale of Irish whiskey by a publican and Scotch whisky by a dealer. In both cases it was alleged that a beverage was sold as whiskey when in fact it was something else. They were blends. The public analyst, Dr Teed, certified that whiskey should come

24. *Truths about Whiskey, op. cit.,* sets out the case for the pot still distillers. *Parliamentary Debates.* The first important debate arose on 4 April 1876 when a request was made to set up a Select Committee (cols. 1185 *et seq.*). It did not succeed, but eventually a *Select Committee on British and Foreign Spirits* reported in 1890–1. Blending in bond was allowed by 23 and 24 Vict., c. 114, sec. 119.

from pot stills using barley malt and other cereals and should contain a certain minimum of secondary products. He found that patent spirit contained only about a quarter of this minimum. The magistrate's decision was that patent spirit and blends with patent spirit could not be classed as Irish or Scotch whiskey and that maize was not a material from which Irish or Scotch whiskey could be derived. Maize was excluded because it was not indigenous to either country. This decision naturally caused consternation amongst blenders and grain distillers. They combined to pay for the expenses of an appeal to the Quarter Sessions. Here the justices were equally divided and the cases were respited. Meanwhile there was pressure through the trade for a full government inquiry and a Royal Commission was appointed. In May 1908, the appeals were withdrawn by arrangement.[25]

The evidence, opinions and arguments given before the Royal Commission in 1908 and 1909 hinged mainly on the fusel oil in different sorts of spirits. Much of it was highly technical, not always easy to follow, and the scientists involved gave conflicting evidence. A brief and admittedly incomplete description might help to understand what was the problem facing the Royal Commission.

Fusel oil is a generic term embracing all the secondary constituents arising during fermentation and distillation. There are a number of these by-products, some of them in measurable quantities and several in very minute quantities, but their total is a very small part of the final spirit. Scientists produced results of their analyses usually in relation to 100,000 parts of absolute alcohol which is rather confusing to the layman. Furthermore their results varied a good deal and they used different methods to get them. Some figures given at the Select Committee inquiry in 1890 give a perspective which is easily understood and is sufficient for the present purpose. It was shown that in relation to proof spirit the fusel oil content in pot still whiskey varied from 0·132 to 0·208 per cent and in spirits from a continuous still from nil to 0·047 per cent. This is not the whole picture because the constituents of the fusel oil also differ in quantity in the two kinds of spirits. In a pot still a part of all the by-products in varying proportions is carried over in the vapours during distillation, even

25. *Royal Comm. on Whisky,* Parl. Pps. 1908 [Cd. 4181], p. 22, and 1909 (Cd. 1796), pp. 1-2.

furfural which has a boiling point of 322°F. In a continuous still each plate is a condenser at temperatures getting lower from the bottom to the top plate. Hence less volatile constituents are largely eliminated as the vapours rise. Thus the constitution of fusel oil is different in the two processes. In both types of still amyl alcohol is the main constituent and butyl and propyl alcohols predominate among the other by-products. There are other so-called higher alcohols in fusel oil, all less volatile than ethyl alcohol and all of an oily character. Some oxidation and interaction occurs to produce aldehydes, acids and ethers associated with the different alcohols, some being more volatile than ethyl alcohol. Subtle changes in the fusel oil take place when spirit is stored in casks for long periods. Not much is known about these changes, but it is thought that air slowly penetrates the wood, some oxidation occurs and secondary aromatic ethers are generated. The more fusel oil present the longer it takes to mature. No satisfactory method to speed maturing has yet been discovered. The contest between pot still and patent still distillers developed during official inquiries into a technical dispute which embraced the raw materials used, methods of converting the starch in the grist, and systems of distilling, but in the end they all led to the fusel oil in the finished product.[26]

While the basic problem facing the Royal Commission in 1908–9 was, if possible, to define the term 'whiskey', they also heard evidence about the manufacture of brandy and rum where similar conditions prevailed. In both cases there were distillations by pot stills and continuous stills and also blending and the terms 'brandy' and 'rum' were used for these blends. They heard also about a foreign high strength pure spirit, generally referred to as German spirit, though much of it came from Russia. This spirit was being used in blends of rum, brandy and whiskey. The trade in all blends had become very large indeed by 1908. Any decision against blended whiskey could not easily be applied to imported rum and brandy unless there was some chemical or other test

26. *S.C. on British Spirits, op. cit.,* 1890, pp. 534–49. Dr Bell explains fusel oil, its commercial uses, and the results of his analysis. The final report, 1890–1, p. 360, gives the percentages found of fusel oil in pot and patent still spirits. *Royal Comm. on Whisky.* In the evidence in 1908 various scientists gave details of the analyses of fusel oil, for example on pp. 123–148. Appendices give the figures of these analyses. See the evidence in 1909, p. 16, on the variations in fusel oil; and 1908, p. 357, on artificial maturing.

which would clearly isolate pot still production from blends and this was shown to be impracticable. Whiskey had become associated with the blended article and was a popular drink. To refuse the term to blends would very seriously affect the trade of many well known brands. Furthermore, whiskey was applied to spirituous liquors made from maize and other cereals in the United States and other countries so a definition based on the cereals used presented a difficulty. These countries might well refuse the title 'whiskey' to British exports if it could not be used in the home country. With all these obstacles the Royal Commission contented itself with a report of the facts, agreed that grain spirit could be called 'whiskey' but gave no definition. Nor would it commit itself to a geographical definition for, at the time, grain spirit was freely passing from Ireland to Scotland to make Scotch whisky. In some cases even English patent spirit not made from cereals was being used in blends.[27]

During the last fifty years the transfer of spirits between countries for blending has practically ceased. Distillers have pressed for, and received legal definitions. In 1938 the term 'Scotch whisky' became legally defined as a spirit made from a mash of cereal grains saccharified by a diastase of malted barley. In 1940 this definition was extended by regulations to Northern Ireland spirits intended for export to the United States of America. The definition includes both pot still and grain spirits and fully accords with distilling practice. In the Republic of Ireland more precise definitions were enacted in 1950 by the Irish Whiskey Act, which distinguished pot still whiskey from blends. To qualify for the title 'Irish Whiskey' the spirits must be distilled in the State from a mash of malt and cereal grains. The title 'Irish Pot Still Whiskey' was reserved for spirits distilled solely in pot stills in the State from a mash of cereal grains normally grown in Ireland and saccharified by a diastase of malted barley. No other spirits were to be described in these terms on official documents. This gave authority to certificates of age and origin for exports.[28]

27. *Royal Comm. on Whisky*, particularly 1908, pp. 100, 197, 200, 208, 225, 242 and 1909, pp. 46–7.
28. Scotch whisky was defined by 23 and 24 Geo. 5, c. 19, sec. 24. The Irish definitions were enacted by 1950, No. 6. See also *Dáil Debates*, vol. 119, 22 February 1950, cols. 531–3.

Rectifying and Compounding

This was never a major industry in Ireland, but it is now growing with the increasing popularity of gin and vodka. In 1914 there were 14 rectifiers each paying a licence duty of £15 15s. a year. They operated with duty paid spirit and could deposit their products on drawback in bonded warehouses. They could then send them out for export or, on paying duty, deliver them for the home market. It is not known what kinds of spirituous beverages were being made, but it is fairly certain that gin was easily the largest market. Since then the independent rectifier and compounder has almost disappeared. Excise regulations have been relaxed to allow manufacture in bond, thus saving the cost of the duty on spirits lost during their operations. The licence duty has also been reduced, in 1933, to £5 5s.[29] At present there are only two important firms in the business. In Dublin, W. and A. Gilbey make gin and vodka, and in Tullamore an Irish whiskey based liqueur, Irish Mist, is made. The latter is now selling well, especially in the United States. The Tullamore firm buys its whiskey from both parts of Ireland. A recent promising addition to the trade is a Waterford firm marketing Irish Coffee.

The principal makers of compounds are now the Irish distillers themselves. Premises and stills have been set aside for the purpose and considerable quantities of gin and vodka are made with all the expertise and care that is devoted to whiskey. Operating in bond enables the distillers to use all the facilities of the premises and modern bottling machinery installed for whiskey. The market is growing rapidly both at home and overseas.

Exports

It is not possible to ascertain reliable statistics of the exports of all Irish whiskey in the century. Before 1922 exports to England, the main market, are not listed since Irish spirits are included in United Kingdom production. There are figures of removals between Ireland, Scotland and England, but these do not necessarily indicate the origin of the spirits. Bearing these facts in mind and that most Irish exports would be distilled locally, Ireland's export trade must have run into millions of proof gallons before the first world war. Thus in 1914 nearly ten million

29. *5th Customs and Excise Report,* Parl. Pps. 1914 [Cd. 7574] xvii, p. 61. 933, No. 15 reduced the licence duty to £5 5s. in the Irish Free State.

proof gallons were distilled and over two million sent to England. After the constitution of the Irish Free State statistics are reliable for that part of Ireland. Removals from Northern Ireland still suffered from the same disabilities and, until the late 1930s, they were important. The same unsatisfactory position applies to exports to overseas markets. Until 1922 all exports were listed simply as British spirits and this continued for spirits from Northern Ireland. In 1914, for example, ten million proof gallons were exported from the United Kingdom. It is fair to assume that Ireland's share would run into millions. All that can be said for Northern Ireland exports after 1922 is that until leading firms ceased production in the late 1930s large quantities of grain spirit were sent to Scotland for blending, blended whiskey was sent to both Scotland and England, and a steadily diminishing quantity of pot still whiskey went to England. At present there is only one distilling firm in Northern Ireland and in recent years their exports to England and overseas have improved. Spirits from the Republic of Ireland are listed in some detail in the annual reports of the Revenue Commissioners and the fortunes of the industry can be traced both in the United Kingdom and overseas markets.

Several factors militated against an expanding export market. First, and probably the most important, was the trend in popularity away from the traditional pot still whiskey and towards blends. Blends only became a serious competitor in the last quarter of the nineteenth century. Irish pot still whiskey was then the favoured drink though some Irish blends did well under this umbrella. In this century the swing towards blends has become more and more marked. Distillers in the North of Ireland and in Scotland fostered and catered for blended whiskey. It was cheaper to make and, though it had a weaker flavour, both the English and overseas markets wanted it. The Irish pot still distillers who had dominated the English and overseas markets for so long with famous names in whiskey were too conservative to recognise the changing fashion as permanent until the blended brands had become firmly established.[30]

Next in importance was the effect of two world wars which thoroughly disrupted trade channels and subjected the production of whiskey to restrictions and rationing so that market demands

30. *Royal Comm. on Whisky,* 1908, especially p. 163.

could not be met. Between the wars there was very great unemployment not merely in the United Kingdom, but in Europe and, more important, in the United States and Canada. With high duties in all countries large numbers of people could not afford to drink whiskey. There was also the prohibition era in the United States from July 1919 to December 1933. In Australia a domestic whiskey industry was established and protected against imports so that market dried up. Scotch whisky interests overcame this by building distilleries in Australia. The same thing happened in Canada. In this depressing period the permanancy of the trend to blended whiskey may have been masked and Irish pot still distillers perhaps pinned their faith on better times ahead when drinkers would be won back to the preference of their fathers. Any such reversal of taste to a costlier drink would need aggressive advertising on a massive scale, an undertaking that would need a combined effort by all Irish distillers to finance it. A Whiskey Association was certainly formed, but it was a loose organisation which never attempted any large and united marketing propaganda in England or overseas. Each firm pushed its own products when the urgent need was to popularise all Irish pot still whiskey. Competition between brands was secondary. In the last decade firms have merged, common agencies for all brands have been established overseas, and the Irish Government has given considerable help in financing and advising on advertising. The Government especially helped to mount a sales campaign in the United States. Together these measures have succeeded in expanding the export trade.[31]

The era of conservatism is over. The disasters of the 1930s, when firms that appeared as soundly based as a central bank had to go out of business, did not immediately jolt those that survived. Fortunately, before it was too late, a new generation of distillers arrived who were realistic and forward looking, and who responded to changing conditions, and this undoubtedly saved the industry. The last thirty years has seen a tremendous expansion in exports of Scotch whisky and the introduction of light blends in the American market with great success. In the United States and Canada domestic whiskeys have been made lighter to suit the changing palates of urban communities. Irish distillers are

31. *Dáil Debates*, vol. 174, 8 April 1959, col. 4; vol. 209, 5 May 1964, col. 943. See also R. Wilson, *Scotch Whisky Industry*, Oct. 1966.

keenly competing for this market. Blending is no longer regarded with some distaste but the distillers are as jealous as ever of their reputation for producing high quality whiskeys. Much research has gone into getting the correct blends. They are also well entrenched in the Irish gin market and were ahead of their British counterparts when they introduced vodka over ten years ago. So they are well based for exports of these beverages. These changes would have been unthinkable fifty years ago, but the younger people now in control of the whiskey have a far more flexible attitude to production processes and more marketing drive. This change was slow in coming, but if anyone tried to fix a time when the change was complete it would probably be 1966 in the Republic of Ireland when all the distillery companies merged. In Northern Ireland the change was a little earlier.[32]

Shannon airport provides an interesting development in the spirit export trade. This airport and an adjoining industrial estate were constituted in 1947 as a customs free zone. Materials for manufacture could be imported free of customs duties and restrictions and a duty charge only arose when goods were delivered from the zone to the domestic market. There was also the usual duty-free shop for outward bound passengers. Exports of spirits have been substantial, amounting in 1960, for example, to about 7 per cent of the total exports to all countries.[33]

Export statistics can only give a general picture of the trade from the Republic of Ireland. If all Ireland is considered, figures of the trade between the Republic and Northern Ireland are available and allowances can be made. Exports from Northern Ireland, however, are swallowed up in the figures for the United Kingdom, and spirits sent to Great Britain are part of the internal trade. All these statistics suffer from the defect already explained; the spirits are not necessarily of domestic origin. It is a fair presumption that the Republic of Ireland exports are nearly all Irish spirits. Before 1937, when the largest Ulster distilling firms were still in business, there was a very large export trade with Great Britain. Since then it has been small, but, in recent years,

32. *Dáil Debates.* The export problem was debated at length and distillers criticised for their alleged complacency about blending. See vol. 138, 29 April 1953, Cols. 787–8; vol. 139, 3 June 1953, cols. 726–36; vol. 140, 8 July 1953, cols. 730–9; vol. 147, 3 November 1954, cols. 352–71.
33. 1947, No. 5. *Dáil Debates,* vol. 197, 31 October 1962, col. 277.

has begun to grow—though this cannot be proved by official statistics. The following figures give a fair idea of the export trade of the Republic of Ireland over the years since 1922, and reflect the depressions of the 1930s and the war years to 1945:

	Proof gallons
1925	1,012,475
1935	127,775
1945	108,040
1955	140,458
1965	300,849

The figures for 1965 are swelled a little by the final sales of considerable quantities of very old whiskey from Kilbeggan distillery which ceased in 1947. Since then recovery of the export trade has set in and, in the fiscal year to 1970, some 340,000 proof gallons were exported, of which about 80 per cent was proprietary whiskey. The main increases have been in the United States and Western European markets.

The principal destinations in 1964, a year when recovery of this trade was just beginning, are also interesting:

	Proof gallons
All countries	216,251
Great Britain	73,089
Northern Ireland	55,619
United States	50,501

There was also a small whiskey trade in each direction with Canada and a small, but growing market in Europe.[34]

The Licensed Spirit Trade

When the century opened the channels to the consumer were through the wholesale dealers, many of them also large blending houses, who sold mainly in casks to publicans and in bottles to off-licence shops. Some of the large publicans bought a few casks and did some blending of their own. The whiskey in casks would be of high strength, up to 11° over proof for Scotch and 25° over proof for Irish. The publican would dilute this to suit his trade. Handbooks were published specially to assist publicans in the

34. Revenue Commissioners' annual reports. *Dáil Debates,* vol. 214, 9 March 1965, col. 1446; vol. 215, 19 May 1965, col. 1619.

arithmetic for dilution. This background favoured grain whiskey, particularly in public houses in working class districts where price was all important. Customers were served by the glass drawn from a cask and a cheap but profitable whiskey could be sold at 2d. a gill glass, with a choice of better whiskey up to 5d. or 6d. a glass. The price would depend on the quantity of grain whiskey in the blend. Obviously this arrangement made misrepresentation easy if customers were not too discriminating. The same price could be charged whether the whiskey was a blend or a self whiskey, with a better profit on the former. Often the customer bought according to the name of the distiller or blender and there was nothing to stop a publican setting up a cask in his bar with the name of a distiller painted on it. It did not follow that the contents came from that firm. The cask could have been re-filled in the publican's cellar. Reputations were apt to suffer when this happened. In the off-licence shop the trade was chiefly in bottles and, although occasionally bottles might not contain the labelled whiskey, in general the customer was better protected.[35]

By the 1920s the spirit duties had reached £3 12s. 6d. a proof gallon and a hogshead at, say, 10° over proof, carried a duty of more than £200. Moreover the wastage in filling glasses was similarly much more expensive. A publican with a cask of spirit in his cellar became extremely rare and the trade had almost entirely gone over to bottles, with measures for serving customers. As all the bottling was done in bond there was no loss on wastage and, with proper capsules, proprietary brands were fully protected except against a determined fraud. The bottled whiskey was diluted with suitable water and ready to serve directly to the drinker. Further dilution in the bar ran the risk of prosecution under the Food and Drugs Acts. With the present duties buying a cask is prohibitive. A hogshead even at proof strength would approach an outlay of £800 in spirit duty. Wastage might run to 3 per cent. Few publicans could finance such a trade.

There were no changes of any consequence in the licensing

35. *Royal Comm. on Whisky.* There are numerous examples of price differences between grain and pot still whiskey and of the practices described. See for example, the evidence in 1908 on pp. 15–16, 22, 61, 64, 74–5, 185, 201 and the final report in 1909, p. 24. One of the handbooks for retailers was by J. J. McBride, *The Spirit Traders' Handbook*, Belfast, 1900.

laws before the political changes in 1922. After the division of the country the same laws continued for a time, but in both the Irish Free State and in Northern Ireland there arose similar problems. The rising spirit and beer duties were altering drinking habits and sobriety was being partly enforced by prices. In consequence public house receipts have fallen and many of their owners, especially in rural areas and in the smaller premises, have found it difficult to make a reasonable living. The right to a licence, however, is a valuable asset not to be surrendered lightly and licence holders can justly expect some compensation where a licence is extinguished because of public policy. Another problem has come to the fore in the last two or three decades. Tourism has become increasingly important commercially and the drinking laws are a factor in its success. Tourism is a two-way business and an influx of visitors provides a welcome income, but this can be offset by a flow outwards. The situation is that the influx must be encouraged or there is a deficit. As a result the tourist industry is concerned that the licensing laws are not too restrictive. Northern Ireland has the problem that temperance pressure groups are strong enough to obstruct easing the licensing laws which still retain the basic restraints necessary in a much less sober age. The restricted drinking hours, drinks only with meals and so on, are probably widely evaded without any feeling of guilt by offenders, a somewhat unhealthy social condition.[36]

There were no radical changes in the licensing laws relating to public houses before the political changes in 1922, but there was a break with tradition in 1910 when spirit grocers disappeared. In that year all existing retail off-licences were abolished and new licences issued in their place at a graduated scale of licence duties according to the annual value of the premises, with a maximum of £50 duty for premises exceeding an annual value of £500. The spirit grocer had been a feature of the trade for over a century and he was now merged with the off-licence retailer. In the following year the trade came within the terms of the Shops Acts, thus bringing the hours of sale into line with all other

36. *Dáil Debates*, vol. 226, 4 February 1967, col. 1113; vol. 229, 7 June 1967, col. 31. The retail trade complained that there were too many licensed houses for the trade available and put forward a scheme to reduce the number. The Government rejected it on the grounds of the cost of compensation. On the problem of evasion see vol. 177, 11 November 1959, and the leading article in the *Belfast Telegraph*, 30 May 1970.

shops. The only other legislation of interest before 1922 was a special measure to meet circumstances resulting from the 'troubles' of 1916. The Dublin Reconstruction (Emergency Provisions) Act, 1916 provided that a licence was deemed to continue for premises destroyed during the fighting. The 1914–18 war brought various temporary restrictions stemming from shortages. In 1922 the British parliament ceased to have any interest in liquor licensing in any part of Ireland.[37]

The new Irish Free State parliament passed its first Intoxicating Liquor Act in 1924. It was a short measure of no lasting importance, but it reflected the undercurrent of turmoil. It gave the district justice, the successor of the resident magistrate, power to close immediately for a short time any licensed premises if in the interests of public order. Later in the year a general Act was passed as an interim measure to deal with certain abuses, mainly concerning hours of sale, shebeens, illicit spirits and methylated spirit drinking. Its main interest centres on the debates in the Dáil during the passage of the Bill. The spirit grocer had only disappeared in name. 'In villages and towns the vast majority of licence holders carry on the retail trade of all commodities necessary for the rural population.' A visit to an Irish village will show that this is true for both on-and-off-licences, though there is a sharp division within the premises between drinking and other sales. The illicit distiller was still a problem and was compared with the evils of methylated spirit drinking. Poteen drinking was said to be widespread in the country. Most poteen was of a poisonous nature 'full of high ethers and all kinds of objectionable poisons, and its effect on human health lamentable'. The speaker attributed this drinking to the high spirit duty. Kevin O'Higgins, speaking for the Government, referred to the difficulties of the police when attempting to enforce the hours of sale, especially on Sundays in remote places. Describing these he said: 'It is the youngster in the tree watching the road for a uniform, what is known as the "cuckoo boy", you have.' He also estimated that there were probably more than twice as many licensed houses than the trade warranted, providing a strong temptation to illegality and abuse. It might be added that the country had only recently

37. 10 Edw. 7, c. 8, sections 51, 53; 1 and 2 Geo. 5, c. 54; 6 and 7 Geo. 5, c. 66, section 8.

emerged from a period when organised rebellion had practically confined the police to defending their barracks and had no chance to do normal police duties; a period when ignoring many laws had become habitual.[38]

Legislation in 1927 covered the whole field of the liquor licence trade. There was very little change in existing law relating to such matters as occasional licences, early closing and six day licences, hotels and so on. The licensee who also ran a non-licence business was required to have a structural division separating the two. If this was not possible both trades had to be confined to the opening hours of licensed premises. The real interest in the Act, however, was the machinery set up for reducing the number of licences. The Act provided for the appointment of a Compensation Authority for each licensing area. The Authority was to be a circuit judge assisted by a qualified assessor, either an auctioneer, surveyor, or valuer. The Authority fixed the sum, within a certain maximum, that was to be paid by every licensee annually into a 'Compensation Annuity Fund'. The police initiated the procedure for closing any licensed premises on the grounds that there were too many in the locality. If agreed, the Authority fixed the compensation payable and granted an abolition order. They could also grant gratuities to employees affected. The essence of the scheme was that it should be self supporting, the existing licensees providing the money to compensate those going out of business, though there was provision for government loans if necessary. How did this excellent scheme work? It got off to a good start in 1928 and 299 licences were abolished, but there were still some 16,000 licences, both on and off, in the country. Thereafter it petered out and in 1941 it was reported that there had been no abolition orders for the previous five years. There had, for some unknown reason, been a larger number of licences lapsed by non-renewal without compensation. There were 609 between 1928 and 1932. Perhaps the police did not initiate the compensation procedure. In 1967 the licensed trade itself prepared a scheme for the extinction of superfluous licences. The Government rejected the scheme as impracticable. The compensation would be enormous and far beyond the ability of licensees to meet by contributions.

38. 1924, Nos. 28, 62. *Dáil Debates,* vol. 7, 20 June 1924, cols. 2787–8, 2790; vol. 9, 20 October 1924, col. 82.

In 1936 there were 16,023 licences and 253 clubs selling intoxicating liquor. By 1965 the number was down to 12,379 of which 11,752 were public houses and hotels. Apparently this reduction was not due to the 1927 Act.[39]

There was a radical change in liquor licence duties in 1960 when all the complications of assessing licence values of premises were swept away and replaced by a flat rate of £4 duty whether the premises were a humble public house in a back street or a splendidly appointed building in the city centre. This change was probably prompted by similar legislation in the United Kingdom a year earlier. There were a number of other reforms in 1960. One of them dealt with the hotel dispense bar which many people must have regarded as an absurdity. Before 1960 a hotel customer could, if the hotel was licensed, order and pay for a drink at a counter where no drinks were on view. The attendant supplied the order from a stock usually kept in an adjoining compartment to which the public had no access. The new law permitted such hotels to install a public bar if the hotel owner arranged for an existing publican's licence to be extinguished. The latter licence could be anywhere in the State.[40]

Most of the Act in 1960 was taken up with hours of sale. The official opinion was that 'there is very little, if any, connexion between opening hours and the problem of excessive drinking'. This may be so, but it is hardly likely that the public would condone unlimited hours, and there is also the welfare of employees in public houses to be considered. On the other hand too much restriction would inevitably lead to abuse and evasion. In 1959 the government view on this subject was 'that in recent years enforcement of licensing laws has proved impossible due to the fact that they have not the force of public opinion behind them'. The existing law was held in contempt. The police were lax and the Courts imposed trivial penalties. Further, contempt of one law may breed a general contempt for the law. The difficulty is that a general rule cannot easily be applied in all cases. It has to be adapted in many instances such as meeting the

39. 1927, No. 15. Part IV deals with the reduction of licences. *Dáil Debates*, vol. 51, 30 March 1934, cols. 1092–3; vol. 65, 18 February 1937, col. 491; vol. 83, 4 June 1941, col. 1426; vol. 226, 4 February 1967, col. 1113; vol. 229, 7 June 1967, col. 31. *42nd Report of the Revenue Commissioners*, 1965, p. 82.
40. 1960, Nos. 18 and 19. *Dáil Debates*, vol. 181, 27 April 1960, col. 210; vol. 217, 15 July 1965, col. 1517.

needs of hotel guests, drinking in clubs, restaurants, aerodromes, holiday camps and so on. All sorts of evasion of drinking hours have long been practised from the outright illegality of serving favoured customers in a back room after closing, to the 'locker lounge' system which was on the fringe of legality. Under this system a publican provided drinking facilities at nearby premises, the customer ordering the drinks in the public house during opening hours. In effect, the customer had his private stock in the nearby premises and it would be very difficult to prove otherwise. Two other changes are worth mentioning. The Food and Drugs Act of 1879 was amended to allow spirits for sale to be diluted to 30° under proof instead of 25° without giving notice to the customer. Also sealed containers had to exhibit the quantity in them. The other change was, in a sense, complementary. Maximum prices were fixed.[41]

The Northern Ireland government quickly began to legislate for the drink trade. In 1923 mixed trading was dealt with in much the same way as in the Irish Free State. The intoxicating liquor business had to be structurally segregated from any other trade, except for hotels. Sometimes conditions such as this are not easily met. In such cases the licence would not be renewed, but compensation would be paid. A Compensation Claims Tribunal was set up to decide on a fair payment and a Claims Fund was instituted to provide the finance. Each licensee contributed to this fund according to the value of his premises and its locality. To begin with Belfast licensees paid considerably higher amounts than other places, the payments ranging from £12 to £60 as against £1 10s. to £10 10s. in the rest of the province. Depending on the state of the fund the amounts varied in later years. There was also a drive to reduce the number of licensed houses and it was decreed that no new licences would be granted unless in a particular town or city there had been an increase of at least 25 per cent in population. Another move in this direction occurred in 1927 when a new licence could be granted if the applicant caused trading to cease in two other licensed houses. Apart from these changes the licensing laws operating before

41. 1960, No. 18, sections 35, 40. Maximum Prices (*Intoxicating Liquor and non-alcoholic Beverages*) Order, 1965. *Dáil Debates*, vol. 177, 11 November 1959, cols. 937, 942; vol. 187, 15 March 1961, col. 609; vol. 195, 29 May 1962, col. 1602; vol. 220, 9 February 1966, col. 1156.

1922 continued. It is fair to say that a more puritan attitude to drinking is taken in Northern Ireland than in the rest of Ireland. This came through in 1959 when all Sunday drinking was stopped. In the same year flat rate licence duties were introduced which made redundant the old six-day reduced licence duty as well as simplifying assessments. Under the new arrangement a publican or a dealer paid £5 a year and an off-licence £2. Hotels still had dispense bars and paid the same rate as publicans. The effect of these various measures on the number of licences, and changes in drinking habits, have probably caused a drop. There appear to be no published statistics in Northern Ireland to confirm whether this has happened.[42]

Beer is the chief competitor to whiskey in the home market. It is not possible to isolate consumption figures for beer and whiskey in Northern Ireland. In the Republic of Ireland the Revenue Commissioners reported in 1965 that in the year ending 31 March 1924 nearly 1·2 million proof gallons of spirit from all sources were retained for home consumption. After that the quantity became less until a recovery set in about 1947. Since then there has been a steady rise. In 1937 spirit consumption was 756,474 proof gallons and beer was 598,542 standard barrels. In 1966 the corresponding figures were 1,182,475 proof gallons and 1,004,154 standard barrels. Thus in the last thirty years there has been a general rise in consumption of alcoholic beverages, probably due to a rising standard of living, but there has been no significant shift in drinking preferences.[43]

42. 13 and 14 Geo. 5, c. 12 (N.I.) sections 3, 6, 9 and First Sched. Part III; 17 and 18 Geo. 5, c. 21 (N.I.), section 3; 1959, c. 1 and c. 9. An example of changes in payments to the Claims Fund can be seen in S.R. and O. 1965, No. 107 which fixed the charge at 11s. in the £.

43. *42nd Revenue Commissioners' Report*, 1965, p. 65. *Dáil Debates*, vol. 48, 7 June 1933, cols. 14–15; vol. 119, 7 March 1950, col. 1292; vol. 227, 20 April 1967, col. 2178.

CHAPTER IX

DISTILLERS PAST AND PRESENT

ALMOST nothing is known about the hundreds of distillers in Ireland in the eighteenth century. There were numerous changes in ownership of these small distilleries and towards the end of the century large numbers ceased to exist because of the impact of the excise still licence duty. Among the few that survived by 1823, when this duty ceased, some developed into very large concerns. During the nineteenth century new and important distilling firms were founded and some of them flourished into the present century. In the decline of the whiskey trade following the 1914–18 war Irish distillers were affected by the depression along with their counterparts in Scotland and a number of well known distilleries ceased. Amalgamations also occurred. The result is that there are now only two distilling companies, the Irish Distillers Group Limited with distilleries in Dublin and Cork, and the 'Old Bushmills' Distillery Company with distilleries in Bushmills and Coleraine.

There is some meagre information about a few distilleries and their owners from about 1780 to the middle of the nineteenth century and rather more knowledge is available as the century progressed but it is still very incomplete. Even information about distilleries that only ceased in the present century is difficult to obtain and there are many gaps. Changes in ownership and the destruction of records makes it impossible to give a full account of most firms of the past, particularly before the middle of the last century. Though original sources, such as a firm's books, hardly exist, a knowledge of some of the early distillers can be gleaned from official returns, street directories and similar publications. In a few cases there are documents in the Public Record Offices in Dublin and Belfast.[1]

1. The following references are common to the histories of a number of distilleries. To avoid repetition a reference to this Note will indicate that these

It would be interesting to know something about the background of the early distillers, how they came into the industry, and how capital was raised in the first place and later by those who were able to expand their production. Again information on these points is rare and vague.

Until late in the century distilleries were usually family businesses so capital was probably found from profits aided, perhaps, by temporary loans from relatives or friends. Occasionally an injection of capital might come from a newcomer to the industry, but there were no public invitations to subscribe for shares till the century was well advanced. An extant deed of partnership contracted in 1824 to start a small business was probably typical for a new venture. E. B. Smith, J. Smith and A. Creighton were to be co-partners as distillers and brewers in Clifden, county Galway. The Smiths were active and Creighton an 'anonymous' partner. The firm was to trade as Edward B. Smith. Each party subscribed £350. Half of any profits was to be shared equally and half re-invested in the firm.[2] In these nineteenth century firms the operative distiller was rarely an employee until about the 1860s when limited liability companies were becoming established in the industry. Even after that time it was customary for the distiller to be a director. In the large distilling companies evolved towards the end of the century important posts had to be created in the administrative, commercial and practical sides of firms. This opened up training and promotion for persons outside the family circle of the founders and a small movement of such men between firms. An account of the development of some of these distilling firms illustrates all these aspects.

---

sources are used. (*a*) *Irish House of Commons Journal*, 1782, appendix, pp. 523–32. (*b*) *Inquiry into Fees, Gratuities, Perquisites . . . in certain Public Offices in Ireland*, 5th Report, Parl. Pps. 1806–7 (124) vi, pp. 204–5. (*c*) *Inquiry into the Revenue arising in Ireland*, 5th Report, Parl. Pps. 1823 (405) vii, pp. 367–9, 378. (*d*) *Inquiry into the . . . Excise Revenue throughout the United Kingdom*, 7th Report, Part I, Parl. Pps. 1834 [7] xxv, pp. 232–4. (*e*) S. Morewood, *A Philosophical and Statistical History . . . of Inebriating Liquors*, Dublin, 1838, p. 725.
2. Public Record Office, Dublin, ref. M5476/20.

A – PAST DISTILLERS

Dublin Distillers Company, Limited

This firm was an amalgamation of three large distilleries: George Roe and Company, The Dublin Distilling Company, and The Dublin Whiskey Distillery Company. The maximum capacity in 1891 was three and a half million proof gallons, all from pot stills, but the output was considerably less than that figure. No blending was done, even from the different distilleries. Each distillery marketed whiskey under its own name and mark. Large quantities of new whiskey was sold to blenders in Dublin, Belfast and London. Some 40 to 50 per cent of the grist used was malted barley with a small proportion of wheat, oats, or rye. The bulk of the whiskey sold under their own mark averaged three years old. There was serious overproduction in the first two decades of this century and by 1923 two of the distilleries had ceased producing and the third ceased in 1926. In the difficult market conditions before the 1939 war, sales were slow and financing the storage of large unsold stocks eventually caused the firm to wind up in the middle 1940s.[3]

The oldest of the three firms in this amalgamation was George Roe and Company. The Company began its life in 1757 when Peter Roe bought a small distillery in Thomas Street. The premises and plant were gradually enlarged as trade expanded and the site spread until it fronted on South Earl Street. Richard Roe carried on from 1766 to 1794, but the distillery laws of the time severely limited any chance of a significant expansion. In 1782 he was working a still of 234 gallons capacity. Meanwhile Nicholas Roe had set up a separate establishment in Pimlico, Dublin, in 1784 on a bigger scale for by 1802 he was working a still of 1,165 gallons which, by 1807, was replaced by a larger still of 1,575 gallons. By 1818, he had, like other distillers, been forced to install a smaller still of only 751 gallons because of the still licence system. After this system was abandoned in 1823 Nicholas Roe expanded his plant rapidly. By 1832 George Roe had succeeded to both distilleries which were close to each other and this marked the beginning of the modern very large business which Barnard saw in 1887. A lease was acquired in 1832 of premises in Mount Brown, Dublin, from J. and C. Hutton,

3. *S.C. on British and Foreign Spirits,* Parl. Pps. 1890–1 (210) xi, p. 412.

former distillers and brewers, and Roe converted the buildings into maltings, kilns, and warehouses. Another addition was in Bonham Street, Mount Brown, where, in 1839, Roe and Meyler were listed as distillers. Meyler disappeared from the scene soon afterwards. George Roe's two sons, Henry and George, succeeded to ownership in 1862 and by now the firm was large and prosperous and the distillers men of wealth and influence. Thus in 1878 Henry subscribed £250,000 for the restoration of Christ Church cathedral. Henry retired about this time and the firm was registered as a limited liability company. A practical distiller was appointed as managing director.

When Alfred Barnard toured round the Irish distilleries in 1887, he gave a picture of Roe's distillery showing it as a large industrial unit using modern equipment and employing very considerable capital. Power was supplied by seven large boilers feeding five steam engines. Water for distilling was drawn from the river Vartry and from the Grand Canal. Grain lofts held 100,000 barrels and conveyor belts were used to transfer grain to the stores. After grinding, continuous screws took the grain to the grist loft to be bagged till wanted. In the brew house there were three very large mash tuns, one of them thirty-six feet across. The wort passed over coolers and Morton's patent refrigerators to 16 fermenting vessels each of 40,000 gallons capacity. In the still house there were eight pot stills ranging from 12,000 to 20,000 gallons capacity. The finished whiskey was made by three distillations. This was the distillery that some fifty years earlier had only a single 751 gallon still and got its power from a windmill. To maintain a plant of this size and handle its production needed a large number of artisans. There was a cooperage, for example, covering nearly an acre. In addition there were workshops for smiths, engineers, fitters and carpenters. Building repairs and similar minor constructions were done within the firm. There were extensive stables and cart houses. The whole premises facing on Thomas Street covered seventeen acres. About 200 were employed which is not large for such a big industrial unit, but distilleries do not lend themselves to large numbers as would be the case, for example, of a textile firm of comparable size. In 1887 the distillery could reach an annual output of nearly two million proof gallons and though its main market was in the United Kingdom, it had an important

M

export trade to Canada, the United States and Australia.[4]

The Dublin Distilling Company was formerly the private firm of William Jameson and Company of Marrowbone Lane. The entry of the Jameson family into the Irish distilling industry started in 1784 when a Jameson of Alloa, Scotland, made a business visit to Dublin. Following this he obtained an interest in a Bow Street distillery and later established his two sons, John and William, in the business, probably with John Stein who owned distilleries in Marrowbone Lane and Bow Street. Eventually a Jameson became a proprietor in each distillery. In 1800 the Marrowbone Lane distillery was run by the firm of Stein and Edgar. In 1802 Edgar had gone and the firm had become Jameson and Stein. By 1822 Stein had also gone and the firm was now William Jameson and Company and worked one 750 gallon still. There was also a James Jameson, perhaps a son, registered as a distiller at the same address. In later years the firm became James Jameson and Company. The first James Jameson was a director of the Bank of Ireland in 1828. In 1833 the distillery output was about 330,000 proof gallons a year. Rapid expansion subsequently followed the pattern of the other Dublin distilleries. The size of the plant in 1887 is well illustrated by the two mash tuns each of 100,000 gallons capacity. Barnard, who visited the distilleries and breweries in Great Britain as well as Ireland, stated that these tuns were the largest in the United Kingdom. Among the thirteen wash backs were some that equalled the mash tuns in size and were said to be large enough to contain a two storey villa complete with garden paths. This seems to be a mild exaggeration, but there is no doubt that to a visitor their size would be impressive. Four pot stills were in use varying in content from 9,000 to 18,000 gallons. Within the distillery premises there were nine warehouses and there were others at the shipping terminal at North Wall, Dublin. About 200 were employed and the annual output was in the region of 200,000 proof gallons. There was an export trade to Australia, British India, Canada and the United States. In 1890 the firm became a limited company under the title of

4. See Note 1 (a) (b) (c) (e). *The Gentleman's and Citizen's Almanack,* Dublin, an annual directory that includes a section on traders and merchants. A. Barnard, *Whisky Distilleries of the United Kingdom,* London, 1887, pp. 366–8. J. G. F. Day and H. E. Patton, *Cathedrals of the Church of Ireland,* London, 1932, p. 90. P.R.O. Dublin, refs. M 4930, 4932.

The Dublin Distilling Company and William Jameson remained as its managing director. In this reorganisation some of the premises became redundant and were sold to H. Medcalf, a linen printer.[5]

The Dublin Whiskey Distillery Company, Limited, was registered on 28 January 1873. The distillery was built at Jones Road, Dublin, and held on a lease of £300 a year which was reduced if water was taken from the Grand Canal Company. Additions of land were acquired in 1886 when the estates of the Butler family were wound up. Maltings worked by Thomas Matthews in Russell Place were bought for £1,750. Further additions remote from the distillery were obtained in Cork Street in 1879 and 1880. The original share capital was £100,000 divided into 200 shares. There were seven foundation subscribers at one share each. As might be expected the plant was of the latest design. This company typifies the changes in management in the industry. This was no family concern; its directors were all business men with little knowledge of the distiller's art. The practical side of making whiskey was left to an employed distiller. The annual output in 1887 was just over half a million proof gallons which was well below the capacity of the plant. The principal market was in England.[6]

The Dodder Bank Distilleries, Dublin

There were two distillery firms operating at Dodder Bank, but neither survived beyond the middle of the nineteenth century. Robert Haig, who owned one of them, said that his distillery began in March, 1795. He also ran a spirit store at 16, Temple Bar in the city. By 1802 this distillery was among the largest in Dublin with two stills of 1,117 and 1,547 gallons capacity. Haig, like all the other distillers, was forced to reduce the size of his plant because of conditions created by the distillery laws. In 1823, the last year of the still licence system, he was working only one still of 500 gallons. Under the more liberal laws after

5. See Note 1 (c) (d). P.R.O. Dublin, ref. M 4936. Barnard, *Whisky Distilleries, op. cit.,* pp. 369–73. *Gentleman's and Citizen's Almanack. The Dublin Directory,* 1838, 1890. *The History of a Great House,* published by John Jameson and Sons, Dublin, 1924.

6. P.R.O. Dublin, refs. M 4926, 4937. Two of the original subscribers were W. G. Craig and R. Gardiner, leading Dublin accountants. Barnard, *Whisky Distilleries,* pp. 375–7.

1823 he expanded and ten years later he was using a Coffey still as well as pot stills and was producing over 330,000 proof gallons a year. He was a prominent witness at the Government revenue inquiries in 1823 and 1834. The distillery had ceased by the middle of the century and there appears to be no extant evidence why this happened.[7]

The other distillery was small by Dublin standards and was owned by Aeneas Coffey, who also had offices at 27, South King Street, Dublin. After some twenty-five years in the excise service and reaching the rank of inspector-general of excise, he retired to become a distiller. He had a distinguished career and on one occasion received bayonet wounds in an encounter with illicit distillers. He was responsible for several innovations in excise distillery control, particularly the perfection of the indicator used on spirit receivers. He was a strong advocate for enclosing the worm end of the still in a safe and helped to devise suitable revenue locks. This was a period of widespread frauds in distilleries. Later he designed the successful continuous still which bears his name and is in use in present day distilleries. This probably decided him to become a distiller. He does not appear to have been successful for, by 1839, the Dodder Bank enterprise had ceased. Meanwhile in 1838 he had established himself as a patent still manufacturer under the title of Coffey & Son of 3, Barrow Street, Dublin. In 1840 the manufacturing firm was under the name of Aeneas Coffey, junior; but by 1847 the firm had disappeared from the Dublin scene. It appears that the firm had moved to England.[8]

Phoenix Park Distillery

This distillery has a special interest as it was an incursion into the Irish scene of the Distillers Company Limited of Scotland. A spinning mill was bought and converted in October, 1878 on the banks of the river Liffey at Chapelizod. It was a distillery of

7. See Note 1 (*b*), (*c*). *Irish Revenue Inquiry, 5th Report*, 1823. *op. cit.*, pp. 294. *Excise Revenue Inquiry, 7th Report, Part I*, 1834, *op. cit.*, pp. 119, 421–2, 438. *Gentleman's and Citizen's Almanack.*

8. *Experiments in Distillation by the Excise Department*, Parl. Pps. 1821 (538) xix, pp. 369–72. A. J. V. Underwood, *Historical Development of Distilling Plant*, a paper read to the Institute of Chemical Engineers, 22 February 1935, p. 28. *Irish Revenue Inquiry, 5th Report*, 1823, pp. 321, 329, 331. *Gentleman's and Citizen's Almanack.*

moderate size compared with the larger plants in the city, with four pot stills with a capacity of 350,000 proof gallons a year and employing sixty persons in 1887. Its chief market was in London. It ceased producing in 1921 following a policy of the company to reduce output and concentrate its activities to Scotland. At the time the danger of over-production was a serious menace. It was also a time of serious civil strife and uncertainty which would doubtless greatly influence the decision of a Scottish based firm.[9]

The Belfast Distilleries

Next to Dublin, Belfast and nearby Comber became the second largest concentration for distilling by the late nineteenth century. At the beginning of the century whiskey production was negligible with two small Belfast distilleries in 1802 that ceased soon afterwards. This is understandable as the town was small and a strong local market did not arise till the rapid expansion of population occurred in the middle of the century. In 1807 another small distillery had started using a 504 gallon still. In 1823 there was only a small 300 gallon still worked by James Shaw. The improved distillery laws encouraged enterprise and, with a view, perhaps, of reaching out beyond local needs, Michael Ferrar established himself as a distiller and maltster at 39, Barrack Street, Belfast. Details of his plant are not available, but in 1833 he was charged duty on 266,000 proof gallons. In 1835 Shaw acquired this distillery. At that time there was one Coffey still at work and a pot still in reserve. Output was over half a million proof gallons a year by 1842. In the following year the distillery had become the property of Alexander McKenzie, but, as Shaw was still the licensed distiller, it seems that McKenzie had merely invested in the enterprise. At the time the Lisburn excise collector reported on a complaint from Shaw that he was being harassed by the excise supervisor.[10]

Alexander McKenzie appears to have been related to the Alexander family, Dublin bankers, and this may have been the

9. Barnard, *Whiskey Distilleries*, pp. 379–81. Ross Wilson, *Seventy Years of the Scotch Whisky Industry*, articles appearing monthly in *The Wine and Spirit Trade Record*, see February and March 1967.

10. See Note 1 (*b*), (*c*), (*d*). *Metier's Belfast Directory*, 1835–6. *Belfast Excise Historical Records*, Custom House, Belfast, Book 6, pp. 1–4, 83.

source for capital. In 1843 the firm of John McKenzie and Company was founded to run the distillery. Alexander McKenzie must have held a lien on the property for his will discloses that the distilling firm owed him over £10,000, and he bequeathed the distillery to his grandson, Alexander McKenzie Shaw. The distiller's licence, however, was held by John Shaw and an application was made for this licence to be held jointly by John and Alexander McKenzie Shaw. From the evidence it seems that John Shaw and John McKenzie became related by the marriage of their children. The distillery prospered and in 1844 the excise collector reported that production was increasing, but he also regarded the firm as fraudulent and that there had been a number of convictions. A new Coffey still was installed in 1846. The firm continued in business as the Belfast Distillery until 1868 when it ceased, and thereafter there is no record of any distillery in Barrack Street. There seems to be no extant record showing the reason for the disappearance of this distillery. The spirit market was strong so it may have been due to deaths of the principals or just inefficient management.[11]

The McKenzie and Shaw families branched out in other directions of the trade in intoxicating drinks. Thus in 1846 an application was made for a brewer's licence by Henry Shaw and A. Wallace to work a Belfast brewery which was run by Alexander McKenzie Shaw. Wallace was the principal clerk at the distillery and Henry Shaw was a cousin of Alexander Shaw. Another earlier venture by Alexander McKenzie, who acquired the Belfast distillery, was a distillery in Dungannon. This distillery was conveyed jointly to John Falls and John McKenzie in 1811. In 1832 a co-partnership was formed between Alexander McKenzie and four others to operate as brewers and distillers at Donoughmore brewery and Dungannon distillery. In none of these various businesses does Alexander McKenzie appear in an active role. Apparently he merely supplied capital and helped to set up members of his family in the undertakings.[12]

11. P.R.O. Dublin, refs. D 17421, T 7128. *Belfast Excise Records*, Book 5, pp. 4 23, 105. *The Belfast Directory*, 1864, shows the distillery company as still in business, but later directories indicate that the premises were unoccupied and by 1868 they had disappeared.

12. P.R.O. Dublin, refs. D 17423, 17430. *Belfast Excise Records*, Book 5, p. 105 See also the *Irish Revenue Inquiry, 5th Report*, 1823, p. 317.

The Royal Irish Distilleries

This distillery firm was founded by William Dunville, J.P. The history of the Dunville family interest in whiskey goes back to the beginning of the nineteenth century; to William Napier who owned a wine and spirit store in Bank Lane, now Bank Street, Belfast. His son, Sir Joseph Napier, became Lord Chancellor of Ireland. John Dunville, after an apprenticeship, became a partner in the business in 1808 and the firm was re-named Napier and Dunville. By 1863 William Dunville had succeeded to the business which was now known as John Dunville and Company. The firm had moved from Bank Lane and were trading from 10, Callender Street, Belfast. William Dunville brought into the business his nephew, Robert J. Dunville, also J. Bruce and James Craig. The main business of the company was blending whiskeys bought from various distillers. After blending and bottling, these were sold under their own brand names. Thus 'V.R.' brand had been marketed since 1837 to mark Queen Victoria's accession, and a still older brand was 'Three Crowns'.[13]

In 1869 the firm decided to enter the distilling business and started building on what was then the outskirts of the city near the Grosvenor Road. There was no distillery in Belfast at this time. The excise laws forbad a distiller from dealing in spirits within two miles of his distillery, so, to overcome this rule, a separate company was formed having the same directors and personnel. Thus William Dunville and Company were distillers, and Dunville and Company were spirit dealers. Both companies had their offices in Callender Street. The distillery, known as 'The Royal Irish Distilleries', began operations in 1870. Considerable capital must have been raised by public subscription for the premises were extensive and equipped with a large and modern plant. The grain lofts could store 6,000 tons. The still houses, mills, malt floors and warehouses were all on a massive scale, much beyond any previous development in Belfast. The fermenting vessels, for example, ranged from 27,000 to 35,000 gallons, and there were sixteen of them, increasing to eighteen

13. *Royal Commission on Whisky and other Potable Spirits,* Parl. Pps. 1908 [Cd. 4181], p. 297. *Belfast Newsletter,* 23 June 1921; 8 December 1936. *Belfast Telegraph,* 31 December 1936; 1 June 1937. *Belfast Directories.* The company also published an illustrated brochure.

by 1900. Three furnaces heated pot stills rising in capacity from 5,255 gallons to 11,240 gallons, and later two new type pot stills were erected and were heated by steam coils. A Coffey still was also installed. By 1908 the plant had been altered to three pot stills and two patent stills. In the 1890s a new office block was built in Arthur Street and now houses a bank. The distilling company was incorporated in 1879 with Robert J. Dunville as chairman. In 1887 Barnard wrote that the output was running at one and a half million proof gallons a year, which rose by another million by 1890. Branch offices and storage premises were opened in London, Liverpool, Newcastle-on-Tyne and Glasgow. At the beginning of this century the firm acquired Bladnoch distillery in Scotland, founded in 1818 and formerly owned by T. & A. McClelland. Extensive improvements were made in this distillery in 1912.[14]

Robert Dunville died in 1910 to be succeeded by his son, Colonel John Dunville. John had two sons, Captain Robert L. Dunville who became chairman of the company till his death in 1931, during a visit to South Africa on the firm's business. The second son, John Spencer Dunville, died of wounds in June 1917 and was posthumously awarded the Victoria Cross. With the passing of Captain Dunville in 1931 the name disappeared from the board of the firm. He was succeeded as chairman by the Right Honourable Captain C. C. Craig, a relative of Lord Craigavon, Prime Minister of Northern Ireland. Probably the main architect of the firm's prosperity was Robert Dunville who joined the firm in 1863 and became its chairman in 1879. In the late nineteenth century he built Redburn House in Holywood near Belfast. His will was proved at £916,200.[15]

The firm emerged from the 1914-18 war in a strong position with ample stocks. There were then 10,000 shares at £10 each and, by 1929, the financial state was so good that it was proposed to repay shareholders by reducing the capital by £5 a share. This was defeated, but in a slightly varied form, the proposal came up again in 1932. Captain Craig, the chairman, proposed

14. Barnard, *Whisky Distilleries*, pp. 426–7. *S.C. on British and Foreign Spirits*, Parl. Pps. 1890–1 (210) xi, p. 423. *R.C. on Whiskey*, 1908, pp. 297, 304. *Belfast Telegraph*, 31 December 1936. *Belfast Newsletter*, 23 June 1921.

15. *Belfast Evening Telegraph*, 8 August 1917. *Belfast Telegraph*, 17 January 1958; 28 March 1958. *Belfast Newsletter*, 18 December 1932.

a special distribution of surplus capital and this was agreed. The firm thereupon petitioned the Court who allowed the change in capital structure on the grounds that it would not prejudice creditors. Share values were reduced from £10 to £1. Each shareholder got £5 in cash per share and some ordinary and preference new shares. This diminution of reserves certainly imperilled the company's position when the depression in trade hit the market in the next few years.[16]

All major whiskey firms had their eyes on the United States in 1933. The repeal of the 18th Amendment to end prohibition was expected and, with it, the opening of a vast market for legitimate trade. It was thought that large quantities of immature and poor quality whiskey would pour into that country from the British Isles and Canada. The policy of Irish distillers, however, was to protect the reputation of their product and send only properly matured whiskey. Dunville had ample suitable stocks and were optimistic. Prohibition ended in November, 1933 but quota restrictions were imposed. These did not work and were virtually abandoned by about May 1934. Thus Dunville were very well placed to invade a very large market which ought to have offset the slump in the whiskey trade in the home market. What really happened is not clear.

Distilling grain spirit was halted in 1935 because stocks were large in relation to sales. About this time the directors appeared to become nervous about the future. During 1936 overtures were made to William H. Ross, chairman of the Distillers Company Limited, with a view to the Scottish company taking over Dunville as a going concern. Ross apparently had no faith in the future of Irish whiskey and turned down the offer. His attitude was understandable. The Scottish firm were having their own difficulties about over-production and would gladly discourage production of a rival product. J. C. Brownrigg, a director of Dunville, considered that Irish whiskey was a 'dead trade'. The trustees of the Dunville estate held the same view. The directors decided to sell out while the firm was solvent and still making good profits, rather than continue and risk disaster. Their first step was to sell Bladnoch distillery in Scotland for a mere £3,500, representing a considerable loss on premises and

16. *Belfast Telegraph*, 29 November 1929; 8 and 15 November 1932. *Belfast Newsletter*, 21 April 1932.

plant; but this loss was more than recouped by the sale of whiskey stocks. Next, in December 1936, the whiskey stocks still held by the two firms—Dunville and McClelland—were transferred to Dunville and Company, the wine and spirit merchants. At a directors' meeting on 31 December 1936, a resolution was agreed to go into voluntary liquidation. This was later passed at an extraordinary general meeting. After approval by the Court liquidators were appointed. Thereafter the property and stocks were sold piecemeal over the next 12 years. A final distribution on liquidation brought the total to £850,000, making £3 8s. 2d. for each £1 share. The distillery premises and warehouses are now owned by a tobacco firm. The names of the nearby streets show the origin of these premises: Distillery Street, Excise Street and Malt Street. Dunville claimed to be the largest distillery unit in the United Kingdom and it is sad to see such a thriving business end so abruptly. Ireland could ill afford its loss, for its product was of high quality and eminently suited to meet the strong competition from Scotch blended whisky. Also, some 400 persons lost their employment. After overcoming a legal difficulty, most of them got some compensation.[17]

The United Distilleries Company Limited, Belfast

Though registered in Belfast in 1902, this company included two distilleries in Londonderry. The company was an amalgamation of the Irish Distillery Limited of Connswater, Belfast, the Avoniel Distillery in Belfast and David Watt and Company of Londonderry, with distilleries in Abbey Street and Waterside in that city.[18]

The deeds of the Connswater property show that in 1872 Lord Templemore granted the land to Daniel and Thomas S. Dixon, Belfast, timber merchants. Three Belfast firms, Kirker, Greer and Company, Mitchell and Company, both blenders, and James Wilson and Sons, distillers, combined to enter distilling. Dixon leased the land to the new United Distillery Company on 8 April 1886 and erected the distillery. Additional land, including some adjoining streets, was leased on 16 January 1889. The managing

17. P.R.O. Belfast, ref. 2132/1/7. *Northern Whig,* 5 October 1933; 15 December 1936. *Belfast Telegraph,* 23 November 1933; 2 April 1935; 14 December 1936; 1 November 1941; 31 November 1960. *Belfast Newsletter,* 22 January 1937.
18. *R.C. on Whiskey,* 1908, p. 152.

director of the new distillery was A. M. Kirker. Very little is known about the early years of this distillery. When Barnard visited it soon after it began operations, he found that there were two Coffey stills each with a capacity of 4,000 gallons an hour and some pot stills. The expected output was two million proof gallons a year.[19]

Practically no information appears to be available about the distillery in Avoniel before it became merged into the United Distilleries Company in 1902. The owner, William Higgins, did not admit Barnard in 1887, but Barnard was able to write that the distillery was built in 1882 and that it was producing 850,000 proof gallons annually, wholly from Coffey stills. Pot stills must have been installed later because W. Virtue, managing director of the United Distilleries Company, stated that such stills were operating in 1908.[20]

The history of the two Londonderry distilleries goes back to the early nineteenth century. In 1823 James Robinson was working a seventy-six gallon still and using a limited number of utensils which entitled him to a reduction in the still licence duty. Alexander Stewart owned the other distillery and worked a sixty-four gallon still. Both these distilleries came into being under the special laws designed to encourage small legal stills to combat illicit distillers. The sites of these distilleries are not certain, but were probably in Abbey Street and Waterside.[21]

From 1833 information becomes more precise. In that year Ross T. Smyth worked the Abbey Street distillery and James Mahon a smaller distillery at Waterside. Smyth was producing yearly between 80,000 and 100,000 proof gallons and Mahon about 14,000 gallons. Smyth estimated it would cost £10,000 to build a new distillery with a capacity of 60,000 gallons. About this time Andrew Alexander Watt appears on the distilling scene. In 1830 he appears to have been a wine and spirit merchant and also dealt in grain and general provisions. Extant sales ledgers of 1829 record sales of puncheons of whiskey and brandy, as well as tea, cider, salmon and other goods. He acquired

19. Barnard, *Whisky Distilleries*, pp. 428–9. All the property of Connswater distillery is now occupied by Gallaher Limited and is their principal Belfast tobacco warehouse.

20. Barnard, *Whisky Distilleries*, p. 430. *R.C. on Whiskey*, 1908, p. 152.

21. 52 Geo. 3, c. 48; 57 Geo. 3, c. 110. See Note 1 (*c*).

Mahon's Waterside distillery and contemplated brewing beer. He then entered into partnership with Smyth in the business of distillers and brewers at Abbey Street, but brewing never materialised. The agreement is interesting as it shows how capital was raised. It specified equal shares in half the profits, the rest to be returned to the business. This clearly shows that Watt must have brought in additional capital to get these terms. Watt became very active in the distilleries and on one occasion in 1847 crossed swords with authority over a duty charge on the loss of spirit in transit to England. Watt retained his interest in the retail business and was a leader in 1845 in a movement to boycott wholesalers illegally selling small quantities, an infringement of the licensing laws apparently ignored by excise officials. Later he merged his retail interests with John Steel in an agreement dated 17 July 1854 and this, no doubt, enabled him to devote more time to distilling for, from that year, there was no further mention of Ross Smyth. The distilling firm became A. Watt and Company; Andrew had gone and David Watt was head of the firm. Other directors were H. O'Donnell and Edward Kelly. This was a period of rapid growth in the business. Watt received two-thirds of the distributed profits. His share in 1876 was £1,371, but rose to £10,188 by 1880. The two distilleries were developed along different lines. At the Waterside plant only pot stills were used and malt spirit was made. The Abbey Street distillery was equipped with two Coffey stills and Barnard recorded, in 1887, that it was the largest distillery in Ireland with a capacity of two million gallons. It was a claim that might well be disputed, but there can be no doubt that Londonderry had become an important distilling centre.[22]

An interesting law suit occurred in 1885. Watt sued O'Hanlon, a spirit merchant, accusing him of selling whiskey labelled 'Watt's Old Innishowen'. There was some complicated argument and wrangling, but it emerged that the excise had objected to the label on the grounds that spirit sold under Watt's name was a grain whiskey and that his malt whiskey was marketed as 'Stewart's Malt', a confirmation that in 1823 Alexander Stewart owned the Abbey Street distillery. O'Hanlon alleged that his

22. P.R.O. Belfast, refs. D 1506/2–1, 7; D 1506/4–1, 2. *Excise Revenue Inquiry, 7th Report, Part I*, 1834, *op. cit.*, pp. 233, 431, 433. See Note 1 (c) (e). *Thom's Directory of Manufacturers*, 1908, p. 252.

label was 'O'Hanlon's Old Innishowen Malt' and that 'Stewart's Malt' was a Scotch whisky masquerading as Irish. The interesting point in this acrimonious dispute was that, in a number of affidavits, the words 'Old Innishowen' were regarded as synonymous with poteen and fetched a better price. In 1908 the firm was trading as David Watt and Company Limited, and was still working both distilleries.[23]

The history after the merging of the three firms in 1902 becomes very important from the standpoint of the Irish distilling industry as a whole. The new company became one of the largest producers of whiskey in the United Kingdom and was in direct competition with the rising dominance of Scotch whisky. Its disappearance, along with Dunville, was a devastating blow. Some 90 per cent of whiskey production in the north of Ireland ceased with the loss of these two producers. The events leading to the closure of the Belfast and Londonderry distilleries are complex and not easily reduced to a short description.

Evidence given before a Royal Commission in 1908 showed that each of the Belfast distilleries had both pot and patent stills and in Londonderry the Abbey Street distillery had a patent still and Waterside distillery had pot stills. The yearly output was five to six million proof gallons of grain spirit divided equally between three distilleries, and about 250,000 gallons of pot still whiskey. The patent stills were worked throughout the year and used malt, rye and maize. The pot stills worked for about six months during winter, using malt and barley and occasionally a little rye, wheat or oats. In Londonderry yeast was produced in Abbey Street. The company had a big market for its grain spirit with blenders in Scotland and England. This was the position when events began which ended the life of the company.[24]

The Distillers Company Limited of Scotland was worried about the uncontrolled flood of grain spirit being thrown on the market and became clearly disturbed when the United Distilleries Company contemplated invading the Scottish distilling industry by buying a bankrupt Edinburgh brewery in order to convert it into a grain spirit distillery. The Scottish company made several vain attempts to get their Irish rivals to agree

23. P.R.O. Belfast, ref. D 1506/8.
24. *R.C. on Whiskey*, 1908, pp. 152, 159.

production limits so as to prevent a saturation of the market and a catastrophic fall in prices. Eventually the two companies agreed to divide the trade and proportions were fixed. As part of the deal there was an exchange of shares which later was to become the 'Achilles heel' of the United Distilleries. The Scottish company received half the shares of the United Distilleries Company and the latter got the equivalent value in the Distillers Company shares. The next move was the creation, in 1913, of the Distillers Finance Corporation in which the Irish distillers were involved. The Scottish firms were not consulted though they had members on the United Distilleries board. This unfriendly act must have rankled. The new Corporation had a half interest in United Distilleries, the Belfast blending houses of Brown Corbett, Young King and Company, and Mitchell and Company, Ferintosh distillery in Dingwall, Mitchell Brothers, blenders in Glasgow, and Tanqueray Gordon, rectifiers in London. The new arrangement meant a partial sharing of capital without any member company surrendering control.

One of the consequences of the Immature Spirits (Restriction) Act, 1915, was that the Distillers Finance Corporation got into difficulties and asked the Distillers Company of Scotland to take them over. The offer was shelved. A new situation arose over yeast production during and after the 1914-18 war and this was the background of later developments. A distiller making yeast also makes high strength grain spirits suitable for industrial use. Thus any severe imbalance in the yeast market may well involve a similar difficulty with spirits. Fleischmann and Company of New York were yeast manufacturers with a European market and in conjunction with the United Distilleries formed the International Yeast Company with the object of competing with the United Yeast Company, a subsidiary of the Distillers Company. The latter were naturally concerned, but they were also afraid that the intrusion of the American company might attract United States distilling interests to make whiskey in Scotland. They therefore determined to acquire the remaining half of the United Distilleries shares and gain control of their Irish rivals. In 1922 the offer to take over the Distillers Finance Corporation was resurrected and accepted. Nearly £3,000,000, in the form of shares, was paid, partly by borrowing. They also acquired Fleischmann's interest in the International Yeast Company. With the half interest already held in the United Distilleries Company, plus the shares held by the Distillers Finance Corporation, the Scottish company now had control of the Irish company. By 1925 the Londonderry distilleries had ceased and the Belfast distilleries were silent by 1929.[25]

Comber Distilleries

In Comber, a few miles from Belfast, there were two distilleries: the upper and lower. The upper distillery was established following the changes in the distillery laws and reduction of duty in 1823. A brewery and malt house were converted in 1825 at a cost of £8,000 by Johnston and Millar, and John Millar, J.P., was licensed as the distiller. In 1833 the output was over 33,000 proof gallons. The lower distillery was much smaller. Byrne and Giffikin converted a paper mill in 1825 and traded as Byrne and Company. The excise collector had a poor opinion of this firm and reports a case of the illegal removal of spirit in 1845. Later, John Millar bought out his rival and worked both distilleries as a single firm, though the accounts and records of the two establishments were kept distinct. In 1871 ownership in both distilleries passed to Samuel Bruce who appears to have taken no active part in the distillery activities. The records of the firm in 1908 show it to be a private company. Of the 10,000 shares, Bruce held 8,173 and was living in Gloucestershire. The distiller was J. McBlizzard, who held 1,666 shares. The remaining 161 shares were divided among six others, all connected in some way with the working of the firm. For example the firm's solicitor held one share. There were fifty-three employees in 1908 and an examination of the wages book reveals that there was no provision for training anyone to assist or replace the distiller. The highest paid employees were two coopers at 5s. 7d. a day. The four still men got from 2s. 8d. to 3s. 4d. a day and others such as malt men, brewers and grain men were in or near this range. Artisans like the blacksmith and carpenter got a little

25. The story of these complicated moves as seen through Scottish eyes is included in monthly articles by Ross Wilson in *Seventy Years of the Scotch Whisky Industry* in the *Wine and Spirit Trade Record*. See specially the articles in September 1966 and February, March and April 1967. *The Customs and Excise Reports* of 1921, p. 59; 1926, p. 130; and 1930, p. 34, show the disappearance of the distilleries. The Belfast distilleries are listed under County Down.

more. Women in the bottling plant were the lowest paid at 2s. od. a day. Another interesting feature in these records is the purchase of yeast. In 1872 the firm was buying yeast from breweries as far away as Bass and Company, Burton-on-Trent, the Trent and Valley Brewery Company in Lichfield and, almost inevitably, from Guinness's brewery in Dublin. The firm's warehouse ledgers for 1890 show that a considerable part of their sales was bottled spirits and it is about this period that a transition was in progress in the industry from sales in casks to sales in cases. In 1914 the firm produced 110,000 proof gallons from both distilleries.[26]

Between the two great wars production remained at about the same level. During and after the second war many local people thought the quality declined, but this might be attributed to tastes changing from pot still whiskey to blends. Their market now was sales to independent blenders and the latter were also declining in the face of competition from the great whiskey combinations of distillers and blenders. Whatever the reason the firm were only selling their whiskey with difficulty and in the early 1950s the number of distilling periods each year became less and less. In February 1953 the distillery ceased working. Attempts to sell the distillery as a going concern all failed. It was well equipped, but the firm were now in a world where a small independent company making a pot still whiskey and with limited resources to finance modern marketing methods would not easily survive, no matter how good the product.

The Glen Distilleries, Cork

The difficulties of giving a coherent account of early nineteenth century distillers is well illustrated in the Cork distilling industry. Official returns give lists of names in different years but, where an address is stated, it is insufficient to establish successive owners. Nor are there adequate directories. In the latter half of the century the picture becomes less cloudy. Cork history also gives clear examples of the close association of some distillers with rectifying houses; a situation so objectionable to the excise authorities because it made fraud easier. Thus Thomas and Francis Wise

26. P.R.O. Belfast, refs. D 1808–8/1, 16/1, 25/1–4, 28/1. *Belfast Excise Historical Records, op. cit.*, Book 5, pp. 78, 89. *Excise Revenue Inquiry, 7th Report, Part I.* 1834, pp. 233, 444, 446. Barnard, *Whisky Distilleries*, pp. 430–1.

were distillers in North Mall and Henry Wise was a rectifier in North Abbey. In Milfield, Morgan Caldwell was a distiller and William Caldwell a rectifier. In Watercourse, Dennis Corcoran was a partner with Robert Allan in a distillery and also ran a rectifying house.[27]

Probably the most distinguished distiller in Cork in the early part of the century was Daniel Callaghan who owned a distillery at Dodges Glen, Kilnap. In 1806 this distillery was run by Sir Anthony Perrier who worked a 1,555 gallon still. By 1818 P. W. Callaghan is listed as the distiller, but Perrier may have continued his interest, for in 1822 he was granted a patent for a continuous still. This still was not a success and no more is heard of him as a distiller. Callaghan, who by now must have become the sole proprietor, used a still of 500 gallons content, probably because of the abnormal conditions prevailing under the still licence system. By 1834 Callaghan had succeeded to the distillery and, probably with improved plant, was producing over 200,000 proof gallons a year. In addition to his distilling activities he was a member of parliament and a Cork harbour commissioner. He was particularly outspoken on corruption in the excise service in his evidence before a Government inquiry in 1834. A striking example of Callaghan's enterprise emerged during a similar inquiry in 1823, for it was disclosed that he had established a rectifying house in London to receive and process spirits from the Cork distillery, thus circumventing the prohibitive import laws against Irish rectified spirits and the monopoly practices of English distillers and rectifiers. The English distillers bought him off on terms ensuring a market for a substantial quota of his production at favourable prices. Callaghan's distillery is listed in a Cork directory of 1845 as the Glen distillery, but after that year there is no further record.

Some old buildings can be seen in the Kilnap district which are shown on the 1907 ordnance survey map as the 'old Glen distillery'. They are now being used for other purposes. These buildings were the premises of the Glen Distillery Company owned by the Sugrue family. Barnard visited this distillery in

27. See Note 1 (b). *Inquiry into Fees in Ireland, 5th Report,* 1806-7, pp. 165, 244. The law forbad distilling and rectifying on the same premises, but a surveyor-general of excise said that some of these businesses were contiguous and had associated names.

1887. He wrote that it was a small distillery employing twenty men and had an annual output of 60,000 proof gallons. He states that the buildings had been converted from a mill a few years earlier and that the mill had worked for a century. He may have been mistaken and it is probable that here was the site of Callaghan's distillery which was, perhaps, used as a mill for a few years.[28] By 1925 the later Glen distillery had discontinued.

Bandon Distillery

The improved distillery laws after 1823 not only encouraged expansion in existing distilleries, but occasionally tempted new-comers. In Bandon, about eighteen miles west of Cork, James C. Allman started a new distillery. There is no record of any previous distillery in Bandon and there is no information about Allman's previous experience in distilling. Nor is it known whether he financed the enterprise himself or raised capital from others. The buildings had been used as a mill and were converted to distilling in 1826 using the same water power that had driven the mill. In the early years a large part of the profits were ploughed back and the business rapidly expanded. For the first few years the output was about 60,000 proof gallons annually, but by 1836 this had risen to 200,000 proof gallons and by the 1880s, to half a million proof gallons. By 1846 Richard Allman had succeeded to the business and by 1881 the distillery was owned by R. L. and James C. Allman in partnership, trading as Allman and Company. James was a local Justice of the Peace. Barnard visited this distillery in 1887 and remarked on the large malt house and the pot stills, two of which had a capacity of 26,000 gallons each. The firm made the traditional Irish mixed grain pot still whiskey and a pure malt whiskey. The main markets were in Great Britain and the Colonies. About 200 persons were employed. This distillery continued into this century, but by

28. *Inquiry into Fees, op. cit.*, pp. 204, 292. See Note 1 (c). *Irish Revenue Inquiry, 5th Report, Supplement*, Parl. Pps. 1823 (498) vii, pp. 667–8. *Excise Revenue Inquiry, 7th Report, Part I*, 1834, pp. 176, 179–80, 232. Morewood, *Inebriating Liquors*, pp. 643, 677, 725. *Aldwell's Cork Directory*, 1844–5, pp. 54, 163. Sir Antony Perrier became secretary for the Commercial Buildings and for the Pipe Water Trustees. *Cork: Its Trade and Commerce*, 1919, handbook of the Cork Chamber of Commerce. Barnard, *Whisky Distilleries*, pp. 412–3. A. J. V. Underwood, *Historical Development of Distilling Plant*, p. 27. Some early 19th century directories and the 1907 Ordnance Survey map are in the Cork Public Library.

1925 it had ceased and Allman was in business in the firm of Allman, Dowden and Company, whiskey agents, particularly for Allman's whiskey. They were probably marketing the stocks that had built up in bonded warehouses. The distilling company wound up in 1929.[29]

Limerick Distillery

One other Munster distillery is worth a note. There appears to have been no legal distillery in Limerick city before the nineteenth century and in the first two decades of that century legal distilling was intermittent. In 1802 White and McSweeney worked a 514-gallon still, but this was not operating in 1807. By 1818 there were two distillers: John Brown, working two stills each of 501 gallons content, and George Connell with a smaller still. In 1823 only John Brown had survived with one 500-gallon still, and he continued after the changes in the distillery laws. By 1846 the distillery was owned and run by the firm of James Stein, junior, and Company and became known as the Thomond Gate distillery. There was another Limerick distillery in 1846 in St. James's Square, but it had only a brief existence. By 1881 the Thomond Gate distillery had passed to Archibald Walker, a Scot who also worked the Adelphi distillery in Glasgow and the Vauxhall distillery in Liverpool. The latter was equipped with four Coffey stills. Ownership in all three distilleries had become vested in the firm of A. Walker and Company by the early 1900s and this must be amongst the earliest examples of a distilling firm branching out into all three parts of the United Kingdom. Archibald Walker, junior, joined the board of the Distillers Company Limited and this resulted in the Limerick distillery becoming absorbed and closed down.[30]

Burt Distillery, County Donegal

Small distilleries were licensed in the Londonderry excise collection in 1782. They were meeting the full force of the

29. See Note 1 (*d*). *Slater's Directory*, 1846, p. 153; 1881, Munster, p. 11 *Macdonald's Irish Directory*, 1915, p. 337. Barnard, *Whisky Distilleries*, pp. 415–18. *Ham's Inland Revenue Year Book*, 1900, pp. 318–19. *Dáil Debates*, vol. 29, 25 April 1929, col. 911.

30. See Note 1 (*c*) (*d*) (*e*). *Slater's Directory*, 1846, p. 273; 1881, Munster, p. 94. *Thom's Directory of Manufacturers*, 1908, p. 252. Barnard, *Whisky Distilleries*, pp. 400–3. Ross Wilson, *Seventy Years of the Scotch Whisky Industry*, February 1967.

upsurge in illicit distilling at the time, and by 1802 all had ceased legal operations. Seizures of illicit stills and apparatus for this excise collection in 1833 accounted for a third of all the seizures in Ireland and is a measure of the severe competition from poteen. In 1808 and later years, laws encouraged small stills in poteen areas and three legal distilleries were set up. In 1823 two small distilleries in the city worked stills of forty-nine and sixty-four gallons content, and another similar distillery was established at Burt in the barony of Innishowen.[31] The Burt distillery, under the ownership of William Leathem, though unimportant in relation to the whole industry, was remarkable. It was situated in the heart of the most notorious poteen area in Ireland and challenged the poteen monopoly. Leathem survived this competition for nearly twenty-five years. This was probably because he avoided a direct clash with poteen, a malt whiskey, by making a grain pot still whiskey, for which there would be some local preference and he sought a wider market. He developed a trade with England. His yearly output in the 1830s was over 40,000 proof gallons. He gave important evidence on illicit distilling practices, based on first-hand knowledge, before a Government inquiry in 1834. His evidence was very critical of the excise administration, particularly the posting of incompetent English officers to Ireland. The Burt distillery had ceased by 1840, probably because of the rise of two large distilleries in Londonderry.[32]

Limavady Distillery

As a result of the encouragement given to erect small stills in notorious poteen areas, a distillery began in Newtown-Limavady, midway between Coleraine and Londonderry. In 1818 William Cathar worked a forty-nine gallon still. Unlike many other distilleries, there was no immediate expansion following the revision of the distillery laws in 1823, and even ten years later Cathar was producing only about 19,000 proof gallons a year. The reason for this static position is not known. It may have

31. See Note 1 (*a*) (*c*). 49 Geo. 3, c. 99, relaxed the laws restricting the minimum size of stills. *Excise Revenue Inquiry, 7th Report, Part I*, 1834, p. 238, shows a return of seizures.

32. See Note 1 (*c*). *Excise Revenue Inquiry*, 1834, pp. 184, 194, 207, 233. *Return of Licensed Distillers, 1835–1850*, Parl. Pps. 1851 (369) i, p. 659.

been simply a lack of capital, or the pressure of poteen competition in a purely local market may have rendered further capital investment too risky. Cathar himself may not have been ambitious and been content to run a small business, perhaps risking an occasional run through the still which he overlooked entering with the excise! He had disappeared from the scene by 1846 and the distillery was being worked by Peter Rankin. Information on the fortunes of Rankin and the distillery for the next few years is not available, but there may have been some expansion. By 1887 the firm of Young, King and Company Limited had acquired the distillery, had set up a head office in Belfast and were producing half a million proof gallons annually. The firm prospered for some years, but after the outbreak of war in 1914 distilling ceased. The reason cannot be traced, but it may have been due to war-time difficulties. For example, the Immature Spirits (Restriction) Act of 1915 imposed a three-year minimum in warehouse and, if the firm was selling younger spirit, this regulation would involve more capital in warehouse space and delayed return for the expense of manufacture.[33]

Nun's Island Distillery, Galway

A thriving distilling industry never developed in Connaught. In the early years of the nineteenth century this was probably partly due to the competition from poteen and as the century progressed there came the competition from the large distilleries in Dublin as railways developed. A notable exception was the Nun's Island distillery in Galway which expanded while the traditional wine trade declined. There had been at least eleven small distilleries in the city towards the end of the eighteenth century, some of them owned by women, but most of them had disappeared by 1800. In 1802 there remained only two stills, the larger being 355 gallons content. Both these had gone by 1807. The laws encouraging small stills in poteen areas induced Michael Ryan to set up a still of ninety-eight gallons, and Bartholomew Finn one of fifty-three gallons. By 1823 both these gentlemen had ceased, but Patrick Joyce was working a still of eighty-nine gallons using turf fuel. It is not known whether he acquired one of the former distilleries or started anew. By 1833

33. Barnard, *Whisky Distilleries,* pp. 438–9. *Slater's Directory,* 1846, p. 513. *Belfast Directory,* 1913, p. 1832. In the 1915 edition this distillery is not shown.

Joyce had prospered and had an annual output of over 100,000 proof gallons. By this time there were two other Galway distillers: Richard Lynch producing nearly 80,000 proof gallons, and Burton Persse with two distilleries, one at Newton-Smith and the other at Newcastle, producing a total of 120,000 proof gallons. In 1840 Henry Persse, who had succeeded to the distilling business, bought from the Encumbered Estates Court the property formerly owned by the Joyce family. The Joyce distillery had, in the meantime, been converted into a woollen factory. By 1846 the Newcastle distillery was being run by Thomas Moore Persse and Company, but shortly afterwards the Newcastle lease expired and Persse restored the old Joyce distillery which became known as Nun's Island distillery. In 1881 Henry Persse was the proprietor, and by 1887 this distillery had a yearly output of 400,000 proof gallons. The plant used water power taken from the river Corrib. The distillery was still working in 1908, but ceased at the beginning of the first world war.[34]

Dundalk Distillery

Despite the dominance of Dublin, several distilleries thrived in small towns in Leinster. It is not always easy to account for success in one town and failure in another not far away. In Dundalk a distillery was first established at the beginning of the nineteenth century and was active till 1923, whereas in Newry, only fourteen miles further north, a distillery run by Caulfield and Company in 1802, later by the Thompson family, and finally by Denis Maguire, had ceased by 1846. Both towns were ports and Newry had the added advantage of inland transport by canal. It can only be surmised that there was no room for both distilleries in a market that was largely local, and that success or failure depended chiefly on efficient management and marketing. The first Dundalk distillery was owned by Godbey and Gilligan who, in 1802, worked a 1,514-gallon still, quite a large still for the period. The operation of the still licence system made this size impracticable and by 1807 the still was replaced

---

34. Note 1 (a) (b) (c) (d) (e). In Note 1 (b) no Galway distillery is shown in 1807. Note 1 (d) shows the duties paid at 3s. 4d. a gallon and the quantities have been calculated from this data. *Slater's Commercial Directory*, 1846, p. 124; 1881, Connaught, p. 45. *Thom's Directory of Manufacturers*, 1908, p. 251. *Macdonald's Irish Directory*, 1915, does not show any Galway distillery.

by one of 520 gallons and the owners were now Read, Brown and Company. Read disappeared soon afterwards and by 1818 Malcolm Brown was the distiller. Like so many others his production expanded after 1823 and, ten years later, his output had reached more than a quarter of a million proof gallons. Later in the century the owners are shown as M. Brown and Company of Roden Place. In 1887 both pot and Coffey stills were used and the yearly production had reached 700,000 proof gallons. The distillery by now was well equipped with the usual cooperage and workshops for engineers, smiths, carpenters and harness makers, and the whole plant employed about 100 men.[35]

At the beginning of this century the distillers concentrated on grain spirit with yeast as a profitable by-product. Apparently pot still whiskey was no longer made. The distillers' concentration on yeast resulted in producing an industrial spirit which they were satisfied to unload on the London market at a low price. This disturbed the Distillers Company of Scotland as their London-made spirit was being undersold. In 1912 the Dundalk distillers decided to sell out and approached the United Distillers Company of Belfast. The latter were willing to buy but wanted to pay in the form of shares in their company, but the Dundalk distillers wanted cash. While negotiations were going on the Scottish Company stepped in with a cash offer of £160,000 which was accepted. Thus the supply of industrial spirit outside the control of the Distillers Company was stopped. The distillery continued working until it was closed down in 1926. In 1927 the Irish Government tried to get the Scottish firm to re-open the distillery in the interests of local employment, but were told that the distillery was uneconomic to work as most of the product had to be sold in England. The company said that re-opening would be considered if they were granted an increased drawback on spirits exported and an import tariff on yeast. This proposal was rejected and the distillery finally wound up in 1929.[36]

35. See Note 1 (b) (c) (d) (e). Barnard, *Whisky Distilleries*, pp. 423–5. *Slater's Directory*, 1846, p. 36; 1881, Leinster p. 399. *Thom's Directory of Manufacturers*, 1908, p. 251. *Macdonald's Irish Directory*, 1915, p. 284.

36. Ross Wilson, *Seventy Years in the Scotch Whisky Industry*, article in March 1967. *Dáil Debates*, vol. 20, 29 July 1927, col. 1134. The reference to drawback is not quite accurate. Spirits are normally exported under bond. Perhaps the Distillers Company wanted an export bounty.

Drogheda Distillery

Drogheda had a distilling tradition in the eighteenth century and in 1782 there were no less than fifteen small distilleries, but the still licence system caused a drastic reduction. In 1802 there were only three distilleries all with stills in the range of 500 to 600 gallons in size. Five years later only one was operating, owned by Delahoyde and Company and working a single 500 gallon still. The squeeze of the still licence system forced a new owner, Robert Codd, to reduce the size of his still to 101 gallons. At this stage the distillery came into the possession of John Woolsey who must have been an enterprising man. Steam engines had been imported by brewers and distillers from the beginning of the nineteenth century, but the Drogheda distillery had the distinction of installing the first steam engine made in Ireland. Woolsey appeared on the scene at an opportune time, just before the changes in the distillery laws. From working a modest 300-gallon still in 1823 he was, by 1833, producing 300,000 proof gallons a year. In 1840 the output exceeded half a million proof gallons. By 1850 five stills were at work, over half a million proof gallons were charged duty at the still and over three quarters of a million gallons were deposited in bond. The distilling firm ceased within the next few years. The firm of John Woolsey and Company were, however, ale and porter brewers at Castle-bellingham in County Louth and in the 1870s had offices in Middle Abbey Street, Dublin; so it seems that they merely dropped out of distilling to concentrate on brewing. Woolsey may have sold out to John Jameson of Dublin, who acquired maltings in Drogheda about this time. The buildings were sold in the 1930s to Cairns, the brewing firm.[37]

Wexford Distillery

The town of Wexford did not develop into a distilling centre until 1827, though there had been a little distilling in the late eighteenth century when John Devereux worked two small stills

37. See Note 1 (a) (b) (d) (e). *Return relating to Spirits Distilled*, Parl. Pps. 1842 (238) xxxix, p. 545. *Return of Licensed Distillers, and Spirits Distilled*, Parl. Pps. 1851 (386) liii, pp. 269, 459. G. O'Brien, *The Economic History of Ireland from the Union to the Famine*, London, 1921, p. 414. *Thom's Directory*, 1865, does not show Woolsey as a distiller, but the 1873 edition lists him on p. 1876 as an ale and porter brewer.

at Bishop's Water, but these did not last long. A group of local gentlemen erected a new distillery at Bishop's Water in 1827, but by 1833 this business had been acquired by Nicholas Devereux and in that year he was charged duty on nearly 200,000 proof gallons. The Devereux family were prominent in the town and another member, John Thomas Devereux, was a maltster and Wexford's member of Parliament from 1847 to 1859. In 1847 Richard Devereux worked the distillery and as a gesture towards the relief of famine, he temporarily closed down the distillery. By 1881 the distillery was in the name of Nicholas Devereux and Company working three pot stills and an annual output of over 100,000 proof gallons. The firm never expanded like many others and it had a limited local market, hence it was not in a strong position to fend off competition from the spreading markets of firms in Dublin. By 1914 the distillery had ceased operations.[38]

Birr Distillery

There were four inland distilling centres in Leinster that are worth mentioning. At Birr the pattern of decline and revival noticeable in other centres was repeated. Towards the end of the eighteenth century there were four distillers working between them seven small stills. In 1802 there was only one small still and even this had gone by 1807. By 1818 two distillers had started up: Robert Hackett and Arthur Robinson, each working a still of 101 gallon capacity. Barnard states that one of them was established in 1805. This is not shown in the 1807 official return, but there may have been a period of inactivity. Between 1845 and 1850 one of the distilleries ceased. In 1887 the remaining distillery was in the hands of R. and J. Wallace, it had an output of 200,000 proof gallons and employed forty men. In the last decade of the century this, too, ceased to exist.[39]

38. See Note 1 (a) (d). Barnard, *Whisky Distilleries*, pp. 420–2. *Belfast Commercial Chronicle*, 6 January 1847. *Thom's Directory*, 1833. *Thom's Directory of Manufacturers*, 1908. *Macdonald's Irish Directory*, 1915, omits this distillery, but it is included in earlier years.

39. See Note 1 (a) (c) (e). *Return of Licensed Distillers*, 1851, *op. cit.*, p. 659. Barnard, *Whisky Distilleries*, p. 419. *Ham's Inland Revenue Year Book*, Effingham Wilson, London publication, 1890, p. 253. No distillery is shown in the 1900 edition.

Monasterevan Distillery

Monasterevan, in the excise district of Naas, boasted two small distilleries in 1782: one worked by Robert Kelly with a 202 gallon still and the other a 253 gallon still run by Edward McDonagh. John Goslin is said to have had a still in the town in 1784, so that either there was a change in ownership or there was a third still not working when the excise return was made. John Cassidy became owner of one of these distilleries in 1784, but this was destroyed within a year and re-built. He entered into partnership, in 1788, with Robert Harvey of Dublin who may have provided some of the money needed for re-building. Harvey was to receive half the profits and, in return, he paid the rent of the private house and distillery premises. Harvey also undertook to sell the whiskey without commission. The millstones used to grind the malt and grain in the new distillery were powered by a water wheel. In 1802 Cassidy was working a 608-gallon still heated by turf, but probably because of the still licence duty he had reduced his plant by 1818 to a still of 200 gallons. Like other distillers he expanded after the change in the distillery laws in 1823 and ten years later was producing 165,000 proof gallons a year. By 1887 the distillery contained a substantial plant. The wash still had a capacity of 26,000 gallons and there were seventeen warehouses on the premises in which the best whiskey was matured for six years. The market was mainly local, but there was also an export trade handled by the London firm of Twiss and Browning. Some of the Monasterevan whiskey was sold to Irish blenders to blend with other Irish pot still whiskeys.[40]

John Cassidy sealed his partnership with Harvey by marrying Mary Harvey. He also served on the Church of Ireland vestry which discloses one of the peculiarities of Irish local government because he was a Roman Catholic. The reason was that in those years the vestries performed certain county council functions and for this purpose were not strictly ecclesiastic. He died in 1834 and was succeeded in the distillery by his younger son who died five years later. The elder son, Robert, then took over to be succeeded on his death by his two sons, Robert and James. Robert died early and James continued till his death in 1890.

40. See Note 1 (a) (c) (d) (e). Barnard, *Whisky Distilleries*, pp. 383-6. *Slater's Directory*, 1846, p. 70. *Thom's Directory of Manufacturers*, 1908, p. 251. *R.C. on Whiskey*, 1908, p. 337.

James extended the premises and installed steam power to replace the water wheel. His son Robert succeeded him. He died in 1918 leaving a young son, James, so the widow ran the business. It did not prosper and finally went into liquidation when, in 1921, an overdraft of £400,000 was called in. During its last few years the distillery was silent and the firm were probably disposing of their warehoused stocks. The war-time difficulties during 1914–18 were no doubt a deciding factor. The premises were acquired by the engineering firm of Samuel E. Holmes.[41]

Kilbeggan Distillery

It is claimed that the Kilbeggan distillery had existed since 1757. This cannot be verified from official sources, but there were three small distilleries in 1782, each with a 230-gallon still. One of those continued into the nineteenth century and was then worked by William and John Codd. This distillery may well have been founded in the mid-eighteenth century. No distillery was licensed in 1807 and the next clear information is that Patrick Brett and Company were distillers in Kilbeggan in 1833, producing a little over 40,000 proof gallons, a modest quantity by contemporary standards. By 1846 Brett had gone and John Locke had established himself in a distillery on the river Brusna, directly connected with the Grand Canal. Probably this was the former Brett distillery. Under Locke's ownership the distillery flourished and by 1887 the sons, John and James, were working a much enlarged plant. The output was 150,000 proof gallons a year from four pot stills installed by Millar and Company of Dublin. About seventy men were employed. Private ownership ceased in 1893 when the firm was registered as John Locke and Company, Limited. It continued successfully well into the present century, but its fortunes declined in the 1940s, probably because of war conditions.[42]

In 1947 the distillery was offered for sale as a going concern, but there was no response. At this time the managing director was Mrs. Hope-Johnson and the other two directors were her

41. John Holmes, *Monasterevan Distillery* in the *Journal of the Co. Kildare Archaeological Society*, 1969, xiv, No. 4.
42. See Note 1 (a) (c) (d). Barnard, *Whisky Distilleries*, pp. 392–4. *Slater's Directory*, 1846, p. 50; 1881, Leinster p. 432 *Macdonald's Irish Directory*, 1915, p. 305.

sister and Thomas Coffey. The proposed sale gave rise to allegations in the Dáil that there had been an indiscreet association by
some ministers of the Government with undesirable Swiss
nationals, two of whom had since been deported. It was said
that these persons were trying to buy the distillery in order to get
possession of 66,000 gallons of matured whiskey. They would
then sell it on the black market at £11 a gallon to a Mr. Jameson
of James Stewart and Company, Park Lane, London. The Swiss
syndicate apparently had no intention of working the distillery.
The shortage of whiskey at the time gave currency to these
allegations and a judicial tribunal was set up. Their report went
into details of the firm's history and the facts surrounding the
proposed sale, but was indeterminate on the main issue of
ministerial involvement, and no further action was warranted.
The distillery continued operations, but its future as an independent unit was very uncertain. Distilling finally ceased in 1953.[43]

Tullamore Distillery

This distillery does not boast the antiquity of Kilbeggan, but
there were two small distilleries in the town in the late eighteenth
century and one of them continued under different owners until
1822. There were some silent periods when, perhaps, some distilling occurred without the cognisance of the excise authorities.
In 1829 Michael Molloy erected a distillery in Bridge Street.
A visitor today can see for himself the date of its foundation for
it is incorporated in the wrought iron gates of the premises.
Molloy may have used the site of an older distillery since it is
situated conveniently on the banks of the river Clodagh which
was probably a clearer stream than at present. It was a medium
size distillery for, in 1833, duty was paid on 20,000 proof gallons
to which must be added whiskey put into bonded warehouses
and also sold in bond. At that time there was a second distillery
in the town paying duty on half as much again, but it did not
last long. On Molloy's death in 1857 the business passed to his
nephew, Bernard Daly. In 1887 Daly's son, Captain Bernard
Daly, took charge of the distillery. He was a man with many
outside interests. He was Master of the Hounds in the County,

43. The National Library, Dublin, ref. Mss. 949–52, vol. 1. *Dáil Debates*, vol.
108, 22 October 1947, cols. 682–3, 828–39; 5 November 1947, cols. 1338–1421.
Irish Times, 6 October 1947.

an international polo player, and a prominent racehorse owner. These claims on his time, and probably his chief interests, led to changes in management. An employee, Daniel E. Williams, who began in the firm at fifteen years of age, had risen to be the distillery engineer. Captain Daly, recognising the ability of his engineer, promoted Williams to general manager and retired from distilling activities to devote his time to his social duties. The change had a marked effect on the business; the distilling premises were enlarged and additions and improvements made to the plant. Thereafter production expanded and the brand name 'Tullamore Dew' became well known in domestic and foreign markets. One factor that helped this expansion in the early years was the proximity of the Grand Canal connecting Tullamore and Dublin. At one period coal for the distillery was imported from England in chartered ships and transported from Dublin by barge, and naturally, casks of whiskey travelled in the reverse direction. At that time, haulage of heavy vehicles along indifferent roads was slow and uncertain, and the railway system was still developing. Captain John Williams, son of Daniel, entered the distillery in 1918 on his return from service in the 1914–18 war and took charge of the business on the death of his distinguished father in 1921. Other changes in the distillery management stemmed from the registration of the firm in 1903 under the name of B. Daly and Company Limited, Captain Daly holding some of the shares and the Williams family the remainder. In 1931 Captain Daly resigned as a director and the Williams family acquired all the shares.

When Alfred Barnard visited the distillery in 1887 he saw two wash stills, each of 16,000 gallons capacity, and two large stills for low wines and for spirits, the latter for a third distillation. All the malt used was made on the premises. There were also large, bonded warehouse facilities. The buildings are still there, but the firm of D. E. Williams, Limited has interests outside distilling and kindred activities, and the premises no longer resound to the 'flogger' of the cooper. B. Daly and Company are still in being, but as maltsters.

The cessation of distilling at Tullamore in 1954 is bound up with the introduction and success of 'Irish Mist', a whiskey-based liqueur. It is also the only Irish example of a distilling firm with an uncertain future having the foresight to seek energetically for an

alternative related product should the whiskey market seriously decline. As has been shown, when other firms were hit by adverse conditions they had no such ammunition to fight off the liquidator.

The story of Irish Mist really began in the time of Daniel E.
Williams. He explored the possibility of reviving an old Irish
beverage known as heather-wine, a concoction of whiskey,
heather honey and herbal flavourings. He tried many recipes,
but all were found wanting. His successors did the same. These
researches had led Daniel Williams to think that the secret of this
traditional Irish drink was taken to the Continent, either during
the exodus after the defeat of the Irish armies in 1692 or during
the forced emigrations of the eighteenth century. He instituted
research facilities in the hope that the formula may have survived.
Austria was one of the countries involved in this search as some
Irishmen had distinguished themselves in that country. One had
become a field marshal. The Williams family were not, therefore,
surprised in 1948 when an Austrian refugee arrived in Tullamore
with a recipe which came very close to their own researches.

A separate company was formed in 1948 to make this re-
discovered liqueur which they labelled 'Irish Mist'. The distillery
supplied the whiskey base. In 1953 the new company incorporated
its liqueur in its name as The Irish Mist Liqueur Company
Limited. By 1954 whiskey stocks had built up substantially and
the market was not absorbing the quantity being produced. Nor
were there immediate prospects of improvement. This was
a situation all too familiar in the distilling world. Decisions were
taken year by year to postpone distilling. Meanwhile Irish Mist
flourished. The Williams family therefore decided to use available
capital to expand production of the liqueur rather than tie up
money in whiskey while it was ageing for an unpredictable
market. So Irish Mist was conceived, born and became a sturdy
successor while its parent, whiskey, gracefully bowed out at
Tullamore. The well known Tullamore Dew did not die,
however. It was too good for that. Irish Distillers Limited,
after some research and skilful blending, were able to reproduce
the characteristics of Tullamore Dew and are now successfully
marketing this famous whiskey.[44]

44. See Note 1 (a) (c) (d). Barnard, *Whisky Distilleries*, pp. 387–9. *Slater's Directory*, 1846, p. 93; 1881, Leinster p. 505. *Thom's Directory of Manufacturers*, 1908, p. 251. *Thom's Directory*, 1966. Information from D. E. Williams Limited.

Other Distilleries

A number of distilleries not mentioned might have had some interest, others were unimportant. In all these cases there is no information of consequence beyond that already given in the history of the industry as a whole. For example, the Roscrea distillery worked by John Birch is noteworthy because of his attempts to save fuel by encasing his still with a steam jacket. Little is known about John Birch himself. The great majority of Irish distillers had disappeared by 1823 when the still licence system was abolished. The survivors flourished and new distillers appeared. Early nineteenth-century distillers depended heavily on a local market and there were, in effect, several distinct markets in the country. As transport facilities improved these markets merged until all Ireland became a single market. Prices in Belfast would not differ materially from those in Cork. During these changes some distilleries prospered, others failed. There is not enough information to give specific reasons for successes or failure in most cases. Sometimes there might be a special cause, such as the death of the owner and no adequate successor, but in general, distilling skill, sufficient capital and business efficiency would be determining factors. Sheer size was not so important before the present century.

B – THE PRESENT DISTILLERIES

In 1966 the three distilling firms operating in the Republic of Ireland decided to amalgamate in order to strengthen themselves for export promotion, particularly in the American market. This would also make them stronger to face the impact of entry into the European Economic Community. The merger increased their facilities for research and development. The three firms concerned were—Cork Distilleries Company, John Jameson & Son, and John Power & Son who had recently acquired Tullamore Dew whiskey. The new parent company was first registered as the United Distillers of Ireland, Limited, but this was later changed to the Irish Distillers Group Limited. Directors of each of the three firms formed the Board of the new company. They included Norbert Murphy of Cork Distilleries Company as president; Francis J. O'Reilly, former chairman of John Power & Son as chairman; and Alexander C. Crichton, former chairman of John

Jameson & Son. In 1968 Kevin C. McCourt joined the Board as managing director, bringing in experience in other fields.

John Power & Sons, Limited

The oldest of these firms is John Power and Sons operating a distillery in John's Lane, Dublin. The firm began its life when James Power owned an inn and was distilling in 1796, probably earlier, at 109, Thomas Street. In 1804 the business was in the name of James Power and Son, but from 1802 there was also a John Power, distiller, of John's Lane, Thomas Street. In 1809 the firm was listed in the directories as John Power and Company of John's Street. By August of 1841 the firm had greatly prospered and the head of the firm was created a baronet. In 1854 he laid the foundation stone of the O'Connell monument in Dublin.[45]

The firm's expansion dates from the abolition of the still licence system in 1823. In that year they worked one small pot still of 500 gallons assessed at a monthly charge of 33,075 gallons of spirit and probably worked it for some six or seven months a year. In 1833, with better equipment, the firm was producing 300,000 proof gallons. The distillery was expanding and modernising as business increased and there was a major rebuilding in 1871. Barnard, on his visit in 1887, found a distillery covering over six acres and extending from Thomas Street to the quay on the river Liffey. There were the latest inventions and devices, including patent grain-cleaning machines, and the arrangements of the building and equipment were carefully designed for economical handling from grain to whiskey. Two mash tuns, each capable of mashing thirty-five tons a day, fed wort to eight fermenting vessels each with a capacity of 35,000 gallons. There were two wash stills, each 25,000 gallons content, and three 20,000 gallon low wines stills. A prominent feature was the can-pit room with its glass safe encased in mahogany and brass. It is still a point of interest to visitors. The firm had acquired additional warehouses at Westland Row and under the new city markets. Barnard specially noted the white enamel bricks lining the walls of these warehouses and the efforts made to ventilate them efficiently and maintain an even temperature.

45. See Note 1 (c). *Gentleman's and Citizen's Almanack. Thom's Directory*, 1842, p. 106.

The firm were in the vanguard of improvements which would be treated as commonplace today. At this period, 1887, the well-appointed office buildings included a lunch hall for employees, an unusual amenity at the time. There was also an internal telephone. The distillery was self-contained for all maintenance work, coopering and extensions or alterations, except major building or repair programmes. Barnard made an interesting comment on the Vartry river water used. It seems that some customers sent with their orders, two empty casks, one for whiskey, probably at about 25 per cent over proof, and the other for Vartry water to dilute the spirit as desired. The annual output in the 1880s was 900,000 proof gallons. The firm employed 250 men in the distillery and a staff of twenty-five in the office.[46]

James Talbot Power, who died in 1932, was the last of that name in the firm. The present directors, F. J. O'Reilly, and C. J. and J. A. Ryan, are grandsons of Power's two sisters. In evidence before a Royal Commission in 1908 Power stressed the conservative nature of the firm. Having discovered by long experience how to make first class whiskey, the firm was not prepared to risk its reputation by using cheaper methods. He was referring to patent stills. This conservative attitude was attacked in parliament in 1953 and, with the clear evidence that blends were generally preferred, especially in the export trade, the firm finally installed a patent still of the bubble cap type in order to add blended whiskey to the firm's products. Pot still whiskey is still made and marketed, blended whiskey has merely been added to the firm's products. So also have gin and vodka to cater for changing public taste. As far as possible Irish grain only is used. The grist for whiskey contains about 40 per cent of malted barley. Malting on the premises ceased towards the end of the nineteenth century. Supplies formerly from outside firms now come wholly from the Malting Company of Ireland, Ballincollig, county Cork, in which the Irish Distillers Limited are part owners. The distillery went over to electric power in the 1920s, but not everything became modern in haste. Malt and grain were ground by millstones until very recently, but when the miller retired a powered hammer mill was installed.

46. See Note 1 (c) (d). Barnard, *Whisky Distilleries*, pp. 357–64.

N

One view was that the firm preferred this old method, but there was no one expert enough to follow him. The position might also have been consideration for an old and loyal employee who did the job well and the change deferred till he left. In 1908 James Power instanced a case before the Royal Commission of the family of Whitty who had been their distillers for four generations.

Distilling has always been seasonal to coincide with the harvest and also, in earlier years, because of the difficulty of controlling temperature in hot weather. Hence a larger labour force was needed in the winter months. Powers had a unique arrangement to meet the labour problem. They employed river fishermen from county Wexford to work in Dublin during winter and return to their homes in the summer. The firm built a village at Oylegate on the river Slaney in the late 1890s and the men came up to Dublin each year when distilling began.[47]

John Jameson and Son Limited

There is some uncertainty about the origin of the Bow Street distillery of John Jameson & Son. Towards the end of the eighteenth century the area between Bow Street and Smithfield, where the present distillery buildings are situated, became a distilling centre. Thus in 1783 John Swan was a distiller at 52, Smithfield. Edmond Grange, then Dublin's foremost distiller, worked two stills in Smithfield and a still of 1089 gallons capacity in Bow Street. Another Bow Street distiller was John Stein working a small still. Stein came from a family well known in distilling circles both in Ireland and Scotland and became connected, through marriage, with the Jameson family in Scotland. A book published by John Jameson & Son states that a Jameson of Alloa visited Dublin in 1784 and, as a result, his two eldest sons became associated with Stein. John, the older of the two, married Isabella, daughter of Stein, and later became owner of the Bow Street distillery, and brother William, ran the other Stein distillery in Marrowbone Lane across the river Liffey on the south side. William left his distillery to a younger brother, James. James married a Woolsey of Dundalk, a brewery family that, for a time, tried their hand at distilling. An old accounting record,

47. *Royal Comm. on Whisky*, 1908, p. 62. *Dáil Debates*, vol. 139, 3 June 1953, col. 729. Information about present distilling practices and labour relations were given during a visit to the firm.

dated 1806, shows the distribution of profits, the major part of which were received by John and William Jameson and John Stein. Another younger brother of the Jamesons became concerned with a distillery at Fairfield, near Enniscorthy. The main interest here is that his daughter, Anne, married Guiseppe Marconi, and their son was the inventor of wireless telegraphy. Thus the roots of the Jameson family go deep and long in distilling history. When the first John Jameson of Bow Street said in evidence in March 1823 that his distillery was erected 18 years earlier, he clearly must have referred to some re-building or the installation of new plant. The title John Jameson & Son appears to have been adopted in 1810. In that year he was working a 1,256 gallon still.[48]

When the shackles of the still licence system were removed in 1823 Jameson estimated that conversion of the plant to meet the changes would cost from £3,000 to £4,000. The firm, like other successful distillers, expanded rapidly. By 1833 they were paying duty on 334,284 proof gallons and putting a lot more into bonded or distillers' warehouses. By 1887 the firm had become very large with extensive premises and plant. The annual output was in the region of a million proof gallons and about 300 were employed. Malting ceased very recently and supplies are now obtained from Ballincollig, but the malt floors, grain lofts and many other features dating from the last century, can still be seen. The expansion of the firm in the latter half of the nineteenth century led the proprietors to look for more facilities and three large maltings and two kilns were acquired in Drogheda which were said to be larger than those in Dublin. This development may have been the result of the extinction of distilling in Drogheda. In the 1930s these were sold to a brewery company. In 1891 Jamesons became a private limited company and in 1902 it was reorganised as a public company.[49]

48. See Note 1 (b) (c) (e). Jameson's statement about the erection of the distillery appears in the evidence given before the *Irish Revenue Inquiry, 5th Report*, 1823, p. 308. The record of the profit distribution in 1806 is with the company. *Gentleman's and Citizen's Almanack*. In some years John Swan is shown as a brewer. With the kind of plant then used such a switch was simple. All that was necessary was to use the brewing vessels to make ale instead of distiller's wash and partially dismantle the still. Clandestine distilling was also easy. John Jameson and Sons, *The History of a Great House*, Dublin, 1924.

49. See Note 1 (d). Barnard, *Whisky Distilleries*, pp. 353–6. *Thom's Directory of Manufacturers*, 1908, p. 435.

During the nineteenth century John Jameson built up a world wide reputation for the excellence of their whiskey, but, from about 1880, they were having difficulties with some blenders. They sold their pot still whiskey in casks to reputed bottlers who marketed the whiskey under a Jameson label. There were, however, some blenders who used this whiskey in blends with grain whiskey, mainly in England, and sold the result as Jameson's Irish Whiskey. After analysis to get proof, the firm always prosecuted. The firm were staunch defendents of pot still whiskey and, in the early years of this century, were accused of sticking to tradition because they would neither make nor use grain whiskey. They resisted outside advice which allegedly would bring in a fortune. The same charges of complacency were repeated in the Dáil debates in 1953 and 1954. There is no question that there had been a very marked change in public taste to lighter whiskey, and their product, undeniably of high quality, was unlikely to succeed in a mass market. In recent years and after much research, Jameson whiskey has now been adapted to the modern market.[50]

The distillery at Bow Street was greatly enlarged towards the end of the nineteenth century. Plans were made for doubling its capacity, but these were scrapped by Andrew Jameson who foresaw the future changed conditions of the industry. The Right Honourable Andrew Jameson was one of the original senators of the Irish Free State and was a director of the Bank of Ireland for 53 years.

The distillery ceased operations in 1971, but the Irish Distillers Limited have been able to reproduce the characteristics of all the Jameson brands. When the distillery became silent it had four large pot stills with lyne arms which had been there longer than anyone could remember. All the stills had been converted from furnace heating to steam coils. The 30,000 gallon wash backs complete with attemperator pipes, mash tuns and other utensils, were commensurate with this large production capacity. Grinding grain and malt by millstones was replaced, in 1904, by more modern methods and, by 1971, this was being done by a hammer mill capable of very fine adjustment to get any desired size of particle.

50. *Truths about Whiskey,* published in 1878 by John Jameson and Son, William Jameson and Company, John Power and Son, and George Roe and

The Cork Distilleries Company, Limited

This company was incorporated on 23 December 1867 to facilitate merging into one group the Cork distilleries at North Mall, the Green, Watercourse Road and John's Street, and the distillery at Midleton, the last being the largest in the group.

The North Mall distillery in the early nineteenth century was owned by the brothers Thomas and Francis Wise and, at that time, was the largest in Cork. It is said that the distillery was founded in 1779, but no Wise appears amongst the eight licensed distillers in 1782. There is, therefore, some doubt about the date this distillery began. There was a small distillery in 1782 with a 208 gallon still in North Abbey run by Samuel Newson. The brothers Wise may have acquired this since their distillery is said to have been built on the site of a friary. By 1802, however, the Wise distillery was firmly established and was using a new 1,112-gallon still, a large still for that period. This was replaced by an even larger still of 1,516 gallons in 1807, and there was also a Henry B. Wise working as a rectifying distiller in North Abbey. Onerous distillery laws caused large stills to be abandoned and by 1818 William Wise, who was now the licensed distiller, was using a 501 gallon still rated by the excise at a weekly production of 8,285 gallons, but probably had an output of at least half as much again. For a time there was a second still of 200 gallons capacity, but by 1823 this had ceased. It was uncommon then for any distillery to have more than one still. The more sensible laws after 1823 enabled Wise to erect larger and more stills and to expand production. By 1833 output was running at about 400,000 proof gallons annually. In 1845 the distillers are listed as Thomas and Francis Wise, and Francis was still in business when the distillery was grouped into the Cork Distilleries Company. When Francis died in the 1880s he left £1.6 million and large estates in counties Cork and Kerry.[51]

Alfred Barnard visited the North Mall distillery in 1887 and

Company. See p. 4 regarding the origin of John Jameson and Son, pp. 36–50 on blending with grain spirit, and pp. 96–103 on misrepresentation of Jameson's whiskey. *R.C. on Whiskey*, 1908, pp. 52, 60. *Dáil Debates*, vol. 139, 3 June 1953, col. 729; vol. 147, 3 November 1954, cols. 352–71.

51. See Note 1 (a) (b) (c) (d). S. Morewood, *Inebriating Liquors, op. cit.*, pp. 677 725. *Aldwell's Cork Directory*, 1844–5, p. 264. *Cork; Its Trade and Commerce*, the handbook of the Cork Chamber of Commerce and Shipping, 1919, p. 153.

gives an impressive picture. The premises and adjoining land covered twenty-three acres with additional warehouses at Wise's Hill and Morrison's Island in the city. The plant was powered by two engines built by Rowan of Belfast. Three conventional pot stills ranged from 16,000 to 22,000 gallons capacity. Mash tuns, fermenting and other vessels were commensurate in size to deal with the output of these large stills. One fermenting vessel had a capacity of 45,000 gallons. The distillery employed some 250 persons. Its best known brand was 'Wise's Old Pot Still Whiskey', bottled at 10° under proof when five years old. There was a disastrous fire in 1920 which destroyed the mill and ended distilling. Relics of the old water mill can still be seen, also the old strong room with massive thick walls, built at a time when large amounts of gold coin were used in business. The Cork Distilleries Company converted for storage the buildings that survived the fire. New buildings were erected within the extensive grounds in 1964 and fully automatic bottling plant installed with glass lined vats and every modern device. All the beverages from the distilleries in the company are bottled here.[52]

The Green distillery in Thomas Davis Street began its career on 12 May 1796 when Bartholomew Foley, a draper, sold a dwelling house and malthouse to Robert Allan and Denis Corcoran, distillers. The malthouse was formerly owned by Thomas Wood, a maltster in 1780. Allan and Corcoran were working a 762 gallon still in 1802. About 1812 the business was being carried on by the brothers Thomas and Joseph Shee, Benjamin Hodges and others, with Thomas Shee as the distiller working a 201 gallon still. His brother Joseph acted as marketing agent in London. Hodges and others in the group soon disappeared. They probably put up capital and were not active in the distillery. In June 1830 the Shee brothers got into financial difficulties and the distillery was made over to Joseph, who continued distilling using capital supplied by James Kiernan under a mortgage, but Thomas remained as the licensed distiller. An excise record of the year ending 5 January 1833 shows a duty charge of £26,716, equal to about 160,000 proof gallons, which indicates that there had not

52. When visiting Cork the company kindly supplied much of the information about their distilleries, the present-day activities and the history of the men who had worked them since the distilleries began. See also Barnard, *Whisky Distilleries*, pp. 405–8.

been much expansion of production after the 1823 changes in the distillery laws. By 1835 Kiernan had acquired the distillery and when he died in December 1844 his will directed that the distillery was to be sold. On 27 July 1850 the executors sold the Green distillery to George Waters, a distiller, who had previously owned the Riverstown distillery on the outskirts of Cork. When Waters retired in November 1868 this left the way open for the property to be conveyed to the Cork Distillers Company. Distilling ceased in the 1880s, future production being transferred to the distillery at North Mall. In recent years the Green distillery has had new plant installed and is now producing gin.[53]

Joseph Shee has special interest because he patented a continuous still which Morewood described in 1838. The still was not widely adopted, but one was in use at the Green distillery in 1850. It consisted of a series of four connected pot stills, each one set higher than the one before it. The first and lowest still contained water and was heated by a fire. The steam passed up to the next still and on to the third and fourth stills. Wash entered the fourth still and flowed counter to the steam down to the first still. The rising vapours passing through the wash became rich in alcohol and were tapped off and condensed from the fourth still. The exhausted wash in the first still would provide vapours to keep the whole apparatus going. This apparatus appears to have been a variant of a still invented by Adams a little earlier.[54]

John Teulon and Thomas Hewitt, merchants of Cork, and Richard T. Blunt, distiller from London, became partners on 2 October 1792 as maltsters and distillers. Land was taken in the northern suburbs of the city, a distillery built, plant installed and business began 'with every prospect of success'. This enterprise became known as the Watercourse distillery. The partnership, operative from 1 October 1793, was confirmed in August of the following year for periods of 7, 14 and 21 years. Each partner was

53. See Note 1 (*e*). *Irish Revenue Inquiry, 5th Report,* 1823, pp. 294, 302, 369, 378. *The Cork Directory,* 1844–5, shows the occupant of the Green distillery in York Street (now Thomas Davis Street) as James Punch. He may have been licensed in the period between the ownership of Shee and that of Waters, between 1844 and 1850. Information about the transfers of ownership was supplied by the Cork Distilleries Company.

54. *Return of Licensed Distillers . . . distinguishing stills not sanctioned by law,* Par, Pps. 1851 (386) liii, p. 269. S. Morewood, *Inebriating Liquors,* p. 643. Underwool. *The Historical Development of Distilling Plant,* 1935, p. 24.

to subscribe £5,000 towards the cost of buildings, plant and stock before 25 March 1795. Net profits were to be shared equally and notice of one year was to be given before retirement at the end of seven or fourteen years. A new partnership deed in October 1799 brought in James Morrough, each partner subscribing £10,000. Morrough died leaving his share to his son John, a minor, and his mother acted for him. On 1 October 1805 he gave the required notice and sold his share to Hewitt and Teulon and from 1 October 1806, the partnership traded as Hewitt and Company. By 1816 the Teulon share had been assigned to James Morrough. He, in turn, assigned his share on 18 August 1834 to Charles Hewitt. There were no further changes. In 1846 the firm was trading as Thomas Henry Hewitt and Company. The distillery was now wholly owned by the Hewitt family who, on 24 August 1868, conveyed it to the Cork Distilleries Company.

No record is extant about the activities or output during the first few years of the Watercourse distillery. An excise return for 1802 shows Teulon, Hewitt and Blunt as operating two stills of 1,514 gallons and 643 gallons capacity, which placed this distillery as amongst the largest in the country. By 1807 only the larger still was working. James Morrough was the licensed distiller in 1822 working a 500 gallon still, the most economical size in view of the distillery laws then in force. After these laws changed in 1823 the firm expanded its production and in 1833 paid duty on nearly 365,000 proof gallons, second only to Cork's largest producers, the brothers Wise. In the 1880s the Cork Distilleries Company concentrated production in the North Mall distillery and ceased distilling at Watercourse. In 1916 new plant was installed and the distillery re-opened to make grain spirit and baker's yeast. Today there are two modern continuous stills, one producing potable grain spirit and the other industrial spirit. A subsidiary, the Cork Yeast Company Limited, was formed to market this yeast.[55]

Daly's distillery of 32 John's Street, the fourth of the Cork distilleries to merge into the Cork Distilleries Company, is said to have been founded in 1807. James Daly was working this distillery in 1833 and in the previous year was charged excise duty

55. See Note 1 (b) (c) (d). *Cork: Its Trade and Commerce,* 1919, p. 155. *Slater's Commercial Directory of Ireland,* 1846, pp. 211–2 (second series).

on 39,000 proof gallons, which indicates that it was a small business. Earlier records do not show any Daly as a licensed distiller in Cork and none of the licensed distillers in the early nineteenth century fits in conclusively as a forerunner of Daly. There was a rectifying distiller, William Lyons, in John's Street in 1807 and it is possible that these premises passed to Daly. After incorporation into the Cork Distilleries Company, Daly's distillery was closed and sold. The main buildings became Shaw's flour mill and the rest of the property passed to J. J. Murphy and Company of Ladyswell brewery, Cork.[56]

Midleton lies about fourteen miles east of Cork. After the changes in the distillery laws in 1823 two distilleries were founded in this small market town. William Hackett's distillery was small and did not prosper. It lasted for about 20 years and its main claim to distilling history was the extensive frauds uncovered in the 1830s which resulted in the removal of the excise staff who had all been involved. The other distillery was destined to be much more important and is still working. It was founded by the Murphy family who, after nearly 150 years, still control its operations.

The history of Murphy's distillery really starts on 20 May 1796 when Viscount Midleton leased lands to Marcus Lynch. In partnership with two London merchants, Lynch erected a considerable building for woollen manufactures. Marcus Lynch became the sole owner when his partners were adjudged bankrupt. Under the pressure of the Napoleonic wars the Government bought the property in December 1803 for £20,000 and used it for stabling horses and accommodating troops. Part of the premises was leased back to Lynch. Eighteen years later Lynch had gone and the barracks were redundant. The Government sold the whole property to the Archbishop of Cashel, a brother of Lord Midleton, for £1,750, which seems like a bargain for the prelate. When the Archbishop died in January 1824, Lord Midleton bought the property for the same price. He sold it on 20 December 1825 to James Murphy and his two brothers, Daniel Nicholas and Jeremiah James, for £4,000. The Murphy brothers 'expended large sums erecting a distillery on the premises.' Two years later they acquired the full use of a waterway

56. See Note 1 (*b*) (*d*). Other information came from the Cork Distilleries Company.

from the nearby Dungourney river which, to this day, turns an undershot iron water wheel. The pulleys and shafting are still in good order and the water power is able to drive the mechanical rakes in the huge mash tuns. Daniel retired from the partnership in August 1828, the property was vested in James and the firm traded as James Murphy and Company. There were various changes subsequently owing to deaths, but no interest went outside the Murphy family. Thus in October 1857 the partners were James, John Nicholas and Nicholas Murphy. Two other Murphys left the firm, under a financial arrangement, to become brewers in Cork. James conceived the idea of amalgamating his distillery with four Cork distilleries to make one strong financial and economic unit, and so the Cork Distilleries Company was registered in 1867. James Murphy was the first managing director. The Midleton distillery was formally sold to the new company in June 1868.[57]

It is interesting to compare the distillery visited by Alfred Barnard in 1887 with the present plant and premises. In outward appearance Barnard would not find any striking difference other than the absence of drays and horses. The distillery covers the same area and there is still the surrounding farmland. In 1887 there were three pot stills and a Coffey still. The wash still, the largest in Ireland and perhaps in the world, was described by Barnard as having a capacity of 31,648 gallons. This very large still remains in full operation, though naturally any worn plates or parts have been replaced or repaired. Two other stills worked efficiently from their erection in 1880 until 1949 when they were replaced by the same firm, Daniel Miller & Company of Dublin. The boilers admired by Barnard have gone and no solid fuel is now used. Electric power is employed and steam coils heat the pot stills. The Coffey still has gone. In 1962 a new German-made continuous still with bubble cap plates was erected. It is usually referred to as the Hamburg still and produces a higher strength spirit with less fusel oil than did the old Coffey still. One curious feature that Barnard would have seen is still there. It is an ingenious arrangement for diverting the flow from the pot stills

57. *Excise Revenue Inquiry, 7th Report, Part I,* 1834, pp. 234, 267. Both Midleton distilleries were then in the Mallow excise collection. *Cork: Its Trade and Commerce,* 1919, p. 153. *Ham's Inland Revenue Year Book,* 1888, see the section relating to excise stations.

to the appropriate receivers. Normally this is done by turning cocks on a manifold. In Midleton there are small troughs in a glass compartment, the outlets from the base of each trough leads to a receiver. Only one pipe supplies the extract to the troughs, but on the pipe is a moveable sleeve so that the outlet can be directed to any desired trough. A familiar name to Barnard would be that of the distiller himself: Mr Sandy Ross, the present distiller is the latest of that family who have been distillers at Midleton for about 120 years. The first Ross came here from the Riverstown distillery which was worked in the 1830s by John Lyons.[58]

About three years ago malting ceased in Midleton and the group now obtains its malt from the Malting Company of Ireland with maltings at Ballincollig. This malting undertaking is owned jointly by the Irish Distillers Limited, the Cork brewers Beamish and Crawford, and the Associated British Maltsters. All the barley and oats used at Midleton is grown locally.

The best known whiskey made in Cork is marketed under the brand name of 'Paddy'. In 1941 the Company branched out on a new venture when they began to market Cork Dry Gin, the first Irish gin in modern times. In 1960 Nordoff Vodka was introduced. After some ten years of research to get the best blend of malt and grain whiskey, 'Hewitt's' came on the market in 1964. With these various beverages, plus industrial spirit, making baker's yeast, and sales of fusel oil and spent grains, the Cork Distilleries Company can fairly claim to be a complete industrial unit. The head offices are in Morrison's Island, Cork. There are a number of warehouses, all kept at an even temperature and the right humidity where casks of spirit lie silently maturing for several years. Selected casks of matured whiskey are tasted before blending, either for a pure pot still or a blended whiskey. All go to the modern bottling plant at North Mall to receive Cork's whiskey accolade, the label 'Paddy' or 'Hewitt's'. The vodka and gin receive similar care. The reward for all this trouble is an expanding market at home and abroad, especially in the United States.[59]

58. Barnard, *Whisky Distilleries,* pp. 409–11.
59. Facilities to visit all the Cork distilleries and warehouses, and information from the Company's records, were freely given. For much of this information there is no other source.

Irish Distillers Group Limited

Since the formation of this company in 1966 there have been some notable changes. A very modern bottling plant now operates in the Fox and Geese district of Dublin and caters for the Dublin production. There is a change in attitude towards marketing. There is now less concern about production since the products are good and the methods for making them satisfactory and efficient. Any problems can be solved, but marketing is another matter. It is the problem of persuading uncommitted people. The company's marketing department has been re-organized and, backed by wide market research, there has been a greatly increased expenditure on advertising. New blends have been created and new brands introduced, such as a white rum under the brand name 'Kiskadee'. The company have also spread their interest by acquiring a well-established wine and spirit importing firm.

The last few years have witnessed a notable expansion. A good index for measuring this is the pre-tax profit for each year since amalgamation:

1967	£606,000
1968	£522,000
1969	£828,000
1970	£1,188,000
1971	£1,265,000

The most important change is now in progress. A new distillery complex is to be built at Midleton, county Cork. It will have a variety of pot stills and modern continuous stills. The intention is to replace the existing distilleries.

The 'Old Bushmills' Distillery Company Limited

This is the only distilling firm now operating in Northern Ireland and works distilleries at Bushmills in County Antrim and at Coleraine, some eight miles away on the river Bann. The company also own the former Killowen distillery in Coleraine which has been converted for use as warehouses.

In the north and north west of Ireland there was such an impact from illicit distillers that it becomes impossible to trace the fortunes of either distillers or distilleries until the nineteenth century was well advanced. From about 1780 many licensed distillers ceased or turned to illicit manufacture. Occasionally a new licensed distillery might appear as the result of laws designed to tempt illicit distillers to mend their ways; or a determined man might persist in legal manufacture with periods when his still was silent and, therefore, was not shown in official returns. In the last case it did not necessarily follow that there was no distilling, it meant that there was no legal distilling. The distillery at Bushmills is an example. It is claimed that the present distillery was founded in 1743 for illicit distilling and that it became a legitimate distillery in 1784. In 1782 there were five licensed distilleries in Bushmills with stills in the range 200 to 252 gallons. Official returns of distillers do not show any distiller in Bushmills in the following years until 1833. This does not mean that no distillery existed during these years. Circumstances were so abnormal because of the extent of illicit distilling that any legal distillery would have great difficulty in marketing a regular production. It is probable that at least one distillery was maintained, but was silent for long periods and these may have coincided with the times of the official returns. Perhaps there was a little illegal manufacture as a side line to keep alive. Bushmills malt whiskey had a good reputation in the early nineteenth century which supports the view that a distillery did operate from time to time, and there might have been a few unofficial runs through the still. Nevertheless, the information is too meagre to trace which one of the five distilleries in 1782 survived into the next century or who owned it. In the booklet issued by the present owners it is claimed that the first legal distillery was owned by Hugh Anderson, perhaps at some time before 1782 as his name does not appear amongst the five distillers. In 1835 there was only one Bushmills distillery, but from 1840 to 1845 there were two.[60]

There is no doubt that Bushmills has been a distilling centre for a very long time, due in large measure to the suitability of the water from the river Bush. The present owners exhibit in their booklet a certified copy, issued by the Public Record Office of Ireland, showing a grant to Sir Thomas Phillips in 1608 to distil in this district. During the nineteenth century there was a suc-

---

60. See Note 1 (a). *Return of Licensed Distillers, 1835–50*, Parl. Pps. 1851, *op. cit.*, p. 659. *Excise Revenue Inquiry, 7th Report, Part I*, 1834, pp. 190, 446. *S.C. on extending the functions of the Constabulary in Ireland to the suppression of Illicit Distillation*, Parl. Pps. 1854 (58) x, p. 56.

cession of proprietors and very little is known of their activities. In 1833 James M'Kibben paid duty on 10,216 proof gallons and was still the owner in 1846. In 1881 the owners were Corrigan and Company. By 1884 the distillery had passed to the Bushmills Old Distillery Company, Limited. In 1887 the firm had established a head office in Belfast and was registered as The 'Old Bushmills' Distillery Company. Samuel W. Boyd became head of the firm, which remained a family business until very recently.[61] The main market at this time was local families who preferred malt whiskey. The only other legal distillery that catered for this taste was at Gorton in County Tyrone in the first half of the century. It was a small undertaking and did not last long. Poteen was a malt whiskey for most of the early years of the century and this undoubtedly competed with Bushmills. The decline in illicit distilling after 1860 helped the Bushmills distillery to prosper after Boyd became its owner. There were two pot stills of 1,500 and 2,500 gallons in 1887, and two further stills were installed soon after. Grain lofts, malt floors, kilns and other apparatus matched this distilling capacity. By contemporary standards the distillery was not large, but its product was good and became so well known that its market became very much wider. Four large warehouses were erected in the distillery premises and another bonded warehouse was built in Hill Street, Belfast, adjoining the head offices. The annual production of about 10,000 proof gallons in the 1830s had increased tenfold by the end of the century. Like most Irish distilleries the supervision of distillery operations in the latter part of the century was the direct responsibility of a director, but in the 1890s the firm employed Allan Swan as manager, a distiller of wide European experience. Unlike other Irish distilleries its success was based on the type of whiskey made in Scotland.[62]

Coleraine, some eight miles from Bushmills, had been a

61. See Note 1 (*d*). *Slater's Commercial Directory*, 1846, p. 6 (second series); 1881, Ulster, p. 239. *Belfast and Ulster Directory*, 1884, p. 64; 1887, p. 239. The Company issues a booklet giving a foreword on its history.

62. *Irish Revenue Inquiry, 5th Report,* 1823, p. 328. In the returns on pp. 367, 378, Bushmills is not shown as licensed in 1802 or in 1823. *Excise Revenue Inquiry, 7th Report, Part I,* 1834, p. 307. *S.C. on Constabulary functions,* 1854, pp. 51, 56. *S.C. on British and Foreign Spirits,* Parl. Pps. 1890–1 (210) xi, pp. 417–9. Barnard, *Whisky Distilleries,* pp. 432–3. The Belfast warehouse was destroyed in an air raid in 1942, but has since been rebuilt.

distilling centre until the latter part of the eighteenth century, but after that distilling was intermittent and severely handicapped by competition from poteen. In 1782 there were two small stills working in Killowen on the outskirts of the town. By 1802 there remained only one distillery with a 570 gallon still worked by McPeak and Hopkins, and this had disappeared by 1807. For some years there was no registered distiller. By 1833 the Bann distillery in Coleraine was being worked by James Moore and producing nearly 50,000 proof gallons. He was still active in 1846, but thereafter knowledge of him ceases. The next reliable information about Coleraine appears in 1881 when Robert A. Taylor was listed as a distiller in Newmarket Street, the site of the present distillery. Barnard wrote in 1887 that this distillery was founded by the conversion of a mill in 1820 so it is probable, but not certain, that Taylor acquired the same premises earlier used by Moore. Taylor was a man of many business interests, most of them associated with the distilling trade. In Londonderry he was a grain merchant. In Coleraine he ran a business under the name of D. and R. Taylor, family grocers, and grain and seed merchants, at premises in the Diamond, Coleraine. He bought port and sherry by the cask for this business. The connection of this trade with the local distillery is clearly indicated in some of the transactions. For example, on 17 July 1868, he sold a case of 'fine old malt' whiskey for £2 3s. 6d. excluding duty, direct from the Coleraine distillery. This is not clear proof that he owned the distillery, but is a probability. By that time whiskey sales in bond were a common feature. Taylor's other activities included a cloth shop, farming a few acres for barley and, trading under the name of Gailey and Taylor, as a flax commission agent in Londonderry. Despite this variety of interests the distillery must have got special attention, though of necessity he had to rely on employees rather more than was customary in other distilleries. The Coleraine malt whiskey gained a high reputation and, on the strength of supplying the House of Commons, he incorporated H.C. in his trade mark. By 1887 a bottling plant was operating in the distillery and no whiskey was bottled till it was ten years old.

The distillery in Newmarket Street continued under the firm of A. R. Taylor until 1935 when ownership changed and the distiller is shown in directories as W. Boyd, head of the Bushmills Company.[63]

In nearby Killowen distilling revived in the first years of this century under the ownership of Brown, Corbett and Company. They were a large-scale blending firm in Belfast who became linked in the 1920s to the Distillers Company of Scotland through shares held by the Distillers Finance Corporation. By this time Coleraine had become a much larger town, absorbing Killowen, and the distillery is listed as in Captain Street. The contraction of the distilling industry in the 1930s led to the premises coming on the market and in 1937 they were acquired by the Bushmills Company. They have since been used to warehouse whiskey made at Bushmills and Newmarket Street, Coleraine.[64]

The Bushmills and Coleraine distilleries are now managed as a single unit. The brand name 'Old Bushmills' and the trademark, a small pot still, applied to whiskey from either source. Malt is made at Bushmills for both distilleries, and locally grown grain is used as far as possible. If Barnard could re-visit these distilleries he would see the same pot stills that were working in 1887, plus some additions installed shortly afterwards, but all are now heated by steam coils instead of furnaces. The malt floors are still the same. Barnard would find that the arduous and hot work of turning over the malt in the kilns has been eliminated by the use of mechanical rakes. In 1954 a Coffey still was erected at Coleraine and since then there has been some blending, but the proportion of grain whiskey in blends is small. Some of this grain spirit is sold to rectifiers and blenders. Until very recently all whiskey was bottled on the premises of the Coleraine distillery. This ceased in 1968 when a modern bottling plant was installed in Bushmills. An interesting new feature at Bushmills is a new warehouse adjoining the bottling floor. In it casks are stacked in tiers on steel racks up to the roof and are easily accessible for inspection or removal with the aid of special mobile mechanical lift trucks.

63. See Note 1 (a) (c) (d). P.R.O. Belfast, ref. D 1435/2–4. Barnard, *Whisky Distilleries*, pp. 434–7. *Slater's Directory*, 1846, p. 440 (second series); 1881, Ulster p. 295. *Thom's Directory of Manufacturers*, 1908, p. 251. *Macdonald's Irish Directory*, 1915, p. 505.

64. The changes in ownership are clearly seen under the heading Coleraine in the *Belfast and Ulster Directories*, 1934–9. The connexion of Brown, Corbett and Co. with the Distillers Finance Corporation is explained in the history of the United Distilleries Company of Belfast, and in Note 25.

Since the second world war ended there have been changes in ownership and development in marketing 'Old Bushmills' whiskey, due in some measure, to the difficulties of a small firm to survive in the modern, commercial world. The Boyd family had owned and managed the business as a private company from 1884, but after the war they sold their interest to the group of companies making up the Great Universal Stores. There was no outward change: management and staff remained as formerly and the change in ownership had all the appearance of an investment only. It was an unstable arrangement since distilling was not the business of the new owners. In July 1964 there was a more fundamental change when the Charrington United Breweries of England bought the 'Old Bushmills' Distillery Company from Great Universal Stores. Since then the distilling company has been grouped with the old established Northern Ireland wine and spirit merchants of Lyle and Kinahan, and with the Ulster Brewery Company, both subsidiaries of the very large Bass-Charrington brewery group. Sir Robin Kinahan is the present head of the Northern Ireland group. These changes have had a marked impact on the fortunes of Bushmills whiskey. Its sale is promoted in the hundreds of English tied public houses and there is far greater financial backing in overseas markets, particularly in north America. Special attention has been given to the selection of agencies in other countries and to advertising. All these factors have resulted in an increased share of the whiskey market and, as this prosperity is based on the sound foundation of a good product, the future of the Bushmills distilleries is both secure and good.[65]

65. Information about recent ownership changes have been supplied by the Company.

CHAPTER X

ILLICIT DISTILLATION

MANY writers, politicians, travellers and sometimes reports to parliament make no distinction when referring to illicit spirits between spirit clandestinely distilled at a licensed distillery and the poteen coming from the unlicensed still. All this spirit is, of course, illicit, but it is convenient to confine the term 'illicit' to unlicensed distilling and refer to spirits evading duty at licensed distilleries as illegal spirits.[1]

The illicit distiller has been the subject of many travellers tales, often giving him a romantic halo and a glowing description of his operations coloured, perhaps, by the distiller's hospitality. It is doubtful if most of these writers had any real acquaintance with the techniques of distilling. More serious writers gave factual accounts which show the illicit distiller to be anything but a romantic figure and his mode of living as well as his apparatus were truly primitive. As the enforcement of revenue laws became stronger in the latter half of the eighteenth century so the illicit distiller was driven from the towns. Sometimes he could operate with fair safety in a country cottage using the chimney, if there was one, to convey away the smoke from his still fire without arousing suspicion. More often the illicit distiller would seek out a place in the mountains where he could conceal his operations in a cave or among rocks. Alternatively he might establish himself in open bogland where it would be very difficult for revenue officers to approach unobserved. His essentials were an adequate water supply, such as a mountain stream, and easy access to fuel and there was usually plenty of peat available. His apparatus would be simple, cheap and preferably portable.

The illicit distiller's method of operation did not change very much over the eighteenth and nineteenth centuries and among the

1. Sometimes illegal spirits are referred to as smuggled spirits, but this term is apt to be confusing as it usually applies to something imported illegally.

best descriptions of an illicit still at work is that given by Dr
Donovan, a professor of chemistry and well versed in distilling
practices, who visited a still in 1830. His description tallies with
those given by revenue officers closely concerned with suppressing
illicit distilling. He wrote that 'the distillery was a small thatched
cabin, at one end was a large turf fire kindled on the ground and
confined by a semi-circle of large stones. Resting on these stones,
and over the fire, was a forty gallon tin vessel, which answered
both for heating the water and the body of the still. The mash tun
was a cask hooped with wood, at the bottom of which, next the
chimb, was a hole plugged with tow. This vessel had no false
bottom; in place of it the bottom was strewed with young heath;
and over this a stratum of oat husks. Here the mash of hot water
and ground malt was occasionally mixed for two hours; after
which time the vent at the bottom was opened and the worts
were allowed to filter through the stratum of oat husks and heath.
The mashing with hot water on the grains was then repeated and
the worts were again withdrawn. The two worts being mixed
in another cask, some yeast added and the fermentation allowed
to proceed until it fell spontaneously, which happened in about
three days. It was now ready for distillation and was transferred
into the body, which was capable of distilling a charge of forty
gallons. A piece of soap weighing about two ounces was then
thrown in to prevent its running foul; and the head, apparently
a large tin pot with a tube at its side, was inserted into the rim of
the body and luted with paste made of oatmeal and water. A
lateral tube was then luted into the worm, which was a copper
tube of an inch and a half bore, coiled in a barrel for a flakestand
(a worm tub). The tail of the worm where it emerged from the
barrel was caulked with tow. The wash speedily came to the boil
and water was thrown on the fire; for at this period is the chief
danger of boiling over. The spirit almost immediately came over;
it was perfectly clear; and by its bead, this first running was
inferred to be proof.' Donovan did not test the strength and it is
unlikely that it was as strong as proof. He went on to describe
how the water in the worm tub was kept cool by dashing in large
pailfuls of cold water sufficiently violently to get into the lower
levels and overflow the warmer water at the top. Singlings came
over in about two hours and four such distillations made up a
charge for producing poteen in a further distilling. Donovan

thought the flavour excellent and considered that it might well have passed for whiskey three months old. He does not go into any detail about controlling quality by discarding foreshots and tailings, but his verdict on quality would infer that the distiller was well skilled.

This particular distiller apparently used a mixture of malt and grain. Donovan describes illicit malting by this distiller who had no kiln of his own and used that of a licensed country maltster, who was unlikely to have been wholly ignorant of the illicit malt. The distiller made his malt by soaking a sack of barley in bog water, draining it and causing germination, usually by spreading it on the floor of his cabin. When sufficiently germinated the grain was taken to a licensed kiln along with a sack of raw corn. 'The raw corn was spread out on the kiln; but during the night when the kiln owner had retired to rest, the raw corn was removed, and malt spread on, dried, and replaced by the raw grain before day. The owner of corn drying on a kiln sits up all night to watch it. In this way discovery was eluded, and the malting completed.'

Donovan thought that part of the character of poteen was due to making it entirely from malt, but that lately one-fourth raw corn was generally added. The product of this mixed grist gave the distiller about one gallon of spirit at three-to-one strength for a bushel of grist. By three-to-one strength he meant that by adding one part of water to three of spirit the result would be proof spirit. He considered this to be much below the produce that should be obtained. He gave the following costs of the apparatus: Still body £1, head 4s., worm 25s., mash tun and flakestand 12s., a total of about £3. Donovan explained that the still was purposely constructed on this cheap plan as it held out no inducement to informers or excise men. At the time rewards for seizures were based on their value. He did not think that the flavour of poteen had any relation to the turf smoke at the kiln and the distiller told him that his spirit had the same smell and taste when coal was used. He thought that the taste was related to rapid fermentation which carried over much of the essential oils. He was referring to fusel oil. However, he did think it possible that smoke might be absorbed from the turf fire when spirits were running and that some bog extract might be charred in kiln drying. This was a description of illicit distilling in 1830 and while there were variations in practices in other cases and in other periods, the basic conditions were similar.[2]

At the beginning of the eighteenth century there were three kinds of legal distillers. There were privileged persons who could distil spirits for use in their households; there were keepers of inns and taverns who distilled spirits for sale to their clients; and there had emerged specialist distillers making spirit for sale generally. The privileged class was expanded to allow any household to distil for its own use provided the size of the still did not exceed twelve gallons content. The division between the vintner and the specialist distiller was blurred until separately distinguished in 1761 when distillers had to be registered, but the prescribed minimum sizes of his vessels were too large for the retailing distiller.[3] This was the legal field, but it is certain that, with the imperfect machinery for collecting the revenue and indeed the difficulty of paying duty if any distance from an excise office, there would be very many persons distilling small quantities of spirits outside the law. Clearly, also, knowledge of the distiller's art would be widespread. As new laws were passed to embrace all distilling within closer excise control so would the numbers illicitly distilling increase since more small household stills would become illegal. This process of converting the small legal still into an illicit still was slow and even as late as 1763 the household twelve gallon still could remain legal if its owner was prepared to register the still with the excise and notify the gauger before making spirit.[4] It is probable, therefore, that illicit distilling did not become a major problem until the latter part of the eighteenth century. If the pressure of excise regulations in an area became too great much domestic distilling would cease, but much would also continue either surreptitiously or by retreating to quieter spots in the surrounding countryside beyond the prying eyes of revenue officers. In this way the professional illicit distiller would

2. M. Donovan, *Domestic Economy*, Dublin, 1830, i, pp. 252–5. Compare with the *Commission of Inquiry into the Excise Establishment and the Management of the Excise Revenue throughout the United Kingdom, 7th Report, Part I*, Parl. Pps. 1834 (7) xxv, p. 400; and *S.C. to consider extending the functions of the Constabulary in Ireland to the suppression of Illicit Distillation*, Parl. Pps. 1854 (53) x, pp. 30–1.

3. 1 Geo. 3, c. 7, sections 7–8. There was a distinction in 1661 for under section 38 of 14 and 15 Car. 2, c. 8, a vintner could not sell spirits to another retailer. On the other hand a distiller could have a shop on his premises for retail sales and could also sell to retailers. There must have been many border-line cases.

4. 3 Geo. 3, c. 21, sections 5–6.

emerge. He would at first accommodate local farmers who would, perhaps, malt some of their grain and either take it to the illicit distiller or the latter might carry his still from farm to farm. Eventually the more ambitious illicit distillers would work in much the same way as legal distillers and buy grain, malt and grind it and distil for sale, all outside the law. The extent of illicit distilling would depend on the power of the authorities to stop it, local drinking habits, grain prices and the rate of duty. Thus illicit distilling in Ireland evolved naturally from the domestic nature of making spirit.

Understandably there is practically no information about illicit distilling in the first half of the eighteenth century and with many hundreds of small legal stills as well as the legal facility for persons to distil their own spirits in stills not exceeding twelve gallons content, it is probable that illicit distilling was nothing like the problem it became later. Nevertheless there must have been enough to make the authorities take notice for in 1731 an Act prohibited distilling 'in the mountainous parts of the Kingdom, remote from any market town'. An official return in 1757 of the net spirit duties for each excise district shows that there was a general distribution of licensed distilleries throughout the country except along the southern coast. Certainly in Ulster and Connaught the return shows considerable legal distilling in relation to population, which might be taken to indicate that legal distillers were successfully competing with the private still. Even as late as 1782 the distribution of licensed stills does not suggest a concentration of illicit distilling in any particular area.[5]

The interaction of legal and illicit distilling is clearly revealed in the changing pattern following alterations in the laws governing legal distilleries in the late eighteenth century. Returns laid before parliament disclose a fairly rapid decline in the numbers of legal distilleries in some areas without a corresponding increase in size of those remaining. In other places the decline was compensated for by increased production from larger stills. Since it can be presumed that there was no significant change in drinking

5. *House of Commons Journal*, 29 October 1757; 7 June 1782, app. pp. 523–32. See also 28 January 1791 where it is stated that there were 50 legal distilleries in Connaught even as late as 1784, an area later notorious for illicit distilling. It is possible that the term 'private' still is a relic of the time when much distilling was in private houses. The Act of 1731 was 5 Geo. 2, c. 3, sections 13–14.

habits the reflection of changes in legal distilling would correspond
with changes in the opposite direction in illicit distilling. A return
in 1782 shows that the distilling industry, apart from Dublin,
consisted of hundreds of small licensed stills, most of them in the
range of 200 to 300 gallons content, widely spread throughout
the country. In most cases there was only one such still in each
small town or village.[6] In country areas, particularly in the northwest and west, road links between market towns were poor and
the transport of merchandise in primitive carts was difficult. Thus
the distiller in a small town had a very localised market and was
not likely to be in serious competition with another distiller in a
neighbouring town. The scale of production would be geared to
local needs. The licensed distiller might and often did, have to
contend with local illicit distilling and to prevent being undersold
the licensed distiller would have to rely on better quality coupled
with some evasion. He received two blows from the legislators
that almost eliminated legal distilling in large areas. In 1775 the
duty was raised to 1s. 2d. giving the illicit distiller a decided
advantage which he was not slow to exploit. In 1780, however,
the still licence duty was imposed as the minimum spirit duty and
while some evasion might have helped many licensed distillers
to survive a higher rate of duty per gallon, this new measure was
a mortal blow to large numbers.[7] If the local market was large
enough the licensed distiller could manage, but if small he would
be driven out of business because the minimum production
required from him was more than his market could take. Nor
could he easily expand his market to neighbouring towns in
sparsely populated areas with poor transport facilities and perhaps
served by a similarly placed licensed distiller. The field was thus
left wide open to the illicit distiller and it is probable that many a
licensed distiller took his small still out of the town to a quiet
spot and used his skill to make poteen. He had very little to fear
from the law; there was no organised police force, magistrates
were unlikely to be active against him and no excise officer could
safely pursue him without the protection of a military escort. It

6. *H. C. Journal,* 7 June 1782, app. pp. 523–32.
7. 15 and 16 Geo. 3, c. 8, section 5; 19 and 20 Geo. 3, c. 12, section 20. See
Parliamentary Register, ed. Byrne and Porter, Dublin, xi, p. 76. Beresford stated
on 2 February 1791 that the addition of 4d. to the spirit duty in 1775 caused a
general increase in clandestine distilling. He was referring to both unlicensed
distilling and evasion at licensed distilleries.

was a period of continuous unrest and occasional open rebellion.[8]

The switch from licensed to illicit distilling was not dramatic. It came by degrees as the minimum from the still licence duty rose. At first the duty did not bear too heavily as the distiller was not expected to charge his still more than four times in twenty-eight days, but it was not long before this became eight times and steadily rose until by the close of the eighteenth century the small still was being assessed at thirty charges; far more than many licensed distillers could possibly meet with their limited markets. Thus the government in their efforts to counteract evasion in legal distilleries were driving distillers into illicit distilling. The reaction of the legal distilling industry as a whole was a contraction in the number of distilling units, but this bare statement masks the full results. A distiller faced with elimination naturally seeks some way to survive. He can either turn to illicit distilling, or enlarge his plant, or work his existing plant more rapidly. In the northwest and west there was very little choice as in most cases increasing production was out of the question. In the Cavan excise district, for example, there were thirty-nine stills in 1782, all between 200 and 234 gallons content. In 1790 this number fell to five and in 1796 to two. In the Killybegs excise district, which stretched to Enniskillen, eighteen small stills in 1782 fell to three in 1790 one of which was just over 500 gallons. In the Armagh district seventy-four stills in 1782 fell to nine by 1796. Londonderry and Strabane excise districts were even more dramatically affected for from nineteen and seventy-four stills respectively in 1782 none survived by 1796. There is no indication either of changing drinking habits or of spirits being imported into these areas so the conclusion is inescapable that the gap in the market was filled by illicit spirits.

In most of the rest of Ireland the picture was different. Here it is likely that transport facilities were better, population less sparse and the possibility of larger scale production better. Larger local markets would enable the more efficient distillers to expand by larger stills or more rapid production and there was no room for the ousted lesser skilled distiller to revert successfully to illicit distilling. Lower priced poteen was severely handicapped by

8. J. A. Froude, *The English in Ireland in the Eighteenth Century*, London, 1874, ii, p. 316. He quotes Lord Carlisle, Viceroy, whose opinion in 1782 was that no magistrate or revenue officer would venture to enforce the law. See Chap. V, p. 125.

spirits made in excess of the still licence duty and which were rarely charged. In the Clonmel excise district there were forty-seven stills in 1782 ranging from 200 to 479 gallons content, the latter size indicating that there was a sufficient local market. By 1796 this number had fallen to twenty-four, but two of them were more than 1,000 gallons content.

There was, of course, no clear-cut change from licensed to illicit distilling in any area and in some districts there was both a concentration of legal distilling and a switch to illicit practices. In the Ennis excise district, for example, twenty-five small stills in 1782 became five small stills and one still of 1,078 gallons in 1796. The Lisburn excise district, which embraced Belfast, did not appear to be involved in these changes. In 1782 there were only two small stills both under 250 gallons, yet the market was large enough to support much more. There is no record of any excessive illicit distilling so it is probable that spirit was supplied from Dublin or Drogheda by sea through Belfast. By 1796 there were two stills, of 536 and 1,007 gallons, so that in this case local distillers were expanding at the expense of imports rather than competing with illicit distillers. The large cities of Dublin and Cork were special cases. The numbers of stills in these cities did not vary greatly between 1782 and 1796, but they increased in size and it is doubtful if there was any increase in illicit distilling; the probability is that there was a decrease.[9] Thus it is a fair conclusion that in areas where it was not possible to meet the minimum duty charge by increased production, illicit distillers took the place of the licensed distillers. Where the market could be enlarged the more successful distillers increased the size of their plant or worked more rapidly and evaded more duty, the others went out of business and there was no large gap for the illicit distiller. There were, of course, other circumstances, such as changes in drinking habits. In Cork and Dublin, for example, a good deal of porter was drunk and did compete with the spirit market, and in Galway wine drinking had been traditional for a long time.[10]

9. *H.C. Journal.* All the statistics are taken from appendices dated 7 June 1782, pp. 523–32; 7 February 1792, pp. 140–4; 26 February 1796 pp. 372–6.
10. *H.C. Journal*, 23 February 1792. Reference is made to a thriving brewing trade in Cork, but less elsewhere. T. Newenham, *A Statistical and Historical Inquiry into the Population of Ireland*, London, 1805, pp. 140, 234. He refers to the increase in porter and ale breweries in the past 20 years and the growing consumption of

In the late eighteenth century revenue officers did what they could with military protection to combat illicit distilling, but there were far too few of them to spare from their normal duties. The work was dangerous and they were often attacked when still hunting, but violence was not always one-sided. Howard wrote in 1776 that revenue officers frequently assaulted, wounded and sometimes killed in the execution of their duties.[11] The report of a particular seizure in 1788 in the Ennis excise district gives a vivid picture of the kind of war existing between the revenue and the illicit distiller. It runs:

'Limerick, February 25. On the 20th instant, John Downes, esquire, inspector of excise, accompanied by some other civil officers and a detachment of the 27th regiment with two field pieces, proceeded to attack the Castle of Ognolly, in which has been carried on for some years an immense distillery in open defiance of the laws; but on the first appearance of the military force the castle surrendered without the least resistence. In it was found one of the most compleat distilleries in the Kingdom, which they totally destroyed.'

Evidently violent resistance was expected and only avoided by using overwhelming military assistance. There were probably innumerable instances on a lesser scale that would be too common-place to be worth reporting.[12]

Military assistance involved employing large numbers of soldiers on work that the army viewed with some apprehension as likely to lead to drunkenness and indiscipline. Army regulations restricted the duties of soldiers to protecting the person of the excise officer and to give him no other assistance. The military officer in charge of a party of soldiers would not, for example, detach some of his party to guard the rear of a house being raided and the distiller could often escape while the officer was forcing an entrance at the front, the distiller perhaps carrying away his apparatus. If a seizure was made, soldiers would not remain to guard it if the excise officer had to leave to get a conveyance; they would all go with him. In some districts an

beer in Munster. *Parliamentary Register,* xi, p. 69, 2 February 1791, statement by Grattan; and xii, p. 258, 5 March 1792.

11. G. E. Howard, *A Treatise of the Exchequer and Revenue of Ireland,* Dublin, 1776, ii, p. 321.

12. *The Annual Register,* Dublin, 1788, The Chronicle, p. 199.

excise officer would get over the difficulty by hiring reliable men to go with him. In 1788 seven armed parties were privately raised under the authority of the Lord Lieutenant, each of a dozen men under two officers. They operated in areas in the counties of Fermanagh, Sligo and Leitrim. It was said that these parties succeeded in suppressing illicit distilling in the areas in which they operated, but only because these distillers moved to adjoining districts. These early efforts resulted in the formation in 1818 of the revenue police, armed and equipped, living in barracks and employed almost wholly against the illicit distiller. In 1855 this work was taken over by the constabulary. The effect of all these measures was to make illicit distilling more hazardous and to drive the trade into more remote and inaccessible places and with a very localised market.[13]

The effects of the new distillery laws in 1780 on illicit distilling must have been alarming to the Government for they were spurred into taking exceptional measures that proved very unwise and led to much lawlessness and even bloodshed. The land laws of the period enabled land owners to exact as much rent from tenants as they could get and in many cases tenants could only avoid eviction if they practised or permitted illicit distilling in order to meet the rent. Landlords, therefore, had an interest in encouraging such distilling. The Government took the view that not only the landlord, but the people living in the barony or parish would be fully aware of any illicit distilling. It was considered that it was their collective duty to support the Government by information and assistance to suppress the trade. This they had failed to do, which is not surprising since the local inhabitants bought the poteen at cheaper prices than legal whiskey and in some areas there was no legal spirit to be had. Furthermore, many farmers had from time beyond memory made their own whiskey and if they expanded into selling some to their neighbours or commercially they were better able to pay their rents. In 1783 the Government attempted to force the assistance of all persons in their fight against illicit distilling by imposing on the

13. *Excise Revenue Inquiry, 7th Report, Part II*, Parl. Pps. 1835 (8) xxx, pp. 58, 84–5, 88. 17 and 18 Vict., c. 89, sections 13–15. *13th Inland Revenue Report*, Parl. Pps. 1870 (c. 82) xx, p. 234. The constabulary began to act in 1855 in Donegal and Cavan. Their success decided the Government to extend their activities to the whole country.

county or town, a fine of £20 for any 'still, alembic or blackpot found,' the fine to be raised by a grand jury presentment, or in modern terms by an addition to the rates. The Revenue Commissioners determined each case and they were empowered to swear in collectors of excise as sub-commissioners to undertake this task for them.[14] Thus the excise judged the case and determined the county or town liable. The inhabitants who would have to pay the fine were not cited as defendants and had no opportunity of rebutting liability. All that was necessary was proof of discovery usually given by a revenue officer or an informer who were both interested in getting a reward. It was not necessary to prove that illicit distilling had occurred where the still or utensils were found nor to accuse any one of distilling. It was a most iniquitous Act open to great abuse and a measure of the helplessness of the Government to deal with illicit distilling.

To fine a whole county or town was manifestly unjust. It could not, for example, be expected that the inhabitants of south Donegal would have any knowledge of a still found in Innishowen in north Donegal, so after pressure in parliament the area to be fined was reduced in 1785 to the parish or townland and the grand jury presentment was to be confirmed by the judge at the next assize. The judge, however, could not determine a case or hear an appeal, he merely had to be satisfied that the process of levying the fine was in order. Some grand juries had refused or omitted to include these fines in their presentments so it was decreed that the judge could not confirm any presentments for public works unless the townland fines were included.[15] This system of fines does not appear to have had the desired effect. Large sums were levied, but as one Revenue Commissioner remarked 'so large a sum due for fines for illicit distilling means that landed people took too little care to suppress them' (the distillers). Allegations were made that fines often arose through collusion between the excise officer and the distiller for the sake of the reward. The revenue authorities ridiculed this on the grounds that the reward was less than the fine, but frequently no person was made amenable and an old worn out still could be planted and information given leading to its discovery by the gauger. The only losers would be the inhabitants of the barony.

14. 23 and 24 Geo. 3, c. 29, sections 2, 13.
15. *H.C. Journal,* 12 March 1784. 25 Geo. 3, c. 34, sections 67–9.

In 1791 the fine was reduced to £10 in country districts, but as the fine applied to each discovery, a barony in an illicit distilling area could well run up a large bill for fines. Far from enlisting the inhabitants as unpaid excise men this law banded them together to prevent the discovery of stills. Nor did the law have much effect on landlords whose first interest was their rents. Illicit distilling to the landlord sometimes meant getting a good rent for poor land. The Act of 1791 did, however, try to remedy one serious injustice. It made provision for objections to be raised to the imposition of a fine, but it was not very effective.[16] This was the position to the end of the century, but from 1800 the system was further developed as an important feature of government policy and came in for very severe criticism.

The private still described by Donovan in 1830 was obviously favourably placed and not in an area where the excise or revenue police were very active. In most cases these stills were in open country, either mountainous or bogland. Morewood relates the artful construction of distilleries on townland boundaries where the danger of interference by a landowner or the inhabitants, who would become liable to fines, was possible. Any threat from them and the apparatus was quickly moved over the boundary. In the case of a seizure by the excise it was sometimes difficult to decide on which townland the fine should be levied. He also describes the situation of stills in mountain caverns, on islands in lakes or even on boats on rivers. In one case a still was discovered in a cavern with a tube to convey the smoke to the distiller's dwelling and up the chimney. Smoke was similarly conducted to discharge at nearby lime kilns. Smoke was also made to issue as if from burning heath or sods of peat ignited for manure. Lookouts were posted to act as messengers or blow a horn at the approach of revenue officers upon which the pot-ale was either destroyed or run into a previously prepared underground receptacle. The apparatus was easily portable and the site usually on a commanding eminence or the centre of a bog and not easily approached.[17] Coffey, an inspector-general of excise who had for

16. 31 Geo. 3, c. 16, sections 101, 104–6. *Parliamentary Register,* vi, 26 January 1786. Other debates occurred on 31 January 1786, pp. 61–6, and 8 March 1786, pp. 252–4. In xi, 26 January 1791, p. 39, Beresford denounced landowners.
17. S. Morewood, *A Philosophical and Statistical History of . . . Inebriating Liquors with the present practice of Distillation in all its varieties,* Dublin, 1838, p. 674.

some years been actively engaged against illicit distillers in
Donegal, testified that the trade 'was chiefly, if not entirely,
carried on by persons of a very low rank in life, who generally
fermented not more than one sack of grain at a time; they made
weak wash of it, fermenting in a short time and distilling it off
rapidly, making about ten or twelve gallons of illicit spirit with
it and before the individual made any more he generally brought
it to market; perhaps half a dozen or at times a dozen men would
come to market, armed with heavy cudgels, riding together; so
that no officer would attack them, unless he had a military party,
and he could hardly ever come up with them, unless his party
were cavalry.' Where the revenue police were successful they
caused the illicit distillers to change their tactics and go singly
carrying the spirit on their backs. Their works consisted of a few
sods of turf near a convenient stream. These descriptions of illicit
distillation in the early nineteenth century differ very little from
descriptions towards the end of the century. Le Fanu visited an
illicit distillery in 1873 and he wrote that because of the difficulty
in concealing smoke when drying malt, this was often done in
July when the police were busy dealing with riots in Londonderry.[18]

Illicit stills were made by itinerant tinkers. In some cases the
tin was bought in sheets and given to tinkers to make stills. The
worm, was, if possible, made of copper. Sometimes stills were
hired to illicit distillers. In other cases stills were owned by
travelling distillers who went from farm to farm. The cost of a
still varied with its size and the material used. The size did not
normally exceed fifty to sixty gallons. Cost also differed according
to locality. In Mayo and Galway a tin still in 1834 cost from 15s.
to £1. In the Londonderry area the cost was from 30s. to 50s.
If made of copper a still and worm could cost £6, but this may
have included a couple of flax seed casks for fermenting and a

Morewood was a senior excise official serving in Ireland. *S.C. on Constabulary
functions,* 1854, *op. cit.,* p. 170. A head constable describes an incident where the
dispersal of equipment was done by a line of men relieving each other so that the
still was passed on to the next man after 2 or 3 miles and none would tire, till
the still was safely beyond the reach of the revenue police. See also p. 46.

18. *Inquiry into the Revenue arising in Ireland,* 5th Report, Parl. Pps. 1823 (405)
vii, pp. 325, 331, 336. *Excise Revenue Inquiry,* 7th Report, Part I, 1834, *op. cit.,*
p. 400. W. R. le Fanu, *Seventy years of Irish Life,* London, 1896, p. 290. His visit
was made about 1873.

sugar hogshead for use as a mash tun, and would indicate a well established and safe distillery.[19] The complete distillery was not always in one place. An excise official said that in order to escape detection the pot-ale was buried in casks perhaps 300 or 400 yards from the still and so cleverly concealed that revenue police coming upon a still with fires still burning had to spend two or three hours looking for the pot-ale. They had to scour the countryside prodding the ground with the ramrods of their muskets.[20]

Illicit spirits in 1823 were normally made from malted barley and of a strength of from 4° to 8° over proof, but sometimes as high as 15° over proof. By 1834 illicit distilling was so extensive in north Donegal that there was insufficient local barley and malted oats was also used. In addition there was a regular barter trade at Magilligan Strand where distillers exchanged spirits with Scottish importers of barley. To prepare his spirits for sale the illicit distiller reduced his spirit with water till it made a froth in the glass. This he deemed as proof. Later before final sale to a customer, the spirit was further watered down to about 11° under proof.[21] The distillers themselves were often men of no property, 'a species of migrating contrabandistes', and sometimes employed by persons of substance, the distiller being prepared to accept the consequences of discovery to protect the employers from any odium. In a slack season the distiller might sometimes do other work such as spinning. A witness in 1812 said that women were found working stills in the belief that they would not be prosecuted.[22] The usual fine on conviction was the minimum penalty of £6 or three months imprisonment and release

19. *Report from a Committee on Distilleries in Ireland*, Parl. Pps. 1812–13 (269) vi, pp. 12, 22. *Irish Revenue Inquiry, 5th Report*, 1823, *op. cit.*, pp. 325, 331. *Excise Revenue Inquiry, 7th Report*, Part I, 1834, *op. cit.*, p. 400. *S.C. on Constabulary functions*, 1854, *op. cit.*, pp. 29, 68. A witness said that flour barrels were used for making pot-ale and then used as worm tubs.

20. *Irish Revenue Inquiry, 5th Report*, 1823, *op. cit.*, p. 334. *S.C. on Constabulary functions*, 1854, *op. cit.*, p. 28.

21. *Report on Distilleries in Ireland*, 1812–13, *op. cit.*, p. 9. *Irish Revenue Inquiry, 5th Report*, 1823, *op. cit.*, pp. 332, 337. *Excise Revenue Inquiry, 7th Report*, Part I, 1834, *op. cit.*, p. 430. *S.C. on Constabulary functions*, 1854, *op. cit.*, p. 48. An illicit distiller estimated strength from the bubbles produced when pouring poteen into a glass, he then added water to reduce the spirit to about 3° over proof.

22. *Report on Distilleries in Ireland*, 1812–13, *op. cit.*, pp. 11, 20, 22–3. *Irish Revenue Inquiry*, 5th Report, 1823, *op. cit.*, p. 331. Rev. E. Chichester, *Oppressions and Cruelties of Irish Revenue Officers*, London, 1818, p. 11.

could be obtained at the rate of £2 a month for part of an unexpired sentence. If a gaol was any distance from the courthouse there were times when it was so hazardous to convey a prisoner on remand that he was released without bail. Fines were rarely paid in full as prison was often preferred to the distiller's usual wretched cabin, especially in winter. In addition a prisoner might be able to earn a little money breaking stones.[23] The illicit distiller was far from the romantic figure of popular conception.

Where illicit distilling was conducted in remote areas the risks of discovery were small, but bringing the spirit to a market involved greater risk and required lookouts to be posted on the route. The spirit would be carried from mountain stills in kegs of eight to ten gallons, two to a sack straddled across a horse with a man using this as a saddle and another ahead of him on foot to give warning of any revenue police party. In parts of Innishowen, however, it was a different story. Here the illicit distillers were so contemptuous of the ineffective measures taken against them that they openly transported their spirits to Londonderry where, so it was said, practically the whole population were supporting them. In one instance these distillers loaded their spirits on a ship for Scotland with a magistrate looking on. These distillers from Buncrana and Culdaff were armed and would resist any magistrate or revenue officers who had no military support. One witness in 1833 said that poteen was sold in the streets as openly as a loaf of bread. Sometimes the illicit distiller sold cheaper at the still to another person who then took the risk of transporting the spirit to the dram shops and shebeens.[24] Later in the century when the authorities had a better grip on controlling the transport of illicit spirits, the distiller's market was extremely local and generally confined to persons too poor to buy duty paid spirits. It was either poteen or nothing. In the first half of the century, however, this was not so and as some of this poteen was equal if not better than malt spirit from legal stills, the latter had great difficulty in surviving. In Sligo the largest legal distiller had to

23. 1 and 2 Will, 4, c. 55, sections 39, 42. *Report on Distilleries in Ireland, 1812–13, op. cit.,* p. 24. *Excise Revenue Inquiry, 7th Report,* Part I, 1834, pp. 387, 393, 400, 405–6.

24. *Report on Distilleries in Ireland,* 1812–13, p. 25. *Irish Revenue Inquiry, 5th Report,* 1823, pp. 327, 372. *Excise Revenue Inquiry, 7th Report, Part I,* 1834, pp. 205, 416. *S.C. on Constabulary functions,* 1854, p. 34. See also *S.C. on Illicit Distillation in Ireland,* 2nd Report, Parl. Pps. 1816 (436) ix, p. 26.

cease operations for a time and a Coleraine distillery went bankrupt. Bushmills also could only work intermittently. An excise collector did, however, say in 1854 that Bushmills was superior as the illicit distiller usually allowed more impurities to distil over.[25] Poteen found its way in the first quarter of the century into markets some considerable distance from where it was made. Innishowen spirit was sold even as far away as Dublin, though it might be suspected that this was a special market to suit particular demands as Dublin had no taste for malt spirits. Belfast certainly got a fair supply and a number of seizures are recorded in the excise records. In one instance fifty gallons of illicit spirit was seized in Belfast. The excise collector believed that it was distilled on the Isle of Scuddy, Lough Neagh, near Toomebridge. The smoke from this illicit distillery was conveyed through the chimney in the distiller's house.[26] There is no record of any illicit still being found in or near Belfast at this period. It is at least probable that some sales of poteen in towns remote from the illicit distilling areas were to persons of standing who liked to boast their cellars to friends rather than because of the quality of the spirit. A Dublin distiller, for example, said in 1823, that in his view the quality of illicit spirit was no more than his low wines, but he was probably a biassed witness as it is doubtful if poteen was quite as bad as that.[27]

The price of poteen varied with the price of barley and oats. If there was a good harvest and prices were low, the illicit distiller prospered. If corn was scarce and prices high he might have to suspend operations because it might pay the farmers to send the

25. *Inquiry into Fees, Perquisites . . . received in Public Offices in Ireland, 5th Report*, Parl. Pps. 1806–7 (124) vi, p. 204. A list of licensed distillers in 1807 shows only two in Ulster, in Belfast and Newry, and none in Connaught. *Report on Distilleries in Ireland 1812–13, op. cit.,* p. 10, illicit whiskey was preferred in Northern Ireland; p. 18, the Coleraine bankruptcy was caused by cheaper poteen. *Irish Revenue Inquiry, 5th Report,* 1823, p. 308. On page 280, Pakenham, M.P. gave his view that illicit whiskey was 'without comparison better than legal whiskey'. *Excise Revenue Inquiry, 7th Report, Part I,* 1834, p. 190. A magistrate asserted that some poteen could pass off as Bushmills or Scotch Isla. See also p. 407. *S.C. on Constabulary functions,* 1854, p. 50.

26. *Report on Distilleries in Ireland,* 1812–13, *op. cit.,* p. 7. *Belfast Excise Historical Records,* Custom House, Belfast. Mss. book 5, p. 20, report dated 16 March 1844. Other seizures are recorded in Book 5, pp. 22, 25, 28–30, 34 and Book 6, p. 52.

27. *Irish Revenue Inquiry, 5th Report,* 1823, p. 296. *S.C. on Constabulary functions,* 1854, pp. 49, 72. An example is given of illicit spirit supplied to a gentleman who prided himself on giving his guests some 'mountain dew'.

P

grain to market instead of direct sales to the illicit distiller. In 1834 a Londonderry legal distiller gave current prices and costs. At that time poteen was selling at 1s. a gallon below legal grain spirit and 2s. to 2s. 6d. below duty paid good quality malt spirit. He gave figures on the basis of producing a spirit of 25° over proof. The total cost of producing was shown as £1 1s. using eighteen stones of oats at 7d. a stone, the average price in 1833. In a legal distillery this would produce ten gallons, but the illicit distiller would get a little over eight gallons, so that the latter's costs would be almost 6d. a gallon more, but the legal distiller would have the addition of the duty at 3s. 4d. a proof gallon. There would be a return for the sale of spent grains in both cases which is not shown in the account. In 1854 this sale was estimated at 7s. for every ten gallons of spirit and, indeed, buyers of this spent grain attended illicit distillations and were sometimes arrested along with those interested in the spirit.[28]

Some interesting figures of costs and prices were given by witnesses at the revenue inquiries in 1823 and 1834. The quotations for illicit spirit should be treated with caution for most of the evidence comes from licensed distillers who were trying to make out a case for reducing the duty in order to compete with illicit distillers. A Dungannon distiller said that duty paid spirit sold at 9s. a gallon at the mouth of the still and illegal spirit from a licensed distillery at 6s. to 7s. a gallon. He said that poteen was selling at 4s. to 5s. a gallon in Londonderry. He estimated the risk value of transporting poteen between country and town at 6d. a gallon. A Londonderry distiller put the price of poteen a little higher at 4s. 6d. to 6s. and if sent to a more remote market it might reach up to 10s. to 12s., but the latter prices, which appear to have been paid in Belfast, had an element of prestige value for the buyer amongst his friends. A Belfast distiller alleged that this price, which was higher than the price of legal spirit, was due to better quality and a smokey flavour and before 1823 this may well have been the case. After that year the distiller was free to ferment and distil at his preferred speed so that any excuse

28. *Excise Revenue Inquiry, 7th Report, Part I,* 1834, *op. cit.,* pp. 205, 395. *S.C. on Constabulary functions,* 1854, *op. cit.,* p. 75. The cost figures for an illicit distiller are given net. He would have to add something for seizures in his selling price. See p. 263 where the Excise Board stated that illicit distillers did not mind the low yield of spirits in view of the recovery of costs from the sale of spent grains for cattle food.

that poteen was superior was a reflection on his skill. In country areas poteen prices were said to be lower in 1834 than in 1823, and a Belturbet licensed distiller selling his legal whiskey at 7s. a gallon said that poteen was being sold to publicans at 3s. He does not say if this was a normal price or some special transaction, but it seems very low and would indicate a low risk value.[29]

Illicit malting was 'part and parcel with illicit distilling'. 'The prevalence of illicit manufacture of malt will always vary with the extent of unlicensed distillation and whatever tends to the suppression of one will produce a proportionate effect on the other.' These were opinions expressed in 1808 and 1854.[30] The illicit distiller could get his malt either by making it himself, by taking germinated grain to a registered mill normally used for drying and grinding corn for bakers and others, by taking it to a licensed maltster willing to finish the processes clandestinely, or if necessity pushed too hard by buying duty paid malt. The last case would be rare. At the beginning of the nineteenth century evasion of the malt duty by licensed maltsters was widespread in all parts of Ireland and this illegal malt was supplied to licensed distilleries and breweries as well as illicit distillers. It was the opinion of the inquiry into the excise department's activities in 1834 that illicit malting in Ireland prevailed to an immense extent. In the illicit distilling areas the main source of malt supplies came from illicit malting.[31]

Barry, an inspector of revenue police with over twenty years experience, gave a description of the methods used for illicit malting in 1854. The grain was steeped for twenty-four hours and then put into an excavation for up to ten days, the grain being turned occasionally until germinated sufficiently. It was then removed to a kiln for drying. The kiln was a temporary affair,

29. *S.C. on Illicit Distillation, 2nd Report*, 1816, *op. cit.*, p. 27. The costs and selling prices of poteen show a profit of 5s. a gallon, but this appears much too high in view of the evidence in 1823. *Irish Revenue Inquiry, 5th Report*, 1823, *op. cit.*, pp. 268, 308, 318–9. *Excise Revenue Inquiry, 7th Report, Part I*, 1834, *op. cit.*, pp. 75, 395, 406, 442.

30. *Inquiry into Fees in Ireland, 6th Report*, Parl. Pps. 1808 (4) iii, p. 477. *S.C. on Constabulary functions*, 1854, *op. cit.*, p. 22.

31. *Excise Revenue Inquiry, 7th Report, Part I*, 1834, *op. cit.*, p. 382, and *Part II*, 1835, *op. cit.*, p. 74. *10th Report*, Parl. Pps. 1834 (11) xxv, p. 591. See also *Report on Distilleries in Ireland*, 1812–13, *op. cit.*, p. 23, where it is stated that in Cavan there were 190 corn mills and that most of them ground corn for private distilleries, 40 of them exclusively.

usually formed with turf in a ditch. The turf was laid in a circle
and built up to the required height and a few branches of trees or
sticks placed over the circle and more sods of turf on top. The
under part was the hearth and the grain was spread out on top.
After drying it was ground, often by mountain hand mills called
querns. Thereafter the brewing and distilling processes were
conducted and the refuse from the first distillation sold for cattle
food.[32] There were other variations. Some distillers might do all
the processes from raw grain to finished spirit. Remote farms
might malt their grain and sell it to illicit distillers rather than
carry the grain to the market. Prices and ease of transport would
be deciding factors for the farmers.[33] As with illicit distilling
revenue officers faced the same hostile opposition when attempting to suppress illicit malting, but they had the complication that
a raid on a registered mill at work might well result in finding
that it was legitimately grinding corn. Sometimes encounters
with illicit maltsters could be just as serious as with illicit
distillers.[34]

During the period before 1823 when licensed distillers were
making whiskey of indifferent quality and when there were
stringent laws governing both distilling and malting and against
the illicit trade, H. R. Pakenham, MP, was impelled to express
himself vigorously. He said: 'I confess I am at a loss for a proper
term to apply to a system that offers to supply the community
with a bad article at an expensive rate, and then endeavours to
force consumption of the stuff, rendered pernicious by their own
regulations; by multiplying gaugers, revenue police, employing
military and so on.'[35] This was a valid criticism, but the prevalence
of illicit distilling after 1823 cannot be attributed to the poor
quality coming from legal stills. There must be some explanation
also, why persons, even of the low class of illicit distillers, should

---

32. *S.C. on Constabulary functions,* 1854, *op. cit.,* pp. 30–1. On p. 51 a mountain
quern is described as two horizontal stones, one of which is moved by hand.

33. *Excise Revenue Inquiry, 10th Report,* 1834, *op. cit.,* p. 593.

34. *S.C. on Constabulary functions,* 1854, *op. cit.,* p. 14. In an incident in Naas
a woman was killed in a shooting affray between the revenue police and illicit
maltsters. *Belfast Historical Excise Records, op. cit.,* Book 5, pp. 17–18, 34–5, 80,
85. There was an illicit still in a corn mill in Carrickfergus; yet another variant
in illicit traffic. Illicit malting reported from Hillsborough was probably for
licensed distillers.

35. *Irish Revenue Inquiry, 5th Report,* 1823, *op. cit.,* p. 280.

continue in their trade in the teeth of very repressive laws. It is not enough to say that they were following 'a trade so congenial with their habits, constitution and propensities.' They were harassed by revenue officers supported by military and by some landowners and inhabitants who would suffer fines if illicit practices or distilling utensils were found in their townlands or parishes. Continued illicit distilling over a long period could only survive if the distiller's activities were fairly safe, if there was some encouragement from the growers of cereal crops and if alternative employment did not exist. In 1819 it was reported that 'amongst the positive evils resulting from the want of employment and the impassable state of the mountain districts, is the facility under the present circumstances of the country of illicit distillation, with its consequent depravation of morals and loss of revenue.'[36]

The northwest and west of Ireland contained large tracts of poor land and there were many remote but suitable places to conduct illicit distilling. Also there were few other means of obtaining a livelihood. If landowners had taken active steps against illicit distillers the latter could not have survived, but many landlords did the opposite. Coffey testified that many landowners were hostile to revenue officers, that they could get a rent of as much as three guineas an acre for a barren waste where little grain would grow, and that their tenants would not be able to pay this rent but for illicit distilling. He was speaking chiefly of Innishowen barony where landlords possessed large areas mostly of poor land and where poteen could be marketed in nearby Londonderry. His view was that reducing the spirit duty would not stop illicit distilling which would persist in places where otherwise 'not a blade of grass would be grown'. He thought many landlords would resist a reduction of duty or any other means for helping legal spirit to compete with poteen. Logie, another senior excise official, said that illicit distillers were chiefly drawn from smallholders of three to fifteen acres of bad land. The families did spinning, but the rents could not be paid except for illicit distilling. These smallholders of marginal land were mainly concerned with marketing their barley and oats; if grain prices were low poteen was a profitable way of doing this. If they

36. *S.C. on the State of Disease and Condition of the Labouring Poor in Ireland,* 2nd Report, Parl. Pps. 1819 (409) viii, p. 461. *Irish Revenue Inquiry, 5th Report,* 1823, *op. cit.,* p. 289.

were prevented from making poteen the land might go out of cultivation and the landowner would lose his rent. Hence both tenant and landowner supported illicit distilling.[37] There were exceptions to this general statement. In some cases the real landowner may well have been helpless; for instance the Marquis of Donegal owned a very large tract of land he had let on long leases and the real power to restrain illicit distilling was in the hands of these leaseholders who had let lands to small holders. A good deal of church property was similarly placed. A suggestion was made that a conviction for illicit distilling should give the landowner power to terminate the lease and Morewood quotes the action of the Earl of Kingston who effectively stopped illicit distilling in county Cork by putting an appropriate clause in all leases.[38]

The system of townland fines inherited from the previous century became so oppressive as to lead to open and violent opposition to the law. Attempts to root out illicit practices assumed the proportions of a military operation. Planting stills or utensils, usually worn out, for reward or for revenge was common and in the opinion of an inspector-general of excise in 1806 the 'bounties to revenue officers and military for detecting private stills are generally very fraudulently obtained.' Elderly widows, minors, military officers serving overseas and even members of parliament attending their duties in London were all mulcted because stills or parts had been found on their lands, usually without any evidence that distilling had taken place where these items were found. It mattered not that these items were obviously discarded. One landlord, Lucius Carey, tried to stop distilling on his lands and was beaten; he tried to prevent the discovery of stills by using man-traps and was denounced in parliament. His

---

37. *S.C. to inquire how far it may be practicable to confine Distilleries to the use of Sugar and Molasses*, Parl. Pps. 1808 (178) iv, p. 74. Chichester, *Oppressions by Revenue Officers*, 1818, *op. cit.*, p. 10. *Irish Revenue Inquiry, 5th Report*, 1823, *op. cit.*, pp. 326–8, 331, 372. *Parliamentary Debates* (Hansard), 2 July 1804, col. 900, an appeal to the Irish gentry to assist the revenue authorities. 26 May 1816, col. 706, a landowner stated that he would not get his rents if it were not for illicit distilling. See also T. Reid, *Travels in Ireland*, London, 1823, p. 341.

38. *Irish Revenue Inquiry, 5th Report*, 1823, *op. cit.*, pp. 272, 328. *Excise Revenue Inquiry, 7th Report, Part I*, 1834, *op. cit.*, p. 399. See also p. 85. In the north of Ireland almost all landlords either supported illicit distillation or remained neutral. The Londonderry excise collector said 'we have scarcely in any instance found any co-operation on the part of landed proprietors'.

case was typical of the helpless position of many landlords unless they were themselves involved with illicit distilling, generally by condoning the practice and profiting from higher rents.[39] Some landlords better able to protect themselves did not permit illicit distilling and occasionally took vigorous steps to suppress it, urged on, perhaps, by the probability of townland fines and amongst the instances quoted was the Marquis of Abercorn on his estates at Strabane. Young of Culdaff in the barony of Innishowen, in a drive to put down private distilling on his lands, seized twenty-seven to thirty serviceable copper stills and brought them to the excise in Londonderry. These were exceptional land-owners and very often their efforts merely drove the illicit distiller to a neighbouring property where he might be 'more than welcome' to an impecunious landlord.[40]

Accounts by travellers and official testimony show that energetic measures combined with townland fines made little impression on illicit distilling itself, but did result in confining the practice to the lowest social classes to whom prison was no stigma. The threat of these fines often led to the most lawless acts. Revenue officers were not only attacked when still hunting, but were sometimes wounded, murdered or abducted in efforts to prevent them from giving evidence that could lead to a fine. A fine fell heavily on the occupier of the land on which the distilling apparatus was found and the townland as a whole was liable if the fine could not be recovered from the occupier. The fines themselves sometimes built up through several seizures to a total which might equal the value of the property and all the cattle of a smallholder might also be distrained. This in turn led to corrupt practices by excise officers buying in such cattle through a third party at absurdly low prices. The ruin of a small farmer could be so great that in order to escape the debt he fled to America and the country must often have lost a good man whilst the rootless distiller remained. The cost to society of attempting to suppress the illicit distiller through townland fines must have

39. *Inquiry into Fees in Ireland*, 5th Report, 1806–7, *op. cit.*, p. 229. S.C. on *Illicit Distillation*, 2nd Report, 1816, *op. cit.*, pp. 52, 69. *Parl. Debates*, 6 May 1818, cols. 532–3; 30 May 1818, col. 1014. E. Wakefield, *Account of Ireland, Statistical and Political*, London, 1812, i, p. 729. Chichester, *Oppressions of Revenue Officers, op. cit.*, pp. 22, 28, 61.

40. *Irish Revenue Inquiry*, 5th Report, 1823, *op. cit.*, p. 328. S.C. on *Illicit Distillation*, 2nd Report, 1816, *op. cit.*, p. 122.

been great indeed and the excise man of the period became the
most despised and hated of all government officials. Magistrates,
who were drawn from the ranks of the landlords gave no help
even if they did not openly obstruct.[41]

The apparent advantage to landlords of getting better rents for
their lands if they encouraged or ignored illicit distilling on their
lands may well have been ephemeral. As one witness said at an
inquiry in 1823, any landlords who thought this 'must admit that
their tenantry and the peasantry in general have been seriously
injured in their moral and industrial habits, and that those private
distilleries are meeting places for all the loose and disorderly
characters in the neighbourhood, where, half intoxicated, they
discuss politics and regulate rents, tithes and taxes'. These were
not the words of a temperance reformer, but a licensed distiller
in Roscrea where illicit distilling was not a serious problem.[42]
Thus the system of townland fines, ill-advised though it may have
been, was partly, if not mainly, forced on the Government by
laggard landlords themselves and the evidence of witnesses at
parliamentary inquiries tends to show that the fines did act as a
brake on illicit distilling. The alternative was stronger and
incorrupt enforcement agencies and these did not exist until after
1820 when the still fines ceased.

The laws relating to townland fines were revised and improved
a number of times by the United Kingdom parliament. The trial
of a case was removed from the jurisdiction of an excise court.
A case began by an information laid before a justice of the
peace who, if satisfied, bound over the informant to appear at the
assize court where the case was decided. No inhabitant of the
offending parish, barony or townland could serve as a juror. The

41. 55 Geo. 3, c. 151, section 11, provided that a court could proceed and
impose a fine even if the officer serving the court notice was killed, wounded or
abducted. Chichester, *Oppressions of Revenue Officers, op. cit.* This reverend
gentleman was bitterly opposed to townland fines and his opinions must be
treated with reserve. His facts regarding violence, however, were not disputed
in an official rebuttal by Coffey. Chichester describes many cases of murder,
wounding, the destruction of property, and abduction even in one case of an
excise officer from a military camp (pp. 68–84). A bad case of emigration appears
on pp. 74–5. See also *S.C. on Illicit Distillation, 2nd Report,* 1816, *op. cit.,* p. 69,
and *Irish Revenue Inquiry,* 5th Report, 1823, pp. 331–2, 372. A witness said that to
permit an excise officer to make a seizure alone would be an affront to the young
men of Donegal. Military aid saved them from disgrace. *Parl. Debates,* 30 April
1819, Col. 1513. A force of 140 infantry and 40 cavalry was successfully resisted.

42. *Irish Revenue Inquiry,* 5th Report, 1823, *op. cit.,* p. 286.

scale of fines was £25 for the first offence, £40 for the second and £60 for each subsequent offence. Thus in places like Innishowen the standard fine would be £60. In 1814 half of the fines collected were paid to the excise officer and his assistants or, if a private informer, this half was paid to him. The other half was to be paid to anyone prepared to erect and work a licensed still of less than 1,000 gallons content in the vicinity, or failing that a quarter went to the Crown and a quarter to the local infirmary. In the following year this was changed and half was paid to the excise collector to disburse amongst those responsible for the seizure and half to the informer. It was these payments which had led to so much abuse for it was clearly profitable for ill-disposed and dishonest persons to manufacture evidence.[43]

The informer could be in real danger of his life and to ensure his appearance in court he was bound over to prosecute at the assize. He committed a misdemeanour if he failed and a warrant would be issued for his arrest. It was also a misdemeanour for the townland inhabitants to insure against fines.[44] The grand jury cess collector still retained the duty of recovering the fines inflicted or if he neglected this duty the Excise Commissioners could appoint their own collectors. This was a necessary precaution because in some places a cess collector could well suffer personal violence. The method of levying a fine was left to the inhabitants who were required to call a meeting within thirty days to apportion the fine amongst themselves and if they did not do so the levy was put on the whole parish. The inhabitants were encouraged to protect themselves and were given power to appoint inspectors at a salary of £20 a year whose duty it was to prevent or discover illicit distilling and prosecute offenders, but it is unlikely that much use was made of this provision. There was a further inducement in 1816, for if an offender was convicted on the evidence of an inhabitant the penalty was halved, payment suspended for twelve months and if there was no further offence it was remitted. Another inducement was to impose no townland fine if an inhabitant gave the initial information leading to a conviction.[45]

43. 54 Geo. 3, c. 150, sections 2–3, 5, 8; 55 Geo. 3, c. 151, Section 9.
44. 54 Geo. 3, c. 150, sections 12, 34.
45. 54 Geo. 3, c. 150, sections 22–3; 55 Geo. 3, c. 12, section 5; 56 Geo. 3, c. 112, sections 3–4.

For a short period from 1811 to 1813, and in response to criticism, the townland fines were respited, but this resulted in such an upsurge in illicit distilling that they were revived. Following this revival a combination of these fines and a drive by revenue officers brought about a great number of convictions. In the words of an Act in 1816 'from the great number of dissolute and disorderly persons who have been convicted and imprisoned for the offence of carrying on illicit distillation, many gaols in Ireland are so crowded as not only very much to endanger the health of prisoners, but also to increase the depravity of their morals'. The authorities resorted to confining some of them in hulks. Coffey supplied official figures showing more than a sixfold increase in the duty paid consumption of spirits in the Londonderry area in the three years immediately following the resumption of townland fines and similar large increases in Strabane and Sligo. In evidence he said that the fines had caused landlords to make a special effort to rid themselves of the illicit distiller.[46]

The distribution of illicit distilling in 1816 is clearly seen from the returns of townland fines inflicted in the different counties by assize courts. At the Spring assizes, the number of fines were:

Clare	83	Meath	26	Antrim	55
Limerick	12	Westmeath	15	Down	1
Cork	1	King's County	9	Louth	1
Waterford	3	Queen's County	9	Monaghan	13
Tipperary	54	Carlow	23	Armagh	4
		Kildare	10		

At the Lent assizes:

Longford	3	Tyrone	151	Roscommon	26
Cavan	46	Donegal	531	Leitrim	74
Fermanagh	24	Londonderry	127	Sligo	54
Mayo	108	Galway	86	Leinster	5

46. Townland fines were respited by 50 Geo. 3, c. 15, section 18, and revived by 52 Geo. 3, c. 97. The 1816 Act was 56 Geo. 3, c. 112, Section 2. *Report on Distilleries in Ireland, 1812–13, op. cit.,* pp. 3, 16–17. A. Coffey, *Observations on Chichester's pamphlet entitled 'Oppressions and Cruelties of Irish Revenue Officers',* London, 1818, appendices 1, 3, 4. *S.C. on Illicit Distillation, 2nd Report,* 1816, *op. cit.,* pp. 121–2. *Irish Revenue Inquiry, 5th Report,* 1823, *op. cit.,* pp. 332–3. It was alleged that the resumption of fines almost banished the illicit distiller from Innishowen and that he barely survived in the Rosses region of Donegal.

Leinster included Dublin. In towns the fine was levied on the house where the offending articles were found and if it could not be recovered in full the balance fell on adjoining property. The returns show firstly that some illicit distilling occurred in most parts of Ireland and secondly, that Donegal stands out far above other counties.[47]

Mounting criticism of townland fines and their patent encouragement to lawlessness eventually convinced the Government of the futility as well as the injustice of the system. In a last effort to make the system work the Chancellor of the Exchequer presented a Bill in 1819 which he hoped would remove some of the worst features of townland fines. Under this Bill no fine would be imposed unless a complete still was found. It would no longer be possible for an informer or other ill-disposed person to split up the parts of a still and get more than one reward for planting the head and worm separately. Nor would there be any townland fines where revenue police were taking effective action and he referred specially to Innishowen where, apparently, illicit distilling was being checked. In other areas where there were no revenue police, or too few to be fully effective, townland fines would continue unless the grand jury applied to the Lord Lieutenant to proclaim the district. In that case he would appoint a chief magistrate and a chief constable with up to fifty sub-constables all armed and equipped. No townland fines were to be imposed in a proclaimed district. These constables would be part of the new constabulary which had so far shown no desire to become involved with illicit distilling and retained this attitude until this work was forced on them in 1855. The Act of 1819 provided that a barony or other district asking for the area to be proclaimed was to pay half the cost of the additional constabulary so there was no inducement to apply for them. It was a compromise Act, but it had the effect of silencing the critics especially as there was a provision that fines were to cease in 1820. They were never renewed though the final repeal was not enacted until 1831.[48]

47. *Return of Townland Fines*, Parl. Pps. 1816 (281) ix, pp. 557–62.

48. *Parl. Debates*, 20 May 1819, col. 593. The Chancellor of the Exchequer explained the purpose of the Bill which later was passed as 59 Geo. 3, c. 98. Final repeal of these fines was enacted by 1 and 2 Will. 4, c. 55, section 54. Other debates took place on 7 May 1819, cols. 253 *et seq.*, and 27 June 1819, cols. 1420–2.

The laws for suppressing illicit malting and distilling were consolidated in 1831 and the Act remained in force for the rest of the century. Among minor improvements the Act extended excise control over all kilns, including those used for drying corn for purposes other than distilling. They were now to be entered and any found unentered were to be destroyed. Kilns used for drying corn or grain were not be be used for drying malt thus meeting the case of the illicit distiller using the country kiln with the connivance or in the absence of the kiln owner.[49] Some of the preventive regulations were repeated or improved. Small stills used by chemists, for example, that were not supposed to be used to make spirits had to be licensed, a provision which is simple enough for a manufactured still, but would be difficult to enforce in cases where a retort could be made up and dismantled easily in a laboratory. However, the Act provided powers of inspection and penalties for breaches. The rules for still makers were strengthened. They had to be licensed and the maker's name and other details stamped on the breast of each still. If a small still was imported the local excise were to be promptly notified. The conveyance of any still required a permit. Thus a tinker making stills for illicit distillers would contravene a number of regulations, each with its own penalty.[50] The special powers of excise officers to search for and destroy any still, utensil or materials were extended to any justice of the peace, landlord or bailiff. The onus of proving duty payment was put on anyone possessing or conveying spirit. Further, any containers, wagons or horses used to transport illicit spirits were forfeit and forcibly obstructing an officer was a felony.[51] The Act provided for severe penalties, but permitted magistrates to mitigate them to a minimum of £6 or three months imprisonment for a first offence or double this for subsequent offences. As in former Acts the offender could go to prison and reduce his term in prison at the rate of £2 a month or £4 if not a first offender. In practice magistrates usually mitigated to the mini-

---

For reluctance of the constabulary to suppress the private still see *Excise Revenue Inquiry, 7th Report, Part I,* 1834, *op. cit.,* pp. 407–8, and *Part II,* 1835, *op. cit.,* p. 70. See also *Irish Revenue Inquiry, 5th Report,* 1823, *op. cit.,* p. 370.

49. 1 and 2 Will, 4, c. 55, sections 1–6.
50. *Ibid.,* sections 9–14.
51. *Ibid.,* sections 17–29, 48.

mum and the offender stayed in prison to suit his convenience,
buying himself out, perhaps, when the distilling season was
beginning.[52] This is a bare outline of the Act. Its terms gave the
authorities all the powers they could reasonably expect and
sufficient deterrents, but there is sometimes a wide gap between
drafting an Act and enforcing its provisions. Illicit distilling
continued to be a problem for many more years particularly in
the west and northwest.

The question arises as to why there should be this concentration
of illicit distilling in Donegal, Tyrone and to a lesser extent in
other counties in the west of Ireland. In the last two decades of
the eighteenth century the operation of the still licence duty
introduced by the Irish Government had resulted in this concentration, but this does not explain why it continued to a considerable extent for at least the next half century. So far as
terrain is a factor there were equally favoured areas in counties
like Kerry or Cork with mountain streams and turf fuel at hand
and cereals could be grown just as well as in Donegal. Illicit
distillers in the vicinity of cities like Limerick, Cork or Waterford
had a nearby good potential market. Even near Dublin there
are mountainous parts to the west and south of the city sufficiently
remote to suit the needs of illicit distillers. In all these areas the
inhabitants had no greater respect for revenue or any other laws
than the people of Donegal or Mayo. There is no single explanation that is completely satisfactory. One minor reason was the
influence of Scottish immigrants in Ulster, for illicit distilling
had been a major problem in Scotland, and their skill with small
stills; indeed at one time they were barred from obtaining a
licence to work a small still legally.[53] Another reason might be
that in Ulster and perhaps parts of north Connaught, oatmeal
was more an article of food than in other places where the potato
predominated, and oatmeal is a raw material for poteen. This is
not a convincing reason for there was a good deal of depopulation
in these parts as a result of the potato famines in 1844-5. The two

52. *Ibid.*, sections 36–42. *Excise Revenue Inquiry, 7th Report, Part I, 1834, op.
cit.*, pp. 393, 400.
53. *Irish Revenue Inquiry, 5th Report, 1823, op. cit.*, p. 379. A Treasury minute
dated 29 May 1812 directed the Board of Excise to 'allow no expert Scotch
distiller who can do rapid work'. The prohibition was primarily directed against
rapid distilling, but obviously such persons would make very useful illicit
distillers

principal reasons seem to be the power of the larger scale distilling units that developed after 1780 except in Ulster and Connaught to maintain their markets and keep the illicit distiller at bay. The second reason was the drinking preferences in the two sectors. In Ulster and much of Connaught the preference remained for malt whiskey and for the first three decades of the nineteenth century poteen was a malt spirit, but there is evidence that some illicit distillers were using some raw grain in their grist from about 1830 onwards.[54] In the rest of Ireland grain whiskey had supplanted the malt spirit that all legal distillers had to make until 1800, so much so that imported Scotch malt whiskey was difficult to sell in Dublin and any Dublin distiller who had tried making malt spirit had no success in marketing it. Coffey put the situation clearly when he wrote in 1818 that 'Donegal disliked legal spirit and Dublin and Cork disliked poteen though both may be of the same purity'. He stated that the best poteen seized could not be sold in Dublin by the excise even at 2s. 6d. a gallon below the price of legal whiskey.[55] Thus there were two distinct markets.

There still remains the puzzle of the preference for poteen in the north over the malt whiskey coming from licensed distilleries, the best known of which was at Bushmills. Price would, of course, be a factor, and not all poteen was of high quality. Among the peasantry price was probably a deciding factor, but there must be other reasons to account for so much illicit distilling. The preference probably dates from the period before 1823 when the distillery laws forced the legal distiller to work rapidly regardless of quality or economy. On the other hand the illicit distiller, unless harassed by revenue police, could take his time and thus compete successfully with the legal distiller both in quality and price. His reputation continued long after it was deserved, when the legal distiller, under better distillery laws, was able to control his operations with a view to quality. It was

54. M. Donovan, *Domestic Economy*, op. cit., i, p. 253. *Excise Revenue Inquiry, 7th Report*, 1834, op. cit., p. 446.

55. A. Coffey, *Observations on Chichester's pamphlet entitled 'The Oppressions and Cruelties of Irish Revenue Officers'*, op. cit., pp. 82–3. *Excise Revenue Inquiry, 7th Report, Part I*, 1834, op. cit., pp. 71, 377, 379. *S.C. to inquire into the Effect upon the Trade in Spirits in Ireland of the Repeal of the Malt Drawback*. Parl. Pps. 1842 (338) xiv, p. 442.

said in 1808 that not one-fiftieth of the spirit consumed in the illicit distilling areas was duty paid, but there were no licensed distillers in these areas. In 1842 the reputation of poteen was still high, though with less reason, and it seems that the gentry in Connaught and northern Ireland still preferred it.[56] In other parts of Ireland some illicit distilling occasionally arose in a few isolated places such as in Carlow, but the practice never took root. Some people thought that there was a connexion between politically disturbed areas and illicit distilling, but this is not apparent and in some notorious poteen areas there were no 'whitefeet' or other rebel movements.[57]

So far illicit distilling has been considered in its relation to licensed distilling, but both could be affected by preferences for other beverages, particularly beer. Breweries use the same raw materials and are an alternative market for the cereal grower. In 1790 there were three kinds of breweries, those making strong beer, those making small beer, and retailer-brewers. The difference between strong and small beer depended on the selling price per barrel, the latter being a weaker and probably inferior beer. In the whole of Ireland in 1790 there were 236 breweries making strong beer, fifty-five making small beer and 646 retailer-brewers. For the present purpose the breweries making small beer can be ignored as they were unlikely to affect spirit drinking. Of the strong beer breweries there were only thirty in the northwest and western counties. In the south there were fifty-nine, in the east eighty-two, and the remaining sixty-five were distributed in the midland counties. The retailer-brewers show a reverse picture for out of 646 there were 388 in the north and northwest. These would be publicans making their own beer for sale in their taverns along with spirits and their numbers indicate that the strong beer breweries in the west and northwest were not only few but that they did not have a large trade. It would not be surprising also if the retailer-brewer

56. *S.C. to inquire how far it may be practicable to confine distilleries to the use of Sugar and Molasses*, Parl. Pps. 1808 (178) iv, p. 74. *S.C. on the Malt Drawback*, 1842, *op. cit.*, p. 444.

57. *Excise Revenue Inquiry, 7th Report, Part I,* 1834, *op. cit.*, p. 410. This connexion is alleged by the inspector-general of the coast guard. On pp. 381, 396 the opposite view is taken by the excise solicitor and the collector, Galway. See also *S.C. on Constabulary functions,* 1854, *op. cit.*, p. 39.

did not, on occasion, use his apparatus to make some poteen.[58]
This background militated against the emergence of any large
brewery in this part of Ireland. In the south and east, however,
and especially in Cork and Dublin where capital was available,
large breweries were likely to arise and did, in fact, arise in the
early part of the next century. The market for beer was there
to be developed and, aided by legislation designed to favour
beer and against spirit drinking, it did expand. The development
of larger breweries was greatly assisted by the development of
canals for transporting bulky cargoes which enabled brewers
like Guinness of Dublin to penetrate into the midland counties.
Beer drinking, in Munster, in the form of porter was said by
Newenham in 1805 to be growing and this was also the opinion
of Wakefield in 1812. The trade of these large breweries with
Ulster was negligible.[59] Thus the illicit distiller in northwest
Ulster and in Connaught had to contend only with malt spirit
from legal distilleries and in many areas he was fairly safe from
molestation by revenue officials. The local farmers in these areas
had a convenient market for their cereal crops and landlords
benefited from increased rents. In the rest of Ireland the illicit
distiller had to compete with the large legal distilleries which,
after 1823, could make better quality spirit at lesser costs, and
both had to compete with the brewer. The farmer had a much
greater market for his crops and there was not the same incentive
for illicit malting for poteen; nor had the landlords the same need
for illegal practices to maintain their rents.

As the nineteenth century progressed illicit distilling varied in
intensity if the rise and fall of excise detections is used as a guide.
Some authorities related these variations to the rise or fall of
the spirit duty and obviously this would be an important factor.
Others, however, thought that grain prices were the main reason.
When examining these variations it is important to bear in mind

58. *H.C. Journal*, 27 February 1792, app. pp. 190–1. The principal brewing
excise districts were Clonmel with 10 breweries, Dublin and Dublin county 43,
Cork 20, Maryborough 14, Naas 21 and Lisburn 10. The output is not known as
the duty was in part chargeable on the malt and this revenue would be shared by
distillers' malt.

59. T. Newenham, *Statistical and Historical Inquiry into the Population of Ireland*,
op. cit., p. 234. E. Wakefield, *An Account of Ireland, Statistical and Political*, London,
1812, i, pp. 743–6. *Irish Revenue Inquiry, 5th Report*, 1823, *op. cit.*, p. 658. P. Lynch
and J. Vaizey, *Guinness's Brewery and the Irish Economy*, Cambridge, 1960, pp.
90, 93.

the markets of the illicit and legal distiller. Poteen was made with primitive apparatus, one still serving to distil both wash and low wines and fermentation imperfectly controlled. The result was generally a harsh spirit with a bad flavour. The market was mainly amongst the peasantry who would find it difficult to afford legal whiskey. Some skilled illicit distillers made poteen of good quality and they were able to sell some of their product in the market of the legal distiller. The latter, however, had no market amongst the peasantry addicted to poteen. Thus the rate of spirit duty would affect only the competition of the few skilled illicit distillers and legal distillers. The bulk of illicit distillers would only be marginally affected by variations in the duty. Changes in grain prices would have a much greater effect on illicit distilling. Cheap grain prices would be a great incentive for farmers to sell to illicit distillers nearby rather than transport it to market; or else convert the grain into spirit which is more easily transported if the farmer could get a market for it. In places like Londonderry this market did exist, but in country areas the market for illicit spirit was very limited. With high grain prices, a sure market for his crops would reduce the desire to make poteen. The risk of seizure also had to be taken into account. The Galway and Londonderry collectors of excise gave their opinion that when grain prices fell the illicit distiller prospered, when the prices rose he failed and might even be driven out of business. A similar view was expressed by others. Thus a good harvest was expected in 1854 with consequent low grain prices and revenue officials were apprehensive that there would follow an increase in illicit distilling. The Commissioners of the Revenue Inquiry in 1834 thought the rate of duty was the dominating factor, but the Inland Revenue Board reviewing a longer period, reported in 1870 that 'there have been constant variations in the extent of smuggling in Ireland, without any other apparent cause than an abundant or deficient crop'.[60]

The following figures give the relationship between barley prices, rate of duty and the illicit stills seized from 1830 to 1840 when the rate of duty rose and fell within the limits of 1s. a gallon and when illicit distilling was rife. The barley prices are

---

60. *Irish Revenue Inquiry, 5th Report*, 1823, pp. 308–9. *Excise Revenue Inquiry, 7th Report, Part I*, 1834, *op. cit.*, pp. 84, 86, 393–5. *S.C. on Constabulary functions*, 1854, *op. cit.*, p. 37. *13th Inland Revenue Report*, Parl. Pps. 1870 (c. 82) xx, p. 234.

the average for all Ireland and therefore no more than a guide since it would be the local prices that would matter. Seizures also are merely a guide for they only represent success or otherwise of the excise authorities.[61]

Year	Barley per quarter	Rate of duty	Seizures
1830	31s. 7d.	2s. 10d.–3s. 4d.	804
1831	38s.	3s. 4d.	723
1832	33s.	3s. 4d.	974
1833	27s. 6d.	3s. 4d.	1,549
1834	29s.	3s. 4d.–2s. 4d.	1,525
1835	29s. 11d.	2s. 4d.	956
1836	32s. 10d.	2s. 4d.	590
1837	30s. 4d.	2s. 4d.	395
1838	31s. 5d.	2s. 4d.	368
1839	39s. 6d.	2s. 5d.	168
1840	36s. 5d.	2s. 4d.–2s. 8d.	148

It will be apparent that during this period there is a strong correlation between grain prices and seizures and a weaker connexion between the rate of duty and seizures, which rather supports the views of the Board of Inland Revenue in 1870. In the latter half of the century illicit distilling dwindled away until the figures for seizures, which look so impressive, really represented a great many trivial offences, or even no offences at all because of manufactured cases for purposes of reward.[62]

The full impact of the distillery Act of 1823 in the illicit distilling areas was almost dramatic. The legal distilling industry, released from the tyranny of speed, soon expanded. In 1822 there were only two small licensed distilleries in the Galway excise

61. The figures are taken from the report of the *S.C. on Constabulary functions*, 1854, pp. 284, 363. A similar pattern continued in the next decade. Thus in 1847 the price of barley rose to 44s. 2d. a quarter and seizures were 132, but in 1850 when the price fell seizures rose to 518. The duty was constant at 2s. 8d. During these latter years the revenue police were reorganised and the extent of illicit distilling was falling.

62. *13th Inland Revenue Report*, 1870, op. cit., p. 235; *23rd Report*, Parl. Pps. 1880 (c. 2770) xxix, p. 96. *Parl. Debates*, 15 July 1902, cols. 341–9.

district, three in Londonderry, one in Coleraine and one in
Buncrana. In no case did any of these stills exceed 100 gallons
content. Most were making grain spirit and all were operating
on a scale comparable with the host of illicit distillers around
them. Ten years later there had been increases in the spirit duties
from 2s. 4d. to 3s. 4d. a gallon, yet despite this rise the new laws
had resulted in four licensed distilleries in the Galway excise
district, six in the Londonderry district, six in Coleraine and
four in Sligo. The sizes of the stills are not known since they no
longer had any relation to the spirit duty charged, but their
production far exceeded that of the licensed distilleries in 1822.
One of these distilleries, established at Burt in the barony of
Innishowen, was producing 40,000 to 50,000 gallons a year. This
is not a large quantity for a licensed distillery in 1832, but its
situation was such that it could not have been in closer competition with the heart of illicit distilling.[63]

In a most thorough and searching inquiry over about three
years the Commissioners appointed by parliament gave a great
deal of their attention in 1834-5 to the problem of illicit distilling
in Ireland. They heard evidence from licensed distillers that
poteen tended to be better than legal whiskey and a few excise
officials supported this claim to the limited extent that some
poteen reached the standards of legal whiskey. In the latter case
this opinion might well have been merely a preference for a
malt whiskey and poteen could only be fairly compared with a
Bushmills or similar spirit and not the normal Irish mixed grain
whiskey. The claim by the Irish distillers was, however, on a
different basis. They were now saying in 1834 that their product
was inferior despite the advantages of the Act of 1823. These
same distillers had said before 1823 that they could produce
superior whiskey and this during the former system of rapid
working. This apparent admission of inefficiency was simply a
means of pressing a case for reducing the spirit duty on the plea
that they could better compete with poteen, so their opinions
on the merits of poteen should be treated with some scepticism.
The Inquiry Commissioners seem to have ignored these opinions,

63. *Irish Revenue Inquiry, 5th Report,* 1823, *op. cit.,* p. 369. *Excise Revenue Inquiry, 7th Report, Part I,* 1834, *op. cit.,* pp. 232-4, 423. An excise district, now known as a collection, comprised a large area round the headquarters town and the distilleries quoted were not necessarily in the towns named.

Instead they concentrated on the existence of the revenue police and probed witnesses to support their disapproval of this force. The distillers got their way and on the recommendation of the Commission the duty was reduced from 3s. 4d. to 2s. 4d. a gallon, but it made little difference to illicit distilling. So narrow was this concentration on the revenue police that the Commissioners were trapped into making the surprising statement that 'distilling is not in itself an offence and the force is used exclusively against a class of offence which are offences merely because of transgressions of the law'.[64]

There may have been several reasons for the Inquiry Commissioners' dislike of the revenue police. There was no similar body in other parts of the United Kingdom, but then Ireland had a unique problem in 1834. Also the calibre of men in the force was not good. If, however, illicit distilling was an evil to be suppressed there must be some agency to do it. In the early part of the century the excise officer using military support had failed and the revenue police was an alternative. No help was given either by the constabulary or the coastguard which at that time had shore based parties as well as revenue cruisers patrolling off-shore islands. Both forces feared unpopularity though it is not easy to agree that combatting smuggling was higher in popularity than still hunting.[65] No doubt the criticisms made led to the reorganisation of the revenue police by Colonel Brereton in 1836. Elderly or incompetent men were discarded, a proper training depot established in Dublin and a new structure of command among the police parties set up. The force quickly became an effective instrument against the illicit distiller and seizures of complete stills fell rapidly. In 1835 there were 956 stills seized, but by 1840 the number had fallen to 148 without any change in the rate of duty. The number of detections is a less reliable guide as these would include numerous trivial offences and probably a good many cases of discovery of abandoned or

64. *Ibid.*, pp. 79, 204–5, 407 are a few examples of opinions on the quality of poteen. Condemnation of the revenue police appears in *Part II*, 1835, *op. cit.*, pp. 59–65. The quotation appears on pp. 59–60. This lapse by the Inquiry Commissioners was exceptional. Their reports were of the highest quality. In parliamentary debates on 3 December 1852 Disraeli described them as 'the most valuable documents in our Parliamentary library'.

65. *Excise Revenue Inquiry, 7th Report, Part II*, 1835, *op. cit.*, pp. 60–1, 63, 69. See also *S.C. on Constabulary functions*, 1854, *op. cit.*, pp. 6, 15, 23, 64, 276–9.

planted worn out still parts, but nevertheless detections fell from 4,904 to 1,004.[66] Brereton claimed that the reorganised force put a stop to gangs of illicit distillers operating in open defiance of the law and therefore had stopped violence and it is true that after 1840 there were no more reports of armed conflict with the authorities. Brereton did concede that small scale illicit distilling still prevailed, but it was no longer a threat to the legal distiller. The private still had been driven into the wilder parts of the country with greater risks in marketing the poteen beyond a small area around the scene of operations. One result from this success was that the rate of duty began to climb. There was a small rise to 2s. 8d. in 1840. By 1855 the rate had risen to 6s. 2d. a proof gallon and by 1858 to 8s., equalling the rate in Great Britain.[67]

It required constant vigilance by the revenue police to keep illicit distilling subdued. The threat of a reversion to wholesale illicit practices was never far distant and from time to time the Treasury were asked to increase the size of the force. By 1852 it had reached 1,100 officers and men, all accoutred, armed and trained on the pattern of light infantry and living in numbers of small barracks. They got no assistance from the police or customs and even the excise officers in localities where the revenue police operated took no further interest in illicit distilling. Their very success began to raise the question of continuing the force. As they overcame the illicit practices so the force became uneconomic since they could turn to no other duties. The Government began to ask whether the constabulary doing peace duties in the same areas should not include illicit distilling and also why the customs should not assist. The first move was a Treasury direction that the customs coastguard were to help suppressing illicit distilling in an area within six miles of the coast. Then a Select Committee examined the possible use of the constabulary who already covered all the country for every other kind of crime. These moves resulted in disbanding the revenue police and handing over their duties to the constabulary. The personnel

66. *S.C. on Constabulary functions*, 1854, *op. cit.*, pp. 4, 7–9, 284. *13th Inland Revenue Report*, 1870, *op. cit.*, p. 390.

67. *S.C. on Constabulary functions*, 1854, pp. 9, 28. *13th Inland Revenue Report*, 1870, p. 387. Food shortages from about 1838 onwards may have helped the satisfactory revenue results. 21 Vict., c. 15, section 1.

were either pensioned off or merged into the constabulary. The police were given the powers of excise officers in relation to illicit distilling and this situation continues to the present day.[68]

The new arrangement did not escape criticism, which may have been inspired, so strong were the constabulary objections to doing this work. A member of parliament alleged that 'one of the most deep rooted feelings in Ireland was a hatred of the exciseman, and to make the same body of men both policemen and revenue officers was calculated to render the police peculiarly obnoxious in the eyes of the people'. Another member thought that if police came upon poteen 'instead of destroying a seizure they would drink it'. The amalgamation of the forces was, however, a good move and with a force of some 12,500 deployed over the whole country illicit distilling had little chance of ever reviving to become the menace it was in the first three decades of the century. The revenue police had broken the distillers' resistance for convictions fell from 1,100 persons in 1849 to 140 in 1856 and the constabulary took over a waning task in 1857.[69]

In the early years of the century shebeens were a part of the illicit distilling scene. They were to be found everywhere in Ireland and sold both legal and illicit spirit, the latter being their main trade in parts like Donegal. These houses of 'entertainment' were usually found on the outskirts of towns and advertised their trade by hanging up some turf outside. Some legal spirit received on permit would normally be kept on the premises as a cover for poteen. The customers in shebeens were beggars, itinerant dealers and similar characters and the shebeen, therefore, was not wholly disliked by the licensed publican since it drew off unwelcome drinkers. Clearly the suppression of the shebeen was as much in the interest of both the revenue and the constabulary as was the illicit distiller. The revenue interest in shebeens was very

68. *Excise Revenue Inquiry, 7th Report, Part II,* 1835, *op. cit.,* p. 60. *S.C. on Constabulary functions,* 1854, pp. 70, 78–81, 83, 94, 265–8, 354. On p. 26 it is stated that the revenue police acquired their own steamer to visit islands. The Acts governing the changes were 17 and 18 Vict., c. 89, sections 6, 13–16; and 20 and 21 Vict., c. 40, section 7. See *Parl. Debates,* 17 July 1857, cols. 1683–4.

69. *Parl. Debates,* 27 July 1857, cols. 415–7. *S.C. on Constabulary functions,* 1854, *op. cit.,* p. 301. See also p. 347. In 1834 the four provincial inspectors–general of constabulary seem to have based their objection to suppressing illicit distilling on the supervision of local constabulary by magistrates. The magistrates were mostly landed gentry and many got better rents because of illicit distilling. The constabulary, therefore, might become unpopular with the magistrates.

much reduced as the quality of legal whiskey improved because from about 1830 the shebeen owner could buy legal spirit from a publican at 25° over proof whereas his illicit supplies might be as much as 12° under proof by the time the illicit distiller had reduced his spirit for marketing. By watering down the legal spirit to the level of the poteen it would cost the shebeener no more.[70]

As in the case of illicit distilling the constabulary were very reluctant to take strong action against shebeens and relied on an alleged gap in the law as their reason. The laws relating to spirits up to 1854 gave the excise power to search for illicit spirits wherever it was suspected that they may be stored, including private premises, but the revenue police rarely exercised these powers to inspect shebeens on the grounds that it would take them away from their primary duty of still hunting. In any case their interest was limited as some or all spirit being sold might well be duty paid. The excise ride officer apparently did not pursue the fact that no licence duty was paid, possibly because to do so single handed might not be safe.[71] The constabulary maintained that they had no right to entry because a shebeen was, after all, a private dwelling. If they desired entry it was necessary to get a justice's warrant which, according to their regulations would only be granted to a sub-inspector or chief constable. If after these preliminaries the constabulary visited a shebeen they had their entry obstructed long enough to allow customers time to hide their drinks and also to claim that they were lodgers. Sometimes forty or fifty might be in a shebeen. Under government pressure there was correspondence between the Treasury, Inland Revenue and Constabulary and it was ruled that evidence of sale was not essential and that a constable's evidence of the reputation of the house and the presence of spirit intended for sale was sufficient. Fear of becoming unpopular as well as difficulties of gaining entry and establishing proof of unlicensed sales seems to have obsessed some of the police officials. They certainly regarded the suppression of shebeens as necessary in the interests of keeping the peace, but their view was that a shebeen owner was not regarded by the people as a smuggler and any constable visiting the house was thought to

70. *Ibid.*, pp. 11, 32, 45, 56.
71. *Ibid.*, pp. 32, 56.

be an excise informer. The desire seems to have been to put the
duty wholly on the excise. This unsatisfactory position was
cleared up by the Act authorising the constabulary to undertake
the suppression of illicit distilling which included clauses laying
a duty on them to be more active against the shebeen. The combination of better legal spirit and the extension of repressive
measures to the constabulary virtually ended the shebeen.[72] The
effect of these unlicensed sales on legal distilling and selling had
declined to almost vanishing point by 1854. There was a resur-
gence of shebeens from time to time, for example, following the
Sunday Closing Act in 1878, but it was of no real importance
and had little effect on legitimate trade.[73]

The annual reports to parliament by the Commissioners of
Inland Revenue from 1856 to 1909 and of the Commissioners of
Customs and Excise after 1909 give the numbers of detections
relating to illicit distilling in each of the three countries in the
United Kingdom. Detections in Ireland are out of all proportion
with those of the other two countries. In 1900, for example,
there were 1,828 in Ireland and only twelve in England and five
in Scotland. In the latter countries any illicit distilling was
handled entirely by the excise. The numbers of detections in
Ireland for each tenth year before the political division of the
country are:

1860	— 2,396	1900	— 1,828
1870	— 2,215	1910	— 1,139
1880	— 685	1920	— 947
1890	— 1,819	1922	— 172

Two important points should be borne in mind. Firstly, these are
detections of all kinds, not stills at work, and could range from
a small bottle of illicit spirits to a complete still with utensils and
materials. Secondly, the Revenue Commissioners reported in
1880 that the detections were mainly trivial so that the numbers
do not represent the extent of illicit distilling. Two essentials
are necessary to assess this, the number of stills seized and the
number of persons convicted of actually distilling. There is no
information on either point. In relation to the distillery industry

72. *Ibid.,* pp. 56, 99, 108, 166, 217–20. 17 and 18 Vict., c. 89, sections 2–5.
73. 41 and 42 Vict., c. 72. *Royal Commission on the Liquor Licensing Laws:
Evidence taken in Ireland.* Parl. Pps. 1898 (8980) xxxviii, p. 598.

the Revenue Commissioners reported in 1870 that the consumers of illicit spirit were too poor to buy duty paid spirit and that such illicit distilling as did occur did not affect the revenue yield.[74]

A system of rewards had always been a basic feature in the preventive measures against illicit distilling and was always an administrative problem. In fixing a scale of payment a balance had to be struck between the advantages of incentives to the staff and informers against the abuses of fictitious detections. If rewards were generous, abuses would arise; if niggardly, the private still would be safer. Until the middle of the nineteenth century indifferent recruitment of staff, low pay and arduous working hours all contributed to a poor sense of civic duty and rewards were a severe and almost irresistible temptation to indulge in dishonest practices. Efficient supervision was essential. Thus the still hunter was in turn hunted, but not very efficiently in the first half of the century. Later, when the constabulary took over the duty of suppressing the private still the Revenue Commissioners continued to pay rewards to police, but had no control over the validity of claims. There is at least a strong suspicion that supervision within the constabulary over rewards paid by another body for work which at first many thought was not police work, was not very strict. The scale of rewards for the revenue police in 1830 was:

Still head and worm with worts and vessels £3 3s.
Still and head £2 2s.
Still 10s.
Head or worm 5s.
Pot-ale or worts and vessels £1 1s.

There were also smaller rewards per bushel of malt destroyed or brought to store. The lieutenant of the party received one-third and the rest of the party shared the remainder equally. These rates were reduced by one-third in 1830 and with small modifications were the rates paid to the constabulary. From time to time

74. *Inland Revenue Reports*, *5th*, Parl. Pps. 1861 (2877) xxxi, p. 113; *13th Report*, P.P. 1870 (c. 82) xx, p. 235; *14th Report*, P.P. 1871 (c. 370) xvii, p. 657; *23rd Report*, P.P. 1880 (c. 2770) xxix, p. 96; *34th Report*, P.P. 1890–1 (c. 6537) xxvi, p. 317; *44th Report*, P.P. 1901 (Cd. 764) xviii, p. 460; *Customs and Excise Reports*, *2nd*, 1911 (Cd. 5827) xv, p. 215/28. *12th Report*, P.P. 1921 (Cmd. 1435), p. 60.

there were allegations that because of rewards it did not pay the enforcement officers to press the illicit distiller too hard or put him out of business. It was in their interest to 'scotch the snake, not kill it.'[75]

The very large number of detections in Ireland, reported annually by the Inland Revenue, as compared with the rest of the United Kingdom, was bound to attract criticism. Appearing before a Select Committee of the House of Commons in 1890 the Chairman of the Inland Revenue Board said that 'for the most part these cases are very small, but they are detections, and that they were mostly 'wretched little cases'. He was repeating the view of the Board in 1880. By 1901 the reward system and the distorted picture given by merely quoting detections came under severe criticism. The Chancellor of the Exchequer stated in 1901 that rewards ranged from 6s. to 10s. but were sometimes £2 to £3. He refuted allegations that large numbers of seizures were manufactured for purposes of reward, but he refused information of details essential for the critics, including the number of persons charged, the actual rewards paid, prosecutions and results.[76]

In the following year Irish members of parliament again attacked the statistics of illicit distilling detections. It was said that constables persuaded persons to establish illicit stills, probably men of the vagrant class. One member alleged that one seized still was used over and over again to provide for 200 seizures and gave the name of the place privately to Chamberlain, then Chancellor of the Exchequer, who admitted that the problem was new to him. He did say, however, that the Board of Inland Revenue and the Constabulary had assured him that there were no malpractices. Naturally this was not accepted by the critics. Chamberlain still refused detailed information, but went so far as to admit that many seizures were of a trivial kind and that it would be 'an abuse of language to call them illicit stills'. He also admitted that many of the trivial cases did not justify any reward and there was not sufficient endeavour to bring home cases. A member for Cork remarked that he was sure that Chamberlain

75. *Excise Revenue Inquiry, 7th Report, Part I*, 1834, *op. cit.*, pp. 239, 445.

76. *S.C. on British and Foreign Spirits*, Parl. Pps. 1890 (316) x, p. 499. *Parl. Debates*, 7 June 1901, col. 1339; 25 November 1901, cols. 1410–11.

'did not know what an illicit still was', and that the whiskey produced was vile. It was so easy to plant still parts or materials for reward. All that was necessary to get a reward was to find them on unenclosed land so that nobody was amenable and there would be no prosecution or any other inquiry. Some 'inside' information appears in the *Revenue Review*, a journal privately published and circulated in the excise service and not under the control of the Board of Inland Revenue. It is stated that of the 1,828 detections in 1900 there followed only twenty prosecutions, a clear indication that the extent of illicit distilling was very much smaller than would be supposed from the numbers of detections. It was said in parliament that ever since the Irish constabulary had replaced the revenue police the planting of stills and parts had been going on and it appears that the Chief Secretary for Ireland had in 1901 admitted that the charges against the police were well founded.[77] *The Revenue Review* reported that the allegations in parliament had at least caused one genuine seizure of a still complete with worm and utensils in south Londonderry. It also reported the conviction in Mayo of a householder where a bottle containing a trace of poteen was found in his field, but does not know how the prosecution proved that this was illicit spirit. Correspondence published was from excise supervisors and others stationed in Ireland and in close touch with the police and inhabitants. One supervisor wrote that two constables on patrol found a pint bottle of illicit whiskey in a newly made hole on an unenclosed mountain. Nobody was, or could be, made amenable, but a reward of £2 was paid. Another supervisor throws light on illicit distilling in 1902. He wrote that stills of twenty gallons content were used, running some twenty to forty gallons of wash. Very little reached publicans as it was nearly all drunk on the spot by persons who would not be able to buy spirits otherwise. He also wrote that he had often been told by policemen that they would 'not press so-and-so too hard or he would give up'. He did not blame the constabulary so much as the system of rewards that encouraged

77. *The Revenue Review*, ii, July 1902, p. 356. Edited by J. T. Mulqueen, Inspector of Inland Revenue, printed in Falkirk. *Parl. Debates*, 14 April 1902, col. 155; 15 July 1902, cols. 341–9. The second debate followed a motion to reduce the vote of the Board of Inland Revenue. Rewards were totalling £3,000 a year.

these practices.[78] The system of rewards was revised. There were to be no rewards for discovering still parts or small quantities of liquor, but a considerable area remained for abuse. For example, illicit distillers, who were no more than vagrants as a rule, could still be cultivated as before. On rare occasions a worthwhile discovery was made, not always in mountain wastes. An illicit still was found at work in Little Donegal Street, Belfast, on 13 August 1902 together with twenty five gallons of singlings, ten gallons of proof spirit and 176 gallons of wash.[79] In relation to the legal whiskey being produced in the city this was infinitesimal, but it was news, and that seems to be the picture elsewhere. In the early part of the century only an exceptional seizure was reported and it is some indication of the prevalance of the private still that it was not 'news' at that period.

The three principal objections to rewards are (*a*) that it is wrong in principle to reward an official for doing his duty and indirectly gives the idea that still detections are outside ordinary duties; (*b*) that hope of reward may result in oppressive treatment of citizens; and (*c*) that they may lead to special attention to work leading to rewards and the neglect of other work. There was no reason to regard illicit distilling detections as different to larceny or any other police duty and this is now the case. Fewer detections are made and rewards are very restricted.

Looking back over the history of illicit distilling it is clear that it emerged from domestic distilling when duties on spirits were imposed in the seventeenth century and that such distilling was widespread in most parts of the country till the late eighteenth century. After 1780 there was a fairly rapid change in this picture owing to the introduction of the still licence charge on legal stills and a steady increase in the number of these charges. In the northwest and west the small legal stills were displaced by the illicit distiller and in the rest of the country there was severe competition between the legal distiller evading the duty and the illicit distiller, with the former generally winning. Nevertheless in the whole of Ireland at this time large quantities were coming

78. *The Revenue Review*, i, September 1901, pp. 434–5; November 1901, pp. 578–9. In ii August 1902, p. 422 it reports an inquiry being opened at Castlebar against 3 district inspectors and 4 constables accused of not destroying seized stills and later planting them for re-discovery.

79. *The Belfast Newsletter*, 22 August 1902.

from illicit stills and they were a real threat to the legitimate industry as well as the revenue. There was a turning point in 1823 when the method of charging duty was changed though it is very doubtful if this was realised at the time. Licensed distillers could use better apparatus and increase the size of their operations. Their produce, too, was greatly improved and their working much more economical. Licensed distilleries were established in notorious illicit distilling areas and competed successfully. Better methods for suppressing the private still were evolved, the revenue police strengthened and reorganised, and the illicit distiller driven into remote areas where he was harassed first by the revenue police and later by the constabulary. The illicit distiller degenerated into a small-time distiller with a strictly local market generally of persons who could not afford to buy legal whiskey. In the latter half of the nineteenth century any threat to the distilling industry from illicit distillers had disappeared. Detections were, for the most part, trivial cases of no more consequence than poaching. So far as the distilling industry was concerned, illicit distilling could be ignored.[80] The industry's main competitors were, as fundamentally they had always been, the spirit importer and the brewer.

In the present century the story of illicit distilling is devoid of much interest except to the romantic and the tourist. It makes interesting material for the fiction writer, but the illicit distiller himself generally belongs to the itinerant class or is a local odd job man. Sometimes he is a farmer with a small holding. His spirit trade is entirely local and very small. The penalties in relation to his financial standing are heavy; up to £50 fine for a first offence and double thereafter in the Republic of Ireland. This penalty also applies to anyone having materials for making illicit spirit. Poteen made from malt and grain would be a rarity today. The usual base for poteen is treacle and in the Republic its sale has been controlled in poteen areas. The spirit is cheap, sold to people of very limited means and in one sense it has a

---

80. K. H. Connell, *Illicit Distillation: An Irish Peasant Industry,* Historical Studies, III, 1961. An account is given of illicit distilling practices and the position of the illicit distiller in Irish peasant life. W. Carleton, *Traits and Stories of the Irish Peasantry,* Dublin, 1846. The story of *Bob Pentland* is a good tale about illicit distilling which has an authentic ring about it and is obviously based on first-hand knowledge.

social value because otherwise some of these consumers might resort to methylated spirits. Poteen has a limited appeal to tourists. Some will buy the stuff at a high price compared to its proper value and in a suitable atmosphere of secrecy. It is displayed with pride to friends at home and drunk with the same relish as a boy eating stolen immature apples.[81]

Statistics of illicit distillation obviously give only a partial picture, but they do put the extent of the problem in perspective. Until very recently official reports gave the number of detections, but these can include anything from the discovery of a glass of poteen to a full scale plant. The few stills found have been very small and inefficient. Detections in all Ireland in 1930 were 436. In 1950 they had fallen to 74 despite the great increase in spirit duties. What is more significant, however, is the number of convictions and this is the figure now officially recorded. The total in 1960 for both parts of Ireland was twenty. In that year there were 170 detections in the Republic alone. Thus it is clear that detections are not a reliable guide to the extent of illicit distillation. One indication that the practice is small is evident from newspapers. Wholly unimportant seizures appear as news items in papers with more than local circulation. Very occasionally there is a news value unrelated to the size of the seizure. For example, in December 1957, D. Finch, a Bangor jeweller, was making illicit spirit in his flat, perhaps for Christmas. He left his plant working for a short time and there was an overflow which seeped through to the office of the local newspaper below. A visit from the office disclosed the still and the police were called. Even the bath was in use to hold the wash.[82]

Illicit distilling is likely to persist as long as there is a duty on spirits. It is poor stuff compared with the legal article, but it is cheap and will always have its advocates who will praise it with the zeal of eccentrics.

81. 1924 No. 62, sec. 26. *Dail Debates*, vol. 7, 20 June 1924, cols. 2787–8; vol. 22, 20 February 1928, col. 466.

82. *Annual Reports of the Revenue Commissioners*, Dublin, and the *Customs and Excise*, London. *Belfast Newsletter*, 12 December 1957.

CHAPTER XI

CONCLUSIONS

IRISH distilling and the spirit trade for more than two centuries has had to develop within the rigid framework of revenue laws designed not only to counteract fraud, but to restrain the activities of distillers and discourage consumption in the interests of public morals. Its history, therefore, is so inseparable from these laws that it is also a history of revenue administration. Unlike other industries, government controls over manufacture and marketing cannot be treated as on the fringe of the story. With spirits these controls become an intimate part of the industry at all stages.

Whiskey is, and always has been, the solid foundation of the Irish distilling industry, but it is well to bear in mind that, over the centuries, there have been great changes in the product itself. The usquebagh of the seventeenth and much of the next century would be considered almost unpotable today. Early writers described it as fiery, virulent spirit requiring raisins and other additions to make it drinkable. As the art and knowledge of distilling improved, so the spirit approached our conception of whiskey. For a long time, however, imported rum and brandy were better beverages and more popular. By the early nineteenth century the modern whiskey was emerging, particularly when made from a mash of malted barley and unmalted cereals, but it was marketed with little, if any, maturing. Whiskey a few months old was regarded as a special treat. These harsh, immature whiskeys would certainly not find favour today. The mild, blended whiskey now so much preferred would have been treated with disdain by our ancestors who wanted something with a bite in it and well flavoured; something that would stand use as a base for punch as well as a drink in its own right.

A history of the Irish distilling industry suffers more than the record of most other industries from the lack of sources of information, and also the difficulty of separating folklore from fact. Travellers' tales have to be treated with some reserve and stories about poteen especially, often display more imagination than truth. Before the nineteenth century there were no substantial distilling concerns. The vast majority were one-man affairs, and these small distilleries frequently changed ownership. In a few cases distilleries of the late eighteenth century developed into large undertakings and a little of their early beginnings can be unearthed. For the rest there is nothing except a few names. Almost the only sources until the late eighteenth century were the laws, parliamentary papers and similar official documents. Even parliamentary debates in Ireland were not recorded until 1780. Information from private sources, novels and the like, was sparse indeed. As the nineteenth century progressed, much more information came from these latter sources, sometimes from distillers themselves, particularly in their evidence before official inquiries. Newspapers and books also swell our knowledge. Thus the pattern of this history shows a marked reliance on distillery laws, excise returns, House of Commons journals and similar material during the early years. Information from a wider field developed later.

The features which, perhaps, catch the attention most are the fraudulent practices of distillers and spirit dealers, and the overt corruption of officials until about the middle of the nineteenth century; the growth and wane of illicit distilling; and some of the disastrous attempts by governments to frustrate the various ways of evading the malt and spirit duties. When passing judgement on these features it is well to bear in mind the conditions of the time, the state of technical knowledge and the level of civic morality. The fees and bribes openly demanded and paid to revenue officers in the eighteenth and early nineteenth centuries were not so outrageous as they appear, for they occurred in an era when similar practices were common in public life from the highest office holder to the doorkeeper. At the time, fraudulent practices in trade usually excited no comment and brought no disgrace unless there was some exceptional feature. A fraud against the revenue would be regarded as almost legitimate and was so widespread that distillers found fraud necessary in order to keep in business. On the other hand, the revenue from spirits was growing so important that governments were bound to take strong legal measures though, because of ineffective execution, these were only partially successful. The same atmosphere extended to the commerce in spirits where various forms of adulteration were practised such as adding vitriol in order to give the spirit a spurious strength. Distillers had no difficulty in selling spirits that had evaded the duty if they accommodated on the price, and the relative permit was manipulated by both the distiller and spirit dealer, often with the active assistance of the gauger who would be suitably rewarded. In this environment the stringent laws and severe penalties were rendered almost useless. Witness, for example, the smuggling of brandy through Dublin with the full knowledge of the Revenue Commissioners; or the fact that a regular scale of bribes to excise officers had the connivance of the Revenue Board.[1] Only occasionally was there a stand to curb these evils, and then it came from within the industry when these practices became intolerable as, for instance, when distillers in County Cork made a pact to refrain from revenue frauds and report to the excise if they became aware of them. This pact was not very successful for frauds were discovered in Midleton, despite the pact.[2]

Illicit distilling has always carried an aura of romance which it scarcely deserves. Some illicit spirit was of good quality, but most of it, because of the techniques employed, must have been poor in comparison with legal whiskey. The practice was a natural outcome of early domestic distilling and for much of the eighteenth century the distinction between illicit spirits and spirits from registered distillers that had evaded duty was blurred. Until late in the eighteenth century it was perfectly legal for a householder to possess a twelve-gallon still and make spirits for his own consumption without paying duty. He did not even have to register his still with the excise until 1763. Obviously it would be difficult to stop such spirits having a wider consumption than the household, and there was no real difference between these spirits and those made by the illicit distiller in the mountainous bogs. The privilege disappeared in 1779 when the minimum size of all stills was fixed at 200 gallons. From then on

1. J. A. Froude, *The English in Ireland in the Eighteenth century*, London, 1874, i, pp. 448–9. *Inquiry into Fees, Gratuities and Emoluments . . . received in Public Offices in Ireland*, 5th Report, Parl. Pps., 1806–7 (124) vi, p. 153.
2. *Inquiry into the Excise Establishment and . . . Revenue throughout the United Kingdom*, 7th Report, Part I, Parl. Pps. 1834 (7) xxv, p. 267. Frauds in Kilkenny appear on p. 268.

all distillers had to be licensed and the unlicensed distiller was outlawed, whether the still was in a mansion or on the mountain.[3]

Extensive illicit distilling as distinct from the illegal spirit manufacture in legal stills really became a serious problem after 1780 when the still licence duty was imposed.[4] The Government had the laudable intention of encouraging larger manufacturing units and eliminating small distilleries. This did result, but it forced large numbers of these distillers into the ranks of the illicit distillers and there is no indication that this was anticipated by the Government. They certainly had no adequate machinery for dealing with the problem. The full effects of this unexpected result was mainly felt in the northwest and west of Ireland where, for topographical reasons, large-scale distilling was impracticable. Distilling in these regions was an outlet for cereal crops, frequently from poor land and, therefore, it continued illicitly. In the early part of the nineteenth century the revenue police force was created and severe punitive measures to suppress illicit distilling drove the unlicensed distiller into remote places. Eventually the principle consumers were mainly confined to those who could not afford legal whiskey. One writer, describing poteen-making in Connemara in 1824, stated that it was the custom 'for all neighbours to attend when a still is run off and never quit until all is consumed'.[5] In these circumstances it is fair to assume that, after about 1830, illicit distilling had very little effect on the main distilling industry. In general, the unlicensed distiller was 'a man of straw' drawn from the lowest social strata and well used to periods in gaol for his activities. He was sometimes merely the tool of wealthier persons, greedy to get better rents from their lands.

3. The registration of 12 gallon stills was enacted by 3 Geo. 3, c. 21, section 6. 31 Geo. 2, c. 6, section 8, imposed a minimum of 200 gallons on the size of stills from 1758, but exempted the 12 gallon household still. The exemption lapsed when all stills had to be 200 gallons or more under 19 and 20 Geo. 3, c. 12, section 30.

4. A number of historians have assumed that illicit distilling prevailed to a great extent before 1780. Thus A. E. Murray, *Commercial and Financial Relations between England and Ireland*, London, 1903, p. 287, writing on the late eighteenth century comments that 'illicit distilling was probably more widespread in earlier years'. The evidence available is far from conclusive. Revenue statistics before and after 1780 do indicate that much spirit evaded duty at legal distilleries in the earlier period.

5. Hely Dutton, *Statistical Survey of the County of Galway*, Dublin, 1824, pp. 368–9.

Despite the decreasing importance of poteen as a threat to the legal distillers, to such an extent that even the shebeens preferred buying duty-paid whiskey, while the threat was real, the industry had reason to be grateful to the illicit distiller. He was always there as a potential danger if the Government thought of raising the spirit duties.[6] It was not till after the middle of the nineteenth century that this threat had receded sufficiently for the duties to be raised until they reached the level of those in Great Britain. In the latter part of the century the poteen maker was merely a social evil that could be restrained by ordinary police methods. Today poteen is no more a threat to the legal distiller of whiskey than methylated spirits. To the journalist, illicit distilling is always good for a story.

Other less spectacular, but more important features, affected both distillers and the revenue authorities. From the revenue standpoint probably the earliest effective measure was in 1761 when all distillers had to enter their premises with the excise. It gave the gauger a much firmer grip on the distilling going on in his locality. This entry was elaborated from time to time until the gauger was fully informed, not only of all those legally distilling spirits, but exactly what plant was being used.[7] One of the most important innovations affecting both the revenue and the distiller occurred in 1804 when Irish spirits could be deposited without paying duty in customs warehouses. The warehousing system had modest beginnings but developed over the next seventy years, sometimes against official resistance, to a point where the spirits could be stored duty-free in privately owned warehouses under official supervision. The spirits could be bought and sold, bottled and generally prepared for the consumer market, the duty being levied only on the quantity delivered to the home market. Dealers could also operate in bond on a large scale. This single facility enabled large quantities to be made for stock to be released to the consumer market in an orderly, regulated manner. Distillers could plan their production two or more years ahead. Indeed, large-scale distilling units

6. This restraint to raising spirit duties was brought out on several occasions in parliament. Thus in *Parliamentary Debates,* 6 May 1836, col. 669, the Chancellor of the Exchequer said that 'the only plan is to fix the duty below the insurance on smuggling'. He was referring to illicit distilling when he used the term 'smuggling'.

7. 1 Geo. 3, c. 7, section 7.

could not have operated economically without duty-free warehousing. The beneficial effect of the system in helping to build
up an overseas trade cannot be over-stressed. These large stocks
were there, ready for shipment as soon as a foreign order was
received. Within the United Kingdom the warehousing system
gave a much greater freedom in the intercourse of spirits between
Ireland and Great Britain before the duties in the three countries
were equalised and the trade was completely freed. The revenue
authorities, slow at first to realise the full importance of the
system as an aid to effective revenue control, finally acknowledged
its value, especially as a cushion when there were budgetary
changes. Bonded warehousing enabled the Government, in 1915,
to ensure a three-year maturing period. The full importance of
bonded warehousing can be seen at the present time rather more
dramatically than was the case in the nineteenth century. The
spirit duty in 1970 reached £13 9s. 9d. a proof gallon and it
needs little imagination to see how impossible it would be for
a distiller to finance this duty on even a modest scale of production
if he had to pay the duty as soon as he produced his spirit.

The other outstanding landmarks in the history of the distilling
industry are without doubt the changes in the distillery laws in
1780 and 1823. The first introduced a duty charge on the capacity
of stills and the presumed speed of working them. This inaugurated an incredible race between distillers and legislation. It
also wiped out hundreds of small distilleries. The distilling
methods adopted involved a great waste in fuel and drew the
attention of inventors to find means for fuel economy. Chief
attention was directed to some way of constructing a continuous
still and the result in Ireland was the Coffey still in 1830. This, in
turn, caused distillers in many cases to resort to blending. The
changes in the laws in 1823 freed the distiller from the bonds of
the still licence duty and left him free to develop distilling
apparatus to suit the needs for producing good quality spirit instead
of apparatus designed solely to distil at great speed almost without
regard to economic working or quality. Much larger distilling
firms emerged as a result of these changes.

Some developments in the distilling industry depended heavily
on advances in scientific and technical knowledge, and this was
specially so with the measurement of alcohol in a mixture. In a
distillery the control over fermentation rests on a proper assess-

ment of the alcohol being formed. Assessment by sight is a crude method and can be fairly satisfactory if the distiller is skilled in his art. The invention of the saccharometer and its perfection over the eighteenth and nineteenth centuries changed guesswork into precise knowledge. Judgement of the condition of wash still relies on inspection, but any doubts can be dispelled with the use of the saccharometer and appropriate action taken before it is too late. The other, and probably more important invention was the hydrometer which was improved and developed during the eighteenth century until, in the early nineteenth century, the Sikes hydrometer emerged and is still used. For practical purposes the hydrometer is necessarily coupled with a definition of proof spirit and this resulted only after extensive scientific research into the physical properties of alcohol. With an accurate hydrometer, convenient to use, the distiller could control with more precision the flow of his extract and divert unwanted fractions of his distillates to feints receivers and so get a maximum return of good quality spirit from his wash. Further, it enabled all trade and revenue trans-actions to be based on one standard, the alcohol content of the beverage. Without these two instruments, the saccharometer and hydrometer, the beneficial changes in the distillery laws in 1823 would not have been possible.

The development of a suitable hydrometer was, of course, bound to come, for in a world where improving transport facilities meant expanding trade, spirits, like any other article of commerce, must have a satisfactory standard of measurement. With all doubts on the strength of a spirituous beverage being removed it left flavour as the deciding factor in successful market-ing. This is a factor that cannot be measured so the competition between beverages and between one whiskey and another has come to depend to a large extent on conditioning the public taste by advertising and other marketing devices. The competi-tion between spirits and other alcoholic beverages, chiefly beer, is, of course, also influenced by discriminating excise duties which directly affect the price.

The invention of the Coffey still had a most important influence on flavour and price. The spirit it produces has very little flavour and is much cheaper to make. In its early years the main outlet for the spirit was probably for industrial use and undoubtedly undersold the spirits of wine made by rectifiers. This spirit is also well suited to dilute the harsh taste of raw pot still whiskey. Thus a cheaper and more palatable drink could be made. There is no evidence that this blending was customary before the middle of the nineteenth century, though it is fairly certain that some distillers would practice a little diluting as it would be more profitable. The public taste at the time would not tolerate any more. This picture changed fairly quickly in the latter half of the nineteenth century. Blending was accompanied by lower prices and aimed at the working class market where a cheap, strong, alcoholic beverage was a considerable attraction, especially in England. The traditional pot still distillers in general held their market in Ireland, but fought a losing battle in their English market. Blended whiskey steadily increased its hold in England from about 1870 and made great inroads into the market in the north of Ireland and in Scotland. It also gained a strong hold on the markets overseas. Many conservative Irish distillers stuck to the pot still product which had dominated all markets for a long time. By amalgamation of firms a few very large distilling companies emerged in Scotland and in the north of Ireland. They concentrated on blended whiskeys and, with lower prices and good marketing techniques, finally replaced the old pot still whiskeys in the public favour. The companies in the north of Ireland disappeared during the economic depressions between the two world wars leaving Scotch whiskey by far the largest influence in the whiskey trade. Irish distillers have now discarded their distaste for blending. They have fully accepted the change in the public preference and are competing with success in the whiskey trade. They face a formidable task to make headway into the well entrenched Scotch whiskey market as well as retaining some of their self whiskeys. They produce a high quality product under a virile management and their prospects are good.

A feature of the distilling industry, not only in Ireland, but in the United Kingdom as a whole, has been the cycles of expansion and depression in their markets. There have probably been cycles of this sort throughout its history, but they were not very evident until this century. Failures and successes in earlier years depended chiefly on efficient management. In this century, however, compulsory maturing in bond has been imposed both in home and foreign markets and this has added greatly to the difficulty of forecasting future demands. Uncontrolled production by competing firms was disastrous and amalgamations of firms took place to prevent markets being flooded. Great increases in excise duties at home and protective measures in other countries have accentuated the penalties of over-production. The Australian market, for example, has been virtually closed to United Kingdom distillers. There has also been the impact of two world wars and the prohibition era in the United States. The final result of these forces has been the merging of distilling firms in Ireland into two companies, the Irish Distillers in the Republic of Ireland and the 'Old Bushmills' Company in Northern Ireland.

The United Distillers, now known as the Irish Distillers Limited, have changed their marketing policy since the company was formed in 1966. Whiskey is no longer sold in bulk. A dealer cannot now buy whiskey to make up his own blends. In the past some such whiskeys blended and bottled outside the control of the distiller were very good, but there were also blends of indifferent quality which did not enhance the reputation of Irish whiskey. Since there is now only one distilling company, this quality control is very effective and all whiskey from the Republic of Ireland now has the guarantee of the distillers. Another, and possibly more important change was the decision, in the 1940s, to enter the market of the rectifier and compounder. Not since the first years of the nineteenth century has an Irish distiller made anything other than plain spirits because of restrictive laws and because making spirituous compounds had become a specialised industry. The distillers are now well established in the markets for gin and vodka. These beverages have become very popular in recent years, and since the Irish products compare favourably with those made elsewhere, there is every prospect of a successful future. It may be argued that the Irish Distillers Limited have a monopoly in the Republic of Ireland and that this is not in the best public interest, but can the manufacture of spirituous beverages be regarded as a tight monopoly? The distiller has to compete with imported spirits though he has the advantage of a protective duty except for imports from the United Kingdom. More important, however, is the competition of locally made beer that has a world wide reputation for its excellence.

The sole distilling firm in Northern Ireland is differently placed. It is within the domestic market of the United Kingdom and therefore cannot be protected from the large Scottish firms. Bushmills whiskey is malt-based and in recent years there has been some blending with spirits from a Coffey still. The proportion of grain spirit used is much less than in most Scotch whiskies, because the pot still whiskey is thrice distilled. Thus Bushmills can be regarded as similar to Scotch whisky and therefore must retain a high standard to be successful. Furthermore, in its own local market blending firms still operate, buying whiskey from any source they please and marketing under their own brand names. The only restriction on these blends is that the label 'Irish Whiskey' cannot be used unless all the spirit is of Irish origin. This distilling firm is now closely associated with large brewery interests in England. This protects it from possible extinction by mergers and helps in marketing. All this reduces competition to satisfying a public demand with a high quality product at a competitive price. A long reputation of excellence helps, but only in the short term. This is being maintained and the whiskey from Northern Ireland is making substantial headway in both domestic and overseas markets.

The question arises as to the possibility of the Irish distilling industry attaining again the position it held as late as 1900 when it was producing ten million proof gallons a year and had a large hold on the English and overseas markets. By far its most important rival is Scotch whisky. Both the Irish and Scottish products are of high quality and both are marketed at similar strengths and prices. In both cases there is efficient management, modern equipment and economic use of materials. Both cater for the popular taste for blends and both have a solid local market. There are variations in flavour amongst the different brands, but it is fairly narrow and, except for the extremes, it would need an expert to distinguish the source of the whiskey. For example, the mild blends made in Ireland approximate in lightness with the proprietary Scotch blends. The self whiskeys are at the extremes where the Scottish product is usually much heavier than the Irish counterpart. It seems inescapable that success depends not on the whiskey itself, but on marketing techniques. The distillers are well aware of this and in the past decade or so have energetically pursued a policy of market research, advertising in various forms, appointing efficient agencies abroad and so on. Exports are rising steadily and the future looks promising. Whether they will reach the eminence of their Scottish rivals is perhaps unlikely, but not impossible. In the 1880s the position was reversed and few people at that time could have foreseen a Scottish expansion of such proportions in a market then dominated by Irish distillers. Business efficiency rather than the product changed the picture.

Not much can be said about the retail home market. The usual economic rules are overwhelmed by the whims of politicians, the pressure of excise duties, the activities of temperance and similar groups, and the quite proper attempts by governments to restrain excessive drinking. After a distiller has expended so much skill and care to produce a quality beverage that can be enjoyed and is satisfying, it is sad to see it wasted on a drunkard to whom any sort of potable alcohol is good enough.

The history shows clearly how closely the excise service is bound up with the distillers' activities. At the present time the friction between the exciseman and distiller is so small as to warrant no comment. As has been shown, this was far from the case until about the mid-nineteenth century. When that century opened the two departments, the customs and the excise, represented by far the bulk of the Irish civil service. Members of their Boards and nearly all senior officials were political nominees owing their position to political jobbery. The vast number of lesser officers, the genuine civil servants, were underpaid and appointed as a result of influence. The former made policy, the rest were their dependent servants with no avenue to reach the senior posts. A more ineffectual civil service could hardly be imagined. Inefficiency and corruption were a natural consequence. After the Act of Union in 1800 there was a slow improvement until, in the middle of the century, a civil service as we know it emerged. The establishment of the Civil Service Commission ensured that officials were adequately educated and free from dependence on some political or influential figure. Salaries were improved, there was proper provision for promotion to all posts and an assured pension. These measures practically wiped out corruption, the bane of the excise service and distillers alike in earlier times. A much healthier relationship between distillers and officials was established.

AUTHORITIES CONSULTED

Calendar of Documents, Ireland, 1293–1301; 1302–7, ed. H. S. Sweetman, London, 1881.
Calendar of State Papers, Ireland, 1598–9. ed. E. G. Atkinson, H.M. Stationery Office, 1891.
1615–25. ed. C. W. Russell and J. P. Prendergast, London, 1880.
1663–5. ed. R. P. Mehaffy, London, 1907.
Carew Mss., Calendar of State Papers, 1575–88, 1589–1600, 1603–24; ed. J. S. Buller and W. Bullen, London, 1868.
Carew Mss., Book of Howth, ed. Buller and Bullen, London. 1871.
Statutes at Large of the Irish Parliament.
English and United Kingdom Statutes.
Statutes of Saorstát Éireann.
Irish House of Commons Journals.
Parliamentary Register of the History of Debates in the Irish Parliament, ed. Byrne and Porter, Dublin.
Parliamentary Debates (Hansard).
Dáil Éireann Debates.
Parliamentary Papers:
   Report on Scottish Distilleries, 1799.
   Instructions for Collecting Customs and Excise duties, 1805 (23) vi.
   Accounts presented to Parliament, 1806 (162) (191) xiv.
   Inquiry into Fees, Gratuities, Perquisites and Emoluments . . . received in certain Public Offices in Ireland. 5th Report, 1806–7 (124) vi. 6th Report, 1808 (4) iii.
   Committee appointed to inquire and report how far . . . it may be practicable and expedient to confine distilleries in the United Kingdom to use sugar and molasses only . . . , 1808 (178) iv.
   Select Committee to inquire into the Regulations governing the drawbacks and countervailing duties on the Import and Export of Spirits made in Great Britain and Ireland from one country to the other, 1809 (199) (235) iii.
   Report from the Committee on Distilleries in Ireland, 1812–13 (269) vi.

Return of Officers of Excise: Troops cantoned for assisting the Excise, 1816 (231) ix.

Fines on Townlands, 1816 (281) ix.

Select Committee on Illicit Distillation in Ireland, 2nd Report, 1816 (436) ix.

Return of Revenue Accounts, 1819 (209) ix.

Select Committee on the State of Disease and the condition of the Labouring Poor in Ireland, 2nd Report, 1819 (409) viii.

Inquiry into the Warehousing System, 10th Report, 1821 (25) x.

Experiments in Distillation by the Excise Department, 1821 (538) xix.

Inquiry into the Revenue arising in Ireland:
    2nd Report, 1822 (565) xii; 3rd Report, 1822 (606) xiii;
    4th Report, 1822 (634) xiii; 5th Report, 1823 (405) vii;
    5th Report Supplement, 1823 (498) vii;
    7th Report, 1824 (100) xi;
    15th Report, 1824 (141) ix; 16th Report, 1824 (429) ix.

Detailed Account of the Excise Establishment, Ireland, 1823 (203) xii.

Select Committee on petitions complaining of additional duties on Malt, 1821 (598) viii.

Numbers in the Public Service, 1828 (552) xvi.

Memorials addressed to the Treasury by Corn Distillers, 1830 (370) xxii.

Select Committee to inquire into the effects of allowing a Malt Drawback on Spirits, 1831 (295) vii.

Report of the Board of Excise on the Malt Drawback, 1831–2 (150) xxxiv.

Select Committee to inquire into Drunkenness, 1834 (559) viii.

Return of Deficiency Duties on Whiskey, 1834 (414) xlix.

Inquiry into the Excise Establishmnet and into the Management and Collection of the Excise Revenue throughout the United Kingdom:
    7th Report, Part I, 1834 (7) xxv; Part II, 1835 (8) xxx; 10th
    1834 (11) xxv; 19th Report, 1837 (83) xxx; 20th Report, 1836
    (22) xxvi; Digest of Reports, 1837 (84) xxx; Report of . . . the
    Board of Excise, . . . upon . . . the 20th Report, 1837 (96) xxx.
    Return of recommendations . . . carried into Effect, . . . 1842
    (75) xxvi.

Establishment in the Excise Department, 1835 (593) xlviii.

Inquiry into the State of the Poor in Ireland, 1st Report, 1836 (369) xxxii.

Return of Spirit Licenses, 1837–8 (717) xlvi.

Compensation for losses sustained by the fire at the Custom House, Dublin, 1835 (481) xxxviii; 1837 (312) xxxix.

Accounts relating to proof spirits distilled and exported, 1840 (623) xliv.

Memorial from Licensed Victuallers in Ireland, 1841 (275) xxvi.

Return relating to spirits distilled in each Collection of Excise, 1842 (238) xxxix.

Select Committee to inquire into the effect upon the Trade in Spirits in Ireland of the Repeal of the Malt Drawback, 1842 (338) xiv.

Report from the Board of Excise to the Treasury on the use of barley... in Breweries and Distilleries, 1847 (26) lix.

Statements of evidence before the Sugar and Coffee Planting Committee showing transit losses on . . . spirits imported into London, 1847–8 (518) lviii.

Return of proof spirits distilled; Return of Licensed Distillers, 1851 (263) (380) liii.

Returns of Licensed Distillers, 1851 (369) 1; 1854 (175) lxv; 1866 (435) lxvi.

Select Committee to consider the consequences of extending the functions of the Constabulary in Ireland to the suppression of Illicit Distillation, 1854 (53) x.

Accounts of proof spirits distilled, removed and in bond . . ., 1856 (326) lv; 1861 (144) lviii.

Select Committee to inquire whether it would be practicable to consolidate any establishments governed by the Boards of Inland Revenue and Customs, 1862 (370) vii.

Select Committee on the operation of the Malt Tax, 1867 (470) xi; 1867–8 (420) ix.

Select Committee on British and Foreign Spirits, 1890 (316) x; 1891 (210) xi.

Royal Commission on the Liquor Licensing Laws, 1898.

Statistics relating to licensed premises, 1898 (c. 8698) xxxvii;

Evidence taken in Ireland, 1898 (c. 8980) xxxviii.

Royal Commission on Whiskey and other Potable Spirits, 1908 (Cd. 4181); 1909 (Cd. 4796).

Reports of the Commissioners of Inland Revenue, from the 5th, 1861 (2877) xxxi; to the 52nd, 1909 (Cd. 4868) xxvii.

Reports of the Commissioners of Customs and Excise:
2nd, 1911 (Cd. 5827) xv, and later years.

Reports of the Revenue Commissioners, Dublin.

Official Reports:

Profs., Graham, Hofman and Redwood, *Report on Original Gravities*, addressed to the Board of Inland Revenue on 16 August 1852. Customs and Excise Library, London, ref. 1101.

Drs. Hope, Thomson and Coventry, *Report on the proportional value of Malt made from Bere or Bigg and Malt made from Barley*. Customs and Excise Library, London, ref. Treasury and Scottish excise, No. 1817. 1085–11, p. 117.

Report of the Government Chemist, year ending 1912.

Manuscript records:
Historical Excise Records, Custom House, Belfast, and Custom House, Londonderry.
List of the Commissioners of Customs appointed by patent in 1772, Linenhall Library, Belfast, ref. N. 2060.
Private diary of F. Montgomery, J.P., Lin. Lib. Belfast. Relates to Comber, Co. Down, in the early 19th century.
Customs and Excise Library, London. Miscellaneous correspondence and reports.

Public Record Office, Dublin.
Creighton papers, ref. M 5476/20.
Roe distillery, refs. M 4930, 4932.
Dublin Whiskey Co., refs. M 4926, 4937.
Alex. McKenzie, refs. D 17421, 17423, 17430. T 7128.

Public Record Office, Belfast.
Dunville and Co., refs. D 2132/1–3.
Comber distillery, refs. D 1808 and sub refs.
R. A. Taylor, ref. D 1435/2–4.
D. Watt and Co., refs. D 1506 and sub refs.

National Library, Dublin.
Kilbeggan distillery, refs. Mss. 949–52.

Books:
Mainly scientific or technical:
W. Speer, *Enquiry into the causes of Errors and Irregularities which take place in ascertaining the strengths of spirituous liquors by the Hydrometer,* London, 1802.
F. Acum, *Treatise on the Art of Brewing,* London, 1821.
W. Symons, *The Practical Gager,* London, 1821. Methods for measuring the various distillery vessels are explained.
M. Donovan, *Domestic Economy,* i, Dublin, 1830.
E. G. Hooper, *Manual of Brewing,* London, 1882, pp. 18 *et seq.,* describes brewing apparatus.
J. E. Thausing, *Theory and Practice of the preparation of Malt . . . ,* London, 1882, translated from German, ed. A. Schwarz, pp. 272 *et seq.,* deals in detail with malting processes. Later chapters explain brewing processes. Opinions are expressed on the merits of different types of utensils.
W. T. Brannt, *Practical Treatise on the Raw Materials and Distillation*

and Rectification of Alcohol, London, 1885. Chap. 2 deals with alcoholometry.

E. R. Moritz and G. H. Morris, *Textbook of the Science of Brewing*, London, 1891. Brewing apparatus is described in Chap. 2.

J. A. Nettleton, *The Manufacture of Spirit*, London, 1893.

J. Scarisbrick, *Spirit Assaying*, Wolverhampton, 1898.

C. Simmonds, *Alcohol*, London, 1919. The whole range of spirit manufacture is covered, from the enzymes in grain and yeast, alcoholometry, right through to descriptions of pot, patent and rectifying stills.

S. Young, *Distillation Principles and Processes*, London, 1922.

A. Harden, *Alcoholic fermentation*, London, 1925.

W. H. Nithsdale and A. J. Manton, *Practical Brewing*, Glasgow, 1924. Intended for brewers, but some of the brewing problems are of interest to distillers.

C. Elliott, *Distillation in Practice*, London, 1925. Distillery apparatus is described in Chap. 7.

F. G. H. Tate, *Alcoholometry*, London, 1930. Contains an historical introduction.

A. J. V. Underwood, *Historical Development of Distilling Plant*, London, 1935. A paper read before the Institute of Chemical Engineers, 22 February 1935.

J. Reilly, *Distillation*, London, 1936. Chap. 5 explains azeotropic mixtures in connextion with alcohol.

The Philosophical Transactions of the Royal Society, London.

Legal works:

L. MacNally, *The Justice of the Peace for Ireland*, Dublin, 1810.

S. J. Douglas, *Manual of Summary Proceedings*, London, 1853. Chiefly concerned with revenue cases.

A. Reed, *The Liquor Licensing Laws of Ireland*, Dublin, 1889.

C. Molloy, *The Justice of the Peace for Ireland*, Dublin, 1890.

J. O'Connor, *The Licensing Laws of Ireland*, Dublin, 1904.

Sir N. J. Highmore, *The Customs Laws*, 3rd ed. London, 1922. *The Excise Laws*, 3rd ed. London, 1923.

Other books:

A. Barnard, *The Whisky Distilleries of the United Kingdom*, London, 1887.

J. Bateman, *The Excise Officer's Manual*, London, 1840. 3rd ed. 1865, revised by J. Bell.

E. Borlase, *History of the Irish Rebellion*, London, 1680.

E. Campion, *History of Ireland*, Dublin, 1633.

W. Carleton, *Traits and Stories of the Irish Peasantry*, Dublin, 1847. *Amusing Irish Tales*, London, 1889.

E. Chichester, *Oppressions and Cruelties of Irish Revenue Officers*, London, 1818.

   A. Coffey, *Observations on Chichester's Pamphlet*, London, 1818.

   E. Chichester, *Reply to Coffey's Observations*, London, 1818.

K. H. Connell, *Illicit Distilling*, Historical Studies, III, 1961. *Ether Drinking in Ulster*, Studies in Alcohol, Vol. 26, 1965, New Brunswick, U.S.A. *The Population of Ireland*, Oxford, 1950.

L. M. Cullen, *Smuggling in Galway in the seventeen-thirties*, Galway Archaeological and Historical Society Journal, 1962.

E. Curtis, *A History of Ireland*, London, 1936.

J. G. F. Day & H. E. Patton, *Cathedrals of the Church of Ireland*. London, 1932.

R. Dunlop, *Ireland under the Commonwealth*. Manchester, 1913.

P. Egan, *Real Life in Ireland*. London, 1829.

W. R. le Fanu, *Seventy years of Irish life*. London, 1896.

J. Forbes: *Memorandums made in Ireland in 1852*. London, 1853.

T. W. Freeman, *Ireland*. London, 1950.

P. Froggart, *The Census of Ireland, 1813–15*. Irish Historical Studies, III. 1965.

J. A. Froude, *The English in Ireland in the Eighteenth Century*. London, 1874.

C. H. Hall, *Economic Writings of Sir William Petty*. Cambridge, 1899.

C. Hannah, *Impartial review of the true causes of existing misery in Ireland*. Dublin, 1822.

J. Holmes, *Monasterevan Distillery*. Jnl. Kildare Archaeological Soc., xvi, No. 4. 1969.

G. E. Howard, *A treatise on the Exchequer & Revenue of Ireland*. Dublin, 1776.

J. Hely Hutchinson, *The Commercial Restraints of Ireland considered*. Dublin, 1779.

John Jameson & Sons, *The History of a Great House*. Dublin, 1924.

W. H. Johnston, *Revenue Officer's Manual*. Loftus publications. London, 1873.

P. W. Joyce, *Social History of Ancient Ireland*. Dublin, 1906.

C. Leadbetter, *The Royal Gauger*. London, 1785.

A. Lecky, *A History of Ireland in the Eighteenth Century*. London, 1896.

A. K. Longfield, *Anglo-Irish trade in the Sixteenth century*. London, 1929.

P. Lynch & J. Vaizey: *Guinness' Brewery in the Irish economy*. Cambridge, 1960.

J. J. McBride, *The Spirit Traders' Handbook*. Belfast, 1900.

M. J. F. McCarthy, *Irish land & Irish liberty*. London, 1911.

C. McCoy, *Dictionary of Customs & Excise*. London, 1938.

R. B. McDowell, *The Irish Administration, 1801–1914*. London, 1964.

J. F. Maguire, *Father Mathew*. ed. R. Mulholland, Dublin. No date.

L. W. Marrison, *Wines & Spirits*. Penguin series. London, 1957.

W. S. Mason, *A Statistical Account or Parochial survey of Ireland*, Dublin, 1816.

C. Maxwell, *Dublin under the Georges*, London, 1946.
  Country and Town under the Georges, Dundalk, 1949.

O. A. Mendelsohn, *Dictionary of Drink and Drinking*, London, 1965.

John Milton, *Prose works*, ii, ed. J. A. St. John, London, 1875.

S. Morewood, *Inventions and Customs in the use of Inebriating Liquors*, London, 1824.
  A Philosophical and Statistical History of the . . . use of Inebriating Liquors with the present practice of Distillation, . . . Dublin, 1838.

M. G. Mulhall, *Dictionary of Statistics*, London, 1809.

J. Mullala, *A View of Irish Affairs*, ii, Dublin, 1795.

A. E. Murray, *The Commercial and Financial Relations between England and Ireland*, London, 1903.

T. Newenham, *Statistical and Historical Inquiry into the Population of Ireland*, London, 1805.
  A view of the National, Political and Commercial Circumstances of Ireland, London, 1809.

G. O'Brien, *Economic History of Ireland in the 17th Century*, London, 1919.
  Economic History of Ireland in the 18th Century, London, 1918.
  Economic History of Ireland from the Union to the Famine, London, 1921.

J. Owens, *Plain Papers*, London, 1879.

J. Pim, *Conditions and Prospects of Ireland*, London, 1848.

F. Plowden, *Historical Review of the State of Ireland*, ii, London, 1903.

T. Reid, *Travels in Ireland*, London, 1823.

P. Rogers, *Father Theobald Mathew*, Dublin, 1943.

J. Scarisbrick, *Spirit Manual*, 2nd ed., Wolverhampton, 1891.

E. Spenser and others, *Ireland under Elizabeth and James I*, ed. H. Morley, London, 1890. The writings of Fynes Moryson are relevant.

R. Twiss, *A Tour of Ireland*, Dublin, 1776.

E. Wakefield, *An Account of Ireland, Statistical and Political*, London, 1812.

Ross Wilson, *Seventy Years in the Scotch Whisky Industry*, articles in the *Wine and Spirit Trade Record*, October 1964 to July 1967.

Arthur Young, *A Tour in Ireland*, London, 1780.

Miscellaneous references:

Department of Agriculture and Technical Instruction, Ireland, *Industry and Agriculture*, Dublin, 1902. Article on distilleries.

Ulster Journal of Archaeology, Belfast, 1858 and 1859.

Studia Hibernica, No. 6, 1966, *Peel and Police reform in Ireland, 1814–18.*

Tobacco Year Book, London, 1920. Survey of the Government Laboratory.

Ham's Year Book for Inland Revenue Officers from 1879 and for Customs and Excise Officers from 1909. Ham's Year Book was published for Customs Officers from 1876.

The Revenue Review, a monthly journal for Inland Revenue Officers, published from 1900. The journals contain a wide range of technical articles and current revenue problems. The early years were edited by J. T. Mulqueen.

Handbook for Officers of Excise, Loftus publication, London, 1857.

Truths about Whiskey, Dublin, 1878. Published jointly by four Dublin distilling firms: John Jameson and Son, William Jameson and Co., John Power and Son, and George Roe and Co.

Scotch Whisky, Scotch Whisky Association. Published in the form of questions and answers. It explains the blending of patent and pot still spirits which began on a large scale between 1860 and 1870.

The Dublin Society's statistical surveys with particular reference to counties where illicit distilling was prevalent, namely:

    J. McParlan, *County of Donegal*, Dublin, 1802.
      County of Sligo, Dublin, 1801.
    H. Dutton, *County of Clare*, Dublin, 1808.
      County of Galway, Dublin, 1824.
    G. V. Sampson, *County of Londonderry*, Dublin, 1802.

The Annual Register, Dublin, 1788.

The Newry Magazine, iv, 1818.

J. R. McCulloch, *Dictionary, Practical, Theoretical and Historical of Commerce and Commercial Navigation*. Published annually.

The Irish Year Book.

Mss. Sources of the History of Irish Civilisation, ed. R. T. Hayes, Boston, U.S.A., 1965.

Appropriate reports in the *Irish Times*, the *Belfast Newsletter*, the *Northern Whig*, the *Belfast Commercial Chronicle*, and the *Belfast Telegraph*.

Cork: Its Trade and Commerce. Handbook of the Cork Chamber of Shipping, 1919.

Directories:
 Thom's Irish Directory.
 Thom's Directory of Manufacturers.
 Macdonald's Irish Directory.
 Slater's Commercial Directory of Ireland.
 The Treble Almanack, published yearly in the late 18th century
  by W. Wilson, Dublin.
 The Gentleman's and Citizen's Almanack, late 18th century.
 The Dublin Almanac, 18th and early 19th centuries.
 Belfast and Ulster Directory.
 Metier's Belfast Directory.
 Cork Directory. Photographic copies of two early directories in
  the Cork public library.
 Cork Directory, 1845–6, published by A. Aldwell.

INDEX